WALL IS THE MOST BASIC TOOL
ARCHITECTURE.
TADAO ANDO

ARCHITECTURE IS A TERRIBLY FOOLISH PROFESSION TO GO INTO.
I THINK MOST STUDENTS KNOW THAT.
AT LEAST I ALWAYS TELL THEM.
PHILIP JOHNSON

AL STRIPTEASE."
LUIS BARRAGÁN

THE GETTY IS NOT A WHITE BUILDING.
RICHARD MEIER

I HAVE THE BUILDING IN MY HEAD
LIKE A COMPOSER HAS HIS SYMPHONY.
JØRN UTZON

BY THE WORLD OF LIGHT
DOW THAT EXISTS FREE OF ASSOCIATIONS
ECIFIC COLORS OR MATERIALS.
RICHARD MEIER

YOU WILL KNOW THAT THE HOUSE IS SUCCESSFUL
IF YOU GET UP ONE MORNING
AND FIND YOURSELF DANCING BAREFOOT THROUGH IT.
PAULO MENDES DA ROCHA

I FIND IT VERY MYSTERIOUS,
CHITECTURE. IT IS FILLED WITH DEATH
ISM—THE ARCHETYPES
D DARKNESS.
VERRE FEHN

I AM INTERESTED IN THE SHAPE OF THE BUILDING
ONLY AS A CONSEQUENCE OF THE ISSUES
ABOUT THE RESPONSIBILITY TOWARD MATERIALS,
PROCESS OF PRODUCTION, THE ABILITY TO RECYCLE, LIGHT, VENTILATION,
THE RELATIONSHIP TO THE OUTSIDE AND THE NATURAL LANDSCAPE.
GLENN MURCUTT

M MUST BE TO ACHIEVE
DYNAMIC EQUILIBRIUM
SOCIETY, CITIES, AND NATURE.
RICHARD ROGERS

TWO ISSUES THAT I BELIEVE ARE PARTICULARLY IMPORTANT
IN THE FUTURE GROWTH OF CITIES: THE ROLE OF PUBLIC SPACES
AND THE QUEST FOR MORE ECOLOGICALLY RESPONSIBLE ARCHITECTURE.
NORMAN FOSTER

CANNOT MAKE ARCHITECTURE
HOUT STUDYING THE CONDITION
LIFE IN THE CITY.
ALDO ROSSI

NEITHER ARCHITECTS
NOR ANYONE WHO IS CONCERNED ABOUT THE FUTURE
CAN IGNORE THE EFFECTS OF CLIMATE CHANGE
NOR THE WIDENING GULF BETWEEN RICH AND POOR.
RICHARD ROGERS

ECTURE SHOULD NOT BE A PERSONAL GESTURE.
NGS TO THE CITY.
NEEDS AN ARTISTIC INVESTMENT.
CHRISTIAN DE PORTZAMPARC

LAST,
A RELATIONSHIP WITH THE PEOPLE
WHO ARE TO USE THE BUILDINGS.
JØRN UTZON

SHOPPING IS ARGUABLY THE LAST REMAINING FORM
OF PUBLIC ACTIVITY. . . . THE VORACITY BY WHICH
SHOPPING PURSUES THE PUBLIC HAS, IN EFFECT,
MADE IT ONE OF THE PRINCIPAL— IF ONLY—
MODES BY WHICH WE EXPERIENCE THE CITY.
REM KOOLHAAS

RESPONSIBILITY OF THE ARCHITECT
BEHIND BUILDINGS THAT ARE ASSETS TO CULTURE.
FUMIHIKO MAKI

AS WE HAD LEARNED FROM THE SPACES OF ROME,
WE LEARNED FROM THE SYMBOLISM OF LAS VEGAS.
ROBERT VENTURI

I HAVE NO MESSAGE TO TELL EVERYBODY
YOND SAYING WE'VE GOT RESPONSIBILITIES
TO DO THINGS PROPERLY.
THAT'S THE LEAST WE CAN DO AS ARCHITECTS.
GLENN MURCUTT

ANYONE WHO DOES NOT HAVE THE STRENGTH TO SIN
WILL NOT NECESSARILY BE A SAINT OR A GOOD ARCHITECT—
MORE LIKELY A BORE.
GOTTFRIED BÖHM

CHITECTURAL PROJECT IS A VOCATION
N EITHER CASE, IT IS A CONSTRUCTION.
AN HOLD ONESELF BACK IN THE FACE OF THIS VOCATION
R, BUT IT WILL ALWAYS REMAIN AN UNRESOLVED THING.
ALDO ROSSI

THE ROLE OF AN ARCHITECT IS SERVICE.
YOU ARE A SERVANT OF THE COMMUNITY.
YOU ARE, IN A WAY, "A HANDYMAN."
KEVIN ROCHE

# ARCHITECT

RAFAEL ARANDA, CARME PIGEM, RAMON VILALTA
ALEJANDRO ARAVENA
FREI OTTO
SHIGERU BAN
TOYO ITO
WANG SHU
EDUARDO SOUTO DE MOURA
KAZUYO SEJIMA + RYUE NISHIZAWA
PETER ZUMTHOR
JEAN NOUVEL
RICHARD ROGERS
PAULO MENDES DA ROCHA
THOM MAYNE
ZAHA HADID
JØRN UTZON
GLENN MURCUTT
JACQUES HERZOG & PIERRE DE MEURON
REM KOOLHAAS
NORMAN FOSTER
RENZO PIANO
SVERRE FEHN
RAFAEL MONEO
TADAO ANDO
CHRISTIAN DE PORTZAMPARC
FUMIHIKO MAKI
ALVARO SIZA
ROBERT VENTURI
ALDO ROSSI
FRANK O. GEHRY
GORDON BUNSHAFT AND OSCAR NIEMEYER
KENZO TANGE
GOTTFRIED BÖHM
HANS HOLLEIN
RICHARD MEIER
I. M. PEI
KEVIN ROCHE
JAMES STIRLING
LUIS BARRÁGAN
PHILIP JOHNSON

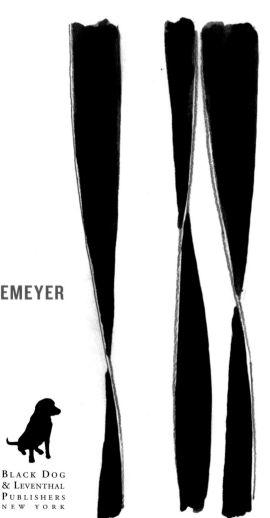

BLACK DOG
& LEVENTHAL
PUBLISHERS
NEW YORK

RUTH PELTASON AND GRACE ONG YAN
FOREWORD BY MARTHA THORNE, EXECUTIVE DIRECTOR, THE PRITZKER ARCHITECTURE PRIZE

# ARCHITECT

## THE PRITZKER PRIZE LAUREATES IN THEIR OWN WORDS

### REVISED AND UPDATED

Editor: Ruth Peltason, Bespoke Books
Designer: Johan Vipper
Research assistance, revised edition: John Kerner

Black Dog & Leventhal Publishers
Hachette Book Group
1290 Avenue of the Americas
New York, NY 10104

www.hachettebookgroup.com
www.blackdogandleventhal.com

First Edition: October 2010

Revised Edition: November 2017

Print book interior design by Eight Communications

ISBNs: 978-0-316-50505-5 (hardcover), 978-0-316-47369-9 (ebook)
LCCN: 2017938101

Printed in China

IM

10 9 8 7 6 5 4 3 2 1

**" WHAT SURPRISES ME MOST IN ARCHITECTURE, AS IN OTHER TECHNIQUES, IS THAT A PROJECT HAS ONE LIFE IN ITS BUILT STATE BUT ANOTHER IN ITS WRITTEN OR DRAWN STATE. "**
ALDO ROSSI

2017

2016

2015

2014

2013

2012

2011

2010

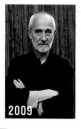
2009

2008

2007

2006

2005

2004

2003

2002

2001

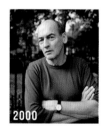
2006

2005

2004

2003

2002

2001

2000

1999

1998

1997

1996

1995

1994

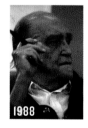
1993

1992

1991

1990

1989

1988

1988

1987

1986

1985

1984

1983

1982

1981

1980

1979

# CONTENTS

**FOREWORD** Celebrating 40 years of recognizing outstanding architecture around the world, the Pritzker Prize is perhaps the most revered, talked about, and anticipated independent architecture award granted each year. After four decades, its position is well established, even if the jury's decisions have, at times, caused surprise. This anniversary publication, which allows a close-up understanding of the laureates through their own writings and words, as well as carefully selected images of their buildings, is a window to the most important thinkers and makers of architecture of our time.

The Pritzker Architecture Prize was established by the Hyatt Foundation in 1979 to annually honor a living architect or architects whose built work demonstrates a combination of those qualities of talent, vision, and commitment that has produced consistent and significant contributions to humanity and the built environment through the art of architecture. The prize takes its name from the Pritzker family, whose international business interests are headquartered in Chicago. The Pritzkers have long been known for their support of educational, scientific, medical, and cultural activities. Jay A. Pritzker (1922–1999) founded the prize with his wife, Cindy. His eldest son, Thomas J. Pritzker, the chairman of The Hyatt Foundation, and wife, Margot Pritzker, are currently the most active patrons of the prize. While their roles never intersect with the nominations and selection processes, they choose the venue for the ceremony and maintain the stability and vision of the prize over time. Tom Pritzker explains, "As native Chicagoans, it's not surprising that our family was keenly aware of architecture, living in the birthplace of the skyscraper, a city filled with buildings designed by architectural legends such as Louis Sullivan, Frank Lloyd Wright, Mies van der Rohe, and many others."

The granting of prizes for significant accomplishments in the arts and sciences is not new. Academies have a long tradition of rewarding excellence by inducting outstanding professionals into their ranks and granting awards and medals for special purposes. All awards seek to honor and recognize achievement. Some may also try to set standards, either clearly stated or simply implied. Without a doubt, however, some awards are more distinguished and valued than others are. The Pritzker Architecture Prize is often known as the Nobel Prize of Architecture, and each year the name of the new laureate is eagerly awaited by all—architects, students, critics, journalists, and the general public. Several factors contribute to the strength, longevity, and prestige of this award. The Pritzker Prize began with a clear and ambitious mission. The Pritzker family, patrons of the arts and attuned to architecture through their business interests, established the award to honor living architects from around the world who have contributed in a significant way to the built environment. They realized that architecture was one of the few areas that was not sufficiently acknowledged or widely discussed, in contrast with other arts. Therefore, it is possible to identify three main goals of the Prize: to recognize excellence; raise public awareness about the field; and encourage other architects to achieve high standards.

Unlike many other architecture awards, the Pritzker Architecture Prize is truly independent. It is not part of nor controlled by any professional association, school, or company. The jury is comprised of independent experts and ranges in size from five to nine members. Members serve for multiple years, with a minimum three-year term, which assures a balance between past and new members. No members of the Pritzker family or outside observers are present at or participate in jury deliberations, which usually take place during the first months of the calendar year. The jury members, who are solely responsible for selecting the laureate, are highly respected professionals in their own specific fields of architecture, business, education, publishing, and culture. Some of the guidelines for the prize were loosely modeled after the Nobel Prize procedures, such as its international nature, open nominations process, independent jury, generous purse (US $100,000), and a ceremony and medal to honor the new laureate each year. The nominations procedure is extremely straightforward. Each year, the Executive Director requests suggestions from more than 200 people who are knowledgeable about architecture, such as critics, architects, past laureates, museum directors, academics, business professionals, and others. Additionally, any licensed architect from any place in the world may send in a suggestion for the prize. In this day of easy and fast communication, a name simply e-mailed to the Executive Director constitutes a nomination. There are no forms to fill out or portfolios to submit. The Pritzker Prize organization assumes research on potential candidates. The Pritzker Jury also travels together each year to look at examples of contemporary architecture. This is, without a doubt, a distinguishing and significant feature of the Pritzker process. Site visits to experience buildings firsthand enable the jury to analyze real works within their contexts and to make informed decisions based on direct observation.

The jury citation, written each year and published when the winner is announced in the springtime, explains the rationale for granting the award to a specific professional and enumerates some of the important characteristics of the laureate's architecture. In recent years the citations have become longer and more in-depth. These explanations are an attempt to go beyond a simple headline of merely stating that an architect from a certain country has received the Pritzker; instead, the citation highlights the design intentions of the laureates and places the Prize within the broader context of architecture.

Each year the award ceremony is held at a different and architecturally significant site to publicly honor the winner. While the location of the ceremony is not linked to that year's winner, it does provide the opportunity to reinforce the international nature of the prize and to address our message of the importance of architecture to communities around the world. Past ceremony venues have included the Campidoglio in Rome, Italy (ceremony site for laureate Glenn Murcutt, 2002); Todai-ji Temple at Nara, Japan (Frank Gehry, 1989); the Palace of Versailles in France (Tadao Ando, 1995); Altes Museum in Berlin, Germany (Norman Foster, 1999), the State Hermitage Museum in St. Petersburg,

Russia (Zaha Hadid, 2004); the White House in Washington, D.C. (Renzo Piano, 1998); the Palace of the People in Beijing, China (Wang Shu, 2012); the Rijksmuseum in Amsterdam, the Netherlands (Shigeru Ban, 2014); as well as sites in Mexico, Turkey, the Czech Republic, Argentina, Great Britain, Israel, Spain, and other venues in the United States. At the yearly ceremony, the architect or architects are requested to speak about architecture from a personal point of view, in contrast to the lectures they may normally give related to their work.

Without a doubt, the built works are the main testimony of the Pritzker laureates. When reviewing the illustrations of buildings within the pages of this publication reflecting more than 40 years of architectural production, the great variety of approaches becomes apparent. It is clear that architectural excellence is not limited to any one definition, type, or style. Perhaps even more important, the written words—the architects' own voices—contained in this book add a unique and important dimension and contribute greatly to understanding the meaning of the prize and the oeuvre of the recipient architects. Pondering the architects' own words and thoughts brings them even closer to us. The carefully selected texts reveal the laureates' views, not just about architecture, but on other matters such as social responsibility, sustainability, education, or people and experiences that have influenced them throughout their lives.

As the jury citation for the 2017 winners said, "they help us to see, in a most beautiful and poetic way, that the answer to the question is not 'either/or' and that we can, at least in architecture, aspire to have both; our roots firmly in place and our arms outstretched to the rest of the world." The Pritzker Prize winners through their own words and voices reflect the talented individuality of each, at the same time they uncover the universality of architecture and the many connections that unite us.

Martha Thorne
Executive Director
The Pritzker Architecture Prize

**NOTE TO THE UPDATED EDITION** The updated edition of *Architect* arrives on the cusp of 40 years of the Pritzker Architecture Prize. There is much to celebrate and acknowledge. Since our book was originally published in 2010, nine more laureates have been named and now added to this anniversary edition: Eduardo Souto de Moura (2011), Wang Shu (2012), Toyo Ito (2013), Shigeru Ban (2014), Frei Otto (2015), Alejandro Aravena (2016), and, at the time of publication, architects Rafael Aranda, Carme Pigem, and Ramon Vilalta (2017). Geographically, the forty-four laureates encircle the world—from our home base in the United States to Australia, Austria, Brazil, Chile, China, Denmark, France, Germany, Italy, Japan, Mexico, the Netherlands, Norway, Portugal, Switzerland, Spain, and the U.K. Their built works represented here cast an even wider circumference of the globe.

This "wider circumference" brings with it a discernible emphasis in the works of these recent laureates, chiefly a response to natural disasters and societies in crisis. About this, Alejandro Aravena is declarative: "The advancement of architecture is a way to improve people's quality of life." Shigeru Ban, who worries less about the form and more about the inhabitants, speaks of "meaningful architecture": "If the structure is loved by the people, it will stay forever." With erudition and grace, Toyo Ito addresses the "fluid order in nature" and, in his Home-for-All projects, seeks "a new community architecture."

Materials encoded with meaning and memory turn up in the work of Wang Shu. His reclamation of bricks and tiles from ruins is "a way of preserving time" and of "containing values that we must keep alive." The architect-poet Souto de Moura escalates the selection of materials and style of architecture to the canvas of creativity itself: "the greatest aspiration of an architect is to . . . create, in a given time, a space that will possess the wisdom accumulated over thousands of years." Architects Aranda, Pigem, and Vilalta address the quality of life, of connecting the global and the local: "Because although we are passionate about globality, we want our architecture to sink its roots deeply into its specific location. We often say it is good to have roots and wings."

Aspiration is often expressed in the words of the beloved, late Frei Otto: "Whether it will be possible in the future to contribute to world peace by means of good residential and urban planning is something we can only hope."

Each of the Pritzker Prize laureates engages in a dialogue, both in words and in the making of architecture, in what Aravena describes as the "doing" of architecture. And each laureate, in his or her inimitable way, considers the role of architecture and our world "then, now, and tomorrow." With characteristic eloquence and ease, Souto de Moura says of architects, "Our role is to improve the world, perhaps by design."

R. P. and G. O. Y.
Spring 2017

**INTRODUCTION** Architecture is at the core of our contemporary culture. When we look at the distinguished buildings of our time— some that we may inhabit in our everyday lives, seek out as tourists, or regard intellectually—the physical architectural features draw us in. But there is so much we don't know, beginning with, What did the architect intend? Why is a building a given shape, or made with certain materials? What about the landscape, or the constraints of a city? And what about us—how much were we, the public, considered when the architect began to first imagine the work?

This is an uncommon book of architecture. So often writing on architecture is through the lens of a critic, scholar, or journalist. But in *Architect,* we look through the other end of the telescope: this time it is the architect—35 Pritzker Prize laureates, to be specific—who speak to us and share their thoughts, dreams, philosophies, inspirations, and influences about their built work. Here the outsider is silenced and we listen instead to the creators themselves. The results are illuminating. On the whole, architects tend to be intensely thoughtful and verbal. There is Peter Zumthor (2009), the architect's poet, who can make stone as seductive as a steamy art film (of the Thermal Baths in Vals, Switzerland, he writes: "mass, large and serene, should be left alone so that the presence of the stone is felt, so that it can exert its own effect on our bodies."). Contrast that with someone like Frank Gehry (1989), who is to the point about his work and his legacy (of Guggenheim Bilbao: "the most important thing to me is to build the buildings." And, "In the end my work is my work; it's not a critic's work."). Or Thom Mayne (2005), who speaks emphatically of "the music of reality." And there is the intensely personal aspect of architecture, its emotive quality, summed up simply but heroically by Luis Barragán (1980): "my architecture is biographical." Now look at works by each of these architects and you will be looking as a privileged insider—with the eyes of the architect him- and herself.

The architects presented here are not only hugely influential and leaders in their field, they are the Pritzker Prize laureates, deemed the best architects in the world. Collectively, they have shaped the field of architecture, architectural history, and our built environment at the end of the twentieth century and the first decade of the twenty-first. The annual Pritzker Prize has been called architecture's Nobel Prize, a comparison supported by both prizes' use of an open nominations procedure and independence of the jury. It was only in 1979 that the

Pritzker family of Chicago through the Hyatt Foundation established the prize. Though relatively young as prizes go, its impact has been enormous and significant. Its stated purpose is "to honor a living architect whose built work demonstrates a combination of those qualities of talent, vision, and commitment, which has produced consistent and significant contributions to humanity and the built environment through the art of architecture." The prize is not given for a specific built work, but rather for what is considered to be the accumulated excellence of a career. From the first laureate, Philip Johnson, in 1979, to Kazuyo Sejima and Ryue Nishizawa, the 2010 laureates, the arc of architectural accomplishment is both impressive and potent.

In focusing on what architects have to say about their work, we chose to present the Pritkzer Prize laureates because they not only provide an extraordinary and wide-ranging international selection of contemporary architecture of the past three decades, but also because many of them, at least in name, are familiar to a broad audience. Their prominence extends well beyond more cloistered architecture circles. A list of major landmarks impresses in scope and place, including I.M. Pei's glass pyramid for the Louvre in Paris, Norman Foster's profound response to the historically loaded Reichstag in Berlin, Jørn Utzon's melodic Sydney Opera House, Herzog & de Meuron's triumphant Beijing National Stadium, Tange's deeply respectful Hiroshima Peace Memorial Museum, Kevin Roche's long-lasting affiliation with New York's Metropolitan Museum of Art. The list goes on and on. The differences in the architects' approaches, interests, and locations are great, but the connective tissue is that each is a strong individual with well-honed philosophies, intensely focused in the practice of architecture. In the work of these laureates we see reflected the trajectory of changing tastes over time.

As we began our research, one of our early questions was, Does an architect follow through—is there a connection from an architect's ideas to the execution of those ideas? In other words, does an architect walk the talk? Although it's often said that a work speaks volumes, we turned the tables and asked, But how about the words themselves? What do they tell us?

*Architect* is organized chronologically, taking as its starting point today, 2010, and retracing the laureates back to the debut of the Pritzker Prize in 1979 of that outspoken sophisticate, Philip Johnson ("I don't think ideology has anything to do with architecture. . . . You see, I have no convictions, but do have taste.") Each chapter features approximately four to six major built works that are both awe-inspiring and important in defining each architect's body of work, as well as their contributions to the field. The projects were carefully chosen to demonstrate the depth and richness of repertoire, for in sum they profile the diversity of our lives, our interests, and our needs: schools, places of worship, shops, airports, museums, courthouses, stadiums and sports arenas, corporate headquarters, residences, embassies, memorials, spas, libraries, hotels, banks, and cemeteries. But in this book we look at the built work with the architects themselves talking in our ear, leading us into the privileged and often private terrain of their own thoughts, gathered from a variety of sources including interviews, lectures, and writings. As the title of this book makes clear, this is the Pritzker Prize laureates "in their own words."

They had plenty to say on a number of topics, beginning with the most important issues over the past three decades, including materiality, regionalism, and sustainability. Indeed, one of the most urgent issues of our time is the practice of ecological architecture and the use of sustainable technologies. Glenn Murcutt (2002), Richard Rogers (2007), and Norman Foster (1999) are leaders in incorporating sustainable technologies at the core of their architecture, setting new standards for practicing architects as well as for society. Murcutt, for example, is both a leader and teacher in ecological architecture, pioneering such concepts as, "climate-responsive architecture," as well as showing us that sustainable practices need not be overly technical, but that in fact, ethics, as well as ordinary and simple things, are very much part of this approach.

As our research continued, there were many surprises too. The importance of the cinema as a lens through which to view the human condition influences Aldo Rossi (1990), Herzog & de Meuron (2001), and Christian de Portzamparc (1994). As Jean Nouvel (2009) observes, "there are a lot of crossovers between the two disciplines." A number of the laureates have express opinions about the pros and cons of generating a design using the computer or other digital technology and architectural software, including AutoCAD, as well as three-dimensional modeling tools like Rhino, 3D Studio Max, and Maya. (Hadid, yes; Utzon, never; Gehry, grudgingly.) From architects like de Portzamparc and the late James Stirling (1981), we learn that architecture does not exist in isolation—that it is instead vitally informed by its context, be it urban or natural. Cities and nature are dramatis personae to be reckoned with (clients, too, but less glowingly). Aldo Rossi writes, "A knowledge of the city enables us not only to understand architecture, but also, as architects, to design it." Kevin Roche and Fumihiko Maki (1993) each intone the value of public service and the greater good, for as James Stirling once said of the architect, "it is his unique responsibility to raise the human spirit by the quality of the environment which he creates, whether in a room, a building, or a town." Personalities emerge in delightfully unexpected ways, most notably Gordon Bunshaft (1988), who was famously reticent on the topic of his architectural process and theories, having once said flatly, "I like my architecture to speak for me." Contrast this with the eighty-year-old Bunshaft who told his interviewer, Betty Blum, "I'm old. And I can reminisce for the next ten years." On the Beineke Rare Book & Manuscript Library at Yale University, Bunshaft recalled, "I've had ladies write me about the Beinecke saying that they just shivered when they saw it." As for the pitfall of becoming or being labeled a starchitect, Mayne is unambiguous on the subject.

Another frequent topic among the architects was their indebtedness to the modern masters. Tadao Ando (1995), Kenzo Tange (1987), and Sverre Fehn (1997), to name a few, reference the significant influence of Swiss architect Le Corbusier (1887–1965). German architect Ludwig Mies van der Rohe (1886–1969) was another influential figure. So too were Louis Kahn (1901–1974) and Walter Gropius (1883–1969). Among the laureates, Jørn Utzon (2003) is frequently upheld as an example of an architect wronged by local politics, but whose vision for the Sydney Opera House is one of the great architectural designs of the modern age.

Among these architects, you will find tastemakers, manifesto-writers, and intellectuals. They are the kinds of particularly influential architects who devote their energies to academia and cultural institutions as well as to building architecture. Rem Koolhaas (2000), Rafael Moneo (1996), Robert Venturi (1991), Aldo Rossi, and James Stirling are architect-theorists who, through their architecture, writings, and teaching have influenced many generations of young architects. As Thom Mayne has remarked, he hopes to engage "virtual territory—that is, the territory of the mind of the student."

A significant change since 2000 is that women have won the Pritzker Prize. In 2004, Zaha Hadid became the first woman named a laureate and in 2010, Kazuyo Sejima, with her male partner as SANAA, also won the prize. While there are many women architects practicing today in the traditionally male-dominated profession of architecture, the percentage that lead their own firms is still surprisingly small. As Sejima says, "There is an image that it is only men who make big projects, but I think that's just because there weren't many women in architecture in the past. Hadid, characteristically, is more forthright: "If I was a man, they wouldn't call me a diva."

And where does Architecture intersect with Art? Many architects, including Renzo Piano (1998), believe that while architecture is a kind of art, its material, structural, and functional aspects make it unique. By contrast, Philip Johnson sees it as a no-contest debate: "Architecture is art, nothing else."

Regarding the prosaic matters of editing and such, we kept changes to a minimum throughout, preferring to preserve natural cadence and syntax, hoping that in this regard readers can most directly experience any of the architects in their glorious diversity. For matters of internal consistency, we Americanized spelling and punctuation, and corrected obvious errors when necessary.

As the editors of this massive body of work, we have brought together two satisfyingly divergent views of architecture. We like to think that together we represent a broad audience of interested readers: Ruth Peltason is an editor and writer, with years of experience editing art and illustrated books, among them *100 Contemporary Architects* by Bill Lacy, former executive director of the Pritkzer Prize. Grace Ong Yan, Ph.D., is an architectural historian, educator, and architect who specializes in modern and contemporary architecture.

Despite our different skills and interests, we have each been moved and enriched by the experience of compiling this publication. Each of the architects, through their own words, has given us a greater appreciations of their work. Our hope is that *Architect* offers interested readers fresh meaning and ideas, and serves both to elevate *and* humanize the process of making great architecture.

Ruth Peltason
Grace Ong Yan, Ph.D.
May 2010

**ORIGINS** We believe that well-harmonized architecture means having a good understanding of the environment around it. Because although we are passionate about globality, we want our architecture to sink its roots deeply into its specific location. We often say it is good to have roots and wings. _ R. A., C. P., R. V., courtesy RCR Arquitectes

We all have "our origins," which remain constant within us, even when we move from one place to another. We are the result of a place, a climate, a culture. Distances in the world are becoming smaller and smaller, but we believe it is essential to understand and respect these origins, which ought to strengthen a shared creativity in which everyone should feel represented. _ A + U: Architecture and Urbanism 542, Special Issue, November 2015

# RAFAEL ARANDA, CARME PIGEM, RAMON VILALTA

**BORN:** Rafael Aranda, May 12, 1961, Olot, Girona, Spain; Carme Pigem, April 18, 1962, Olot, Girona, Spain; Ramon Vilalta, April 25, 1960, Vic, Barcelona, Spain

**EDUCATION:** (All three laureates) Diploma, School of Architecture, Vallès (Escola Tècnica Superior d'Arquitectura del Vallès, or ETSAV), Sant Cugat del Vallès (Barcelona) Spain, 1987

**OFFICE:** RCR Aranda Pigem Vilalta Arquitectes, C. Fontanella, 26, 17800, Olot, Girona, Spain Tel: +34 972 269 105, www.rcrarquitectes.es

**PROJECTS FEATURED:** Soulages Museum, Rodez, France, 2014; Les Cols Restaurant Marquee, Olot, Girona, Spain, 2011; Barberí Laboratory, Olot, Girona, Spain, 2008; Bell-Lloc Winery, Palamós, Girona, Spain, 2007; Tossols-Basil Athletic Track, Olot, Spain, 2000

**"WE SHALL BUILD MORE TEMPORARY, WASTE LESS POWER, AND ABANDON THE IDEA OF ACCUMULATION."**

**Bell-Lloc Winery, Palamós, Spain, 2007**
The interior of the winery, looking toward the tasting room. The slats not only allow air and light to enter the winery but also generate a variety of shadows throughout the day.

## COLLABORATION

*Aranda, Pigem, and Vilalta are distinctive for the intense and enduring collaborative nature of their work together. They are, de facto, architects with one voice.*

 **WE HAVE CREATED TOGETHER SOMETHING SPECIAL.**

When we graduated, we decided to share the experience of entering the real world, and we're still at it. So we started just like that. None of us three have ever worked in any other office, and we've grown together, talked a lot, done in-depth research into the issues we are interested in, travelled, all of which has facilitated our mutual understanding. _ *A + U: Architecture and Urbanism* 542, Special Issue, November 2015

Ideas arise from dialogue and conversation by more than one person. We have believed in dialogue. In a way it's like spoken jazz. One says something, another one continues. This type of conversation takes you to unexpected places. It's almost a reaction against the contemporary world that has promoted, in an exaggerated way, the value of the individual. We have always appreciated this idea of sharing. _ R. A., C. P., R. V., video, Pritzker Architecture Prize, 2017

To share this journey is to talk, to feel relieved, not indispensable, to be enriched in a collective way, to perceive the presence of the whole and acknowledge its relevance, to put aside individual reason and push shared creativity into levels of excellence where individuality cannot arrive. _ R. A., C. P., R. V., courtesy RCR Arquitectes

To quote the Spanish philosopher J. A. Marina, we like to say that "shared creativity" is something that lets a group of not necessarily extraordinary people produce extraordinary results. _ *A + U: Architecture and Urbanism* 542, Special Issue, November 2015

First thing in the morning, there's a brief exchange between us three. Then with our staff, meetings or site inspections. We share our discussions on every project, regardless of the scale. If we have disagreements, we reiterate our conversations and our trials to get a better idea, even if it requires more time and it's a common idea. _ *A + U: Architecture and Urbanism* 542, Special Issue, November 2015

Our collaboration was always easy and flowing. We've always talked a lot. Little by little we've learned to communicate simply with a look. At first it was a slow process, but with time, now we are working together for forty years. We are able to communicate with many parts of our bodies. _ R. A., C. P., R. V., video, Pritzker Architecture Prize, 2017

When we begin a project, we are very interested in visiting the place. . . . We are used to reading the place as if it spoke to us with its own alphabet, an alphabet established between the site and us. . . . We like to think about the program, the needs that we can detect. This is the beginning for us. We don't like to start with a typology or assumptions. We ask, "What is this?" Building in places far from home encourages us to understand those places. We are passionate about this. We do not want to do the same that we do at home and just transplant it. Rather, the way we understand space and spatial relationships is a search to arrive at the essential of each different place. This what drives us. _ R. A., C. P., R. V., video, Pritzker Architecture Prize, 2017

## SELECTIONS

*In a special issue of* El Croquis, *the architects were posed eighty-four "exam" questions, to which they replied with sincerity and wit. The following are excerpts.*

Test for an Architecture Exam

1. Architecture is a very long word. Can it be abbreviated?
The art of materializing dreams on a long journey.

2. Do architects construct architecture?
Not always; sometimes we destroy it.

3. What do you learn from?
From our senses, and from an intense, selective gaze.

4. Who do you learn from?
From anybody who has allowed a work to speak for itself.

28. Is new good?
No, but neither is old.

33. Is silence music?
Definitely!

36. Digital world: instrument or matter?
We use the instrument and we investigate matter.

82. Is 3 better than 1?
Undoubtedly.
_ *El Croquis* 115/116 (III), 2003

## OLOT

In 1988, most recent graduates tended to stay in the capital, Barcelona, and work in a prestigious office at a time when most architects in

Catalonia wanted to be part of a project for the 1992 Barcelona Olympic Games. But we took a very natural initiative and decided to return to experience and work with the architecture of our homeland, where all our families resided, Olot. _ *A + U: Architecture and Urbanism* 542, Special Issue, November 2015

Just a short stroll takes you into the heart of the landscape, the forest, the river. Your experiences are very different here from in a big city, because knowing something about nature isn't the same as experiencing it directly. And that difference is present in our daily lives and in the way we regard architecture. _ *A + U: Architecture and Urbanism* 542, Special Issue, November 2015

 **IDEAS ARISE FROM DIALOGUE AND CONVERSATION BY MORE THAN ONE PERSON. WE HAVE BELIEVED IN DIALOGUE. IN A WAY IT'S LIKE SPOKEN JAZZ. ONE SAYS SOMETHING, ANOTHER ONE CONTINUES.**

### OLOT, GIRONA 2008
# BARBERÍ LABORATORY
We were captivated by "Espai Barberí" when we visited it ten years before. So in 2008, we moved to this old foundry, and now we have already been here for 7! It's an old complex with references dating back to 1550. It was always the Barberí art foundry, where bronze church bells, pots and artists' sculptures were cast. It's so easy to feel the power of fire, earth, water, air, light, time, and nature in this space. Although we are in the town center, this is a breathing space for us, a world of silence, a microcosm. _ *A + U: Architecture and Urbanism* 542, Special Issue, November 2015

The shared workspace, a feature of the collaborative environment of Barberí Laboratory, is actually a large library table around which the three principals discuss projects.

## ❝❝ A PLACE TO PERFORM ACTS OF MAGIC, WHICH ULTIMATELY IS TO BRING IMAGINATION TO REALITY. ❞❞

The original Barberí foundry, which dates to the beginning of the 20th century, inspired the present iteration. The original wood, stone, and ceramic materials contrast with the added steel and glass, creating the light, open environment. Glass-enclosed pavilions also function to bring nature into the work space.

Basically there are three zones. The first zone, which we call the "Workshop," is a space that all three of us share alongside another one, which is the space for our staff and management. All the zones are connected visually and spatially to facilitate communication. The second zone is the "Hall of Dreams," which is a pavilion with a garden. Here you can sense nature, internally as well as externally. You enjoy a great sense of peace and tranquility. The garden is for contemplation, with the spontaneous vegetation that has grown here on the basis of ferns and a plantation of beech trees, which are local native species. It's a place to dream

and think, a place to perform magic tricks, which essentially involves the power to turn imagination into reality. It's a place for corrections, big meetings and analytical work. The third area is the main pavilion, which is linked to a cultural and creative project. It's a large multipurpose space for events, presentations, screenings, exhibitions, conferences, and so on, with the idea of opening it up to the public. _ *A + U: Architecture and Urbanism* 542, Special Issue, November 2015

**Work Environment**  We have a core of 12 people. Some are locals, and others have settled here from other countries, France, Portugal etc. There's a sense of trust. _ *A + U: Architecture and Urbanism* 542, Special Issue, November 2015

The old, long-awaited Barberí foundry has smoke-laden walls, ceilings and floors from quenched fires, with bronze, a mineral pre-existence in the garden, together with the smells, the colors, and the furnace chimneys. Earth and fire are present, along with the increasingly ethereal air, gaining ground. _ R. A., C. P., R. V., courtesy RCR Arquitectes

Our world is established here, putting down roots and raising minds. Trees and ferns in the garden. Independent supplies. Letting the atmosphere surround us and adding our mark to the history of this space that has forged so many sculptures. Quietly getting on with our work. _ R. A., C. P., R. V., courtesy RCR Arquitectes

## MATERIALS

In our architecture, we try to select a few materials in order not to disturb the space with materials. It's trying, with one material, very different subtle changes, but with only this one material to make the space appear in a very pure way. _ R. A., C. P., R. V., video, Pritzker Architecture Prize, 2017

> **SPACE IS BEST EXPRESSED WITH THE EXPLORATION OF ALL THE DIFFERENT REGISTERS OF A SINGLE MATERIAL.**

Whenever possible, we try to select natural materials. We speak honestly about materials. We are also very interested in using few materials. Ones that are authentic. We have believed in trying to do the maximum using the minimum. By using just one material, we hope to be able to create an atmosphere. And this is positive for us. Therefore, within this uniformity of materials, but with different and subtle changes, we believe that it creates a framework for space, that allows the space to emerge with greater strength. _ R. A., C. P., R. V., video, Pritzker Architecture Prize, 2017

## NATURE

For us, landscape is more than green. It's also the sky, the trees, the atmosphere, it's a place that we want to be in relation with. _ R. A., C. P., R. V., video, Pritzker Architecture Prize, 2017

We believe that nature will be fundamental to the needs of the contemporary man and woman, along with the elements—air, fire, water, and earth—which will become basic for working on a new architecture. They will take the place of—or at least regain the same value as—concrete, glass, steel, and so on. _ R. A., C. P., R. V., courtesy RCR Arquitectes

We like to speak of creating "atmospheres." We have always tried to create architecture that makes people "feel" it, to evoke feelings and transmit a sensation of well being and beauty. We like to speak of beauty. We believe in this—architecture that conveys beauty. . . . We have learned a lot from nature, even from an early age. Our relation with it is frank, direct. It's difficult to explain, but it has instilled in us many of the values that we have tried to apply to our architecture and to our lives. _ R. A., C. P., R. V., video, Pritzker Architecture Prize, 2017

From the outset we have always believed in the value of a good relationship with the landscape. Now we understand that it is not only a question of creating a good relationship with the environment, but also of creating symbiosis, in other words, of establishing as deep a relationship as possible and also emotional, transcendental experi-

ences. It is no longer just a relationship with the nearby context and landscape, but also with the universe. _ A + U: Architecture and Urbanism 542, November 2015

## JAPAN

Since their first visit to Japan in 1990, the architects have traveled there four times, each stay deepening their regard for the country.

This serene time that one experiences in Japan has certainly left a mark on our lives, which is definitely present in our architecture. _ A + U: Architecture and Urbanism 542, Special Issue, November 2015

If we are talking about traditional Japanese architecture, we are fascinated by its connection to nature, which is the result of a profound refinement over the decades. The relationship between interior and exterior is ambiguous and soft; it is a whole, and it gives the impression that nature and architecture interact with each other. We are moved by the perfection of its solutions, its capacity and its wisdom. _ A + U: Architecture and Urbanism: 542, Special Issue, November 2015

> **HUMILITY AND FRAILTY SHOULD ALWAYS BE PRESENT ON OUR EPHEMERAL PATH ON THIS EARTH.**

[Japan] is a society whose people know that the collective still has priority over the individual. This translates into a deep sensitivity and respect for people and nature. You have a sense of perfection and beauty, effort and commitment that shines out in every corner, in a rich, lush landscape. _ A + U: Architecture and Urbanism 542, Special Issue, November 2015

## LOCAL / GLOBAL

Distances in the world are becoming smaller and smaller, but we believe it is essential to understand and respect these origins . . . . _ R.A., C.P., R. V., courtesy RCR Arquitectes

In this ever-changing life, we want to keep looking for an architecture that is more in keeping with our time. Maybe that's more possible now, with a broader, more humanistic vision, not only through art but also through science and humanities. _ R. A., C. P., R. V., courtesy RCR Arquitectes

[Global problems involve] understanding the common problems that have to be addressed specifically. Understanding that globality is on a common level of discussion and complexity, but that the particularities and specificities are a global value which requires specific solutions. _ A + U: Architecture and Urbanism: 542, November 2015

## PALAMÓS, GIRONA 2007
# BELL-LLOC WINERY The Approach

To build a warehouse for the private production and consumption of wine in a unique setting; the start of a valley at the foot of the mountain of a protected space, is the engine of the project. _ "Bell-Lloc Winery/RCR Arquitectes," *Arch Daily*, August 13, 2014

The approach is fluid: we follow a path which descends from place to place in the border between the vineyard and the woods, and are drawn along by it. _ R. A., C. P., R. V., courtesy RCR Arquitectes

This is not a single site but a promenade for discovering different spaces whose undulating route, in plan and section, becomes their dimension. _ "Bell-Lloc Winery/RCR Arquitectes," *Arch Daily*, August 13, 2014

Cellars for private wine production and tasting are located between the vineyards and the woods, and designed in such a way that part of it is under-

ground, thus creating a union where landscape and buildings become one. A promenade is defined by tilted recycled steel sheets with slits between them to allow natural light to penetrate. Visitors descend into the underground world of wine where there are large recycled steel vats, suspended barrels, and bottles in racks. There is also a chapel at the foot of the slope and a small auditorium. _ R. A., C. P., R. V., courtesy RCR Arquitectes

**The Senses** This is an experience for all the senses. The silence can be "heard," the aroma of the wine can be perceived, the strength of the materials and the changes in temperature can be felt, the minimal light and shadows are experienced. Finally, there

> **ARCHITECTURE IS OFFERING SOMEONE AN EXPERIENCE OF BEAUTY AND EMOTION.**

is the tasting of the wines. The winery's unusual appearance is the result of its spatial geometry and the materials—recycled steel and stone—which embraces visitors and carries them to a concealed world where they can feel and taste a different time. _ R. A., C. P., R. V., courtesy RCR Arquitectes

Matter dissolves, thanks to the light which bathes the void of this wine-tasting room; the atmosphere changes, although the actual limits remain the same. The boundaries of the space dissolve into shadows. _ R. A., C. P., R. V., courtesy RCR Arquitectes

The mind is unaware of the boundaries and levels but the body has discovered hidden and unexpected spaces by following this path: a refuge which only the curious and the intrepid know how to find for themselves. _ R. A., C. P., R. V., courtesy RCR Arquitectes

**Material Resolution and Repose** This excavated environment is used to avoid energy consumption. _ "Bell-Lloc Winery/RCR Arquitectes," *Arch Daily*, August 13, 2014

One mineral, iron, supports another material, stones and earth, with its strength. _ R. A., C. P., R. V., courtesy RCR Arquitectes

The entry is . . . by means of a recessed piece which slides: the threshold to a dark, underground world of oblique angles perceived gradually as the eye adjusts and the pupil opens. In turn we begin to sense the weight of earth and rock which envelopes us, leaning and bending, upwards and downwards, left and right. The space dug out by hand is tilted and curved. . . . In contrast to this obliqueness, a larger space reveals itself. Here human skills resist the surrounding pressure by making the walls lean, thus creating a sense of resolution and repose. _ R. A., C. P., R. V., courtesy RCR Arquitectes

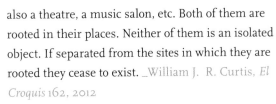

Both projects [Bell-Lloc and Marquee] have this is common. They are both about landscape and both have ambiguous identities. At Bell-Lloc there is ambiguity of use. It is a bodega (a winery) but it is also a theatre, a music salon, etc. Both of them are rooted in their places. Neither of them is an isolated object. If separated from the sites in which they are rooted they cease to exist. _William J. R. Curtis, *El Croquis* 162, 2012

*Opposite:* **From the forest, the valley extends toward the sea. The vineyards cover the cellar and the folded roof protects the laboratory and the walkways. The concept is that of a promenade from the outdoors into an underworld of winemaking. Half-light marks the pathways along the interior; even the tasting room, farther in, receives light, air, and rain from the surrounding area.**

**▌▌ LIVING A CELEBRATION. A GATHERING FOR AN EVENT WHICH EVOKES TIME, OUTDOOR LIVING, THE CULINARY ARTS, ESSENTIALITY, AND THE FUTURE. ▐▐**

### OLOT, GIRONA 2011
# LES COLS RESTAURANT MARQUEE

In all of our projects, the relationship between the interior and the exterior is a key component. Bringing the outside inside is a recurrent obsession. . . . The pavilions which we constructed a few years ago for the restaurant Les Cols were all about the weaving together of interior and exterior spaces. The program for the marquee at Les Cols was all about the people passing through. We wanted people to have a sense of the exterior, for it to be a part of their experience. We wanted to create a space which could not exist inside a building; a place where people could sense the changing time of the day and weather, how rain or light vary minute to minute. We wished to develop a relationship between life and nature. That is what we were looking for. _ William J. R. Curtis, *El Croquis* 162, 2012

With our architecture it is not a question of establishing limits with walls, but by other means. Yes, certainly the marquee pulls together themes of

many earlier works. One of these concerns the ambiguity of limits. Another concerns the ambiguity of definitions. One is not sure if this is an architectural project, a landscape project, a "natural" project, or an "ecological" project. There is ambiguity as well in the experience of its dimensions and its uses. It can serve many purposes. It was built for one function but it is sufficiently ambiguous that it can serve many others. _ William J. R. Curtis, *El Croquis* 162, 2012

Moreover this ambiguity comes out of a particular attitude to materiality, as is the case in many of our projects. We are interested in dematerialization but also in the directness of materials. The steel is steel without any painting. The structure creates optical vibrations. The concrete is very much concrete. . . . This project, the marquee, is both material and immaterial. _ William J. R. Curtis, *El Croquis* 162, 2012

In the case of our marquee, the human figure activates the entire space. With the Villa Mairea [Aalto, 1939] we had the impression of an architecture which can exist without people. In our scheme this

is not the case. People are needed to bring it alive.
_ William J. R. Curtis, *El Croquis* 162, 2012

Evocation of essentiality. The removed stone is
returned in the form of walls, embankments,
and pavements. Steel pipes hold up and shape the
marquee, while the dense, transparent membrane
provides shelter from the sun and the rain. _ R. A.,
C. P., R. V., in *El Croquis* 162, 2012

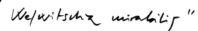

## SKETCHES

Here we present the sketch, one of the techniques
among many that we use, and that has allowed us
over the years to present the force of a concept in a
concise and inviting way. This concept can be at different scales and at different stages of the project. Its
technique is watercolor. Where a brush, now thick,
now thin, with black ink, or perhaps with colors,
usually on a pencil drawing, led by a strong hand,
allows with the freshness of the technique and the
solidity of the marks and strokes, the translation of
endless suggestions: ultimately, a drawn calligraphy
that communicates the project. _ R. A., C. P., R. V.,
courtesy RCR Arquitectes

In our opinion, there is no better way to express the
crystallization of an initial idea than through ink-
wash sketching. We think that it is a wonderful tool,
well-suited to the process of materialization. _ R. A.,
C. P., R. V., courtesy RCR Arquitectes

Sketching is fundamental to establishing common
criteria for both ourselves and the shared growth of
the project. Sketching is both intuitive and suggestive; nothing is off limits; it is not a particularly intellectual form of representation. It is a way to begin the
journey from darkness into light, it is an unspecific
specification, it is incipient, it symbolizes an opening,
growth. _ R. A., C. P., R. V., courtesy RCR Arquitectes

> ❝ A SPACE DOESN'T HAVE TO BE ACTIVATED BY FURNITURE OR OBJECTS. THE PRESENCE OF A PERSON IS WHAT SHOULD ACTIVATE A SPACE AND GIVE IT MEANING. ❞

The inspiration was both simple and noble: the first Olympic games in Greece. The track and overall outdoor facility provides the athlete as natural a setting as possible while also preserving the landscape.
Soulages, *opposite,* was designed only with Cor-Ten steel, which over time will change. The decision was in response to the concept of a building to house art. "Museum and landscape thus have a mutual feedback, like the painter and his work."

### OLOT, GIRONA 2000
# TOSSOLS-BASIL ATHLETIC TRACK
New architecture does not have to impose itself on the landscape: it has to coexist in it and make the most of all its beauty. The new landscape must once again become the landscape. Any runner can enjoy it. _ R. A., C. P., R. V., from the exhibition "RCR Arquitectes Creativitat Compartida," February 2015

The stadium, located in natural surroundings, enhances the existing landscape and brings track and field competitions closer to nature.

The facility stands in an oak forest clearing and establishes a relationship of both proximity and distance with its immediate woodland environment, the seating arrangement for spectators enhancing this relationship by adopting the form of small-scale tiers or slopes between clearings.

We conceived the Tossols-Basil area, at the border between the city and the park along the river, as a lei-sure and sports area, an architectural response to the natural park/artificial city dichotomy. At the time of writing we have built a section of the path, the swimming pavilion, the 2 x 1 pavilion, and an athletics track.

The site, in fact, consists of two clearings in the oak forest separated by a volcanic outflow, and serious problems had to be solved when it came to siting the athletics track, due to its large dimensions. We therefore decided to openly reconsider the track as a place where athletes may run, as in ancient times, in entirely natural surroundings.

The track is clearly visible in the clearing. The project aroused protest from athletes on the one hand and from ecologists on the other, since the former objected to there being trees in the way and the latter demanded that no trees be felled.

The trees in-between act as filters that change according to the seasons, ranging from opaque through translucent to semi-transparent. There is something else in the distance: beyond our intuition the clearing, a former cultivated field, opens out as a positive space that breaks through its own boundaries.

The lights, like watchtowers, emerge observantly from among the dense clusters of tree trunks; the tiered seating adapts to the slope to serve the spectators. _ miesarch.com/work/2496

## RODEZ 2014
# SOULAGES MUSEUM [To design] a
museum for Soulages, the French painter of "light"
who has inspired us so often was—and still is—a
cherished dream. In the town of his birth, Soulages
can be seen for what he is: his approach, his attitude, and his involvement. _ Dan Howarth, *Dezeen*,
March 13, 2017

Museum and landscape thus have a mutual feedback, merging into one, like the painter and his
work, displaying a wealth of relationships where
nothing can be removed, because everything that
belongs to this new created world is inherent. Work,
museum and landscape: Soulages and Rodez.
_ R. A., C. P., R. V., courtesy RCR Arquitectes

We wanted to find a site that interfered as little as
possible with the park, and to relate the project to
the circulation around it. _ David Cohn, *Architectural
Record*, August 16, 2014

## "ROOTED ARCHITECTURE"

It is essential to understand that architecture is not an object, not a
hermetic unit superimposed into a location; it is rather a system of spatial relations, and with this we mean the whole: the constructed form,
the landscape, the location, the people, and the architectural brief.
They all merge together in order to create a rooted architecture, an
architecture that is a landscape. _ The University of Western Australia,
online news, March 15, 2017

## THE FREEDOM OF UNCERTAINTY

The unknown is the realm of all possibilities. Without uncertainty, risk,
and the unknown, life is repetition, and without change, life is dead.
The known is the past, and the past is dead. Uncertainty is the path
that leads to freedom. And security can be found by understanding
uncertainty. _ R. A., C. P., R. V., courtesy RCR Arquitectes

Innovation will only be possible if it is present in the very first stage
where necessity becomes a question that requires an answer, and if

it is referred to by all participants in its response. _ The University of
Western Australia, online news, March 15, 2017

## THE FUTURE

We believe it is extremely important to try to understand the world
around us and see ourselves as part of that world; to understand the
key aspects of the basic dynamics of nature, to continue and live in
the best possible way with the natural order. _ A + U: Architecture and
Urbanism 542, November 2015

Perhaps the main goal could be to stop regarding architecture as a
creator of unique, independent objects that are finished and enclosed
on themselves . . . In other words, not only as a visual thing but also as
something that aims to stimulate a total reaction with the human body,
where the material—the tactile—regains value while at the same time,
the immaterial—silence—is perceived as well. _ A + U: Architecture
and Urbanism 542, November 2015

**LIVING CONDITIONS** Architects like to build things that are unique. But if something is unique it can't be repeated, so in terms of it serving many people in many places, the value is close to zero. _ Michael Kimmelman, *T: The New York Times Style Magazine*, May 23, 2016

Here in Chile, we are faced with very concrete issues and that's why I am very critical of arbitrary gestures in architecture. . . . I am doing architecture for a reason. I want to build projects better than they were done before. Not just different, but better. Better, meaning not just as far as design, but better in terms of the living conditions. _ Vladimir Belogolovsky, *Conversations with Architects: In the Age of Celebrity*, Berlin: DOM Publishing, 2015

# ALEJANDRO ARAVENA

**BORN:** June 22, 1967, Santiago, Chile

**EDUCATION:** Catholic University of Chile, Santiago, Chile, 1991; History and Theory, IUAV, Venice, Italy, 1992–93; Engraving, Academy of Fine Arts in Venice, Venice, Italy, 1992–93

**OFFICE:** Elemental, Av. Los Conquistadores 1700, Piso 29 A, 7520282 Providencia, Santiago, Chile
Tel: +56 229-637-500, info@elementalchile.cl
www.elementalchile.cl/en

**PROJECTS FEATURED:** UC Innovation Center—Anacleto Angelini, San Joaquín Campus, Universidad Católica de Chile, Santiago, Chile, 2014; Villa Verde Housing, Constitución, Chile, 2013; St. Edward's University Dorms, Austin, Texas, 2008; Siamese Towers, Santiago, Chile, 2005; Quinta Monroy Housing, Iquique, Chile, 2004

"WE DON'T THINK OF OURSELVES AS ARTISTS."

**UC Innovation Center, Santiago, 2014**
In order to avoid what Aravena described as the greenhouse effect of using a glass skin, he chose instead a thermal mass on the perimeter to accommodate the heat in Santiago.

## ELEMENTAL

I said, "We want to build, not just to discuss"; that's why we call Elemental a "do-tank," and one of the conditions was to accept the policy as it was. _ Ken Tadashi Oshima interview with Alejandro Aravena in Alejandro Aravena, *Alejandro Aravena: The Forces in Architecture*, Tokyo: Toto Publishing, 2011

We're a small enough office to still be able to work on the projects we want. What I want to do is make a contribution by having a pen in my hand and drawing things. I don't want to spend my day as an administrator. The kind of office that we have is small enough that I can still be involved in each project that we take care of. Yet we have to be big enough to address complex projects, like the reconstruction of our entire city, Santiago, after an earthquake. _ Alejandro Aravena interview by Rocky Casale, *Surface*, July 13, 2016

The way we comment on reality is not by writing a letter to a newspaper, but by doing a project. My way of improving the reality is by building. _ Vladimir Belogolovsky, *Conversations with Architects: In the Age of Celebrity*, Berlin: DOM Publishing, 2015

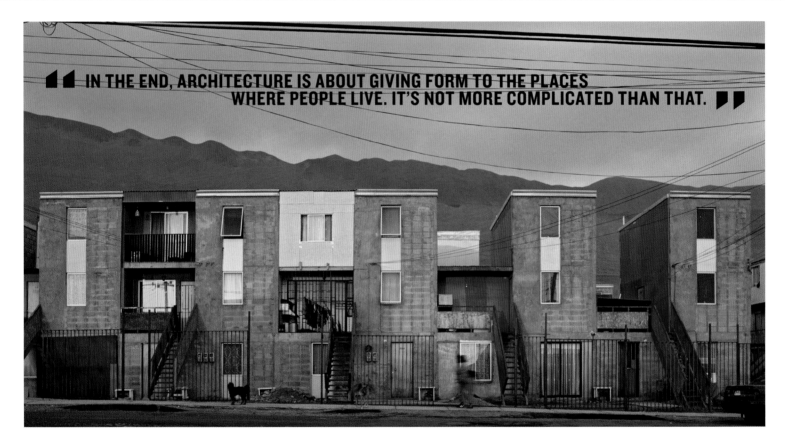

**IN THE END, ARCHITECTURE IS ABOUT GIVING FORM TO THE PLACES WHERE PEOPLE LIVE. IT'S NOT MORE COMPLICATED THAN THAT.**

### IQUIQUE 2004
# QUINTA MONROY HOUSING

I want to make it clear that we are far from being housing experts, and we were even less knowledgeable when we started the Quinta Monroy development in Chile. _ Matthew Roman and Tal Schori, eds., *Perspecta 42*, 2010

$$X = \frac{150 \text{ familias} \times 30 \text{m}^2 \times US\$7.500}{1 \text{ ha}}$$

**Arriving at the Question** *Aravena met Andres Iacobelli, a transportation engineer, while at Harvard University in 2000. They subsequently founded Elemental and began addressing subsidized housing.*

I would say that when this firm Elemental initially started, we wanted to change the approach of design to social housing, which is always seen as something negative or what you have to do because you don't have enough means and enough resources. Somehow, an elementary project is something that you would like to do no matter how many resources you've got. So this capacity of filtering what is superfluous is a desirable thing, and we wanted to enter social housing not by complaining or dreaming what we cannot do, but by really appreciating the need of answering with what is strictly the case and going straight to the core, one shot and no chance for mistakes nor for two hits— just one. _ Ken Tadashi Oshima interview with Alejandro Aravena in Alejandro Aravena, *Alejandro Aravena: The Forces in Architecture*, Tokyo: Toto Publishing, 2011

Our ignorance forced us to be extremely rigorous. Not knowing about something makes you double-check everything and allows you, eventually, to ask seemingly stupid questions that might move a project forward. _ Matthew Roman and Tal Schori, eds., *Perspecta 42*, 2010

And the objective we came up with was this: do something that gains value over time. The design had to be used as a tool for people to overcome poverty. My job as an architect was to be able to translate these ideas into forms. _ Vladimir Belogolovsky, *Conversations with Architects: In the Age of Celebrity*, Berlin: DOM Publishing, 2015

**Incremental Housing** *Quinta Monroy was the first project in which Aravena introduced the concept of incremental housing.*

The challenge of our first project was to accommodate a hundred families using a subsidy of $7,500 dollars that in the best of the cases allowed for thirty-six square meters of built space in a 5,000 square meter site, which cost three times what social housing could normally afford. None of the solutions in the market solved the equation. So we thought of a typology that, as buildings, could make a very efficient use of land and as houses allowed for expansion. After a year, each property value was beyond $20,000 dollars. Still, all the families have preferred to stay and keep on improving their homes, instead of selling them. _ Alejandro Aravena, courtesy Elemental

If one proposes that the core of a housing project is to increase its value over time, the fact that it is an investment and not an expense should be seen as a major attribute which is what we propose in Elemental. _ Source unknown

**" IN PUBLIC POLICY, THE MORE ANCHORED YOU ARE IN THE SOCIETY, THE BETTER. . . . YOUR OUTCOME SHOULD BE AS REPLICABLE AND REPEATABLE AS POSSIBLE. "**

Instead of thinking of 40 square meters as a small house, why don't we consider it half of a good one? When you rephrase the problem as half of a good house, instead of a small one, the key question is, "Which half do you do?" And we thought that with public money we had to do the half of the house which families wouldn't be able to do individually. _ "My Architectural Philosophy? Bring the Community into the Process," lecture by Alejandro Aravena for TEDGlobal, Rio de Janeiro, October 9, 2014

We provide a full house and frame and enclose just half of it, leaving the other half for future growth. . . . This guarantees structural integrity as well as visual order and coherence. _ Vladimir Belogolovsky, *Conversations with Architects: In the Age of Celebrity*, Berlin: DOM Publishing, 2015

In fact, a tight budget is not the only factor that led us to providing half of a house; even with more money, we prefer to deliver more quality per square meter of construction than more square meters. _ Matthew Roman and Tal Schori, eds., *Perspecta 42*, 2010

**" WHAT IS MAINLY DONE IN CHILE IS HOUSING UNITS WITH EXTREMELY LIMITED RESOURCES. "**

The brief for this project was challenging, under the best of circumstances. But as a first project, it also permitted the young firm a certain creative freedom. The result was housing that engaged the residents and offered them equity in the outcome. Aravena's seemingly simple diagram, *opposite*, expresses the challenge.

## AUSTIN 2008
# ST. EDWARD'S UNIVERSITY DORMS

The real theme and challenge of this project was not architectural but personal. This is the first project I do outside Chile. And it happened to be not in another Latin-American country but in the United States, a country very different from Chile. _ Fabrizio Gallanti, ed., *Abitare* 495, September 2009

**"The Specificity of Matter"** *Aravena has long placed importance on meeting with those who will directly benefit from what he builds. In so doing, he eschews the insular confines of the architectural community.*

But there was also an underlying task. It had to do with the debate of how to determine the appropriate architectural language of the building in order to relate to the rest of the campus, particularly the old buildings.

This discussion took place mainly with and within the Board of Trustees, where none of them was an architect. I say this not to disqualify those other speakers, but to clarify that the discussion was held in a transversal and common (in the sense of shared and normal) way. It was not a disciplinary discussion of how to deal with history that could have happened among architects, a debate that would have been mainly ideological and based on abstract principles.

This one took place among citizens, so it became very concrete. Not better, nor worse: concrete. . . . It's not about the openings of the volume, but about the windows in the wall. It's not about how to crown an object, but about how the roof is going to appear or not. It's not about the quantity of lines necessary to define a solid, but about its decoration. _ Fabrizio Gallanti, ed., *Abitare* 495, September 2009

We tried to escape figurative languages: no pastiche or aping 90-year-old buildings, but no antiseptic "look-at-me-how-cool-I-am" boxes either. _ Fabrizio Gallanti, ed., *Abitare* 495, September 2009

We thought that a dorm is like a monastery: it's about how to organize a collection of repetitive small cells and how to relate them with larger special pieces. In the case of the monastery, it's about the monks' cells and how they relate with the refectory and chapel. Here it was about the rooms and the dining hall and common facilities. Both of them have to do with old atavist situations: sleeping, studying and eating. Or to put it in a more suggestive way: feeding the body and the soul and digesting. _ Fabrizio Gallanti, ed., *Abitare* 495, September 2009

We also created an articulated footprint, but instead of making it as a reaction to a geographic event, we

> ❝ I REALLY BELIEVE THAT IT IS CITIZENS TO WHOM WE SHOULD BE GIVING EXPLANATIONS, NOT OTHER ARCHITECTS. ❞

From Aravena: "To be able to resist a tough environment, we opted for a sequence of skins that are hard and rough in the outer layer and become softer and more delicate towards the core."

did it to increase the perimeter of the building so that every single room could have a view and natural light without having to compromise their intimacy. And we also wrapped the strip around a void, but instead of doing it to conform the special pieces, we made it in order to introduce and mediate outdoor space, adding one topological dimension to a campus that only had solids displayed on a field. Actually, we placed all the common rooms of the dorm's program facing this "Cartesian canyon," so that the entire project could be seen as an order of degrees, from public, to intermediate, to common, to private. _ Fabrizio Gallanti, ed., *Abitare* 495, September 2009

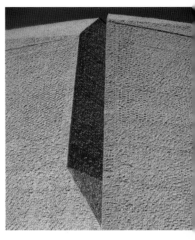

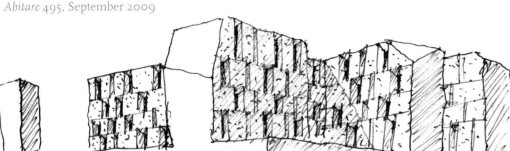

**❝ CHILEAN ARCHITECTURE IS A BIG SOURCE OF INSPIRATION FOR ME. ❞**

## EDUCATION UNDER A DICTATORSHIP

*Aravena brings clarity to becoming an architect under Pinochet.*

Maybe the only positive side of Pinochet was that the information control saved us from Post-Modernism. . . . Before that, it was very hard to know what was going on in the rest of the world. There were almost no architectural magazines available; there was almost even no access to Western music. . . . What we did have though were books. They were considered less dangerous than magazines. The only contemporary architecture we were looking at were Portuguese architects, such as Alvaro Siza or Souto de Moura. _ Vladimir Belogolovsky, *Conversations with Architects: In the Age of Celebrity*, Berlin: DOM Publishing, 2015

By default, we were left to find our own identity. Our professors were practitioners, not theorists, who taught how to get buildings built. It was, in retrospect, a very useful education. _ Michael Kimmelman, *T: The New York Times Style Magazine*, May 23, 2016

## POST-GRADUATE TRAVEL

I graduated in 1991 and the first thing I did I went to Italy, Greece, and Turkey on scholarship to visit ancient temples for the first time. You have to understand that at that time in Chile we only studied architecture through images. _ Vladimir Belogolovsky, *Conversations with Architects: In the Age of Celebrity*, Berlin: DOM Publishing, 2015

I feel I really began to study architecture when I moved to Venice in 1992. I was on a completely different planet there. I could go to a building for a week just to draw it. I spent a month drawing Doric temples in Sicily. I was measuring everything, absorbing all this history we didn't learn in Chile. I saw Romanesque buildings and Palladio's buildings and Alberti's and Brunelleschi's buildings, all of which finally made me realize what architecture could aspire to be. _ Michael Kimmelman, *T: The New York Times Style Magazine*, May 23, 2016

## CHILE

Chile is an interesting place. We are, in a way, an island nation because we have the Pacific Ocean on one side and the Andes Mountains on the other. We are quite far away and cut off from everyone else. So remoteness protects us from arbitrariness and trendiness. _ Vladimir Belogolovsky, *Conversations with Architects: In the Age of Celebrity*, Berlin: DOM Publishing, 2015

You wouldn't draw something more complex than what can be built. We have to get things built rather than speculate intellectually on the nature of architecture. _ Vladimir Belogolovsky, *Conversations with Architects: In the Age of Celebrity*, Berlin: DOM Publishing, 2015

We young architects [in Chile] did not have the weight of any architectural heritage on us. We were not afraid to innovate in the most radical way. _ Vladimir Belogolovsky, *Conversations with Architects: In the Age of Celebrity*, Berlin: DOM Publishing, 2015

A scarcity of means forces you to have an abundance of meaning. . . . You have to justify it and that somehow tempers projects in the global south. _ Alejandro Aravena interview by Rocky Casale, *Surface*, July 13, 2016

I'd say that the most interesting challenge—beyond making speed and quality compatible—is to export our experience in a field about which there is little know-how elsewhere in the world. If Chile is able to show what it is to do something well, with the quality befitting the architecture of developed countries and with few material resources, we will have made the most of the opportunity at hand. _ Antón García-Abril, *Arquitectura Viva*, January 2010

## THE CITY

The more elites in a certain place, the more chances there are of creating knowledge. For poor people, on the other hand, the city is a shortcut to equality. . . . As a result you have a city for rich and poor, who, more than ever, need one another. _ Juan Pablo Corvalán, Manuel de Rivero, and Francisco J. Quintana, *Archis 3*, 2009

What we have seen is that the city is a shortcut toward equality. You can, by identifying strategic projects in the city, improve the quality of life for people without having to wait for income redistribution. _ Samuel Medina and Avinash Rajagopal, *Metropolis 35*, April 2016

## DEGREES OF PERFECTION

I like being very precise and by that I don't mean everything has to be straight or aligned. Sometimes a project is missing life precisely because something is too perfect. Slight misalignments in someone's face can be more attractive than a perfect computer-generated face. _ Vladimir Belogolovsky, *Conversations with Architects: In the Age of Celebrity*, Berlin: DOM Publishing, 2015

In Chile to achieve perfection it is very expensive. . . . In the developed world, you're required to be perfect for many reasons. . . . Of course now we're practicing in different places, we're not necessarily trying to bring in what we're doing in Chile to other places. We just read the situations and try to understand. _ Ken Tadashi Oshima interview with Alejandro Aravena in Alejandro Aravena, *Alejandro Aravena: The Forces in Architecture*, Tokyo: Toto Publishing, 2011

Today many architects build around the globe as if it were a natural thing; for me it's not. I've had to design in English not in Spanish. I've had to learn to think in inches and feet instead of meters. I've had to transit from a culture of scarcity to a culture of abundance (where I want tightness, my clients may see meanness; where I want compression, users may see invasion). But mainly I had to go from the third world to the first one and lead a project there. This is not obvious for me at all and I still don't get used to it. _ Fabrizio Gallanti, ed., *Abitare 495*, September 2009

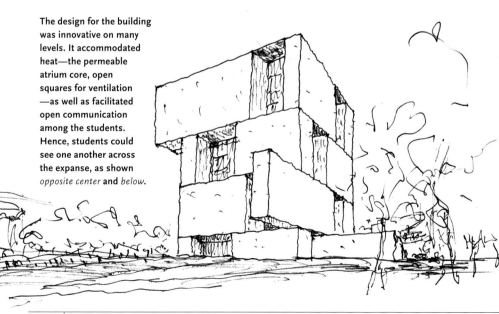

The design for the building was innovative on many levels. It accommodated heat—the permeable atrium core, open squares for ventilation—as well as facilitated open communication among the students. Hence, students could see one another across the expanse, as shown *opposite center* and *below*.

## UC INNOVATION CENTER— ANACLETO ANGELINI
We wanted to have a building that you could say does not have any style. It is as neutral and out of fashion as one can imagine. The biggest threat to any innovation center is that it may become obsolete too soon. That's why the building was not about a particular style, but about how it functions. _ Vladimir Belogolovsky, *Conversations with Architects: In the Age of Celebrity*, Berlin: DOM Publishing, 2015

The aim was a . . . building where companies, businesses and more in general, demand, could

converge with university researchers and outputs.
_ Alejandro Aravena, courtesy Elemental

There are five main points that affected the form of this building. First, the objective was to make an efficient building from the point of view of the environment. In this climate, it makes sense to have solid building in the perimeter, not to let the heat from the sun come inside. Our building consumes just a third of the energy compared to a similar building with glass façade. So instead of following the trend we wanted to make common-sense choices. Therefore, the building has massive façades and a hollowed core.

The second point is conditioned by the program, which works well with the first point. The building is conceived as an infrastructure complex rather than a piece of architecture. There is an industrial crane operating within the internal shaft that can bring up to your office anything you might want.

The third point is about social interaction. The hollowed core allows people inside to be aware of what everyone is doing and interact with one another, which may lead to collaborations, and so on. We created many opportunities for such incidental face-to-face meetings—wider corridors, seating areas in front of the elevators, public exterior terraces, and so on.

Point number four is the character or appearance. We wanted to make it very stable, severe, neutral, and an industrial-looking place. . . .

And finally, we wanted to use permanent materials that would not deteriorate with time. Concrete is an excellent material for that. With time it only gets harder. We want this building to serve for at least 50 years, or more, so we addressed a simple question—will this building look better with time or worse? Concrete, wood, and steel tend to look better as they age. _ Vladimir Belogolovsky, *Conversations with Architects: In the Age of Celebrity,* Berlin: DOM Publishing, 2015

**The Design** The rejection of the glass façade, along with the use of rather strict geometry and strong monolithic materiality, was also a search for a design that could replace trendiness by timelessness.
_ Alejandro Aravena, courtesy Elemental

## ◀◀ THE INNOVATION CENTER IS ALL STRUCTURE, ALL MUSCLE. ▶▶

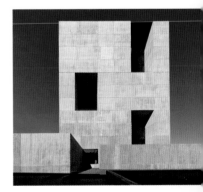

**Sustainability** When you have an open atrium inside, you are able to see what others are doing from within the building, and you have a better way to control light, and when you place the mass and the walls in the perimeter, then you are preventing direct sun radiation. You may also open those windows and get cross-ventilation. We just made those openings of such a scale that they could work as elevated squares, outdoor spaces throughout the entire height of the building. None of this is rocket science. You don't require sophisticated programming. It's not about technology. This is just archaic, primitive common sense, and by using common sense, we went from 120 kilowatts per square meter per year, which is the typical energy consumption for cooling a glass tower, to 40 kilowatts per square meter per year. So with the right design, sustainability is nothing but the rigorous use of common sense. _ "My Architectural Philosophy? Bring the Community into the Process," lecture by Alejandro Aravena for TEDGlobal, Rio de Janeiro, October 9, 2014

## ASKING THE RIGHT QUESTION

In the 60s, when everybody was saying that technology was going to be the answer, [British architect] Cedric Price asked, "What is the question?" _ Samuel Medina and Avinash Rajagopal, *Metropolis* 35, April 2016

Our buildings have to function. They have to be within budget, they have to fulfill a purpose. We begin by trying to understand all the threats: laws, environment, time frame, materials, expectation. We start by designing the question before going into the answer. This is mainly about trying to understand the forces at play. _ Alejandro Aravena interview by Rocky Casale, *Surface*, July 13, 2016

Training yourself to respond to a problem within its real restrictions is what allows you to simultaneously maintain distance while having a mechanism that, when you go work in the outside world, will make what you studied and trained for worthwhile. I mean restrictions that in general lead you toward new questions which consequently leads to new answers. _ Juan Pablo Corvalán, Manuel de Rivero, and Francisco J. Quintana, *Archis* 3, 2009

## ❝❝ SUSTAINABILITY IS NOTHING BUT THE RIGOROUS USE OF COMMON SENSE. ❞❞

As with the UC Innovation Center, heat was an important factor in the design, and yet Aravena was specifically asked to design a glass tower. He decided to put two buildings into one: an energy-efficient interior encased with a glass shell, through which air could circulate.

### SANTIAGO 2005
# SIAMESE TOWERS

We were asked to build a glass tower to host everything that had to do with computers in the university. We saw 3 problems in this: the computers, the glass, and the tower. The university asked us to question the type of architecture required for teaching now that everything depends on digital technology. Should architecture change now that we have computers? Does the notion of room (be it for work or to attend a class) still make sense? Our answer was, of course, Yes and No.

Yes, because the paradigm for working spaces has been reversed; if until now a good room was the one that had a good natural light (library, class-room, etc.), now that we work on screens, a good space is the one that has achieved a good half-light (to avoid uncomfortable reflections). This fact led us to explore a relatively hermetic volume, with very controlled perforations towards the outside.

But on the other hand, we were not that optimistic regarding computers and their influence in education, or the transmission of knowledge; in the end nothing will defeat a good conversation of two persons (be it between a professor and a student, or between students) under a good shadow, drinking a nice cup of coffee or having a casual conversation in a corridor. (We had in mind Louis Kahn's old notion of institution in this case that of a school.) . . . So, instead of moving forward thinking about the next step in education, we thought we had to move back as much as possible, to more archaic and primitive ways of being. Wood slopes, a natural public bench, or a 10-story-high corridor were those spaces where we expected old good conversations to take place.

Regarding the glass, the problem was that building a glass tower in Santiago means automatically to take care of the greenhouse effect. We had no money for a curtain-wall, able to solve all the issues in 1 single skin (double, reflective, and colored glass). Even if we had the money, the amount of energy that has to be spent afterwards for air conditioning is obscene. Finally we did not like mirror glass for the façade, because it is vulgar.

So instead of thinking about a skin capable of doing all the job . . . we thought that it would be cheaper to do several skins, each of them doing well 1 thing at a time. So we designed an outer single glass skin, very bad in energetic terms, but very good against weathering, and then an internal building made out of fiber-cement, bad against weathering but energetic wise. In between them: air. All we had to do was to avoid the greenhouse effect generated after the sun trespassed the glass, before it reached the second building inside. So we allowed the space in between the 2 buildings to perform as a perimeter chimney, letting the hot air to leave the system, ascending by convection to a void in the top.

Finally, there was the problem of trying to have a tower, because we had just 5000 m² to achieve it. Didn't matter how much we reduced the surface of each floor, the resulting figure was pretty hefty; it was a high building, but it didn't look like a tower. So the only solution we thought of was to cut the volume in two from the 7th floor up. For each of the resulting parts we used almost width-less aluminum pieces of slightly different colors. So if seen from the front, the building was a unique bi-cephalous volume, but seen as a foreshortened figure, the color difference could show a couple of really vertical figures that happened to share great part of their bodies, as if they were Siamese creatures.

_ Alejandro Aravena, courtesy Elemental

**❦❦ TO ME, CREATIVITY COMES FROM OVERCOMING CONSTRAINTS. ❧❧**

## SYNTHESIS
## "SOLUTIONS SHOULD BE DIRECT AND SIMPLE."

Be it the force of self construction, the force of common sense, or the force of nature, all these forces need to be translated into form. And what that form is modeling and shaping is not cement, brick, or wood, it is life itself. Design's power of synthesis is just an attempt to put at the innermost core of architecture the force of life. _ "My Architectural Philosophy? Bring the Community into the Process," lecture by Alejandro Aravena for TEDGlobal, Rio de Janeiro, October 9, 2014

## A MATTER OF BEAUTY

Actually no one deliberately wants to raise ugly buildings. But when your work aims primarily at beauty, the thinking is that you have better taste than average, and that's what they pay you for. The danger lies in the fact that you need to have complete control over the result, but without it, your taste will not live up to expectations. . . . [as opposed to] open systems where your success depends on your capacity to activate a beginning, and simply on future development having started off in the right direction. _ Antón García-Abril, *Arquitectura Viva*, January 2010

# ❝ IF THERE'S ANY POWER IN DESIGN, THAT'S THE POWER OF SYNTHESIS. THE MORE COMPLEX THE PROBLEM THE MORE THE NEED FOR SIMPLICITY. ❞

Poverty doesn't belong to architecture. I mean space eventually belongs to architecture, but poverty does not. So that's outside architecture. . . . I would say that in general, our challenges will come from those non-architectural issues treated through the lens of architecture, which is its power of synthesis and strategic use of form. _ Ken Tadashi Oshima interview with Alejandro Aravena in Alejandro Aravena, *Alejandro Aravena: The Forces in Architecture*, Tokyo: Toto Publishing, 2011

The start of any project must have no architectural component. Architecture must come into play only when time to give a synthetic response to the problem at hand. So how much architecture at the starting point? The answer is this: zero architecture, 100% of other disciplines. Halfway through synthesizing the complexity, how much architecture? The answer: 100%. And in the verification of the result, how much architecture? Again, zero, because zero is where we started out. _ Antón García-Abril, *Arquitectura Viva*, January 2010

## XV VENICE ARCHITECTURE BIENNIAL

*Aravena was chair of the XV Venice Architecture Biennale and the first South American to have this position. He titled the theme "Reporting from the Front."*

We believe that the advancement of architecture is not a goal in itself but a way to improve people's quality of life. Given life ranges from very basic physical needs to the most intangible dimensions of the human condition, consequently improving the quality of the built environment is an endeavor that has to tackle many fronts: from guaranteeing very concrete, down-to-earth living standards to interpreting and fulfilling human desires, from respecting the single individual to taking care of the common good, from efficiently hosting daily activities to expanding the frontiers of civilization. _ Alejandro Aravena, *AV Monographs* 185, 2016

We would like to show that in the permanent debate about the quality of the built environment, there is not only need but also room for action. _ Alejandro Aravena, *AV Monographs* 185, 2016

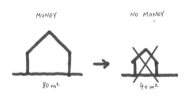

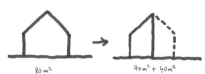

## CONSTITUCIÓN 2013
# VILLA VERDE HOUSING
*Constitución was heavily damaged after a tsunami in 2010. Aravena was hired to help with the reconstruction of the area, specifically with new housing for the thousands of residents left homeless. Villa Verde is the largest reconstruction project in Constitución.*

COPEC owns Arauco, the forest company in the south of Chile in the city of Constitución. After the 8.8-magnitude earthquake in 2010, the company asked us to try and create new housing for its workers with the Elemental approach. . . . _ Asad Syrkett, *Architectural Record* 201, March 2013

**Participatory Design** Residents in Constitución naturally suspected, because we were working for the forestry company, that all the benefits of reconstruction would go to the company, not them. That's why we knew from the start that the people had to participate in the reconstruction process. In effect, we needed to create the right client. So we devised a consortium: Arauco, the government, the public, and us. We were taking an intuitive approach because we actually knew nothing about planning. In the end, ignorance helped. _ Michael Kimmelman, *T: The New York Times Style Magazine*, May 23, 2016

## ❝ WHENEVER AND WHEREVER THERE IS SCARCITY, THERE IS ROOM FOR ELEMENTAL'S APPROACH. ❞

Participatory design is not a hippie, romantic, let's-all-dream-together-about-the-future-of-the-city kind of thing. It is actually not even with the families trying to find the right answer. It is mainly trying to identify with precision what is the right question. There is nothing worse than answering well the wrong question. _ "My Architectural Philosophy? Bring the Community into the Process," lecture by Alejandro Aravena for TEDGlobal, Rio de Janeiro, October 9, 2014

A common problem in participatory design is to invite people to complain about where we are, so channeling those particles of a problem into one direction is the crucial factor. _ Justin Harvey, Architecture New Zealand 4, 2015

We need the best people in the entire chain of production, from the politicians to the social worker to the designer. What we've been trying to do is communicate that architecture, instead of an extra cost, is an added value. _ Robin Pogrebin, "Pritzker Prize for Architecture Is Awarded to Alejandro Aravena of Chile," New York Times, January 13, 2016

**Social Housing** Social Housing is not only an ethical question, it is a difficult problem; it requires professional quality more than professional charity. _ Ken Tadashi Oshima interview with Alejandro Aravena in

Alejandro Aravena, Alejandro Aravena: The Forces in Architecture, Tokyo: Toto Publishing, 2011

I'm not sure that a private house is especially interesting as architecture, in that it's either the client's vision or the architect's. A school or public housing project operates in a more complex space where everything becomes negotiable, which I think is more creative, more difficult, more challenging for an architect and more rewarding. _ Michael Kimmelman, T: The New York Times Style Magazine, May 23, 2016

Our model for building subsidized housing quickly and cheaply has become a real laboratory and model for other Third World countries. _ Vladimir Belogolovsky, Conversations with Architects: In the Age of Celebrity, Berlin: DOM Publishing, 2015

Only to focus on the projects we are building today is more than enough. We've done only a few thousand units and there [are] a couple billion needed in the world. So on the one hand, we might have had some achievements; on the other hand I feel we are a failure in that we are not mainstream, we are an interesting exception on the periphery of what is being built nowadays, so I would say we have a lot to do. _ Curry Stone Design Prize, video, Can Public Housing Be Designed to Encourage Resident Ownership?, 2010

## ❝ THE PARTICIPATORY PROCESS REVEALED PRIORITIES. ❞

The lessons from earlier social housing projects informed the plan for Villa Verde's employee development. The incremental housing concept, shown in the diagram, *opposite*, was now adapted to a greater budget yet with the aim of engaging residents and giving them possible ownership in their housing community.

**SURVIVAL** I have seen whole cities burning. As a pilot flying over the burning cities, especially the city of Munich, the city of Ulm, and also partially the city of Stuttgart, the strongest first semester for a student of city planning and architecture is to see a burning city. You will never forget it, that what generations have built and made and developed could be in a few hours destroyed. To talk on those things, to learn what you could learn from a war is very important. Yes, my architecture is an architecture of survival. Very simple. To survive, also, is all that we are doing. _ *Frei Otto: Spanning the Future,* documentary, 2015

# FREI OTTO

**BORN:** 1925, Siegmar, Germany; Died: March 9, 2015, Leonberg, Germany

**EDUCATION:** Technical University of Berlin, 1948; Doctorate of Civil Engineering, Technical University, Berlin, 1954

**OFFICE:** Atelier Frei Otto + Partner, Künstler + Ingenieure, Lucas-Cranach-Weg 5, D-71065, Sindelfingen, Germany www.freiotto.de

**PROJECTS FEATURED:** Manufacturing Pavilions for Wilkhahn, Bad Münder, Germany, 1988; Multihalle, Mannheim, Germany, with Carlfried Mutschler and Joachim Langner, 1975; Munich Olympic Park for the 1972 Summer Olympics, Munich, Germany, with Günter Behnisch and Fritz Leonhardt, 1972; German Pavilion, Expo 67, Montreal, Canada, with Rolf Gutbrod and Fritz Leonhardt, 1967

" I AM FREI.
I AM FREE.
I AM FREI OTTO. "

**Munich Olympic Park, 1972**
With the war as a constant reminder of man's ability to destroy and the fragility of cities, Otto made it a lifelong mission to employ a light hand, to make gentle inroads on civilization. As he said, architects "must help that catastrophe cannot kill people, it's that simple." In this regard, temporary exhibitions were his ideal platform.

<blockquote>❝ THE FORM OF SOAP FILM LASTS ONLY A FEW SECONDS, BEFORE IT DISAPPEARS, SO I CAN'T SHOW IT TO ANYONE. ❞</blockquote>

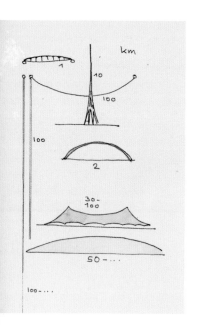

Otto studied "accident" and nature with as much precision and calculation as weight and mass. As he discovered, a slight tug on a soap bubble took a circle and made of it a point at top—not unlike the tented structure of the German Pavilion and other structures he built over time.

**World War II** I must say the philosophical aspect of my work is to make not only a new kind of architecture, to make an *other* architecture. Under Hitler it was a very strong, heavy architecture, and I wanted a new thinking, a real new kind of thinking. _ *Frei Otto: Spanning the Future,* documentary, 2015

The biggest enemy of buildings is man. When we started to rebuild our country, other countries, middle Europe, we started thinking there is no building which can be stable for centuries or longer. Buildings must always change to be perfect. But some buildings should be protected because they should show what people have done and should be a help so that man can go into the future. _ "Fundamental Architectural and Philosophical Ideas," lecture by Frei Otto at AA School of Architecture, November 5, 2003

**Seeking Lightness** Grateful to have survived the war unscathed, the wish to be useful to society was embedded in me right from the beginning of my professional life. From the abundance of available tasks, I tried to select those that I hoped would make a difference. But most of all, I had the urge to develop the lightest of all houses—shells and tents. _ Irene Meissner and Eberhard Moller, *Frei Otto: Forschen, Bauen, Inspirieren / A Life of Research, Construction and Inspiration,* Basel: Birkhäuser, 2015

<blockquote>❝ GOOD ARCHITECTURE SHOULD GROW IN FREEDOM. ❞</blockquote>

### MONTREAL 1967
### GERMAN PAVILION, EXPO 67
*Given Frei Otto's ongoing interest in experimentation and work with tensile structures, this early important project and other subsequent commissions over the years provided him with a living laboratory. So-called temporary structures gave Otto the freedom to explore ideas without the concerns of permanence, although in fact many of his tensile structures have remained intact for decades.*

On the one hand, exhibitions provided the opportunity to realize things I had only started to think about. I was able to advance my research and invention through exhibitions because I received official funding for my research only after 1968–69. And on the other hand, I realized that my work was not in opposition to society, that new things were accepted. Our success in the Expo 67 in Montreal with the German Pavilion made it clear. That was my way. _ Hans Ulrich Obrist, *Hans Ulrich Obrist: Interviews,* Vol. 1, Milan: Charta, 2003

<blockquote>❝ THE TRUE PROBLEM COMPRISES WITHIN ITSELF THE CORE OF THE SOLUTION. ❞</blockquote>

*Written in 1965, with great optimism about the future of civilization and world peace.*

The great expansion that has occurred in every department of science since 1945—a rate of development unique in history—is leading to a gradually emerging fresh understanding of the world. A new relationship of each individual human being to the community, to his own environment, to the universe . . . is manifesting itself. . . . At the present time, we are, in all countries, in the midst of a period of progressively extending liberation from one-sided doctrines with universal claims. We are in a period of reorientation. _ Conrad Roland, *Frei Otto: Tension Structures,* New York: Praeger Publishers, 1970

**Soap Bubbles** *Frei Otto famously experimented with soap bubbles, beginning as early as 1961.*

In the soap bubble if you put a little hair inside and put the soap bubble in the middle then you get an exact round circle, but if you pull on one point in the circle you get a shape. I used the shape for many buildings— the Montreal pavilion, and also for the Munich, [where] you get a wonderful curve. _ "Fundamental Architectural and Philosophical Ideas," lecture by Frei Otto at AA School of Architecture, November 5, 2003

We hang soap film, we let a string fall, we break the film remaining inside the string, and then a perfect circle is generated; afterwards, we take the string, we try to pull it outside, and then this minimum surface

**WE HAVE KNOWN THE FUTURE. THE FUTURE IS NOT TOMORROW. THE FUTURE IS TODAY.**

**ARCHITECTURAL ART NEED NOT BE EXPENSIVE —BUT ITS VALUE IS ALWAYS HIGH.**

is generated. Now it can be calculated, but for more than forty years it was impossible to calculate it. _ Juan Maria Songel and Frei Otto, *A Conversation with Frei Otto*, New York: Princeton Architectural Press, 2010

**Achieving Calculations** The engineering is still not perfect, especially in architecture, because very seldom was proved what the calculations said . . . because it was so difficult to measure these stresses and forces in buildings. [When] I started my Montreal building, I put a hydraulic press under the mast and I measured the force in the mast, and we measured all cables, and we knew that the calculation done by Fritz Leonhardt would fit together. _ "Fundamental Archi-

tectural and Philosophical Ideas," lecture by Frei Otto at AA School of Architecture, November 5, 2003

We developed the pattern of the roof of the German Pavilion in Montreal by hand and later we did the calculations using a computer, a novelty back then. The swimming pool pavilion and the Olympic Stadium of Munich were also done by hand. _ Juan Maria Songel and Frei Otto, *A Conversation with Frei Otto*, New York: Princeton Architectural Press, 2010

## A DESIRE TO INVENT

Ever since I was a child it has been a pastime and an obsession: I always had to be inventing something, and I built the strangest inventions, which didn't have anything to do with architecture. When I was seven or eight years old, I invented inline skates, which are so common today. . . . An invention always has to arise at the right time and place and with the right people; if all these conditions aren't present, the invention fails. _ Juan Maria Songel and Frei Otto, *A Conversation with Frei Otto*, New York: Princeton Architectural Press, 2010

My father was a sculptor and stonemason (like my grandfather) and was very interested in medieval stonework, in finding out how vaults were built so they wouldn't collapse, as neither Hooke nor Newton had yet existed then, nor current mathematics or computer programs; nevertheless, people knew how to build. _ Juan Maria Songel and Frei Otto, *A Conversation with Frei Otto*, New York: Princeton Architectural Press, 2010

## WET PLASTER CLOTHS

*In his father's studio Otto experimented with soaking a wet cloth in plaster.*

Yes, it was simply part of a sculptor's work. It was there when I tried to build these inverted forms for the first time, and even today I continue to play with this: a marvelous toy. _ Juan Maria Songel and Frei Otto, *A Conversation with Frei Otto*, New York: Princeton Architectural Press, 2010

## RESEARCH

*Research was a lifelong part of Frei Otto's work. In 1961, Otto and Johann-Gerhard Helmcke founded the Biology and Building research group at the Technical University of Berlin, where Helmcke taught.*

A new world opened up to us, an entirely new perception of nature. Our work now became more important to me than building houses. We wanted to do pure basic research. We wanted to know how the world of animate and inanimate nature came to exist, how its forms developed and which constructions hold these forms together or modify them. . . . We wanted to learn about nature and understand its creation a little more. _ Irene Meissner and Eberhard Moller, *Frei Otto: Forschen, Bauen, Inspirieren / A Life of Research, Construction and Inspiration*, Basel: Birkhäuser, 2015

I was always involved in interdisciplinary foundation research that was independent of projects and was intended to benefit natural science in general. My colleagues from biology particularly challenged me with inquiries on how to explain living organizations with the help of our knowledge. We searched for answers, but not to invent a new architecture or to imitate living objects. _ Hans Ulrich Obrist, *Hans Ulrich Obrist: Interviews*, Vol. 1, Milan: Charta, 2003

## INSTITUT FUR LEICHTE FLACHENTRAGWERKE (INSTITUTE FOR LIGHTWEIGHT STRUCTURES)

*In 1964, Otto founded the interdisciplinary Institute for Lightweight Structures [IL] at the University of Stuttgart. It was here that Otto worked on the 1967 German Pavilion for the Montreal Expo and for the 1972 Olympic Park in Munich. His nickname for the institute was "Spinnerzentrum"—a riff on the German "spinner" for someone who is crazy—which signaled the sense of play and experimentation that he encouraged among his dedicated students. Otto taught at the IL until his retirement nearly three decades later, at the end of March 1991.*

The institute has generated knowledge, which was published and which makes up a body of general knowledge, although it's not applied. The institute today doesn't exist as it did before. _ Juan Maria Songel and Frei Otto, *A Conversation with Frei Otto*, New York: Princeton Architectural Press, 2010

## FINDING SOLUTIONS

Some also call me an engineer. At heart, I am a form-seeker and sometimes also a form-finder, who is fully aware of the imperfection of his actions and products. I only see the ideal form with my inner eye, while the finished project usually differs significantly. _ Irene Meissner and Eberhard Moller, *Frei Otto: Forschen, Bauen, Inspirieren / A Life of Research, Construction and Inspiration*, Basel: Birkhäuser, 2015

## NATURE

I try to understand nature, although I have come to realize that it is not likely that nature can be understood by a creature that is itself a product of nature. _ Irene Meissner and Eberhard Moller, *Frei Otto: Forschen, Bauen, Inspirieren / A Life of Research, Construction and Inspiration*, Basel: Birkhäuser, 2015

## EXHIBITIONS

For the "Federal Horticultural Exhibition" in 1957 in Cologne, my Berlin team—Siegfried Lohse, Dieter Frank, and Ewald Bubner—and I designed more experimental tent structures, which were all related to each other: the Dance Pavilion, the Entrance Arch, the Riverside Shelter, and several mobile fountains. Every building was constructed from simple cotton and was meant originally to last for just one summer. We thought the buildings would disappear after the exhibition, and the environment would not be harmed. . . . One very special experience for us was the enormous popularity of the Entrance Arch and the Dance Pavilion, which, as a result, remained in Cologne for many years. _ Hans Ulrich Obrist, *Hans Ulrich Obrist: Interviews*, Vol. 1, Milan: Charta, 2003

**MUNICH 1972**
# MUNICH OLYMPIC PARK FOR THE 1972 SUMMER OLYMPICS, MUNICH

*The Olympia Baugesellschaft commissioned Otto in partnership with Günter Behnisch and Fritz Leonhardt to design and manufacture various coverings for the more than 70,000 square meters of the Olympic Park. The resulting structures included a tensile structure arena; fabric roof over the swimming pool; coverings for the track and field stadium; the general stadium; and hyperbolic membrane canopies to connect the buildings and provide protection for visitors from the sun and rain.*

Exhibition architecture can have an enormous impact, because the temporary statement can be more intense than the permanent one. _ Hans Ulrich Obrist, *Hans Ulrich Obrist: Interviews,* Vol. 1, Milan: Charta, 2003

My hope is that light, flexible architecture might bring about a new and open society. _ Source unknown

Using air as a building material means that the amount of material you need is very minimal so you can dedicate your forces to the relation between animals and man, and man and plants, and make an environment which is in equilibrium. _ *Frei Otto: Spanning the Future,* documentary, 2015

In the case of Munich we measured the real stresses in each cable; it is probably the first building where we really know what happens inside. We also know the dangers that can arise from overloads and what happens in the structure when we overload it. _ Juan Maria Songel and Frei Otto, *A Conversation with Frei Otto,* New York: Princeton Architectural Press, 2010

"I regard the architecture of the new century as part of nature"—a statement as simple as it is profound. Tethered to that was Frei Otto's desire that light, flexible architecture "might bring about a new and open society." His soaring structures resonated with the public, and often what was meant to be temporary remained in situ for decades.

## MAJOR 20TH CENTURY ARCHITECTS

I met Walter Gropius, Mies van der Rohe, Frank Lloyd Wright, Erich Mendelsohn, and Fred Severud (this last person thanks to Eero Saarinen) during a long study trip to the United States between 1950 and 1951. I continued developing relationships with some of them until their deaths, especially Walter Gropius and Mies van der Rohe—very important and beautiful relationships for me. _ Juan Maria Songel and Frei Otto, *A Conversation with Frei Otto*, New York: Princeton Architectural Press, 2010

I met [Josef] Albers when he taught a seminar at Yale University during my stay in the United States in 1960, but I was more interested in Walter Gropius. Gropius came to visit me in Berlin when Gropiusstadt was being built [c. 1965–66]. During that visit he told me that I was the only one who continued working in the line he had established, mainly because I did not start from any formal approaches but searched for the future architectural form through experiments. I could almost say that Gropius was a passionate enthusiast of my work (which was reciprocal) and he was very well informed of what I did. _ Juan Maria Songel and Frei Otto, *A Conversation with Frei Otto*, New York: Princeton Architectural Press, 2010

## GROPIUS AND MIES

Gropius didn't want architecture based on form, but architecture based on natural sciences. Mies van der Rohe was another world, and, although we understood each other very well, he tended more towards creation, elaboration, or construction of form; he designed architectonic forms. Gropius didn't search for form but for the essential, the substantial. That is the difference between these two greatly successful characters with very different paths.

I went to Mies van der Rohe's studio in Chicago when they were working on the Neue Nationalgalerie in Berlin. He was already very sick at the time, and his collaborators asked me for my opinion, because it seemed that Mies had requested it. . . . I proposed they put at least two pillars on each side, that is, to support the roof on a total of eight pillars, and that is how it was done. I met Mies van der Rohe for the last time in Berlin a few weeks before his death, when the roof was being assembled, and he was very happy with the decision of the pillars. _ Juan Maria Songel and Frei Otto, *A Conversation with Frei Otto*, New York: Princeton Architectural Press, 2010

## GAUDÍ AND THE WAR

I must say that it [the Bauhaus] didn't really influence me; I have followed my own path. Even the influence of Antoni Gaudí came much later, when I had already done investigations with models in the prisoner of war camp that could be considered Gaudían, without even having known Gaudí. One can follow this path simply based on logic, especially when it comes to inverting structures that function by traction so they function by compression. I learned this from an engineer friend in the prisoner camp who was in my work group. _ Juan Maria Songel and Frei Otto, *A Conversation with Frei Otto*, New York: Princeton Architectural Press, 2010

## BUCKMINSTER FULLER

I knew his work and we saw each other for the first time in 1958, in St. Louis, when I was teaching at Washington University. We had a long conversation, which at times became a heated but friendly discussion on wide-span constructions, especially wide-span grid shells. Later he traveled frequently to Germany and came to visit me at the institute [the IL] and we spoke about biology. When he saw Helmcke's works [Johann-Gerhard Helmcke], especially the radiolarian and diatomic stereomicroscopic images, he stood up and wanted to grab them! It was very funny. He was amazed when he saw how animate nature was faster at inventing than he was. _ Juan Maria Songel and Frei Otto, *A Conversation with Frei Otto*, New York: Princeton Architectural Press, 2010

We [Fuller and Otto] discussed necessary minimum building weights and their possible maximum span, and if he could actually build one of his geodesic domes around the entire surface of the earth. Only much later he agreed with me about the impossibility of such a project. _ Hans Ulrich Obrist, *Hans Ulrich Obrist: Interviews*, Vol. 1, Milan: Charta, 2003

## ARCHITECTS AND ENGINEERS

I'm an architect, I'm not an engineer. I always was interested in a good relationship between architects and engineers. _ "Fundamental Architectural and Philosophical Ideas," lecture by Frei Otto at AA School of Architecture, November 5, 2003

When architects and engineers work together to achieve a common goal, their efforts are more likely to result in a work of architectural art than when each group works alone. _ Winfried Nerdinger, ed., *Frei Otto Complete Works: Lightweight Construction, Natural Design*, Basel: Birkhaüser, 2005

Since the separation between engineers and architects took place, it's always been the architects who have been more concerned with the qualitative vision and the meticulous study of buildings and structures, while the engineers have focused on calculations; both focuses are necessary. I place myself both on the side of the engineers and on the side of the architects; for me there is no separation. All possible separation is erroneous, because experimental physics is as necessary as theoretical physics; it's not about separating but about integrating. _ Juan Maria Songel and Frei Otto, *A Conversation with Frei Otto*, New York: Princeton Architectural Press, 2010

## ❝ I TELL [MY STUDENTS], 'LET'S NOT DRAW ANYTHING, LET'S JUST LOOK FOR THE UNKNOWN.' ❞

### TEACHING

The teaching commitment demanded a certain order. . . . I have always considered the attention to history the responsibility of my specialist colleagues . . . my job is to work for the future. _ Juan Maria Songel and Frei Otto, *A Conversation with Frei Otto*, New York: Princeton Architectural Press, 2010

### MODELS

Depending on the type of problem posed one has to invent the methods of experiment. In experiments one can use string, water, egg yolk, or anything else; the important thing is to be able to extract knowledge based on the results. The best trials with models don't cost much. _ Juan Maria Songel and Frei Otto, *A Conversation with Frei Otto*, New York: Princeton Architectural Press, 2010

I have always combined systematic experimentation with the fortuitous or casual, where chance plays a role; if something is accidentally discovered, it would be stupid to reject it simply because it doesn't fit within the systematization. _ Juan Maria Songel and Frei Otto, *A Conversation with Frei Otto*, New York: Princeton Architectural Press, 2010

I have said to some engineers that although not everything can be calculated, we can do very precise experiments with models, and knowing the formulas of the laws inherent in the models, I can and have the right to verify bridges, shells, and lattices with carefully built models. _ Juan Maria Songel and Frei Otto, *A Conversation with Frei Otto*, New York: Princeton Architectural Press, 2010

You have to be very careful, especially if you have large spans, in concrete, in stone, in earth, then you have to be careful in enlarging the models. We make many models, one to look, one to test, and very seldom also static test models, but also to prove what is their final limit of taken forces. In my office we have done as many as 200 models . . . and always it is a problem to make them in such a way so that they can be used also as a tool for the engineers. _ "Fundamental Architectural and Philosophical Ideas," lecture by Frei Otto at AA School of Architecture, November 5, 2003

In the '80s and '90s, the model was out of style: people thought it could be replaced by the computer. But good architects always built models. When Norman Foster designed the Bank of Hong Kong (Hong Kong and Shanghai Bank Tower, Hong Kong, 1986), I saw about a hundred different skyscrapers on a table in his office, all of them attempts at the design of this bank. _ Hans Ulrich Obrist, *Hans Ulrich Obrist: Interviews,* Vol. 1, Milan: Charta, 2003

### STABILITY

The most interesting phenomenon is the buckling of superficial structures. At what moment does a piece of paper buckle? _ Juan Maria Songel and Frei Otto, *A Conversation with Frei Otto*, New York: Princeton Architectural Press, 2010

The less mass a form has, the more stable it will be. . . . The most stable construction is the one that doesn't exist or has already collapsed. I always said to my students that a collapsed building is the most stable; the standing building has a degree of instability. . . . [A]ll architecture tries to do is to temporarily make stable what in principle is unstable. _ Juan Maria Songel and Frei Otto, *A Conversation with Frei Otto*, New York: Princeton Architectural Press, 2010

In my opinion some computer programs used to calculate structures don't have a physical verification process, therefore buildings can collapse and kill people today. _ Juan Maria Songel and Frei Otto, *A Conversation with Frei Otto*, New York: Princeton Architectural Press, 2010

### INVENTION: NATURE AND MODELS

It's not very scientific to take nature as a model; nature can't be imitated because it's very complex. In principle it seems very simple but it is actually very complicated and should not be interpreted mistakenly. _ Juan Maria Songel and Frei Otto, *A Conversation with Frei Otto*, New York: Princeton Architectural Press, 2010

I continue to believe that the direct imitation of objects of animate nature for the construction of buildings is an erroneous path. _ Juan Maria Songel and Frei Otto, *A Conversation with Frei Otto*, New York: Princeton Architectural Press, 2010

### ❝ SHELLS ARE SHELLS AND MEMBRANES ARE MEMBRANES. ❞

### SHELLS AND MEMBRANES

To tell you the truth, all stress analyses done so far have been imprecise. To say that stress in buildings can be calculated is not true, because these calculations are only approximate methods. _ Juan Maria Songel and Frei Otto, *A Conversation with Frei Otto*, New York: Princeton Architectural Press, 2010

## SOAP: INFINITE POSSIBILITIES

I claim that you can construct an individually designed environment for every individual human being. Such infinite variety has biological reasons, which I studied in detail. It could be compared to soap foam: there are no two bubbles exactly alike. _ Hans Ulrich Obrist, *Hans Ulrich Obrist: Interviews*, Vol. 1, Milan: Charta, 2003

I have been focusing more on those processes that contain an optimization from the beginning, like soap bubbles, minimum sur-

faces, and fluid forms, which, being very sensitive, can only exist in very few forms. Based on those, we found a universe of infinite possibilities. The membranes of soap bubbles have infinite forms. _ Juan Maria Songel and Frei Otto, *A Conversation with Frei Otto*, New York: Princeton Architectural Press, 2010

## CURVES

People know what a circle is, but there are also, among other curves of constant curvature, the spiral and helicoidal lines. . . . You can also make an unequal curve, but only the exact curve of constant curvature provides infinite possibilities. . . . If you modify the connection, then infinite possibilities arise. _ Juan Maria Songel and Frei Otto, *A Conversation with Frei Otto*, New York: Princeton Architectural Press, 2010

## ❝❝ I ARRIVED AT GRID SHELLS THROUGH BUILDING FUSELAGES OF GLIDERS AND NOT BY CONSTRUCTING BUILDINGS. ❞❞

Multihalle gave Otto an opportunity to use wood, which he felt was a material well suited to lightweight structures, given that it could be bent or compressed. For this project, models were a necessary "approximation of reality."

### MANNHEIM 1975
### MULTIHALLE (MULTI-PURPOSE HALL), WITH CARLFRIED MUTSCHLER AND JOACHIM LANGNER
My largest building was the so-called Multihalle, done with the architects Mutschler and Langner in Germany. It is a problematic building because the span is more than 80 meters and the

wood is very thin. There are lattices of long-grain wood, the hemlock pine of Canada, and the lattices are 47–40 millimeters, not centimeters, and I said that we could build this building just as the lattice of the roof is out of the structure underneath. So we did it, and we are happy that the building is standing still. It was planned for only one summer. It is now a protected building. _ "Fundamental Architectural and Philosophical Ideas," lecture by Frei Otto at AA School of Architecture, November 5, 2003

**Grid Shells and Meshes**  People don't think about why some buildings have been standing for centuries and continue to be stable, while nowadays a well-calculated structure suddenly collapses. The majority of the collapses today concern grid shells—the type of structures I have worked on—because people don't act carefully enough. _ Juan Maria Songel and Frei Otto, *A Conversation with Frei Otto*, New York: Princeton Architectural Press, 2010

I learned to avoid hexagonal meshes: they are very dangerous and expensive because the knots require extraordinary care. They lack safe points, because no element crosses them continuously, other than in the Mannheim pavilion. _ Juan Maria Songel and Frei Otto, *A Conversation with Frei Otto*, New York: Princeton Architectural Press, 2010

I tried to make a larger experiment in compression structure. The Multihalle was not using tension structure. These are structures in compression. I have done several experiments with compression structures but the Multihalle was the largest. Compression is much more difficult to build than tension. Tension is always stable, compression is very seldom stable. This is the main knowledge of our century. _ *Frei Otto: Spanning the Future,* documentary, 2015

**When the Temporary Endures**  I was really amazed at being able to build this work, a structure that, on the other hand, supported a load test that we carried out well. The building is still standing and soon it will turn thirty years old, if I'm not mistaken. [Otto made this remark in c. 2007.] It's the work I've been the most afraid of; the most audacious work that really went beyond my knowledge back then and perhaps even my current knowledge. Originally, the pavilion was supposed to remain only during the Federal Garden Exposition. . . . Nevertheless, the older it gets, the more anxious I become. I don't know what I should do: Should I warn the owner that it would be better to tear it down so that I can sleep better? _ Juan Maria Songel and Frei Otto, *A Conversation with Frei Otto,* New York: Princeton Architectural Press, 2010

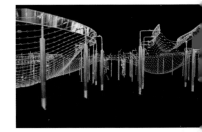

## AESTHETICS, ETHICS, AND NOTIONS OF BEAUTY

Something that is beautiful is not necessarily ethical too. Beauty is not equal to goodness. Beauty can be cruel, and ugliness can be good. And sometimes the beautiful grows ugly over time, while the ugly grows beautiful. In art, beauty is always original and new; it is an invention and an innovation. A work becomes a work of art through a wealth of inventiveness. _ Winfried Nerdinger, ed., *Frei Otto Complete Works: Lightweight Construction, Natural Design*, Basel: Birkhäuser, 2005

## CONTRIBUTING TO HUMANITY

Today, the task of the architect is not simply to provide shelter from the forces of nature, but to create conditions which allow people to live in harmony with nature and at peace with one another. _ Winfried Nerdinger, ed., *Frei Otto Complete Works: Lightweight Construction, Natural Design*, Basel: Birkhäuser, 2005

## ❰❰ THERE ARE NO RULES OR SCHOOLS FOR AESTHETICS. ❱❱

Even if architects, urban planners, and engineers recognize a shared code of professional ethics, this does not mean that they are all above reproach. . . . [A]rchitects, in addition to producing buildings that give shelter and solving technical problems with technical means, [should be] prepared to go the extra mile and produce beautiful structures that give their owners a sense of being at home. _ Winfried Nerdinger, ed., *Frei Otto Complete Works: Lightweight Construction, Natural Design*, Basel: Birkhäuser, 2005

However, what we do need is unequivocal dedication to the ethos of the builder; without this dedication, a house may be beautiful, but will never be humane. _ Winfried Nerdinger, ed., *Frei Otto Complete Works: Lightweight Construction, Natural Design*, Basel: Birkhäuser, 2005

**❝ ECOLOGICAL CONSCIOUSNESS**—TO PROTECT NOT ONLY THE MAN, BUT ALSO LIFE AS A WHOLE—IS A NOVELTY IN THE AREA OF ARCHITECTURE. ❞

**❝ I WAS KNOWN AS THE YOUNG TENT BUILDER. ❞**

**BAD MÜNDER 1988**
## MANUFACTURING PAVILIONS FOR WILKHAHN
*For Wilkhahn, a furniture manufacturer, Otto returned to his earliest structure, the tent, to create four buildings for employees that combined aesthetics with humanitarian considerations.*

"Less is more" is something that fascinates me: use fewer houses, consume less material, less concrete and less energy, but build in a humane way using what's available: earth, water, air. Build in harmony with nature and make a lot out of little, observe and think critically from the very first line of a drawing. Better not to build at all than to build too much! These are old and new goals. _ Irene Meissner and Eberhard Moller, *Frei Otto: Forschen, Bauen, Inspirieren / A Life of Research, Construction and Inspiration,* Basel: Birkhäuser, 2015

And frequently it is those buildings that were created at low technical and financial cost which acquire the unique beauty of something original. _ Winfried Nerdinger, ed., *Frei Otto Complete Works: Lightweight Construction, Natural Design,* Basel: Birkhaüser, 2005

Many friends have helped to provide the driving force and create the driving conditions for my work—above all, Peter Stromeyer. He turned tent-making into an experimental field for building construction characterized by low expenditure of effort, materials, and cost. The results, however, are not confined to impermanent tent structures. _ Conrad Roland, *Frei Otto: Tension Structures,* New York: Praeger Publishers, 1970

The dazzling skins and soaring lightness of Otto's structures expressed a constant clarity of vision and calculation. But experimentation in the laboratory never eclipsed Otto's lifelong philosophy that architecture was meant to co-exist "in harmony with nature."

## CASTLES IN THE AIR AND THE PRITZKER PRIZE

*Frei Otto died shortly before he was to attend the 2015 Pritzker Architecture Prize award ceremonies in his honor that May. Fortuitously, he had met with members of the Pritzker Prize in early 2015 when he shared his thoughts on being made the 40th laureate.*

I have never done anything to gain this prize. My architectural drive was to design new types of buildings to help poor people, especially, following natural disasters and catastrophes. So what shall be better for me than to win this prize? I will use whatever time is left to me to keep doing what I have been doing, which is to help humanity. You have here a happy man. _ *Frei Otto*, video, Pritzker Architecture Prize, 2015

I would like to give paradise to everyone: to foreign people, to poor people, even to the rich, but especially for foreign people. . . . I don't know how many years I will have, if it's one day or one year or one decade I don't know, but I have to do something. I am not looking forward to sleep, I will work every day and this is the beauty I learned from my family what is beauty. I learned that you cannot make beauty, ever. "Sit down and make beauty"—that's not possible, but you can *live* beauty. _ *Frei Otto*, video, Pritzker Architecture Prize, 2015

Architects live within their own world of ethics. Architects help people to live on earth, to create houses and residences. They practice brotherly love even towards people whom they do not know. . . . This means that architects must be able to say "no" when they are asked to perform a service which they cannot support, because their work can cause harm to human beings in body and spirit, and can even kill. Saying no at the right moment and in the right place is necessary whenever a building project is harmful to nature and the environment. _ Winfried Nerdinger, ed., *Frei Otto Complete Works: Lightweight Construction, Natural Design*, Basel: Birkhaüser, 2005

I built little. But I devised many "castles in the air." Why the few real constructions I built myself or was involved in turned out to be so famous is a mystery to me, because the majority only existed for a short period of time. _ Irene Meissner and Eberhard Moller, *Frei Otto: Forschen, Bauen, Inspirieren / A Life of Research, Construction and Inspiration*, Basel: Birkhäuser, 2015

**MEANINGFUL ARCHITECTURE** Even in disaster areas, as an architect I want to create beautiful buildings. I want to move people and to improve people's lives. If I did not feel this way, it would be impossible to create meaningful architecture and to make a contribution to society at the same time. _ Emilio Ambasz, *Shigeru Ban*, New York: Princeton Architectural Press, 2001

Whether the structure is temporary or permanent is not dependent on what kind of material it is made of. If the structure is loved by the people, it will stay forever. _ Brad Pitt and Shigeru Ban, "Paper Architecture & Make It Right: A Conversation between Brad Pitt and Shigeru Ban," in *Shigeru Ban: Humanitarian Architecture*, 2014

I don't think a building is important, I think the human life is more important. That's why even if the building is destroyed by earthquake, doesn't matter, as long as people are safe. _ "Architect Shigeru Ban's Temporary Cathedral for Christchurch," *Urbis* 64, October 2011

# SHIGERU BAN

**BORN:** August 5, 1957, Tokyo, Japan

**EDUCATION:** Southern California Institute of Architecture, 1977–80; , Cooper Union, New York, 1984

**OFFICE:** Shigeru Ban Architects, 5-2-4 Matsubara, Setagaya, Tokyo, 156-0043 Japan
Tel: +81-(0)3-3324-6760, Fax: +81-(0)3-3324-6789
www.shigerubanarchitects.com

**PROJECTS FEATURED:** Aspen Art Museum, Aspen, Colorado, 2014; Temporary Cathedral, Christchurch, New Zealand, 2013; Onagawa Temporary Container Housing and Community Center, Miyagi, Japan, 2011; Metal Shutter House, New York, 2011; Paper Art Museum, Shizuoka, Japan, 2002; Curtain Wall House, Tokyo, 199

"PERSONALLY, I'VE NEVER CLAIMED TO HAVE INVENTED ANYTHING. MY WORK IS BASED ON OBSERVATION, ON EXPLORING THE POTENTIAL OF WHAT EXISTS. I HAVE ALWAYS USED EVERYDAY MATERIALS AND TECHNOLOGIES, THOUGH DIFFERENTLY TO HOW THEY ARE NORMALLY EMPLOYED. IT'S A QUESTION OF STRIPPING ONESELF OF PREJUDICES."

**Temporary Cathedral, Christchurch, New Zealand, 2013**
Ban's design for the cathedral is one of his many works to help communities in distress. Beauty and a respect for materials is immediately apparent here. Ban writes, "The equilateral triangle façade is an important load-bearing wall, but as it was also the front triangle window, we decided to divide it into small triangles of 2.3m on each side and reconfigured the motif of the old cathedral rose window to make a triangle 'rose window.'"

## STUDENT DAYS

I believe my own fate was decided in secondary school. At the time, I was trying to gain admittance to the architecture school at the Tokyo University of Fine Arts and Music, and was taking classes at the Ochanomizu University. There, while neglecting to prepare for my entrance examinations, I threw myself into solving design problems. Students were called on to create a structural frame out of different materials— wood, paper, bamboo—each week. I would always produce two solutions for each assignment. _ Emilio Ambasz, *Shigeru Ban*, New York: Princeton Architectural Press, 2001

To enter the Japanese art school, we had to create a tower higher than one meter just using cardboard, and without wasting materials. Working with strict rules and a limited amount of materials was something I was very good at. I saw my teacher again a few years ago, and he said to me: "You are still doing the same things." _ Philip Jodidio, *Shigeru Ban, Complete Works 1985–2015*, Cologne: Taschen, 2015

## SOUTHERN CALIFORNIA INSTITUTE OF ARCHITECTURE (SCI-ARC) AND COOPER UNION

I visited a few schools in California and enrolled at SCI-Arc, the Southern California Institute of Architecture. It was a terrific experience because we had case studies, which included Raymond Kappe and Wright and Neutra, who mixed Modernism with Japanese influences. Then when I did enroll at Cooper, I learned history: Corbu, Mies, Palladio, Schinkel. I started with Hejduk's geometry, and Mies and Corbu became my gods. _ Michael Kimmelman, *New York Times Magazine*, May 20, 2007

## COOPER UNION

It was at Makabe's home [Tomoharu Makabe, Ban's professor at Ochanomizu] that I happened to see the issue of *A+U* on the Whites and the Greys and the issue on John Hejduk. My future was decided then and there. Even though I knew nothing about architecture, I was instantly attracted to the work of the New York Five. . . . I decided I wanted to study in the United States at the Cooper Union where three of the New York Five (Hejduk, Peter Eisenman, and Richard Meier) had graduated from or were on faculty. _ Emilio Ambasz, *Shigeru Ban*, New York: Princeton Architectural Press, 2001

## ARATA ISOZAKI

I took a leave from Cooper Union in 1982 and joined Arata Isozaki & Associates for one year. . . . An architect usually affects the atmosphere or style of the atelier they belong to. However, in Isozaki's atelier, no one tried to inherit his style, and we tried to learn the spirit behind his works, I think. It was significant to see that Isozaki was competitive overseas, without any sense of inferiority. I feel like I learned my stance as an architect from him, rather than how to design. Even now, he doesn't easily side with authority and that attitude is outstanding. _ Koh Kitayama and Shigeru Ban, "Architecture for Nurturing People: A Conversation between Koh Kitayama and Shigeru Ban," in *Shigeru Ban: Humanitarian Architecture*, 2014

I studied in the United States, not in Japan, and I am aware that that is where most of my influences come from. But then, when I think about those influences—the Case Study Houses in California, for instance—I see in them direct references to Japanese culture. So it could be said that my relationship with Japanese architecture takes the form of an American reinterpretation. _ "Interview with Shigeru Ban," *Quaderns* 226, July 2000

## ❝ ARCHITECTURE IS MY LIFE. ❞

The spatial continuity of interior and exterior spaces drive the design: the curtains, made of simple cotton, hang from the base of the roof and can either screen or reveal the verandah and rooms. Sliding glass panels extend both floors of the house; inside, cardboard tubes were used for some of the specially designed tables and chairs.

**TOKYO 1995**
# CURTAIN WALL HOUSE "Physical Continuity"
Curtain Wall House, 2/5 House, and Wall-Less House are works revolving around spatial rather than structural themes. One of my favorite buildings is Mies van der Rohe's Farnsworth House. This was a revolutionary work that took Western architecture, previously enclosed by masonry walls, to the realization of interior/exterior continuity by means of a glazed exterior. However, the windows on the perimeter are all fixed, and though a visual continuity between the inside and outside is achieved, there is no physical continuity as in traditional Japanese homes, where spaces can be exposed or enclosed by the use of

screens. _ Emilio Ambasz, *Shigeru Ban*, New York: Princeton Architectural Press, 2001

The Curtain Wall House was formed with an actual exterior curtain wall. The idea was to create a contemporary interpretation of traditional Japanese spaces with contemporary materials. _ Emilio Ambasz, *Shigeru Ban*, New York: Princeton Architectural Press, 2001

**"Physical Transparency"** I wanted to make a transparent house, according to Japanese traditional way, open-close, so not only visually transparent but also physically inside and outside spaces are connected. I call this "physical transparency." _ Tom Pritzker and Shigeru Ban interview by Charlie Rose, *Charlie Rose*, March 25, 2014

Instead of thick, heavy walls, traditional Japanese houses are enveloped in wafer-thin membranes— *shooji, fusuma, amado,* and *sudare*—which are added or removed to suit the weather and the season. My curtain provides these same features of Japanese indoor climate control so my clients will continue to enjoy the calm, outward-looking, people-centered lifestyle of Old Japan. _ Shigeru Ban, *Abitare* 364, July/August 1997

## DESIGN

I'm not interested in making trendy shapes. My designs naturally emerge from solving some problem or dealing with some condition or developing some technology—it's not just making a form. If you design a building made from steel, you can do anything. You create the structure, add some cladding, and you can produce any shape. But once you start doing that, it's like a drug. You want to take stronger and stronger drugs. There is no limitation. I'm not interested in such freedom. I'm looking for limitations and for ways to take advantage of these limitations. _ "Architect Shigeru Ban's Temporary Cathedral for Christchurch," *Urbis* 64, October 2011

In order to make a better building you have to have more time for designing and more time for building. But if you save time, especially using a computer, and spend less time designing and less time in construction, architecture gets worse and worse. It's a repetition of the same kind of building everywhere. You can make a strange shape, but it's just strange, it's just unusual, it doesn't mean it's beautiful. _ Andrew Barrie, "Christchurch Transitional (Cardboard) Cathedral," *Architecture New Zealand* 3, May 2013

## THE CHINESE HAT

I happened to buy a Chinese hat in 1998 in Paris. I was working at that time on the Japanese pavilion in Hanover but I was coming almost every weekend to Paris. I saw this hat in a Chinese crafts shop in Saint-Germain-des-Prés and I was astonished at how architectonic it was. The structure is made of bamboo, and there is a layer of oil paper for waterproofing. There is also a layer of dry leaves for insulation. It is just like architecture for a building. Since I bought this hat, I wanted to design a roof in a similar manner. _ Philip Jodidio, *Shigeru Ban, Complete Works 1985–2015*, Cologne: Taschen, 2015

Museums have to be very practical. They can't just be sculpture. _ Carolina A. Miranda, *Architect*, March 8, 2014

**The Choice of Wood** Wood is the most ecological thing. Steel, concrete—we are just consuming from a limited amount. Timber is the only renewable material. A concrete building stays only a hundred years, and it's very difficult to replace or repair, where timber is very easy to repair. _ Dana Goodyear, *The New Yorker*, August 11 and 18, 2014

**NEW YORK 2011**
# METAL SHUTTER HOUSE
There were originally many warehouses in Chelsea in New York, and a lot of galleries moved from Soho in the 1980's because the rent had been raised there. Most wide entrances of warehouses and gallery windows were covered with shutters. That impression of the area is the context in which this building is set. _ Shigeru Ban, courtesy Shigeru Ban Architects

It's a work on the idea of transparency. Because the site is in the shadow of high-rise buildings for much of the day, each residential unit has been designed with doubly high spaces on the southern side with retractable glass shutters. _ Judith Benhamou-Huet, *Interview Magazine*, April 28, 2009

The north façade features screens made of roll-up perforated security shutters to provide privacy while helping to create a distinctly unique openness to the city beyond. The living room with a double-height ceiling connects to a terrace outside, and the double-height façade is able to open entirely using bi-fold doors. _ Shigeru Ban, courtesy Shigeru Ban Architects

**Manufacturing Challenges** In the original design, we proposed to use glass shutters which I have used many times in several projects before, but it was not manufactured in the United States. Therefore, we developed the bi-fold door with mullions of glass, which has been modified from the horizontal folding door normally used for airplane hangars at airports in the U.S. _ Shigeru Ban, courtesy Shigeru Ban Architects

Ban paired the practical design of the gallery spaces with the beauty, craftsmanship, and striking use of wood throughout the structure.

**ASPEN 2014**
# ASPEN ART MUSEUM
The site is in the middle of downtown, and it was quite disappointing when I first saw it. I couldn't see mountains or anything. _ Ted Loos, *Cultured Magazine*, July 2015

The site was small in terms of having a big foyer, so I made the foyer on top of the roof. You take the grand stair or the elevator up there to enjoy the view of the mountains and then come down to look at the galleries and art. It's the same sequence when you ski. _ Ted Loos, *Cultured Magazine*, July 2015

In designing the Aspen Art Museum, I wanted to create a site-specific sequence that took into account the mountain views and the building's purpose as an art museum, and to open the building to the outside so visitors could appreciate the beauty of Aspen from inside the building. _ Anna Winston, *Dezeen*, August 6, 2014

In a traditional Western downtown, the street fabric is controlled—all the buildings are the same height, the same material. In Aspen, there are many nice, old brick buildings. I wanted to make this a traditional volume, a brown boxlike building, to be part of the downtown fabric. _ Dana Goodyear, *The New Yorker*, August 11 and 18, 2014

Space was a major factor in the design, requiring that Ban consider how to best maximize floor area ratio. Each unit became a maisonette having double-high spaces.

> **I WANTED TO OPEN THE LIVING ROOM TO THE CITYSCAPE BECAUSE MOST APARTMENTS IN NEW YORK ARE VERY CLOSED.**

## PAPER ARCHITECTS

The Cooper Union has a long tradition of paper architects, very well-known architects who have produced important theoretical and conceptual work. . . . In fact, it is because their contributions are essentially in the fields of theory and teaching that they have been called paper architects. I am carrying on this tradition of Cooper Union architects, though in a different way. _ "Interview with Shigeru Ban," *Quaderns* 226, July 2000

## JOHN HEJDUK

His works shocked me. They looked like toys, with simple colors and geometry, totally different from what I saw in Tokyo. _ Michael Kimmelman, *New York Times Magazine*, May 20, 2007

## INFLUENCES
## FREI OTTO

*Shigeru Ban asked Frei Otto to collaborate with him on the design of the Japan Pavilion at the Hanover Expo 2000.*

When most people think of Frei Otto, they think of a structural engineer; but in fact, he is an architect. My first meeting with Otto occurred on July 1, 1997, when I visited him at his atelier in the town of Warmbronn. I have had great respect for Otto ever since my first years in college: I will never forget the excitement I felt on my first encounter with his Munich Olympic Stadium and his multipurpose hall in Mannheim, Germany. _ Matilda McQuaid, *Shigeru Ban*, London: Phaidon Press, 2003

I also dreamed of designing expo structures. When I got the commission to design the Japanese Pavilion at the Hanover Exhibition, I immediately thought that I need a local strong architect or engineer to help me. _ Philip Jodidio, *Shigeru Ban, Complete Works 1985–2015*, Cologne: Taschen, 2015

I don't like to be influenced by the fashionable style of the day. Always, in architecture, there are many styles that are fashionable or very popular, but I like architects like Frei Otto or Buckminster Fuller, who made their own styles. _ David Basulto, *Arch Daily*, March 25, 2014

## ALVAR AALTO: "COMPASSIONATE APPROACH TO ARCHITECTURE"

I went to Finland, in 1985, and it was there that I understood that the contribution of Alvar Aalto was capital. To understand his work, you have to go to the sites in question, because he really created buildings that function in their environments. . . . The most important thing, in order to forge one's own creative personality, is to travel, to see different environments, different cultures. _ Judith Benhamou-Huet, *Interview Magazine*, April 28, 2009

## LOUIS KAHN

He was striving in India and Bangladesh to make their own cities and capitals without being paid. He's really the one who worked in the country where the people needed dignity. _ Tom Pritzker and Shigeru Ban interview by Charlie Rose, *Charlie Rose*, March 25, 2014

### SHIZUOKA 2001
## PAPER ART MUSEUM
*This project includes the museum, referenced as "A" by the architect, and contemporary art gallery, "B." The client, an important paper manufacturer, wanted the museum as an homage to paper, including his own collection as well as other Japanese art and graphic design.*

Striking in its simplicity, yet compelling for the ease in which each of the features work in seamless elegance. The design reinforces Ban's regard for the dialogue between interior and exterior spaces.

Paper Art Museum A is the private museum of a paper manufacturer. All the façades are composed of fiberglass reinforced panels. The square floor plan is divided into three rows, and the middle is a three-story-high atrium. By opening stacking shutters and awnings (*shitomido*), a spatial continuity of the interior and exterior is achieved. Paper Art Museum B is formerly the laboratory and has been renovated as a gallery for contemporary art. By reversing the rails of the overhead sliding doors, when they are opened they act as a large shading device and create a comfortable shaded patio space. The idea in both buildings was to recreate, using contemporary materials, spaces for contemporary life while maintaining continuity between interior and exterior in a very Japanese manner. _ Shigeru Ban, courtesy Shigeru Ban Architects

## THE USE OF MATERIALS

My development was using more humble material, or weaker material. The strength of the material has nothing to do with the strength of the building, even nothing to do with durability. I knew logically that even using a weaker material like a paper tube I could make a strong building. _ Dana Goodyear, *The New Yorker*, August 11 and 18, 2014

I have always used everyday materials and technologies, though differently to how they are normally employed. _ "Interview with Shigeru Ban," *Quaderns* 226, July 2000

## “ ANYTHING CAN BE A STRUCTURE. WATER, AIR, GRASS, PAPER. ”

Wood is such a wonderful material, and it's the only renewable one. Once you start using steel connections, the timber becomes an ornament. It's more interesting to explore the limitations of the material. _ Ted Loos, *Cultured Magazine*, July 2015

## PAPER TUBES: AN ACCIDENTAL OPPORTUNITY

I came to develop paper tubes in the 1980s more by chance than anything else. No one was talking about environmental issues in those days, but I had a strong desire to respect material values and reduce waste. _ Koh Kitayama and Shigeru Ban, "Architecture for Nurturing People: A Conversation between Koh Kitayama and Shigeru Ban," in *Shigeru Ban: Humanitarian Architecture*, 2014

I do not know the meaning of "Green Architect." I have no interest in "Green," "Eco," and "Environmentally Friendly." _ Dana Goodyear, *The New Yorker*, August 11 and 18, 2014

I think it's impossible to reach "no waste," to reach "zero." My purpose of architecture is to recycle the material as much as possible—to minimize waste. _ Eugenia Lim, *Assemble Papers* 5, April 2016

## “ I DON'T CONSIDER THE ENVIRONMENTAL PROBLEM AS MY STRATEGY. ”

While working on the Emilio Ambasz exhibition in Tokyo's Axis Gallery [in 1985] I used transparent fabric to partition the space. _ Vladimir Belogolovsky, *Conversations with Architects: In the Age of Celebrity*, Berlin: DOM Publishers, 2015

## “ I USED PAPER TUBES IN ORDER TO STOP CUTTING TREES. ”

When we had finished hanging the fabric, only the paper tubes remained. Instead of throwing them away, I brought them back to my office. _ Philip Jodidio, *Shigeru Ban, Complete Works 1985–2015*, Cologne: Taschen, 2015

A year later, in the same gallery, I was working on an exhibition of the works of Alvar Aalto, who is well known for using natural wood in his warm and cozy interiors. But the use of natural wood for the exhibit would have been prohibitively expensive. Then I remembered the tubes, went to a local paper factory and found out that cardboard tubes can be manufactured to any diameter and length. That is how this cheap material, imitating wood, appeared in the show and then again and again in so many other of my projects. _ Vladimir Belogolovsky, *Conversations with Architects: In the Age of Celebrity*, Berlin: DOM Publishers, 2015

Any building, regardless of what it is made of, has to be fireproof and isolated from bad weather. So what difference does it make what a building is made of? The paper that I use for construction is specially treated to make it fireproof and waterproof. _ Vladimir Belogolovsky, *Conversations with Architects: In the Age of Celebrity*, Berlin: DOM Publishers, 2015

## “ BUCKMINSTER FULLER USED PAPER TUBES IN HIS FAMOUS GEODESIC DOMES. BUT NO ONE BEFORE ME BUILT PERMANENT STRUCTURES PRIMARILY OUT OF PAPER. ”

## EARLY PAPER ARCHITECTURE

I began to design a multi-purpose hall for an event celebrating the fiftieth anniversary of the city of Odawara. [This was in 1990.] I finally had the opportunity to design a true piece of paper architecture, albeit a temporary one. I decided to ask Gengo Matsui to do the structural design. . . . My collaboration with Matsui eventually produced the Odawara Pavilion and Gate, Library of a Poet, paper gallery, and the Paper House. The paper tube structure developed for the Paper House was approved by the Minister of Construction and added to the Building Standard Law. . . . I learned that anything is possible if the design is credible and one has the will. _ Emilio Ambasz, *Shigeru Ban*, New York: Princeton Architectural Press, 2001

## "I SENSE THAT THIS MONUMENT IN CHRISTCHURCH WILL BE LOVED AND USED BY THE CITIZENS OF NEW ZEALAND FOR A LONG TIME."

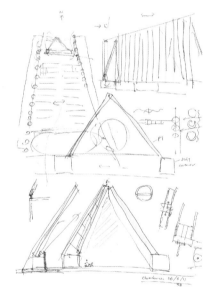

Although intended to be temporary, the beauty of the completed cathedral and the community's response far exceeded the initial need. The shelter is supported with 196 paper tubes with 15cm gaps in between, which also result in myriad plays of light and shadow throughout the day.

**NEW ZEALAND 2013**

# TEMPORARY CATHEDRAL, CHRISTCHURCH

*On New Zealand's South Island, a magnitude 6.3 earthquake struck on February 21, 2011. The town of Christchurch, with a population of about 400,000, was heavily damaged, including the land-marked cathedral, its spire sent careening into the village square. The earthquake occurred barely five months after a previous one in New Zealand, on September 4, 2010.*

Eighteen days before the Japanese earthquake, there was a big earthquake in New Zealand. They lost their most important Anglican church. I was asked to design a church to be the symbol for the recovery from the earthquake and using locally available paper tubes. _ Tom Pritzker and Shigeru Ban interview by Charlie Rose, *Charlie Rose*, March 25, 2014

The news on the earthquake in Christchurch had a huge impact on Japanese people, especially that it had caused the death of many Japanese language students there. . . . There is no word to describe the hopelessness in losing precious lives of the Japanese students who would have played an active part in the world, especially knowing that this resulted as the consequence of ignoring structural reinforcement suggestions made when an earthquake had just hit Christchurch the previous year. Christchurch was a place I wished to visit for that reason. . . .

The former neo-Gothic style Christchurch Cathedral had experienced earthquake three times during its construction, completed in 1904. It was one of the most visited tourist destinations in New Zealand. Unfortunately, the aftershock had demolished the cathedral, its front stained glass rose window left without hope and possibility whatsoever of repair or reconstruction. The cathedral was barely keeping its form by huge steel reinforcements, but we could still imagine the previous iconic façade which had been formed by the strong form of the equilateral triangle roof. . . .

As per request from the church at the very beginning regarding materials and structure, we were expecting to use paper tubes. We fortunately found out that there was a paper tube factory within [the city of] Christchurch itself. In order to meet the church ideal of having 700 seats as well as constructing the paper tube structure at low cost, I designed an A-frame structure as it is also convenient for repro-ducing the front roof of equilateral triangle and the back side isosceles triangle of the old cathedral. . . .

The cathedral happened to be the first public building to be built after the earthquake and due to its unique material being paper, the cathedral was given the nickname "Cardboard Cathedral." Before its completion, the cathedral naturally became the symbol of New Zealand's restoration. I have heard that besides religious ceremony, the cathedral has been a place of gathering for the community where concerts and dinner parties were held since its opening. _ Shigeru Ban, "Disaster Relief as a Monument"

**The Christchurch Design**  Many people connected my design with Maori meeting house structures. . . . They saw my design as somehow relating to New Zealand's architectural history, but it was by accident. But we explained that the geometry of the new building was derived from the original cathedral. _ "Architect Shigeru Ban's Temporary Cathedral for Christchurch," *Urbis* 64, October 2011

**Funds for Construction**  The important thing for me is that I never wait until all the funding is in place to start a project. Always, I start first and then, during the design and construction, keep searching out the funds. If you wait until the funding is ready, any emergency project will be too late. Also, once something is happening, it becomes easier to gather funding. _ "Architect Shigeru Ban's Temporary Cathedral for Christchurch," *Urbis* 64, October 2011

❝❝ **I'M PLEASED WHEN THE INHABITANTS ARE HAPPY.** ❞❞

## DISASTER WORK

*In 1994, upon seeing photographs of the refugee camps in Rwanda depicting two million people in poorly assembled shelters, Ban contacted the Office of the United Nations High Commissioner for Refugees (UNHCR).*

I had no experience with this sort of problem, but I went to Rwanda and went to see the high commissioner. My timing was good. Many companies had been trying to sell him their products, to make money. With my proposal, the [paper] tubes could be made cheaply and simply and by the people on site, if they got a little training with equipment that even Rwanda had. _ Michael Kimmelman, *New York Times Magazine*, May 20, 2007

❝❝ **YOU NEED LOVE**
**TO CARRY OUT GOOD PROJECTS.** ❞❞

I have been working on several emergency housings projects in the past starting with developing the refugee camp in Rwanda after the civil war in 1994. I have also worked on improving shelters and building temporary houses for victims who lost their homes due to earthquakes and tsunamis which are constantly happening around the world each year. Amongst these projects, I worked on bigger scale projects for larger public such as the temporary church, Paper Church, in Kobe after the 1995 earthquake (although it was only a total of 150m²) as well as a temporary concert hall in L'Aquila in Italy. Although these couple of projects were of larger scales, there were not monumentality buildings and the facilities were meant for a small community. _ Shigeru Ban, "Disaster Relief as a Monument"

I look for people who have a particular problem. Always I take care of smaller groups of people. My capacity is not big enough. The bigger number of people has to be taken care of by the government. _ Dana Goodyear, *The New Yorker*, August 11 and 18, 2014

Initially, I had a feeling of "do something out of kindness" for those in trouble. So I expected gratitude since I am doing something for them out of kindness. But I came to realize this wouldn't work well unless you know that you are doing it for yourself, even though your actions might do good for others as a result. _ Koh Kitayama and Shigeru Ban, "Architecture for Nurturing People: A Conversation between Koh Kitayama and Shigeru Ban," in *Shigeru Ban: Humanitarian Architecture*, 2014

## "TEMPORARY BUILDINGS" AND LOVE

Architecture does not have to exist permanently anymore. Environments are changing around us; we can work anywhere with an internet connection; we have diverse means of transportation and our way of life, such as living in the same place permanently, is surely changing. In such an age, there is no difference between temporary and permanent architecture. Even a concrete building is temporary in that a developer buys the site and destroys the building to replace it with another for the purpose of making money. On the other hand, something temporary can have a permanent existence, as when the Paper Church in Kobe was taken down and moved to Taomi Village. In that sense, whether something becomes permanent or not isn't decided by architectural materials. Whether people come to love a structure or not determines if it becomes permanent or remains merely temporary. _ Eugenia Lim, *Assemble Papers* 5, April 2016

*In 2000, Shigeru Ban built Paper Log House following an earthquake in Turkey in 1999. Some local architects feared the public would not embrace the new structures. In fact, they welcomed their relief homes.*

People said they felt more comfortable in the paper houses because the concrete and brick houses had collapsed and people were killed in their sleep. The paper houses wouldn't fall on them in the middle of the night. _ Michael Kimmelman, *New York Times Magazine*, May 20, 2007

closets and shelves in all of our houses with the help of volunteers and with the donation fund. It will become a breakthrough and precedent to new government standards of evacuation facilities and temporary housing. _ Shigeru Ban, courtesy Shigeru Ban Architects

The area of the house is exactly the same, but much more comfortable. Many of the people want to stay here forever. I was very happy to hear that. _ "Temporary Shelters Made from Paper," lecture by Shigeru Ban for TEDx Tokyo, May 13, 2013

To provide more space to store, Voluntary Architects' Network (VAN) assembled shelves and installed them to each room. About 200 people gathered from all over the country to volunteer in Onagawa, Miyagi, prefecture. _ Shigeru Ban, courtesy Shigeru Ban Architects

We built a market in the center of the site. Stores are not located in this neighborhood, and daily necessities are not accessible. The market is also for locals to open their shops. The big tent creates space in the market where people get together. _ Shigeru Ban, courtesy Shigeru Ban Architects

## ❜❜ I HOWEVER BELIEVE THAT IF ARCHITECTS WERE MORE INVOLVED IN DISASTER RELIEF, WE COULD BUILD BETTER QUALITY TEMPORARY EMERGENCY HOUSES. ❛❛

Creativity and high-quality design characterize Ban's emergency relief housing. Innovative materials—paper tubes, bamboo, and shipping containers for Onagawa—are deployed with skill, invention, thrift, and ease of execution. There is one other word that applies to all the architect's disaster relief housing: *respect*.

### MIYAGI 2011
# ONAGAWA TEMPORARY CONTAINER HOUSING AND COMMUNITY CENTER
Since the 3.11 earthquake [in Japan], we have visited more than 50 evacuation facilities and installed over 1,800 units (2m x 2m) of our Paper Partition System, to ensure privacy between families. During that time, I heard the news that the town of Onagawa was having difficulty to construct enough temporary housing due to the insufficient amount of flat land. Therefore, we decided to propose three-story temporary housing made from shipping containers. By stacking these containers in a checkerboard pattern, our system creates bright, open living spaces in between the containers. . . . We installed built-in

**Using Shipping Containers** *Shigeru Ban learned that in addition to limited housing for disaster relief, much of it is suitable only for level terrain. The challenging topography in Onagawa led him to find a more adaptable solution by using shipping containers for the following reasons.*

- Shorten the construction period by usage of existing containers
- Wide interval can provide parking area, community facility and privacy of families
- Placing containers in a checkerboard pattern creates open living space in between
- Excellent seismic performance
- Can be used as a permanent apartment
_ Shigeru Ban, courtesy Shigeru Ban Architects

## RESPONSIBLE ARCHITECTURE

I was thinking: How can we use our experience and knowledge for the general public, or for someone like a victim of an earthquake? And that is why I became interested in making temporary structures for victims. _ Brad Pitt and Shigeru Ban, "Paper Architecture & Make It Right: A Conversation between Brad Pitt and Shigeru Ban," in *Shigeru Ban: Humanitarian Architecture*, 2014

**" I HOWEVER BELIEVE THAT IF ARCHITECTS WERE MORE INVOLVED IN DISASTER RELIEF, WE COULD BUILD BETTER QUALITY TEMPORARY EMERGENCY HOUSES. "**

I started working on disaster relief projects and temporary buildings because I felt a strong sense of discomfort with the traditional function of architects—that is to build monuments for the privileged social class. However I think that I, myself, ended up building monuments, only this time not for the privileged social class, but for people to love them. _ Shigeru Ban, "Disaster Relief as a Monument"

I always want to work with a community to find out their particular problem, especially after I worked for the UN in refugee situations. The UN cannot solve the problem of the minority people, so I always go there to find out the particular problem of the minority people to show by design. Even the temporary shelter has to be beautiful and comfortable. _ Tom Pritzker and Shigeru Ban interview by Charlie Rose, *Charlie Rose*, March 25, 2014

Natural disasters could actually be defined as "man-made disasters." For instance, people are not directly killed from an earthquake, they die being hit by collapsing buildings. That is the responsibility of architects. _ Shigeru Ban, "Disaster Relief as a Monument"

## TEACHING

*Since the early 1990s, Shigeru Ban has taught architecture in Japan and in the United States.*

I received a good education in the U.S., but I wasn't able to give anything back to my teachers. I thought that the only thing I would be able to do was to teach those younger than me. I also supposed that educating the next generation would be significant for me as an architect since I'm convinced that good education made me what I am now. _ Koh Kitayama and Shigeru Ban, "Architecture for Nurturing People: A Conversation between Koh Kitayama and Shigeru Ban," in *Shigeru Ban: Humanitarian Architecture*, 2014

## VAN

*In response to his disaster relief work following the Kobe earthquake of 1995, Ban formed Voluntary Architects' Network [VAN], a coalition of volunteer students and others to provide help worldwide. To date, VAN has worked in areas such as Turkey, India, Nepal, Haiti, New Zealand, Italy, and of course Japan.*

Students often consult with me and express the desire to join VAN, but we don't have full-time staff. Although such attitudes are laudable, I always tell them to first achieve a degree of competency as architects. They have realized the importance of architecture's social responsibility and are trying to work for an organization that supports this idea. However, they won't be of use if they don't have the necessary architectural skills. _ Koh Kitayama and Shigeru Ban, "Architecture for Nurturing People: A Conversation between Koh Kitayama and Shigeru Ban," in *Shigeru Ban: Humanitarian Architecture*, 2014

I no longer teach in Japan, but as soon as I organize a project, my former students get together with my office and take steps to intervene quickly. . . . I want to emphasize that the students are indeed the heart and engine of reconstruction as well as the hope for the future. _ Francesca Picchi, *Domus*, May 9, 2011

**" THE WORK OF ARCHITECTS IS CREATING BUILDINGS, BUT I KEENLY BELIEVE THAT WHAT IS TRULY SIGNIFICANT IS FOSTERING PEOPLE. "**

## JAPAN: NURTURING ARCHITECTURE

It is often said overseas that many good architects are produced in Japan. I suppose one of the factors is the Japanese system for fostering young architects. Japan could be the only country where the middle-class people pay, even if it's a low price, for architects to create interesting architecture. . . . Japan must certainly be a place of experimentation for young architects and a good environment for their training. _ Koh Kitayama and Shigeru Ban, "Architecture for Nurturing People: A Conversation between Koh Kitayama and Shigeru Ban," in *Shigeru Ban: Humanitarian Architecture*, 2014

## WHEN A PROJECT IS PLEASING

I am happy when I can meet the people who will move into my houses. That is why I don't like working on apartment complexes, since I don't know who is going to live there. Occasionally, I like visiting my museums or churches, and hide behind one of the paper columns simply to observe the visitors. I enjoy doing that a lot. _ Vladimir Belogolovsky, *Conversations with Architects: In the Age of Celebrity*, Berlin: DOM Publishers, 2015

**TRANSFORMING MEMORIES** People of every age have tried to preserve in their domestic space memories of the land that are inscribed in their bodies. This transformation of memory into space happens not just with personal memories but also with those of families and whole local communities. Houses built in this way pass through generations of desperate struggle with nature until they become almost like extensions of the human skin. At the same time, however, people have always striven to build another kind of home to house their memories of the future.... When people try to slip into skins made of steel, glass, aluminum or plastic, they experience a liberation of their bodies as if they were moving into another dimension.... It would not be an unnatural body, but one accustomed to a new nature, and one which would still be able to accept the old. It is only when these two natures come together that houses seeking new bodies will start to speak a positive language. _ Andrea Maffei, ed., *Toyo Ito: Works Projects Writings*, London: Phaidon Press, 2002

# TOYO ITO

**BORN:** June 1, 1941, Keijo (Seoul), Korea

**EDUCATION:** Tokyo University, Department of Architecture, 1965

**OFFICE:** Toyo Ito & Associates, Architects, Fujiya Building, 1-19-4, Shibuya, Shibuya-ku, Tokyo, 150-0002 Japan
Tel: +81 3-3409-5822, Fax: +81 3-3409-5969
www.toyo-ito.co.jp

**PROJECTS FEATURED:** Home-for-All, Rikuzentakata, Japan, 2011; Tama Art University Library, Hachioji, Japan, 2007; Meiso no Mori Municipal Funeral Hall, Kakamigahara, Japan, 2006; Serpentine Gallery Pavilion, London, with Cecil Balmond and Arup, 2002; Sendai Mediatheque, Sendai, Japan, 2001; Tower of Winds, Yokohama, Japan, 1986

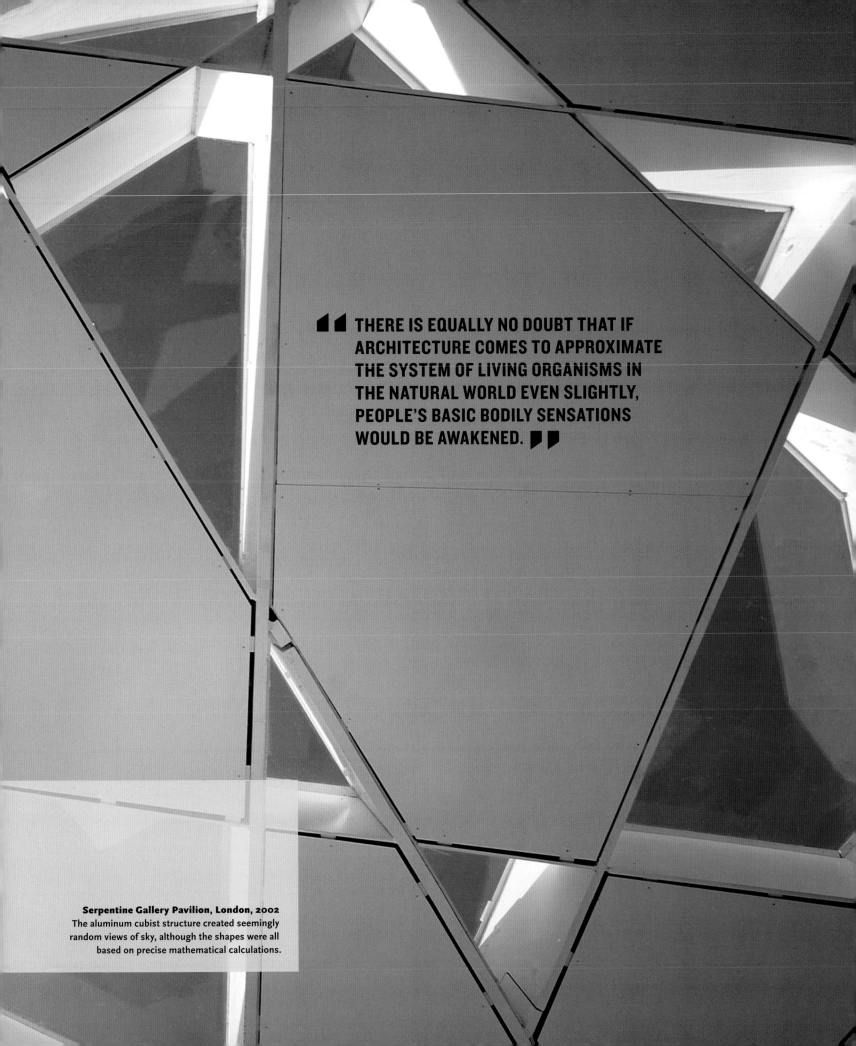

" THERE IS EQUALLY NO DOUBT THAT IF
ARCHITECTURE COMES TO APPROXIMATE
THE SYSTEM OF LIVING ORGANISMS IN
THE NATURAL WORLD EVEN SLIGHTLY,
PEOPLE'S BASIC BODILY SENSATIONS
WOULD BE AWAKENED. "

**Serpentine Gallery Pavilion, London, 2002**
The aluminum cubist structure created seemingly
random views of sky, although the shapes were all
based on precise mathematical calculations.

## INFLUENCES:
## LE CORBUSIER

I don't know exactly why, but over the course of my career I have kept stumbling across Le Corbusier, even though I have never consciously followed in his footsteps. . . . I only become aware of his influence when people point it out to me, after looking at my models or my plans. Le Corbusier has played an important role in the works that I have designed so far. Although I am not aware of the end result that I am going to attain right from the outset, the fact is that the architecture of the Swiss master is always somewhere along the line of the route to be followed in order to get there. It is strange, but every time I deviate from the course I have laid down for myself and am then forced to change direction, I run into Le Corbusier again. _ Andrea Maffei, ed., *Toyo Ito: Works Projects Writings*, London: Phaidon Press, 2002

## MIES VAN DER ROHE

Mies's Barcelona Pavilion (1928–29) stands out as the most remarkable of all twentieth-century works of architecture. This is overwhelmingly true even in relation to all of the same architect's subsequent works. Nowhere else do we find a space filled with such "fluidity." . . . This not simply because of the spatial composition, but owes a great deal to the brilliance of the materials. . . . The sensation created by the space is not the lightness of flowing air but the thickness of molten liquid. _ Toyo Ito, "Tarzans in the Media Forest," in *Tarzans in the Media Forest*, London: Architectural Association Press, 2011

### ❝❝ BOTH LE CORBUSIER'S HOUSES AND MY OWN SEEK TO ESTABLISH A POSITIVE RELATIONSHIP WITH NATURE. ❞❞

I would claim what the transparency in Mies van der Rhoe's buildings and spaces display is something intrinsically different from the transparence we usually find in modernist architecture. . . . In my view, no architect equals Mies van der Rhoe in his passionate exploration and through understanding of the materiality of glass and steel. _ Toyo Ito, "Tarzans in the Media Forest," in Sylvia Liska, ed., *The Secession Talks, Exhibitions in Conversation 1998–2010*, Koln, Germany: Verlag der Buchandlung Walther König, 2012

## MIES AND LE CORBUSIER

According to Terunobu Fujimori's theory about the white and red schools of architecture, white describes Mies, and red describes Le Corbusier. . . . If one pole is abstract and the other is real, I am interested in the middle space. _ Blaine Brownell, "The Emerging Grid," in *Matter in the Floating World: Conversations with Leading Japanese Architects and Designers*, New York: Princeton Architectural Press, 2011

## AS A JAPANESE ARCHITECT

I was influenced in my early works by Kazuo Shinohara and Arata Isozaki. These were the only two figures in Japanese architecture at the time whose work contained a critical social message. _ "Toyo Ito 1986–1995," *El Croquis* 71, 1995

## EAST-WEST DESIGN PROCESS

I think the process of my design thought is much closer to the Japanese tradition than to Western architectural culture. Look, I can barely speak English, but I can express my architectural attitudes by a comparison between the English and Japanese languages, as I understand them. In English the words, as well as the interaction between words, are very definite and stabilized. It is certainly not so in the Japanese language, where the same types of word arrangement can be flexible. And I may say that I design space in the same way as I use words in the Japanese language. _ Georgi Stanishev, *World Architecture* 34, 1995

## SEEKING SYSTEMS THAT ENABLE CHANGE

Modernist architecture is all too familiar to both architects and users alike. We'd convinced ourselves that plain, unadorned, transparent, abstract spaces were ultimate beauty. That's how we designed buildings, and that's how we used them. Can't we by now have architecture based on different values? Isn't it time for buildings to offer "dynamic delight over aesthetic purity"? _ Toyo Ito, "Dynamic Delight over Aesthetic Purity," in *Tarzans in the Media Forest,* London: Architectural Association Press, 2011

The act of design begins with a personal expression of my unbearable frustration with regard to the state of society and the city. _ Toyo Ito, "Shedding the Modern Body Image: Is a House without Criticality Possible?" in *Tarzans in the Media Forest,* London: Architectural Association Press, 2011

## TOKYO

The act of creating, or rather, choreographing a piece of architecture in a city like Tokyo is akin to playing chess. It is a completely unpredictable game. _ Toyo Ito, *Architectural Design* 62, September/October 1992

### ❝❝ ONCE WE DON'T UNDERSTAND THE WORLD, THAT'S WHEN WE ARE CREATIVE. ❞❞

Moreover, when I participate in an overseas competition, I feel free and I am able to develop a bold proposal because the place is far away and I do not have any direct knowledge of the client at first. I have to compete while working under many constraints in proposal-type or limited competitions in Japan. That is the crucial difference. I feel I have been liberated considerably by my experiences overseas. _ Toyo Ito and Kumiko Inui, *A + U: Architecture and Urbanism* 5, May 2004

## HACHIOJI 2007
# TAMA ART UNIVERSITY LIBRARY

I don't make any distinction between a library and a museum. I'm mainly interested in softening up the rigid programs of conventional libraries and museums, making them more ambiguous. _ Toyo Ito and Thomas Daniell, *Volume* 15, 2008

The new library is located to one side of the main gate; many students will pass by it on their way to various university buildings. That's why our aim is to create not only a place for reading and studying, but a center for the student community. We decided therefore to make the new library as low as possible, even though buildings on the campus are nearly all four to five stories in height. _ Toyo Ito, *A + U: Architecture and Urbanism* 6, June 2005

On the first floor . . . the space is like an extension of the garden which stretches from the main gate. A large portion of the floor is gently inclined to reflect the slope of the site. _ Toyo Ito, *A + U: Architecture and Urbanism* 6, June 2005

While designing the Tama Art University Library, I worried every day whether spaces with sloping floors would be safe for the future users of the library. . . . The furniture is custom-made for the slope—the magazine racks have sloping tops and the legs of the computer tables have different lengths to support the horizontal tabletops. _ Toyo Ito and Thomas Daniell, *Volume* 15, 2008

I was inspired by the l'Institut National d'Histoire de l'Art in Paris. That's not because it's also a library. I just liked the slenderness and elegance of the steel arches and the stimulating space they create. I also found it very interesting that although the arch is an ancient architectural element this project was built using a technology that was very innovative at the time. _ Toyo Ito and Thomas Daniell, *Volume* 15, 2008

There is no question that I have used a lot of ovals in my recent projects. And I am somewhat concerned they might be a bit too expressive. But I believe the ideal of architecture is to provide the minimum required to cover one's immediate needs. Places where people gather to communicate with each other are like little whirlpools. The oval functions symbolize the area which accommodates this whirlpool. _ "Toyo Ito 1986–1995," *El Croquis* 71, 1995

In Tama, the arches are repeated, but I believe both movement and stillness can be expressed by curving and changing the span of the arches. _ Toyo Ito, *A + U: Architecture and Urbanism* 6, June 2005

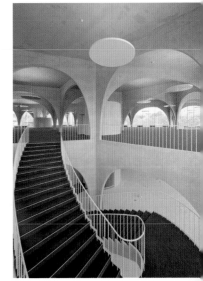

Curves, arches, slopes are all manifest throughout Tama, creating what Ito called its "most distinctive characteristic . . . rhythm."

## ARCHITECTURE AS A GARDEN

I have always conceived my architecture by superimposing it on a garden, which means that I saw my works as gardens and not that my aim was necessarily to create an architecture that blended into the landscape. . . . I have attempted to conceal the volume of the buildings or to establish a positive relationship between the individual buildings and the space outside by removing or adding earth. _ Andrea Maffei, ed., *Toyo Ito: Works Projects Writings*, London: Phaidon Press, 2002

## GARDENS OF LIGHT

Yet my first attempt to produce a work like a garden, the House at Nakano or the White U [1976], resulted in a space that resembled a *kaiyu* garden. A "garden of light" was created between two concrete walls that curved to form a U. A luminous space rich in effects of light and shade, produced by the natural illumination from above and the sides, was formed within this tubular ring of spotless white. The phenomenon of light was used to create a space filled with currents and vortices. _ Andrea Maffei, ed., *Toyo Ito: Works Projects Writings*, London: Phaidon Press, 2002

## GARDENS OF WIND

What the two projects [Silver Hut, 1984, and the Municipal Museum of Yatsushiro, 1991] have in common are their continuous light and thin vaulted roofs, constructed out of a framework of steel slats, and the free space between the independent columns that support them. Should not such a space be regarded as a garden that induces currents of air, like the wind blowing through a wood? _ Andrea Maffei, ed., *Toyo Ito: Works Projects Writings*, London: Phaidon Press, 2002

Like clouds, or currents of air, or plants growing, the undulating roof of Meiso No Mori offers organic tranquility.

### KAKAMIGAHARA 2006
# MEISO NO MORI MUNICIPAL FUNERAL HALL
Our idea was to respond not with a conventional crematorium, but with a space formed by a roof that is like a cloud which, drifting through the sky, has come to settle upon the site, creating a pleasantly soft atmosphere. _ Riken Yamamoto, Dana Buntrock, and Taro Igarashi, *Toyo Ito*, London: Phaidon Press, 2009

The final shape of the roof structure was determined by an algorithm that generates the optimum structural solution. Since this type of structural analysis resembles the growth patterns of plants which keep transforming, following simple natural rules, the process is called "evolution." . . . The curved line becomes landscape, in harmony with the contours of the surrounding mountains. _ Riken Yamamoto, Dana Buntrock, and Taro Igarashi, *Toyo Ito*, London: Phaidon Press, 2009

Since the early 1980s, I've desired, on the one hand, to create pure, modernist spaces and, on the other hand, to create buildings making abundant use of more organic, three-dimensionally curved surfaces that are apt to be labeled expressionistic. When one desire has been satisfied, the other inevitably becomes more urgent. As a consequence, I seem to have repeatedly alternated between these two tendencies. This is accounted for in part by a desire I have long had to create fluid spaces. _ Toyo Ito and Kumiko Inui, *A + U: Architecture and Urbanism* 5, May 2004

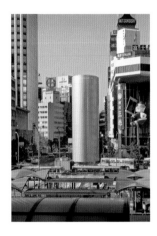

## YOKOHAMA 1986
# TOWER OF WINDS
My interest in electronic phenomena commenced with the Tower of Winds in 1986. The project cannot exactly be defined as a work of architecture, but it was the precursor of a series of works in which both light and images have been utilized. At the base of the Tower of Winds lay the intention of selecting the air (wind) and sound (noise) from the various currents flowing through the surroundings and turning them into luminous signs, i.e., into visual information. To put it briefly, it was a question of introducing information into the environment. _ Andrea Maffei, ed., *Toyo Ito: Works Projects Writings,* London: Phaidon Press, 2002

**❝ DESIGNING ARCHITECTURE IS AN ACT OF GENERATING VORTEXES IN THE CURRENTS OF AIR, WIND, LIGHT, AND SOUND.... ❞**

All the lights are managed by computers, which correlate them according to signals coming from two main sensors in the tower: one reacting to the strength of the wind, the other to the intensity of the outside noise. _ Georgi Stanishev, *World Architecture* 34, 1995

People had the impression that the air was purified only around the tower. It is clear that in this case a substance could not have been expected to emit light into the air. Instead, the air itself became light. _ Andrea Maffei, ed., *Toyo Ito: Works Projects Writings,* London: Phaidon Press, 2002

**❝ AN EXPERIMENTAL INTERACTIVE SCULPTURE. ❞**

Ito covered the cylinder walls with semi-transparent sheets of aluminum and installed 20 neon rings and more than 1,000 fixed lights, which are visible at night. He described the interactive project as being a "design of the air."

## SPIRALING GEOMETRIES

If I am to go beyond modernism, I must retain the norms of modernism and disseminate them. I am also concerned about geometry—not the pure forms that Le Corbusier talked about—but a dynamic geometry, such as spirals and complex three-dimensional surfaces that recognize the concept of movement. _ Toyo Ito and Kumiko Inui, *A + U: Architecture and Urbanism* 5, May 2004

Why do so many life forms of the biosphere, plant and animal, embody spiral forms, yet architecture subsists on circles and ovals? . . . We had long wanted to incorporate spiraling geometries into our structures to realize more dynamic spaces. . . . Riken Yamamoto, Dana Buntrock, and Taro Igarashi, *Toyo Ito,* London: Phaidon Press, 2009

## VORTEX AND FLOW

It is critical to aim at spaces of unstable states which may be conducive to a movement or flow. Such spaces are also analogous to the physical movement of humans. _ Toyo Ito, *Architectural Design* 62, September/October 1992

Today we are able to create architecture based on the rules in the natural world by using computer technologies. However, we should use these rules not to make forms that imitate nature but instead to create architecture that breathes and is congruous with the environment. _ Pedro Gadanho and Phoebe Springstubb, eds., *A Japanese Constellation,* New York: Museum of Modern Art, 2016

## FLEXIBLE ORDER

Humanity developed its classical geometric shapes and grid spaces by seeking an absolute order against the world of natural phenomena, a world of animals and plants regarded as having no conceivable order because of its constant repetition of the cycle of fluid growth, decay, and death. What today attracts our attention most compellingly is exactly this fluid order in nature that constantly grows and changes. . . . This order is relative, flexible and soft. It is constantly and dynamically repeated self-organization. _ Riken Yamamoto, Dana Buntrock, and Taro Igarashi, *Toyo Ito*, London: Phaidon Press, 2009

## VIRTUAL BODIES, REAL PEOPLE

*Over the years, Ito has been actively engaged in thinking about the role of the virtual in his work, and how ideas of "home," "community," and what he calls "real nature" intersect.*

Prior to the Sendai Mediatheque I truly thought that spaces and facilities for the virtual body might be possible. That's what I intended in my Sendai Mediatheque competition proposal: the transparent, almost weightless sense of a virtual body, an array of computers in some kind of fantasy forest. However, right from the outset there was a huge pro-test against this imagery from people in the city. "Stop the construction of that building!" they yelled (laughs). That's the moment I stopped talking about the virtual body. I realized that I had to make real things for real people. _ Toyo Ito and Thomas Daniell, *Volume* 15, 2008

Electronic media are extending and connecting our closed-off individual selves to the social/outside world. . . . the new media has by imperceptible degrees blurred the dividing line that separates inside from outside. Even though we are dealing with seemingly antinomical concepts, we have to recognize that the entities we call our "real" and our "virtual" bodies are in fact overlapping and congruent. _ Toyo Ito, "Tarzans in the Media Forest," in Sylvia Liska, ed., *The Secession Talks, Exhibitions in Conversation 1998–2010*, Koln, Germany: Verlag der Buchandlung Walther König, 2012

Thus, each of us today possesses two bodies that allow us to respond to and cope with these two different forms of nature. Our real, or primitive, body linked to the natural world as a member in which water circulates, and our virtual body linked to the natural world as a member in which an electronic flow—information—circulates. _ Christian Schittich, *Detail* 50, no. 9, 2011

**❝ IF THE IDEAL LIFE IN THE AGE OF ELECTRICITY FOUND CONCRETE EXPRESSION IN 'MODERN LIVING,' WHAT WILL BE THE IMAGE OF THE IDEAL LIFE IN THE ERA OF THE COMPUTER? ❞**

### SENDAI 2001
## SENDAI MEDIATHEQUE
The building greeted the dawn of the new millennium with a countdown to zero hour on 1 January 2000, when the big glass doors in front opened and in rushed throngs of cheering people. _Riken Yamamoto, Dana Buntrock, and Taro Igarashi, *Toyo Ito*, London: Phaidon Press, 2009

**❝ SURELY ONE OF THE HIGH POINTS OF MY CAREER. ❞**

My early work was about lightness and delicacy. For the Sendai Mediatheque, however, I wanted to speak to the strength of architecture. . . . I wanted to convince people that architecture has significance to society. _ Blaine Brownell, "The Emerging Grid," in *Matter in the Floating World: Conversations with Leading Japanese Architects and Designers*, New York: Princeton Architectural Press, 2011

## ❝ I THREW OFF MY INHIBITIONS AT SENDAI. ❞

**Fostering Communication** People use the Mediatheque similarly to a public park: Young couples meet here, school children and seniors congregate, spontaneous conversations emerge. The architecture supports communication—that is very important to me. In Sendai, we have confronted numerous challenges that were, in return, received by the users in a surprisingly positive way. _ Christian Schittich, *Detail* 50, no. 9, 2011

If you talk to students in Sendai they say that even though the university library is a great resource, they prefer going to the Sendai Mediatheque. There is somehow a sense of relaxation there. I think it allows people to gain an understanding of many things—that is, of society itself.... _ Toyo Ito and Thomas Daniell, *Volume* 15, 2008

When I designed the Sendai building, I used the metaphor of water to guide my approach. The metaphor had two meanings for me. In one sense, I was thinking of water as, basically, the Internet: the fluid network that links the building to the rest of the world. At the same time, I was thinking about water in a more literal sense: Before modernization, the entire world was connected by water; water was the network for all transportation and communication. I wanted to incorporate both of these modes of exchange into the architecture, because balancing these two types of connection—one virtual, one physical—is probably one of the most important considerations for the architecture of the coming century. _ Julian Rose, *Artforum*, September 2013

**Like Planting a Grove of Trees** I began to want to show the material strength of such abstract, inorganic spaces only after the Sendai Mediatheque began construction. The strong contrast between organic-shaped "tubes" and thin, highly abstract "plates" almost seems like planting a grove of trees across an otherwise manmade expanse. _ Toyo Ito, "The New 'Real': Toward Reclaiming Materiality in Contemporary Architecture," in *Tarzans in the Media Forest*, London: Architectural Association Press, 2011

**Biomorphic Structures** What characterizes the Sendai Mediatheque project is the tubular columns that support the floors in six tiers. The slabs, measuring about 50m on a side, are supported by 13 tubes that act as the structure.... Natural light enters from the top of the tube. The tubes have different sizes and shapes depending on the functions they house. The design can be modified to adapt to the plan of the corresponding floor. In other words, these tubes are organic in nature, resembling plants in their forms and actions. They can be said to be biomorphic structures. _ Toyo Ito, "Tarzans in the Media Forest," in *Tarzans in the Media Forest*, London: Architectural Association Press, 2011

**Living Steel** Steelworkers had told me that "steel is a living thing," which sounded like utter nonsense until I actually witnessed those masses of steel stretching and bending with heat: the raw dynamic of real material was much more appealing than any pure, abstract beauty. _ Toyo Ito, "Dynamic Delight over Aesthetic Purity," in *Tarzans in the Media Forest*, London: Architectural Association Press, 2011

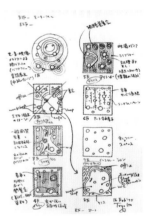

In Sendai, handling the steel plates was very difficult. We relied on ship builders for this task. They were very proud of their work, and their attitude expressed this: the Mediatheque would not happen without them.... While we use more and more sophisticated computer programs, at the end of the day, successful building depends very strongly on human manual labor on the construction site. _ Christian Schittich, *Detail* 50, no. 9, 2011

## ❝ THE SPATIAL EXPERIENCE IS NOT UNLIKE WALKING THROUGH THE WOODS. ❞

Water is one of the driving metaphors in Sendai's morphology, exemplified not only in the spiral shapes and tubular columns, but as flowing energy uniting technology and nature, the virtual and the real.

## FLUID BODIES

Underwater, organisms have far greater flexibility than on dry land. On dry land, gravity makes it necessary for fauna and flora alike to be armored with a rigid and self-supporting framework. Animals can never overcome the rigidity of motion imposed by this framework. But in water, the bodies of animals are subjected to pressure as well as the effects of buoyancy. Pliant and flexible structures stand up better to the flow or pressure of the water. It is better to be receptive and surrender to the forces than to resist them. Thus aquatic flora and fauna tend to sway and dance gracefully. These motions define the forms of living beings. The forms of aquatic creatures represent motions more explicitly than those living on the land. The forms of living beings are the loci of their motions. Indeed, they are "fluid bodies." _ Toyo Ito, "Tarzans in the Media Forest," in *Tarzans in the Media Forest*, London: Architectural Association Press, 2011

## THE INFORMATION ENVIRONMENT

The information environment significantly replaces the natural one.

Information and computer technologies are multiplying our possibilities of being present in many points simultaneously, condensing time and making it more efficient. _ Georgi Stanishev, *World Architecture* 34, 1995

Contemporary architecture needs to function, in addition, as a means of adapting ourselves to the information environment. It has to function as an extension of our skin in relation to both nature and information. Architecture today must be a media suit. _ Andrea Maffei, ed., *Toyo Ito: Works Projects Writings*, London: Phaidon Press, 2002

Our architecture has traditionally been linked with nature through the figuration of the vortices that occur in water and air. In contemporary architecture, we must link ourselves with the electronic environment through the figuration of vortices of information. The question is how can we integrate the primitive space linked with nature and the virtual space linked with the world through the electronic network. _ Andrea Maffei, ed., *Toyo Ito: Works Projects Writings*, London: Phaidon Press, 2002

## " IN A CATASTROPHE, A PUBLIC BUILDING REALLY NEEDS TO REMAIN OPEN, SO THAT PEOPLE CAN GATHER THERE. "

As Ito, in collaboration with three other architects, considered how to rebuild areas destroyed by the Great Earthquake of 2011, a few factors were manifest: to make use of existing materials when possible; to engage the community in building the new structures; and to create a genuine "home for all."

### RIKUZENTAKATA 2011
# HOME-FOR-ALL Social Responsibility

One of the most important lessons I took from the 1995 earthquake [in Kobe] was that it helped me understand the crucial role public architecture plays in the response to natural disasters. From that point on, I have thought as much about the social function the building will fulfill after a natural disaster as about how its structure will respond to an earthquake itself. In a catastrophe, a public building really needs to remain open, so that people can gather there. _ Julian Rose, *Artforum*, September 2013

My goal is not to reestablish the way of life that existed before the tsunami hit; it is to create a new social life for the next generation that will be growing up in the aftermath of the catastrophe. _ Julian Rose, *Artforum*, September 2013

**The "Home" in Home-for-All** *In March 2011, Japan's Pacific coastline was struck by an earthquake with a magnitude of 9.0–9.5, with a concurrent tsunami that generated waves as high as 130 feet, or 40 meters. Near-total destruction and damage included homes, fishing ports, commercial areas, airports, and the Fukushima nuclear power plant. In the aftermath of the Great East Japan Earthquake, Toyo Ito spearheaded an effort to build temporary community centers for those residents who had lost virtually everything. The Home-for-All project in Rikuzentakata was designed as a collaborative effort with three other architects: Sou Fujimoto, Akihisa Hirata, and Kumiko Inui. Today, in response to the 2011 earthquake, Ito + Partners and other leading architects have built sixteen Home-for-All buildings along the east coast of Japan.*

When I first launched the Home-for-All project, there were three objectives. One, it needs to provide people living in temporary housing a place to eat together and chat with one another. Two, it needs to be made by everyone—residents, architects, volunteers—all together. And three, it needs to serve as a base for local residents to discuss community regeneration. _ "Architecture after 3.11," lecture by Toyo Ito at the University of Tokyo, September 25, 2011, in "'Home-for-All' in Rikuzentakata, and the Venice Biennale International Architecture Exhibition," *Wochi Kochi Magazine*

The Home-for-All buildings create a different sense of place, more like that of a house in pre-modern Japan. They have northern and southern exposure and good natural light, which gives you a sense of contact with your surroundings. When possible, they use local materials. . . . And all the functions are gathered in one room: The living spaces are continuous with the kitchen and the hearth. The buildings don't have bedrooms, because they are not intended for a single family to inhabit, but placing one of them within a complex of temporary houses in the communities affected by the earthquake and tsunami offers a homelike atmosphere for everyone. By offering this kind of informal shared space, I am trying to establish conditions that will increase meaningful interaction between residents and encourage the development of new relationships. _ Julian Rose, *Artforum*, September 2013

### Influence of a Survivor: Mikiko Sugawara  The idea started to take concrete shape on November 26, 2011, when all of the team members visited Rikuzentakata together. There, we met Mikiko Sugawara. Despite having lost her mother and elder sister in the disaster, this woman was dedicating herself to a multitude of activities supporting her new community and its residents. Inspired by her energetic spark, we decided to build a Home-for-All on the grounds of her temporary housing site. [Later] Ms. Sugawara called, saying that she had found a perfect site, and wanted to take us there. The site was symbolic—a vast plain at the foot of the mountain where the tsunami had washed away

everything, an empty flatland that commanded a clear view all the way to the ocean.

After the finding of this symbolic site, the project made a remarkable progress. The team members gradually developed common goals. For one, we wanted a vertical structure, like a fire tower, overlooking the entire city of Rikuzentakata. For another, we wanted the building to resemble a grove, making use of Japanese cedar salt-damaged by the tsunami. _ "Architecture after 3.11," lecture by Toyo Ito at the University of Tokyo, September 25, 2011, in "'Home-for-All' in Rikuzentakata, and the Venice Biennale International Architecture Exhibition," *Wochi Kochi Magazine*

> ## ❝❝ A DISASTER ZONE, WHERE EVERYTHING IS LOST, OFFERS THE OPPORTUNITY FOR US TO TAKE A FRESH LOOK, FROM THE GROUND UP, AT WHAT ARCHITECTURE REALLY IS. ❞❞

Ms. Sugawara's activities thrive on one abstract question—How are we going to rebuild our lives? And the architects who are there to help answer that question also face an essential question—What is architecture? _ "Architecture after 3.11," lecture by Toyo Ito at the University of Tokyo, September 25, 2011, in "'Home-for-All' in Rikuzentakata, and the Venice Biennale International Architecture Exhibition," *Wochi Kochi Magazine*

> ## ❝❝ WE WANTED THE BUILDING TO RESEMBLE A GROVE, MAKING USE OF JAPANESE CEDAR SALT-DAMAGED BY THE TSUNAMI. ❞❞

### Cedar Wood, a Symbolic Purpose  Nineteen cedar logs were used to build the Home-for-All in Rikuzentakata. These logs were trees ravaged by tsunami and left standing dead. If the cedars had been left abandoned, they could only be used as firewood. By resurrecting the logs as columns, they carry a symbolic meaning, representing the revitalization of the community. The rising verticality of these columns symbolizes growth and initiation from an empty land. I like this strong expression. _ Åsne Maria Gundersen, Einar Bjarki Malmquist, and Toyo Ito, *Arkitektur 95*, no.4, 2013

## SERPENTINE GALLERY PAVILION (WITH CECIL BALMOND AND ARUP)

The Serpentine was articulated out of line art elements to form a cube structure of surfaces only. Taking what would ordinarily would have been a grid-form horizontal plane and algorithmically rotating concentric squares within it, then extending those lines down the vertical faces, we generated a rotational form enlivened by spatial rhythms that avoided typical Euclidean geometries and so created a curiously dynamic "impossible object." This dynamism was its fascination. _ Riken Yamamoto, Dana Buntrock, and Taro Igarashi, *Toyo Ito*, London: Phaidon Press, 2009

### The Spiraling of a Square

We began with two images: the image of a straight line continuing forever like the path of a billiard ball, and an aluminum honeycomb structure that was an extension of what had been tried in the Bruges Pavilion. . . . The idea of a spiraling square was subsequently conceived. I felt it could be more random, but he [Cecil Balmond] was quite particular about this algorithm based on a spiraling square. _ Toyo Ito and Kumiko Inui, *A + U: Architecture and Urbanism* 5, May 2004

The surface of the Serpentine Pavilion, seemingly a random network of tangled lines, comprises a structure of flat steel bars formed according to Balmond's precise algorithms, which embed squares in rotating concentric succession, a dynamic twist that transforms the pure geometric shapes into a spiraling environment. _ Toyo Ito, "The New 'Real': Toward Reclaiming Materiality in Contemporary Architecture," in *Tarzans in the Media Forest*, London: Architectural Association Press, 2011

Step inside the structure, and one hardly feels enclosed in a cube; the space seems simultaneously interior and exterior, as if all six faces could easily flip inside-out. _ Toyo Ito, "Dynamic Delight over Aesthetic Purity," in *Tarzans in the Media Forest*, London: Architectural Association Press, 2011

> ❝❝ I SEARCH FOR FORMS THAT TELL PEOPLE A STORY, THAT ENTERTAIN THEM, THAT ENRICH URBAN SPACE. ❞❞

The complex pattern of triangles and trapezoids that seem to intersect randomly in the Serpentine were based on an algorithm developed by Cecil Balmond. The result is anything but mathematical.

**"A Curious Art Object"** For a fact, the experience of being inside the pavilion with no visible columns and beams or windows and doors, none of the usual hierarchy of architectural forms, is that of space itself—an ever-fluctuating, self-recursive abstract space whose interior and exterior are contiguous, not at all organic yet filled with a curious vitality. _ Toyo Ito, "The New 'Real': Toward Reclaiming Materiality in Contemporary Architecture," in *Tarzans in the Media Forest*, London: Architectural Association Press, 2011

A curious art object that is clearly architecture, yet at the same time non-architecture. The reason being that, while offering the bare minimum of functions as a space for people's activities, it on the other hand has no columns, no windows, no doors—that is, it has none of the usual architectural elements. Does this cube offer hints toward a new vision in architecture to come? _ Cecil Balmond and Toyo Ito, *Casabella* 67, May 2003

**Liberation** There is something very attractive about the idea of it existing only temporarily for three months. Whereas just the thought that the buildings I design might stand for a hundred years or more wears heavily on me, the notion of a temporary project is liberating in many ways. One need not be so strict about function nor worry about how it will age. And it seems to me, it just might offer the clearest expression of the concepts I habitually imagine. _ Cecil Balmond and Toyo Ito, *Casabella* 67, May 2003

> **ARCHITECTURE ALWAYS CREATES ORDER, YET I AM ALWAYS LOOKING FOR FREEDOM.**

## THE NATURAL AND MAN-MADE

Our way of life is still based in twentieth-century ideas, specifically a modernist philosophy that assumes we can use science and technology to conquer nature. . . . For instance, in 2011, many parts of the Japanese coast were protected by huge retaining walls that were built to withstand a tsunami. The nuclear plant itself was supposedly designed to resist even a massive earthquake. Yet the walls were easily broken and the plant was irreparably damaged. The catastrophe showed that you cannot isolate a building or a city from the environment. That kind of modernist thinking has reached its limit.

But before Japan's modernization, we used to think of ourselves as part of nature, and also of architecture as part of nature. . . . timber construction was inherently adaptable to the forces of nature because it could be easily repaired or rebuilt after an earthquake. I'm not suggesting we can simply return to the past, but to get beyond the limitations of modernism, we probably need to look for new approaches, some of which might be suggested by our own culture and history. _ Julian Rose, *Artforum*, September 2013

## PUBLIC ARCHITECTURE

Public architecture should serve as the basic unit of communal space and provide the essential idea of public life. And this is not about the size of the building—the Home-for-All project is small, but the ways in which it brings people together, and the results of this exchange, are the same as in the Sendai Mediatheque. These structures might offer not only a new community architecture, but also—if on a small scale—a new kind of society. _ Julian Rose, *Artforum*, September 2013

**TRADITION IS CONTINUITY** A good architect should have a thorough experience of the society he comes from. Between 1990 and 2000 I had no commissions, and I did not want a government or academic position either. I just wanted to work with craftsmen, gain experience on the ground and take no responsibility for the design—only for the construction. So I worked in the lowest levels of our society. . . . While working and eating with the craftsmen, I started to wonder what had happened to our experience of tradition. Gradually, I gained confidence while learning everything about construction methods. Continuity is very important in my opinion. Tradition is continuity. During those years I began studying the history of art in Europe, India, Africa and America; as well as philosophy, movies and contemporary art—a practice I continue today. I believe in starting with a broad vision and condensing it to fit the local situation.

_"Wang Shu: Local Hero," *Mark Magazine* 19, April–May 2009

# WANG SHU

**BORN:** November 4, 1963, Urumqi, Xinjiang Province, China

**EDUCATION:** Nanjing Institute of Technology, Jiangsu, China, 1985 and 1988; Ph.D., Tongji University, Shanghai, China, 2000

**OFFICE:** Amateur Architecture Studio, 218 Nanshan Road, 310002 Hangzhou, Zhejiang, China
Tel: +86 571-8716-4708, Fax: +86 571-8716-4708

**PROJECTS FEATURED:** Wencun Village, Huangpo, Wuchuan, Guangdong, China, 2016; Tiles Hill Guesthouse and Reception Center, China Art Academy, Xiangshan Campus, Hangzhou, China, 2012; Ningbo History Museum, Ningbo, China, 2008; Xiangshan Campus, China Art Academy, Hangzhou, China, 2007; Ceramic House, Jinhua, China, 2006

**“** I'M JUST A LOCAL ARCHITECT. **”**

**“** IF WE LOSE OUR TRADITIONS,
I BELIEVE THAT WE HAVE
NO FUTURE. **”**

**Ceramic House, Jinhua, 2007**
"There are two doors for the house; one is
on the east and the other on the west. On
the north of the house lays a tree-meter-
high earth bank running from east to west.
The house is anchored on the earth bank,
which prevents the hustle and bustle
from the road on the north. The shallow
pool in the south catches the reflection of
the house in the water."—Wang Shu

## WANG SHU, APPRENTICE

From 1990 till 1998, I did not accept any architectural commissions. I didn't want to work as an architect. Instead, I worked with the craftsmen to gain experience from actual construction work. Day after day, from eight in the morning till midnight, I worked with them, ate with them and learnt everything I could from a construction site. At that time my work involved renovating old buildings. _ Claudia Fuchs, *Detail* 5, 2012

> **I CALL MY PRACTICE A STUDIO; IT'S NOT AN OFFICE, IT'S NOT A COMPANY, IT'S JUST A SMALL STUDIO.**

### THE WORD "AMATEUR"

In my view, the dignity of life comes from the construction of the sense of existence, and this is what the mission of architecture should be. . . . Before criticizing the society, architects have to criticize themselves first, and that is why I named my studio "Amateur Architecture Studio." _ Wang Shu and Hsieh Ying-chun, *Illegal Architecture*, Taiwan: Garden City Publishing, 2012

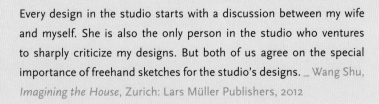

Before becoming an architect I was a writer. Architecture is only one of my activities. If I choose the term "amateur," 业余, it is to differentiate myself from "professionals." "Amateur," in its traditional Chinese meaning, is closer to notions of "erudite" or "well read." . . . I am not an architect! (laughs) _ Rafael Magrou, *L'architecture d'aujourd'hui* 375, December 2009

In the long Chinese tradition, there are many ways of being an architect: floral art, painting, etc. Only a few artists are professionals. But to be amateur is very important. This allows you to question the professional system and to be independent. _ Rafael Magrou, *L'architecture d'aujourd'hui* 375, December 2009

### WANG SHU AND LU WENYU

My office generates few overheads. There are only six of us, counting my wife Lu Wenyu [pictured above] and myself. This allows me to adopt a really independent attitude. _ Rafael Magrou, *L'architecture d'aujourd'hui* 375, December 2009

I am the person that has many dreams, but my wife is more connected to reality. _ Anna Tweeddale, *Australian Design Review*, November 2012

Every design in the studio starts with a discussion between my wife and myself. She is also the only person in the studio who ventures to sharply criticize my designs. But both of us agree on the special importance of freehand sketches for the studio's designs. _ Wang Shu, *Imagining the House*, Zurich: Lars Müller Publishers, 2012

We make all of the important decisions together after discussing them. I am mainly in charge of the conceptual drawings; Lu Wenyu plays a crucial role in realizing the designs, including specifications and construction management. People often underestimate how important creativity is in these stages. There would be no designs in our studio without me, and no realizations of the designs without Lu Wenyu. _ Claudia Fuchs, *Detail* 5, 2012

### A DIALOGUE

Lu Wenyu: We do the first prototype ourselves in the office. But then we bring the construction workers in early on. . . . Every time the client and the construction company must agree to the collaborative methodology, otherwise we will refuse the project. It's very important for us.

WS: I am more focused on the workers; Wenyu is more focused on the students. She is also a professor of architecture, teaching a first-year course about traditional joinery and carpentry. . . . The construction workers are more afraid of her.

Lu Wenyu: He's very kind to the workers. Every worker likes him. They are afraid of me. The client, too!

WS: Yes, and I know that. If the client or craftsmen want to make something easier, but it means it won't be right, they can't say it to her. They say it to me. But I just say, "No, no, no. Everyone should listen to Lu. She's the one in charge of this." _ Toshiko Mori, Rosalie Genevro, and Anne Rieselbach, "In Conversation with Wang Shu, Lu Wenyu, and Toshiko Mori," The Architectural League NY, April 2, 2013

> **EVERY DAY, I PRACTICE MY CALLIGRAPHY.**

### THE TRANQUILITY OF CALLIGRAPHY

Compared with the contemporary fast pace of Chinese society, calligraphy always helps lead me into a tranquil inner world, a focused but very natural and relaxed state of mind. The writing of every character is like constructing a living place or part of a garden. _ Wang Shu, *Imagining the House*, Zurich: Lars Müller Publishers, 2012

## DRAWING: ACTIVE RESTRICTION

To us [Lu Wenyu and I], times past and the memories associated with them can only be reawakened through real personal experience, and they can only be reflected in freehand drawing. From my point of view, the hand directly connects the feelings in my inner world and my body. _ Wang Shu, *Imagining the House*, Zurich: Lars Müller Publishers, 2012

Freehand drawing tends to produce plainer buildings. It is an active restriction that prevents over-showy spaces and the loss of scale that usually results from computer design. _ Wang Shu, *Imagining the House*, Zurich: Lars Müller Publishers, 2012

You draw without fixing your thoughts. It is similar to writing or painting. Your project ripens over three or four months of study, by means of a large number of sketches, and one day, it is time to draw it. There is an auspicious moment for that. _ Rafael Magrou, *L'architecture d'aujourd'hui* 375, December 2009

## INFLUENCES: CHINESE LANDSCAPE PAINTING

I think your experience really counts. Mine has been a careful study on paintings of the Song Dynasty [960–1279]. Although I became interested in this kind of art at an early age, this interest didn't translate into language for immediate use. . . . When I looked back, I found my finished works of art were indicative of this influence and I deepened my understanding of painting while creating architecture. _ Fang Zhenning and Wang Shu, *Abitare* 495, September 2009

Architecture, too, must be thought of not as just the building itself, but as a picture that strikes harmony with all the surrounding environment. _ Jane Misun Shim, *Space* 540, November 2012

I think that this is my concept of architecture, I think it's a cultural expression . . . a cultural tradition. Here I am hidden behind the trees, the trees are more beautiful than I am, but I think this is the way forward. I am here, but I am behind the trees. _ "Plenary II: Culture for Sustainable Cities," lecture by Wang Shu at the International Conference on Culture for Sustainable Cities, Hangzhou, China, December 10–12, 2015

## PRESERVING LIVING TRADITIONS

It is very difficult to do preservation in China. . . . Now very few craftsmen know this way of rebuilding around older structures, very few. The last generation of craftsmen who know it are 60 years old; they will work 10 more years and they will die. But the younger generation cannot do it. . . . We should connect (vernacular knowledge) to that (modern) system. _ Julia Mandell, Pei Zhu, Wang Shu, and Qingyun Ma, *Cite* 88, April 2012

On the one hand, we demolish to the extreme. On the other, we build excessively and rebuild fake historical villas for the tourist industry. _ Rafael Magrou, *L'architecture d'aujourd'hui* 375, December 2009

The current generations copy everything they see elsewhere. They have wiped their own ancestral models from their memories. . . . If we do not keep our living traditions, then we have no future. Demolishing old buildings is like getting rid of the teachers, and cutting education. _ Rafael Magrou, *L'architecture d'aujourd'hui* 375, December 2009

**❝ I WANT TO OFFER THE CHANCE TO REDEVELOP CRAFTWORK IN ARCHITECTURE. IT'S ALMOST A LAST CHANCE AND I WANT TO PARTICIPATE. ❞**

## CHINESE HANDICRAFT

It is in the tradition of the [Chinese] society that tens of thousands of craftsmen can work together, a characteristic architects here should take advantage of, as we could still combine handicraft and machines to have large-scale productions. _ Wang Shu and Hsieh Ying-chun, *Illegal Architecture*, Taiwan: Garden City Publishing, 2012

In my studio we do many small experiments. Through this process we build friendships and an understanding of the ways of craftsmen. Finally we have what I call the "architect-directly-working-with-craftsmen-together" way. _ Julia Mandell, Pei Zhu, Wang Shu, and Qingyun Ma, *Cite* 88, April 2012

**❝ IF WE MANAGE TO RECYCLE MORE OF CERTAIN CONSTRUCTION MATERIALS, WE MIGHT BE ABLE TO BETTER PRESERVE RESOURCES. ❞**

## RECYCLING AS HISTORY

I like to build with old recycled bricks and tiles in the tradition of the region in which I live. . . . In a number of projects we have used materials salvaged from demolished buildings—and mixed them with modern materials and technology. _ Claudia Fuchs, *Detail* 5, 2012

Early on, people hated the Xiangshan Campus. They thought it was ugly. Only a few people found it interesting. Then as time went by, they ended up appreciating it. It was the same thing for the Ningbo History Museum. In the beginning, they reacted to the use of scrap material in a brand-new modern district, but not any more. These turnarounds are satisfying for me. _ Rafael Magrou, *L'architecture d'aujourd'hui* 375, December 2009

## THE NINGBO HISTORY MUSEUM WAS THE MOST **DIFFICULT PROJECT** I HAVE EVER DONE.

"The internal structure is made up of three valleys that contain three escalators, one of which is exterior and the other two connect the interior space. Four caves are arranged at the entrance, the lobby and the cliffs of the exterior valley. Two sunken courtyards dominate the center and two more discreet ones are hidden further inside."—Wang Shu

**NINGBO 2008**
# NINGBO HISTORY MUSEUM

**Designing Ningbo** I design very similarly to the traditional Chinese painter. I don't sketch very much, but I do study cities, valleys and mountains. Then I stop. I think for about a week and don't draw. In the case of this museum, one night I couldn't sleep and suddenly it emerged. To me, every design is about both poetic thinking and mathematics. I sat on the bed, drew it in my mind and calculated the size of the building. When that was done, I took a small piece of paper and a pencil. I drew everything directly: numbers, structure, size, space, stairs, where to locate the entrance, functions and so on. Then I drank tea. _ "Wang Shu: Local Hero," *Mark Magazine* 19, April–May 2009

The issue thus became how to design something that had a life of its own; the building therefore was treated as an artificial mountain—a Chinese way of looking at things that has its long tradition. _ Wang Shu and Hsieh Ying-chun, *Illegal Architecture,* Taiwan: Garden City Publishing, 2012

From a distance you can only see a simple box. As you approach the museum, the volume appears more complex, resembling a mineral block, half natural, half artificial. It is an abstraction of old Chinese paintings, with their mountain landscapes. _ Rafael Magrou, *L'architecture d'aujourd'hui* 375, December 2009

The path through the building reveals a sequence of framings of the environment, while the exhibition spaces converge onto a central courtyard. _ Rafael Magrou, *L'architecture d'aujourd'hui* 375, December 2009

The upper part is a mountain-shaped structure, and as public space is always with multiple paths, it branches upward from the ground floor, forming a root-like labyrinth, which is in tune with exhibitions that are never permanent. _ Wang Shu and Hsieh Ying-chun, *Illegal Architecture*, Taiwan: Garden City Publishing, 2012

**Materials** The inner and outer walls of the structure is a mixture of bamboo, concrete and more than twelve kinds of recycled bricks and tiles, feeling like grand, simple and light matter, which is alive and half artificial, half natural. _ Wang Shu and Hsieh Ying-chun, *Illegal Architecture,* Taiwan: Garden City Publishing, 2012

**Adapting Wapan to the Site** The materials in the exterior walls refer to the historic fabric, and in this way evoke memories of it. They are inspired by Ningbo's traditional construction system, the "*Wapan* wall," in which material that has been amassed is stacked in layers. We used bricks and tiles from demolished buildings—more than 20 different types of bricks and roof tiles. _ Claudia Fuchs, *Detail* 5, 2012

Implementing the *Wapan* technique on such a building is a completely different task to that of a house or a fine arts campus. So I did some research and tests to check that the *Wapan* was adapted to this type of construction and particularly to the scale of the façades. _ Rafael Magrou, *L'architecture d'aujourd'hui 375*, December 2009

I did design the pattern on the walls of this museum. When the construction process started, people worked behind a scaffold. It was very secretive. Nobody saw what was happening, including me. Obviously, they changed my design, but when they took the scaffold down I loved it, precisely because it was beyond my control. _ "Wang Shu: Local Hero," *Mark Magazine 19*, April–May 2009

**Community Response** Before this development, I had to look for the materials to implement this technique. Now, people automatically call me to say, "I can offer you a few million tiles and bricks. Are you interested?" (laughs) _ Rafael Magrou, *L'architecture d'aujourd'hui 375*, December 2009

When the museum was completed, many local residents went to visit repeatedly, only because in here they can try to find their lost memories. I am very moved by this. _ Edward Denison, Guang Yu Ren, and Wang Shu, *Architectural Design 82*, November 2012

## JINHUA 2007
# CERAMIC HOUSE
*The Chinese artist Ai Wei Wei developed Jinhua Architectural Park in homage to his father, a poet, who was from Jinhua. Wei Wei invited 16 Chinese and international architects to each design one of the 17 pavilions planned for the park. [He designed one as well.] Wang Shu's Ceramic House was among the earliest of his projects to bring him international attention.*

The small house of one hundred square meters—like a café—I decided to make a container. Whether it will hold wind or water is completely determined by intuition.

Where a design will start is often accidental. For instance, in this case I can explain it by the form of an ink stone from the Song Dynasty [960–1279]. The ink stone is made for the function only. Its surface is made of two parts. One is comparatively plain and the other is a slope. The plain part is for storing ink and the slope is for dripping ink. I asked myself what I would see standing on the surface of the ink stone and what from the bottom. As it is a pottery ink stone, it reminded me of my friend Zhou Wu, who makes earthenware. He made a piece of porcelain the size of 40 x 80, having a slope on the bottom of the piece. The curving part is to prevent the glaze from dripping when it is in the kiln. He made thousands of such pieces, which amazed me. The ink stone and Zhou Wu's porcelain became the inspiration for this small house. _ Wang Shu, courtesy Amateur Architecture Studio

**"THE INK STONE AND ZHOU WU'S PORCELAIN BECAME THE INSPIRATION FOR THIS SMALL HOUSE. "**

The enamel tiles were pasted on the inner and outer walls of the house. The glazes are a combination of 40 different colors, representing all the colors in Chinese ceramics.

## THE BUILDING PROCESS

There are three very difficult stages during the building process. The first is how to convince the government. The second deals with designing working details and with other construction issues. . . . The third stage is the hardest of all. When a building is finished, the Chinese rarely think of it as a work of art. They treat is as a container with many functions that they can change randomly and at will. This is very difficult for me. I can control the first and second stages, but I have no influence on the third. _ "Wang Shu: Local Hero," *Mark Magazine* 19, April–May 2009

## ILLEGAL ARCHITECTURE

Once, all the illegal constructions [in Hangzhou, where Wang Shu's practice is located] were ordered to be removed, and the building was turned into a featherless chicken in a few days. But, what was amazing was that, in the following year, these small-scale constructions, like mushrooms, grew out again. Though somewhat different from how they used to look, it was still possible to recognize them, and life, again, regained its implicit order and meaning. _ Wang Shu and Hsieh Ying-chun, *Illegal Architecture*, Taiwan: Garden City Publishing, 2012

## ARCHITECTURE IN CHINA TODAY

In China, there are two movements. One is very strong and powerful, represented by the professional companies of Chinese architects. The other, my approach, is a minority. However, the two can coexist perfectly in the development of cities. _ Rafael Magrou, *L'architecture d'aujourd'hui* 375, December 2009

> ## ARCHITECTURE IS NOT UNIQUELY ENCAPSULATED IN THE HOUSE, BUT THE WHOLE OF THE LANDSCAPE.

Architects are fanatically copying the West. They were fanatic about huge, strong, shining, smooth, high-tech, symbolic and monumental public buildings, and commercialized high-rise residential apartments. . . . Architects seldom question the damage their pursuit of so-called modernity inflicts on tradition, nature and culture. _ Edward Denison, Guang Yu Ren, and Wang Shu, *Architectural Design* 82, November 2012

## BOTTOM-UP ARCHITECTURE

What's shocking is, no matter whether in Hangzhou or in Taipei, though illegal constructions often look piling up and messy, if we examine them carefully, they are actually not chaotic but direct and distinguishable, as all the reusable materials in the surroundings are recycled and the lightest structure and simplest methods are adopted. _ Wang Shu and Hsieh Ying-chun, *Illegal Architecture*, Taiwan: Garden City Publishing, 2012

## "THE DIRTY WAY"

In China architects usually don't go to the site. So working on-site is quite a different way of doing things. But you should understand what your workers and your craftsmen can do. . . . My way, I call it the "dirty way." A little bit dirty, a little bit imperfect. I like the feeling. I don't like perfect things. The feeling is perfect, but you can see many small mistakes. _ Julia Mandell, Pei Zhu, Wang Shu, and Qingyun Ma, *Cite* 88, April 2012

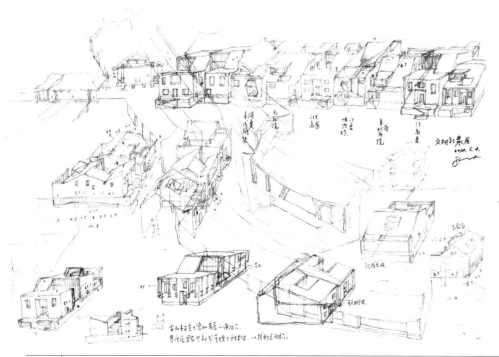

### HUANGPO 2016
# WENCUN VILLAGE
*Wang Shu was invited by the Fuyang municipality to build a cultural complex in this historic area, a kind of prototype for improved rural life in China. After a search of hundreds of old villages in the area, and in part because of its proximity to the Heshan Stream, in the Fuchun River Valley, Wang Shu chose Wencun. The resulting community includes fourteen new residential buildings plus public pavilions and refurbishment to some existing structures.*

I wanted to design new houses for the farmers and . . . keep the diversity of traditional villages with new houses, or keep the real life feeling in the villages, instead of designing for the tourists. _ Wang Shu, courtesy Amateur Architecture Studio

The most important thing is to make the villages attractive to people again. The farmers have lost confidence in their own way of life. They think villages are backward and that cities are good. _ Amy Qin, "Architects Seize on Potential in Countryside," *New York Times*, June 17, 2016

Everyone, including the local government, is interested in this topic of how to revive China's villages. _ Amy Qin, "Architects Seize on Potential in Countryside," *New York Times*, June 17, 2016

**The Housing Design** We insisted to apply the traditional courtyard type and developed eight different types by making slight changes. Every type developed several variations with different locations, neighborhood and materials. _ Wang Shu, courtesy Amateur Architecture Studio

We also wanted to ensure that there was a main room on the axis where, for example, ancestral spirits remained, and this large room is also disappearing slowly but surely because people are no longer believing in the same things as in the past. . . . As architects, we have to do something to make sure, to ensure that tradition comes back to the fore and that is the reason for which this main room remains within our constructions. _ "Plenary II: Culture for Sustainable Cities," lecture by Wang Shu at the International Conference on Culture for Sustainable Cities, Hangzhou, China, December 10–12, 2015

**Materials** The materials used are a combination of traditional materials and modern construction materials. For example, we used mud, bamboo, etc.,

which we have been able to combine with cement and even with solar panels. _ "Plenary II: Culture for Sustainable Cities," lecture by Wang Shu at the International Conference on Culture for Sustainable Cities, Hangzhou, China, December 10–12, 2015

**Wencun as a Model** Our ambition is to build similar projects in the Zhejiang province, in other villages, over the next 10 years. We're really trying to take things in a new direction. If we can build one project per year, that would be 10 projects over the next 10 years. _ "Plenary II: Culture for Sustainable Cities," lecture by Wang Shu at the International Conference on Culture for Sustainable Cities, Hangzhou, China, December 10–12, 2015

With Wencun, we've created a research and work method that can be copied, but the challenge is still scalability. In terms of implementation, every village has different traditions and vernacular architecture. There's no one template. _ Amy Qin, "Architects Seize on Potential in Countryside," *New York Times*, June 17, 2016

**❝❝ WE INVITED LOCAL ARTISANS TO BUILD THE VILLAGE. ❞❞**

**❝❝ ITS PICTURESQUE QUALITY IS ONE OF THE MAIN REASONS TO USE THIS AS THE SAMPLE VILLAGE. ❞❞**

For Wencun Village, Wang Shu wanted residents to experience the beauty of the old and the new, of preservation and restoration. As with all his projects, a keen sensitivity to landscape and water informs the design.

## GARDENS

Many of my buildings are similar to the Chinese garden: they have many entrances, and it's not clear where the main entrance is. _ "Wang Shu: Local Hero," *Mark Magazine* 19, April–May 2009

Chinese gardens do not mimic nature's forms or patterns from the human standpoint, but rather echo the pleasurable experiences people derive from natural hills and bodies of water. The houses are thus interwoven with natural elements such as stones, ponds, streams, trees, and flowers, which in turn influence the house's spatial layout. . . . _ Wang Shu, *Imagining the House*, Zurich: Lars Müller Publishers, 2012

## HANGZHOU

In Chinese tradition Hangzhou is the perfect example for big cities. The city's name means half city and half landscape. For the Chinese dream of the traditional city, Hangzhou is the perfect model. They call it paradise. _ Julia Mandell, Pei Zhu, Wang Shu, and Qingyun Ma, *Cite* 88, April 2012

So from the year 1000 to 1955, the city [Hangzhou] really hasn't changed. . . . In the past, this would be the typical model of a Chinese city. . . . Any other city would have adopted the same configuration with the mountains, the lake and the city. _ "Plenary II: Culture for Sustainable Cities," lecture by Wang Shu at the International Conference on Culture for Sustainable Cities, Hangzhou, China, December 10–12, 2015

> ❯❯ **CHINESE GARDENS ARE HOUSES IN WHICH THE HUMAN BODY HAS AN INFINITE EXPERIENCE OF THE NATURAL LAWS.** ❯❯

### HANGZHOU 2007
# XIANGSHAN CAMPUS, CHINA ACADEMY OF ART
*For this major project, Wang Shu was asked to design numerous buildings for the prestigious China Academy of Art. This was accomplished over two design phases, back to back: Phase I, completed 2004, and Phase II, completed 2007. Overall, the expanded campus included schools for architecture, design, film, an art museum, gymnasium, student dormitories, and dining hall, and needed to accommodate more than 500 instructors and 5,000 students. Ultimately, the campus was situated around a hill, known as "Xiangshan."*

In my design for the Hangzhou campus, for instance, I positioned the buildings at the foot of the Xiangshan (Elephant) Mountain in such a way that each building enters into a different dialogue with the mountain, offering various views of it. _ "Wang Shu: Local Hero [2008]," *Mark Magazine* 19, April–May 2009

All the academy professors, artists and architects involved thought that, in accordance with Chinese tradition, mountains and rivers in the surroundings are more important than the architecture in choosing a site. _ Wang Shu and Hsieh Ying-chun, *Illegal Architecture*, Taiwan: Garden City Publishing, 2012

**Phase I and Phase II** This is the largest project I've ever designed—within six years, on a site with an area of around 533,333 square meters, encompassing a hill, two streams, and over thirty buildings. The second project phase, for the south campus, contains thirteen large buildings and two small ones; every building is different, but belongs to one of four types. It was like an encyclopedic method of design. _ Wang Shu, *Imagining the House*, Zurich: Lars Müller Publishers, 2012

The architecture in Phase I is plain and simple, like a pure and extensive object. I racked my brains on the internal structure for Phase II, especially high-lighting what I called "the small places" designed accidentally and stuck in a maze. . . . You might see some great settings in Phase I, but fail to find a private place to talk and chat. I think, even if this is where an academy is located, you are able to experience that which an interesting city can give to you. Phase II is much more like a combined structure with urban features incorporated. _ Fang Zhenning and Wang Shu, *Abitare* 495, September 2009

After borrowing [from] the traditional Chinese gardens and courtyards commonly seen in the first Chinese universities, Xiangshan campus eventually is composed of a series of courtyards built on different elevations on the hill. The buildings sensitively turn and tilt along the hill and by the river. The farmlands, rivers and fish ponds originally there are carefully preserved, and delicate, poetic traditional Chinese gardens and space language are tentatively transformed into [a] modest, open rural scene. _ Wang Shu and Hsieh Ying-chun, *Illegal Architecture*, Taiwan: Garden City Publishing, 2012

**Diversity of Design** Concerning the mixture of languages, this project is like city design. For me, one type in a city won't work. So I made a rule—there were at least four basic types on Xiangshan Campus. Then, I made another rule: every type would be repeated at least twice, not just once. In addition, we would use four major building materials and every material would be used at least twice. _ Fang Zhenning and Wang Shu, *Abitare* 495, September 2009

**Bamboo** I had already developed the technique on the Xiangshan campus. It was a first in China. I wanted to use a local and inexpensive material. _ Rafael Magrou, *L'architecture d'aujourd'hui* 375, December 2009

## The Size of the Windows, the Depth of the Stairs

Indeed, this design explains my understanding of light in Chinese architecture—that is, a combination of dark and bright. This is not a technical question. Rather, I call this translucent light "You Ming": "You" means black, so *You Ming* means bright black. Of course, this light will bring about an effect—I want to build a university with quiet rooms for contemplation. One more thing, the windows can't be opened wide; in addition, their positions tend to be irregular. This is what I mean when I talk about "self-awareness"; that is to say, we have to be aware of the existence of windows. . . . Windows enable you to see from inside to outdoors. If the outside is nature, then windows are a man-made medium between you and the nature.

When a sensitive friend of mine went upstairs in Xiangshan Campus, he said surprisingly: "It's not right. How come there is a big difference in the height between two stairs? This is a mistake." Then, I answered: "Now you know you have feet! You are able to feel where your feet are." _ Fang Zhenning and Wang Shu, *Abitare* 495, September 2009

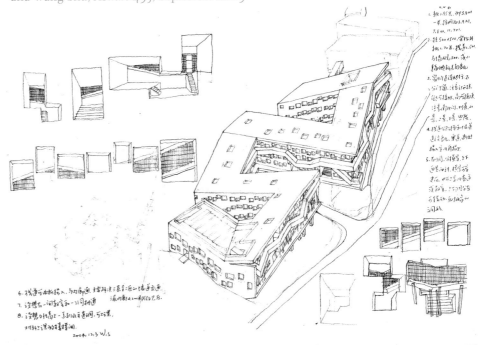

**" FOR THE XIANGSHAN CAMPUS, I HAVE ALREADY SUGGESTED A NEW MODEL WHICH COULD BE THE CONTEMPORARY CHINESE CITY. "**

For this vastly complex project, which was executed over several years, Wang Shu felt he had to "dissolve its power by breaking it down into smaller components."

> ❝ **WHAT IS MOST IMPORTANT TO ME IS THE USE AND LIFE OF MY BUILDINGS.** ❞

In designing Tiles Hill, Wang Shu was moved to realize the poetry in nature, to have the buildings engage in "silent conversation" with the environment.

HANGZHOU 2012
## TILES HILL GUESTHOUSE AND RECEPTION CENTER, CHINA ART ACADEMY, XIANGSHAN CAMPUS

For this final project, I wanted to express my deep understanding of the Chinese spirit. Maybe I touched it this time. _ Clare Jacobson, *Architectural Record*, December 16, 2013

**Inspiration**  This assumption [solution] was also derived from the architect's travel experience in the west mountain area of Hunan Province twenty years ago. A village had been constructed along the river. There were hundreds of traditional residential houses with sloping roofs, connected by a winding tile cover and the streets and lanes were all covered with a huge continuous tiled roof.

This smart solution to the rainy and extremely hot summer climate also implied imagination and poetry. _ Wang Shu, courtesy Amateur Architecture Studio, April 27, 2012

**Rammed Earth**  I decided to use rammed earth for all construction. The significant change in material finally led to the overturning of the original design. . . . The rammed earth method of construction especially emphasized simple walls. But the Chinese way of expression especially emphasizes implicit poetry. Therefore, all these elements would be covered with Chinese black tiles. The general impression of the building from the entrance would be tiles. _ Wang Shu, *Imagining the House*, Zurich: Lars Müller Publishers, 2012

**Experiencing the Building** Viewed from the south and north, the building looks like a hill-shaped ventilating screen; people could see through the building so that the volume of the building reduces visually. _ Wang Shu, courtesy Amateur Architecture Studio, April 27, 2012

People would be invited to experience a sequence of surprising feelings in various segments and finally enter into a very quiet bedroom with an atmosphere of meditation. _ Wang Shu, *Imagining the House*, Zurich: Lars Müller Publishers, 2012

You go outside, then inside, outside, inside. Finally, you go to the top of the hill and you see back. The building is not about the form or the shape: it's about the discovery. _ Clare Jacobson, *Architectural Record*, December 16, 2013

## TEACHING

*In 2001, Wang Shu developed an architecture school in Hangzhou, and was joined there in 2003 by Lu Wenyu.*

Lu Wenyu: So we teach the students in the first year, how to work with real materials. Wood, brick, concrete, bamboo, metal. Real materials. _ Toshiko Mori, Rosalie Genevro, and Anne Rieselbach, "In Conversation with Wang Shu, Lu Wenyu, and Toshiko Mori," The Architectural League NY, April 2, 2013

My dream, as a teacher, is to include craftsmen in order to be in closer contact with the materials, so that students may practice these techniques and be continuously in contact with the building site. _ Rafael Magrou, *L'architecture d'aujourd'hui* 375, December 2009

Lu Wenyu: The students often mix together and collaborate. And it is very hands-on environment. The students are learning very different skills, and sharing with one another. _ Toshiko Mori, Rosalie Genevro, and Anne Rieselbach, "In Conversation with Wang Shu, Lu Wenyu, and Toshiko Mori," The Architectural League NY, April 2, 2013

Design instruction is divorced from Chinese tradition with respect to philosophical issues, but also from its materials and construction methods. There is blind imitation of Western styles and disregard for the cultural and social context. . . . Our academic goal is to provide a contemporary, vernacular architectural education that emphasizes philosophy and craftsmanship. _ Claudia Fuchs, *Detail* 5, 2012

Our students learn Chinese calligraphy. . . . In the first year of the course our students learn about traditional carpentry skills. It's important that they learn how to construct with bricks, with rammed earth and with concrete. The first two years are all about construction. _ Helen Norrie, *Architecture Australia* 101, September 2012

**▌▌ I AM INTERESTED IN THE DEVELOPMENT OF LIFE, CLOSELY LINKED TO THE REVIVAL OF THE PAST. ▌▌**

## THE FUTURE

What is the future of Beijing, the future of China? Do we really believe that urbanization on a massive scale is the future for all our cities in China? Cities can make use of nature and make the best of nature, but they can also destroy it.

. . . Of course, everybody aspires to a better life, but culture takes millennia to develop, and yet it can very easily be destroyed in an instant. _ "Plenary II: Culture for Sustainable Cities," lecture by Wang Shu at the International Conference on Culture for Sustainable Cities, Hangzhou, China, December 10–12, 2015

One day someone asked me the following question, "What is the finality of your work?" I answered, "An echo in an empty valley." _ Rafael Magrou, *L'architecture d'aujourd'hui* 375, December 2009

**BEAUTY AS TENSION** One thing is to show the contradictions, because architecture is rich and good. Beauty is the tension between two different things. We can show this tension sometimes as writers, or we can work in architecture. _ Luciano Basauri, Ana Dana Beroš, and Vera Grimmer, *Oris* 11, no. 60, 2009

For me, architecture is a global issue. There is no ecological architecture, no intelligent architecture, no fascist architecture, no sustainable architecture—there is only good and bad architecture. There are always problems we must not neglect; for example, energy, resources, costs, social aspects—one must always pay attention to all these. _ Eduardo Souto de Moura interview by Lara Braun, *Meaning People Concepts Future Forum*, LafargeHolcim Foundation for Sustainable Construction, 2004

To say that nature is architecture and culture is nature constitutes the highest stage we can reach. I believe that the greatest aspiration of an architect is to be anonymous; to be anonymous not out of false modesty but by managing to create, in a given time, a space that will possess the wisdom accumulated over thousands of years. . . . _ Xavier Güell, "Interview with Eduardo Souto de Moura," *Nexus* 2G, 1998

# EDUARDO SOUTO DE MOURA

**BORN:** July 25, 1952, Porto, Portugal

**EDUCATION:** School of Fine Arts (ESBAP), University of Porto, Portugal, 1980

**OFFICE:** Souto Moura Arquitectos SA, Rua do Aleixo, no. 53, 1° A, Porto 4150-043, Portugal
Tel: +351 2261-87547, Fax: +351 2261-08092
geral@soutomoura.pt

**PROJECTS FEATURED:** Kortrijk Crematorium, Antwerp, Belgium, 2011; Paula Rego Museum, Cascais, Portugal, 2008; Braga Municipal Stadium, Braga, Portugal, 2003; House in Serra da Arrábida, Portugal, 2002; Santa Maria Do Bouro Convent, Amares, Portugal, 1997

**"I HAVE AN EMPATHY WITH THE ANGUISH AND THE CREATIVE SEARCH OF CONTEMPORARY ARTISTS."**

**Paula Rego Museum, Cascais, 2008**
Souto de Moura attributes his use of red for the concrete based on buildings he saw in Pakistan and India. The two pyramid volumes also function as skylights, and recall the kitchen chimney at the Alcobaca Monastery in Portugal.

## BEAUTY IN CONTRADICTIONS

A sculptor recently said there is nothing we make in the world but architecture. He said that nature, the creation of God, is what exists in the world, and that everything which is not nature is architecture: ships, houses, graveyards, bridges, roads, and everything else we make. So architecture is non-natural. But being non-natural is not necessarily being against nature. The relationship between the natural and the non-natural should be a natural one; there must be an empathy between the two for both to coexist in harmony. If the relationship is not harmonious, the architecture is not sustainable. _ Eduardo Souto de Moura interview by Lara Braun, *Meaning People Concepts Future Forum*, LafargeHolcim Foundation for Sustainable Construction, 2004

Architecture is something artificial. . . . "Natural" means it was made by God, "architecture" is made by man. I'm not religious, but I had a religious education, I respect it, but I prefer things made by man to things made by God. I prefer the Parthenon to the marble stone in the mountain made by God. _ Luciano Basauri, Ana Dana Beroš, and Vera Grimmer, *Oris* 11, no. 60, 2009

You need to manipulate the site; if you don't manipulate it, it's natural. _ Luciano Basauri, Ana Dana Beroš, and Vera Grimmer, *Oris* 11, no. 60, 2009

## ❝ I LIKE RUINS BECAUSE THEY ARE THE ONLY THING IN ARCHITECTURE THAT IS TRUE. IT'S SO TRUE THAT IT IS NATURAL. ❞

### AMARES, 1997
## SANTA MARIA DO BOURO CONVENT

What interests me most about Santa Maria Do Bouro is the radicalism and youth of the work. That was my first renovation. I visited the building with Fernando Távora and took heed of his observations about what was authentic and what was a pastiche. Távora said that sometimes a good pastiche is better than poor new work. I showed him the project and he was very critical: he had quite contrary views about my work. All the same, his advice helped me during my work. We tend to rely on the idea that when an architect works on an historic building, he has to do so in a very dichotomous, a very dual way—old here, modern there—and the consequence is that the modern part is glass and stainless steel and the old part is stone. But that's not necessarily true. Santa Maria do Bouro is a modern work built with old stones. _ José Morales, *El Croquis* 176, Special Issue, 2015

It's the reason why I like the ruins, because it's like studying anatomy. The French architect Auguste Perret said that a good building gives always a good ruin. _ Luciano Basauri, Ana Dana Beroš, and Vera Grimmer, *Oris* 11, no. 60, 2009

I like ruins because they are the only thing in architecture that is true. It's so true that it is natural. I went to see the place where the project would be made; it doesn't matter for architecture but it is important to me. It was a monument that I knew from childhood. My mother lives there, and I always visited this monument in ruins. _ Luciano Basauri, Ana Dana Beroš, and Vera Grimmer, *Oris* 11, no. 60, 2009

. . . the question of our architectural patrimony must be dealt with in a different way and in different conditions than it has been until now. . . . What is ancient is precisely the succession of time and space throughout time, and as my intervention was just one of many, it wasn't necessary for me to confront the monument. Realizing this allowed me to soften my approach over time. . . . _ Xavier Güell, "Interview with Eduardo Souto de Moura," *Nexus* 2G, 1998

Souto de Moura has written that closed designs also permit an openness for experimentation. To him, the rigidity of a monastery—corridors and cells, for example—work well when made into other spaces such as bedrooms and pubic spaces. *Opposite:* Rather than try to reconstruct the actual convent, Souto de Moura decided to use the original stones and adapt them to the new building. *Opposite below:* An early concept sketch for the corridors in the convent.

**SANTA MARIA DO BOURO IS A MODERN WORK BUILT WITH OLD STONES.**

*Corredor dos Quartos.*

I recommended installing a heating system but no air conditioning. Those massive walls had enough thermal mass and thermal lag to keep the rooms cool. But there is a standard in Portugal that requires every five-star hotel to have air conditioning. So I was forced to cut open the walls and install air conditioning units. Not only was the exercise costly and needless, the historic fabric of the building was destroyed in the process. _ Eduardo Souto de Moura interview by Lara Braun, *Meaning People Concepts Future Forum*, LafargeHolcim Foundation for Sustainable Construction, 2004

**"I like America and America likes me," Joseph Beuys, 1974** *This seminal Action took place over seven days in May 1974. Beuys spent the entire time in the company of a wild coyote, during which time man and beast created a dialogue, a dual performance.*

[D]uring the work on Santa Maria do Bouro, Fernando Távora told me that we had few monasteries, and that I was destroying them. He told me that when you're young, you want to be a star and make your mark in print, but that all that was nonsense and instead, I ought to discover what the building needed. He advised me to visit the site every week, and that the work itself would provide a solution for the problems that had to be solved; that by living with the "animal" I would truly understand what the building needed because the building dictates the rules. That is what I mean when I talk about domesticating the "beast." That's why I like Beuys' installation, because it's mine. In his performance, Beuys lives with the coyote for seven days, during which time the coyote stops being aggressive and shares its food with him. _ José Morales, *El Croquis* 176, Special Issue, 2015

# " I LOVE MIES, BUT HE'S THE MOST CONTRADICTORY ARCHITECT I KNOW. "

## ARCHITECTS OF ENDURING INFLUENCE
### ALVARO SIZA

Architects lose quality with age because architecture requires a lot of physical energy. Siza, on the other hand, has maintained his quality and he has been surprising in a very positive way. Nobody imagined that he would produce the Iberê Camargo Museum, "dancing samba" as the headline of an article put it. He is an infallible personality in his answers, he has a grammar that he refreshes on the basis of every situation, and that means being very contemporary. _ Nuno Grande, *El Croquis* 146, 2009

I work a lot with a team. If I have a problem between stucco and concrete, I phone the engineer. And then if I have nothing, in the end I ask Siza. _ Luciano Basauri, Ana Dana Beroš, and Vera Grimmer, *Oris* 11, no. 60, 2009

I remember that when I was working with Siza, there was a tendency to deal with buildings as if they were animals, I can acknowledge that. When we were designing the solution for the Serpentine Gallery Pavilion, in London, Siza often used biological terms. Once he sent a fax to me in London before I presented the project, which said, "Eduardo, the animal has to walk." And he had added some drawings: feet. _ Nuno Grande, *El Croquis* 146, 2009

### MIES VAN DER ROHE

There is a way of reading Mies, which is to just regard him as a minimalist. But he always oscillated between classicism and neo-plasticism. He lived with that uneasiness. You only have to remember the last construction of his life, the IBM building, with that powerful travertine base that he drilled through to produce a gigantic door. Then on the other hand, he arrived in Barcelona and did two pavilions, didn't he? One was abstract and neoplastic, and the other one was classical, symmetrical, with closed corners. Why? Because of the brief? No, he was experimenting, and if a structure seemed ugly to him, he covered it with a skin in successive operations. _ Nuno Grande, *El Croquis* 146, 2009

### FERNANDO TÁVORA

Távora was my teacher, one of the few that asked us to work on designs.

. . . But the first thing that struck me about Távora was his habit of drawing, because I'd never seen anyone do it. Then I was struck by his culture, because Távora already knew everything we thought was the future of architecture, everything we read about in books or studied in math lessons, the principles of Rossi or Le Corbusier, he knew all that, and so to us he was the personification of the cultivated architect. Everything we were beginning to study and understand, Távora understood it already. _ Antonio Esposito and Giovanni Leoni, eds., *Eduardo Souto de Moura*, Milan: Electa, 2003

### SIZA AND TÁVORA

To Siza's architecture I attribute the fundamental quality of naturalness, a term fallen into disuse. In Távora I also look above all at an aspect not much in vogue nowadays, the sense of comfort that his works transmit, the result of a set of qualities that architecture needs to have, not bound up with taste or form. _ Antonio Esposito and Giovanni Leoni, eds., *Eduardo Souto de Moura*, Milan: Electa, 2003

### THE ARTS

For me, producing a detail is like writing: a comma, a period or a stroke appears. I work on the theme: if it's big, it's a book, if it's a small, it's a short story, if it's less, it's an essay, and if it has five lines, it's poetry. I arrive at the scale and the proportion early on. The detail is what unites, locks in, what staples and articulates, what ultimately provides the meaning. I like Mies because the detail in his work lends coherence to the idea. He doesn't draw too much or too little, he just does the right amount of detail—it's like writing, a text can't be full of commas, or have none, like [José] Saramago's prose. Mies is exact, precise. _ José Morales, *El Croquis* 176, Special Issue, 2015

The problem is that everyone wants to build a monument and create a work of art. But the intention of producing a work of art can never be a conscious one. A writer sits down and says, "I'm going to write." He doesn't say, "Now I'm going to write a classic novel." Then he writes like a volcano. It comes from the inside. If it is good, his work can become a work of art. _ Eduardo Souto de Moura interview by Lara Braun, *Meaning People Concepts Future Forum*, LafargeHolcim Foundation for Sustainable Construction, 2004

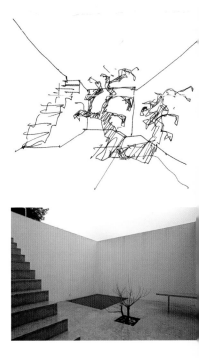

## PORTUGAL 2002
# HOUSE IN SERRA DA ARRÁBIDA

The project for the House in Arrábida has been in progress for almost four years [this was written in 1986] and so far I have only obtained the building permit from the municipality. At the present moment I surpassed "the permanent crisis," the personal difficulties with language definition, and the construction project is now ready to go ahead. The problem was that it was not compatible, neither with the client, nor with the topography, not even with "myself," to adapt a previous experience to this particular project. The "simple" solutions were exhausted, and quickly turned out "simplistic." The "form" was becoming "formula." _ Eduardo Souto de Moura, courtesy Souto Moura Arquitectos

**Programs for Designing Houses** In 1998 I wrote a text exemplifying my conceptual intentions at the time. . . . I verify that, in spite of the diversity of places and briefs, there is a permanent obsession with a building "type," a kind of design persecution. . . . In the north the houses are narrow and long, with a corridor closed to the exterior, with a perimeter wall that continues and defines the lot. Whereas in the south the houses are usually isolated units sited at the top of a small mount ("monte") with the various interior spaces laid around a central courtyard. It was this theme of the

> ❝ **IN THE HISTORY OF ARCHITECTURE, THERE IS PROBABLY NO MORE DIFFICULT TYPOLOGY THAN THE ONE OF THE 'HOUSE.' TO DESIGN A HOUSE IS THE EQUIVALENT —CLOSE TO PARANOIA—OF REDUCING THE WORLD TO A VITAL OBJECT.** ❞

topography that led me to break the unitary volume into fragments, for better adaptation to the site topography. Today [written in 2003], I still design houses, and I verify that they are different. . . . The houses that I am now designing are less "black and white," they have variations: sometimes the volume "decomposes" in parts, the plans are no longer with full straight angles. . . . In some cases detail is "interrupted," omitted, as it were, to reinforce the indispensable design. _ Luisella Gelsomino, ed., *Eduardo Souto De Moura: Case, ultimi progetti*, Florence: Alinea, 2001

Sometimes I do two projects, two models and two teams in the studio. One team does one house with the doors and windows, and the other one does something more abstract. _ Luciano Basauri, Ana Dana Beroš, and Vera Grimmer, *Oris* 11, no. 60, 2009

If you have different families, different places of life, it's stupid to make them equal. _ Luciano Basauri, Ana Dana Beroš, and Vera Grimmer, *Oris* 11, no. 60, 2009

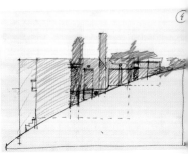

References to literature and art provide context for much of Souto de Moura's explorations and ways of processing design. Of residential work he says, "One designs houses for oneself, like writers who write books they want to read themselves."

## RESIDENTIAL ARCHITECTURE

There were no architects in my family, I had no contacts in political parties, and I was 20 years old. What could I do? My first projects were houses for my family and friends. Then they were published, and people started asking me for that type of house. But I didn't want to repeat myself; I didn't want to reproduce the same models. Later on, I entered competitions and got some public contracts. I was tired of just doing houses. _ José Morales, *El Croquis* 176, Special Issue, 2015

When I visit my houses I also see certain advantages and disadvantages. It's not that they're not elegant or that people are not at ease in them, but I think, for example, that they are lacking in something that I have been discovering over time, and that was almost impossible for me to perceive when I started out as a professional. I call that something *comfort*, not in the English sense of the term, or in the decorative sense, but rather understood as the capacity or the disposition of the users of the house to be able to experience different situations with regard to light, to space, to different points of view, to the landscape (both exterior and interior), and to changes in color. So I decided to introduce errors, things that wouldn't look right. That's how I lost my fear of making new mistakes in the sense of plastic composition. _ Xavier Güell, "Interview with Eduardo Souto de Moura," *Nexus* 2G, 1998

## ❝❝ ONE DESIGNS HOUSES FOR ONESELF, LIKE WRITERS WHO WRITE BOOKS THEY WANT TO READ THEMSELVES. ❞❞

## HOME AS A "NEUTRAL SPACE"

Perhaps it's worth repeating why Mies didn't want to move house. I'm studying the reason why some artists live and work in very conservative environments, in old houses. They write, work and paint in those houses. Well, I've come to the conclusion that those architects and artists are so obsessed with their work that they don't want anything to disturb them. To produce their work and build the "vanguard," they need to inhabit a neutral space that is already encoded, without transgressions, without vanguards. It has to do with wanting a more neutral, more anonymous space. _ José Morales, *El Croquis* 176, Special Issue, 2015

No one has ever lived in many of the great houses of modern architecture. Villa Savoye is one example. There are several houses that are true manifestos. You just don't sleep inside history. I can't sleep in a house that changed the course of twentieth century history. _ Eduardo Souto de Moura interview by Lara Braun, *Meaning People Concepts Future Forum*, LafargeHolcim Foundation for Sustainable Construction, 2004

## SOUTO DE MOURA HOME

. . . it's a house I did for an architect who didn't want to design the house herself, and I understand that. It's not easy. In the end, she didn't live there because her family moved to another city, so I was able to buy it. And there was no problem, because I design houses as if they were for me, not for my clients, which I find a good criterion—I was widely criticized at the time for that statement. . . . So in the house where I live, I didn't change anything except the way some of the kitchen cabinet doors work, under instruction by my wife. _ José Morales, *El Croquis* 176, Special Issue, 2015

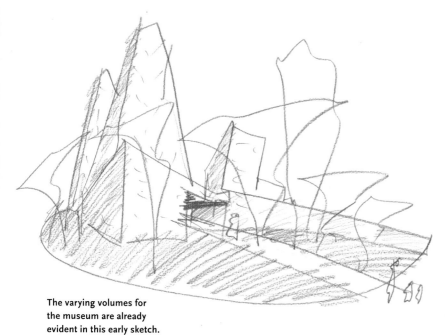

The varying volumes for the museum are already evident in this early sketch.

**CASCAIS 2008**
# PAULA REGO MUSEUM
I had a chat with Paula Rego. We spoke in Portugal, and then in London, where she showed me her exhibition at the Tate Gallery. She likes big rooms, with space between the paintings. When we finished wandering around the exhibition, she opened the door of a room that was closed off to the public and said, "Actually, what I like is this," and we entered a room painted purple that only contained works by Francis Bacon in orange shades, beautiful. I think that was when I was able to get a glimpse of her imagination. _ Nuno Grande, *El Croquis* 146, 2009

I was lucky enough to choose the site, a circumstance that increased my responsibility after the painter Paula Rego had chosen me to design the project. The site

was a wood, surrounded by a wall, with a void in the middle, old tennis courts from a local club that had disappeared with the Carnation Revolution [April 25, 1974]. With a survey taken of the trees, especially their crowns, I developed a set of volumes with different heights to respond to the plurality of the program.

The disposition of boxes acts like a mineral positive, from the leftover negative space that remains from the treetop perimeter. This "Yang and Yin" game between artifact and nature helped to decide the exterior material, red concrete, the opposite color to the green of the wood. . . . Truth remains, that it is never too much to juxtapose the abstract and totally artificial reality of contemporary art with the daily and harsh reality that surrounds us. _ Eduardo Souto de Moura, courtesy Souto Moura Arquitectos

When architecture is completely abstract, made of walls, boxes or panes of glass, it is harder to say whether something is on or off scale, because everything is based on a positive/negative relationship. But when I build a "chimney," as in the case of this museum, I certainly can codify it with domestic spaces and I can measure and see whether I am mistaken. I am always asking myself, "Has that thing ended up being too high, ridiculously monumental? Has it ended up being just wishful thinking?" _ Nuno Grande, *El Croquis* 146, 2009

**▌▌ TO ME, IT IS A TOTALLY NEW PROJECT FROM A GRAMMATICAL POINT OF VIEW, WHICH IS WHY I SENSE THAT IT HAS SPELLING AND CALLIGRAPHIC MISTAKES. ▌▌**

The red concrete was meant to contrast with the surrounding landscape, accomplishing a yin-yang of color, whereas light penetrating the pyramids from within conveys calm and purity.

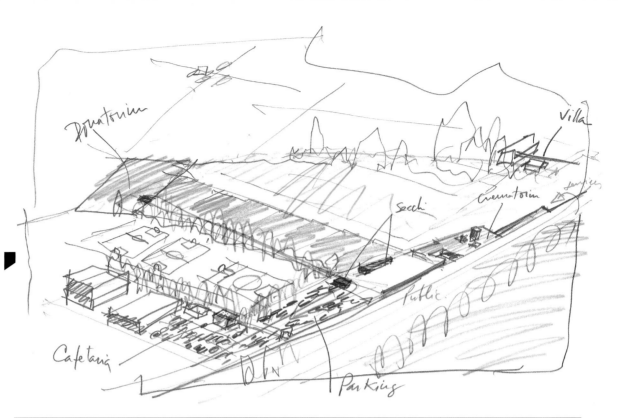

❝ **ARCHITECTURE IS MEANT TO SERVE FUNCTIONALITY FIRST AND FOREMOST.** ❞

The rich detail of the sketch, *above*, provides the many functions of the crematorium, including how it eases into the existing cemetery in the overall space. For the architect, serenity was both ubiquitous and essential for Kortrijk.

### ANTWERP 2011
## KORTRIJK CREMATORIUM
It is a matter of searching for calm and making peace with the impressive landscape of Hoog-Kortrijk. The cemetery of Hoog-Kortrijk is a serene place that unfolds on the landscape, with plateaus that slip rhythmically over the slope. The strength of this place results specially from its extension and vastness. It is very important to maintain the perspective and silence. The new crematory is covered with earth and green as the landscape, being part of it. On the roof of the crematory one can recognize some figures of light and sky, in granite, metal, glass and stone. The new crematory will breathe light and sky, water and landscape—for us the essential things. The crematory will not become a church or chapel, with a religious or mysterious ambiance. Nor will the crematory be a house with a familiar ambiance. The new crematory that we propose will become an extremely sober building, for a clear and dignified last farewell. _ Eduardo Souto de Moura, courtesy Souto Moura Arquitectos

# "" NOTHING SHOULD BE SO BEAUTIFUL THAT IT BECOMES NONFUNCTIONAL. ""

## DESIGN

If you are interested, you're drawing a lot and deciding what is good and what is not. You make details to check a color. You make a model, perhaps the height is not good and so on, because you are interested. If you are not interested, you don't check. _ Luciano Basauri, Ana Dana Beroš, and Vera Grimmer, *Oris* 11, no. 60, 2009

I arrive at form via image. I do a lot of sketches. It's a working method that owes a lot to the tradition that Siza inculcated in us. When we had doubts about some aspect of the project, we had to draw to explain ourselves. . . . When we explained the circumstances to Siza, he always resolved the problem with sketches. _ José Morales, *El Croquis* 176, Special Issue, 2015

When I work with Siza and I continue working with him, when I ask some questions like "Why do you want this cube?" he said, "Because I like it." _ Luciano Basauri, Ana Dana Beroš, and Vera Grimmer, *Oris* 11, no. 60, 2009

I like structures: there are no good buildings with poor structures. For me it's a sacred triangle: material-construction system-language. I mean, a stone building has to be in stone: a concrete building has to be in concrete . . . you can't supplant the relationship between language, material and construction. However, there are times when that is not possible. As Einstein said, "The shortest distance between two points is a straight line, when the medium is uniform. If the medium is not uniform, it can be different, for example, a curve." _ José Morales, *El Croquis* 176, Special Issue, 2015

## SCALE

The scale is the most difficult aspect. It is what provides the precision—the "click" for the whole project. If architecture is always made of the same stuff—walls, doors and windows—why is there such a difference between good and bad architecture? For me, above all it's a question of scale. . . . I love the way Robert Venturi played with it in the competition for the National Football Hall of Fame, for example, with that huge façade which hid the stadium. . . . I also love Aldo Rossi's changes of scale, for example the transformations between furniture and buildings. I wrote about this issue once, comparing tables with buildings, how the tables were like small models of big houses. _ José Morales, *El Croquis* 176, Special Issue, 2015

The elevation is a drawing of a face, the first expression of a person; it is what makes us fall in love. The section reveals the truth and displays the intrinsic rules that prove the congruence of things. _ Nuno Grande, *El Croquis* 146, 2009

## "OPEN WORK"

I'm interested in the concept of open work. Art has a social function. I have to help people, and that has to do with my worldview. I believe that nature is not as well made as we imagine. Our role is to improve the world, perhaps by design. _ José Morales, *El Croquis* 176, Special Issue, 2015

## MATERIALS

I do sometimes like to provoke with my materials and make people think about their lightness or heaviness. I enjoy all that, even more with structures. _ José Morales, *El Croquis* 176, Special Issue, 2015

I avoid using endangered or protected species. I think we should use wood in moderation and replant our forests as we use the wood. We have to use wood because it is one of the finest materials available. _ Rose Etherington, *Dezeen*, March 29, 2011

---

This project is the result of a competition held to build a new crematorium in an existing cemetery designed by Bernardo Sechi. There are few opportunities in the history of architecture to witness the invention of a typology. Just think, for example, of how little the house typology has changed down to the present day. It is no coincidence that "astronauts like to come home." Building a crematorium does not mean building an incineration machine or a church; nor does it mean building a meeting hall or a café. Yet while it is none of that, it has to be able to adapt to each one of those uses. Designing a crematorium was a unique chance to invent a typology that will be fundamental for our future, the way we will go on living, in the knowledge of how we are going to end up after we have lived. _ "Crematorium Uitzicht in Kortrijk," *El Croquis* 146, 2005

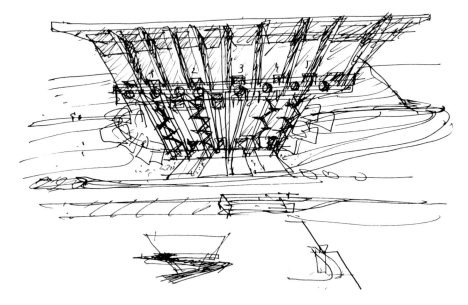

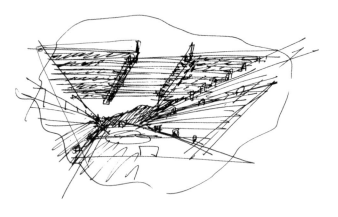

# ❝❝ THIS JUXTAPOSITION OF THE NATURAL AND THE MAN-MADE EXPRESSES **THE ESSENCE OF THE STADIUM.** ❞❞

In June 2011, President Barack Obama delivered a speech in New York at the Pritzker Prize ceremony for Souto de Moura. In particular, the president applauded Braga Stadium because it showed that the architect "took great care to position the stadium in such a way that anyone who couldn't afford a ticket could watch the match from the surrounding hillside."

### BRAGA 2003
## BRAGA MUNICIPAL STADIUM

When we were invited to make the project, we went to see the site, to see whether it is interesting, and to decide whether we would accept or not. The only way to make a good decision is to visit the site after the work and say whether it is better now, or better without the stadium. I prefer the stadium there because I like this game. _ Luciano Basauri, Ana Dana Beroš, and Vera Grimmer, *Oris* 11, no. 60, 2009

Harmony can be achieved only through conflict. At Braga Stadium, it was a drama to break down the mountain and make concrete from the stone. The concrete is the mountain, no longer in natural form, but in manmade form. _ Eduardo Souto de Moura interview by Lara Braun, *Meaning People Concepts Future Forum*, LafargeHolcim Foundation for Sustainable Construction, 2004

Ultimately it is the mountain that supports the roof. It is this encounter, this meeting point between the natural and the manmade that I find interesting to deal with. . . . Thus having the stone wall of the mountain terminate the southeast end of the stadium instead of the usual seating is a fitting reminder that the stadium owes its existence to the mountain. _ Eduardo Souto de Moura interview by Lara Braun, *Meaning People Concepts Future Forum*, LafargeHolcim Foundation for Sustainable Construction, 2004

## MODERNISM, POSTMODERNISM, MINIMALISM

[In Portugal] during fifty years of fascism, modern architecture was forbidden, it was considered communist. . . . I started my profession in a country without housing, hospitals, schools and so on. There were some programs after the revolution, to rebuild the country. . . . Modernism was not a choice of language but a possibility to rebuild the country. I said I don't have to work with this postmodern language because I have no money, and I think it is stupid for a country like Portugal to have columns and so on. . . .

Modernism is not against history, it isn't against classicism. It's a new classicism with other materials, other technologies, but the types are the same. It's another way to see, like Picasso. He repainted the classic pictures about the history of Spain in another way. _ Luciano Basauri, Ana Dana Beroš, and Vera Grimmer, *Oris* 11, no. 60, 2009

. . . for a long time now I have been irritated by the use of the term *minimalism*. People said that minimalism was quite appropriate for cleansing and mental health, to get away from postmodernism. But the truth is that they turned it into a style, a series of tics, something with no substance. Many architects produce a "box," they paint it white and they say it is minimalist. And I find them exasperating. There are no universal languages, just as there are no universal places; there is just *adaptation*. That is one of my favorite words, because architecture is a problem of adaptation. _ Nuno Grande, *El Croquis* 146, 2009

## DESIGN WORK IN PORTUGAL

Oporto today lacks initiative. It gets excited about nature projects but it's not interested in quality architecture. . . . Because of a false idea of the heritage, if you touch a church there's a scandal, but an ugly building, badly designed, passes without comment. _ Antonio Esposito and Giovanni Leoni, eds., *Eduardo Souto de Moura*, Milan: Electa, 2003

## FAME

In Portugal, when architecture became politicized in the 1950s, the 1960s and then after the April 74 Revolution, architects were somewhat reluctant to stand out and have their work published. I still remember the modesty of some colleagues who are now published quite widely. Alvaro Siza, who had more international contacts, phoned his colleagues to tell them that foreign journals were interested in publicizing the social housing projects they were producing at the time. Their answer was, "Publish? That's for the bourgeoisie. What we need to do is to build for the people." _ Nuno Grande, *El Croquis* 146, 2009

## SUSTAINABILITY

Some years ago, when high-tech enthusiasts transformed buildings into machines, they called them intelligent buildings and coined the phrase "intelligent architecture," as if buildings without such systems are stupid. It's like saying the Pantheon, which has no equipment, is stupid architecture. So I'm quite critical when it comes to such slogans and labels attached to buildings. That's why I'm wary of those slogans of sustainable architecture. _ Eduardo Souto de Moura interview by Lara Braun, *Meaning People Concepts Future Forum*, LafargeHolcim Foundation for Sustainable Construction, 2004

Nature can be altered in the service of man and community, but there are limits. . . . Changing the course of a river, temporarily interrupting the flow and restoring it later is one thing, but it is quite another thing to relocate a river and thereby change the microclimate, the topography, the local environment. That's what I'm against. _ Eduardo Souto de Moura interview by Lara Braun, *Meaning People Concepts Future Forum*, LafargeHolcim Foundation for Sustainable Construction, 2004

## GLOBALIZATION

Globalization of course has advantages, like communication and speed, but when it comes to architecture I don't think globalization can play such an important role. . . . It is incorrigible to build a glass skyscraper in Ecuador and the same building in Moscow. The climates are different, the customs are different. _ Eduardo Souto de Moura interview by Lara Braun, *Meaning People Concepts Future Forum*, LafargeHolcim Foundation for Sustainable Construction, 2004

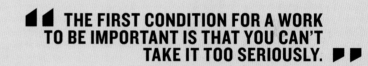

**THE FIRST CONDITION FOR A WORK TO BE IMPORTANT IS THAT YOU CAN'T TAKE IT TOO SERIOUSLY.**

## CHANGE

I am critical, but I am not pessimistic. Architecture, for instance, hasn't changed very much, although it appears quite different nowadays. Since its infancy, in Mesopotamia, the concept of the house has evolved very little. You can change the materials, add or take away glass, but in the end the house is still a sort of second layer of clothing for the fundamental social unit—the family. The hierarchy and organization of the family hasn't changed that much over time and houses haven't either. There are things that have never changed and never will. _ Eduardo Souto de Moura interview by Lara Braun, *Meaning People Concepts Future Forum*, LafargeHolcim Foundation for Sustainable Construction, 2004

I'm not terribly worried about the issue of change. Einstein said that the future arrives too fast to think about it. . . . In spite of everything, I have an optimistic outlook—we haven't got much choice. _ José Morales, *El Croquis* 176, Special Issue, 2015

## IMAGINATIVE PRINCIPLES

I think that in our design, what lie at the root of everything are not just our desires to better solve the programs or come up with extraordinary space structures, but to go beyond them to eventually create imaginative principles of our own. It may be that when we are creating a building we are also trying to create the principles of the building at the same time.

_ Ryue Nishizawa, *GA Architect 18,* November 2005

For the time being the method we are using is premised on the extremely modern idea of making the content of the building the human actions that take place within [to] kind of create the architectural form.

_ Kristin Feireiss, ed., *The Zollverein School of Management and Design, Essen, Germany,* Munich: Prestel, 2006

# KAZUYO SEJIMA + RYUE NISHIZAWA

**BORN:** Kazuyo Sejima: October 29, 1956, Ibaraki Prefecture, Japan;
Ryue Nishizawa: February 7, 1966, Kanagawa Prefecture, Japan

**EDUCATION:** Kazuyo Sejima: M.Arch, Japan Women's University, Toyko, Japan, 1981;
Ryue Nishizawa: M.Arch, Yokohama National University, Yokohama, Japan, 1990

**OFFICE:** Kazuyo Sejima + Ryue Nishizawa / SANAA, 1-5-27, Tatsumi, Koto-ku, Tokyo, 135-0053 Japan
Tel +81 0-3-5534-1780, Fax +81 0-3-5534-1757, press@sanaa.co.jp

**PROJECTS FEATURED:** Rolex Learning Center, Lausanne, Switzerland, 2010; New Museum of Contemporary Art, New York, 2007; Glass Pavilion at the Toledo Museum of Art, Ohio, 2006; Zollverein School of Management and Design, Essen, Germany, 2006; 21st Century Museum of Contemporary Art, Kanazawa, Japan, 2004

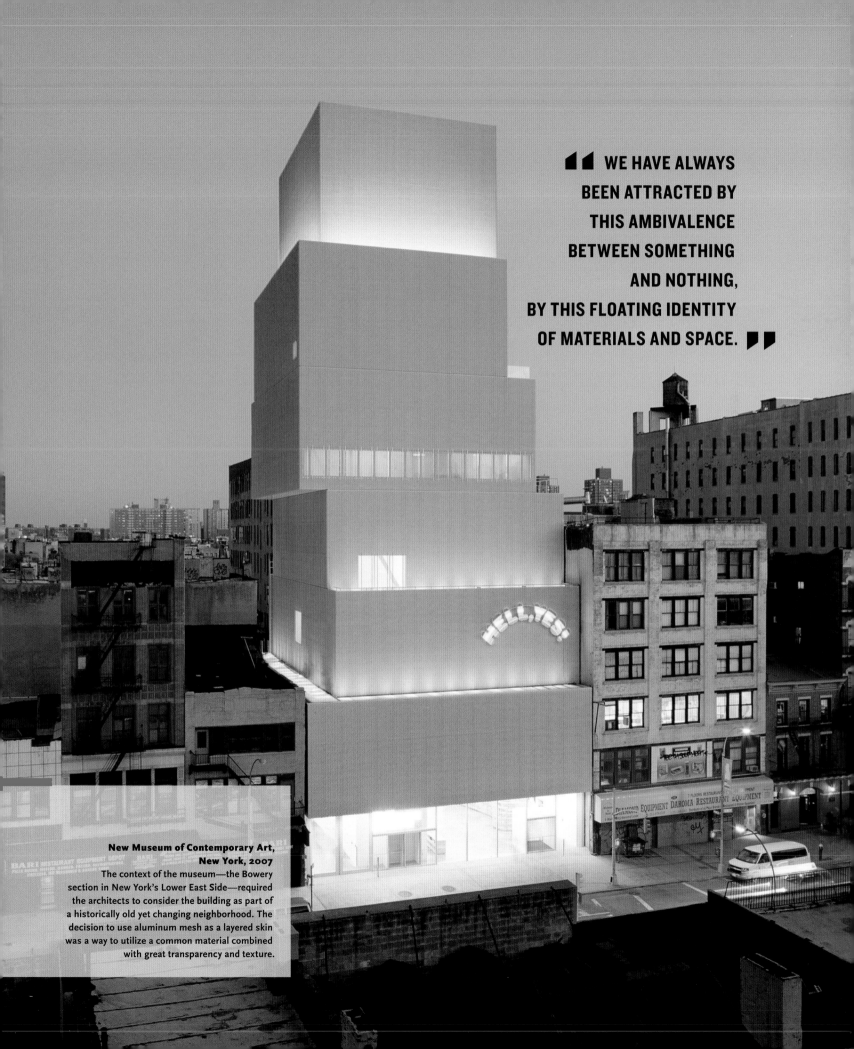

“ WE HAVE ALWAYS
BEEN ATTRACTED BY
THIS AMBIVALENCE
BETWEEN SOMETHING
AND NOTHING,
BY THIS FLOATING IDENTITY
OF MATERIALS AND SPACE. ”

**New Museum of Contemporary Art,
New York, 2007**
The context of the museum—the Bowery
section in New York's Lower East Side—required
the architects to consider the building as part of
a historically old yet changing neighborhood. The
decision to use aluminum mesh as a layered skin
was a way to utilize a common material combined
with great transparency and texture.

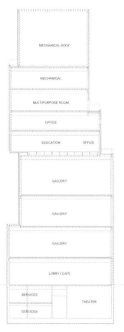

With a limited footprint, the variable stack, seen in the section above, permitted the introduction of terraces and natural light into the exhibition galleries.

### NEW YORK 2007
## NEW MUSEUM OF CONTEMPO- RARY ART

New York, compared with the rest of America, is a really special place. I find it a really special city. Things are always changing in New York. . . . When you look at New York, most of it was built in the nineteenth century. We wanted to make a really new, twenty-first-century building—appropriate for a museum in a city that is always in the business of defining what is new. _ Ryue Nishizawa interview with Edan Corkill, *Japan Times,* January 6, 2008

First, with a plot of land as small as that 740 square meters, there was no alternative but to stack the galleries on top of each other. But when you put galleries on top of each other, you end up with a high-rise building, right? In that situation the most cost-effective method is to make what's known as a "typical floor plan." In other words, all the floors end up the same and, as a consequence, the building ends up looking more like an office tower than a museum. So we decided that each floor needed to look differ-

ent from the others, and to achieve that we needed to vary their sizes. _ Ryue Nishizawa interview with Edan Corkill, *Japan Times,* January 6, 2008

The different-sized floors also made terraces on the middle floors possible, and they were important too. In galleries it's difficult to make windows, because you need walls for the art. So we came up with the skylight and terrace idea. _ Kazuyo Sejima interview with Edan Corkill, *Japan Times,* January 6, 2008

There are two things we paid a lot of attention to. One was the building's surface and the other was the height and the overall proportions of the building. The layered mesh skin and stacked volumes give the building a very specific identity. _ Joseph Grima and Karen Wong, eds., *Shift: SANAA and The New Museum,* Baden, Switzerland: Lars Müller Publishers, 2008

**"Texture"** I was deeply struck—especially in the early days of the project—by the roughness of the Bowery. I couldn't believe it was so close to

Broadway. Broadway is another world. The use of mesh was inspired by our desire to acknowledge the "texture" of the surroundings. . . . Mesh is the most common industrial material. Our objective was to use it in a subtler, more poetic way without sacrificing its qualities. For this reason we decided to use an aluminum mesh instead of the more common steel variety. Aluminum gives a very different impression—it's bright and white and translucent. It gives the building a totally different feeling of lightness, subtlety, and permeability. _ Joseph Grima and Karen Wong, eds., *Shift: SANAA and The New Museum*, Baden, Switzerland: Lars Müller Publishers, 2008

Its appearance also changes depending on the weather. When it's cloudy it looks gray and flat, but when the sun shines the aluminum reflects the sun, and the shadows of the mesh are visible on the internal wall. _ Ryue Nishizawa interview with Edan Corkill, *Japan Times*, January 6, 2008

I think the double-façade system is one of the most successful parts of the building. One of our greatest concerns was that the building could appear too harsh, too opaque, just a pile of stacked boxes. The double façade gives depth and transparency to the surface of the volumes. _ Joseph Grima and Karen Wong, eds., *Shift: SANAA and The New Museum*, Baden, Switzerland: Lars Müller Publishers, 2008

## TRANSPARENCY

Mainly we think about borders. A reflection is not a real wall, but it signals a different space. The meaning of transparency is to create a diversity of relations. It is not necessary to always see through. Transparency also means clarity, not only visual, but also conceptual. There are many relations. _ Augustin Pérez Rubio, *Houses: Kazuyo Sejima + Ryue Nishizawa, SANAA*, Barcelona: Actar, 2007

Usually, transparency and lightness, in terms of mass, are not the ultimate goals. What we are trying to do is to organize the components in a clear way. _ SANAA, *Lars: Cultura y Ciudad*, May 2005

## ATMOSPHERE

One of our interests is how to create atmosphere, a landscape for people. _ Ryue Nishizawa interview by Juan Antonio Cortés, *El Croquis, SANAA 2004–2008*, 2008

I think all our architecture has a very intimate relation with the atmosphere. We are always trying to find the way to relate. There are no buildings that have no relation with the atmosphere. _ Augustin Pérez Rubio, *Houses: Kazuyo Sejima + Ryue Nishizawa, SANAA*, Barcelona: Actar, 2007

Atmosphere has two meanings for us. One relates to the surroundings of the building and the other has to do with space. One is the atmosphere that a building creates, outside and inside, that does not exist before the building is constructed. The other is the atmosphere that exists before the building is constructed. Both are very important. In any case, we have no idea at the start of the project about which is

the most important aspect that we have to react to: program, atmosphere, dimensions . . . _ Christina Diaz Moreno and Efrén Garcia Grinda, *El Croquis*, vol. 121/122, 2004

## SIMPLICITY

A lot of discussion and work is required to make a simple project. We never start from a simple base, even in the schematic design phase. We seem to start from very complicated things that gradually become simple. _Christina Diaz Moreno and Efrén Garcia Grinda, *El Croquis*, vol. 121/122, 2004

We are minimalists. But we distinguish between two directions in the minimalist movement. We don't want to make formally minimal architecture which might be very strict and rigid. In other words, we try to make our buildings very simple and straightforward, but the most important thing for us is that people enjoy the spaces we create. _ Kristin Feireiss, ed., *The Zollverein School of Management and Design, Essen, Germany*, Munich: Prestel, 2006

## EXPERIENCING ARCHITECTURE

The transparency [of the architecture] depends on the comprehension of the person experiencing it. On the other hand, it would be boring if one could understand it without experiencing it. It is like discovering how to relate to the building through experiencing it. One receives suggestions from the building up to a certain point, but after that, one discovers the building oneself so that one can freely walk around in it. _ SANAA, *Sejima Kazuyo + Nishizawa Ryue Dokuhon*, Tokyo: A.D.A. Edita, 2005

### KANAZAWA 2004
# 21ST CENTURY MUSEUM OF CONTEMPORARY ART

In the competition phase of the Kanazawa Art Museum, we proposed a circle because the site is in the center of the city, and the people approached the site from all directions. A rectangular or square plan cannot make the entire façade a front, as we could with a circular plan. _ Christina Diaz Moreno and Efrén Garcia Grinda, *El Croquis*, vol. 121/122, 2004

In Japan, the client usually requires that the architect create big exhibition spaces which use movable walls. But we decided against making two or three big galleries, and designed eighteen smaller spaces. _ Hans Ulrich Obrist, *Domus*, December 2004

At the beginning of our study, we might consider that we have a round option or a rectangular option. We compare and wonder which must be taken. There might be many reasons to take the round one. This is not so difficult, because there is a clear difference between both options. But once we choose the round option, for instance in Kanazawa, we face a situation with thousands of different options that look almost the same. This brings different qualities we have to choose from. . . . What we do during the study process is to try to create local rules or "regulations" to define the building. For instance, for Kanazawa, we created many models, and gradually we found the idea of having a long visual connection that penetrates the building from one side to the other to give a feeling of transparency. At some point somebody found this idea, that we must have this kind of penetration. We create many "small regulations" that also include visual impressions. We might decide that we will have five shapes repeated. This is the kind of thing that happens during our study to define a direction. _ Augustin Pérez Rubio, *Houses: Kazuyo Sejima + Ryue Nishizawa, SANAA*, Barcelona: Actar, 2007

While working on Kanazawa, another item entered the stage besides "separating the rooms": the

The elegant, extended circle has become a defining element of Kanazawa, and for the architects was a meditative response to the museum's placement in the center of the city and adapting to the environment. The transparency of the museum departments further unites the various activities within the large space and is an example of what the architects call "the equivalence of spaces."

transparent curved glass wall. This also became a major subject theme. This idea was already there at the very early stage, but the moment it was given the significant size of 4.5 by 3 meters and a large curvature radius, its presence was suddenly brought under the spotlight. A curve in which an expansive piece of transparent glass would stretch to the edge of the site, close in, then move off. Also, it made an extremely strong impact in terms of the relationship between environment and building. _ Ryue Nishizawa, *GA Architect 18*, November 2005

We are trying to inject a different sense of space, and also a different sense of time, into the experience of walking through the passages. Some passages have openings, but most don't. _ Hans Ulrich Obrist, *Domus*, December 2004

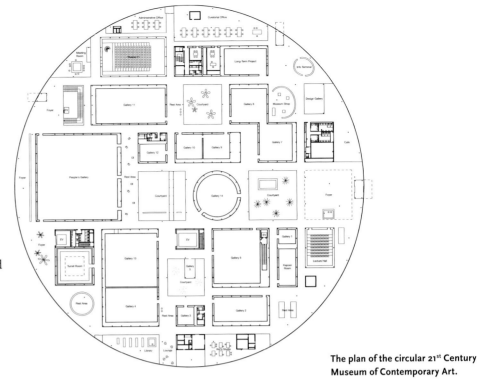

The plan of the circular 21st Century Museum of Contemporary Art.

## ❝ WE ARE VERY MUCH INFLUENCED BY JAPANESE ARCHITECTURE. WE JUST HAVE NEVER TRIED TO QUOTE DIRECTLY FROM THE JAPANESE PAST. ❞

### JAPANESE ARCHITECTURE

We never refer to anything from Japanese traditional buildings. We don't have a different attitude to our projects in Japan and Europe. It is all about the context. That is the decisive factor. We do not transform Japanese elements into our own architectural language. We might be inspired by history or tradition, but this could come from any country or culture. _ Kristin Feireiss, ed., *The Zollverein School of Management and Design, Essen, Germany,* Munich: Prestel, 2006

We are obviously influenced by Japanese culture because we grew up in a Japanese atmosphere, which is made up of many translucent, transparent, light things. If you go to a soba noodle shop, you will see a very light fabric hanging from the entrance door, and you can go through it. We are very interested in the way of creating a relationship between two sides, in using something that does not divide too much and somehow maintains the relationship, and I think that is why we often use translucent or transparent elements in our projects . . . _ Ryue Nishizawa interview by Juan Antonio Cortés, *El Croquis, SANAA 2004–2008,* 2008

### INSIDE/OUTSIDE

We are always very interested in how to forge a relationship between outside and inside. _ Kazuyo Sejima interview with Juan Antonio Cortés, *El Croquis, SANAA 2004–2008,* 2008

One of the trends that is happening in downtown Tokyo is that architects don't think about the relation between city and the building. They just make buildings within the regulations to create the maximum volume. Buildings in Tokyo are getting more and more enclosed. They don't believe in the outside, so they try to do everything inside. This kind of tendency creates very big opaque volumes on the street. This gives the street very dark shadows, which make the street even worse. If the streets get very bad, people will want more enclosed houses. This kind of vicious cycle is happening. _ Augustin Pérez Rubio, *Houses: Kazuyo Sejima + Ryue Nishizawa, SANAA,* Barcelona: Actar, 2007

### GARDENS

There are differences between Western and Asian cities. I think Western cities can be artificial, but in Asia it is different. Here, natural things and artificial things live together and there is a kind of mixture. . . . I think we can encourage a more open lifestyle by using gardens as well as the buildings. We can make the most of having this kind of tradition of living with nature right in the center of the city, in contrast to what happens in the West. _ Ryue Nishizawa interview by Juan Antonio Cortés, *El Croquis, SANAA 2004–2008,* 2008

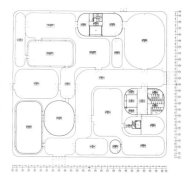

Glass is an apt metaphor and material for the Toledo annex, for the museum has long been renowned for having one of the best glass collections in the country. Again, there is the prevailing sense of transparency, but this time each individual cavity is encased in glass, maintaining the overall concept and permitting continued dialogue within the pavilion (including a glass-making facility) and the outdoors. The plan, directly above, shows the interior glass bays or rooms and resulting double membranes.

**TOLEDO 2006**

# GLASS PAVILION AT THE TOLEDO MUSEUM OF ART

The spatial organization of the Glass Pavilion at the Toledo Museum of Art came from the idea of the wall and its relationship with space, not from a desire to search for a new idea of transparency. Normally, one wall has two sides, so if you define the shape of the wall, this will affect two adjacent spaces. This relationship between the wall and the two adjacent spaces is always accepted and not discussed. We decided to make a wall with two thin membranes, not necessarily linked together, and we found that this created a kind of double wall between these two spaces and marked the independence of each room. Both are close, and you can perceive one from the other, but they keep their independence. _ Christina Diaz Moreno and Efrén Garcia Grinda, *El Croquis*, vol. 121/122, 2004

The important thing for us was that each space, each functional space, would be outlined on the plan by one line. That is why there are so many layers of glass, which sometimes are quite transparent and sometimes, on account of the visual overlap of the curved glass, become translucent. That produces an atmospheric effect, although that is not the main reason. The most important reason why we use glass here is to clarify our idea (of the organization).

_ Kazuyo Sejima interview by Juan Antonio Cortés, *El Croquis, SANAA 2004–2008*, 2008

## LAUSANNE 2010
# ROLEX LEARNING CENTER We

somehow imagined a park—a space where people can communicate. _ Kazuyo Sejima, *Building Design*, March 2010

The building has a multiple program, with a restaurant, a library, exhibition space, offices, and others, all different. First we produced a diagram of the building with many stories to house all the different programs. But we were not happy with that solution because the plan became very conventional with stacked floors. . . . We felt it was a a bit strange for one floor to be a library, another floor to be a café, and we thought we ought to discover a nicer architectural shape. Finally we reached the idea of housing all the different programs in one space, but with the continuity divided by patios, some big and others small. And we gave the shape a deformation (a warp or a wave) to create different levels for the occupants. They can be set in a slightly higher area without being disconnected from the floor, and you can move to a higher part of the floor to see the lake and the mountain. Another thing is that this kind of distortion of the floor provides a desirable distance between these programs. This formation of hills and valleys in the building gives rise to a separation between them. But it is not a total separation, because the relations and continuity are maintained.
_ Kazuyo Sejima interview by Juan Antonio Cortés, *El Croquis, SANAA 2004–2008*, 2008

We imagined that this type of open space might increase the possibility for new meetings or trigger new activities. In comparison to traditional study spaces, where corridors and classrooms are clearly separated, we hope that there will be many different ways to use the new space and that there will be more active interaction, which in turn will trigger new activities. _SANAA, domusweb.it, February 2010

In my opinion, this project reflects our aspiration to move further beyond the framework of plane structure. The building presents itself as an unusual single-volume space in which the presence of lots of patios seems to cause each space and each corner to connect with one another while keeping some distance from one another at the same time. _ Ryue Nishizawa, *GA Architect 18*, November 2005

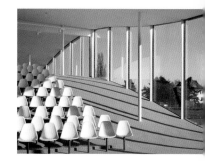

The undulation of the Rolex Learning Center may seem to mimic the surrounding Alps, but its stated purpose is one of unfettered movement and flexibility. The curved glass-and-concrete volume is spread over 20,000 square meters.

The scattered windows or openings (in three sizes) immediately confer an openness to the concrete volume. Moreover, the windows serve to bring in light and maintain connection with the outdoors. The open floor plan allows for activities specific to each level. *Opposite:* Sejima and Nishizawa with models of the Zollverein project. The photo at center shows the building's multiple interior levels.

## ESSEN 2006
# ZOLLVEREIN SCHOOL OF MANAGEMENT AND DESIGN

The Zollverein site is dynamic and the scale overwhelming, yet the building structures in themselves are delicate. Our aim was to design a new building which refers to the scale of the former coalmine buildings. _ Kristin Feireiss, ed., *The Zollverein School of Management and Design, Essen, Germany*, Munich: Prestel, 2006

The big volume of the building was necessary not only as a reaction to the site but also so that a dialogue with the remarkable historic buildings could be created. We have tried to make one volume which shows continuity with the other big buildings, and we have kept a wide open space around our building as a reference to the site. _ Kristin Feireiss, ed., *The Zollverein School of Management and Design, Essen, Germany*, Munich: Prestel, 2006

It sounds like a paradox, but it was our intention to make the concrete transparent by adding a number of openings, but this transparency is totally different from the transparency achieved using glass. For us the thickness of the concrete wall, or rather the thinness, is as important as the penetration of windows to achieve a feeling of transparency. _ Kristin Feireiss, ed., *The Zollverein School of Management and Design, Essen, Germany*, Munich: Prestel, 2006

Massiveness and light—both were important qualities for us to achieve continuity on the site. The windows, or rather the holes or openings, are a strong element in achieving this aim. We always checked the different elevations with the client and the users, because the windows naturally have an impact on the interior as well as the exterior expression. _ Kristin Feireiss, ed., *The Zollverein School of Management and Design, Essen, Germany*, Munich: Prestel, 2006

## THE SANAA STUDIO

*SANAA was founded in 1995 by Kazuyo Sejima and Ryue Nishizawa. Although Sejima and Nishizawa work together under the name SANAA, they also have studios under their own names. Sejima worked for Toyo Ito before setting up her own studio in 1987, while Nishizawa set up his own office in 1997.*

The reason why we originally established SANAA was to tackle foreign competitions and major Japanese projects together. We would continue to do small houses or interiors individually, but there are exceptions like the Issey Miyake shop by Naoki Takizawa. _ Christina Diaz Moreno and Efrén Garcia Grinda, *El Croquis,* vol. 121/122, 2004

We both think that it is very important to have three offices close to each other so that people can move around from here to there in five seconds or so. We have the Sejima office here, part of the SANAA office here, the Nishizawa office there, and another part of the SANAA office over there. We have the studio space in one building, and we think this is very important. Another idea for our studio is having one room, allowing people to be together. . . . However, we understand it is important for the people who work here to be connected to the other projects that do not relate directly to them. That's one of the ideas for the studio. _ Augustin Pérez Rubio, *Houses: Kazuyo Sejima + Ryue Nishizawa, SANAA,* Barcelona: Actar, 2007

## WORKING METHODS

Each project has its own method of adjustment; the process in itself constitutes the creative act. _ Kristin Feireiss, ed., *The Zollverein School of Management and Design, Essen, Germany,* Munich: Prestel, 2006

We get asked a lot if there is any division of the responsibilities between us. But there isn't! Our way of working was never that one of us would lead with a sketch, and then our staff would work from that. Rather, from the very beginning, all our staff throw in ideas—how's this? how's that?—and then we decide on the direction through a process of dis-

cussion. But when it's time to decide on something, Nishizawa and I do it together. _ Kazuyo Sejima interview with Edan Corkill, *Japan Times,* January 6, 2008

Between the two of us there is not a design leader. Inside of our office there is a responsible person who comes to us when decisions need to be made. This person is the leader. We collaborate as equals, but we are not the same. We keep each other from losing our way more than anything. We sometimes argue, but usually we give each other pause to think and then quietly agree on a new direction. Often one of us is allowed to be emotional while the other stays rational. Who is feeling one way or the other changes every day. Mostly, we sit together in the office at a very big table discussing ideas. We rarely decide anything. We like to think about different possibilities until late at night. _ Culture Zohn, *Huffington Post,* April 1, 2010

## WOMEN ARCHITECTS

Women love making big things too! And small things. With large buildings there are so many people who get involved—and so many people who use the buildings. On the other hand, I make small things too; I like designing objects, such as spoons and private residences, which is a very personal process. There is an image that it is only men who make big projects, but I think that's just because there weren't many women in architecture in the past. Now that is really changing. There are more women architects now—but people often say that women have a softer image, a softer exterior. We make things through discussion.

So, rather than saying it's difficult to be a woman, I think maybe there is just a difference of nuance in how we make something. And yes, it is a male-dominated society, and there are good and bad things there. Because I'm a woman, maybe where a man might start yelling I would not yell, and instead say calmly, "I can't have you doing that." On the other hand, because there aren't many women, then sometimes men go easy on us a bit. _ Kazuyo Sejima interview with Edan Corkill, *Japan Times,* January 6, 2008

**AN IDEAL OF PERFECTION** I do not work toward architecture from a theoretically defined point of departure, for I am committed to making architecture, to building, to an ideal of perfection, just as in my boyhood I used to make things according to my ideas, things that had to be just right, for reasons which I do not understand. It was always there, this deeply personal feeling for the things I made for myself, and I never thought of it as being anything special. It was just there.

Today, I am aware that my work as an architect is largely a quest for this early passion, this obsession, and an attempt to understand it better and to refine it. And when I reflect on whether I have since added new images and passions to the old ones, and whether I have learned something in my training and practice, I realize that in some way I seem always to have known the intuitive core of new discoveries. _ Peter Zumthor, *Thinking Architecture*, Basel, Switzerland: Birkhäuser, 2006

# PETER ZUMTHOR

**BORN:** April 26, 1943, Basel, Switzerland

**EDUCATION:** Studied at the Kunstgewerbeschule, Vorkurs and Fachklasse, 1963–67, Basel, Switzerland; Pratt Institute, New York, 1966

**OFFICE:** Atelier Peter Zumthor & Partner, Architekturbüro, CH-7023 Haldenstein, Süsswinkel 20
Tel: +41 81-354-92-92, Fax: +41 81-354-92-93, arch@zumthor.ch

**PROJECTS FEATURED:** Kolumba Art Museum of the Cologne Archdiocese, Cologne, Germany, 2007; Brother Klaus Field Chapel, Mechernich, Germany, 2007; Bregenz Art Museum, Bregenz, Austria, 1997; Swiss Sound Box, Hanover, Germany, 2000; Thermal Bath, Vals, Switzerland, 1996; Saint Benedict Chapel, Sumvitg, Switzerland, 1988; Zumthor Studio, Haldenstein, Switzerland, 1986

> ❝ ASSOCIATIVE, WILD, FREE, ORDERED, AND SYSTEMATIC THINKING IN IMAGES, IN ARCHITECTURAL, SPATIAL, COLORFUL, AND SENSUOUS PICTURES— THIS IS MY FAVORITE DEFINITION OF DESIGN. ❞

**Thermal Bath, Vals, 1996**
The building is constructed of local Valser quartzite and concrete. Zumthor used design and the natural surroundings to create a sensual and spirutal experience.

Water, light, steam, and heat bring a new dimension to the primal ritual of the bath. *Above:* Thermal Bath, Vals, block study.

### VALS 1996
# THERMAL BATH
The beginning was easy. Going back in time, bathing as one might have a thousand years ago, creating a building, a structure set into the slope with an architectural attitude and aura older than anything already built around it, inventing a building that could somehow always have been there, a building that relates to the topography and geology of the location, that responds to the stone masses of Vals Valley, pressed, faulted, folded, and sometimes broken into thousands of plates—these were the objectives of our design. _ Sigrid Hauser, Peter Zumthor, eds., *Peter Zumthor Therme Vals,* Zurich: Verlag Scheidegger and Spiess, 2007

The meandering internal space with its sunken springwater basins and gulleys must appear, we imagined, as if it had been chiseled out of a homogenous stone mass. _ Sigrid Hauser, Peter Zumthor, eds., *Peter Zumthor Therme Vals,* Zurich: Verlag Scheidegger and Spiess, 2007

So our bath is not a showcase for the latest aqua-gadgetry, water jets, nozzles, or chutes. It relies instead on the silent, primary experiences of bathing, cleansing oneself, and relaxing in the water; on the body's contact with water at different temperatures and in different kinds of spaces; on touching stone. _ Peter Zumthor, *Peter Zumthor Works: Buildings and Projects 1979–1997,* Baden, Switzerland: Lars Müller Publishers, 1998

And for the stone to caress the human body, it has to be heated, made to feel as if it had been warmed by the sun. _ Sigrid Hauser, Peter Zumthor, eds., *Peter Zumthor Therme Vals,* Zurich: Verlag Scheidegger and Spiess, 2007

**"We staged the daylight"** The idea of hollowing out a huge monolith and providing it with caves, sunken areas, and slots for a variety of uses also helped to define a strategy for cutting up the stone mass toward the top of the building, to bring in light. _ Peter Zumthor, *Peter Zumthor Works: Buildings and Projects 1979–1997,* Baden, Switzerland: Lars Müller Publishers, 1998

Right from the start, there was a feeling for the mystical nature of a world of stone inside the mountain, for darkness and light, for the reflection of light upon the water, for the diffusion of light through steam-filled air, for the different sounds that water makes in stone surroundings, for warm stone and naked skin, for the ritual of bathing. _ Peter Zumthor, *Peter Zumthor Works: Buildings and Projects 1979–1997,* Baden, Switzerland: Lars Müller Publishers, 1998

We staged the daylight by cutting small openings into the ceiling slabs suspended between the pillar blocks of the indoor pool, an idea inspired by the cupolas in Turkish baths. In the Rudas Baths in Budapest the points of light are multicolored; in Vals they are of blue glass. _ Sigrid Hauser, Peter Zumthor, eds., *Peter Zumthor Therme Vals,* Zurich: Verlag Scheidegger and Spiess, 2007

**❝ . . . MASS, LARGE AND SERENE, SHOULD BE LEFT ALONE SO THAT THE PRESENCE OF THE STONE IS FELT, SO THAT IT CAN EXERT ITS OWN EFFECT ON OUR BODIES. ❞**

## RESONANCE IN MATERIALS

My idea of architecture is always very physical. I like materials that wear, keep, and have resonance. _ Hanno Rauterberg, *Talking Architecture: Interviews with Architects,* Munich: Prestel, 2008

**❝ THERE ARE NO IDEAS EXCEPT IN THINGS. ❞**

I believe that the real core of all architectural work lies in the act of construction. At the point in time when concrete materials are assembled and erected, the architecture we have been looking for becomes part of the real world.

I feel respect for the art of joining, the ability of craftsmen and engineers. I am impressed by the knowledge of how to make things, which lies at the bottom of human skill. I try to design buildings that are worthy of this knowledge and merit the challenge to this skill. _ Peter Zumthor, *Thinking Architecture,* Basel, Switzerland: Birkhäuser, 2006

## MATERIAL PROXIMITY

There's a critical proximity between materials, depending on the type of material and its weight. You can combine different materials in a building. _ Peter Zumthor, *Atmospheres: Architectural Environments—Surrounding Objects,* Basel, Switzerland: Birkhäuser, 2006

The reality of architecture is the concrete body in which forms, volumes, and spaces come into being. There are no ideas except in things. _ Peter Zumthor, *Thinking Architecture,* Basel, Switzerland: Birkhäuser, 2006

I've always had the feeling that as an architect, as a master builder, he [Palladio, Italian Renaissance architect] must have had an extraordinary sense of the presence and weight of materials, indeed of the very things I'm trying to talk about. _ Peter Zumthor, *Atmospheres: Architectural Environments—Surrounding Objects,* Basel, Switzerland: Birkhäuser, 2006

. . . the first and the greatest secret of architecture, that it collects different things in the world, different materials, and combines them to create a space. . . . To me it's a kind of anatomy we are talking about. . . . It's like our own bodies with their anatomy and things we can't see and skin covering us—that's what architecture means to me, and that's how I try to think about it. As a bodily mass, a membrane, a fabric, a kind of covering, cloth, velvet, silk, all around me. _ Peter Zumthor, *Atmospheres: Architectural Environments—Surrounding Objects,* Basel, Switzerland: Birkhäuser, 2006

## ATMOSPHERE

Quality architecture to me is when a building manages to move me. What on earth is it that moves me? How can I get it into my own work?

One word for it is *atmosphere.* This is something we all know about. Our first impression of a person. What I learned was: don't trust it—give the guy a chance. Years passed. I got a bit older. And I have to admit that I'm back to believing in first impressions. It's a bit like that with architecture, too. _ Peter Zumthor, *Atmospheres: Architectural Environments—Surrounding Objects,* Basel, Switzerland: Birkhäuser, 2006

**❝◀ IT HAS AN AIR OF DURABILITY AND QUALITY. ▶❞**

The Kolumba Art Museum of the Cologne Archdiocese was constructed on top of ruins, becoming the sum of the old and the new. The unexpected, such as a bright red walkway over ruins or the introduction of natural light in a gallery are part of the design experience.

### COLOGNE 2007
# KOLUMBA ART MUSEUM OF THE COLOGNE ARCHDIOCESE

The buildings on the site, formally heterogeneous and fragmented but, in substance, a historical unit, yielded the image of a special edifice for Kolumba. The new building rises on the old foundations and acquires form by using its substance to incorporate, complement, and unify the fragmented parts of the existing buildings. _ Peter Zumthor, *Peter Zumthor Works: Buildings and Projects 1979–1997*, Baden, Switzerland: Lars Müller Publishers, 1998

The new architectural concept is reconciliatory and integrative. . . . It integrates and shelters the old structure. It does not eliminate traces or destroy without necessity. It supplements and leads onwards in the search for an idiom of its own. No architectural wounds are to be kept open, nor shall the architecture be used to make a statement about them. Instead, the aim is to be as straightforward as possible in dealing with what has survived within the matter-of-fact framework of a new building that has a program of its own. _ Peter Zumthor, *Peter Zumthor Works: Buildings and Projects 1979–1997*, Baden, Switzerland: Lars Müller Publishers, 1998

This attitude is that of the *Baumeister,* of the architect as a master builder. It aims at the wholeness of architectural expression, or more precisely, at the wholeness of a new architectural body. _ Peter Zumthor, *Peter Zumthor Works: Buildings and Projects 1979–1997*, Baden, Switzerland: Lars Müller Publishers, 1998

The material of the new building is open brickwork. The design proposes producing a special brick for Kolumba whose color, format, and bond are designed to match the old buildings, the coloring of the existing stone and brick masonry, and the structure of the cement blocks used by Gottfried Böhm. _ Peter Zumthor, *Peter Zumthor Works: Buildings and Projects 1979–1997*, Baden, Switzerland: Lars Müller Publishers, 1998

## "MAGIC OF THE REAL"

People interact with objects. As an architect that is what I deal with all the time. Actually, it's what I'd call my passion. The real has its own magic. _ Peter Zumthor, *Atmospheres: Architectural Environments— Surrounding Objects*, Basel, Switzerland: Birkhäuser, 2006

I wonder: what is this "Magic of the Real"—café at a students' hostel, a thirties picture by Baumgartner. Men, just sitting around—and they're enjoying themselves too. And I ask myself: can I achieve this as an architect—an atmosphere like that, its intensity, its mood. And if so, how do I go about it? _ Peter Zumthor, *Atmospheres: Architectural Environments—Surrounding Objects*, Basel, Switzerland: Birkhäuser, 2006

## THE GENTLER ART OF SEDUCTION

"Between Composure and Seduction." . . . There is also the gentler art of seduction, of getting people to let go, to saunter, and that lies within the powers of an architect. The ability I am speaking of is rather akin to designing a stage setting, directing a play. _ Peter Zumthor, *Atmospheres: Architectural Environments—Surrounding Objects*, Basel, Switzerland: Birkhäuser, 2006

I'd be standing there, and might just stay a while, but then something would be drawing me round the corner—it was the way the light falls, over here, over there: and so I saunter on—and I must say I find that a great source of pleasure. The feeling that I am not being directed but can stroll at will—just drifting along, you know? And it's a kind of voyage of discovery. _ Peter Zumthor, *Atmospheres: Architectural Environments—Surrounding Objects*, Basel, Switzerland: Birkhäuser, 2006

---

## SUMVITG 1988
# SAINT BENEDICT CHAPEL
The church is a one-room building. The shape of the interior corresponds to that of the exterior. This correspondence is both simple and complex. The slim external shape of the building develops from a leaf or drop-shaped plan. This interior space recalls older centrally planned churches of the region like those at Disla or Vattiz, yet it is softer and more flowing because of its biomorphic leaf shape. _ Peter Zumthor, *Peter Zumthor Works: Buildings and Projects 1979–1997*, Baden, Switzerland: Lars Müller Publishers, 1998

The form of this sheltering space seems to be moving, due to the east-west directional leaf-shaped plan which can actually be felt in the forward-thrusting curve of the choir. _ Peter Zumthor, *Peter Zumthor Works: Buildings and Projects 1979–1997*, Baden, Switzerland: Lars Müller Publishers, 1998

Reflection and composure. Whoever goes into the church leaves the land and climbs into the wooden vessel as if into a boat. The gently curved floor of wooden boards, which floats freely on the joists, is slightly springy underfoot. Thirty-seven freestanding structural timbers surround the leaf form of the floor and define the space. They support the roof, which is a structure of wooden struts, conjuring up the image of the veins of a leaf or the ribs on the

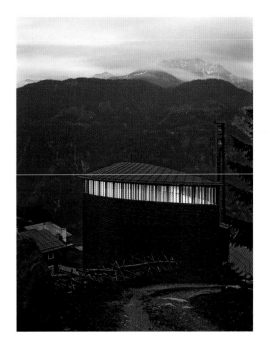

inside of a boat. _ Peter Zumthor, *Peter Zumthor Works: Buildings and Projects 1979–1997*, Baden, Switzerland: Lars Müller Publishers, 1998

. . . the unity of the roof and the columns suggest a huge baldachin. Delicate slats in front of the windows under the baldachin modulate the light that falls in from above. _ Peter Zumthor, *Peter Zumthor Works: Buildings and Projects 1979–1997*, Baden, Switzerland: Lars Müller Publishers, 1998

Zumthor's shingled chapel replaced a Baroque stone chapel destroyed in an earthquake in 1984. *Right:* A view of the leaf-shaped interior.

The interior of the Brother Klaus
Field Chapel was formed with 112
tree trunks, configured like a giant
tent. Photos, above, show how
Zumthor adapted the small chapel
to the field. *Opposite:* **Bregenz Art
Museum, daylight study.**

MECHERNICH 2007
# BROTHER KLAUS FIELD CHAPEL

*This chapel, which was commissioned by an elderly
farm couple, Hermann-Josef and Trudl Scheidtweiler,
both devoted Roman Catholics, is an example of
Zumthor's dedication and commitment to a project.
He began work in 1998, and in May 2007 the chapel
was consecrated. When Zumthor learned that it was
to be dedicated to the Swiss saint Nikolas von der Flüe
(1417–1487), known as Brother Klaus, he did the chapel
for a nominal fee because Brother Klaus was also his
mother's favorite saint.*

Brother Klaus is everybody's favorite saint in Switzerland. Half of the population is Catholic. He only
became a saint in the 1940s, four hundred years
after his death. For me he represents an upright figure who does not make any wrong compromises—
any compromise. And also he is staying himself. He
is a positive figure for me also in his opposition to
the church at that time. . . . The main thing was that
there is no altar (in the Brother Klaus chapel), so it is
not a space for the church. To seek to make a new . . .
tiny little space in a field that in the end expresses

hopes about human existence. . . . At the end it was
the chapel and the material and the rain and the
water and whatever. . . . I wanted to take this commission to make something really contemporary.
_ Peter Zumthor interview by Patrick Lynch, *Architects' Journal,* April 2009

I want to make good buildings. When I have an
idea, I look at what can help. [When researching the
charred interior of the Brother Klaus Field Chapel
near Cologne,] I went to charcoal makers because
I thought they would know, but they didn't know
anything. It was a romantic notion. I had to go to a
completely different person: a chimney sweep. So I
don't care whether I find solutions in the Iron Age or
in the future. To be innovative is an object of modernism. _ Peter Zumthor interview by Rob Gregory,
*Architectural Review,* vol. 225, no. 1347, 2009

People go there and are deeply moved. I get books
of poems from all levels of people—intellectuals
and academics, ordinary people, farmers . . . _ Peter
Zumthor interview by Patrick Lynch, *Architects'
Journal,* April 2009

*Zumthor is architecture's poet, both in his built works and how he expresses himself in language. His use of words parallels the eloquence and singular focus of his buildings—they are clear, sensuous, articulate, and deeply felt. Just as there is no wasted anything in a Zumthor building, words, too, are well chosen and evocative. Word and deed are integral to Zumthor.*

## DRAWING AS ANATOMY

Among all the drawings produced by architects, my favorites are the working drawings. Working drawings are detailed and objective. Created for the craftsmen who are to give the imagined object a material form, they are free of associative manipulation. They do not try to convince and impress like project drawings. They seem to be saying: "This is exactly how it will look."

Working drawings are like anatomical drawings. They reveal something of the secret inner tension that the finished architectural body is reluctant to divulge: the art of joining, hidden geometry, the friction of materials, the inner forces of bearing and holding, the human work which is inherent in manmade things. _ Peter Zumthor, *Thinking Architecture,* Basel, Switzerland: Birkhäuser, 2006

I continue working on my drawings until they reach the delicate point of representation when the prevailing mood I seek emerges, and I stop before inessentials start detracting from its impact. _ Peter Zumthor, *Thinking Architecture,* Basel, Switzerland: Birkhäuser, 2006

There is a magical power in every completed, self-contained creation. It is as if we succumb to the magic of the fully developed architectural body. Our attention is caught, perhaps for the first time, by a detail

## ❝ WORKING DRAWINGS ARE LIKE ANATOMICAL DRAWINGS. ❞

such as two nails in the floor that hold the steel plates by the worn-out doorstep. Emotions well up. Something moves us. _ Peter Zumthor, *Thinking Architecture,* Basel, Switzerland: Birkhäuser, 2006

## MUSEUMS: PROMOTING TRANSCENDENCE

The way I imagined a museum is like this: I believe in the spiritual values of art, and have myself experienced that works of art can promote transcendence. They intimate to us that we are incorporated in something greater that we don't understand. I'm fascinated by this nonrational, mental or spiritual element, such as appears most clearly in early German Romanticism, for example, by Novalis or Caspar David Friedrich. _ Hanno Rauterberg, *Talking Architecture: Interviews with Architects,* Munich: Prestel, 2008

## "THE LIGHT ON THINGS"

Thinking about daylight and artificial light, I have to admit that daylight, the light on things, is so moving to me that I feel it almost as a spiritual quality. When the sun comes up in the morning . . . and casts its light on things, it doesn't feel as if it quite belongs in this world. I don't understand light. It gives me the feeling there's something beyond me, something beyond all understanding. And I am very glad, very grateful that there is such a thing. _ Peter Zumthor, *Atmospheres: Architectural Environments—Surrounding Objects,* Basel, Switzerland: Birkhäuser, 2006

### BREGENZ 1997
# BREGENZ ART MUSEUM From the
outside, the building looks like a lamp. It absorbs the changing light of the sky, the haze of the lake—it reflects light and color and gives an intimation of its inner life according to the angle of vision, the daylight, and the weather. _ Peter Zumthor, *Peter Zumthor Works: Buildings and Projects 1979–1997,* Baden, Switzerland: Lars Müller Publishers, 1998

The outer skin of the building consists of finely etched glass. It looks like slightly ruffled feathers or like a scaly structure of large glass panels. The glass panels, which are all the same size, are neither perforated nor cut. They rest on metal

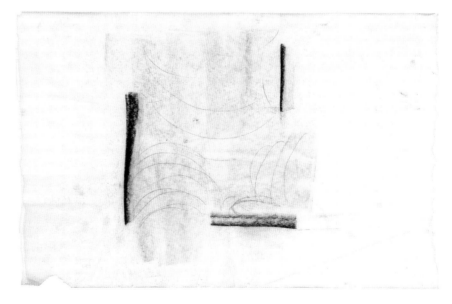

**❝ THE CONSTANTLY FLUCTUATING LIGHT CREATES THE IMPRESSION THAT THE BUILDING IS BREATHING. ❞**

*Above, right:* **Gallery space in the Bregenz Art Museum. The ceilings in the exhibition rooms show Zumthor's radical idea for moving air through the galleries.** *Top:* **The entrance hall.** *Bottom:* **A café outside allows visitors to watch the building's constantly fluctuating light. Zumthor wanted the building to appear to be breathing.**

consoles, held in place by large clamps. The edges of the glass are exposed. The wind wafts through the open joints of the scaly structure. Lake air penetrates the fine mesh of the space-framework. _ Peter Zumthor, *Peter Zumthor Works: Buildings and Projects 1979–1997*, Baden, Switzerland: Lars Müller Publishers, 1998

The ability to cast concrete to flow into complex shapes, to integrate technical installations, and to assume the appearance of a large monolithic form of an almost sculptural character has been fully exploited. _ Peter Zumthor, *Peter Zumthor Works: Buildings and Projects 1979–1997*, Baden, Switzerland: Lars Müller Publishers, 1998

We believe that the works of art will benefit from the sensuous presence of the materials that define the space. _ Peter Zumthor, *Peter Zumthor Works: Buildings and Projects 1979–1997*, Baden, Switzerland: Lars Müller Publishers, 1998

The ceilings of the exhibition rooms on the upper floors . . . consist of light trapped in glass. Open-jointed glass panels with exposed edges hang individually from the concrete ceiling on hundreds of thin steel rods. A sea of glass panels, etched on the downside, with subtly shimmering surfaces and edges, distributes the daylight throughout the room. _ Peter Zumthor, *Peter Zumthor Works: Buildings and Projects 1979–1997*, Baden, Switzerland: Lars Müller Publishers, 1998

The spatial constellation of the slabs varies the orientation of the light, generates shadows and reflections. It tempers the mood of the light and gives depth to the room. The constantly fluctuating light creates the impression that the building is breathing. Everything seems permeable—permeable to light, wind, and weather, as if the building could manage, up here, without an airtight skin. _ Peter Zumthor, *Peter Zumthor Works: Buildings and Projects 1979–1997*, Baden, Switzerland: Lars Müller Publishers, 1998

## MUSIC

... what also comes to mind when I think of my own work is the verb "to temper"—a bit like the tempering of pianos perhaps, this search for the right mood, in the sense of instrumental tuning and atmosphere as well. So temperature in this sense is physical, but presumably psychological too. It's in what I see, what I feel, what I touch, even with my feet. _ Peter Zumthor, *Atmospheres: Architectural Environments—Surrounding Objects,* Basel, Switzerland: Birkhäuser, 2006

We know all about emotional response from music. The first movement of Brahms's viola sonata [Sonata No. 2 in E Flat Major for Viola and Piano], when the viola comes in—just two seconds and we're there! I have no idea why that is so, but it's like that with architecture, too. _ Peter Zumthor, *Atmospheres: Architectural Environments—Surrounding Objects,* Basel, Switzerland: Birkhäuser, 2006

I sense similarities with contemporary compositions where you have to listen the same way you look at a picture, i.e., they work with density, space, movement, and tonal color. Being a composer is something I'd go for. Perhaps in my next life. _ Hanno Rauterberg, *Talking Architecture: Interviews with Architects,* Munich: Prestel, 2008

## HANOVER 2000
# SWISS SOUND BOX

*Zumthor's use of wood native to Switzerland was an ode to sustainability and eco reuse. It was also a dazzling tour de force of architecture based largely on one material yielding a variety of sensations, including smell.*

The most beautiful things generally come as a surprise. We used a great deal of wood, lots of wooden beams, when we built the Swiss Pavilion for the Hanover World's Fair. And when it was hot outside the pavilion was as cool as a forest, and when it was cool the pavilion was warmer than it was outside. . . . It is well known that materials more or less extract the warmth from our bodies. _ Peter Zumthor, *Atmospheres: Architectural Environments—Surrounding Objects,* Basel, Switzerland: Birkhäuser, 2006

Taking the Expo theme of sustainability seriously, we constructed the pavilion out of 144 km of lumber with a cross-section of 20 x 10 cm, totaling 2,800 cubic meters of larch and Douglas pine from Swiss forests, assembled without glue, bolts, or nails, only braced with steel cables, and with each beam being pressed down on the one below. After the closure of the Expo, the building was dismantled and the beams sold as seasoned timber. _ Pritzker Prize online, www.pritzkerprize.com

Interiors are like large instruments, collecting sound, amplifying it, transmitting it elsewhere. That has to do with the shape peculiar to each room and with the surfaces of the materials they contain, and the way those materials have been applied. Take a wonderful spruce floor like the top of a violin and lay it across wood. Or again: stick it to a concrete slab. Do you notice the difference in sound? Of course. _ Peter Zumthor, *Atmospheres: Architectural Environments—Surrounding Objects,* Basel, Switzerland: Birkhäuser, 2006

# " I BELIEVE EVERY BUILDING HAS A CERTAIN TEMPERATURE . . . "

The Swiss Pavilion for the Hanover World's Fair. The entire structure made use of indigenous wood native to the area and through the use of steel supports avoided the need for any other reinforcements.

Zumthor's Studio and Residence in the Graübunden area of Switzerland.

A trellis along the wall is overgrown with grapevines and protects the studio from the sunlight with large sailcloth screens.

The interior consists of one large, open space subdivided by a freestanding "working wall" extending over all three stories and separating the narrow circulation area on the north from the rooms to the south. The artist Matia Spescha painted the inside surface of the exterior walls. _ Peter Zumthor, *Peter Zumthor Works: Buildings and Projects 1979–1997,* Baden, Switzerland: Lars Müller Publishers, 1998

I live and work in the Graübunden in a farming village surrounded by mountains. I sometimes wonder whether this has influenced my work, and the thought that it probably has is not unpleasant. _ Peter Zumthor, *Thinking Architecture,* Basel, Switzerland: Birkhäuser, 2006

**Authorship** I have an office with fourteen people, not 40 or 140—and that's how it will remain, because I want to work the way I want. Because I want to know the door handles in every building. _ Hanno Rauterberg, *Talking Architecture: Interviews with Architects,* Munich: Prestel, 2008

That [the office] is the way it's going to be so that I can be the author of everything. _ Robin Pogrebin, *New York Times,* April 2, 2009

**"I just say no"** I need a genuine interest in the project. So if a rich guy comes to me and says, "I would like a nice house on a ski resort, and money is not a problem. I'd like a nice place for me and my friends to come to stay, could you think about something?" even though he might be a nice guy or is a nice guy I say, No. For me it would mean four years out of my life and for you it is just another weekend house somewhere, so this doesn't go together. _ Peter Zumthor interview by Patrick Lynch, *Architects' Journal,* April 2009

You cannot order a piece of architecture from me. It has nothing to do with shopping and it's not about giving me enough money. I cannot work that way—I just say no. _ Peter Zumthor interview by Rob Gregory, *Architectural Review,* vol. 225, no. 1347, 2009

"The roots of architectural understanding lie in our architectural experience: our room, our house, our street, our village, our town, our landscape . . ." _ Peter Zumthor, *Thinking Architecture,* Basel, Switzerland: Birkhäuser, 2006

**❝ THE ROOTS OF OUR UNDERSTANDING OF ARCHITECTURE LIE IN OUR CHILDHOOD, IN OUR YOUTH; THEY LIE IN OUR BIOGRAPHY. ❞**

**HALDENSTEIN 1986**
# ZUMTHOR STUDIO
The studio house in the center of the village of Haldenstein contains a garden room on the first floor, a drafting room on the second floor, and archives in the cellar. It is built out of wood like the traditional local buildings for trades and craftsmanship but has the appearance of an object-like body of wood. A finely structured shell of larch wood slats, worked like a piece of furniture, encases the façades. A large opening facing south looks onto a decorative garden—a grove of cherry trees.

## A PROCESS OF GREAT NAÏVETÉ

The moment a first design is put to paper, it turns around and begins to exert an effect on its author. We look at the finished drawings and ask ourselves: Which parts work? _ Peter Zumthor, *Peter Zumthor Works: Buildings and Projects 1979–1997*, Baden, Switzerland: Lars Müller Publishers, 1998

For me, the work on the design is a process which begins with and returns to dwelling. In my mind, I envisage what it will feel like to live in the house I am designing. . . . I dream of the experiences I would like us to make in the house as yet unbuilt. _ Peter Zumthor, *Peter Zumthor Works: Buildings and Projects 1979–1997*, Baden, Switzerland: Lars Müller Publishers, 1998

When I'm designing—working—I mainly follow my inclination. It's a process of great naïveté where everyone can have a say regardless of how much idea he has of architecture. The important thing is to be able to imagine things as a picture. Unfortunately, 80 percent of architects can't imagine things three-dimensionally. For them, architecture is only a drawing on paper, and they don't translate that into an idea of what it will one day be. _ Hanno Rauterberg, *Talking Architecture: Interviews with Architects*, Munich: Prestel, 2008

I listen to my inner ear and see what experiences I can call on to tackle a new building job. I often experience that—as writers say—the book writes itself. You make a start and then have to let go to find out where the material is taking you. _ Hanno Rauterberg, *Talking Architecture: Interviews with Architects*, Munich: Prestel, 2008

. . . as the design progresses, it occurs that I wake up and find myself somewhere in the building and think to myself, that wall or this door's not quite right. I don't have to do anything, it just comes. _ Hanno Rauterberg, *Talking Architecture: Interviews with Architects*, Munich: Prestel, 2008

## THE PURSUIT OF STANDARDS

At the age of eighteen, when I was approaching the end of my apprenticeship as a cabinetmaker, I made my first self-designed pieces of furniture. . . . I chose light-colored ash for my bed and cupboard, and I made them so that they looked good on all sides, with the same wood and the same careful work back and front. I disregarded the usual practice of expending less time and care on the back because no one ever sees it anyway. _ Peter Zumthor, *Thinking Architecture*, Basel, Switzerland: Birkhäuser, 2006

It [being a perfectionist] is old; it has always been there. My father, who was a cabinetmaker, was a perfectionist. _ Peter Zumthor interview by Visnja Brdar and Krunoslav Ivanisin, *Oris*, vol. 6, no. 27, 2004

## COHERENCE

[Architecture] is at its most beautiful when things have come into their own—when they are coherent. That is when everything refers to everything else, and it is impossible to remove a single thing without destroying the whole. Place, use, and form. The form reflects the place, the place is just so, and the use reflects this and that. _ Peter Zumthor, *Atmospheres: Architectural Environments—Surrounding Objects*, Basel, Switzerland: Birkhäuser, 2006

I like to be very much grounded in the place but at the same time very much part of the world. . . . All good architecture is regional, and every good building gives identity to a place . . . creating identity; giving identity to the place is one of the noblest tasks of architecture. _ Peter Zumthor interview by Visnja Brdar and Krunoslav Ivanisin, *Oris*, vol. 6, no. 27, 2004

## MATERIAL AND SPACE, NOT FORM

You express yourself at the end with a form. Ultimately, the house must have a form—this cannot be escaped. When I talk about architecture, I prefer not to talk about form. I prefer to talk about material and space. I am working on the substance; I am not working on the form. I am working on space and time, shadow, sound, the materiality, the physicality, the combination of material. When I am putting these things together I am trying to get the feeling of whether I like this kind of combination, whether I like the light on the water. . . . So I would say at the end that it is a simple question of beauty or non-beauty and this has to do with form. _ Peter Zumthor interview by Visnja Brdar and Krunoslav Ivanisin, *Oris*, vol. 6, no. 27, 2004

## "THE BEAUTIFUL FORM"

What I find is that when things have come out well they tend to assume a form which often surprises me when I finally stand back from the work and which makes me think: you could never have imagined when you started out that this would be the outcome. And that is something that only happens sometimes, even after all these years—slow architecture. . . . But if, at the end of the day, the thing does not look beautiful—and . . . if the form doesn't move me, then I'll go back to the beginning and start again. . . . My final aim, probably, is: "The Beautiful Form." _ Peter Zumthor, *Atmospheres: Architectural Environments—Surrounding Objects*, Basel, Switzerland: Birkhäuser, 2006

**LIGHT** Traditional architecture was based on fixing solid and void. This approach overlooked the primacy of light, which is what enables us to see architecture at all! And it overlooks the potential of light, and its variability. For me, light is matter, and light is a material, a basic material. Once you understand how light varies, and varies our perceptions, your architectural vocabulary is immediately extended in ways classical architecture never thought of. An architecture of ephemerality becomes possible—not in the sense of temporary structures, but mutable ones, changed by light and changing with light. Not only through changes in daylight, but through changing the interior lighting of the building, and playing with different opacities and transparencies. Using light effectively is for me a baseline in my architecture. My buildings are planned around five, six, or seven different sets of lighting conditions, from the start. Had I started with just one set—as some other architects still do—the result would be very different, but not acceptable to me! _ Conway Lloyd Morgan, *Jean Nouvel: The Elements of Architecture,* New York: Universe Publishing, 1998

# JEAN NOUVEL

**BORN:** August 12, 1945, Fumel, France

**EDUCATION:** DPLG (degree in architecture), l'École Nationale Supérieure des Beaux-Arts, Paris, 1972; l'École des Beaux-Arts, Bordeaux, France, 1966

**OFFICE:** Ateliers Jean Nouvel, 10 Cité d'Angoulême, 75011 Paris
Tel +33 1-49-23-83-83, Fax +33 1-43-14-81-10
info@jeannouvel.fr
www.ateliersjeannouvel.com

**PROJECTS FEATURED:** Guthrie Theater, Minneapolis, Minnesota, 2006; Quai Branly Museum, Paris, 2006; Agbar Tower, Barcelona, 2005; Cartier Foundation, Paris, 1994; Arab World Institute, Paris, 1987

" ONCE YOU UNDERSTAND **HOW LIGHT VARIES,** AND VARIES OUR PERCEPTIONS, YOUR ARCHITECTURAL VOCABULARY IS IMMEDIATELY EXTENDED IN WAYS CLASSICAL ARCHITECTURE NEVER THOUGHT OF. "

**Agbar Tower, Barcelona, 2005**
Twenty-five different colors comprise
the brilliant aluminum panel façade
that appears behind glass louvers.

# AGBAR TOWER

Agbar Tower is a heritage of Catalan obsessions. A few millenniums ago, in Montserrat [a mountain close to Barcelona that is of symbolic importance to Catalans], the wind created these shapes. For this reason Gaudí and other Catalan architects are really interested in this shape—the pinnacle, the parabola. You can see it in Gaudí's Sagrada Familia. . . . I didn't want to design an International Style tower in downtown Barcelona. I wanted a building linked to the identity of the city. So I revisited this form.

It is a building linked to the climate; a tower where you can open the windows, with more windows on the north side than the south. I created a double skin to create a convection of air so you have the feeling you can breathe the outside air. _ Marcus Fairs, "Icon Eye," *Icon 026*, August 2005

[Agbar] is a fluid mass that has perforated the ground—a geyser under a permanent calculated pressure. The surface of this construction evokes water: smooth and continuous, but also vibrating and transparent because it manifests itself in colored depths. . . . The uncertainties of matter and light make the campanile of Agbar vibrate in the skyline of Barcelona: a faraway mirage day and night. . . . This singular object becomes a new symbol for an international city. _ jeannouvel.com

## The Missing Piece of the Puzzle

Every architecture is an opportunity to create what I call the missing piece of the puzzle, to find how you can create more poetry with the place where you are and the program you have. You research what will be the most emotional, the most perfect, the most natural. _ Arthur Lubow, *New York Times*, April 6, 2008

**Nouvel's bullet-shaped, 31-floor Agbar Tower. Instead of a glass grid, Nouvel chose a seemingly random pattern of red-trimmed windows. Motorized glass blinds open and close automatically in order to regulate temperature in the building.**

I am most receptive to architecture that uses light. The first things that moved me violently—truly amazed me—were religious buildings, because they are often read by the penetration of light by way of stained glass windows and colors. For me, Chartres, the Sainte Chapelle, certain Romanesque buildings are fantastic. But I've seen the same use of light in Japan, too, in the tea houses, at Katsura. . . . You find it in nineteenth-century architecture, too, and in Pierre Chareau's Maison de Verre. I've also found it in the most total abstraction, as in Mies van der Rohe, or in some buildings by Le Corbusier in which he uses light with sculptural precision. _ "Jean Nouvel 1987–2006," *A + U: Architecture and Urbanism*, Special Issue, April 2006

## AN ARCHITECTURE OF SPECIFICITY

My work is always a logical result of what the given situations are. . . . There is a set of problems, and the questions are solved following a very logical order. It's never in terms of a style. I agree with Venturi in the sense that I am against the notion of the heroic architect or architecture for architects, the notion of monuments or of styles. I am against all the pretension that comes along with architecture made by and for architects. _ "Jean Nouvel," *GA Document Extra 07*, 1996

An architect cannot know in advance every element that has to be integrated into a final project. . . . I find myself in favor of a dialogue starting between those who have a right to make demands about the project, for political or social reasons, for example, or those who are going to use or live in the building, and those whose experience gives them information.

I am for this dialogue being participatory because in terms of the uses of the building, I am integrating every properly founded demand. . . . But that doesn't mean I am looking for some impossible cultural consensus—that's a route to gray mediocrity. Not an architecture for the greatest number, rather an architecture of individuality, seeing architecture as a specific response. _ Conway Lloyd Morgan, *Jean Nouvel: The Elements of Architecture*, New York: Universe Publishing, 1998

> **❝ I HAVE MADE MYSELF AN ARCHITECT OF SPECIFICITY AND PARTICULARITY. ❞**

What I really liked [about Arab architecture] was the distillation of light through geometry; the precise light; the precise shadows. But in our country it's not generally possible because sometimes it's cloudy and rainy and sometimes it's sunny. So I decided to adapt the geometry with holes like a camera aperture. Then I had a very precious façade, like the preciousness of moucharabieh [Middle Eastern carved screens] but in aluminum. _ Marcus Fairs, "Icon Eye," *Icon 026*, August 2005

I began to consider the question of light at the Institut du Monde Arabe. The theme of light is reflected in the southern wall, consisting entirely of camera shutters, in the stacking of the stairs, the blurring of contours, the superimpositions, reflections, and shadows. _ Jean Nouvel lecture, London, 1995, in Conway Lloyd Morgan, *Jean Nouvel: The Elements of Architecture*, New York: Universe Publishing, 1998

A moucharabieh in wood or marble is very precious. You have to find the same feeling. If you don't, you have something like Disney. _ Arthur Lubow, *New York Times*, April 6, 2008

### PARIS 1987
## ARAB WORLD INSTITUTE The vocation of the building was to talk about Arab culture. If it is an homage, then it has to use the two main aspects of Arab architecture, geometry and light. _ Arthur Lubow, *New York Times*, April 6, 2008

The interior view of metal lenses at the Arab World Institute. Nouvel wanted to employ geometry and light, two main aspects of Arab architecture.

### Oriental/Occidental: Two Sides of the Same Coin A cultural position in architecture is a necessity. That involves refusing the use of ready-made or facile solutions in order to permit an approach which is both

global in its conception and specific to the site. . . . If the southern side of the building is a contemporary expression of Oriental culture, with the diaphragms, the northern is a literal mirror of Western culture, as images of the nearby Parisian cityscape have been enameled on the exterior glass, like the passage of chemicals over a photographic plate. This pattern of lines and marks on the same façade is also an echo of contemporary art. _ Jean Nouvel, 1986, in Conway Lloyd Morgan, *Jean Nouvel: The Elements of Architecture*, New York: Universe Publishing, 1998

To regulate the light coming into the Arab World Institute, above, Nouvel invented an automated lens system, which operates like the shutter of a camera. A computer monitors both light and temperature and the motorized "shutters" open and close as needed.

## CINEMA AND ARCHITECTURE:
## THE INVENTION OF SMALL WORLDS

*For Nouvel, the creation of a building is similar to making a film, from the sole initial concept to making it more collaborative and integrative.*

There are a lot of crossovers between the two disciplines: For me, the connection between imagery and time came about largely thanks to cinema. Both the architect and the moviemaker create or invent things that interrelate imagery and time. For one, it's a product that plays on total illusion, because there is no physical reality other than the set of pictures; for the other, the product is experienced as a piece of space that works to a sort of scenario, a bit like a small invented world. Both of us—film director and architect—invent small worlds. _ "Jean Nouvel 1987–2006," *A + U: Architecture and Urbanism,* Special Issue, April 2006

I begin always with a very deep analysis and research of all the factors relevant to the case in a way that I believe goes far deeper than the traditional method. I try to put off the formal fixing with pencil on paper until the final minute. I try to find all the good reasons to do it one way and not another. I call this the rules of formation.

Very often I draw the comparison with the cinema. It's a bit like shooting a film in the sense that there are different people who work as a team, each member having a different role. This team takes the project through. As actors don't switch roles midway through a film, each person tries to carry his own weight through the entire process. Though economically it's not necessarily always the best or most functional thing.

I never start a project with saying that here is a certain technology which I will put at work. It's always the idea which comes first, and then we figure out how to do it. _ "Jean Nouvel," *GA Document Extra 07,* 1996

The plastic arts and cinema are substrate; subjects that give life to architecture. I try to make use of all these references and I really do believe that my work has been influenced by filmmakers and artists that I worked with over fifteen years on the Paris Biennial where they often did installations. I see artists just as people who enlighten us. An artist enables us to see whether a particular formal area is usable or not. _ Jean Nouvel, *Architectural Design,* July 2007

## THE COMPUTER

*The computer is a cautionary aide, but never a solution for Nouvel. The active imagination must precede the realization that a computer can help generate. It is, ultimately, what he calls "computer-assisted imagination."*

[The computer] would be the end of my brain. Forget the computer. First for the architect, they need to have the feelings. Then take a pen and explain an idea like this, a little sketch. But not too much drawing. An idea first. _ William Booth, *Washington Post,* June 2, 2008

The computer has brought me what I call computer-assisted imagination, as against simulation imagery or computer-assisted design. I found myself moving against the current followed by most architects and graphic artists; what they liked most in computer imagery was to play with the immaterial aspect, the abstract features, even in handling colors. That is nothing more than the automatic reflexes of the Ecole des Beaux-Arts: the way they made you put the same colors in the same places, with no relationship between the nature of what was represented and what it was in reality. I try to do things so that everything is represented as the eye sees it, so that the representation stays as close as possible to reality, so that it aims at translating an illusion of reality.

I am basically against the computer for everything that concerns the outline phase, which for me, incidentally, is the phase that passes more by words. From time to time, you have to produce a still—and when that happens, I prefer getting out the old pencils and sheets of paper to do it. When you're working up a vague idea, I'm not keen on giving it form via the computer. . . . In the outline stages I like the project to retain something that is random, a degree of haziness. You know that a hand sketch is off the cuff. But as soon as you trace lines on a computer, you get the impression they are definitive. _ "Jean Nouvel 1987–2006," *A + U: Architecture and Urbanism,* Special Issue, April 2006

MINNEAPOLIS 2006
# GUTHRIE THEATER
Here, the theater is a machine for the senses. It creates the stage upon which the city performs before its citizens. It recalls the perspective machines used by painters since the Renaissance. It is a borrowing from the history of painting deployed again in a history of looking, of urban contemplation, sometimes an idealized scene of public life, sometimes a picturesque ensemble, or a vision shattered, distorted, and forever recomposed. _ "Atelier Jean Nouvel, Guthrie Theater," arcspace.com, July 10, 2006

The cantilever bridge overhanging the Mississippi riverfront provides an instrument for experimentation, both visual and physical, with the landscape.

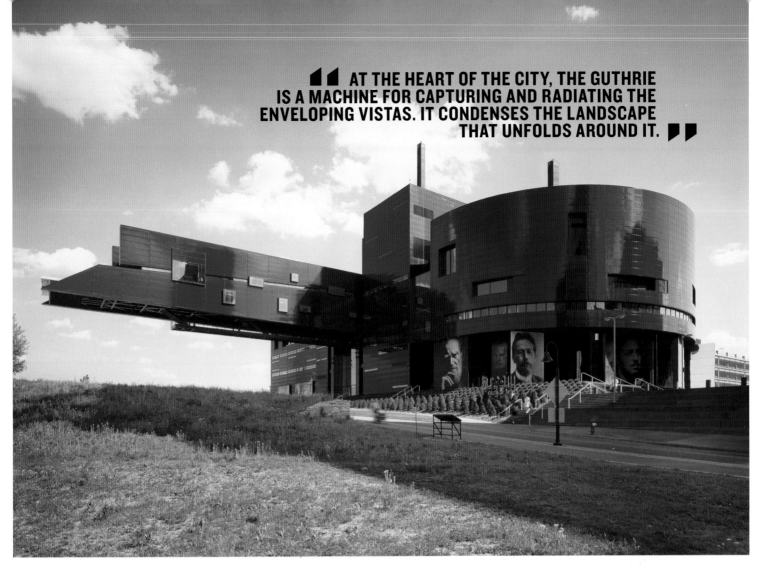

**AT THE HEART OF THE CITY, THE GUTHRIE IS A MACHINE FOR CAPTURING AND RADIATING THE ENVELOPING VISTAS. IT CONDENSES THE LANDSCAPE THAT UNFOLDS AROUND IT.**

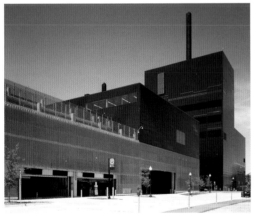

The walk from the lobby to the balcony opening onto the Saint Anthony Falls is an event as much as a promenade. Slits and apertures offer glimpses of the geography; the rhythm of footsteps is modulated by an uneven floor. When the window at the far end is open, the rumble of the falls can be heard (the Dakota Indians used to speak of the "laughing water"). A curtain of warm air blurs the outlook, as in a mirage.

The window is in blue glass. Its color too lends an unreal aspect to the scenery. On reaching the balcony, the floor slips away, plunging to become an open-air theater with a view across the landscape.
_ "Atelier Jean Nouvel, Guthrie Theater," arcspace. com, July 10, 2006

The sleek Guthrie Theater in Minneapolis provides visitors with a sensory experience, drawn especially from the surrounding landscape and Saint Anthony Falls.

## PARIS 2006
# QUAI BRANLY MUSEUM

This museum design is also unique because we were able to design around the collection. Sometimes when you work on a museum you won't know what will be presented. . . . Here we knew exactly. We were able to establish a link between the place and between the art inside. Between the container and the contents. To me, the main attitude at Branly was to create a special place that provided a link for the pieces of art and artifacts of this civilization. So I think it was very important to welcome the visitors in a special area that was protected and mysterious. It is in some ways the opposite of a contemporary art museum, which has its white walls on which you display works like stamps.

Today's museums are about flexibility. But we did the opposite. Everything was premeditated and specific. I established this idea for almost 4,000 pieces. . . . We designed systems that were appropriate for various parts of the collection—I was thinking a lot of Carlo Scarpa. It's not the same vocabulary, but we carefully considered how some things would hang, how things would be suspended. We left nothing to chance. For example, we carefully thought about how to exhibit masks. Orthogonal white walls didn't seem appropriate. I wanted to create a spiritual space because all of these objects are linked to religions we don't know, to the memory of the ancestors, to the rest of humanity. For me, it was very important to keep a sense of ambiguity or mystery, since we don't know everything

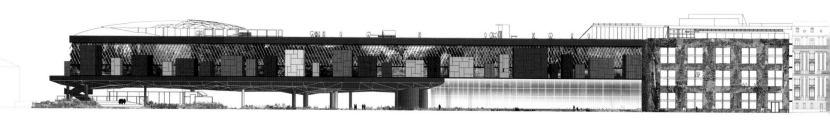

about these civilizations, and create a dialogue that brought all these subjects together. _ Jean Nouvel interview by Yoshio Futagawa, *GA Document*, Special Issue, September 2006

It's not an Occidental building. For me it is a world done with colors and shapes linked to an interpretation of Africa and Oceanic and American culture. _ Arthur Lubow, *New York Times*, April 6, 2008

Some critics say it is like a Disney museum. But I do not think it is the right attitude to show this art on white walls . . . people in Europe have the habit of white walls with a lot of light . . . [but] here every piece of art is done with the exact lighting that you need to see it. That is not what people are expecting. It's a game with the spirits of the dead people, so you see the reflections like ghosts. _ Arthur Lubow, *New York Times*, April 6, 2008

### The Façade: Two Different Vocabularies
The big question today [2006] is the garden. On the north façade we want the continuity of the trees and the trees of the city. In a sense the building is not done until the trees mature a little. I never meant for the façade to be seen in its entirety like it is now. I always imagined it behind a filter, a screen. And the reflection of the trees was meant to be read through the glass from the spaces inside. It was always meant to be both vague and precise at the same time. _ Jean Nouvel interview by Yoshio Futagawa, *GA Document*, Special Issue, September 2006

We had to cut down 90 percent of the light. On the north we have huge stained glass, which is spiritually important, a little bit like a church, to create this spiritual atmosphere. And this wall was in tension with the wall on the south, through which we bring in some natural light. The two very different façades also let you experience the outside differently. You can sense the weather through the quality of light on the south wall, and through the north you can see the vague shadows of trees and Paris outside. They are two very different vocabularies. _ Jean Nouvel interview by Yoshio Futagawa, *GA Document*, Special Issue, September 2006

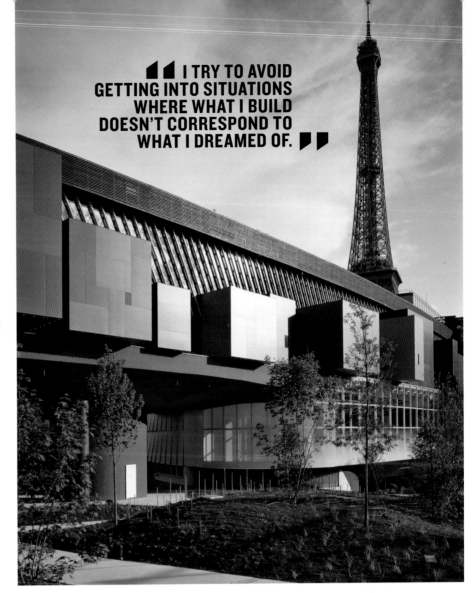

**I TRY TO AVOID GETTING INTO SITUATIONS WHERE WHAT I BUILD DOESN'T CORRESPOND TO WHAT I DREAMED OF.**

## " OF COURSE, YOU CAN FIND A LOT OF CONTRADICTIONS BETWEEN ALL MY BUILDINGS. I HAVE NO GLOBAL REASONS; I HAVE PARTICULAR REASONS. "

### THE DESIGN PROCESS

At the start of any project, there is a series of meetings, discussions, analyses, brainstorming sessions—with the team, with others. Often it can be as simple as making lists—things to do and not to do! That helps me build a mental picture of the possible solutions—and I always remember that architecture is not a matter of single solutions! . . . I then present to the team as a physical interpretation of the ideas, as a narrative of how this aspect meets this requirement, of why this choice of materials, why this handling of light, and so on. Then we discuss further, and the team starts on drawings and models—which in turn throw up new challenges or contradictions, which we must resolve or adapt to. _ Conway Lloyd Morgan, *Jean Nouvel: The Elements of Architecture*, New York: Universe Publishing, 1998

I had a lot of difficulties at the beginning, because some architecture critics said to me, you did three buildings and there is no relationship between them. I said, you're wrong! There is the same attitude. Of course, there are three different kinds of shapes, of vocabulary, but for good reasons. I call that in French *poésie de situation*. I research what is the *pièce manquant*—you have to find the missing piece. To build something is a new opportunity—what would be the singularity of that opportunity? _ Marcus Fairs, "Icon Eye," *Icon 026*, August 2005

### IMAGINATION VS. REALITY

I did a project and all that remains of it is a beautiful image. No thanks. What interests me in this business is building, making dreams pass into reality. . . . It's only interesting when you get the impression you're actually making a contribution. Taking part in a certain idea of the evolution of cities and—philosophically—in creating a certain future. What it boils down to is that I could never have been an architectural

artist. I mean someone who sees architecture as an artwork activity, like Piranesi. The thing that interests me is seeing the images that I design pass into reality. _ "Jean Nouvel 1987–2006," *A + U: Architecture and Urbanism*, Special Issue, April 2006

### HOW IDEAS HAPPEN AND PROGRESS

This is a profession that never leaves you in peace. Your mind is always working. . . . You go out, then you see a brick wall with chimneys, and you say: Hey, that reminds me of something. I can't say what. And then you notice a small detail, a grid between two cement slabs. . . . You're all the time recording sensations that turn into real emotions. . . . Wherever you are, you're constantly spying on the world and listening to it.

Then there is another phase in work—usually a synthesis phase—that takes place more in solitude. You have to be able to resolve things, synthesize, so as to be able to propose something that is already in the order of inventing the form. And you have to know how to control this form, which is something that I do alone, usually at my place, in silence. The thing that I try to avoid is finding myself—due to work pressure—having to look over five or six projects or even ten in a single day, spending half an hour on each. . . . I call that the shaker—it's deadly.

In general, from the month of June through to September, I try to get away. I go down to Saint-Paul-de-Vence. And there we set aside half a day or a whole day for each project. My collaborators come to see me. I stay put. No traveling. . . . As I get older, I'm going to try to work more that way. Because the most violent thing is to have to change state, change the subject when you'd like to stick with it, not have the time and be forced to sidetrack to something else. _ "Jean Nouvel 1987–2006," *A + U: Architecture and Urbanism*, Special Issue, April 2006

### PARIS 1994
# CARTIER FOUNDATION

Art needs to be experienced more widely, not through schemes of patronage like the .01 percent idea, but by a greater public involvement. And the definitions of art are changing continually: The space at Cartier is designed to be entirely flexible. For one exhibition it can be draped, for another open. It can be partitioned, and lit in different ways. _ Conway Lloyd Morgan, *Jean Nouvel: The Elements of Architecture*, New York: Universe Publishing, 1998

The phantom of the park. In its transparency. In inclusion. Trees can be glimpsed behind the high glass enclosure that has taken the place of the long blank wall. Included in an eight-meter-high surface that they lightly touch.

Châteaubriand's cedar tree stands alone, framed by two screens that mark the entrance. The visitor passes underneath the cedar and is faced with the sight of the trees surrounding the exhibition hall, also glazed to a height of eight meters, in an in-depth view of the site.

In the summer, the large sliding bays are drawn aside and the hall turns into an extension of the park, punctuated by tall piles. The longitudinal façades project a long way from the building, blurring its limits. The trees appear to slide behind them, taking on an ambiguous presence. Slender staircases are outlined, lit from behind, against the lateral façades. The glazed façade extends several meters above the terrace. Even the view of the sky is filtered by this transparent wall. From the boulevard, the building looks like a halo against the backdrop of the sky, and real or virtual trees are superimposed on it, reflected and refracted by the glass screens.

The glass is clear. The western and southern façades filter the sunlight by means of their roller blinds. On the eastern façade, elevators of the "climber" type slide along the façade, simple transparent volumes with no apparent mechanism, or even cables. To the south two latticed cages are embedded in the ground, leading cars down to the underground parking lot.

It is an architecture of lightness, of finely ruled glass and steel. An architecture that is based on a blurring of the building's tangible limits and on rendering the sight of a solid volume superfluous in a poetics of soft focus and evanescence. An architecture that gives the quarter the opportunity to enjoy a beautiful garden that has long been concealed from its gaze. An architecture that sets out to make its position clear with regard to the notion of transparency and its alleged lazy neutrality. At a time when virtuality is making an attack on reality, architecture more than ever has to have the courage to assume the image of contradiction. _ Jean Nouvel, *Lotus*, no. 84, 1994

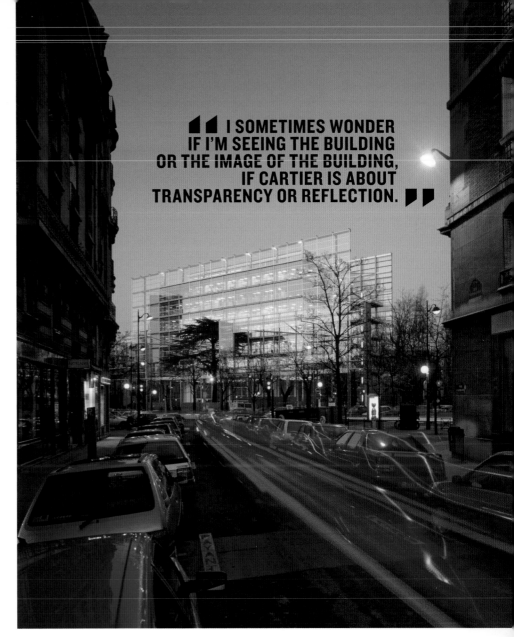

**I SOMETIMES WONDER IF I'M SEEING THE BUILDING OR THE IMAGE OF THE BUILDING, IF CARTIER IS ABOUT TRANSPARENCY OR REFLECTION.**

The immaterial caught in a grid is the theme here. The tree planted by Chateaubriand is a real historical monument. That is why architecture endeavors to emphasize it, to frame it. _ Conway Lloyd Morgan, *Jean Nouvel: The Elements of Architecture*, New York: Universe Publishing, 1998

**Legacy** A testimonial of an attitude—an epoch. I am very different from a lot of architects who use always the same typologies, the same materials and techniques. This is not a criticism—but I am the opposite. When you travel round the world you meet all the clones. All these buildings always the same, they have no roots. I fight against generic designs for specific architecture—that will be my legacy. _ Max Thompson, *Architects' Journal*, April 2, 2008

The Cartier Foundation was completed in 1994, two years before the Quai Branly Museum. The Cartier building is transformed depending on the time of day.

## SUSTAINABLE ARCHITECTURE

Architecture is the art form to which we are continually exposed. It enhances or hinders our lives because it creates the environment in which all our everyday experiences take place, be they commonplace or seminal. There should be no surprise that architecture becomes controversial, nor that it is the art form which the public criticizes the most widely and the most passionately. The special status that architecture holds in our lives demands special vigilance from the citizen, and this requires society to be both informed and prescriptive about quality. . . . The requirement for architecture to contribute to social and environmental sustainability now charges architects with responsibilities that go beyond the limits of an autonomous brief. . . . Buildings should inspire, and compose cities that celebrate society and respect nature. Our present need for sustainable building now offers opportunities to re-establish ambition and to evolve new aesthetic orders—it could provide the impetus for the revival of the profession of architecture. _ Richard Rogers, *Cities for a Small Planet,* London: Westview Press, 1997

# RICHARD ROGERS

**BORN:** July 23, 1933, Florence, Italy

**EDUCATION:** M.Arch., Yale University, New Haven, Connecticut, 1959; Diploma, Architectural Association, School of Architecture, London, 1958

**OFFICE:** Rogers Stirk Harbour + Partners, The Leadenhall Building, 122 Leadenhall Street, London EC3V 4AB
Tel: +44 20-7385-1235, Fax: +44 20-7385-8409
www.rsh-p.com

**PROJECTS FEATURED:** The Leadenhall Building, London, 2006; Madrid Barajas International Airport, Terminal 4, Spain, 2005; National Assembly for Wales, Cardiff, U.K., 2005; Millennium Dome, Greenwich, England, 1999; Lloyd's of London, England, 1986; Georges Pompidou Center, Paris, 1977

"I HAVE ALWAYS BELIEVED THAT A HUMANE AND PROGRESSIVE ARCHITECTURE IS ONE THAT CREATES BEAUTY OUT OF FUNCTION. NOT JUST FOR THE SAKE OF BEAUTY IN ITSELF, BUT BECAUSE BEAUTIFUL BUILDINGS AND PUBLIC SPACES HELP PEOPLE ACHIEVE THEIR POTENTIAL, AS CITIZENS AS WELL AS INDIVIDUALS. ARCHITECTS CANNOT BE APOLITICAL; WE HAVE A DUTY TO ENGAGE."

**Georges Pompidou Center, Paris, 1977**
Curved glass enclosed walkway at the
highest accessible point overlooking Paris.

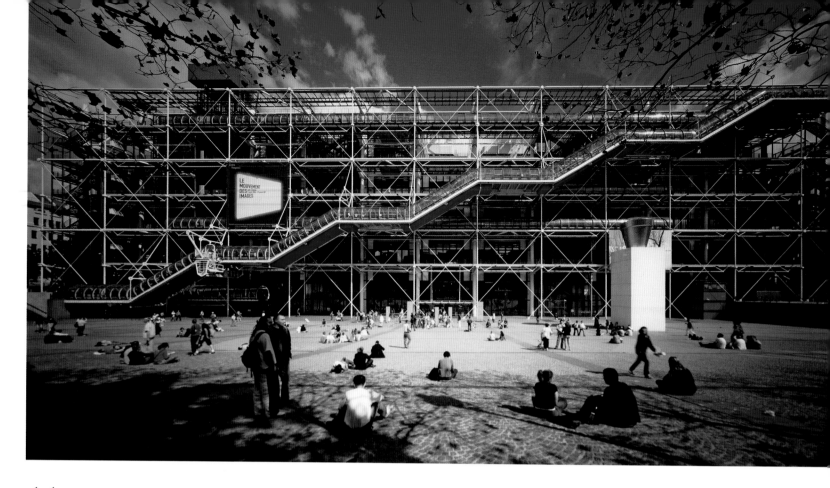

## "... A CROSS BETWEEN AN INFORMATION-ORIENTED COMPUTERIZED TIMES SQUARE AND THE BRITISH MUSEUM, WITH THE STRESS ON

# TWO-WAY PARTICIPATION
## BETWEEN PEOPLE
## AND ACTIVITIES/EXHIBITS. "

The Georges Pompidou Center attracts more visitors than the Eiffel Tower and the Louvre combined. Rogers says he believes it is because of the multitude of things that go on there—from the joy ride up the escalators across the façade, top, to the areas set aside for quiet study. *Above:* The east elevation of the Pompidou Center from rue Renard.

### PARIS 1977
# GEORGES POMPIDOU CENTER

*Richard Rogers and Renzo Piano were partners from 1967 to 1976, and in 1971 they won the Pompidou Center competition. Previously, Rogers had begun an architectural practice in 1962 as Team 4, with his first wife, Su, and Norman and Wendy Foster.*

We were very interested in creating a building that was popular for all people. The aim was to create a framework and to find a way to build a building that was indeterminant, by which I mean the pieces can be changed, even now. Unlike the classical or Miesian, in which you can't add anything to it or take anything away; it's not finite or perfect the day it's finished. It was very important that this building be adaptable. In this way it's worked very well. The framework is a rhythm, and inside it doesn't matter if it's solid, translucent, or transparent as long as it is done intelligently. The pieces, the forms, the departments can all be changed. The building is strong and robust enough to take those changes. _ Richard Rogers interview by Yoshio Futagawa, *GA Document Extra*, 1995

Not a remote monument but a people's place. Our competition report recommended that the Pompidou Center be developed as a live center of information covering Paris and beyond . . . a cross between an information-oriented computerized Times Square and the British Museum, with the stress on two-way participation between people and activities/exhibits. _ Richard Rogers, *Architecture: A Modern View*, London: Thames & Hudson, 1991

In our design for the Pompidou Center . . . we sought to create centers that could appeal to everyone: chil-

dren, tourists and locals, students and workers, users and passersby. We wanted to establish not remote museums but vibrant public meeting places.
_ Richard Rogers, *Architecture: A Modern View*, London: Thames & Hudson, 1991

When we were doing the Pompidou Center, we didn't have a single piece of positive press in the entire six years, other than one very memorable piece in the *New York Times*. We were torn to pieces until the day the doors opened. Then, overnight, the media changed. There's a danger in taking too much to heart what people say about you—the good as well as the bad. Your assessment of what you do has to come from closer to home. _ Geraldine Bedell, *The Observer*, February 12, 2006

The popularity of Centre Pompidou, which draws more people than the Eiffel Tower and the Louvre put together, is, I believe, primarily due to this overlapping of diverse activities ranging from the popular joy ride up the escalators across the façade, to the areas reserved for exclusive and quiet study. These are all contained in a joyful, easily understandable, multipurpose, open-framed building, set in a piazza full of spontaneous activities. _ *Richard Rogers + Architects*, London: Academy Editions, 1985

Initially, the Pompidou Center was bombarded with negative press, although coverage in the *New York Times* was positive. Things changed once it became apparent that the public embraced it as a new icon for the city.

## CITIES

Cities are the heart of our culture, the engines of our economy, and the birthplace of our civilization. There is little that makes me happier than getting lost in a beautiful city: following its narrow passages to the grand tree-lined avenues; stumbling across street theater, sitting in a café with Ruthie [wife Ruth Rogers] watching people go by. This is my idea of heaven. But cities do not just happen—they are made. Designed and managed well, they civilize. Neglected, they quickly lose their vitality. And where cities become run-down, they brutalize. _ Richard Rogers, Pritzker Prize acceptance speech, June 4, 2007

Cities of the future will no longer be zoned as today in isolated one-activity ghettos; rather, they will resemble the more richly layered cities of the past. Living, working, shopping, learning, and leisure will overlap and be housed in continuous, varied, and changing structures. _ Richard Rogers, *Architecture: A Modern View*, London: Thames & Hudson, 1991

We need an architecture that strengthens and enriches the grain of the city fabric by filling in empty spaces so that streets and squares become dynamic rooms without a roof. _ Richard Rogers, "Order, Harmony and Modernity," in *Richard Rogers 1978–1988, A + U: Architecture and Urbanism Extra Edition*, 1989

In urban terms, the most important thing is to make cities more compact, to reuse brownfield land instead of allowing uncontrolled sprawl on greenfield sites. _ "From the Scale of a Lamp to the Scale of a City: An Interview with Richard Rogers," *Detail*, January 2007

## STRADDLING THE IN-BETWEEN

*In 1998 Rogers was invited to chair a government task force charged with translating sustainable urban development principles into strategic advice for planning authorities in England.*

I don't teach, for instance; instead, I work a day a week with the mayor. Everybody does something else, like teaching, which gives you a certain feedback. I work on a bigger scale in London—and here in the office, we work on pieces of London, and pieces like this part of the lamp. So what I do is in between architecture and politics. _ "From the Scale of a Lamp to the Scale of a City: An Interview with Richard Rogers," *Detail*, January 2007

When Terminal 4 opened, it effectively doubled the aircraft and passenger capacity at Spain's largest international airport. But it is about more than just size—the design is meant to be soothing. Glass panels and ceiling domes flood areas with light.

**MADRID 2005**

# MADRID BARAJAS INTERNA-TIONAL AIRPORT, TERMINAL 4

Thirty years later, Barajas Airport in Madrid continues the spirit of the Pompidou: the fun and adventure of travel are expressed in its sweeping roof, its steel structure, and rainbow of colors. _ Richard Rogers, Pritzker Prize acceptance speech, June 4, 2007

Our aim has been to create an airport that is fun, with lots of light, great views, and a high degree of clarity. _ Kenneth Powell, *Richard Rogers: Architecture of the Future,* Boston: Birkhäuser, 2004

## "WE NEVER CALL OURSELVES HIGH TECH"

I certainly don't think of myself as high tech. Most buildings, whether they're Gothic cathedrals or Romanesque ones, were high tech for their time. _ Deborah Solomon, *New York Times,* May 21, 2006

There is no such thing as high technology or low technology—simply appropriate technology. _ Kenneth Powell, *Lloyd's Building, Richard Rogers Partnership,* London: Phaidon, 1994

We never call ourselves high tech; if others have explained our work as high tech, this is fine. As far as this is concerned, it's about finding an appropriate material, and we're more experienced in a certain range of materials. But we try to widen the range all the time. _ "From the Scale of a Lamp to the Scale of a City: An Interview with Richard Rogers," *Detail,* January 2007

Buildings are made of machined pieces, and machines are but modern tools. It is not the machine that destroys the craftsmanship inherent in all good buildings, it is the lack of love and understanding of the machine by those whose responsibility it is to invent, design and control the buildings—primarily the architect. . . . _ Richard Rogers, "Order, Harmony and Modernity," in *Richard Rogers 1978–1988, A + U: Architecture and Urbanism Extra Edition,* 1989

## "LEGIBLE" ARCHITECTURE

. . . buildings which are full of light, which are light in weight, which are flexible, which have low energy, which are what we call legible—you can read how the building is put together. _ Robin Pogrebin, *New York Times,* March 28, 2007

# LLOYD'S OF LONDON

The Lloyd's building is very flexible. The six towers outside are the servant towers, and they all have a short life; in other words, the elevators, the air conditioning, the electricity, all of those elements could be changed quite quickly; you could even add another tower if you wanted to. But the central part—and this like Louis Kahn's idea of servant and served areas—is the warehouse, and that is more static. That's where people live and work; it could be a university, in which the machinery outside would be changed, which is why the towers are outside. It is more vertical whereas Pompidou is more horizontal in its organization, and it is again changing all the time. Lloyd's came to us and said, "we've had three buildings in this century, sixty to seventy years, and we're tired of changing. We want a building that will last well into the twenty-first century." So we had to find a very flexible way of building. And the idea was to have these very simple floor plans, absolutely simple with no vertical interruption, just these clip-on cores. It was a clip-on system with the structure being on the outside or in the atrium. They wanted an atrium because of the way they work, which is like a market or a trading floor, so they had to see each other work but they didn't know how much space they would occupy. . . . It had, like the Pompidou, this immense floor space without real specialized elements, so where the museum goes, where the library goes, where the restaurants go can be anywhere. Lloyd's is much the same thing. _ Richard Rogers interview by Yoshio Futagawa, *GA Document Extra*, 1995

Our intention in the design of the new Lloyd's building has been to create a more articulated, layered building by the manipulation of plan, section, and elevation which would weave together both the oversimplified twentieth-century blocks and the richer, more varied architecture of the past. Approaches to buildings in cities are often long, narrow streets, so that they are seen obliquely. LIoyd's is designed to be approached on the diagonal and viewed in parts. As the viewer approaches the building, the form gradually unfolds, the overlapping elements of its façade opening up to

**❝ IF POMPIDOU WAS A COLORFUL FUN PALACE STANDING IN A GREAT PIAZZA, LLOYD'S OF LONDON WAS A PRIVATE CLUB SQUEEZED INTO THE CITY'S MEDIEVAL STREET PATTERN . . . ❞**

reveal spaces related to the pedestrian scale, spaces that are sheltered from passing vehicles. _ Kenneth Powell, *Richard Rogers*, Zurich: Artemis, 1994

The tall, serrated towers and the rounded atrium form are designed to enrich the skyline, placing the building in its urban environment amongst the spires, domes, and towers of the past. _ Kenneth Powell, *Richard Rogers*, Zurich: Artemis, 1994

Lloyd's of London wanted a building that would last well into the 21st century. The six towers on the outside of the building house the elevators, air conditioning, and electricity, all of which could be easily upgraded and changed. Rogers decided on simple floor plans built around an atrium for ease of use.

# THE LEADENHALL BUILDING Tall

buildings—if sensitively inserted and designed—can function well, especially office buildings built as part of a cluster where the space between towers can be as important as the building itself, the cluster enriching the city and the skyline. One needs only to look at the skylines of Chicago and San Gimignano to be convinced. The winding medieval streets, defining irregular plot sizes, can lead to more dramatic building forms than the grid plan—for example, Washington. Another constraint is the conservation of view corridors to historic buildings. The Leadenhall Building—developed by British Land and designed by Rogers Stirk Harbour + Partners—responds to the view of St. Paul's by sloping back to get out of the view. _ Ian Harrison, *Britain from Above,* London: Pavilion, 2009

The architect's responsibility extends beyond the client's brief into the public realm so that his buildings, whether small or large, give public performances to the user and passerby—the audience of today and tomorrow. They are live theater, which, by means of appropriate technology, reflect and therefore make legible the prevalent social, economic, political, and technical forces. _ Kenneth Powell, *Richard Rogers,* Zurich: Artemis, 1994

As with any new, major building in the City of London, concerns about respecting historic structures are important. An aerial view of Leadenhall Building shows not only how it fits in, but also its keen use of the space among London's skyscraper towers.

## ON SUSTAINABILITY

Today there is a new architectural imperative: not just to complement the urban environment, but also to respect the global environment. _ Richard Rogers, Pritzker Prize acceptance speech, June 4, 2007

Sustainability is about finding more socially cohesive, economically efficient, and ecologically sound ways of producing and distributing existing resources. It is about securing quality of life by establishing the value of goods held in common—the environment and the community—and about recognizing our mutual dependence on both. The planet is perfectly capable of sustaining all humanity if we respect the demands of nature and focus our use of technology. _ Richard Rogers, *Cities for a Small Planet*, London: Westview Press, 1997

Sustainable policies are already reaping visible rewards. On the back of this success and with popular determination, sustainability could become the dominant philosophy of our age. In this way, cities, the habitat of humanity, could be once more woven into the cycle of nature. Cities that are beautiful, safe, and equitable are within our grasp. _ Richard Rogers, *Cities for a Small Planet*, London: Westview Press, 1997

## ❝❝ SUSTAINABILITY COULD BECOME THE DOMINANT PHILOSOPHY OF OUR AGE. ❞❞

### CARDIFF 2005
# NATIONAL ASSEMBLY FOR WALES
The National Assembly building has been recognized as an exemplar of environmental design—we responded enthusiastically to the requirement for a building that maximizes natural daylight and ventilation to reduce energy usage . . .
_ Richard Rogers interview by Leonora Oppenheim, "Richard Rogers Partnership's National Assembly of Wales Sets Environmental Example," Treehugger.com, May 3, 2006

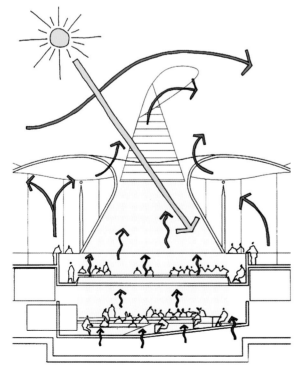

Rogers chose rough slate, smooth concrete, steel, glass, and timber to build the Welsh Assembly. The building was meant to naturally respond to the dynamics of the local environment. There is attention to environmental details like the use of natural ventilation, nighttime cooling, and daylight-linked lighting controls. The building takes advantage of geothermal energy and harvests rainwater. *Near Left:* The assembly's debating chamber.

## THE OFFICE: "THE BIG PIAZZA"

We're an unusual office. We're owned by a charity. I don't believe in ownership of work [so] there's no link between directors and partners and money. _ Louise Jury, *The Independent*, March 30, 2007

*Interestingly, the comment below was made some fifteen years ago, and though the Friday night dinners no longer occur, the "extended family" dynamic continues. Field trips to newly completed projects are arranged for the staff, as are a variety of activities such as quiz evenings, bonfires for staff and their family, and an annual fantasy football league. All of this ensures camaraderie despite the size of the practice.*

I believe in the ideal of community. My wife's restaurant is here, where she's the chef. [Ruth Rogers is chef and co-founder of River Café, a successful Italian restaurant in London.] We work like a big family;

we have office parties every Friday night where everyone comes down here to drink; sometimes we take holidays together. We try to create a community spirit where people enjoy their work. Very few people leave our office; it is unusual. We have people that have been here a very long time. So this is very important to us, and Pompidou, of course, sort of reflects this idea—the big piazza is where the community takes place and the façade was all about people being able to watch each other and enjoy city life. But our own office tries to structure itself around that form of idealized life. _ Richard Rogers interview by Yoshio Futagawa, *GA Document Extra*, 1995

You are leading a team. I've never really understood how architects can think of themselves as an individual. _ Robin Pogrebin, *New York Times*, March 28, 2007

The Millennium Dome was originally used to house a major exhibition to celebrate the beginning of the 21st century.

## GREENWICH 1999
# MILLENNIUM DOME
The dome is essentially a big umbrella for our climate. And I hope it's a very beautiful umbrella. It's big because it marks a big moment in time. It's an optimistic statement about the potential of the present and future; it's about how one can better control one's destiny and at the same time enjoy oneself. _ Elizabeth Wilhide, *The Millennium Dome,* London: Collins, 1999

## "A FAMILY THAT CARED ABOUT THE ARTS"

I had lots of trouble in school as a child, and I lost confidence. Teachers thought I was stupid. I learned to read very late, when I was eleven. Dyslexia wasn't recognized then, and the assumption was you were incapable of thinking. _ Deborah Solomon, *New York Times*, May 21, 2006

The one advantage of being dyslexic is that you are never tempted to look back and idealize your childhood. _ Geraldine Bedell, *The Observer*, February 12, 2006

I was not a good student; in fact I was an appalling student. I was interested in very broad subjects, the philosophical and the political. I was brought up in a family that cared about the arts. _ Richard Rogers interview by Yoshio Futagawa, *GA Document Extra*, 1995

*Although Rogers has lived in England for most of his life, he was born in Florence, where he and his family lived until he was five years old.*

I concentrate well. I love working in cafés. When I was a child in Trieste, there was a little Austrian café opposite our apartment. An accountant used to arrive every day at 9 a.m. and they'd bring him a coffee and a telephone and there he would work all day. When I was about six, I thought that was the ideal life. _ Geraldine Bedell, *The Observer*, February 12, 2006

Culturally I think of myself as an Italian, but I have lived here [England] for 67 years. . . . I love being a Londoner and I love being a Florentine. I'm a European. _ Louise Jury, *The Independent*, March 30, 2007

Visits to Italy put me much more in contact with Ernesto Rogers [a cousin who was editor of major Italian architectural journals including *Domus* and *Casabella*], who was a major influence. When I was nineteen or twenty, it became clear that, as I was interested in social and design problems, architecture would be a good field for me. I decided to become an architect. I worked a little bit at my cousin's office in Milan and would do little houses for myself. . . . After Milan I came back to England, managed to get into the Architectural Association, and spent my next five years there. _ Richard Rogers interview by Yoshio Futagawa, *GA Document Extra*, 1995

I think the AA [Architectural Association, London] is very strong on design. I was in the same year as Peter Cook of Archigram, which was just beginning to form. Cedric Price was there, and was and still is an influential thinker. I left the AA with a scholarship to go to Yale and study under Paul Rudolph and Serge Chermayeff. _ Richard Rogers interview by Yoshio Futagawa, *GA Document Extra*, 1995

In the States I was very influenced by Vincent Scully, a historian [at Yale University] who lectured brilliantly on Frank Lloyd Wright. Norman [Foster], and Su [Rogers], and I went to see 80 percent of Wright's houses and traveled all around the States. The other very strong influence at that time was Louis Kahn. We went to Yale because Louis Kahn was already beginning to finish at Penn; he was teaching less. When we were at Yale our studio was in Louis Kahn's Museum of Modern Art, which was quite influential. We also went to Philadelphia, on an exchange program for a while, because Louis Kahn was there. _ Richard Rogers interview by Yoshio Futagawa, *GA Document Extra*, 1995

## ARCHITECTS AND FASHION

I don't understand why everyone has to wear black, gray, and white. _ Geraldine Bedell, *The Observer*, February 12, 2006

## FRIENDSHIPS: FOSTER AND PIANO

*Richard Rogers and Norman Foster met when they were students at Yale University's School of Architecture. Upon graduating, they returned to London where they formed the partnership Team 4, with their wives Su Rogers and Wendy Foster. After Team 4, Rogers worked with Renzo Piano until 1976. He subsequently opened his own firm, Richard Rogers Partnership, in 1977.*

Probably my closest friend is Renzo Piano. He's a passionate sailor. We go sailing together, and he fills me in on the latest things that have happened in the technology of boats. _ Deborah Solomon, *New York Times*, May 21, 2006

There is always competitiveness with any individual you work with, and with Norman there was always a certain edginess. We were very close friends. . . . I think without any feeling of competition it would be a very strange life. Even when I boil an egg I try to make it good. _ Rob Sharp, *The Independent*, April 23, 2008

My passion and great enjoyment for architecture, and the reason the older I get the more I enjoy, is because I believe we—architects—can affect the quality of life of the people. _ Richard Rogers interview with ScottishArchitecture.com, June 25, 2002

**TERRAIN *IN NATURA*** Leaving the terrain *in natura* can mean a lot today. Shoreline flora and fauna alone are incredibly fertile. And you destroy them all with those famous seawalls, landfills. But I can't say that I will always adopt this or that solution. . . . I therefore have the impression that there'll never be this type of definitive paradigm in architecture, because its beauty is precisely in rallying knowledge in its totality, whether from the perspective of philosophical speculation or in terms of surveying your technical and technological resources and saying: "OK. Now this is what I'm going to do."

_ Paulo Mendes da Rocha, *Paulo Mendes da Rocha Fifty Years,* New York: Rizzoli, 2007

# PAULO MENDES DA ROCHA

**BORN:** October 25, 1928, Vitória, Espírito Santo, Brazil

**EDUCATION:** Architecture degree, Mackenzie University, São Paulo, Brazil, 1954

**OFFICE:** R. Bento Freitas, 306 5 Andar - Conj. 51, São Paulo 01220–000, Brazil

**PROJECTS FEATURED:** The State Museum of São Paulo, Brazil, 1993; Brazilian Sculpture Museum, São Paulo, Brazil, 1988; Forma Furniture Showroom, São Paulo, Brazil, 1987; Brazil's Pavilion at Expo '70, Osaka, Japan, 1970; Paulo Mendes da Rocha Residence, São Paulo, Brazil, 1960; Paulistano Athletic Club, São Paulo, Brazil, 1958

> ❝ ARCHITECTURE IS A HUMAN ENDEAVOR INSPIRED BY THE NATURE ALL AROUND US. WE MUST TRANSFORM NATURE; FUSE SCIENCE, ART, AND TECHNOLOGY INTO A SUBLIME STATEMENT OF HUMAN DIGNITY. ❞

**Paulo Mendes da Rocha Residence, São Paulo, 1960**
The architect's residence is embedded in a small hill and surrounded by gardens. The one-story house, which is on raised concrete piers, excels in maximizing the use of one of his favorite building materials, prefabricated and mass-produced reinforced concrete.

**ESSENTIALLY, THERE IS NO PRIVATE SPACE, THERE ARE ONLY VARYING DEGREES OF PUBLICNESS.**

The Brazilian Sculpture Museum was meant to bring together sculpture and ecology in the same space. *Below:* An early sketch of how the museum would integrate various elements of building and the environment.

**Defining Architecture** For me, architecture is place edified, the spot where the piles were driven in, the straight line of the seafront created so that ships could tie up there. Winds, waters, tides. Physics, mathematics, science. . . . Architecture embraces something larger than building alone; in a wide context it has to do with the determination and construction of a structural basis for human installations. . . .

This dimension of enterprise, of transformation of place, seems to me to be the vital question in architecture. A project . . . has to grow from the whole in every direction. After, using technique, we build each element: solids, fluids, air. That is what architecture should be. _ Armelle Lavalou and Maria Beatriz de Castro, *L'Architecture d'Aujourd'hui*, April 1997

**The Museum as Character** Each of my museums has its specific character, because each stems from very diverse conditions. . . . If I think of the Brazilian Sculpture Museum, it reminds me of a sort of inner microcosm surrounded by walls, with large pools, on multi-levels and covered by a large, reinforced-concrete cantilever. Basically, the built structure has in turn become a gigantic concrete sculpture. . . . The museum concept, however, can also be extended to something broader, beyond the physical boundaries of its spaces. The "museum of museums," in my opinion, is the city with all its contradictions, but also with all its stratifications of time. _ "Concrete Poetry," *Domus*, May 2006

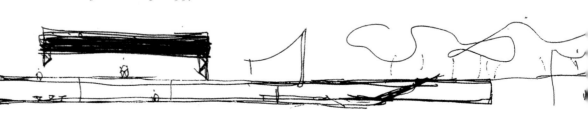

# SÃO PAULO 1988
# BRAZILIAN SCULPTURE
## MUSEUM

The MUBE [Museu Brasileiro da Escultura] was originally conceived as a museum of sculpture and ecology. The concept envisaged the setting up of exchange programs between the MUBE and its near neighbor, the Museum of Light and Sound, supplementing the latter's cultural activities. This led to the idea that the new museum should portray certain special features of the landscape— water features, a large grove of trees, bromeliads and indigenous flowers—within a characteristic Brazilian garden, designed by the landscape architect Roberto Burle Marx. The museum was also to house the city's sculpture collection, taking responsibility for its documentation and subsequent curatorship. In the same field, there was also a plan to mount a large-scale cultural project involving the restoration and relocation of the city's sculptural artifacts and the organizing of temporary exhibitions within the museum complex.

With these considerations in mind, it is possible to see the Sculpture Museum as a garden with a large shaded area and a sunken open-air theater. The main building is not visible from outside except through a portal, symbolic guardian of the garden as well as reference point and a creator of scale for the observer approaching the sculptures. This simple form of protection, a type of loggia or portal, is 12 meters wide, with a span of 60 meters. Taking advantage of the differences in levels at the perimeter of the property, the design presents the museum in a sense as a false basement facing inward and adopts the form of the surface-level terrain. _ Annette Spiro, *Paulo Mendes da Rocha Works and Projects*, Sulgen, Switzerland: Niggli, 2002

In the case of a museum primarily devoted to sculptures, which is something rather charged with symbolism, and for reasons of memory, I thought it best to evoke a cavern, or something like that. But nothing that refers to or produces theories. Not touching the soil was never a stylistic issue. It's just that the soil suddenly assumed a value for us that it didn't have before. _ Paulo Mendes da Rocha, *Paulo Mendes da Rocha Fifty Years*, New York: Rizzoli, 2007

The block it [the museum] stands on has a slope of 4 meters and is in the Jardim Europea, an area of townhouses and luxuriant vegetation. Triangular in form, it is delineated by the avenida Europa, which crosses the city from its center to the Rio Pinheiros, a rift valley omnipresent in the geomorphology of São Paulo. The project rises up from recent road-cut and age-old topography, its construction following the limits of the land. It reveals the tracing of roads and sits on the ground in the movement of the slope.

From the avenue it looks like a garden; from the rua Alemanha, like an edifice. The museum goes beyond narration; it does not emerge from the site like a closed box. The slabs that cover the partly underground internal spaces form perfectly horizontal esplanades. The open-air exhibition garden is one of Burle Marx's last landscaping projects. Set in the transversal axis, perpendicular to the avenue, a beam . . . establishes scale for the sculptures on show. In its shadow, spectacles and events take place. Its free-running aerial line gives the museum its identity and regulates fluid continuity between spaces. _ Armelle Lavalou and Maria Beatriz de Castro, *L'Architecture d'Aujourd'hui,* April 1997

Because the museum is primarily devoted to sculpture, da Rocha wanted a space that was cavelike, while still remaining carefully integrated into the surrounding landscape. *Bottom:* One of the sculpture galleries.

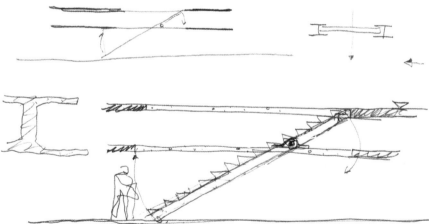

The Forma Furniture showroom features a window strip across the front revealing the contents of the building. *Above:* A concept sketch of the Forma showroom interior.

SÃO PAULO 1987
# FORMA FURNITURE SHOWROOM

The [Forma] store explores the resourcefulness of an architecture which, although discreet and serene, is nevertheless radical. It allows for maximum visibility by displaying products in an elevated showcase window which occupies the building's entire area and looks out, like a billboard, onto an avenue of heavy and rapid traffic. Inside the store, external interference is minimal, as if in a museum, light and silent. The building has clear structural simplicity: the two opposing concrete buttresses are castles that shelter equipment and support functions. The 100-foot space between them is spanned by metal beams which sustain the store's large showroom. This solution frees up the site's total area—900 square yards—for parking. The door to the store is a retractable staircase. _ Paulo Mendes da Rocha, *Paulo Mendes da Rocha Fifty Years*, New York: Rizzoli, 2007

## THE NEED FOR A NEW CONSCIOUSNESS

The rapprochement between America and Europe, and therewith a rekindling of the discussion among architects on an international level, is very important for us all. Before the background of the civilizations that were destroyed, a new consciousness in and about America is urgently needed.

It is deeply interesting how we contemplate the question of human habitation, of architecture and the design of cities. Not only upon the old continent—meaning the Western, Christian culture with all the mistakes that it made—but also upon the American continent and in the countries of Asia and Africa. We live in an age when the formulation of this question is also an eminently political one. The attempt to undertake a critical revision is both deeply interesting and extremely pressing. _ Annette Spiro, *Paulo Mendes da Rocha Works and Projects*, Sulgen, Switzerland: Niggli, 2002

In the Americas, our eyes turn toward the notion of building cities in nature, establishing new rationales about the state of the waters, plains, and mountains, the spatiality of a continent, new horizons for our imagination in the shape and ingenuity of the things we are destined to build. _ Paulo Mendes da Rocha, *Paulo Mendes da Rocha Fifty Years*, New York: Rizzoli, 2007

One never builds something finished. But it is important, however, that there be continuity. Memory is the thread; it is always new. For it is false to think that memory is something that belongs to the past. It is the memory of all things that is capable of surprising history by creating something anew. Therein exists a correlation that I find to be very important: What is missing is a genuine critique of architecture. . . . It gets lost in questions relating to the context, to the meanings, to questions very specific to architecture, forcing one therein toward a systemization that is essentially absurd. It fails to recognize that architecture is much more a discourse that cannot stand independent of the knowledge and conscience of man. _ Annette Spiro, *Paulo Mendes da Rocha Works and Projects*, Sulgen, Switzerland: Niggli, 2002

## "THE ANGUISH OF INFLUENCE"

Maybe it's a sentence, like Harold Bloom said: You can't avoid suffering what he called "the anguish of influence," in the creative sense. But I would prefer to put it as follows: I believe that I have always admired the power of Alfonso Eduardo Reidy, Roberto Burle Marx, Oscar Niemeyer, and Vilanova Artigas, but without forgetting, naturally, my childhood memories—that blustering wind, all that water, the Prata basin, the Amazon basin, eight thousand kilometers of coastline, ships, etc. This awareness, and the joy of being able to live alongside the Arabs, blacks, Iberians, Dutch. . . . This is a country that—like everything good around us—has deep and bitter contradictions, but is nonetheless highly creative, very fertile. _ Paulo Mendes da Rocha, *Paulo Mendes da Rocha Fifty Years*, New York: Rizzoli, 2007

I love the unknown architects who realized Stonehenge, I love the architects who realized the pyramids of Cairo, a machine of its own construction, an inclined plane, which permits one to place a stone 130 meters high—marvelous. I like Palladio, and I'm a very close friend of Luigi Snozzi, an architect who I hold in great esteem. _ Paulo Mendes da Rocha interview by *Design Boom*, July 2, 2007

## THE COLONIAL PAST

Along comes some poor refugee family and rents one of those big mansions, sublets the rooms, and it's there that my father, in the third or fourth chapter of his difficult life, right at the beginning of the crisis of [19]29, sets up home. I was born in 1928. I was born [in] the middle of the crisis and went on to live through the coups, revolutions (1932 in São Paulo), the war, the atomic bomb, but also man's first voyages into space. What bolstered us were the great feats of the twentieth century, as Hobsbawm [Eric Hobsbawm is a prominent British Marxist historian and author] said: a terrible, violent century, but nonetheless the century of the Soviet revolution and the fundamental elucidation of the transformations of labor. And we're still living all this today. The difficulties Brazil, or São Paulo, has today are the same as those faced by Madrid, Paris, London, Lisbon: the blacks, Indians, Algerians, Moroccans, Sumatrans, Borneans are all there. In other words, what we're living today, in the sense of building a new vision for ourselves, is a revision of the colonial past, of colonial imperialism.

Many people might think that these issues lie outside or beyond architecture. But no! They predate it—they helped found it. Any building you see and that somehow moves you has to contain all of this in some form, not explicitly, but in a way you can't quite put your finger on—lyrically, you know? _ Paulo Mendes da Rocha, *Paulo Mendes da Rocha Fifty Years*, New York: Rizzoli, 2007

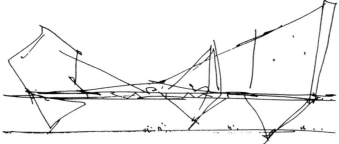

## SÃO PAULO 1958
# PAULISTANO ATHLETIC CLUB The

structure is of reinforced concrete, with steel cables suspending the metal roof. Its overall form generates a sense of lightness and transparency.

The building is distinguished by great clarity of structure. Its spaces have a certain "civic" quality. A long rectangular platform—serving as an esplanade and accommodating peripheral activities—has the actual arena at its center. This is a reinforced concrete ring structure; its six load-bearing supports detach themselves from the space and, pre-tensioned by steel cables, take the load of the central metal element. The combination of these two techniques gives the buildings lightness and three-dimensionality and adds a nuance of technology. The road bustling with traffic and local business activity, the esplanade, and the club's internal gardens made into interrelating areas are designed to encourage other activities not necessarily related to sports programs. _ Annette Spiro, *Paulo Mendes da Rocha Works and Projects,* Sulgen, Switzerland: Niggli, 2002

**Transformative Construction** Construction is a transformation of space. When you build, you need to imagine the universe is something entirely new that didn't exist before. _ Bonnie Churchill, *Christian Science Monitor,* April 13, 2006

**"Blocks in a Cathedral "** A writer is always concerned with seduction, that is, that the person who reads the first paragraph of his book doesn't give up there, but goes on to read the second. . . . It's the same with the construction. What am I going to do to keep the guy's attention long enough to engage him, to hook him so he stays to the end and gets what I'm trying to say? So perhaps you could say that in literature words are like the blocks in a cathedral. It's a construction too. _ Paulo Mendes da Rocha, *Paulo Mendes da Rocha Fifty Years,* New York: Rizzoli, 2007

**❝ THE SENSE OF MOVEMENT COMES FROM THE TERRAIN ITSELF, NOT FROM THE ARCHITECTURAL STRUCTURE. ❞**

## OSAKA 1970
# BRAZIL'S PAVILION AT EXPO '70

The Brazilian Pavilion project . . . is an architectural study on the relationship between nature and construction. Essentially, the pavilion consists of a concrete-and-glass deck, resting lightly on the ground beneath. Instead of perching it on supports in conventional style, the design called for the topography of the plot to be altered to make contact with, and support, the structure at three points. The sense of movement comes from the terrain itself, not from the architectural structure. Except when seen close up, the support used appears to be simply a point of contact between two surfaces, but it is in fact a highly sophisticated device evolved

in response to the frequent earthquakes in Japan and capable of withstanding horizontal forces in addition to normal vertical load. The only support, which looks like a support in the conventional sense, is highly symbolic. It is made of two intersecting arches and provides the pavilion's sole vertical note. This support plays on the building's location and the urbanization of the country-side, denoting a place where people come together—a magnetic attraction, so to speak. _ Annette Spiro, *Paulo Mendes da Rocha Works and Projects*, Sulgen, Switzerland: Niggli, 2002

# THE STATE MUSEUM OF SÃO PAULO

*Da Rocha's design for the State Museum of São Paulo was a renovation of a nineteenth-century neo-Renaissance building.*

The tower of the museum is a new artifact, like a computer or air conditioner that someone wanted to buy. The museum, today, would like to have climate-controlled environments, special precincts in which to store the collection, restoration rooms, etc. From the historical point of view, the right thing to do would be to not touch it and completely restore it. And, if possible, assign it to a certain functionalist void, so that the whole thing can just shine in and for itself, leaving all the gadgets and technical devices for some new building, an annex. What we projected, at the end of the day, is precisely that: an annex. Just that the ideal ground floor in this case was the atrium of the museum, emptied of all the makeshift stop-gaps that were put in there over time . . . so we imagined an intriguing tower rising out of the middle of the palace, more or less like Aldo Rossi's Theatre of the World (1980), a tower you can never quite figure out where it is. It's a kind of phantasmagorical, frightening form, and yet not something altogether strange. In [Rossi's] case, it's as if the steeple of the San Marco had taken a stroll between the canals. In our case, the museum is already surrounded by high towers on all sides, so the appearance of a vertical steel box there—one museum holding up another— is perfectly doable. Preferably a bland tower, without any architectonic character other than its monumental presence as a tower, unavoidably equipped with mechanical lifts, machinery to help mount the exhibitions, linking the galleries to the collection's storerooms. _ Paulo Mendes da Rocha, *Paulo Mendes da Rocha Fifty Years,* New York: Rizzoli, 2007

# ❝❝ THE FLOWER OF ALL KNOWLEDGE IS THE CITY. THE ARCHITECT'S INTENT IS TO IMAGINE A CITY FOR ALL. ❞❞

## ARCHITECTURE FOR HUMAN HABITATION

The ideal of architects is building with precision to support the unpredictability of human life. The objective is dignity—to sustain creativity for all. Buildings are the instruments of life. _ Linda Hales, *Washington Post*, October 27, 2006

Expressions such as dance, speech, poetry, and literature are fundamental. Architecture is, more than one would like to grant it, an exemplary discourse, for human habitation is something fundamental. This is why the idea of architecture in the sense of isolated buildings is so hopelessly dumb. _ Annette Spiro, *Paulo Mendes da Rocha Works and Projects*, Sulgen, Switzerland: Niggli, 2002

Architecture must respond with absolute clarity to pressing issues, all related to the fundamental situations that sustain human life. _ Paulo Mendes da Rocha, *Paulo Mendes da Rocha Fifty Years*, New York: Rizzoli, 2007

Architecture is a discourse of knowledge. I project what I imagine people could desire—I have a delirious vision of what this might be; I don't design for myself—I don't follow my own needs. _ Paulo Mendes da Rocha interview by *Design Boom*, July 2, 2007

## "A CONSTANT SEARCH FOR BALANCE"

The questions remain the same ones; the answers, however, must correspond to the times. One has scruples to be carried away by one's feelings. It is a struggle carried out upon the edge of a knife, because to suppress the feelings would be a stupid act. One should use them, on the contrary, as an efficient instrument. That is the dilemma! Without feelings one cannot work at all, and at the same time they should not enslave one since they can distract one from a project or a plan. It is a constant search for balance. _ Annette Spiro, *Paulo Mendes da Rocha Works and Projects, Sulgen,* Switzerland: Niggli, 2002

## THE FUTURE

We must have hope in the future. For millions and millions of years, we have been constructing the human dimension of man. . . . Shelter is the foundation of the question. Architects have to be in the forum of discussion about the future of humanity. _ Linda Hales, *Washington Post*, October 27, 2006

When da Rocha renovated the classical State Museum of São Paulo, he maintained the exterior, right, and focused on the interior. He put glass roofs over central and side courtyards, left and opposite above. *Opposite:* He reorganized gallery spaces and created metal catwalks on the upper floors.

**ARCHITECTURE IS ESSENTIAL** The most interesting part of my life is that the office has become connected to urbanistic values . . . a completely different level of contribution beyond the formal. If anything, the formal can disappear. What I'm trying to do is submerge the formal into broader ideas. That has changed the practice completely. . . . I've gone full circle. I have opportunities to make certain kinds of contributions because of the magnitude of the work, of the nature of the program, or its position in the city. The work has become explicitly political. _ Thom Mayne interview by Jeffrey Inaba, *Volume*, no. 13, 2007

I'm chasing an architecture that engages and demands inquiry. Architecture is not passive, not decorative. It is essential. . . . It affects us directly and profoundly. It has the potential to impact behavior and the quality of everyday life. _ Thom Mayne, Pritzker Prize acceptance speech, 2005

When architecture engages social, cultural, political, and ethical currents, it has the potential to transform the way we see the world and our place in it. _ Thom Mayne, courtesy Morphosis, February 2007

# THOM MAYNE

**BORN:** January 19, 1944, Waterbury, Connecticut

**EDUCATION:** M.Arch., Harvard University Graduate School of Design, Cambridge, Massachusetts, 1978; B.Arch., USC School of Architecture, Los Angeles, 1968

**OFFICE:** 3440 Wesley Street, Culver City, California, 90232
Tel: +1 424-258-6200
studio@morphosis.net, www.morphosis.com

**PROJECTS FEATURED:** Wayne L. Morse U.S. Courthouse, Eugene, Oregon, 2006; San Francisco Federal Building, California, 2006; Caltrans District 7 Headquarters, Los Angeles, 2004; Diamond Ranch High School, Pomona, California, 1999; Sixth Street Residence, Los Angeles, 1988

**❝ I WORK WITH INERT MATTER. I ORGANIZE IT. ❞**

**San Francisco Federal Building, 2006**
The large government building was part of
the General Services Administration's
Design Excellence program initiated in 1994.

### SAN FRANCISCO 2006
# SAN FRANCISCO FEDERAL
**BUILDING** Our primary interest was to produce a performance-driven building that would fundamentally transform its urban surroundings, the nature of the workplace, and the experiences of the people who use it while making intelligent use of natural resources. _ Thom Mayne, courtesy Morphosis, February 2007

This building's envelope utilizes a dynamic, metabolic skin. It opens and closes. Like the car, a hybrid, it replaces 70 percent of the AC demand with natural ventilation, a first for a tall building in this country.

We did no two-dimensional drawings for this project. Three-dimensional models provided a continuity from the initial concept to construction document. . . . It allows us to continually move back and forth between micro and macro. _ Thom Mayne, "Remarks on Building Information Modeling," AIA Convention, May 2005

**The Significance of Looking Green** *The San Francisco Federal Building was the first office building in the United States to use natural ventilation instead of air conditioning. Mayne has been asked how green a building should "look" to confer its status of being environmentally responsible.*

**Views of the southeast façade of the San Francisco Federal Building,** *above,* **and large picture,** *opposite page.*

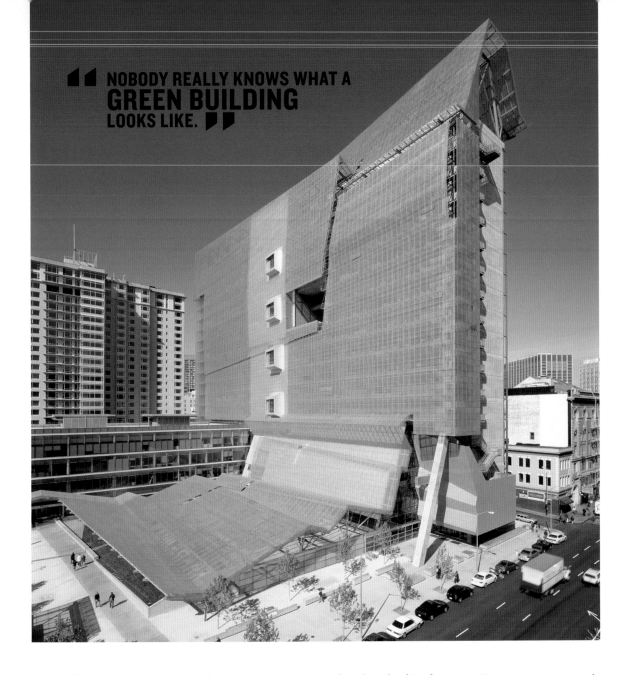

Personally, I think it's irrelevant if it's apparent or not, with the exception of schools or other cases when we've wanted to be didactic about the relationship of a building and its environment, like our NOAA building [National Oceanographic and Atmospheric Administration in Suitland, Maryland]. For the Europeans it's a normal parameter.

It's like fire codes and building codes. Nobody really knows what a green building looks like. I think we will see more different forms. . . . Design is a manifestation of the forces that are driving it, [but] buildings are slower than consumer electronics to reflect change. People are more conservative about them. . . . You can like or dislike the building, but you have to understand its relationship to its purpose and its ecological,

cultural, and political context. We overcame some anti-modern bias because it hit the criteria. . . . Whether a building looks green is irrelevant. What matters is the amount of BTUs per square meter and $CO_2$ per capita or per square meter. _ Thom Mayne interview by Ted Smalley Bowen, *Architectural Record*, November 2007

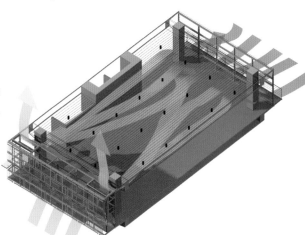

"That stainless-steel cladding allows us to move air and save about $500,000 a year in air-conditioning bills."_ Julie V. Iovine, *New York Times*, May 17, 2004

## STARCHITECTS

I am kind of a shy person, kind of private person, and I like to say what I want to say. I am not that diplomatic. I get many questions like, "How can I become famous?" And I go, "Oh dear, you don't have to worry about it, it won't happen. Do your work." . . . Like my mom said to my brother and me, "Do your work first, don't worry about money, don't worry about anything else, just do your work." The part of it is the absurdity of the expression of the personality, which in itself is an autonomous territory, which has nothing to do with your work and nothing to do with architecture. You have to resist, somehow, capitalistic tendencies, or something like that. . . . They (fame seekers) should not worry about this that much. Just stay with architecture. I don't think this personality issue is useful to architecture. . . . _ Thom Mayne interview by Orhan Ayyuce, archinect.com, July 20, 2007

## MAYNE AND THE MYTH OF THE BAD BOY

The "bad boy" came from one article in *Metropolis* about three years ago. The guy wanted to write a long article, and he asked me if he can stay with me for four days, just following me—meetings, clients. And I did that. He followed me around the clock. At one point somebody asked me if I changed over the years personally. I said yes, I have, I was a much more private person, my position artistically would be much more parallel to that of a poet, or musician, or someone who writes esoteric novels; I could have been a Joyce, or that kind of thing. And I said something like "in my first twenty years you couldn't find a client that would talk to me. They would all say 'arrogant asshole.'" And he wrote that. First of all, I speak in a certain way. I love hyperboles, sometimes, to make a simple point, I radically oversimplify things. It was rhetorical, but he wrote it. And what I've found out about the people who write, very few of them have a fucking clue what they are writing about. They go over what other people write, and if it was said twice it must be true. Three newspapers in Madrid call me *el chico malo*, bad boy. . . .

The "bad boy," or however you want to call him, connects with a certain kind of activism—I am interested in building things. I am interested in making it happen. An architect has to be tough; if you are not, you are in the wrong profession. Architecture is the intersection between the artistic and the social. If you are a politician you have to be tough, but they don't call you a "bad boy," they say you "deal with reality," right? I deal with contractors, builders—if you cannot deal with them and be tough you are going to be beaten down, and there is no architecture. When you get older, you become more relaxed, more comfortable. When you are younger you are fighting harder. _ Thom Mayne interview by Vladimir Paperny, paperny.com, April 2005

I was intoxicated with the idea of autonomy as a young man, and saw architecture as being something against the status quo. In the first twenty-five years, I didn't have a client who would talk to me afterward. They said, "Arrogant bastard." Because I just had to plow through, and I did, to get it done. _ Arthur Lubow, *New York Times*, January 16, 2005

I was totally insistent that I was going to do it the way I wanted to do it. The "bad boy" somehow became part of that, behaving not within the norm of expectations. _ Thom Mayne, *Life & Times*, KCET-TV, May 1, 2006

I think my clients would tell I'm a problem solver. I'm not there to agree with people. I'm there to articulate a point of view. Am I insistent and tenacious? Absolutely. I could not get this work done if I was not. I've grown up a little bit. I understand that importance of the negotiation. It is a collective act. _ Robin Pogrebin, *New York Times*, March 21, 2005

When people attack me, I feel extremely comfortable. I go right to work. I'm just used to that. I don't work for awards. I work for my projects and everybody here knows when we succeed or not. I'm not looking for validation. _ Thom Mayne, *Life & Times*, KCET-TV, May 1, 2006

Although the windows are barely visible on Mayne's Caltrans building, opposite page, there are in fact more than 1,000 of them. Light and temperature sensors on the west side of the building, opposite above, open and close the windows automatically in the morning; similar sensors on the east side of the building take over in the afternoon.

## LOS ANGELES 2004
# CALTRANS DISTRICT 7 HEADQUARTERS
This is a kind of a fascinating project. These are the people that make freeways, design and build freeways. Right? So what can be better than working in Ground Zero? This is at 1st and Main, across from City Hall in Los Angeles. And these people have built infrastructure that make Los Angeles Los Angeles. If you see L.A. as the twentieth-century prototype, like it or not, it is. So we have got a building that totally fits my interest. It's unfinished. It's a continuous line that represents the continuation of a building that represents the development of the freeway. It's made out of tough materials,

concrete and the same materials they use. And everything is infrastructure. The idea of the infrastructure
of the freeway and infrastructure of the building
couldn't be a nicer program for a lot of our interests.
Now we are using light as a medium. The surfaces
are actually light. _ Thom Mayne interview by Charlie
Rose, *Charlie Rose*, December 2, 2005

## MAYNE ON MAYNE

I have no interest in making this world perfect . . . rather, I am interested in contributing to, and sometimes preserving, its imperfections. _ Thom Mayne, *A+U: Architecture and Urbanism*, Special Issue, June 1994

I'm never totally interested in how a work looks. To me, it's already there on its own. It's there by itself. Because of that, in a way, I think after it's completed, after it's done, I'm very much a viewer, and I'm seeing like you are. _ Thom Mayne, in a lecture given at UI-Urbana-Champaign School of Architecture, December 12, 1992

tial assumptions and then continue to investigate and reinvestigate our initial responses. . . . We remain attuned to the in-between conditions—whether in form or in use—to explore an architecture that negotiates a territory for hybridization, for negotiating the contradictory realities that form the basis of our work. . . . _ Thom Mayne, *Fresh Morphosis, 1998–2004*, New York: Rizzoli, 2006

We tend to value discontinuity, randomness, each investigation generated out of a nexus of individual tensions and concerns. . . . Perhaps the only constant in our work has been perpetual mutation. _ Thom Mayne, *Morphosis*, London: Phaidon, 2003

> " ARCHITECTURE IS A DISCIPLINE THAT TAKES TIME AND PATIENCE. IF ONE SPENDS ENOUGH YEARS WRITING COMPLEX NOVELS ONE MIGHT BE ABLE, SOMEDAY, TO CONSTRUCT A RESPECTABLE HAIKU. "

You become interesting because you're doing something compelling, you're doing something that has a broader interest, you're succeeding in certain things, you're uncovering new worlds. I'm ambitious in that sense, if that's ambition. _ Thom Mayne interview by Jeffrey Inaba, *Volume*, no. 13, 2007

What interests me as an architect is trying to appropriate what's idiosyncratic to each particular project. . . . Regardless of this effort to differentiate, there are traces of repetitions. . . . The whole raison d'être for our operational strategies is precisely to challenge the similarities, to push, to evolve. . . . _ Thom Mayne interview by Yoshio Futagawa, *GA Interview*, April 2005

### MAYNE ON MORPHOSIS: "ATTUNED TO THE IN-BETWEEN"

We have long sought to bring more to bear to a problem, not less; to replace and rework problems that have long been solved. . . . Among the threads that I can trace from the beginning are those related to our process: It is a reiterative process whereby we question our ini-

We understand our arena of operation to be one marked by contradiction, conflict, change, and dynamism. And to that end we are interested in producing work that contributes to the conversation, that adds yet another strain to what some may hear as the cacophony of modern life. We hear it as the music of reality. . . .

I suppose that our method does somewhat resemble that of Canetti's doglike writer obsessed with sticking his damp nose into everything, insatiably turning over the earth only to come back to dig it up once again. . . . _ Thom Mayne design philosophy, morphosis.com

What is required now are limitations—an understanding of our work as part of day-to-day ordinary activity, building on what Stravinsky called a "resisting foundation." Architecture rests upon the immutable givens that compose it: places, histories, characters, and the forces of our planet. . . . Rather than reinforcing dominant values we seek recombinations and juxtapositions that might appear to be contradictory—allowing the unrepresentable to be perceivable. _ Thom Mayne, *A+U: Architecture and Urbanism*, Special Issue, June 1994

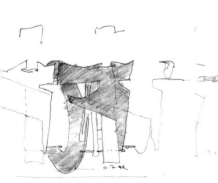

### POMONA 1999
# DIAMOND RANCH HIGH SCHOOL

Most people . . . think this is a private school. . . . And it's proof of the power of architecture, to my mind, that if you are allowed to pursue ideas, you can really kind of take something in a very different direction. What I was so interested in in this project gets back to some of the ideas of what architecture is

or isn't. It was not architecture that's accommodating a school. It was the notion of an architecture which has symbolic value, which participates in education. _ Thom Mayne interview by Charlie Rose, *Charlie Rose*, December 2, 2005

Diamond Ranch High School speaks to its students experientially through a symbolic, physically kinetic

architectural language. Two rows of fragmented forms are set tightly on either side of a long central "canyon" or street that cuts through the face of the hillside like a geologic fault line, marking the status of the campus as a reinterpreted landscape. The buildings' angled walls and canted volumes establish a non-normative yet discernible formal language, a series of discrete and highly ordered forms in the process of becoming. Cantilevered volumes project dramatically into space, roofscapes fold and bend *like shifting geologic plates*. At the top of the narrow entry stair the walls seem to part to provide an unexpected pedestrian highway that manifests the school's sense of community while also connoting an urban environment in stark juxtaposition to the school's suburban context. This interior street is meant to provide an *intensification of experience* parallel to that found in the dense urban spaces of cities such as New York or nearby Los Angeles, where diverse elements interact fortuitously and the energy of street culture is most often found. . . . As with the concern for blurring the boundaries between public and private, we have been engaged in exploring the hybrid territory between building and site, attempting to transcend the traditional figure-ground opposition of passive site versus active building. _ Thom Mayne, *Morphosis,* London: Phaidon, 2003

**Education: "Inspiring Inquiry"** Education is the social glue of our diverse society. I believe that architecture can engage deeply in the act of education both by providing an environment that engenders freedom of thought, creativity, and curiosity, and as a subject of study in its own right.

Inspiring inquiry is at the heart of our responsibility in educating our young people, and architecture has the enormous potential to encourage inquiry and provoke curiosity. As architects, we must address the pragmatic territories at the highest level; but if we fail to capture the virtual territory—that is, the territory of the mind of the student—then we risk constructing another mediocre building that will not spark the creativity, imagination, and optimism that are the birthright of our young citizens. _ Thom Mayne, courtesy Morphosis, March 2007

I have [taught] for thirty years. I can't imagine not doing it. Actually, I'm doing it less and I miss it. I think when you teach, you start over again. It's extremely healthy to have to go back and continually rethink what is it when you ask the simplest questions, what is architecture, what does it mean to start architecture, what does it mean to end architecture, and to go through that process. And it keeps you young. I still think I'm twenty-eight, twenty-nine years old, because I'm always around people that are twenty-five to thirty-five years old. _ Thom Mayne interview by Charlie Rose, *Charlie Rose,* December 2, 2005

**⬛⬛ I WANTED SOMETHING OPTIMISTIC. . . . THE WHOLE IDEA WAS FOR THE BUILDING TO BE A PART OF THE EDUCATIONAL PROCESS. ⬛⬛**

The site for the Diamond Ranch High School was so steeply sloped it was considered by some to be "unbuildable." When Mayne completed the project, the land was shaped in conjunction with the architecture, rather than shaped to accommodate it.

## DESIGN IS A FORM OF POLITICAL NEGOTIATION. ▪▪

Ribbons of steel envelop the Wayne L. Morse U.S. Courthouse in Oregon, above and opposite. For Mayne, building a courthouse for the 21st century was an exceptional opportunity. *Above:* The courthouse atrium.

### EUGENE 2006
# WAYNE L. MORSE
# U.S. COURTHOUSE

We're going to build a glass box. And it's an absolute symbolic statement of a chief justice, [in] Oregon in this case, who refuses to acknowledge the necessity of a defensive strategy. In fact, it is promoting a new openness. _William L. Hamilton, *New York Times,* October 25, 2001

As our working methods became more tangible, transparent, it formed the basis of our relationship, allowing him [U.S. District Judge Michael Hogan] to adjust the many preconceptions he brought to the table. As part of the process, he wanted to see projects that I admired. We met in Paris, spent a week discussing the issues pertinent in developing a twenty-first-century courthouse, visiting Jean Nouvel's courthouse in Nantes and Richard Rogers's law courts in Bordeaux. And through all of this, he's open to exploring with us a future work, with no idea of what the project would end up being, understanding the importance of the early stages of questioning, embracing the inherent potential. _ Thom Mayne interview by Yoshio Futagawa, *GA Interview,* April 2005

Probably the most unique project that we've ever done, and probably the oddest in terms of our kind of firm—kind of redefining a courthouse, working with a fascinating client, Judge Hogan. And believe it or not, this building is based on a series of conventions, and continues those conventions. And it starts with a *piano nobile,* a stair, that takes you to the main level. . . . It's about the shift of our ideas as they move through history but maintain continuities. _ Thom Mayne interview by Charlie Rose, *Charlie Rose,* December 2, 2005

**Designing with Technology** The time compression of digital models allowed us to produce a large number of alternative concepts, responding to the demands of a complex set of variables—programmatic, urban, and human. . . . In this case, we did maybe thirty-four, thirty-five models within a two-month period, which radically changes our ability to look at huge numbers of options. . . . In this project, we wanted fluidity of connections, which we translated into surfaces representing the iconic status of our court, which we tested and modeled, both virtually and physically, using the same medium. Again, we used rapid-prototyping; hands are not touching this. . . . We can produce these kinds of models every evening and work at a pace that's much more connected to how we think, both in terms of detailing and large issues and in terms of the speed that we want to move at, since our minds are always moving much quicker than the mechanical aspects of the work. . . . _ Thom Mayne, "Remarks on Building Information Modeling," AIA Convention, May 2005

**The Public and Architecture** I think one of the issues with architecture that I've come to realize is that architecture is a practice, and the public seems to carry a somewhat conservative kind of sensibility, whereas people would have no problem with a television set or the automobile or set of headphones, or wherever you want to go, in terms of "modern design," or something that's just contemporary. . . . I think we have kind of no histories, we're still looking at buildings as a kind of fake history. You build buildings that look like new, old buildings, and we are uncomfortable with the fact that in Europe, there is no problem. If you're in Italy, there is kind of too much history, and it's alright, you are allowed to build modern buildings and you can attach them to old buildings. _ Thom Mayne interview by Charlie Rose, *Charlie Rose*, December 2, 2005

Most people, for some reason, when it comes to architecture, want a kind of fake nineteenth-century building, and it's not where we are at the moment. You can sense when a building is of its time. It's somehow relevant of who we are and how we live; I'll go back to the values that we live in a time of change and movement. Everything is dynamic, and we actually make a material of it. We make it permanent, right? We take some idea, a snapshot of kind of who we are, and those ideas find their way into the work. _ Thom Mayne, *Life & Times*, KCET-TV, May 1, 2006

## ❮❮ A THRESHOLD PROJECT IN EVERY RESPECT. ❯❯

For the Sixth Street Residence, the architect became an urban archaeologist of sorts, adapting a variety of existing artifacts to a modern space. *Opposite page, from the top:* Mayne in a meeting in the Morphosis conference room; at the Studio Wolf Prix at the University of Applied Arts in Vienna, 2006; and with a model in Morphosis shop in Santa Monica.

### LOS ANGELES 1988
# SIXTH STREET RESIDENCE

The house's conceptual genesis lay in the idea of salvaging industrial artifacts and urban debris—a sort of contemporary archaeology—and reincorporating them within the domestic space. These discarded fragments of spent technology are employed against the grain: They distort scale, subvert typological expectations, and assert functional neologisms. They act both as non sequiturs and as a connective tissue that gives the project its overall coherence. This initial appropriation led immediately to an attack of the cube. . . . The core of the interior space is defined by an oculus that cuts through the main floor, illuminated from above by a giant skylight and inhabited at the ground level by a glass cube enclosing the shower. Acting as the focal point and centerpiece of the living space, the unconventional shower subverts a kind of taken-for-granted domestic prudery, placing functions of hygiene and the body at the center of the home rather than banishing them to its margins. Both lucid and earnest, the shower cube acts as a wry commentary on visibility and invisibility, privacy and secularity. _ Thom Mayne, *Morphosis,* London: Phaidon, 2003

## A CHILD OF THE 60s: "INSTITUTIONALIZED OUTSIDERNESS"

I remember being in this little town below Marrakech, Morocco, in the middle of nowhere and observing this little boy coming out of this village house with a very up-to-date Walkman. As I got closer, I could hear it kind of leaking out of his ears and it was, of course, Mick Jagger and the Rolling Stones. That's extremely interesting to me because what Mick Jagger is talking about is probably a bit more influential than anything we'll do in terms of changing things. _ Thom Mayne, in a lecture given at UI-Urbana-Champaign School of Architecture, December 12, 1992

I think especially in this country, the development of a young architect as you mature moves from something that's more conceptual to something that's more connected to the realities of our political, cultural, social, economic world. . . . _ Thom Mayne interview by Charlie Rose, *Charlie Rose*, December 2, 2005

As a young architect, for me it wasn't about ambition. I had a very naïve, pure idea about architecture. When I started out, I was incredibly naïve politically. I was driven by my interests and they were quite detached from that real world. . . . Somehow I managed to keep that going well into my late thirties, focusing on drawings and small projects. Simultaneously architecture shifted from a more provincial, geographically dominated culture to a global one. At the time I was interested in Jerzy Kosinski's *Being There*. It's a miniature novel about existence. There was an awareness that as architects we didn't exist in the so-called real world and that we were aware that we lived in this kind of cabal.

I didn't emerge out of that into the "real world" with medium-size commissions until I was close to forty. It was a kind of extended childhood. It came with . . . living in your own world and being comfortable with that. . . . Students today live in just the opposite environment:

> **ARCHITECTURE IS THE STORY OF HOW WE SEE OURSELVES. IT IS THE ARCHITECT'S JOB TO SERVICE EVERYDAY LIFE.**

They are hugely aware of Realpolitik while in school and seem to be immediately interested in success, but success as defined by the outside world—that is, in capitalist terms. I look back and somehow we escaped that. We were protected against it both by the era, that unusual time in American history during which the left had a very strong voice, and by a critical mass of architects working in the same way. We had an institutionalized outsiderness and that was what we really aspired to. _ Thom Mayne interview by Jeffrey Inaba, *Volume*, no. 13, 2007

I'm not trying to be different, absolutely no interest in that. . . . To be an authentic person, to be a real person, to be able to somehow integrate your world, your internal world, and the world around you, [and that] has to be one of the most difficult things for human beings. If I'm talking to my boys [Mayne has two sons], that would be the first conversation. This is the difficulty in growing up. How do you maintain some authenticity of your person, including finding out who you are, by the way, because there is no authentic person, you build your own history, you live in your brain, you invent who you are. And matching that with the world, especially this world, today? Tough one. _ Thom Mayne interview by Charlie Rose, *Charlie Rose*, December 2, 2005

[Architecture is] a discipline that's so broad that it's impossible to master, and the good news is that, because you can't master it, there's never any end in sight. _ Thom Mayne, *Life & Times*, KCET-TV, May 1, 2006

**STAYING POWER** It is very important to have the commitment to persevere, and to go back to one's own education in a sense. As a woman you need the confidence that you can carry on and take new steps every time. I believe in hard work; it gives you a layer of confidence. Now we can do a lot of different projects because we have an enormous formal repertoire. The years in isolation, when we were quarantined in a sense, is like research in science. The more research you do, the more and the better the results. It was a very critical period because most people thought I would disappear or give up. _ Zaha Hadid interview by Alice Rawsthorn, for "Frieze Talks," October 21, 2005

# ZAHA HADID

**BORN:** October 31, 1950, Baghdad, Iraq; Died: March 31, 2016

**EDUCATION:** Diploma Prize, Architectural Association, School of Architecture, London, 1977

**OFFICE:** 10 Bowling Green Lane, Studio 9, London EC1R 0BQ
Tel: +44 20-7253-5147, Fax: +44 20-7251-8322
www.zaha-hadid.com

**PROJECTS FEATURED:** Phaeno Science Center, Wolfsburg, Germany, 2006; BMW Plant Central Building, Leipzig, Germany, 2005; Lois & Richard Rosenthal Center for Contemporary Art, Cincinnati, Ohio, 2003; Bergisel Ski Jump, Innsbruck, Austria, 2002; Vitra Fire Station, Weil am Rhein, Germany, 1994

**"IF I WAS A MAN, THEY WOULDN'T CALL ME A DIVA."**

**Painting of Vitra Fire Station, Weil am Rheim, 1994**
Early in her career Hadid came to the conclusion that she could not explain what she wanted to do with a project through the traditional ways of presentation—a plan, a section, an elevation. Painting allowed her to convey her ideas more clearly.

## BEING A FEMALE ARCHITECT

*Since being named a Pritzker laureate, Hadid has frequently been asked about the role that gender plays in architecture. Her responses are characteristically candid and intelligent—not only does she say that being a woman affects her status as an architect and her client relationships, it spills over into what the media writes about her, including her style and manner of dress. But Hadid also uses the Pritzker recognition as a bully pulpit to encourage women, especially students, to topple stereotypes.*

If you're tough, they tell you you're too tough. If you're not tough, you're too soft. And if you're not that then you're pushy. Every pejorative description on Earth is pasted on you. . . . Architecture is a great profession. It is also immensely demanding. But I do think it should be possible for women to survive in it without it finishing them. _ Zoë Blacker, *Building Design*, February 2, 2004

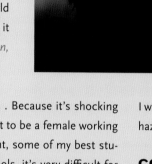

I never thought of myself as a role model. . . . Because it's shocking how in this modern time, it's still very difficult to be a female working in architecture. . . . In all the times I've taught, some of my best students were women. But outside of their schools, it's very difficult for women. . . . A lot of women are part of a team, and even if the woman is the lead person, they're always seen as the second fiddle, no matter how good they are. _ *Perspecta*, no. 37, 2005

*At the opening of the Rosenthal Center in Cincinnati, an interviewer noted that Hadid's team wore T-shirts that read, "Would they still call me a diva if I was a guy?" Was this true, the interviewer asked?*

They certainly would not talk about my rings, nor about my clothes, if I was a man. . . . And it's also the idea that there is something wrong with you if you do well. That's a British thing—if you do well it's as if there's inherently something wrong with your genetic makeup. When I went to the AA [Architectural Association, London] we were always striving to be a failure. _ Zaha Hadid interview by Alice Rawsthorn, for "Frieze Talks," October 21, 2005

One of the liberating situations in my life was that there was no stereotype, and I didn't really care what people thought and how I should dress and how I should behave: That really gave me a degree of freedom. . . . In terms of whether the male and female brains operate differently, I'm sure they do, but I couldn't say how. It depends on the degree of confidence your school or your parents give you, and whether you're male or female has a tremendous impact on that. I think this affects women a lot in their careers—if you try different things it gives you possibilities to make it to the next step. Many women don't have the encouragement and support to do that. _ Zaha Hadid interview by Rem Koolhaas, *Interview*, February 2005

## FAME AND BACKLASH

It's very difficult to think of myself as a well-known person. It always surprises me that people think of me as famous. . . . I have personally never taken it very seriously, the whole fame issue, because I've watched so many people either become hooked to it or desire it so much that it distracts from the real ambition of actually doing good work. Because that's ultimately what it's all about. . . . People always assume that fame is very glamorous, but it's not always, because the real trade of architecture is very hard work. . . . Being well known, actually, has more disadvantages than advantages, personally. . . . For a long time it actually worked against me because I was known for not building or not being able to build. So it became a real hazard. _ *Perspecta*, no. 37, 2005

## CONFORMING

From when I was ten, I wore funny clothes. I said strange things. It wasn't as if I deliberately tried to be outrageous—I was outrageous. . . . I really did not, deliberately or not, decide to conform to what people thought was acceptable. And if you don't conform there is always prejudice and punishment, because everybody wants to put you between brackets. They want you to be made out of the same mold, mass production. And it's the same thing with building. They want everything to be the same. And if you decide not to be the same, then you are crucified. _ *Perspecta*, no. 37, 2005

## FASHION

I think it's a balance, not being a fashion victim but to wear something which you feel comfortable and you enjoy wearing. . . . I think it's important to actually be able to express yourself in the way you dress. And Issey Miyake, particularly, I have a tremendous respect for and Yohji [Yamamoto]. Actually the Japanese are particularly good. And they did travel very light, compact. . . . You can carry lots of things with you when you're traveling. When you're up in your hotel, you don't have to iron them. They're perfect when you open them. So, I mean, all these things, which have to do with, on one hand, practical issues, and on the other hand, you know, fun issues. They can wear them upside down, side— you know, back to front. You have more than one gown. _ Zaha Hadid interview by Terry Gross, *Fresh Air*, National Public Radio, May 26, 2004

**Painting and Drawing** *Much attention is paid to the sci-fi beauty and geometry of Hadid's paintings and drawings, yet for the architect they are functionally important explorations when working on a project. They are laboratory experiments of a sort.*

I'm not a painter. I have to make that quite clear. I can paint, but I'm not a painter. It was clear to me in my fourth year [at the Architectural Association, London] that I could not explain or explore what I wanted to do through a normative method of presentation. Just doing a plan and a section and an elevation was not enough. _ Zaha Hadid interview by Alice Rawsthorn, for "Frieze Talks," October 21, 2005

**Drawings Tell a Story** It all started with me drawing to represent a project in a nonconventional way. I thought about architecture in a different way. I thought the tool we have to represent architecture was not useful to me, and it did not show the meaning of what I wanted to do. So I started off with really trying to devise a way of projection which was useful to me. That's how I started, trying to see it from a different angle. . . . The drawings become a storyboard. They tell you the whole story of the life of this project. _ "Interview with Zaha Hadid," *El Croquis*, no. 52, 1991

My drawings are not the building. They are drawings about the building. They are not illustrations of a final product. You have to look at it like a text. For me they are important tools because they are the only way I can see whether something is right or wrong. _ Zaha Hadid interview by Yukio Futagawa, *GA Document Extra 03*, 1996

I always design with the idea it [a building] should be built. People always thought I just liked to draw. That is not the case. All these works were intended to be built whether it is a competition, a commission, or whatever. Only when we do a drawing for London or New York is it for an idea. All these things were about not the non-possibility of building but the possibility of building. _ "Interview with Zaha Hadid," *El Croquis*, no. 52, 1991

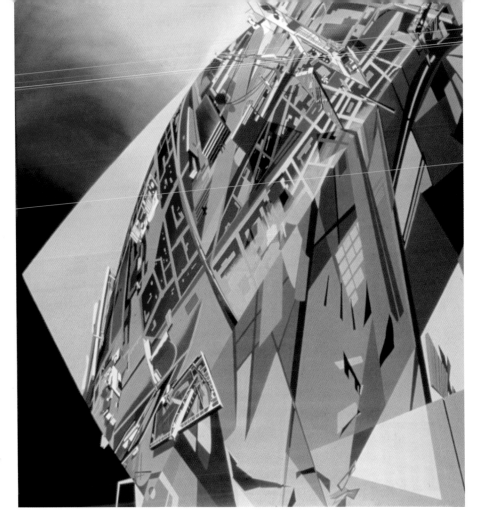

**"The Paintings Were Like Tests"** I still like black-and-white drawings a lot—really crisp line drawings. I have a personal preference for them, but I think color is not necessarily used as a decoration. It shows the temper, in a way. It also unveils the quality of the architecture. . . . Every time we painted a drawing it changed our view of how the building was actually conceived in terms of materials, and of its color. For instance, with the Peak [Hong Kong, 1983] we really had no idea about how it should be finished. By the use of drawings and painting slowly but surely we've developed a confirmed opinion. The paintings were like tests. _ Zaha Hadid interview by Alvin Boyarsky in *Zaha Hadid: Planetary Architecture Two*, London: Architectural Association, 1983

**Representation** They [the paintings] were never to do with representation. They were more to do with the quality of the project. . . . There is also the question of how to achieve transparency through a solid material. This all came through the paintings. _ Zaha Hadid interview by Yukio Futagawa, *GA Document Extra 03*, 1996

About "The World (89 Degrees)," Hadid said, the "drawing is a lens that reveals otherwise imperceptible aspects; it's a method for understanding how things can change and evolve and serve, not for crystallizing a form in a definitive way but to demonstrate the possibilities of what it can become." _ Matilda McQuaid, ed., *Envisioning Architecture: Drawings from The Museum of Modern Art*, New York: The Museum of Modern Art, 2002

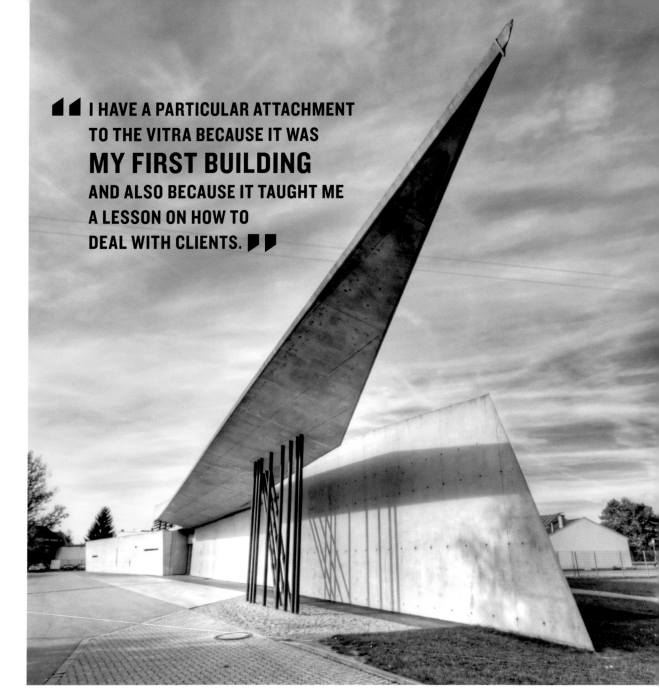

> **❝ I HAVE A PARTICULAR ATTACHMENT TO THE VITRA BECAUSE IT WAS MY FIRST BUILDING AND ALSO BECAUSE IT TAUGHT ME A LESSON ON HOW TO DEAL WITH CLIENTS. ❞**

The Vitra Fire Station was Hadid's first built project and was based in part on a series of paintings, *above* and *opposite*. The station was originally meant to serve just the factory, but when the fire district lines were redrawn, Vitra turned its firehouse into a showplace for part of its chair collection. *Above:* The fire station, as seen from the back, resembles the bow of an ocean liner.

### WEIL AM RHEIN 1994
# VITRA FIRE STATION

We were always interested in a building that could actually transform—not like in the day and the night, but could transform in function. But we always tried to design it as a fire station first, with the idea of functionality centering all the spaces around a single space.
_ Zaha Hadid interview by Yukio Futagawa, *GA Document Extra 03,* 1996

The idea was to create a space dedicated to our facilities. The chair museum and the fire station only. The idea also was for the edge, which becomes the building eventually, to become a shield from the outside. That's how the building was really located.
_ Zaha Hadid interview by Yukio Futagawa, *GA Document Extra 03,* 1996

Vitra was also very precise, like a clock. It had to be close to perfect. It underwent a lot of elimination. Four walls would become three, and then two. . . . The building had to be fit into the frame of the site and all its requirements. It was very interesting because we had to be very careful in interpreting the requirements; it was like designing a glove. How do you fit a building in perfectly with all the site lines and all the regulations? It was an outcome of an elaborate diagram of requirements, and because it was so tight it taught us to be very precise. _ Zaha Hadid interview by Yukio Futagawa, *GA Document Extra 03*, 1996

## The Site

We began to focus and zoom into the site like a lens. In a way the building does that too. The building kind of expands and retracts in both ways—physically in some ways and visually in others. . . . All the ideas became condensed onto this building, although each element was very simple. Once we established the early diagram, the walls became volumes and also became structural walls. It became more than just a play of lines, but a sort of play of volumes and how they begin to weave into each other. The intention was to make the space in the most fluid way possible. . . . We were also trying to achieve transparency not through a transparent material but while using concrete. We looked at it very intensely. Once the diagram was established it was just a matter of going through it.

The idea of landscape also came very early; the idea of what these lines could mean on the site. It was really like land art. We still have this belt—this kind of corridor we called the urban space. _ Zaha Hadid interview by Yukio Futagawa, *GA Document Extra 03*, 1996

## Color

Everybody asked the same question: Did we color the concrete because at first one part looks so much darker? And I said no, it's all the same color. But it was interesting for us also because of our use of painting in the presentation. It also informed us about the quality of the light in the building, not just the color. People always misunderstood this and thought that the color in the paintings was representative, but it was never representative. It had more to do with the quality of the building because it didn't necessarily have to be in bright colors. _ Zaha Hadid interview by Yukio Futagawa, *GA Document Extra 03*, 1996

Originally the idea was to use no color on the outside and color inside. But then I decided to make it very monotone because I felt it required that sense of purity. We wanted to use only light. I discovered that the minute you color the planes you lose the quality of the volumes; it becomes again a planar thing, and I wanted the volumes to read. _ Zaha Hadid interview by Yukio Futagawa, *GA Document Extra 03*, 1996

## Achieving Lightness

I wanted the shed to really have the ability to change. When it's closed it becomes a room, and when it's opened it's just a roof. You don't see the glass walls, they just kind of disappear. You don't feel the metal elements because when open they become very thin. _ Zaha Hadid interview by Yukio Futagawa, *GA Document Extra 03*, 1996

## The Decision to Use Concrete

I decided for this project that concrete was the most appropriate. First of all because of the functionality, but also because there was no duplication. The walls operate as two kinds of walls. The walls become structural walls and also partition walls. I was thinking that one should maintain the integrity of the structure, and they should be in concrete. . . . _ Zaha Hadid interview by Yukio Futagawa, *GA Document Extra 03*, 1996

They [the paintings] were . . . also about how we can modulate light in the building: which wall should be a wall of light and which wall should not be, and how the building transforms from the day to the night. In the day it becomes more volumetric and much harder, and at night it begins to dissolve, and some planes become more accentuated than others, so you only see some of them. What's interesting about concrete in this particular situation is the attempt to make a heavy mass light, not only through the material but through the geometry of the building—how to kind of give it a sense of lightness. _ Zaha Hadid interview by Yukio Futagawa, *GA Document Extra 03*, 1996

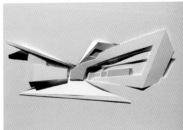

"There is also the question of how to achieve transparency through a solid material. This all came through the paintings." _ Zaha Hadid interview by Yukio Futagawa, *GA Document Extra 03*, 1996

## HONG KONG 1983
## THE PEAK COMPETITION

*Hadid's breakthrough project occurred in 1983, when she won a competition for the Peak, a private club to be located in the hills of Kowloon, overlooking Hong Kong. In a series of large dramatic paintings, Hadid proposed a transformation of the site itself by excavating the hills and using the extracted rock to build artificial cliffs. In this new topography, she interjected architectural forms of cantilevered beams and shardlike fragments. The Peak project established the importance of not only her architectural vision, but the way in which Hadid represents it. The Peak was never constructed.*

Certain drawings do tell a story. For instance, the exploded isometric of the Peak shows the evolution of the building, with the landscape as a backdrop; the beams appear from nowhere and intersect the landscape, ending up with a finished object, which is the building itself. . . . Some drawings . . . have a story which relates to our real intentions. . . . The mountain is removed and reassembled to cause a new kind of geology of the Peak itself. . . . Some drawings are done as if the beams really invaded the site as foreign objects. _ Alvin Boyarsky, *Post-Peak Conversations with Zaha Hadid: 1983 & 1986*, Tokyo: Edita, 1986

I think what is interesting about the Hong Kong project for me is the notion of floating elements within a given space. . . . I almost believed that there was such a thing as zero gravity. I can actually now believe that buildings can float. I know they don't, but I almost believe it—

**Painting from Hong Kong 1983, The Peak Competition.**
**"I almost believed that there was such a thing as zero gravity."**
_ Alvin Boyarsky, *Post-Peak Conversations with Zaha Hadid: 1983 & 1986*, Tokyo: Edita, 1986

except when I see my engineer of course. _ Alvin Boyarsky, *Post-Peak Conversations with Zaha Hadid: 1983 & 1986*, Tokyo: Edita, 1986

## 1983: THE TURNING POINT

Nineteen eighty-three was the critical year. In the span of one week, I was awarded the Peak competition, and Bernard Tschumi won La Villette [Hadid also sought the commission]. At that moment, the AA's importance shifted. It was no longer a school that simply produced radical designs. Its teachers and students were now seen as capable of winning major competitions. Of course, Rem Koolhaas was also very important. . . . All of that work garnered a tremendous amount of press interest. That was the beginning of public interest in alternative fantasies for the city. But the historical project remained quite powerful. _ Todd Gannon, ed., "Zaha Hadid, BMW Central Building," in *Source Books in Architecture, vol. 7*, Princeton: Princeton Architectural Press, 2006

## COMPETITIONS

I personally like competitions because they do lift the standard. . . . I've been grateful to the system because if it wasn't for commissions, I would not have any work. . . . Now these competitions are much smaller and more invited and, let's say, less open. But I still believe in the system. _ Zaha Hadid interview by Terry Gross, *Fresh Air*, National Public Radio, May 26, 2004

---

The Lois & Richard Rosenthal Center for Contemporary Art, is the first American museum to be designed by a woman. Hadid used a variety of materials in combination with one another to enhance both the design and experience of the building. Here, the galleries appear to float over the main lobby. Pictured, opposite, are the roof staircase, the first floor atrium, and one of the staircases to the gallery. *Opposite:* **One of Hadid's early sketches of the center.**

**CINCINNATI 2003**
# LOIS & RICHARD ROSENTHAL CENTER FOR CONTEMPORARY ART

The downtowns of the American Midwest are all dissipating, and the museum was intended to regenerate the downtown. The city wanted to install cultural buildings in the center, and therefore the connection between the building and the city became very critical. . . . This is a museum without a permanent collection, so it would have to accommodate many exhibitions. _ Zaha Hadid interview by Alice Rawsthorn, for "Frieze Talks," October 21, 2005

Most of our work is sometimes horizontal, like layers and so on, but it [the Rosenthal Center] is a stacked building, and the idea that you stretch the space of a museum vertically. . . . So it's like a series of rooms which are juxtaposed over each other, and next to each other, to allow these kinds of spaces to be in concrete or in metal or in glass, to allow light to

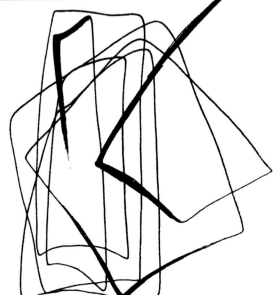

come through the building. It's the idea of transparency and the kind of geometry [that] together provide a[n] . . . interesting impression of that space.

The museum is quite compact, and one thing we just had on the top level is an Un-Museum, which is for children, where you can commission three-dimensional objects or spaces—like a children's museum where you can touch and . . . play. . . . And that was really also great fun. _ Zaha Hadid interview by Terry Gross, *Fresh Air*, National Public Radio, May 26, 2004

> ❝ **WHAT IS INTERESTING ABOUT BUILDING IS THAT THERE IS ALWAYS AN ELEMENT OF SURPRISE. THE SURPRISE IS THE MOST EXCITING PART. IT'S ALWAYS IMPORTANT TO ANTICIPATE THIS CORRECTLY.** ❞

The Phaeno Science Center looks like a spacecraft that is about to touch down, although it rests on ten cone-shaped "feet." Detail photos show a staircase, top, in one of the building's "zones" and, bottom, one of its entrances. *Below:* a Hadid sketch of the building.

### WOLFSBURG 2006
## PHAENO SCIENCE CENTER
If you imagine that the ground is empty and then there are these very large cones in concrete which become the entrances, the theater, the restaurant, you have activity on the ground in the evening and the day.

And then when it lifts up, it becomes one continuous space for the exhibits. So basically it's like a large table, let's say, with very big legs programmed and made active the whole day and all evening. And then the top of the table, the roof, is where the museum is.

The legs are kind of like cones but they, obviously, don't have a point because they have a program. For example, one is a kiosk, one is a bookshop, one is a shop, one is a laboratory, one is the theater, one is restaurants and cafés. . . . There are, like, seven or eight cones, and they're all connected by a roof, and then there's another roof which covers the top of the table. _ Zaha Hadid interview by Terry Gross, *Fresh Air,* National Public Radio, May 26, 2004

# BERGISEL SKI JUMP

The ski jump is a concise piece of functional design, an instrument for high-performance sport, shaped with mathematical precision. The challenge here was to integrate a new, initially alien element into a given formula: the café and sun deck. The assemblage of elements was resolved in the manner of nature, developing a seamless hybrid, where parts are smoothly articulated and fused into an organic unity. The result is a rather unusual silhouette on Bergisel. _ *A + U: Architecture and Urbanism,* no. 3, March 2003

The Bergisel Ski Jump was an unusual project because it had to include public spaces such as a café, middle, and a public viewing terrace.

## "THE FIGURE-GROUND: A METHOD OF INVESTIGATION"

We have been pursuing this sort of investigation [composition, urban organization] for years; it is simply the way we investigate architectural space. From the beginning, we have been obsessive about diagramming context. For us, context ceased to be about historicism or traditional contextual relationships. It became critical. This led to a series of advances in technique. We transformed the figure-ground as a method of investigation. _ Todd Gannon, ed., "Zaha Hadid, BMW Central Building," in *Source Books in Architecture,* vol. 7, Princeton: Princeton Architectural Press, 2006

## CONCRETE

Concrete shows up in some of my early projects very well—for example, Vitra [1994]—as well as in Wolfsburg [Phaeno Science Center, 2006]. I love concrete, but I think we should also look at other things. For instance, there is a preoccupation in my work about what structure can do and how you should be true to the material. . . . Maybe the structure is concrete, but we can begin to look at the skin and how you can interpret that. _ Zaha Hadid interview by Rem Koolhaas, *Interview,* February 2005

You can experiment when you're younger. But it's difficult to predict what happens if your building is built and occupied by people. How does your idea translate into an urban space or a private house? How do people live in it? . . . Building is not architecture. _ "Interview: Alvin Boyarsky Talks with Zaha Hadid (October and December 1987)," *Zaha Hadid,* New York: Guggenheim, 2006

A pattern links Malevich and all the Russians. Mies, Niemeyer, and even Le Corbusier: Through the liberation of the plan they all invent a new kind of space. This realization led me to all kinds of different studies. _ "Interview: Alvin Boyarsky Talks with Zaha Hadid (October and December 1987)," *Zaha Hadid,* New York: Guggenheim, 2006

## LIGHT

I mean around the Mediterranean, although it is not *the* Mediterranean, but around the Mediterranean in that part of the world [where] light is really quite soft, and it's fabulous. And I think particularly when you have so much water, the reflection is also extraordinary. _ Zaha Hadid interview by Diana Nyad, *Savvy Traveler,* Minnesota Public Radio, April 19, 2003

## "" AS LONG AS THERE IS CLARITY IN THE IDEA, YOU CAN CHANGE OTHER THINGS. ""

## SPACE

"'Neutral space' is a wishful oxymoron. All space is colored by individual memory and experience." _ Markus Dochantschi, ed., *Space for Art,* Baden, Switzerland: Lars Müller Publishers, 2005

I always think of a given space—I mean "space" in a broad sense, because you can never perceive small spaces. If you use the term "space," as in public space, you mean a sort of overall concept, like air. _ "Interview: Alvin Boyarsky Talks with Zaha Hadid (October and December 1987)," *Zaha Hadid,* New York: Guggenheim, 2006

## NATURE

I don't like nature very much, but I think that a landscape is not purely to do with a park. I think people go to the countryside not only to see trees but because there is open space. I mean, there's a span of land which is beyond what the eye can see, and this is almost uninterrupted—a very soothing thing. . . . I like water, I like sand, I like all those things. Actually what I do not like is picturesque landscapes. . . . _ Zaha Hadid interview by Alvin Boyarsky in *Zaha Hadid: Planetary Architecture Two,* London: Architectural Association, 1983

## LEIPZIG 2005
## BMW PLANT CENTRAL BUILDING: "A TWENTIETH-CENTURY PROJECT"

Everything moves through the building. The blue-collar and white-collar workers, the public, and, of course, the cars themselves all move through the same space. But actually, with its fascination with the car, with ideas of movement and velocity, BMW really began as a twentieth-century project. _ Todd Gannon, ed., "Zaha Hadid, BMW Central Building," in *Source Books in Architecture, vol. 7,* Princeton: Princeton Architectural Press, 2006

Continuity is crucial for a production facility. You cannot have a factory distributed over eight levels. In this instance, we are responding as much to our own obsessions as to the realities of automobile production. Though the project refers back to Fordism and the lineage of the assembly line, we wanted to create a new field of production. _ Todd Gannon, ed., "Zaha Hadid, BMW Central Building," in *Source Books in Architecture, vol. 7,* Princeton: Princeton Architectural Press, 2006

Hadid's vision for the BMW Plant Central Building turned the conventions of factory design on its ear. Pictured are the northwest façade, *above,* the north façade, *near left,* the interior, *middle,* and the factory foyer, *far right.*

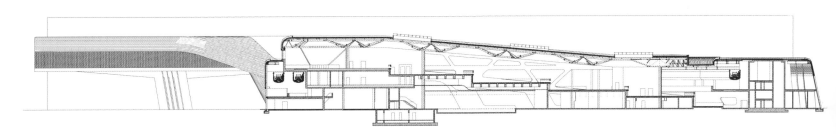

## INFLUENCES:
## THE ISLAMIC WORLD AND FAMILY

What is unique about being part of the ancient world is that history is part of your daily life. . . . In the Garden of Eden, where the Tigris and the Euphrates meet in southern Iraq, you stand there and there is a timelessness. You see the rivers and trees and you know that 10,000 years ago it was like that. _ Dorinda Elliott, *Condé Nast Traveler*, March 2007

Both my parents believed in modernity. The whole connection between Islam and the Arab world, it's so integrated and so intertwined. And it doesn't really matter whether you're Muslim or Christian or Jewish if you live in the Arab world—the dominant force culturally is Islamic, although it's not religious necessarily all the time. _ Zaha Hadid interview by Terry Gross, *Fresh Air*, National Public Radio, May 26, 2004

When I was seven I went with my parents to Beirut to see some new furniture that they had ordered for our home. My father, Mohammad Hadid, was a forward-looking man with cosmopolitan interests. . . . I can still remember going to the furniture maker's studio and seeing our new furniture. The style was angular and modernist, finished in a chartreuse color, and for my room there was an asymmetric mirror. I was thrilled by the mirror and it started my love of asymmetry. When we got home, I reorganized my room. It went from being a little girls' room to a teenager's. My cousin liked what I had done and asked me to do hers, then my aunt asked me to design her bedroom, and so it started. But it was my parents who gave me the confidence to do these things. _ Vinny Lee, *The Times* (London), April 19, 2008

## THE ARCHITECTURAL ASSOCIATION
## AND REM KOOLHAAS

*While attending the Architectural Association, School of Architecture, in London during 1972–77, Hadid studied under Leo Krier, and, significantly in her fourth year, under Rem Koolhaas.*

What was interesting about the AA was that amongst the chaos there were always people who could direct you, but you had to find these people and you had to teach yourself how to do things. . . . You had to be in command of your own destiny. _ Zaha Hadid interview by Yukio Futagawa, *GA Document Extra 03*, 1996

I was a student of Rem's, and our studio unit was very different and new. It wanted to open the door to a world that had yet to be invented. Rem and Elia [Zenghelis] were looking at the city in a new way. . . .

The whole experiment of the AA is to make you lost and confused for three years, and then in the fourth year assume you've been trained enough to choose what you want to pursue and who you want to teach you. . . . _ Zaha Hadid interview by Alice Rawsthorn, for "Frieze Talks," October 21, 2005

## ❝ NEVER WAS THERE IN MY UPBRINGING A FEELING THAT WOMEN ARE DIFFERENT THAN MEN. ❞

Before coming to London I studied mathematics at the American University in Beirut, where I became interested in geometry. It's the mathematics of the Arab world, and I am fascinated by the mind of logic and the abstract. The Russian avant-garde movement of the twenties, the work of Malevich and Kandinsky, brings this together and injects the idea of motion and energy in architecture, giving a feeling of flow and movement in space. _ Vinny Lee, *The Times* (London), April 19, 2008

## PARTNERSHIP WITH OMA

*Hadid joined OMA [the Office for Metropolitan Architecture] in 1977 as partner, with Rem Koolhaas and Elia Zenghelis.*

It took Elia and Rem a long time to convince me that two is bad and one is bad. I now believe that three is better than two and so on. If you are on your own, and don't take any criticism from anyone, you can isolate yourself to such an extent that anybody who says anything about your work appears to attack it. I decided when I left OMA that I would always work with people who can be critical because otherwise you can go on fooling yourself forever and pretend it's all wonderful and it isn't. _ Zaha Hadid interview by Alvin Boyarsky in *Zaha Hadid: Planetary Architecture Two*, London: Architectural Association, 1983

## POST-OMA

*After establishing her own practice in 1980, Hadid entered a competition for the Prime Minister's home in Ireland, which further honed her design sensibility.*

I wanted to push the notion of explosion in architecture, and that's what this project really taught me—pushing something to a certain limit where it doesn't become ridiculous, where you are very much in control, and it erupts only where it is possible. I began to develop my own language. I began to take a different direction, something which was quite personal. _ Zaha Hadid interview by Alvin Boyarsky in *Zaha Hadid: Planetary Architecture Two*, London: Architectural Association, 1983

“ **MY FAMILY SAW EDUCATION AS A PASSPORT TO A BETTER WORLD, BUT I WAS UNSURE ABOUT WHAT I REALLY WANTED TO DO. IT WAS ONLY IN MY FOURTH YEAR AT THE AA THAT I DISCOVERED THE ARCHITECTURE WORLD TO BE EXCITING AND THRILLING.** ”

**Becoming a Significant Architect** I didn't really have a twenty-year plan, but I always planned to change the system and ultimately do the theoretical project, whatever it might be. _ Raul A. Barreneche, *Architectural Record,* January 2003

**A Signature Style** When you build something, people see that you've done something that works, so why can't you do it again? But I also think architecture is like science: If you don't do lab research, you're not going to discover the cures. In terms of research, I think it's a very important point to always expand the boundaries. . . . You learn from your own repertoire, in a sense. Early on . . . we focused so much on the connection between program and site, in untraditional ways, that every interpretation brought us something else. . . . We used to try and invent new rules. Now we have developed a set of things which we can go back to, a lot of available research we can bounce off. . . . You have more experience, and you know how to design things better. And you don't have to reinvent the wheel again every day. . . . Of course the programs are also very different. We have a train station that in no way could be

similar to a ferry station or a science museum or a public school or a factory. No similarities in the program. There may be certain things which you can't repeat. _ *Perspecta,* no. 37, 2005

**The Unconventional Approach** I could never have had a conventional career in architecture. . . . I think you do have to take a certain risk. You have to make a decision when you leave school whether you're going to risk it or play it safe; that is really fundamental, the main thing. If you can take risks, I think it's worthwhile. _ Alvin Boyarsky, *Post-Peak Conversations with Zaha Hadid: 1983 & 1986,* Tokyo: Edita, 1986

**"Luxury on a Bigger Scale"** There is another aspect to architecture which people forget. Architecture should be pleasurable, it should be a pleasure to be in a wonderful space. A nice room, it does not matter how small or big it is. What people misunderstand about luxury is that luxury has nothing to do with price. . . . This is what architecture should do—give you the idea of luxury on a bigger scale. _ "Interview with Zaha Hadid," *El Croquis,* no. 52, 1991

**THE SITE AS PARTNER** At sea you've taken on a partner—the sea itself in ships and boats, large and small; you always have to create the best conditions. It's pure, unadulterated functionalism—you have to propel that ship as fast as you can against the resistance that happens to exist. The partner is thus in the broad sense the place. On land it's about a site and some surroundings—it may be by a forest or on a plain, with the wind conditions and the light that the place happens to offer, but at all events it's a partner that you have to relate to.
_ Jørn Utzon in conversation with Poul Erik Tojner in Michael Juul Holm, ed., *Jørn Utzon: The Architect's Universe*, Humlebaek, Denmark: Louisiana Museum of Modern Art, 2004

# JØRN UTZON

**BORN:** April 9, 1918, Copenhagen; Died: November 29, 2008

**EDUCATION:** Faculty of Architecture, Royal Academy of Fine Arts, Copenhagen, 1942

**PROJECTS FEATURED:** Utzon House, Majorca, Spain, 1994; Kuwait National Assembly, Kuwait City, 1982; Sydney Opera House, Australia, 1973

> **AS AN ARCHITECT
> I BELIEVE IT IS VERY IMPORTANT
> TO FALL IN LOVE WITH
> THE NATURE OF THINGS
> INSTEAD OF FIGHTING FOR
> FORM AND STYLE.**

**The Sydney Opera House, Sydney, 1973**
Utzon has remarked that many people thought
that his design for the opera house was inspired
by sailing. Although his father was a naval architect and so he was familiar with elementary
boat construction, his inspiration was much
more prosaic: the segments of an orange.

# I HAVE THE BUILDING IN MY HEAD LIKE A COMPOSER HAS HIS SYMPHONY.

An early concept sketch by Utzon and an aerial view of the Sydney Opera House. Utzon took advantage of the various ways in which one could encounter the building, and thus decided to develop two theaters rather than one, which would have been more conventional.

### SYDNEY 1973
# SYDNEY OPERA HOUSE

I had the best job anyone could get. I had the possibility with a number of people to concentrate fantastically upon an extraordinarily great structure for a purpose which was not for profit but for the stimulus of the mind. _ Katherine Brisbane, *The Guardian*, October 15, 2007

It was an ideal project for an architect . . . first, because there was a beautiful site with a good view, and second, there was no detailed program. _ Françoise Fromonot, *Jørn Utzon: Architect of the Sydney Opera House*, Milan: Electa, 2000

It was my function as an architect to support the actors in the house and help them present their drama in a better way. . . . When it became clear that our function was to stimulate the audience before the drama, to take them away from their daily lives, the architecture came by itself. _ Katherine Brisbane, *The Guardian*, October 15, 2007

The planning comprises even the smallest detail and is carried out in an unorthodox manner, where the maximum use of models and prototypes ensures that nothing is introduced into the scheme before it has been carefully investigated and has proved to be the right solution to the problem. _ Jørn Utzon, "Descriptive Narrative, Sydney Opera House," January 1965, in *Sydney Opera House: Utzon Design Principles*, 2002

**Influence of Shipbuilding on the Design** I of course had the marvelous thing that we had the shipyard adjacent. . . . You see big ships being built with the ribs, etc. In the shipyard small men made one big steamship every six months, and you would see the whole process. _ Jørn Utzon, Jan Utzon, and Richard Johnson, "Private Records of Discussion," 1999

Many people say my design was inspired by the sailing yachts in the harbor or by seashells. This is not the case. It is like an orange—you peel an orange and you get these segments, these similar shapes. It was like this in my models. It was not that I thought it should be like sails in the harbor. It just so happened that the white sails were similar. I was influenced by the sails only to the extent that my father was a naval architect and I was familiar with

big shapes [ships]. I had never seen Sydney Harbor when I made this design, although I felt quite familiar with it from photographs and naval charts.
_ Eric Ellis, *Good Weekend*, October 31, 1992

It is typical Sydney. Because the site is one you go around, and even sail around, the building needed to be a sculpture, so I spread the two theaters, instead of putting them in a box, and put sails over them to keep the feeling of being on the sea. Underneath I placed this big platform fitting beautifully on the peninsula, repeating the effect of walking on the heads of Sydney Harbor. When you see a hill before you, you want to climb up it, and so I put the wide steps in front of people leading into the foyer. _ Katherine Brisbane, *The Guardian*, October 15, 2007

**❝ NATURE TAUGHT ME TO BE OCCUPIED BY STRUCTURE AND TO REVEAL IT. ❞**

Each element of the design—how the building was sited, the multiple views, the 100 meter-wide staircase—was intended to make visitors feel welcomed and relaxed. Utzon's sketch shows how the podium was to fit within the overall structure.

The feeling you have when you sit on one of the grand staircases in Mexico is a feeling of liberation from daily life. Because I had seen this, the large staircase at the Sydney Opera House was made 100 meters wide and the plateau on top became a very important feature for the feeling of being in another world. This plateau also functions as a gathering place, a town square, and outdoor auditorium.
_ Jørn Utzon, "Descriptive Narrative, Sydney Opera House," January 1965, in *Sydney Opera House: Utzon Design Principles*, 2002

**Shape and Sound** [The concert hall] is like a violin—it has its shape because of its long evolution, and it has attained that shape through evolution toward perfection. _ Jørn Utzon, "Descriptive Narrative, Sydney Opera House," June 2000, in *Sydney Opera House: Utzon Design Principles*, 2002

So rather than changing the acoustics by absorbing certain unwanted sounds or frequencies, it is better to adjust the physical shape of the hall in such a way

that you achieve the perfect acoustical properties.
_ Jørn Utzon, "Descriptive Narrative, Sydney Opera House," June 2000, in *Sydney Opera House: Utzon Design Principles*, 2002

**Near Completion of the Sydney Opera House** *Jørn Utzon won the international design competition for the Sydney Opera House in 1956 and subsequently developed and executed his design. But in 1966, he was replaced by a panel of architects selected by the Minister of Public Works of New South Wales. Ted Farmer, NSW government architect, completed the glass walls and interiors. In 1999, Jørn Utzon was reengaged as Sydney Opera House architect to develop a set of design principles reflecting his original vision and to act as a guide for all future changes to the building.*

If I had finished the building I would have carried through [a] sense of movement. It is treating space like music, almost nonexistent today in architecture.
_ Katherine Brisbane, *The Guardian*, October 15, 2007

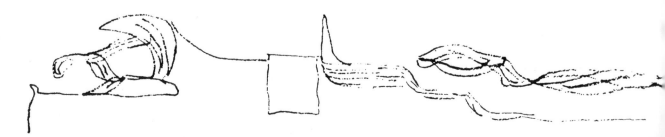

**◀◀ A CLIMAX IN COLOR** UPLIFTS YOU IN THAT FESTIVE MOOD, AWAY FROM DAILY LIFE, THAT YOU EXPECT WHEN YOU GO TO THE THEATER. **▶▶**

## HARMONY WITH THE LANDSCAPE

*A recurring directive in Utzon's thinking was not about architecture as a way of impacting or altering the landscape but of harmonizing with the natural surroundings.*

All the building complexes that have really inspired me—the desert cities in Morocco, for example—have been pushed into position in relation to the place, and in relation to the sun. Then they take on the character that the old cities or Greek temples have. It's about putting the houses and apartments together such that they harmonize with the landscape and thus provide the best conditions for living there.
_ Jørn Utzon in conversation with Poul Erik Tojner, in Michael Juul Holm, ed., *Jørn Utzon: The Architect's Universe*, Humlebaek, Denmark: Louisiana Museum of Modern Art, 2004

## ARCHITECTURE AND PLACE

I went on a very long walk in Morocco, from Ourzazate around the southern side of the Atlas Mountains, and there I experienced a building tradition that was completely in harmony with the place and the materials. They built—now and then—and they sang while they built, stamped out mud houses, you know, in many stories, from clay and grass. It looked like what I knew from the shipyard: A whole swarm of people standing on some scaffolding riveting a hull together. I was quite captivated by the building process. If you'd seen riveters' boys like that standing down beside the slipway, making those rivets red hot, a couple of centimeters thick, with a head on them, and chucking them up with tongs to the fitter, who caught them in the air and stuck them in the holes . . . and then there was a man sitting inside, hammering it all together, you really get captivated by the craftsmanship when you see it like that in reality.
_ Jørn Utzon in conversation with Poul Erik Tojner, in Michael Juul Holm, ed., *Jørn Utzon: The Architect's Universe*, Humlebaek, Denmark: Louisiana Museum of Modern Art, 2004

## THE PROJECT WAS DESIGNED SO IT COULD GROW . . .

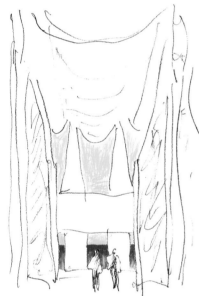

The Kuwait National Assembly contains four spaces: a covered square, a parliamentary chamber, a large conference hall, and a mosque. *Above:* An original color sketch by Utzon.

**KUWAIT CITY 1982**

# KUWAIT NATIONAL ASSEMBLY

All departments of the complex (offices, meeting rooms, reception rooms, library, Assembly Hall, etc.) are arranged along a central street. The departments consist of modules of various sizes, built around small patios or courtyards, connected to the central street via side streets. Each department can be extended at any time by adding modules, so that the building can grow sideways, away from the central street, and its outer boundaries will change as time goes by. These free-flexing outer boundaries of the system are very much related to traditional Islamic bazaar architecture. _ Françoise Fromonot, *Jørn Utzon: Architect of the Sydney Opera House,* Milan: Electa, 2000

Each element gives the building a rhythm. . . . The elements make it possible to build office blocks around a courtyard . . . they radiate like ribs in a flatfish out to the side from the main street. . . . _ Michael Juul Holm, ed., *Jørn Utzon: The Architect's Universe,* Humlebaek, Denmark: Louisiana Museum of Modern Art, 2004

**Clients**   Kuwait was very close to never being realized the way it looks today. . . . I found out that if I put a big shading roof in front, then they [the leaders] could meet [the citizens]. . . . It's a very leader-oriented, patriarchal society, you see, highly group-conscious; it isn't like in a democracy. And at the same time the shade is a very important cultural element. In places like that where the light is so stark, you just can't exist without shade—in Arabia they say that when a leader dies his shade passes away. When we got as far as being ready to build, the leading man among the clients—the Speaker of the Parliament—wasn't willing to spend the money it cost to make that roof. So when at long last I had a chance to meet him . . . I went up to him and explained that in our democracy we didn't have that relationship, that is, the direct contact that I admired, and that this was the basis of that open antechamber. He didn't say anything. Then I took his hand—you aren't supposed to do that, no way!—and shook it. It was as if it was dead, and when I let go the arm just fell down along his side. But a fortnight later we were told that the roof was to be built. _ Michael Juul Holm, ed., *Jørn Utzon: The Architect's Universe,* Humlebaek, Denmark: Louisiana Museum of Modern Art, 2004

**Architecture as a Living Entity**   You never finish with it . . . while you see it against the sky. The interplay with the sun, the light, the clouds is so important that it makes the building into a living thing. _ Geraldine Brooks, *The New Yorker,* October 17, 2005

## BEING AN ARCHITECT
## —AN "ELEMENT OF HUMANISM"

It means having a wonderful profession. For me it has been a gift from God. It is the joy of having a profession with such a strong element of humanism. _ Jørn Utzon and Henrick Sten Møller, *Living Architecture*, no. 14, 1995

If you say that you get an emotional experience of happiness or of depth—in art, in music, and in literature, then you can get it too by entering a room: It can captivate you. My experience is that if a building is good, then I experience the flow of space. _ Michael Juul Holm, ed., *Jørn Utzon: The Architect's Universe*, Humlebaek, Denmark: Louisiana Museum of Modern Art, 2004

Human well-being is something you study all through your life. But none of the relevant courses of education, as an engineer, a technician, or a craftsman, takes in the whole spectrum. . . . _ Jørn Utzon in conversation with Poul Erik Tojner, in Michael Juul Holm, ed., *Jørn Utzon: The Architect's Universe*, Humlebaek, Denmark: Louisiana Museum of Modern Art, 2004

What interested me to begin with was what was built and the relationship between it and those who were to use the houses. . . . All that money we architects are given to work with benefits the people who are to use the building: The building project serves people's well-being. That's why, in the construction process, we study the sources of human well-being more than anyone else. It's all about light and sound, and stairs and outer and inner walls—bits and pieces, and something to have them in. _ Jørn Utzon in conversation with Poul Erik Tojner, in Michael Juul Holm, ed., *Jørn Utzon: The Architect's Universe*, Humlebaek, Denmark: Louisiana Museum of Modern Art, 2004

Today I feel the most important concern is how we can make a better life instead of making more money. An architect can have a great influence on our life quality. Here on this Spanish Island [Majorca, Can Feliz] they have an expression, *"medio dia,"* that is when the old ones sit in open doors and clean vegetables in the blessed warmth of the sun. We shall let the sun in. _ Jørn Utzon and Henrick Sten Møller, *Living Architecture*, no. 14, 1995

First and last, you have a relationship with the people who are to use the buildings. The stronger that relationship is, the better the work will be, and the weaker it is, the more sophisticated it will be, in the bad sense: a poor expression of your own more or less limited imagination. _ Jørn Utzon in conversation with Poul Erik Tojner, in Michael Juul Holm, ed., *Jørn Utzon: The Architect's Universe*, Humlebaek, Denmark: Louisiana Museum of Modern Art, 2004

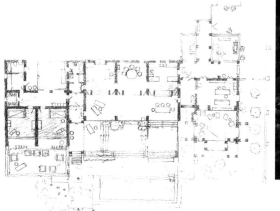

## " I HAVE A STRANGE, INNATE SENSE FOR SPACE. I DREAM A HOUSE AND THEN I HAVE IT IN MY HEAD. "

**Above: Can Feliz expressed Utzon's love of platforms. The house is a sequence of pavilions linked by a wall. The house floor plan has been described as a mini-Acropolis. Utzon used the local limestone as his main building material.**

**MAJORCA 1994**
### UTZON HOUSE, CAN FELIZ: "GRAND SIMPLICITY"
In building this house I have again clarified my relationship to nature, and I chose to direct all my energy on something I really wanted. _ Jørn Utzon and Henrick Sten Møller, *Living Architecture*, no. 14, 1995

See how simple it is. Here are the building materials. From these one can build a house as I have done here with a view over the self-sown landscape, with an old Moorish castle on the mountain behind and the sea in the distance. I prefer looking out over undisturbed nature instead of cultivated fields. It is this grand simplicity I have sought. Nature and empty space, just like the temples. _ Jørn Utzon and Henrick Sten Møller, *Living Architecture*, no. 14, 1995

**Considerations of Site** It wasn't easy to place the house on the site. One shouldn't always place a building on the most obviously beautiful spot. _ Jørn Utzon and Henrick Sten Møller, *Living Architecture*, no. 14, 1995

I have often thought about where one could build here. It would be too brutal to place a house at the top of the site and wrong to place it down along the road. Again and again I sat on this mountainside in different places until one day I found the right spot. A place from which the landscape seemed most powerful. Strangely enough it was also where the house could be integrated with the mountainside in the most beautiful, harmonious way. Then I began to think that this is how a stream trickles through the landscape. Just like a poem. Now, I'm not a poet, and if you ask me why at my age did I build this house, I will answer: This is the only thing I can do. _ Jørn Utzon and Henrick Sten Møller, *Living Architecture*, no. 14, 1995

They [craftsmen on Majorca] have been open to my ideas, but I didn't want to design something they couldn't build. This has influenced the house and its dimensions. A construction site is an incredibly instructive place for an architect. I would rather have spent an hour at the Saint Peter's building site in Rome than have read all the books written about that church. _ Jørn Utzon and Henrick Sten Møller, *Living Architecture*, no. 14, 1995

## EARLY EXPOSURE TO THE MODERN ETHOS

My parents . . . experienced the new and simple white architecture that demanded light and space, that let the sun shine in and rejoiced in the functional, the unconcealed—Functionalism, if you will. It was the Swedish architect Gunnar Asplund's exhibition building, a lightweight structure with an expression then uncommon in Scandinavia. My parents returned home completely carried away by the new ideas and thoughts. They soon commenced in redoing our home. . . . We developed new eating habits: healthy, green, and lean. We began to exercise, get fresh air, cultivate light and the direct, so-called natural way of doing things. . . . That's how much architects can bring about, and it came to influence our whole society. _ Françoise Fromonot, *Jørn Utzon: Architect of the Sydney Opera House*, Milan: Electa, 2000

a house here." And that was hugely important to the two of them. That they had made their own house. It's almost a shame for those architects that they just come in and do computer drawings. The craftsmanship is missing, I think. It was excellent, and now they've given it up. But I'm too old now and I have no idea what can be done about it. _ Jørn Utzon in conversation with Poul Erik Tojner, in Michael Juul Holm, ed., *Jørn Utzon: The Architect's Universe*, Humlebaek, Denmark: Louisiana Museum of Modern Art, 2004

## THE COMPUTER

With the use of computers today, you risk limiting yourself to what can be directly converted into numbers. . . . I sometimes find that rather worrying. _ Jørn Utzon in conversation with Poul Erik Tojner, in Michael Juul Holm, ed., *Jørn Utzon: The Architect's Universe*, Humlebaek, Denmark: Louisiana Museum of Modern Art, 2004

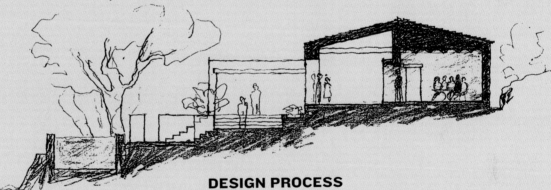

## CRAFTSMANSHIP

In the old days you had to be a craftsman first. We had to work as craftsmen for four months of the first year. . . . I got into the Academy, then we made some simple construction drawings and spatial sketches and we went out and we were carpenters or bricklayers for four months. And the same the next year. In the third year they had bricklayers from the technical school, who could draw and at the same time were craftsmen. I had done carpentry for the first four months in Elsinore, so I was tired of getting up early in the morning. I had a grandmother who had a plot of land down by the beach, and she let me build there. Then I asked my master carpenter: "If I build a wooden house here myself, can I get your signature that I've worked for four months?" I could. So I built myself my first house. And it was a good idea. So I said to Jan, when he was in training . . . and to Kim too, my sons . . . up in Strømstad, we have a little island up there. . . . "Go in and get some planks and make

## DESIGN PROCESS

There is a rumor that I can't draw and never could. This is probably because I work so much with models. Models are one of the most beautiful design tools, but I still do the finest drawings you can imagine. And I made many drawings for this house [Can Feliz] because I wanted to achieve a lightness. _ Jørn Utzon and Henrick Sten Møller, *Living Architecture*, no. 14, 1995

I have known, always said, that one should build a space instead of drawing it. It is also true that one of the greatest experiences is to see what one has drawn in full scale to see it finished. Despite this, I always carry the entire building around in my head, room by room. This is often a strenuous process, especially when it doesn't get built. There are quite simply a number of blocks that I must get out of my head as volumes. Perhaps this is why I am so tied to nature, the sun, trees, and the wind. _ Jørn Utzon and Henrick Sten Møller, *Living Architecture*, no. 14, 1995

**BEING PART OF NATURE** We are instruments. We feel, we touch, we look, we hear. There are things I refer to as the "ings"—arriving, entering, receiving, walking, sitting, smelling, touching, preparing, loving, caring, sleeping, relaxing, watching, observing.

The "ings" of things. We are the instruments. If we cut ourselves off from the elements, the landscape, the abounding beauty of nature around us, we might as well be a brain with a pair of eyes just looking at the world go by. It's wonderful to be able to feel that it's a cooler day today, to know that yesterday was hotter. Our bodies are designed to relate to our environments, and I suspect the body needs this exercise, these changes for our own good. _ Glenn Murcutt interview by Yoshio Futagawa, *GA Houses*, May 2003

# GLENN MURCUTT

**BORN:** July 25, 1936, London

**EDUCATION:** B. Arch., University of New South Wales, Sydney, 1961

**OFFICE:** Glenn Murcutt & Associates, Suite 12, Library Walk, Military Road, Mosman, New South Wales 2088, Australia

**PROJECTS FEATURED:** Arthur and Yvonne Boyd Education Center, Riversdale, New South Wales, 1999; Simpson-Lee House, Mt. Wilson, New South Wales, 1994; Bowali Visitor Information Center, Kakadu National Park, Australia, 1994; Magney House, Bingie Point, New South Wales, 1984

**"MY BUILDINGS ARE A RESULT OF LOOKING AT WHERE I'M LIVING, NOT TRYING TO DESIGN AN AUSTRALIAN ARCHITECTURE, BUT TRYING TO DESIGN AN ARCHITECTURE OF WHERE I AM."**

**Simpson-Lee House, New South Wales, 1994**
Functional, beautiful, and minimally invasive are hallmarks of this house—it's sited facing northeast to block cold winds from the south, temperature can be controlled by the walls and windows, and the materials serve to complement the natural landscape and reflecting pool.

## ETHICS

*Murcutt doesn't disdain outside opinion, but he certainly doesn't court it, either.*

We as architects have ourselves on. I don't care what people do, as long as whatever they're doing is done well. It is what you do as a response to what you say, and the separateness between what you say and what you do, which can be judged. . . . I don't care what people say about me: The fact is I am designing places in the Australian landscape, whether that be the suburban landscape, the urban landscape, or the rural landscape. What I am doing is taking on board place, and that place is about the issues I understand: culture, built form, climate, and all the other things that go to make up place. _ Ian McDougall, *AA: Architecture Australia,* September/October 1992

I won't sit on a jury if I think the principles are wrong, such as changing Jørn Utzon's Opera House around. I feel ashamed of the way my profession has treated Utzon over the years. _ "Spirit and Sensibility," *Architecture,* October 1998

I was raised on the basis that in life you do ordinary things extraordinarily well [*see also the reference to his father, page 196*]. I've never believed that to be successful as an architect you've got to have achieved a multistory building. I couldn't give a damn about any multistory building. I give a damn about the buildings I can do best, and if the regulations and the driving needs of a developer go contrary to my belief system, then I'm not going to take that on.

My life is about doing things other than grandiose things for myself. I'm a very private person, I operate in a very private way. Any awards that come are extraordinary shocks to me. I have no message to tell everybody beyond saying we've got responsibilities to do things properly. That's the least we can do as architects. _ Ian McDougall, *AA: Architecture Australia,* September/October 1992

## ▌▌ IF I OPERATE ETHICALLY, I DON'T HAVE TO THINK ABOUT IT. ▐▐

Modernized countries like Japan, Australia, and the United States consume 90 percent of the earth's resources, and we represent 10 percent of the earth's population. There's something wrong with that. We have to consume less energy. In the first world we consume ten times more than people in the third world. And yet we talk about how the population explosion of third world countries is a worry. We're in no position to say that. That's extremely self-righteous of us. We have to be careful about our moral judgments. _ Glenn Murcutt interview by Yoshio Futagawa, *GA Houses,* May 2003

## ▌▌ VERY ORDINARY AND SIMPLE THINGS CAN ALSO BE ENTIRELY ECOLOGICAL. I WAS RAISED ON THE BASIS OF THAT NOTION. ▐▐

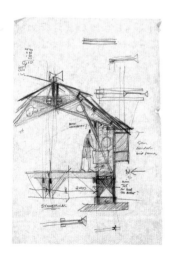

**Sustainable Architecture: Theory and Practice** *For Murcutt, theories about sustainable architecture are inextricably part of the native materials he chooses to work with and his concern for what he calls "climate-responsive architecture."*

Living things can be sustainable if allowed to grow in balance with other organisms and not to consume at a greater rate than is sustainable, as we currently do when we overharvest or poison the land. We don't plan adequately for the future. _ Cynthia Davidson, *Log,* Summer 2006

I am interested in the shape of the building only as a consequence of the issues about the responsibility toward materials, process of production, the ability to recycle, light, ventilation, the relationship to the outside and the natural landscape. All these should be embodied in the design process. These elements all form the basis of thinking in the making of architecture. Just how these elements are combined is the art of architecture. _ "Glenn Murcutt: Thoughts on the Ecology of Architecture," *A + U: Architecture and Urbanism,* August 2007

I'm interested in green architecture, but I'm also interested in structure, space, light, and an architecture that respects the landscape. I'm interested in spaces that achieve both prospect and refuge. I'm interested in the zonal changes in landscape, changes from the water to the land to the hills, the series of ecotones and ecozones. . . . . _ Glenn Murcutt interview by Yoshio Futagawa, *GA Houses,* May 2003

> **"MOST OF IT [SUSTAINABLE ARCHITECTURE] IS BLOODY AWFUL. MUCH OF IT ISN'T ARCHITECTURE, AND SOME OF IT ISN'T SUSTAINABLE."**

It's a way of thinking. The process for determining how elements are connected is also knowing how they can be retrieved and how they can be reused. I'm interested in that because there's very little embodied energy lost in reworking the building material elements. I think that's sustainable.

I have to say, though, that humans are probably not sustainable because we're such destroyers of our environment. If our populations consumed and polluted the earth's resources in balance with the ability of nature to renew, then we'd be sustainable. But we're not sustainable. We destroy. The fact that the planet is in such difficulties shows that we're simply not, as a species, sustainable. _ Cynthia Davidson, *Log,* Summer 2006

There has been a resistance by architects to environmental design, for many regard climate-responsive architecture as being unable to create beautiful work; they see much of the work as ugly. Working with the environment is viewed as a negative constraint. However, from my experience, and by understanding my imposed limitations, I have found that the

opportunities have increased. _ Cynthia Davidson, *Log,* Summer 2006

**Building Sustainable Architecture** My buildings open and close—like an instrument. I'm conscious when I'm designing to include prospect, refuge, observation, and reception. One designs buildings to perceive the changing light levels, temperatures, wind patterns, and sun positions—to perceive all these things so that the building performs as an instrument of the cycles of the day and year. _ Cynthia Davidson, *Log,* Summer 2006

A building that is well related to the geometry of the planet and the sun is a wonderful way of controlling the heat and cooling appropriate to seasonal climatic variations. _ Glenn Murcutt interview by Yoshio Futagawa, *GA Houses,* May 2003

The roofs of my rural buildings are designed to catch rainwater for use: for drinking, extinguishing fire, flushing the toilets, and watering the garden. In some remote, larger projects. wastewater is processed

The Marika-Alderton House in Australia's Northern Territory exemplifies Murcutt's philosophy that his buildings must open and close, like an instrument. Designed for an Aboriginal artist, the house is all about adapting to the hot, tropical climate of the region. Long eaves are meant to shade the house from sun: tubes along the roof vent hot air from inside and special fins direct cool breezes into the living spaces.

The Simpson-Lee house, above, allowed Murcutt to see how much he could meld a home with its surroundings. Water collected from the roof is used for drinking water and to flush toilets. Lighting and ventilation are controlled by closing off the northeast wall of the house.

**"FUNDAMENTALLY, YOU'VE GOT TO HAVE WATER. IF YOU HAVEN'T GOT WATER, YOU'VE GOT TROUBLES."**

for reuse in gardens through rotating biological digesters. _ Cynthia Davidson, *Log*, Summer 2006

**Native Resources** We have huge reserves of iron ore, so steel is a material that is produced locally. Then timber, which is a marvelous, renewable resource. For the first twenty years of its life a tree takes in carbon dioxide and produces an excess of oxygen. After about twenty years the carbon/oxygen ratio is about equal because the fallen old bark and leaves require oxygen to decompose, which cancels out the oxygen excess the tree initially produced. The decomposing bark and leaves produce compost for soil and nutrients for future plants. _ Cynthia Davidson, *Log*, Summer 2006

Australia enjoys five of the world's eight most durable timbers. . . . So long as you protect it where it touches the ground it will last a long time. I'm sure my timber buildings will last well over a hundred years. Maybe two hundred years. _ Glenn Murcutt interview by Yoshio Futagawa, *GA Houses*, May 2003

Of course you can build in the desert, but if you put a building there you've got to have something to support it. You've got to have work. Satellites and computers won't provide that, not at this stage of their development. _ Glenn Murcutt interview by Martin Pawley, *World Architecture*, September 1996

> ❝ THINK OF THE BUILDING AS AN INSTRUMENT. . . .
> IT'S ADDRESSING THE HYDROLOGY, IT'S ADDRESSING
> THE GEOMORPHOLOGY. IT'S ADDRESSING THE TOPOGRAPHY, THE WIND PATTERNS,
> LIGHT PATTERNS, ALTITUDE, LATITUDE, THE ENVIRONMENT AROUND YOU,
> THE SUN MOVEMENTS. IT'S ADDRESSING THE SUMMER, THE WINTER,
> AND THE SEASONS IN BETWEEN. IT'S ADDRESSING WHERE THE TREES ARE. ❞

**Murcutt's Home Near Sydney** As we're in a temperate climate in Sydney, this house and office designed and shared with Wendy Lewin [an architect and Murcutt's wife] is neither heated nor air-conditioned. We rely on opening the windows and doors during the warmer months to receive the air while in winter we close them and put on more clothes. . . . The flooring in the living room is from recycled timber screwed with a timber plug cap, not nailed. So one can drill the timber plug out with a screwdriver and remove each board, so each can be reused. . . . This house is very simple. But remember, simplicity is the other face of complexity. . . . Like a very good stock in cooking, it holds all the qualities of the ingredients in a reduced volume. Simplicity, when it retains complexity, is likely to be resolved by its form.

_ "Glenn Murcutt: Thoughts on the Ecology of Architecture," *A + U: Architecture and Urbanism*, August 2007

Murcutt's home, *above*, is neither heated nor air-conditioned, although Murcutt developed the house to naturally accommodate changes in temperature. Apart from that, the architect and his wife also make certain lifestyle adjustments. *Detail photos:* Interior views of Murcutt's house.

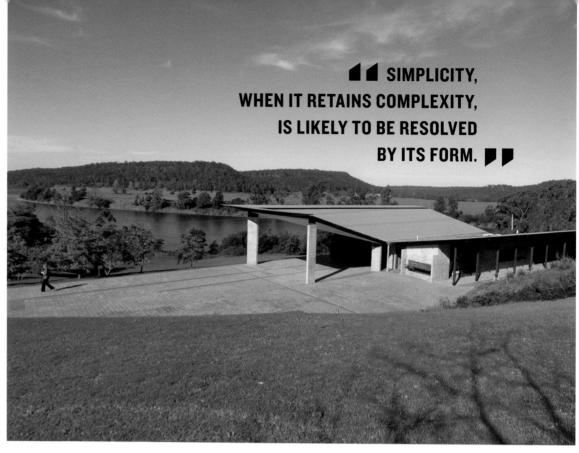

> ❝ SIMPLICITY,
> WHEN IT RETAINS COMPLEXITY,
> IS LIKELY TO BE RESOLVED
> BY ITS FORM. ❞

The center can accommodate up to 32 live-in artists. It also welcomes visiting music, art, and theater students. Large white panels, second from top, block out hot afternoon sun so efficiently that the buildings don't need heat or air-conditioning.

## NEW SOUTH WALES 1999
## ARTHUR AND YVONNE BOYD EDUCATION CENTER

It is probably the most important building I've been associated with in my life. . . . It's about framing views, about relating to the cultivated landscape as well as the native landscape. It's a culmination of thirty years of thinking and private practice. _ Glenn Murcutt interview by Yoshio Futagawa, *GA Houses,* May 2003

## A SENSE OF PLACE

My practice is based on my knowledge of Australia, and my knowledge of Australians, who happen to be Aboriginal Australians, American Australians, European Australians, Japanese Australians. _ Glenn Murcutt interview by Martin Pawley, *World Architecture*, September 1996

Landscape was a very important element in my life from very early on. It was the beginning of the discussion of "place" that is central to my work. It gives you an idea why I'm very interested in how to build a building that is not out of scale or dominating in a large landscape. We're like ants in the landscape in this giant country, and I want my buildings to be quiet within the landscape. _ Glenn Murcutt interview by Yoshio Futagawa, *GA Houses*, May 2003

All of my early experiences had to do with a sense of place, of climate and its patterns, a sense of fear, survival, and danger. We had all sorts of things that were dangerous. In the lowlands there were crocodiles. In the highlands we had scorpions and snakes. All these things were around us, and it gave me a real connection with nature and how to read nature. _ Glenn Murcutt interview by Yoshio Futagawa, *GA Houses*, May 2003

Understanding place is 90 percent of what you've got to achieve. And you've got the 10 percent of understanding the culture, and how that culture works in that place because this country will eventually make us. We won't make it. It is this land that made the aboriginal people, as Lloyd Rees [an Australian landscape artist] said. . . . There is a strength that this landscape possesses, that people can possess, a strength and sensitivity. It is that strength, that toughness, together with a gentleness, that's very important to me. _ Ian McDougall, *AA: Architecture Australia*, September/October 1992

My buildings are a result of looking at where I'm living—not trying to design an Australian architecture, but trying to design an architecture of where I am. . . . For instance, the clarity of light in Australia is phenomenal. On a bright day, it's a very clear light that separates the elements in a landscape. In the Northern Hemisphere the light connects the elements; here the light separates. . . . I'm interested in this legibility, this transparency, this particular kind of shadow, the particular quality of light we get here. It informs me of how to articulate structure and deal with a building as a response to this place. _ Glenn Murcutt interview by Yoshio Futagawa, *GA Houses*, May 2003

**❝ I CAN DESIGN FOR OTHER PLACES, BUT IT'S IMPORTANT FOR ME TO BE WORKING IN MY OWN CULTURE, IN A PLACE THAT IS MY OWN LIFE. ❞**

## VERNACULAR ARCHITECTURE

Vernacular architecture provides a very important basis for the way I work. For instance, I'm interested in the zones of change—from the outside to the inside, from ocean to land, from lowland to highland—and so one element in early Colonial architecture that is significant for me is the veranda. _ Glenn Murcutt interview by Yoshio Futagawa, *GA Houses*, May 2003

As a nation we live not only in cities but also on the edge of Australia. Ninety percent of Australians live on the coast. We live, in a sense, on the veranda of Australia, with most of the country behind us. We're edge dwellers. _ Glenn Murcutt interview by Yoshio Futagawa, *GA Houses*, May 2003

## NEW SOUTH WALES 1984
# MAGNEY HOUSE
From the street it is left absolutely intact. It's my attitude toward buildings that have a character about them. If something before has a quality, then I'll hold onto that quality . . . so it doesn't end up as a façade that's Mickey Mouse. I'm trying to give the space some sort of integrity. And yet I'm opening that space up, so what you're experiencing is the space developing not only in width but in dimension, vertically . . . which you can see runs out through the garden to the north, to the wind, to the ventilation and to the light. . . . This building gives these people a climatic and visual

control, a belonging to its place, to its texture, to its morphology, to its typology.

The spaces are very calm; they can open up to the outside. . . . In the belly of the house there is beautiful light. . . . In the shower, with a window at waist level, you know if it's a windy day, a cold day, a sunny day. And directly above is a roof-light in the shower so that you see the sky in its beautiful form. These are part of the perceptions of living, of the day, of being human.

It's options that I really believe in. I don't believe in designing something specifically for one person. I design something that will allow many people to

> **THIS IS MY STATEMENT: ANY WORK OF ARCHITECTURE THAT HAS BEEN DESIGNED, ANY WORK OF ARCHITECTURE THAT HAS THE POTENTIAL TO EXIST, OR THAT EXISTS, WAS DISCOVERED. IT WASN'T CREATED. OUR ROLE IS TO BE THE DISCOVERER, NOT THE CREATOR.**

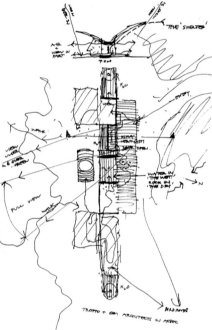

come and occupy it. To be able to give people options in the way they live. . . . I don't want to sit on a triangular balcony, I want to sit in a space. I don't want to be on the bow of a ship, I want to be held within a womb when I am in a state of repose and thinking. Or let me go into the landscape, where I have the freedom. I want to have that freedom and that spirit of freedom, and that, for me, is part of this culture. _ Ian McDougall, *AA: Architecture Australia*, September/October 1992

### KAKADU NATIONAL PARK 1994
# BOWALI VISITOR INFORMATION CENTER
To work with Aboriginal people, if you don't listen, you don't get past base one, because the culture is so different and yet there are so many overlaps in some of our perceptions. . . . They would term 98 percent of the buildings built by the white community as "unhealthy building" because it doesn't breathe properly; you can't have two people and feel comfortable in it, you can't have twenty-five people and still feel comfortable. _ Ian McDougall, *AA: Architecture Australia*, September/October 1992

**Influences** *In most serious discussions with Murcutt, he will often speak about the variety of influences on his life, beginning with his father, from whom he learned about the beauty and qualities of nature. He also cites his formative years spent in New Guinea and regard for Aboriginal culture; architects such as Philip Johnson, Mies van der Rohe, and Alvar Aalto; and both Freud*

*and Thoreau. Understanding this heady stew is entrée to understanding Murcutt and his fierce loyalties.*

**Family** My father said, "In life, most of us are going to do ordinary things. The most important thing about doing ordinary things is to do them extraordinarily well and be able to go to the beach and have nobody know who you are." That was very powerful to me: Ego isn't central.

I'm powerfully influenced by my parents. My father was getting *Architectural Forum* from the United States, documents on Philip Johnson's house, a whole issue on Frank Lloyd Wright. I'd go through these with him and we'd discuss the buildings.

Building boats with my father—racing skiffs, canoes, kayaks, and sailboats—was another influence. Reading a book about the principles of flight, and what creates positive and negative pressure, and how this pressure differential can be applied to architecture. These are very vital: to understand timber, the grain, which way you plane, whether you put timber on a wall horizontally or vertically, what the weathering patterns are, what the durability is, which timbers are for inside and for outside. These are the vocabularies that I absorbed as a kid. _ "Spirit and Sensibility," *Architecture*, October 1998

My father actually propagated native Australian plants where others were planting exotic plants. He took native Australian seeds and put them in the oven and fired them or poured boiling water

*Above*: The Magney House is so far away from the nearest utility it has to be largely self-sufficient; a hearth under the master bedroom helps with heating. The house runs east-west and faces north to take full advantage of the sun. And while the roof is convex, a departure for Murcutt, the rainfall still drains into a central trough. *Opposite*: Murcutt's Bowali Visitor Information Center was designed to look like an Aboriginal rock shelter.

over them to crack them open and then plant them. He was reforesting areas that were depleted by the intrusion of human habitation. _ Glenn Murcutt interview by Yoshio Futagawa, *GA Houses*, May 2003

**New Guinea Upbringing** My parents were great travelers. My father lived in Papua, New Guinea. My mother went up to join him when they were married. . . . We were very self-sufficient and independent. We grew our own vegetables and had our own milk. . . . This lifestyle had a very powerful influence on me, because I learned about independence. I learned about not having to rely on a whole lot of other people living around me. I learned how to live and be by myself. I loved New Guinea very much. But we also lived with a great degree of fear there because the local indigenous people, the Ku Ku Ku Ku, were a very fierce people who sometimes killed Europeans. Because of this, I learned to be aware of what was around me, to always listen to what was happening. . . . All of my early experiences had to do with a sense of place, of climate and its patterns, a sense of fear, survival, and danger. _ Glenn Murcutt interview by Yoshio Futagawa, *GA Houses*, May 2003

**Australia** Another influence is the Australian landscape. Life is so clear in most parts of this country. Drought is a big issue, as is flood, and the trees have adapted. They track the sun throughout the day. . . . I look at the way the landscape feathers at the edges. The flora is so powerful and yet so delicate. I love strength and delicacy as an architectural combination. _ "Spirit and Sensibility," *Architecture*, October 1998

**Architects and Writers** I also read Henry David Thoreau [who] said that the mass of men lead [lives of] quiet desperation: Their resignation is confirmed desperation. I didn't want that quiet desperation. I have to be able to see positive things. . . . Frank Lloyd Wright and Ludwig Mies van der Rohe made a powerful impression on me at university. I saw the Maison de Verre in 1973, and for the first time I saw Modernism without dogma—rationale and poetry as inseparable. _ "Spirit and Sensibility," *Architecture*, October 1998

**❝❝ THE IMPORTANT THING IS TO CHOOSE ONE'S INFLUENCES CAREFULLY BY UNDERSTANDING THE PRINCIPLES BEHIND WHAT PEOPLE DO. ❞❞**

**Education** *Murcutt makes the point that an awareness of nature and natural forms, as well as an understanding of historical forms, makes for the most human sort of architecture.*

Teaching is very important to me. I combine teaching and practice, and the important thing when I teach in other parts of the world is that I'm teaching principles that are transferable. Culture may not be transferable, but principles are. . . . One responds to one's own place and culture. . . . But I try to make them [students] aware. I make them address places, cultures, climate, landscape, and technology. _ Glenn Murcutt interview by Yoshio Futagawa, *GA Houses*, May 2003

**EMPHASIZED MATERIALITY** We are not that interested in telling stories. That is why we do not produce a very narrative or didactic architecture. Rather, we make architecture that, in the most elementary way possible, expresses the being of the materials used, the being of the site, the being of the physical reality of the world. We are interested in such elementary questions as: What is a wall? What is a surface? What is transparency? These questions have an immediate effect on the sensual, perceptual abilities of the observer and the user.

We insist on the world's materiality, on the multiplicity of sense as a central condition of humanity. In our opinion, the spiritual quality of architecture and art lies exactly in this emphasized materiality. . . . We like weight just as much as we like light constructions. We don't have a preference. There is a specific weight to everything that we are interested in, not an absolute weight.

_ Cynthia Davidson, *ANY*, no. 13, 1996

# JACQUES HERZOG & PIERRE DE MEURON

**BORN:** Jacques Herzog: April 19, 1950, Basel, Switzerland; Pierre de Meuron: May 8, 1950, Basel, Switzerland

**EDUCATION:** Diploma, Swiss Federal Institute of Technology, Zurich, 1975

**OFFICE:** Rheinschanze 6, Basel CH–4056, Switzerland
Tel: +41 0-61-385-57-57, Fax: +41 0-61-385-57-58
info@herzogdemeuron.com

**PROJECTS FEATURED:** Beijing National Stadium, China, 2008; de Young Museum, San Francisco, 2004; The Tate Modern, London, 2001; Goetz Art Gallery, Munich, 1992

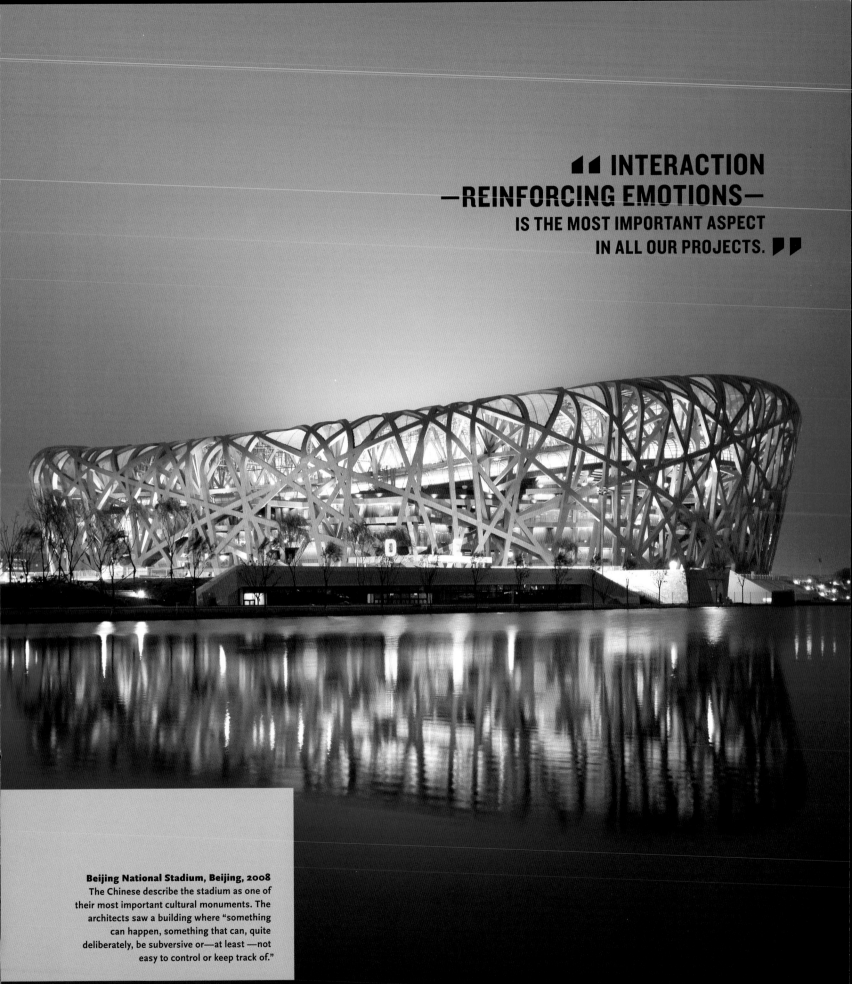

**❝ INTERACTION
—REINFORCING EMOTIONS—
IS THE MOST IMPORTANT ASPECT
IN ALL OUR PROJECTS. ❞**

**Beijing National Stadium, Beijing, 2008**
The Chinese describe the stadium as one of
their most important cultural monuments. The
architects saw a building where "something
can happen, something that can, quite
deliberately, be subversive or—at least —not
easy to control or keep track of."

## PERCEPTUAL ARCHITECTURE AND SENSORY EXPERIENCE

In architecture, "light or heavy" has more of a perceptual than a physical meaning. Something transparent appears light to us; something opaque appears heavy. These categorizations are deceptive; this is why we want to question them and infiltrate them. For this reason we've started making opaque concrete walls look light, using, for example, a thin layer of water flowing over them, as in the Ricola Europe Building in Mulhouse [France]. Another method is printing photographic images on concrete, as we did in the Sports Center Pfaffenholz in St. Louis, France, or in the library project for Eberswalde, near Berlin. "Tattooed" with images, the concrete seems porous and light. . . . To say it simply, the world's physical reality is much more complex and not as clearly tangible as we, out of pure habit, assume it to be. In our architecture, we try to express this complexity. _ Cynthia Davidson, *ANY*, no. 13, 1996

Architecture has to communicate this complex sensuality concentrated in one place and simultaneously have an effect in order to attract us, to convey its meaning to us, and to demonstrate its interpretation. _ Jacques Herzog and Pierre de Meuron, *A + U: Architecture and Urbanism*, February 2002

graphical or entertaining component) that fascinates us, that moves us, that enables us to encounter our own physical presence. _ Gerhard Mack, *Herzog & de Meuron 1989–1991, The Complete Works Volume 2*, Basel, Switzerland: Birkhäuser, 2005

## ARCHITECTURE AND CIVILIZATION

We have no recipe, no ideological basis, as for example [Aldo] Rossi or the modernists had. They formulated a precise idea of what a city should be like. When some years ago we did a study for the tri-national agglomeration of Basel, called "Basel, eine Stadt im Werden?" [Basel, An Evolving City?], we adopted a phenomenological analysis, based on progressive observation more than on a thesis: We noted then that every city has certain tendencies, certain lines of development, certain specific and nonspecific places. And it was these aspects that we wanted to get to know and to understand: Where is nature, where is topography, where is the city in its substance—the historic city, the new city—where are the dynamic zones and the "latent" ones which have a potential; where is the stillness and where is the energy? We wanted simply to understand how we could work on the existing features of a place, and how they can be enhanced. _ Jacques Herzog in conversation with Rita Capezzuto, *Domus 823*, February 2000

## ❞❞ WHAT WE TRY TO APPLY IS A KIND OF TAI-CHI METHOD OF PHENOMENOLOGICAL OBSERVATION, WHICH IN THE FUTURE COULD PRODUCE SUCCESSFUL RESULTS. ❞❞

Architecture is the extension of the body of the architect into a new, projected outward form. It is a kind of reproduction, a copy or rather an expression of the entire sensory experience of the architect. In this it is like a film made by a filmmaker or the picture by a painter, or the song of a musician. It is the physical and sensory presence of the film in the cinema and the sound from the loudspeaker (and not any bio-

Architecture is actually something of no importance. It's only a psychogram of what people are, what cities are, what cultures are. That's what makes architecture interesting, not architecture in itself. Because all the things that you can discover and analyze in architecture can also be found in other areas of our civilization. _ Jacques Herzog and Dietmar Steiner, *Domus 828*, July 2000

BEIJING 2008
## BEIJING NATIONAL STADIUM

We normally don't think in terms of symbols, but the stadium has become one. This building is literally adored. The Chinese themselves describe it as one of their most important cultural monuments, on par with the Great Wall of China. They identify with it and call it the bird's nest. In essence, who built it is no longer relevant. _ Jacques Herzog interview by Ulrike Knöfel and Susanne Beyer, *Spiegel Online International*, July 30, 2008

For us, this stadium is more than just a building. It's a part of a city. Vision is always such a big word, but our vision was to create a public space, a space for the public, where social life is possible, where something can happen, something that can, quite deliberately, be subversive or—at least—not easy to control or keep track of. _ Jacques Herzog interview by Ulrike Knöfel and Susanne Beyer, *Spiegel Online International*, July 30, 2008

The interior of the stadium reveals its massive dimensions: 36 km of wrapped steel embrace nearly 2,196,000 square feet of usable space. *Opposite:* Drawing of the complex building.

> THE SPATIAL EFFECT OF THE STADIUM IS NOVEL AND RADICAL AND YET SIMPLE AND OF AN ALMOST ARCHAIC IMMEDIACY. ITS APPEARANCE IS PURE STRUCTURE. **FAÇADE AND STRUCTURE ARE IDENTICAL.**

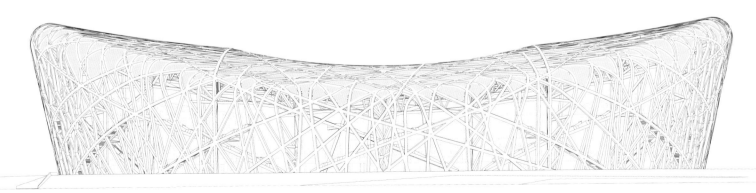

**"NO ONE IN BEIJING ASKED US TO DELIVER AN IDEOLOGICAL BUILDING."**

*Above:* **Inside the Beijing National Stadium and,** *opposite,* **a street-level view.**

**On Building in China** I know that there are architects who now claim that they would never have even considered building in China. This is both a naïve and arrogant position, one that reflects a lack of knowledge of and respect for the incredible cultural achievements this country has continuously provided over the last 5,000 years and still provides today. _ Jacques Herzog interview by Ulrike Knöfel and Susanne Beyer, *Spiegel Online International,* July 30, 2008

We are now convinced that building there [in China] was the right decision. We too cannot accept the disregard for human rights in any form whatsoever. However, we do believe that some things have opened up in this country. We see progress. And we should continue from that point. We do not wish to overemphasize our role, but the stadium is perhaps a component of this path, or at least a small stone. _ Jacques Herzog interview by Ulrike Knöfel and Susanne Beyer, *Spiegel Online International,* July 30, 2008

**Architecture of Contradictions** Before we accept a commission, we ask ourselves whether we can achieve something that goes beyond the commercial. Our strength is to develop buildings that permit contradictions. We refuse to take part in projects that permit only one use, one form of interpretation, perhaps even an ideological interpretation. No one in Beijing asked us to deliver an ideological building. _ Jacques Herzog interview by Ulrike Knöfel and Susanne Beyer, *Spiegel Online International,* July 30, 2008

**" OUR STRENGTH IS TO DEVELOP BUILDINGS THAT PERMIT CONTRADICTIONS. "**

## CONTEMPORARY CONSIDERATIONS FOR ARCHITECTURE

We don't think in historical terms, but in contemporary terms. How are architecture, the city, and the landscape changing today? This affects our lives directly and those of the people who use our buildings. Everyone knows how rarely contemporary architecture functions and is accepted. This is also a constant source of uncertainty for us, which makes the success of a building like the Bird's Nest in Beijing all the more incredible. People have accepted it with an unbelievable amount of joy. No one can force that on them. It's simply there. Even in a dictatorship like China. _ Jacques Herzog interview by Ulrike Knöfel and Susanne Beyer, *Spiegel Online International,* July 30, 2008

## STADIUMS, FOOTBALL, AND ARCHITECTURE

*In addition to the Beijing National Stadium, Herzog & de Meuron have completed a number of other stadiums, including the Allianz Arena in Munich, Germany (2005), and St. Jakob Stadium in Basel, Switzerland (2001). The firm is currently designing the Portsmouth Stadium in England.*

I love football. I grew up next to a football stadium—in the backyard of FC Basel [a Swiss football club based in Basel], so to speak. I also played for a long time myself, and today I am a passionate spectator in the stadium. _ Jacques Herzog interview by Frank Kaltenbach and Christian Schittich, *Detail,* September 2005

## STADIUM DESIGN

Until recently, stadiums were mostly planned by engineers or specialized companies. As far as I know, the Basel stadium was one of the first where genuinely architectural considerations were more important than populist devices like gigantic sliding roofs. The Olympic Stadium in Munich is another example. _ Jacques Herzog interview by Frank Kaltenbach and Christian Schittich, *Detail,* September 2005

**" THE AUDIENCE CREATES THE FOOTBALL STADIUM, NOT JUST THE ARCHITECTURE. EVER SEEN A GAME PLAYED BEHIND CLOSED DOORS? ARCHITECTURE HAS TO BE A SENSUAL INTELLIGENT MEDIUM; OTHERWISE IT'S JUST BORING. . . . "**

## DETAILS

*In contemporary architectural practice, it is common for an architecture firm to focus on one of two major aspects: 1) design or 2) detailing and working drawings. Herzog and de Meuron's firm is exceptional for both aspects in its practice.*

Details are always very important. The construction planning for the stadium [Allianz Arena] was done entirely in our office, as with almost all our projects. _ Jacques Herzog interview by Frank Kaltenbach and Christian Schittich, *Detail,* September 2005

> **" WE THOUGHT THE ART
> SHOULD BE LESS HIERARCHICALLY
> PRESENTED—MORE LIKE
> CONTEMPORARY ART
> THAN LIKE BIJOUX. ""**

### SAN FRANCISCO 2004
# DE YOUNG MUSEUM
The museum project was a chance to create a cluster of different projects, which is always very interesting because you can then test totally different approaches to architecture. . . . The diversity of approach is also a method or a tool to escape your own routine. _ Aaron Betsky, "Interview with Jacques Herzog," in Diana Ketcham, *The de Young in the 21st Century,* London: Thames & Hudson, 2005

Like a protagonist in a novel, the San Francisco fog played a significant role in the design of the de Young. Herzog & de Meuron constructed the museum with warm, earthy materials, including copper and stone.

### Nonhierarchical Presentation of Art
The hierarchy in museums is left over from an elitist way of thinking in which the superiority of our culture over that of the "other" should be demonstrated. Also, within

our specific culture *a priori* positioning was more widespread than open access to the differences of forms and the thinking behind them. San Francisco, which as a city is so much about the diversity of different cultures and cultural influences, should have a new de Young museum that is open to experimental and nonhierarchical presentations of its holdings. _ Aaron Betsky, "Interview with Jacques Herzog," in Diana Ketcham, *The de Young in the 21st Century,* London: Thames & Hudson, 2005

### Atmosphere and Material: Impact and Influence
The fog has inspired us insofar that we wanted the building to deal with it, to use it as a conscious element of the design. It does so in two ways: first,

through the fuzzy, perforated façade panels that seem to blur the edges of the building volume. Clearly the fog enhances this moment of the blur. Secondly, we chose copper as a material because it ages well. We know how it performs and transforms itself over the years. Copper acts almost like a scientific instrument that measures and expresses the impact and change of the climate. The impact of fog, humidity, and heavy sun are likely to transform the embossed and perforated copper panels much more positively than they would any other façade material. _ Aaron Betsky, "Interview with Jacques Herzog," in Diana Ketcham, *The de Young in the 21st Century,* London: Thames & Hudson, 2005

We have used the concept of the blur in many projects for different reasons. One is to express doubt rather than certainty when it comes to defining or positioning volumes in a given context. Here the blur will be enhanced by the fog penetrating through the multiple perforations in the façade panels. It will be especially interesting to see the fog building up in layers, with the lower part of the building hidden in a cloud of fog and the tower twisting out of it, or vice versa. _ Aaron Betsky, "Interview with Jacques Herzog," in Diana Ketcham, *The de Young in the 21st Century,* London: Thames & Hudson, 2005

Another key element for this blur of inside and outside is the large perforated canopy that opens up to the Japanese garden. The Japanese garden thus becomes part of the museum displays in some way. The park, the artwork, and the viewer are involved and bound in a process of looking and being looked at: the viewer becoming aware of the work of art, becoming aware of himself or herself, and becoming aware of his or her presence here and now. This sounds stupidly simple, but, in fact, it is what we always thought a museum space should really achieve. Hence we tried to come as close as we could to this ideal perceptual condition, which was a real challenge because of the diversity of the gallery types. _ Aaron Betsky, "Interview with Jacques Herzog," in Diana Ketcham, *The de Young in the 21st Century,* London: Thames & Hudson, 2005

## MATERIAL LAYERING

One can then see how they are bound to our unmediated sensual life. If, for example, one sees a huge chrome-plated car, one thinks of the 1950s and associates it immediately with the films of that era. Such coded images always inhere to materials. We nonetheless believe that coding of this sort is receding in world culture, whereas overlapping, layering, is gaining the upper hand. _ Jacques Herzog and Pierre de Meuron interview by Lynnette Widder, *Daidalos*, Special Issue, August 1995

entity is comparable to simply coursed stone. When we juxtapose projects based upon their special qualities or structural similarities, we are often astonished that relationships do exist amongst them. For example, we perceive that in an early project, something is already expressed which only later became of real concern to us, or that something quite different is expressed than we had always thought. These categories are ambiguous and overlapping. _ Jacques Herzog and Pierre de Meuron interview by Lynnette Widder, *Daidalos*, Special Issue, August 1995

> **WE WORK WITHOUT BRIGHT COLORS OR DECORATION BECAUSE IN OUR OPINION IT IS IN FACT THIS UNTOUCHED 'NATURAL' STATE OF THESE COMMON MATERIALS, THEIR 'PURITY,' SO TO SPEAK, WHICH GIVES THE BUILDINGS AN EXTRAORDINARY EFFECT.**

Each individual has increasingly easy access to ever more images. In fashion, it has become impossible to say if an item belongs to the 50s, 60s, [or] of another decade, because the stylistic categories have repeated themselves so often that they all exist parallel. We try to work in a similar way, to destroy categories and to avoid stylistic references to the benefit of immediate sensation. We want to disjoin substances from coded concepts in order to use them unrestrictedly. _ Jacques Herzog and Pierre de Meuron interview by Lynnette Widder, *Daidalos*, Special Issue, August 1995

## AMBIGUOUS AND OVERLAPPING CATEGORIES

When we prepare a lecture, we do juxtapose projects according to specific, if often varied, considerations, such as external characteristics or color. We can relate the Blue House to the Stone House in Tavole [Italy] so as to demonstrate that the application of pigment as a visibly material

## IMMATERIAL MATERIALITY

"Firmitas" *was a theoretical essay written by Herzog & de Meuron in 1996. In it, the architects reformulate the concept of* firmitas *from the Vitruvian triad for classical architecture of* firmitas, utilitas, *and* venustas *(stability, utility, and beauty) in a contemporary context.*

It [*firmitas*] is not the fact of the stable materiality, but the immaterial, spiritual quality that is communicated to our sense through the material solidification. It is the dissoluble bond between material and immaterial characteristics of architecture that attracts us and refuses to let go; it is that to which we submit ourselves like to a beloved body that takes us away for a moment into a magical world. _ Jacques Herzog and Pierre de Meuron, *A + U: Architecture and Urbanism*, Special Issue, February 2002

### LONDON 2001
# THE TATE MODERN

This [the urban context of the Tate Modern] is, in fact, a very important component. The building (especially the huge turbine hall, which will work like a covered street where people can walk without necessarily visiting the museum), the galleries, and the landscaping are part of the neighborhood. . . . We will take down small buildings so that some view of St. Paul's and the River Thames is possible and so that you can approach the building. . . . Using both the old bricks from the low-rise buildings and new bricks (we are thinking of using shiny coal-black bricks for some of the new parts), we want to create armlike extensions into the neighborhood. We want to have paving on

the sidewalks that extends to the tube station and deep into the neighborhood—like the string that Ariadne gave to Theseus to guide him out of the labyrinth. We would like to realize this idea of the brick pavement because it evokes a very old London detail and is also a contemporary strategy. _ Cynthia Davidson, *ANY*, no. 13, 1996

**Design Concepts** The large horizontal light box on the building looks like a lantern. It transforms the dark, gloomy brick building. It lights it from two sides: from the outside and toward the inside. This light box is also an important horizontal counterweight to the vertical dominance of the existing brick chimney. _ Cynthia Davidson, *ANY*, no. 13, 1996

We use light like a family, or a language, throughout the building. The light box on top and the glass boxes inside are mostly immaterialized; ideally, they are only light. The boxes (in the turbine hall) are in front of the steel structure, physical, glowing. They cut through the steel, cut away the dominance of steel and the all-too-powerful verticality of the turbine hall. This was very important because you see the boxes mostly from an angle, and you wouldn't see anything new if they didn't come to the front. It has to do with perception and orientation as you walk through the building. _ Jacques Herzog interview by Nina Rappaport, *Architecture*, no. 5, 2000

### Learning from the Tate Modern  *The experience of designing the Tate Modern had an effect on the whole of Herzog & de Meuron's approach to designing for museums.*

We have only now properly understood what a museum actually is. And we have become far more free. It's not the case that we only represent this gallery type that we've created here. Later projects, like the de Young Museum in San Francisco—that's much freer, in its layout too, because it's a quite different collection, a quite different place. And that's an important discovery, namely that perception is dependent on the place and not on the collection culture. We don't think that the white box is the be-all and end-all. Only, for a building like the Tate, a highly restrained [box] is the only correct one. _ Jacques Herzog and Dietmar Steiner, *Domus 828*, July 2000

### Subtle and Subversive Strategy  Even now, when they look at the building, many people think: "What have they actually done?" Because they don't know that actually there was nothing there—it was full up with machinery. A large part of our work consisted in clearing up, after a fashion. And then we actually invented the building as a museum. But this invention of the building always kept close to what was actually there. For whenever we departed—in the dialectically anticipatory sense—from what was there, that always became in a sense quite ridiculous, because the existing fabric was always stronger. And that's why the architecture now plays with subtle, subversive strategy. And this in turn has something

English about it, and that in turn accords with our way of doing architecture. _ Jacques Herzog and Dietmar Steiner, *Domus 828*, July 2000

### England: "Parallelism of Contradictions"  We have discovered a different dimension of English culture, the traditional dimension that suddenly turns out to be something quite different. We accepted that, because we also had to accept this building in many ways, because it is so massive, and then we did turn it into something else after all. This is something I discovered in England, this parallelism of contradictions, which I also feel as liberating. This is also something which Hitchcock celebrated in exemplary fashion. No clear contrasts, the beautiful and the ugly, good and evil, but everything is together in one thing, directly. And that is a central element of our work, and now it has simply grown clearer. _ Jacques Herzog and Dietmar Steiner, *Domus 828*, July 2000

## A MANIFESTO OF SORTS

The architecture we think, draw, imagine, describe; the architecture we photograph and capture on video; the one we define as correct, more correct, or at least more important than other, older or contemporary architectures; the architecture we love, or at least during one phase of our lives loved; the architecture we pursued, the one we accompany with the entire energy of our perception, day and night, into which we penetrate, bodily and in thought . . . without us it does not exist and without it, we do not exist. _ Gerhard Mack, *Herzog & de Meuron 1989–1991, The Complete Works Volume 2*, Basel, Switzerland: Birkhäuser, 2005

know how they relate to real, experienced physical reality. In that respect, the models are also testimony to an archaic understanding of body and reality. . . . Our architecture is highly tailored to the human being, the human being understood as the intersection of challenges and possibilities of the twenty-first century. As soon as architecture is restricted to just visual experience, it is dead. _ Jacques Herzog and Pierre de Meuron, *A + U: Architecture and Urbanism*, August 2006

# ❞❞ THERE IS TOO MUCH IDEOLOGY IN ARCHITECTURE. ❞❞

## PHENOMENA BOTH EXISTENTIAL AND ACTUAL

In our work, the point is always to reflect on the existing world by integrating it into our work. . . . We compare this approach to the strategy of an aikido master who turns the attacker's energies to his own ends. By means of this tactic, something new is produced. . . . _ Jacques Herzog and Pierre de Meuron, *A + U: Architecture and Urbanism*, August 2006

There are places in the world that stay still, and places that are much more dynamic. We study these phenomena from a town planning point of view. As far as architecture is concerned, the changing of elements is very important to us. Time is that of light and that of the seasons, and it interacts with architecture. _ Jacques Herzog in conversation with Rita Capezzuto, *Domus 823*, February 2000

Our concern is the spectrum of sensual capacities through which we test our own perception as well. Our culture tends toward the reduction of sensual impressions, toward the focusing of awareness on specific perceptual poles. . . . It is not a matter of reproducing that which is known, but of expanding again a reduced culture of sensual awareness. _ Jacques Herzog and Pierre de Meuron interview by Lynnette Widder, *Daidalos*, Special Issue, August 1995

## ARCHITECTURE: TAILORED TO THE HUMAN BEING

Glossy depictions of architecture are usually produced after the design—political images, so to speak. Seducing, succeeding politically, deceiving, and misleading are all part of these virtual images, while the models are honest objects, in the sense of archaic and ancient. . . . We don't trust computers, for if we start with virtual images, we don't

Nothing is more boring or stupid than to wake up in the morning naïvely confident in what you already know. _ Jacques Herzog in conversation with Jeffery Kipnis, in Naomi Stungo, *Herzog & de Meuron*, London: Carlton Publishing Group, 2002

## "EXPRESSIONS OF OUR TIMES"

Architecture becomes contemporary the instant you focus your eyes on it, the minute you start to get interested in this or that architecture for any reason—a detail perhaps. It starts to live because you notice something about it that preoccupies you and puts your mind to work. _ Cynthia Davidson, *ANY*, no. 13, 1996

So many people think that contemporary fashion, music, and even art are superficial when compared with the aspirations and responsibilities of architecture. But we disagree. . . . These are practices that shape our sensibilities; they are expressions of our times. It is not the glamorous aspect of fashion which fascinates us. In fact we are more interested in what people are wearing, what they like to wrap around their bodies. . . . We are interested in that aspect of artificial skin which becomes so much of an intimate part of people. _ Naomi Stungo, *Herzog & de Meuron*, London: Carlton Publishing Group, 2002

# ❞❞ WE ABHOR CYNICISM. ❞❞

## VAMPIRE STYLE APPROACH

*Herzog's reference to "vampire style" implies that people are both influenced and transformed by experience or events.*

In a kind of a vampire style, we try to take everything. Everybody is always influenced by, and influencing, things in architecture but also in fashion, and also in art. It's more that kind of history than the traditional sort where you take precedence from a book with recipes. And that specific way of dealing with the existing, and transforming it, and making something new is ultimately what makes the quality and the style of a work. _ Jacques Herzog interview by *Telegraph* readers, *Telegraph*, June 2001

## MUNICH 1992
## GOETZ ART GALLERY
The Goetz Gallery seems to fly away—and at the same time it is like a heavy piece of ice. The glass looks like ice. Because it is slightly opaque, it seems to be very heavy. We like this kind of double aspect: lightness and heaviness at the same time. In fact, architecture is always heavy. It is never really light. _ Cynthia Davidson, *ANY*, no. 13, 1996

**On Art and Architecture** Art is more progressive. Artists react more openly to changes in this world. . . . We don't think that art is superior to architecture. It is just different. We do not have problems with artists or with being architects rather than artists. Our collaborations with artists are very interesting for both sides because we are working at an equal level, making contributions of equal importance to a project. It adds a new dimension to a project. That is what interests us. . . . _ Cynthia Davidson, *ANY*, no. 13, 1996

**Collaboration** *Herzog & de Meuron were the only Pritzker recipients to share the prize as a fully collaborating pair. The 2001 Pritzker jury felt that the two architects work so closely together that each one complements the abilities and talents of the other. While Jacques Herzog tends to be the spokesperson for the firm, their work is the result of a long-term true collaboration.*

Pierre de Meuron and I played together as children and made joint designs. In each project, of course, one of us does a bit more and one a bit less. We have quite different qualities and talents, and neither of us determines his own projects. The vital thing is that we jointly create the product Herzog & de Meuron. _ Jacques Herzog interview by Frank Kaltenbach and Christian Schittich, *Detail*, September 2005

Pierre and I have actually developed our collaboration over thirty years, and it works well without our having ever analyzed it in detail. . . . It is important for us in the future to extend this collaboration with people of disparate creative potential, such as architects, engineers, biologists, and artists, down to the general industrialists and the cost accountants. . . . We are not interested in inflating our own business

to gigantic proportions, as experience has shown that this entails a disproportionate growth in organizational expenditure. _ Gerhard Mack, *Herzog & de Meuron 1989–1991, The Complete Works Volume 2*, Basel, Switzerland: Birkhäuser, 2005

**The Future** For the past two years, Pierre de Meuron and I have been paying more and more attention to one question, namely: How do we work today, and what will we want and be able to do in ten or twenty years? How can we hold younger architects to account? And how do we adjust our organizational form to conform to the changes? . . . Most of all, we want to shock ourselves and our people with such scenarios and questions. _ Jacques Herzog interview by Ulrike Knöfel and Susanne Beyer, *Spiegel Online International*, July 30, 2008

Pierre and I want to continue to be involved in our old age. But that can only happen if the firm is capable of functioning well without us. This means that young people from around the world work for us around the world. This cooperation among different generations could also be a model for society. _ Jacques Herzog interview by Ulrike Knöfel and Susanne Beyer, *Spiegel Online International*, July 30, 2008

**"WE PREFER ART TO ARCHITECTURE, AND FOR THAT MATTER, ARTISTS TO ARCHITECTS."**

The Goetz Art Gallery is located on a quiet residential street in Munich. The idea was to blend the gallery into the leafy suburb while at the same time providing a daylight environment for the art collection.

**FROM JOURNALIST TO ARCHITECT** Well, unlike most architects, I had a profession before I was an architect. I think that being a journalist had an important effect. Journalism is ironically one of the few professions that is almost completely immune to fame. There are almost no famous journalists. The journalist is driven by an insatiable curiosity coupled with the ability to find and condense information quickly. That experience, coupled with the fact that I started relatively late in architecture—I was twenty-five before I even started studying architecture—made it relatively easy for me not to feel intimidated by the architecture world at that stage. The great benefit of writing a book before practicing as an architect was that it helped me get work. But it was bad because it meant that my subsequent work had to meet an unusually heavy burden of proof. I think that my experience exposed me to a number of unspoken prejudices that still operate in the current cultural moment. There's a strange prejudice that says you cannot both think and do architecture at the same time. _ *"Rem Koolhaas," Perspecta*, no. 37, 2005

# REM KOOLHAAS

**BORN:** November 17, 1944, Rotterdam, The Netherlands

**EDUCATION:** Diploma, Architectural Association, School of Architecture, London, 1972

**OFFICE:** Office for Metropolitan Architecture, Heer Bokelweg 149, 3032 AD Rotterdam, The Netherlands
Tel: +31 10-243-82-00, Fax: +31 10-243-82-02
office@oma.com, www.oma.nl

**PROJECTS FEATURED:** Seattle Central Library, Washington, 2004; McCormick Tribune Campus Center, Illinois Institute of Technology, Chicago, 2003; Prada SoHo, New York, 2001; Bordeaux House, France, 1998; Netherlands Dance Theater, The Hague, 1987

**❝ AN ARCHITECT WITH THEORETICAL AND LITERARY INTERESTS, WITH THE NEED TO ANALYZE THE EXACT CONDITIONS AND EXACT POTENTIALS OF THE PROFESSION. THAT IS MY INTERPRETATION OF MY OWN ACTIVITIES. ❞**

**McCormick Tribune Campus Center, Chicago, 2003**
The late architecture critic Herbert Muschamp described this 530-foot-long corrugated stainless steel tube as a "metaphor for absorption, for a receptive frame of mind." The tube not only contained the interfering sound of the train, it also served to suggest the mind itself, through which ideas swirl and form. For Koolhaas, this first project on U.S. soil was a revelatory triumph.

## THEORIST AND ARCHITECT

The relationship for me between the two is incredibly strong, although I never really thought that it would be possible to be a theoretician of architecture and an architect. I always felt [I was] an architect. An architect with theoretical and literary interests, with the need to analyze the exact conditions and exact potentials of the profession. That is my interpretation of my own activities. Ultimately, I wrote *Delirious New York* [1978] to define for myself an agenda of what was interesting and what could be done. And all I can confess is that it was a painful transition: to exercise the profession is almost a bestial activity. _ Alejandro Zaera Polo, *El Croquis*, February 1992

## ❝ IN MY OWN MIND, I AM AS MUCH A WRITER AS AN ARCHITECT. ❞

## ON WINNING THE PRITZKER PRIZE

In no sequence of importance: It's exciting, it's a lot of money, it seems that for the first time in recent memory they gave it to another kind of architect, and they acknowledged that other fields, like writing, are also important. They adopted a certain kind of openness toward the definition of architecture in the twenty-first century, and a modification of the identity of the architect. That will be good for other people. _ Rem Koolhaas interview by Jennifer Sigler, *Interview*, 2000

What almost nobody really understands about architecture is that it is a paradoxical mixture of power and powerlessness . . . the internal shift was based on a criticism of our own work, reinforced by criticism of almost everybody else's work. In the end, it was also the final installment of my transformation from a writer into a building architect that began in the early 80s. _ Alejandro Zaera Polo, *El Croquis*, February 1992

The Campus Center is all metal and glass. History (Mies van der Rohe) meets the present (Koolhaas) in the McCormick Center: the Bauhaus master designed the campus and later Koolhaas significantly added the one-story building and acoustic steel tube.

### CHICAGO 2003
### McCORMICK TRIBUNE CAMPUS CENTER, ILLINOIS INSTITUTE OF TECHNOLOGY

The physical heart of the campus is our project. By not stacking activities, but by positioning each programmatic particle as part of a dense mosaic, our building contains the urban condition itself. _ Rem Koolhaas, arcspace.com, February 2004

To capture the sum of the student flows, the web of lines that connect the eastern and western campus destinations are organized through the campus center to differentiate activities into streets, plazas, and urban islands. Without fragmenting the overall building, each part is articulated according to its specific needs and positioned to create neighborhoods (24-hour, commercial, entertainment, academic, utili-

> **THERE ARE NO WALLS, ONLY PARTITIONS, SHIMMERING MEMBRANES FREQUENTLY COVERED IN MIRROR OR GOLD.**

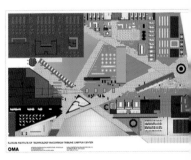

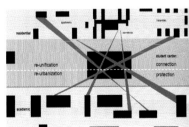

A long glass wall displays portraits of several IIT founders. Detail of the glass wall, right. *Below:* Early sketches of the project.

tarian), parks, and other urban elements in miniature. The main federating element is the roof, a continuous concrete slab that shields the center from the noise of the elevated railway while unifying the heterogeneity below. _ Rem Koolhaas, arcspace.com, February 2004

### Subverting Mies: Explicit Information   *Embedded within a campus designed by Mies van der Rohe, Rem Koolhaas's design conceptually engages it. While Koolhaas has written on his admiration of Mies, the McCormick Tribune Campus Center design demonstrates both an intelligence and subversion of Mies's design ideology.*

. . . when IIT opened [in the 1940s], you could probably assume that everyone would feel very welcome in a highly abstract space such as Crown Hall [designed by Mies]. . . . I think that if the current generation enters a building like that, [it would be] highly dubious. They would kind of feel a weird absence of information . . . given the fact that the student body is now literally from at least four or five continents, it felt very important to try to develop a language of fundamental information that is effective in those circumstances. . . . I think it's really for this explicit purpose and this explicit program, and this explicit condition. _ Rem Koolhaas interview with Lynn Becker, lynnbecker.com

*An important collaboration was with 2x4, a New York–based multidisciplinary studio, which was instrumental in the graphic design and iconography of the project, or what Koolhaas refers to as "explicit"-ness. Koolhaas explains the bold use of color that contributed to the dynamism of the interior space of the McCormick Tribune Campus Center.*

I think that one of my fascinations with Mies is his sense of color, even though at first he is not usually associated with color. But I think that in the 20s and 30s he did some really strong experiments with color, and I can also kind of remember the first time I was in the Chicago Arts Club [designed by Mies in 1951] that there is a kind of really strident and outrageous sense of color. I didn't necessarily want to make it strident or outrageous, but I think that . . . being that color somehow brings out the color in the Mies building, [Koolhaas's design has direct access into a Mies building] also. _ Rem Koolhaas interview with Lynn Becker, lynnbecker.com

. . . it's important to have these vast expanses of exposed sheetrock because this in a way is a kind of return of Miesian Puritanism about steel, but a more abject material. _ Rem Koolhaas interview with Lynn Becker, lynnbecker.com

## WRITING AND ARCHITECTURE: *DELIRIOUS NEW YORK*

*For Rem Koolhaas, writing is symbiotic with architecture. Conceptual ideas that are fundamental to his practice are expressed through writing, research, and architecture. Koolhaas's first book,* Delirious New York, A Retroactive Manifesto for Manhattan, *was published in 1978. In it, Koolhaas recasts Manhattan's history from 1850 onward as a mythical laboratory for the invention and testing of a "Culture of Congestion."*

This book is an interpretation of that Manhattan which gives its seemingly discontinuous—even irreconcilable—episodes a degree of consistency and coherence, and interpretation that intends to establish Manhattan as the product of an unformulated theory, *Manhattanism,* whose program—to exist in a world totally fabricated by man, i.e., to live *inside* fantasy—was so ambitious that to be realized, it could never be openly stated. _ Rem Koolhaas, *Delirious New York,* New York: Oxford University Press, 1978

The structure of the text [*Delirious New York*] is very architectural. . . . Its written structure is analogous to the urbanism it describes. In terms of its layout, its fragmentation, it is also very architectural. . . . It is a book without a single "however," and that to me is very architectural. It has the same logic as a city. Anyway, a crucial element of the work—whether writing or architecture—*is montage.* _ Cynthia Davidson, *ANY,* May–June 1993

### ❝❝ THE DESIGN IS A DEMONSTRATION OF A THESIS OR A QUESTION OR A LITERARY IDEA. ❞❞

I would say that the writing of [*Delirious*] *New York* had one major "aim": I wanted to construct—as a writer—a terrain where I could eventually work as an architect. . . . I was trying to deemphasize the artistic part of being an architect and describe a role that was much more concerned with intellectual issues, where other interventions were possible and therefore, by definition, could not be done through drawing. . . . I would say that almost at the beginning of every project there is maybe not writing but a definition in words—a text—a concept, ambition, or theme that is put in words, and only at the moment that it is put in words can we begin to proceed, to think about architecture; the words unleash the design. All of our projects, or our best projects or maybe our most original projects, are first defined in literary terms, which then suggest an entire architectural program. _ Cynthia Davidson, *ANY,* May–June 1993

### ❝❝ . . . THE WORDS UNLEASH THE DESIGN . . . ❞❞

## *S,M,L,XL*

*Koolhaas's* Small, Medium, Large, Extra-Large *was published in 1995. Far from a typical monograph,* S,M,L,XL *represents the first twenty years of the work of Koolhaas's architecture firm, The Office for Metropolitan Architecture.* S,M,L,XL *is a collection of architectural projects, photos and sketches, diary excerpts, and personal travelogues, as well as critical essays on contemporary architecture and society. The following is an excerpt from the book.*

Architecture is a hazardous mixture of omnipotence and impotence. Ostensibly involved in "shaping" the world, for their thoughts to be mobilized architects depend on the provocations of others—clients, individual or institutional. Therefore, incoherence, or more precisely, randomness, is the underlying structure of all architects' careers: They are confronted with an arbitrary sequence of demands, with parameters they did not establish, in countries they hardly know, about issues they are only dimly aware of, expected to deal with problems that have proved intractable to brains vastly superior to their own. Architecture is by definition a *chaotic adventure.* _ Rem Koolhaas and Bruce Mau, *S,M,L,XL,* New York: Monacelli, 1995

*The writing of* S,M,L,XL *came at a crucial moment. In 1989, the cancellation of a major commission, The Center for Art and Media Technology in Karlsruhe, Germany, led to a major downsizing and financial collapse of OMA. It was at this moment that Koolhaas began work on the book.*

In the pre-'95 period of the firm, we nearly bankrupted ourselves by participating in important competitions that were open to everyone, or competitions where we were only partly paid. They are life-threatening, but the only potential source of future life. _ Arthur Lubow, *New York Times Magazine,* July 9, 2000

## "ABSOLUTE EQUIVALENCE BETWEEN THE UNBUILT AND BUILT"

*S,M,L,XL* is deliberately seamless about this, trying to present an absolute equivalence between unbuilt and built, because in a way I think it's a moot point. Of course, it can be very inspiring to build things. But part of the goal of the book was to explore architecture that didn't come to fruition. I was also interested in showing the implications of failure—showing both the calculations and the miscalculations of projects. _ Rem Koolhaas interview by Katrina Heron, *Wired,* April 2007

I have always had a psychological thing of wanting to re-create or destroy. The book [*S,M,L,XL*] was an initial way of examining what we are doing and have been doing. It was also a deliberate suspension of the office to make a new beginning. _ Arthur Lubow, *New York Times Magazine,* July 9, 2000

## SEATTLE 2004
# SEATTLE CENTRAL LIBRARY A

project always begins with intuition. We play with evidences . . . we prepare a kind of catalogue of prototypes. . . . It's in this way that we transform empty concepts into rich concepts for our project. These inventories of life, of what's topical, are constantly in movement. There's no exclusive territory. . . . I don't establish hierarchies; what counts is the panorama. By means of questions posed, developments, implications, we once again define a situation in permanent transition. . . . And also of coherence, with this awareness we have of the fact that there is no absolutely fixed, completely immobile, value. I mistrust the definitive enunciation of a theoretical position. Our

projects are not born from previously known reflections. _ Rem Koolhaas, *Urban Projects (1985–1990)*, Barcelona: Editorial Gustavo Gili, 1990

I like to do things that on first sight have a degree of simplicity but show their complexity in the way they are used or at second glance. . . . We are flamboyant conceptually, but not formally. _ Arthur Lubow, *New York Times Magazine,* July 9, 2000

I always hesitated between exploding things and making things. And right now it is ten times more interesting to *make* things than to *explode* things, also because explosion lasts one moment, but making takes much longer. _ Alejandro Zaera Polo, *El Croquis,* February 1992

*Opposite: Delirious New York* and *S,M,L,XL* were attention-getting and groundbreaking when first published. Today they are architectural classics. The Seattle Central Library is an example of a city making changes for the betterment of a community. The library not only houses over 1 million books, it has an innovative "Book Spiral" and digital equipment.

> **" MUSEUMS ARE POPULAR, NOT FOR THEIR CONTENT, BUT FOR THEIR *LACK* OF CONTENT: YOU GO, YOU LOOK, YOU LEAVE. NO DECISIONS, NO PRESSURE. OUR AMBITION IS TO CAPTURE ATTENTION AND THEN, ONCE WE HAVE IT, TO HAND IT BACK TO THE CONSUMER. "**

### NEW YORK 2001
## PRADA, SOHO
They asked us to make a proposal for how they could manage their expansion without losing their reputation for adventure and experimentation . . . how they could REMain interesting or surprising in spite of their much greater presence . . . _ Rem Koolhaas interview by Jennifer Sigler, *Interview*, 2000

Expansion can be measured on two levels: quantity and quality. . . . The danger of the large number is repetition: Each additional store reduces aura and contributes to a sense of familiarity. The danger of the larger scale is the Flagship Syndrome: a megalomaniac accumulation of the obvious that eliminates the last elements of surprise and mystery that cling to the brand, imprisoning it in a "definitive" identity. . . _ OMA/AMO Rem Koolhaas, *Prada*, Milan: Fondazione Prada, 2001

. . . we're involved in defining their identity in virtual space. We're also working on technological advances that can make the experience of being in a store better—we're trying to reinvent the dressing room, the cash register: We're trying to REMove some of the traditional irritants of shopping. One of the irritants of shopping is that you always have to know exactly when you're in a store and when you're not, so we tried to blur the limits. _ Rem Koolhaas interview by Jennifer Sigler, *Interview*, 2000

*Koolhaas's approach to retail design or "branding" rejects traditional formulations. Instead of establishing a permanent identity and propagating it repetitively, he defines branding as an opportunity for fluidity in variety and innovation.*

I think there's much more interesting work that you can do with a brand or any identity, which is to make it more variable and less redundant in terms of its significance. If I'm not mistaken—and I may be very mistaken—what is developing is an American ideology of the brand, which is the death knell of further development and therefore ultimate reactionary stability, and a European idea of the brand as something that is alive and that can assume many different identities and incur further development. When Prada briefed us, their key words were *unpredictability* and *variability*. If you look at Disney, there it's a permanent return to the "original," not-too-dangerous condition.

_ "Branding—Signs, Symbols or Something Else?" *Architectural Design,* December 2006

The Prada store is in the former home of the SoHo branch of the Guggenheim Museum. The retail experience banishes any and all competitors.

# "SHOPPING IS SURREPTITIOUSLY BECOMING THE WAY IN WHICH URBAN SUBSTANCE IS GENERATED. "

## SHOPPING

*Rem Koolhaas is a professor at Harvard University's Graduate School of Design, where he conducts "Project on the City," a research program investigating current changing urban conditions around the world. Case studies have included China's Pearl River Delta, Beijing, Rome, Lagos, and Moscow.* The Harvard Design School Guide to Shopping *and* Great Leap Forward, *both published in 2001, resulted from "Project on the City."*

Shopping is arguably the last remaining form of public activity. Through a battery of increasingly predatory forms, shopping has infiltrated, colonized, and even replaced almost every aspect of urban life. Town centers, suburbs, streets, and now airports, train stations, museums, hospitals, schools, the Internet, and the military are shaped by the mechanism and spaces of shopping. The voracity by which shopping pursues the public has, in effect, made it one of the principal—if only—modes by which we experience the city. _ Rem Koolhaas, Jeffrey Inaba, and Sze Tsung Leong, *Harvard Design School Guide to Shopping,* New York: Taschen, 2002

## EFFECTS OF THE MARKET ON ARCHITECTURE

The market economy thrives on spectacle and novelty. Its buildings are ever more dramatic. It offers the promise of total freedom, but in architecture this quickly leads to the danger of grotesqueness. It is hard to do serious, disciplined buildings in such a condition. The media, of course, encourages this teenage architecture; it gives most attention to extreme capitalist buildings, to this ever-growing accumulation of architectural extravagance, to fanciful museums full of shops. We calculated that between 1995 and 2005, OMA was asked to propose designs for thirty-four soccer fields of new museums, all a product of market growth rather than culture. Perhaps there is still a residual nostalgia for refinement, but the pressure is on the other way. _ Rem Koolhaas interview by Jonathan Glancey, *The Guardian,* August 27, 2007

SoHo [in lower Manhattan, until recently a nexus for artists and art galleries] is perhaps the most dramatic territory to document the changes in the city. Ten years ago, this entire domain was a cultural domain or an industrial domain, and now virtually every ground floor is commercial space. _ Arthur Lubow, *New York Times Magazine,* July 9, 2000

The Netherlands Dance Theater was the building in which Koolhaas says he focused on structure. The floating "Skybar," right, can support 200 people. *Opposite:* An elevation of Bordeaux House, a project that required making a new house in Bordeaux, among other things, wheelchair accessible.

### THE HAGUE 1987
# NETHERLANDS DANCE THEATER

The Dance Theater in the Hague is the building where I first became seriously involved with structure. If you see the rook and some of the structural gymnastics in the foyer, you could note the beginnings of an interest in structure. The "Skybar," for instance, supports two hundred people. Depending on whether they stand on the north or the south, the tube that holds it is either stretched or compressed. So, the structural behavior changes completely; it is not a matter of just solving the loads, but a demonstration of unstable structural behavior . . .
_ Alejandro Zaera Polo, *El Croquis*, February 1992

The first issue that interests me enormously is how in any large structure, the distribution of loads becomes bigger and bigger toward the lower part of the buildings, so that on the ground you are literally blocked by a structural and mechanical "inheritance" that comes from "above." You could propose a metaphor of a high-rise building or any big building, as the systematic reduction of freedom toward where it matters most, on the ground. _ Alejandro Zaera Polo, *El Croquis*, February 1992

## COLLABORATION: OMA OFFICE AND EXTERNAL ALLIANCES

It is an insult to me, as well as to the others, to make it all seem like just my work. . . . If I pride myself on one thing, it is a talent to collaborate. _ Arthur Lubow, *New York Times Magazine*, July 9, 2000

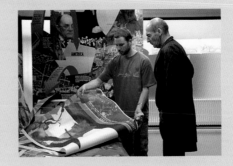

*OMA's international practice for contemporary architecture, urbanism, and cultural analysis includes an important research branch, AMO. As the mirror image of OMA, AMO is the research subsidiary to OMA. Since 2000, AMO has operated as a think tank for areas beyond the boundaries of architecture and urbanism, including sociology, technology, media, and politics.*

## ◀◀ IT'S MORE A KIND OF LAMINATION, A BONDING BETWEEN LAYERS . . . ▶▶

I like Rotterdam. We work here in a cheap office, out of the way with no distractions. We think for ourselves. We are in some ways outside the architectural loop. We do not follow fashion. _ Rem Koolhaas interview by Jonathan Glancey, *The Guardian*, August 27, 2007

I think one of the fatal things that occurs in an architect's career is the moment when he begins to take himself too seriously—where his idea of himself coincides with what the others think of him—when he runs out of secrets. I've always tried to find means and tactics with which to avoid this. Of course, at the beginning one of these was a creation of something called OMA, where my identity was submerged in a group, and that's how we've always worked, as a group. But somehow, the world insists on the individual. Some of the important people who were present in the earlier phases of OMA have been coming back, although not on a permanent basis. This external renewal generated a kind of intellectual discourse, which is otherwise endangered by the unbearable heaviness of the profession. So, rather than suffer alone and put up with your own contradictions, it's essential to insist on these kinds of injections that expand our thinking. _ Rem Koolhaas, *Urban Projects (1985–1990)*, Barcelona: Editorial Gustavo Gill, 1990

. . . what is actually happening is a diffusion or disappearance of the borders of architecture, and just like a corporate merger an increasing connection between architecture and other domains that range from design to politics. . . . The theme is to investigate the unique condition of the previous separation lines between domains like political science, graphic design, and architecture. . . . One of the effects has been of course that I have become much less an architect than I was before and that research has become an increasingly important part of the operation of our office . . . _ "Bigness & Velocity: Rem Koolhaas," *A +U: Architecture and Urbanism*, Special Issue, May 2000

*Collaboration is fundamental to Koolhaas's architectural practice. Structural engineer Cecil Balmond is one of Koolhaas's most important collaborators. His expertise has been crucial to the development of many of Koolhaas's most successful built works, including the Bordeaux House in France (1998), Seattle Central Library (2004), and Casa da Musica in Porto, Portugal (2005).*

Cecil has changed my outlook on structure and enabled me to rethink architecture. _ Koolhaas quoted by Jonathan Glancey, *The Guardian*, July 23, 2007

## BORDEAUX 1998
## BORDEAUX HOUSE
A couple lived in a very old, beautiful house in Bordeaux. They wanted a new house, maybe, a very *simple* house. They were looking at different architects.

Then, the husband had a car accident. He almost died, but he survived. Now he needs a wheelchair. Two years later, the couple began to think about the house again. Now the new house could liberate the husband from the prison that their old house and the medieval city had become.

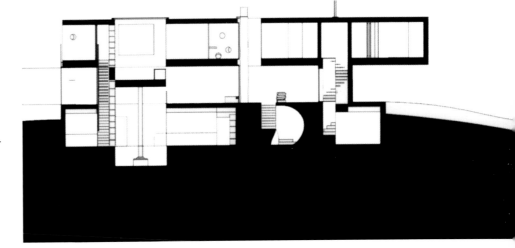

> ❝❝ **THE MOVEMENT OF THE ELEVATOR CHANGED EACH TIME THE ARCHITECTURE OF THE HOUSE [CHANGED]. A MACHINE WAS ITS HEART. ❞❞**

Bordeaux House was actually three houses stacked one on top of the other. The "middle house" was a glass room —half in the house and half out.

"Contrary to what you would expect," he told the architect, "I do not want a simple house. I want a complex house, because the house will define my world . . ." They bought a mountain with a panoramic view over the city.

The architect proposed a house—or actually three houses on top of each other.

The lowest one was cave-like—a series of caverns carved out from the hill for the most intimate life of the family.

The highest house was divided into a house for the couple and a house for the children.

The most important house was almost invisible, sandwiched in between: a glass room—half inside, half outside—for living.

The man had his own "room," or rather "station." A lift, 3-by-3.5 meters that moved freely between the three houses; changing plan and performance when it "locked" into one of the floors or floated above.

A single "wall" intersected each house, next to the elevator. It contained everything the husband might need—books, artwork, and in the cellar, wine . . .

_ "Maison à Bordeaux Text + Credits," courtesy Office for Metropolitan Architecture

## "A PRODUCER OF IDEAS"

In every sense it is important to experiment with things, even if they are dangerous, without knowing where they will end. That is contrary to the very strange aberration of the 80s where architects became so important that the idea of a famous architect failing or doing something wrong was shocking. _ Francesco Bonami, *Flash Art International*, May–June 1995

## ▌▌ *ARCHITECTURE IS BY DEFINITION A CHAOTIC ADVENTURE.* ▌▌

I guess I'm speaking from a position of almost artificial innocence, but in the end, I consider myself to be a producer of ideas. I am more interested in launching ideas and finding reactions to them.... If you are a producer of ideas, it is clearly useful to have access to the *Charlie Rose* show, for instance. [Koolhaas has appeared on *Charlie Rose* five times between 1994 and 2004.] ... Although it was never intended as such, it has enabled me to move beyond the world of architecture, which was what I wanted in any case.... Maybe that's the best characterization of what fame and celebrity have enabled us to do. We have been able to enter territories where architects have not been invited. _ "Rem Koolhaas," *Perspecta*, no. 37, 2005

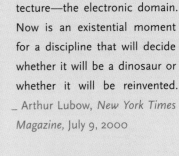

I believe in uncertainty. In order to be really convinced of something you need a profound dislike for almost everything else, so that it's crucial in certain projects to explore your phobias in order to reinforce your convictions. _ Alejandro Zaera Polo, *El Croquis*, February 1992

Our intention could be synthesized in how to turn all that garbage of the present system into our advantage. A kind of democratic King Midas: Try to find the concept through which the worthless turns into something, where even the sublime is not unthinkable. _ Alejandro Zaera Polo, *El Croquis*, February 1992

## ASIA AND AFRICA: THE FUTURE

With globalization, we all have more or less the same future, but Asia and Africa feel much more new. I've been doing research in China recently, investigating cities that emerge suddenly, in eight years or so, seemingly out of nothing. These places are much more vigorous and representative of the future. There, building something new is a daily pleasure and a daily occurrence. _ Rem Koolhaas interview by Katrina Heron, *Wired*, April 2007

## REINVENTING ARCHITECTURE IN THE DIGITAL DOMAIN

There is an extremely new domain being constructed, which partly undermines architecture or eliminates the reason for being of architecture—the electronic domain. Now is an existential moment for a discipline that will decide whether it will be a dinosaur or whether it will be reinvented. _ Arthur Lubow, *New York Times Magazine*, July 9, 2000

## ON HIS FUTURE

It's very simple, and it has nothing to do with identifiable goals. It is to keep thinking about what architecture can be, in whatever form. ... I think that *S,M,L,XL* has one beautiful ambiguity: It used the past to build a future and is very adamant about giving notice that this is not the end. ... That is in itself evidence of a kind of discomfort with achievement measured in terms of identifiable entities, and an announcement that continuity of thinking in whatever form, around whatever subject, is the real ambition. ... To keep thinking about what architecture could be. What I could be. _ Rem Koolhaas interview by Jennifer Sigler, *Interview*, 2000

## NEXT STEPS

Write more. _ Rem Koolhaas interview by Jonathan Glancey, *The Guardian*, August 27, 2007

## ▌▌ A KIND OF DEMOCRATIC KING MIDAS: TRY TO FIND THE CONCEPT THROUGH WHICH THE WORTHLESS TURNS INTO SOMETHING... ▌▌

**1999**

## ARCHITECTURE IS THE ART OF BUILDING

I believe passionately that architecture is a social art—a necessity and not a luxury—that it is concerned with the quality of life and the creation of benefits. This focus on the social dimension acknowledges that architecture is generated by the needs of people—both spiritual and material. It has much to do with optimism, joy, and reassurance—of order in a disordered world, of privacy in the midst of many, of space on a crowded site, of light on a dull day. It is about quality: the quality of the space and the poetry of the light that models it. For me, architecture is the art of building. . . . I am interested too in the way that the design process can question our assumptions about buildings and can reconcile needs which are often in conflict. Sometimes this process can lead through innovation to the reinvention of a building type. In that sense, design is a process of integration. _ Norman Foster, *Reflections,* Munich: Prestel, 2005

# NORMAN FOSTER

**BORN:** June 1, 1935, Manchester, England

**EDUCATION:** Dip.Arch., Manchester University, Manchester, 1961; Cert.TP, Manchester University, 1961; M.Arch., Yale University, New Haven, Connecticut, 1962

**OFFICE:** Foster + Partners, Riverside, 22 Hester Road, London SW11 4AN
Tel: +44 0-20-7738-0455, Fax: +44 0-20-7738-1107, www.fosterandpartners.com

**PROJECTS FEATURED:** Hearst Headquarters, New York, 2006; 30 St Mary Axe (Swiss Re Headquarters), London, 2004; Reichstag, New German Parliament, Berlin, 1999; Hong Kong International Airport, Hong Kong, 1998; Hong Kong and Shanghai Bank Headquarters, Hong Kong, 1986; Sainsbury Center for Visual Arts, Norwich, England, 1978; Willis Faber & Dumas Headquarters, Ipswich, England, 1975

> " ... WHAT GENERATES A BUILDING ... IS SOMETHING THAT **MOVES THE SPIRIT**, OR CREATES SOME MEMORABLE OCCASION, OR GIVES AN ADDED DIMENSION BEYOND THE UTILITARIAN. "

**30 St Mary Axe (Swiss Re Headquarters), London, 2004**
Foster saw the building's aerodynamic form as encouraging the wind to flow around its façades rather than being deflected downward, to the ground level.

The "city within a city" has always been full of surprises!

a reflective solar top · following the ·o· shading ··

The "maypole effect"?

the city grid

The "city grid" is really a 4 storey increment, visually

4

This drawing for the Swiss Re headquarters shows that early on Foster conceived of the building's looming presence. Foster's design, opposite, took into account computer model tests that examined airflow around and through the building.

## LONDON 2004
## 30 ST MARY AXE (SWISS RE HEADQUARTERS)

... ecological factors have played a decisive role in the equally novel form of the building. . . . The profile of this tall tower can be likened to a cigar or a bullet—a cylinder which widens as it rises from the ground and then tapers toward its apex. . . . The building's aerodynamic form encourages wind to flow around its façades rather than being deflected to ground level. . . . "Sky gardens" are central to the building's natural ventilation strategy and build upon the example we pioneered at the Commerzbank Headquarters in Frankfurt [1997]. . . . Each of the forty stacked floors has been rotated so that the voids spiral around the building's periphery. These will be filled with plants

## "THE ECOLOGY OF BUILDING"

Two issues that I believe are particularly important in the future growth of cities: the role of public spaces and the quest for more ecologically responsible architecture. _ "Norman Foster: Building the Future," BBC News, May 9, 2000

To be socially and environmentally responsible any building should work both from the inside responding to the needs that generate it and from the outside in the context of its site—it must be special to its location and the culture that has helped to shape it. One might summarize that as a sense or spirit of the place. That also implies a respect for, and a dialogue with, the natural environment—a feeling for the outside, of the changes in nature and the quality of light: aspects that cannot be quantified. _ Norman Foster, *Reflections*, Munich: Prestel, 2005

. . . in the 70s we were pushing the idea of an ecological architecture—buildings that would consume less energy, not pollute as much, have a softer impact. It was actually the unbuilt projects of that time that set the groundwork for projects that have been able to stretch that agenda much further. _ Norman Foster interview by Soren Larson, *Architectural Record*, May 1999

There are no technological barriers to a sustainable architecture, only ones of political will. The architecture of the future could be the architecture of today. _ Norman Foster & David Jenkins, *On Foster . . . Foster On*, Munich: Prestel, 2000

While technology can help us to control a building's environment, there are also valuable lessons to be learned from regional traditions—for example, using louvered canopies or oversailing roofs to deflect the heat of the sun and offer significant energy savings. There are frequently links between the ecology of building, which is measurable, and the poetic dimensions of architecture—such as the fleeting effects of shadow patterns—which are more difficult to quantify. Perhaps one should define them under the heading of "lifting the spirits." _ Norman Foster, *Reflections*, Munich: Prestel, 2005

## "DESIGN IS ABOUT INTEGRATION"

The best architecture comes from a synthesis of all of the elements that separately comprise a building, from its relationship to the streetscape or skyline to the structure that holds it up; the services that allow it to work; the ecology of the building; the materials used; the character of the spaces; the aesthetic dimension and the beauty of light and shade; the symbolism of the form; and the way in which it signals its presence in the city or the countryside. I think that holds true whether you are creating a landmark or deferring to a historical setting. _ Norman Foster, *Reflections*, Munich: Prestel, 2005

There's always been an interest in the humanizing quality of natural light. And I think there's been the quest to raise the quality of life, the spirit of a building. That might have meant roof gardens, or a swimming pool, or works of art in the office space. _ Norman Foster interview by Soren Larson, *Architectural Record*, May 1999

and will help to purify and oxygenate the air in the building. . . . The slimming of the building's profile at its base reduces reflections, improves transparency, and increases daylight penetration at ground level . . . _ Norman Foster, "Design in a Digital Age," unpublished text, 2000

With Swiss Re, [we subjected] the computer model to "virtual wind-tunnel" tests to examine airflow around and through the building. This was crucial for two reasons: firstly, to assess the impact of wind loads on such a tall structure, and secondly, to test the efficiency of the building's natural ventilation strategy. These studies also showed that the aerodynamic shape of the building will result in improved wind conditions in the locality. _ Norman Foster, "Design in a Digital Age," unpublished text, 2000

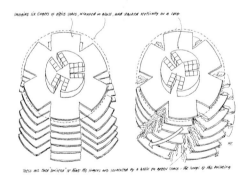

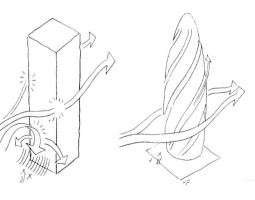

**DESIGN IS NOT JUST ABOUT TECHNOLOGY AND EFFICIENCY.**

Foster's Hearst Tower updates the original six-story building commissioned by publisher William Randolph Hearst in the 1920s. At a stunning 42 stories, it appears to emerge from the existing Art Deco building in midtown.

### NEW YORK 2006
## HEARST HEADQUARTERS

The Hearst Tower is a very important project in terms of its sustainable credentials. . . . It has been a groundbreaking project for the city. It has helped raise green consciousness with respect to the design of new buildings. We . . . achieved a building that not only consumes 26 percent less energy than a conventional building but has also provided Hearst's employees with a light-filled, healthy work environment. _ Norman Foster interview by Stefano Casciani, *Domus*, November 2006

The only truly "invisible" element of this building is the air. The tower is naturally ventilated for up to 75 percent of the year, and the air is filtered and cleaned in a central plant and then distributed throughout the building. This is vital to the energy-saving potential, as it dramatically reduces the need

for artificial heating and cooling. Equally, a significant proportion of the materials we used—including, for example, the carpets—are from recycled material. _ Norman Foster interview by Stefano Casciani, *Domus*, November 2006

The collaboration with Jim Garland (head of Fluidity Design Consultants) on the water feature, and with Jamie Carpenter on the glass, resulted in an animated sculpture that forms an integral part of the entry sequence into the building. The piece also creates a calming acoustic backdrop. . . . The water for the Icefall is 100 percent New York rainwater collected from the tower's roof. It gets filtered, purified, and stored in a tank beneath the sculpture. During summer months, the water cools the lobby space, and during winter, evaporation improves the humidity level of the air. _ Norman Foster interview by Stefano Casciani, *Domus*, November 2006

## "TECHNOLOGY IS NOT AN END IN ITSELF"

*Norman Foster is known for his "high-tech" approach to architecture, and while his work is technologically advanced, the label is misleading. Though he has a firm belief in technological progress, Foster does not see it as an end in itself.*

In each case, to be true to the method of construction is to use materials according to their natural qualities and properties. Pleasure frequently comes from unexpected effects and shifting perceptions: fleeting reflections in a glass façade, smooth planes versus surface patterns, contrasts between old and new, and the changing play of light and shade. _ Norman Foster, *Reflections*, Munich: Prestel, 2005

Technology is not an end in itself, but rather a means to broader goals. High-technology buildings can be created with the same loving care as those crafted from brick or timber. We use technology, but not just for its own sake. _ Norman Foster interview by Yoshio Futagawa, *GA Document Extra 12*, 1999

## ◢◢ I THINK IT [DESIGN] IS AS MUCH ABOUT AN INTUITIVE EYE AS ANY MATHEMATICAL FORMULA. ◣◣

In some societies, there is a gap between tradition and technology, but here there isn't this gap, you just do it. . . . I think there is much more of a continuum, certain things recur over time, but it is an evolution. It is not as though there is a major break between something that is historic and something that is modern, with no communication between the two. I think that particular misconception is a contradiction in terms. There are materials now which didn't exist two hundred years ago, but the basic principles of frame structures, for instance, are the same. _ Staff Writer, *Japan Architect*, May 1991

Since Stonehenge, architects have always been at the cutting edge of technology. And you can't separate technology from the humanistic and spiritual content of a building. _ "Norman Foster: Building the Future," BBC News, May 9, 2000

---

### IPSWICH 1975
# WILLIS FABER & DUMAS HEADQUARTERS

One of the principal challenges of [the headquarters] was to resolve the difficulties of locating a new building on an irregularly shaped urban site; in addition to that was a desire to provide an energy-efficient enclosure. _ Norman Foster, "Design in a Digital Age," unpublished text, 2000

Inwardly social and outwardly contextual—a deep low-rise building that respected the skyline of its market town setting—with a continuous façade that hugged the irregularities of its site and re-created the old medieval street patterns. Although most of the published photographs showed it in wide-angle panorama, the urban realities were of surprise glimpses as you rounded a corner from adjoining streets. _ Malcolm Quantrill, *The Norman Foster Studio: Consistency through Diversity*, London: E & FN Spon, 1999

Willis Faber was . . . radical in the sense that it anticipated the information revolution before it hit, before there were any signs [of it]. Access floors, large spans, central spaces, atria—all those were absolutely radical and revolutionary in the mid-1970s. Now they are absolutely standard practice for development. _ Norman Foster interview by Robert Ivy, *Architectural Record*, July 1999

Our collaborations with Buckminster Fuller—a man who has influenced contemporary thinking about sustainable architecture more than any other—led us to investigate a possible solution in which the site was enclosed within a single, lightweight transparent shell sheltering flexible "trays" of office floors. _ Norman Foster, "Design in a Digital Age," unpublished text, 2000

**The Willis Faber & Dumas Headquarters was one of Foster's earliest commissions after founding Foster Associates.** *Above:* **Escalator to the building's rooftop restaurant.**

## "A SPIRIT OF ENQUIRY"

*Foster + Partners is one of the largest architecture firms in the world, at more than one thousand strong—a considerable size for any architecture practice. As such, it is remarkable that the practice maintains an especially high quality of work. Foster + Partners demonstrates that effective teamwork is built on communication and an ethic of hard work, as well as by a depth of research undertaken for each individual project.*

. . . the way that this office is run . . . is like the School of Architecture at Yale. It is open seven days a week, 24 hours a day. It doesn't close. _ Norman Foster interview by Robert Ivy, *Architectural Record*, July 1999

Communication is the essential flux in a studio. You can literally see it connecting individuals into teams and bridging gaps between us and the many outside specialists and consultants. _ Malcolm Quantrill, *The Norman Foster Studio: Consistency through Diversity*, London: E & FN Spon, 1999

Our work was also socially focused. We explored the idea of a democratic workplace, one that would be rooted in the social realities of the present and the future rather than the past. _ Norman Foster and David Jenkins, *On Foster . . . Foster On*, Munich: Prestel, 2000

We do have extraordinary curiosity about what makes a client tick. We do an incredible amount of research. It's instrumental in terms of breaking down barriers; it's a very revealing process. If you get it right, it commands a tremendous amount of respect from the people who commissioned you because they never expected you to do that. On the other hand, it's very demanding, because if you get it wrong, then you are preaching to somebody whose business it is. _ Norman Foster interview by Robert Ivy, *Architectural Record*, July 1999

## IDEALLY EVERYONE HAS A SHARED SENSE OF VALUES. . . . QUALITY IS MUCH MORE ABOUT AN ATTITUDE OF MIND. IT ALSO HELPS IF THERE IS ENOUGH SHARED RESPECT AND SELF-CONFIDENCE FOR EACH MEMBER OF THE TEAM TO CHALLENGE THE OTHERS' SPECIALIST SKILLS. AGAIN IT COMES BACK TO A SPIRIT OF ENQUIRY.

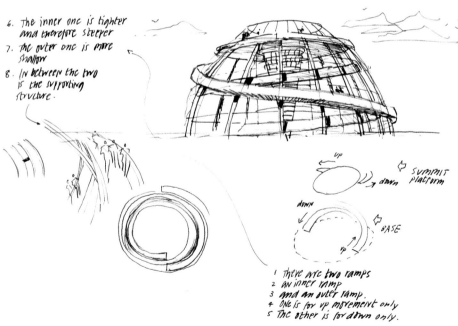

Concept sketch of the New German Parliament. Foster wanted the building to become "a living museum to German history," which included, among other things, preserving graffiti, opposite, written by Soviet soldiers.

### BERLIN 1999
# REICHSTAG, NEW GERMAN PARLIAMENT
What we did was look at really forefront ideas, the role of democracy, the expression of democracy, particularly in a reunified Germany.

What should be its general expression? We suggested a number of conclusions, one of which was that the [parliamentary] chamber should be a public space, should be open to the people. You should be able to look down into the democratic process. We also had a view about history: We felt that the building should be a museum of memories, that history was important and had an active role; it just wasn't a historic show. But we suggested that in [taking] that attitude that you didn't cover up. You revealed. _ Norman Foster interview by Robert Ivy, *Architectural Record*, July 1999

. . . an understanding of how the scarred and graffiti-marked fabric of the Reichstag records the building's troubled past, and how these scars, once revealed, could be preserved, allow the building to become a "living museum" of German history. Throughout our rebuilding we have followed a clear ethos of articulating our new interiors within the surviving historical fabric. We cannot escape history. _ David Jenkins, ed., *The Reichstag Graffiti*, Berlin: Jovis Verlag, 2003

The Reichstag's new cupola, or "lantern," has quickly become a Berlin landmark. Within it, two helical ramps take members of the public to a viewing platform high above the plenary chamber, raising them symbolically above the heads of their political representatives. _ Norman Foster, *Spektrum der Wissenschaft*, February 1999

. . . it has become highly symbolic, the emblematic image of the city. There isn't a day that goes by, either on television or in media, where it isn't featured as the symbol of the elections. It was the background to the elections. It has become completely absorbed into the culture of the place. _ Norman Foster interview by Robert Ivy, *Architectural Record*, July 1999

**❝ . . . HISTORY WAS IMPORTANT AND HAD AN ACTIVE ROLE. ❞**

The philosophical issues facing Foster in his design for the Reichstag were considerable, ultimately leading the architect to balance historical precedent with current thinking. The cupola, seen here, is an inspiring chamber in the redesign.

**IT IS SIGNIFICANT THAT THE BANKNOTES IN HONG KONG ARE DECORATED WITH IMAGES OF THE HONG KONG BANK.**

## HONG KONG AND SHANGHAI BANK HEADQUARTERS

Perhaps the structure might read through on the exterior to impart an urban scale—to profile the building on the skyline of the city. . . . The structure allows the shape of the plan to change at different levels up the height of the building. This articulation creates a hierarchy of order and also resolves the issue of light angle restrictions on nearby streets as effortlessly as it copes with typhoon and seismic forces. Thus constraints are turned into opportunities to sculpt the form of the building and in some cases to create the symbol for the place. _ Norman Foster, "Architecture and Structure," written for the Architectural Association of Japan, November 1994, in Norman Foster and David Jenkins, *On Foster . . . Foster On*, Munich: Prestel, 2000

Hong Kong, even though it is a vertical cluster of buildings, is in many respects an attempt to rediscover certain traditional themes. For example, it strives to produce a sequence and progression of architectural spaces—from the public plaza at the base to the double-height reception spaces located at intervals up the building through to the workplace—a combination of vertical and diagonal movement through the structure by high-speed lift and elevator. . . . The strongest motivation was to provide a more enjoyable way to move around in a building. In a lecture on the project in Paris in 1981, I drew the analogy with the Eiffel Tower—a dynamic experience rather than a passive one. _ "Norman Foster," *L'Architecture d'Aujourd'hui*, February 1986

The sheer visual delight of, say, the cladding details on the bank could not have happened without a shared endeavor, enthusiasm, and dedication which extended from a factory in Missouri through a Chinese workforce on site and a highly mobile design team who were as at home on the shop floor as on the drawing board. I must emphasize that this concern for the quality of how a building is put together is an integral part of a wider total. _ "Norman Foster," *L'Architecture d'Aujourd'hui*, February 1986

## ARCHITECTURE AND AIRPLANES

*As a pilot, Foster's passion for flying has translated into an expertise in the design of airports. In addition to Hong Kong International Airport, 1998, Foster has designed Beijing Airport, 2008, Stansted Airport in London, 1991, and the current design of the Queen Alia International Airport in Jordan, to be completed in 2012.*

Twenty years ago, I learnt to fly, and I've been fascinated by flight ever since. Before that, like many schoolboys, I was obsessed by the world of model aircraft. _ Norman Foster interview by Jonathan Glancey, *The Independent,* October 6, 1996

I am really quite passionate about flying . . . which may explain why I protest that most airports are depressingly more and more like shopping centers. You barely see the aircraft, and when you do you are inside and the experience of flying is almost anaesthetized with drinks, food, and movies. . . . Somewhere there is a missed opportunity here . . . _ Norman Foster, "Building Sights: Boeing 747," in Ruth Rosenthal and Maggie Toy, eds., *Building Sights,* London: Academy Editions, 1995

## "POINTS OF ARRIVAL AND DEPARTURE"

. . . airports are the symbolic gateways to a city. In the past these might have been the portals in the castle walls, the harbor quayside or the train terminus. The need to create imposing and symbolically important structures to celebrate these points of arrival and departure would seem to be a constant over time, from antiquity to the present. _ "Reinventing the Airport," lecture by Norman Foster at the UIA in Barcelona, June 1996, in Norman Foster and David Jenkins, *On Foster . . . Foster On,* Munich: Prestel, 2000

## HONG KONG 1998
## HONG KONG INTERNATIONAL AIRPORT 

In Hong Kong, when the time came to select the site for a new airport, there was no available land. The site itself had to be created. But far from being an obstacle to development, it became instead the catalyst for the largest construction project of modern times. _ "Reinventing the Airport," lecture by Norman Foster at the UIA in Barcelona, June 1996, in Norman Foster and David Jenkins, *On Foster . . . Foster On,* Munich: Prestel, 2000

In Hong Kong, the airport's natural setting is spectacular. To the south is the backdrop of the Lantau mountains, while to the north, across the water, are the New Territories, also with mountains in the distance. Wherever passengers are within the building, they can enjoy unimpeded views . . . and you can see the aircraft. . . . This elemental approach, quite different from the claustrophobic boxes and tunnels that characterize so many airports, brings a sense of pleasure and drama back to the experience of flying. _ "Reinventing the Airport," lecture by Norman Foster at the UIA in Barcelona, June 1996, in Norman Foster and David Jenkins, *On Foster . . . Foster On,* Munich: Prestel, 2000

Nonetheless, the logistics . . . at this scale are awesome. To give just a few examples: The detailed design of the superstructure, including the roof, generated a print run of 125,000 drawings—in excess of 100,000 square meters of paper; at the peak of construction, there was a workforce of 21,000 on site; and the sheer size of this temporary community . . . led to the creation of a "smart card" cashless society . . . _ "Reinventing the Airport," lecture by Norman Foster at the UIA in Barcelona, June 1996, in Norman Foster and David Jenkins, *On Foster . . . Foster On,* Munich: Prestel, 2000

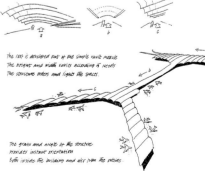

A dramatic view of the airport and surrounding landscape. The actual site was created for the project. The concept sketch shows Foster working out details of the airport.

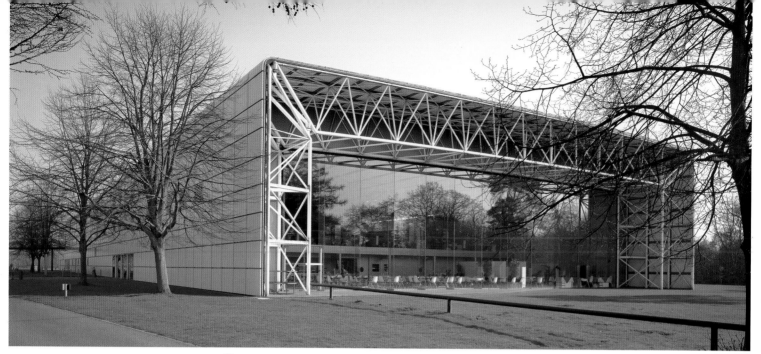

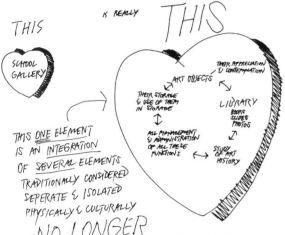

THIS · IS REALLY · THIS

SCHOOL GALLERY

ART OBJECTS — THEIR APPRECIATION & CONTEMPLATION

THEIR STORAGE & USE OF THEM IN STORAGE

LIBRARY — BOOKS SLIDES PHOTOS

ALL MANAGEMENT & ADMINISTRATION OF ALL THESE FUNCTIONS

STUDY OF ART HISTORY

THIS ONE ELEMENT IS AN INTEGRATION OF SEVERAL ELEMENTS TRADITIONALLY CONSIDERED SEPERATE & ISOLATED PHYSICALLY & CULTURALLY —NO LONGER

**NORWICH 1978**

# SAINSBURY CENTER FOR VISUAL ARTS
Well, at the outset there was no brief in the traditional sense of the word—few preconceptions. There was a great deal of discussion and the shared experience of visiting other galleries and museums together. We traveled across Europe with the Sainsburys to see the Louisiana Museum in Denmark, the Mies van der Rohe National Gallery in Berlin, the last museum by Alvar Alto in Jutland—even the hotels we stayed in, such as the one by Arne Jacob-

**The motivation for Sainsbury was to bring all the diverse activities under one roof.**

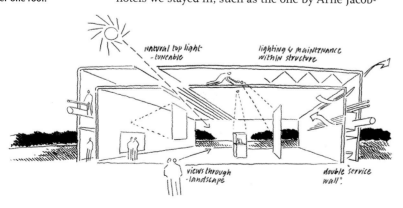

natural top light -tuneable

lighting & maintenance within structure

views through landscape

double 'service wall'.

sen in Copenhagen, were talking points. _ Malcolm Quantrill, *The Norman Foster Studio: Consistency through Diversity*, London: E & FN Spon, 1999

The Sainsbury Center . . . has been labeled a "shed." In that building the concept of a double-layered wall and roof is achieved through a total integration of structure, skin, lighting, and engineering services—each element is interdependent. The space and enclosure are synonymous—the larger total informs all the layers down to the smallest component and vice versa. Yet the motivation to bring all the diverse activities under one roof rather than disperse them in separate buildings was essentially philosophical. I sense that our concern with both strategic design and tactical detail, with the social as well as technological, is a source of bafflement and irritation to certain critics—it upsets their tidy categorizations and "isms." _ "Norman Foster," *L'Architecture d'Aujourd'hui*, February 1986

. . . there would be social gains by grouping all the diverse activities—public and private, teaching and viewing—all under a single roof. For example, the idea that a gallery would, in the morning, be a teaching resource and, in the afternoon, a public space, was revolutionary. Can you imagine the culture shock of teaching an appreciation of art with real masterpieces instead of slides and books?_ Malcolm Quantrill, *The Norman Foster Studio: Consistency through Diversity*, London: E & FN Spon, 1999

## ASPIRATION AND INSPIRATION

As a child I was always interested in sketching and drawing and making things. . . . I was fascinated by model aircraft and construction kits which were called "Trix" or "Meccano." _ Norman Foster and David Jenkins, *On Foster . . . Foster On,* Munich: Prestel, 2000

I think that, irrespective of personal circumstances or environment, if you are passionate about an idea, something can come of it. _ Norman Foster interview by Yoshio Futagawa, *GA Document Extra 12,* 1999

As a teenager at my local library, I discovered the very different worlds of Frank Lloyd Wright and Le Corbusier—imagine the contrast of a home on the prairie with a villa and a Paris boulevard. _ "Norman Foster: Building the Future," BBC News, May 9, 2000

I wasn't able to get a grant to go to university, so I paid my own way. I sold furniture, worked in a bakery, a cold store, and drove an ice-cream van. I also applied for scholarships and entered drawing competitions. In 1959, I won 100 pounds and a silver medal from the Royal Institute of British Architects for a measured drawing of a windmill. I took off to Scandinavia to look at the new architecture and haven't stopped traveling since. _ Norman Foster interview by Jonathan Glancey, *The Independent,* October 6, 1996

I was so highly motivated that when I got into architecture school, nobody was going to stop me. For me, the opportunity to study architecture was the most incredible privilege. I would have paid to do it, which is effectively what I was doing. _ Norman Foster and David Jenkins, *On Foster . . . Foster On,* Munich: Prestel, 2000

America was an incredible experience for me in many ways. It was like coming home because instead of being the odd one out, I suddenly fitted in. . . . Yale is also where

I got to know Richard Rogers, and we became very close friends. . . . And I saw a great deal. I visited other universities, and met Louis Kahn in Philadelphia. I saw all the Frank Lloyd Wright buildings in the Midwest. _ Norman Foster and David Jenkins, *On Foster . . . Foster On,* Munich: Prestel, 2000

At Yale, two teachers polarized for me the cultures of America and Europe. Paul Rudolph had created a studio atmosphere of fevered activity. . . . It was a can-do approach in which concepts could be shredded one day to be reborn overnight. . . . For Serge Chermayeff, debate and theory took precedence over imagery. Analysis dominated action. So it is today that the marriage of analysis with action is at the core of our studio. _ "Norman Foster: Building the Future," BBC News, May 9, 2000

I worry about students who might feel that the power of sophisticated equipment has somehow rendered the humble pencil if not obsolete, then certainly second rate. I have never been embarrassed to state what might be self-evident, so it will come as no surprise to suggest that the pencil and computer are, if left to their own devices, equally dumb and only as good as the person driving them. _ Werner Blaser, *Norman Foster Sketches,* Basel, Switzerland: Birkhäuser, 1992

I don't know how to stop. Like a child's toy, I keep spinning—if I ever stopped, I'd fall over. Recently I took my son, Jay, to Scandinavia. We went sledding with teams of huskies. At first, I thought the dogs were being overworked, but I quickly learnt that they are never happier than when pelting flat out. I'm not very different. _ Norman Foster interview by Jonathan Glancey, *The Independent,* October 6, 1996

**Foster shown in work sessions in his London office.**

**GENIUS LOCI** An architect has a clear social task and is always part of the organization of society. Since ancient times, someone did the hunting and someone made sure there was shelter. The architect is a Robinson Crusoe today, as in the past. . . . You have to take possession of the location, understand the climate, the atmosphere, and the genius loci. You must capture the spirit of that place in order to construct something beautiful and useful there. _ Renzo Piano Building Workshop, *Architecture and Music,* Milan: Lybra Immagine, 2002

Architecture is at the edge, between art and anthropology, between society and science, technology and history. Sometimes memory, too, plays a part. Architecture is about illusion and symbolism, semantics, and the art of telling stories. It's a funny mixture of these things. Sometimes it's humanistic, and sometimes it's materialistic. _ Renzo Piano interview by Robert Ivy, *Architectural Record,* January 10, 2001

# RENZO PIANO

**BORN:** September 14, 1937, Genoa, Italy

**EDUCATION:** Degree in Architecture, Milan Polytechnic, 1964

**OFFICE:** Renzo Piano Building Workshop, via P. P. Rubens 29, 16158 Genoa, Italy
Tel +39 010-61-711
www.rpbw.com

**PROJECTS FEATURED:** New York Times Building, New York, 2008; Beyeler Museum, Basel, Switzerland, 1998; Kansai International Airport, Osaka, Japan, 1994; The Menil Collection, Houston, Texas, 1987; IBM Traveling Pavilion, 20 European Cities, 1984–1986; Georges Pompidou Center, Paris, 1977

**" ARCHITECTURE, CERTAINLY, IS POETRY AND ART, BUT ABOVE ALL, IT IS THE TAKING OF MATERIALS AND TRANSFORMING THEM, TAKING THE WORLD AND CHANGING IT. "**

**New York Times Building, 2008**
Piano is known for this style of rendering, in which elements of the design are constructed in relief onto a two-dimensional drawing. This is a view of the Times rooftop in design development.

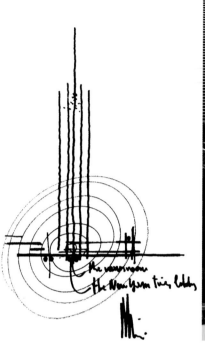

The sketch, however simple, instantly telegraphs Piano's concept for the tower. *Above,* the dramatic main entrance to the Times building. Piano's use of 365,000 small ceramic protrusions serves to reflect light throughout the day as well as partake in the building's efficient use of energy.

# "WHETHER A BUILDING WILL BE LOVED OR NOT, THAT WILL TAKE TIME."

### Architecture: "The Most Material of Trades"  When I was a young architect, I was devoted to developing objects. I was attracted to the physicality. The piece-by-piece approach was essential to me. Then I began to understand that this is not enough. Architecture is more than just putting things together. It's about the organic, about illusions, a sense of memory, and a textural approach. I must admit, though, that I still love the idea of putting parts together. I love the idea that you go from the general to the detail and then from the detail to the general. It's a double process. You cannot think about the presence of the building in the city without thinking about materiality. And when you think about materiality, you start to think about detail. _ Renzo Piano interview by Liz Martin, Archinet.com, January 16, 2006

Design is a trade where you physically make an object; you don't limit yourself to designing it. You build it, you see it, you manipulate it, like when you write a piece of music at the piano, and if you don't like it, you see it, you manipulate it . . . you redo it. When a building is built, it won't allow for any second thoughts; industrial design allows you to reproduce the creative process an infinite number of times. _ Fulvio Irace, ed., "Dialog on Cities," in *Renzo Piano: Visible Cities,* Rome: Electa, 2007

If you make bread every morning and people enjoy it, that's good. That's what architecture should be. A part of life. Discreet, normal, not a pompous discussion about form and expression and art. I'm not saying that architecture is not an art, it is a great art. . . . Don't say it, do it. _ "Renzo Piano talks to Colin Davies," *Architectural Review,* October 1989

### Lightness and Transparency  Lightness and transparency: I do not see these as strictly physical qualities. They are qualities of the spirit, of the mind, of

space. In architecture, the most material of trades, immaterial elements are extremely important. Light and transparency are not elements you touch, yet they are crucial. You do not construct atmosphere just by raising walls; you create it with light and its variations and vibrations. The capacity for metamorphosis that light bestows on architecture is extraordinary! _ Renzo Piano Building Workshop, *Architecture and Music*, Milan: Lybra Immagine, 2002

[Lightness] means creating as much as you can with very little material. The idea of creating a sense of transparency is almost suggesting a more humanistic behavior in people. Architecture is, in fact, the art of creating places where people's behavior is more human. . . . And transparency, in the sense of permeability, [is the] sense of participation between the street and the building. _ Renzo Piano interview by Charlie Rose, *Charlie Rose*, February 17, 2005

Architecture is . . . complicated because it mirrors life. . . . It's almost like a movement between two worlds, the world of massive and the world of lightness, the world of opacity and the world of transparency. _ Christopher Hawthorne, *Architectural Design*, March–April 2004

### NEW YORK 2008
# NEW YORK TIMES BUILDING It's a
very complex city, and rich on a cultural level, even if there is a lot of garbage. New York is the most atmospheric city I know, where the light changes rapidly, because of its being a peninsula in the middle of the sea, exposed to the wind, the sun, the rain. A city turned upward gets the light from all around, and at night all the buildings turn red; just like the New York Times [Building] will; it's made up of three hundred sixty-five thousand little ceramic protrusions that catch the light well. During the sunset, New York is all red; with the rain it turns blue; it's cold; it's hot; it's a city of humors where the buildings follow the weather. Manhattan, because it's windy, has a clean sky and an astounding light. Right after the rain, though, everything is gray, and when the clouds lower, the buildings disappear, along with the sun. In New York, especially along the big, vertical

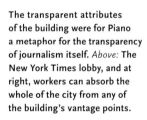

The transparent attributes of the building were for Piano a metaphor for the transparency of journalism itself. *Above:* The New York Times lobby, and at right, workers can absorb the whole of the city from any of the building's vantage points.

avenues, you have the sensation of being in a closed environment because your gaze has a reduced angle of vision, and it doesn't go as far as perceiving the sky. The great perspectives of New York are scenes of interiors, with the sky in the place of the ceiling. . . . _ Fulvio Irace, ed., "Dialog on Cities," in *Renzo Piano: Visible Cities,* Rome: Electa, 2007

The New York Times Building, with its skin that breathes with the environment, is not just a figurative metaphor, but it expresses an energetic reason-ing, because we use glass with a low lead content that is highly transparent, and it does not overheat because it's protected from the wind. Sure it's a technical detail, and yet it contributes to the forming of a vocabulary, the grammar of a language. It's the poetics of lightness, of reactivity and dialogue with the environment; the opposite of the building of stone, of marble, which often is the object of the architect's design. _ Fulvio Irace, ed., "Dialog on Cities," in *Renzo Piano: Visible Cities,* Rome: Electa, 2007

## BUILDING URBANITY FOR AMERICA

The America that asks for my projects is an America seeking urbanity, that particular attitude that we Europeans look for in the relationship between buildings and the city. . . . The United States that we love and admire realizes that the culture of the European city is more human-istic, and deeper. . . . In New York you find beautiful buildings, ones that come down to the earth in such a way that they take possession of the ground and rarely communicate with the city. This finding of the relationship between the inside and the outside of the building, in such a way that the building becomes an integral part of the city, that's the element that, perhaps, justifies my presence in America. _ Fulvio Irace, ed., "Dialog on Cities," in *Renzo Piano: Visible Cities,* Rome: Electa, 2007

## APPROACH TO URBANISM AND THE REAL CITY

The piazza is one of the icons of the city. The city of my dreams is a city made very light, very transparent, full of water and greenery and trees, but also full of piazzas, bridges, and streets. You know, the piazza is the place where people meet, where differences disappear, where fear also goes away. Fear, yes, because it's a place of meeting. _ Renzo Piano interview by Charlie Rose, *Charlie Rose,* February 17, 2005

Some architects imagine perfect constructions, in which clean ash-trays must be put back on the red dot. This is not my style. I believe we have to introduce free values, heretical in the design of a city, to make it more real, more alive. _ Renzo Piano Building Workshop, *Architecture and Music,* Milan: Lybra Immagine, 2002

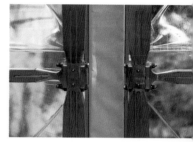

## 1984-1986
# IBM TRAVELING PAVILION
*Renzo Piano Building Workshop's IBM Traveling Pavilion was a demountable exhibition structure. Over a period of three years, it was transported and installed in twenty urban parks in fourteen European cities. The pavilion was a transparent vaulted space, consisting of sixty-eight three-dimensional trusses, each with six polycarbonate pyramids fastened by laminated timber struts with cast aluminum joints.*

The pavilion for IBM wasn't a building that consumed very little, but it did have certain metamorphic qualities which other buildings have subsequently fed off: It marked the limit between a greenhouse and a building. It was a construction that tended to disappear into the environment.
_ Renzo Piano, *Sustainable Architectures*, Corte Madera: Ginko Press, 1998

IBM is very organic because of course everything becomes organic when you look for extreme optimization, lightness, perfection. _ Renzo Piano Building Workshop, *Complete Works Volume One*, London: Phaidon, 1993

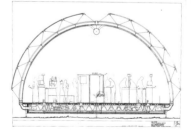

*Above, top to bottom:* **Inside the display hill of the pavilion; detail of the joint and assembling it; the Piano team; and a traversal section of the pavilion.**

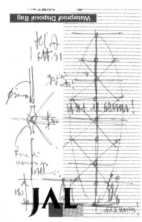

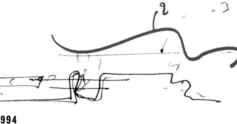

**OSAKA 1994**

# KANSAI INTERNATIONAL AIRPORT

Although concerns such as airflow affected the shape of the Kansai International Airport, for Piano the design of the airport was to convey "an expression reflecting the culture" of Japan. Piano said from the beginning he didn't just have a general concept about the building, but immediately set to including details, like the metallic skin. *From the top:* The departures dropoff was supposed to look dramatic with swooping curves in the roof; Piano's early sketches of the project.

From the beginning we knew that we were going to make a light structure, and lightness is a quality very common to Japan. The first time I came to Japan for this project was when I came together with Nori [Noriaki Okabe, a founding associate of Renzo Piano Building Workshop] and Peter Rice [consulting engineer who often worked with Piano], going out to the site location on a boat when there was no island at all; it was empty. . . . Of course it was already clear at that time that the building would have to be light. This thought came not only because we were floating out there in a boat, but also because it was clear to us that "lightness" is what Japan is about. It's about "temporality" as well. _ "An Idea, from the Generals to the Details," *Japan Architect,* no. 15, 1994

The shape of this building demands very much on the dynamics of airflow. So this building has never been conceived merely as a shape but as a specific system of construction. Even the idea of the skin, the metallic skin, came very early. When you make a scheme, in our experience, it works best to mix up everything from the beginning, not just the general concept but also the detail. _ "An Idea, from the Generals to the Details," *Japan Architect,* no. 15, 1994

To stress so strongly the construction of this airport was a way to recognize the importance of architecture in Japanese society. . . . Every time it happens that big, powerful men decide that architecture is important, I'm very pleased because I believe that it's true. . . . They made the decision to do the airport not like a box, but like an *expression,* an expression representing the culture. _ "An Idea, from the Generals to the Details," *Japan Architect,* no. 15, 1994

**A MUSEUM IS A SPACE FOR CONTEMPLATION.**

## THE MENIL COLLECTION

The Menil Collection is a building whose poetics is linked to the theme of light. And so, once again, beyond the pretext of energy, it's a question of renewed attention, of a poetical sort, toward the physical context that the building resides in. This aspect returns in each project, like a sort of refrain, and I believe it's a sign of a change in tendency. _ Fulvio Irace, ed., "Dialog on Cities," in *Renzo Piano: Visible Cities,* Rome: Electa, 2007

**Emotion and Contemplation: "Galleries Should Be a Place of Silence"** I love building museums. They are magical places—places where you preserve art, enjoy art; everything becomes durable. There's an invisible net of common feeling around them. . . . The success of today's museum is in some ways very dangerous. Crowds may kill the reason why museums were invented. Enjoying art is a very intimate thing. It's about you and the art. The galleries should be a place of silence. _ Renzo Piano interview by Liz Martin, Archinet.com, January 16, 2006

John and Dominique de Menil collected more than 15,000 works of art for the Piano-commisioned building. The roof of the exhibition space is a succession of "leaves."

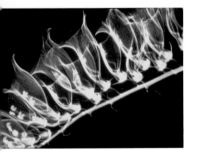

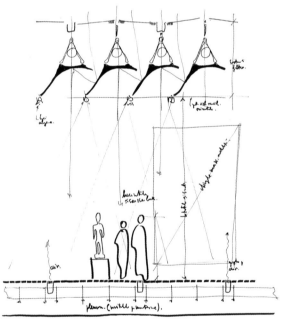

Key elements of the design brief included natural illumination and an unencumbered space to enjoy all of the arts. The thin ferro-cement leaves comprising the roof offered a solution for lighting. *Above,* Piano and Tim Barker with a model of the "leaf" design.

Aside from its sustainability and its intelligence, architecture must be a producer of emotions, and we should never forget that. Light subtly favors contemplation, and it is light, precisely, that makes use of space. I consider that in exhibition spaces the architect cannot impose his style or his intelligence. You must make delicate use of intelligence and technique. _ Renzo Piano, *Sustainable Architectures*, Corte Madera: Ginko Press, 1998

My relationship to the displaying of artworks begins with the design for a Calder exhibition [1982] and gradually takes shape with the Menil collection [1987], the Brancusi Studio [1995], the Twombly Foundation [1995], and finally, the Beyeler Foundation [1998]. The connection between all these projects is natural light and the notion that in a museum contemplative emotion must prevail over any other concept. _ Renzo Piano, *Sustainable Architectures*, Corte Madera: Ginko Press, 1998

# GEORGES POMPIDOU CENTER

*The collaboration between Renzo Piano and Richard Rogers spanned from 1970 to 1977. Together, they produced such notable projects as the Pompidou Center, won by competition in 1971 and completed in 1977, and Institut de Recherche et Coordination Acoustique/Musique (IRCAM), completed in 1977, also in Paris, situated next to and organizationally linked with the Georges Pompidou Center.*

The architect must "disobey" the ordinary, the obvious, and also the customer slightly. When as a youngster I did the Beaubourg in Paris with Richard Rogers [Piano was forty when it was completed], it was our "act of disobedience." In the early 1970s the city was dominated by very serious and intimidating cultural institutions, and we "disobeyed." We introduced this huge piece of meccano [a model construction kit] into the city, this factory, this refinery. The whole Beaubourg is an "act of disobedience," starting from the non-utilization of all the space so as to create a square. We wanted to move away from the cliché of the intimidating museum. If the museum has changed today, if it is no longer an inaccessible place, I think it is partly thanks to that breaking of the rules. _ Renzo Piano Building Workshop, *Architecture and Music*, Milan: Lybra Immagine, 2002

## Piano and Rogers: "We Were Both Bad Boys"

We were convinced that culture is more about curiosity, not about intimidation. And the typical building in that period, the beginning of the seventies, was very intimidating—those kind of monumental stone, marble buildings. So we were genuinely interested in making that provocation, to make a factory, to make a refinery, to make whatever. Everybody was saying this is more like a factory than like a museum, and we were very pleased about that. _ Renzo Piano interview by John Tusa, BBC Radio, July 28, 2004

## The Pompidou Pipes

*The Pompidou Center has been referred to as an example of "high-tech" architecture in which the building's technological and mechanical components are externally displayed.*

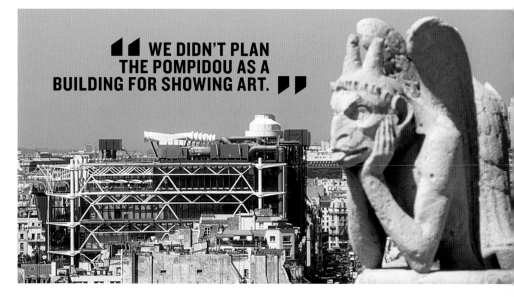

**WE DIDN'T PLAN THE POMPIDOU AS A BUILDING FOR SHOWING ART.**

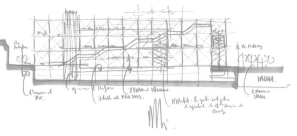

[The Pompidou] is really not high-tech triumphalistic building. It's more about a parody of high-tech, about introducing familiarity of the machine instead of the intimidation of the stone and marble and arches. It was really about welcoming people. And it was also about flexibility. Don't forget, a few years ago big changes were made. After twenty-five years of life with fifty million visitors, some changes were made, and those changes were possible only because the building was really like a machine, like a tool, completely flexible. _ Renzo Piano interview by John Tusa, BBC Radio, July 28, 2004

According to Piano, the Georges Pompidou Center was not intended as a high-tech building. *Above left:* A Piano sketch of the building and the center's famous exterior escalator.

## REBELLION AND FREEDOM

I was always a disobedient youngster. I always used to make my mother cry . . . but artistic "disobedience" is civil disobedience, because if you want to do something you will always end up disobeying. If you obey you are finished. _ Renzo Piano Building Workshop, *Architecture and Music*, Milan: Lybra Immagine, 2002

Architecture is a great adventure and a fight against gravity. I rebel against the obvious, and I hate the idea of style and the formulaic gesture. _ Renzo Piano interview by Michael Webb, *Town & Country*, August 2006

## THE STAR SYSTEM AND STYLE

My problem is that the star concept is not good news for architecture because it doesn't celebrate architecture. It celebrates the architect. . . . If there is an art that is about freedom, it's architecture, because architecture is an adventure. Every time the adventure is different. And in an adventure, you cannot come first. . . . This is very narcissistic. And I think it's wrong. . . . I think the architect must be free. Free from other people, but free from himself as well. _ Renzo Piano interview by Charlie Rose, *Charlie Rose*, February 17, 2005

I don't ally myself to any movement. I dislike movements, not necessarily because I am critical of what they stand for, but because that is not where my ideas come from. _ "Renzo Piano talks to Colin Davies," *Architectural Review*, October 1989

The concept of style . . . seems like a prison cell to me that limits and blocks you, eroding your creative freedom. . . . _ Renzo Piano, *Sustainable Architectures*, Corte Madera: Ginko Press, 1998

## THE PROCESS OF DESIGN

*Piano describes a number of actions he takes as part of his approach to developing a design: walking, listening, sketching, and—surprisingly—distancing. Then, like many of his colleagues, there is the collaborative element of engaging staff.*

When I start a new job I like to walk around the site for a long time with my hands in my pockets, just going around. . . . By doing that you

**" THE TERM 'BUILDING WORKSHOP' DELIBERATELY EXPRESSES THE SENSE OF COLLABORATION AND TEAMWORK THAT PERMEATE OUR DESIGN PROCESS. "**

feel what happens. . . . You get away from the risk of being theoretical, of making something wrong. . . . You go [to the site] once, you go twice, and then you go back. You think, but you *don't* draw. You wait. You start to build up your idea, and then you go back there. And this is quite typical of my behavior. I like to do that. _ Jackie Kestenbaum, *Japan Architect*, November–December 1989

Listening is useful because it is the art of stealing, of taking, of capturing: a theft right before your eyes, but with a noble purpose. There's a world of difference between building a great museum for contemporary art in New York and working on the project of reclaiming a historical center, but in both cases you have to understand, above all, what is left untold. You have to listen to the subtle voices, the voices that are weak and silent; capturing the essence of things implies a training for listening that you don't learn in school [but] rather through life's experiences. _ Fulvio Irace, ed., "Dialog on Cities," in *Renzo Piano: Visible Cities*, Rome: Electa, 2007

. . . the spark that is ignited when someone makes a discovery and which acts a bit like a drug. In those moments, backup from the past does not count. You are an acrobat with no safety net. For example, I start with a sketch—I could never manage without it—but I don't know exactly where I will end up. I let myself be guided, I find that what I have written is not so bad after all, and I go on. It is a sort of "short writing." Your hand leads you to the goal. You lose control of this mechanism once you have discovered it. In those moments you have your back to the wall. Either you do it or you fail. _ Renzo Piano Building Workshop, *Architecture and Music*, Milan: Lybra Immagine, 2002

Architecture is about passion. . . . But you have to have enough lucidity in the passion to understand that something is wrong, so you cannot fall in love with a specific solution or then you never come back. You need the lucidity from time to time to look and to say no, that's wrong. _ Renzo Piano interview by John Tusa, BBC Radio, July 28, 2004

. . . the technique of forgetting, of distancing yourself and making the unconscious work, is highly productive. I believe it is the technique used by the masters of the Ravenna mosaics; for a certain length of time they had to work focusing on the space they were decorating, then now and again they moved away to understand what they were doing with a glance at the whole. I used this technique out of necessity, when I moved from one office to another, from Paris to Berlin, or to some other worksite. _ Renzo Piano Building Workshop, *Architecture and Music,* Milan: Lybra Immagine, 2002

## INFLUENCES:
## PIANO'S FATHER AND JEAN PROUVÉ

I learned from [Marco] Zanuso, from [Jean] Prouvé, from my father, from [Franco] Albini how to make scale-size prototypes for every project. _ Fulvio Irace, ed. "Dialog on Cities," in *Renzo Piano: Visible Cities.* Rome: Electa, 2007

I think my father, a builder, was the most influential. What you learn when you are seven, eight, nine years old stays with you for all your life. . . . My real passion . . . is not just building but *making* the building. . . . _ Renzo Piano, Jean Nouvel, Zaha Hadid, and Frank Gehry interview by Charlie Rose, *Charlie Rose,* June 5, 2008

[Jean] Prouvé and Buckminster Fuller had an attraction on me, and a determining influence, along with Konrad Wachsman, too. But Fuller was a sort of distant star, a shaman of geometry, whereas Jean Prouvé

**❝ THE ARCHITECT IS A BUILDER FIRST AND FOREMOST. IF HE DOES NOT GET HIS HANDS DIRTY HE IS NOT AN ARCHITECT. ❞**

was a simple person, a craftsman. I grew up with the idea of being a builder, like my father; at the same time, though, I wanted to get out of Genoa, and Jean Prouvé, who was my father's age, was a model for me of a builder: intellectual, very determined socially. In 1964, I went to his school in Paris . . . the École des Arts et Métiers. . . . He taught the young people how to work with their hands. _ Fulvio Irace, ed., "Dialog on Cities," in *Renzo Piano: Visible Cities,* Rome: Electa, 2007

I still remember one of his [Prouvé's] exercises: He gave you a sheet of paper and told you to make a bridge that would join together two points that were beyond the extremes of the paper! Then he came back and rested his pencil on top of your model bridge, and if it collapsed, you had to start over again. In this way, the youngsters entered into the logic of the material's behavior and understood that a fold will give greater resistance in one direction and less in the other. So the search for form was linked to its static performance, and not to the volatility of a spontaneous idea that might have been fascinating, but impossible.

Thanks to these antibodies, I passed unscathed through the most difficult periods of my youth as an architect, when you're easy prey for formal and academic obsession. _ Fulvio Irace, ed., "Dialog on Cities," in *Renzo Piano: Visible Cities,* Rome: Electa, 2007

## BECOMING AN ARCHITECT

Probably it's quite true for all the professions, but in architecture, you really have to spend the first fifty years just learning, learning and understanding. . . . _ Renzo Piano interview by Charlie Rose, *Charlie Rose,* February 17, 2005

## TOWARD A SUSTAINABLE ARCHITECTURE

Good architecture is a question of balance. I always cite the example of the pianist. To be a genius one must metabolize one's scientific abilities in front of the piano and then contrive to forget them. The opposite would be a robot playing the piano. Sustainability and ecology are a bit like that. It's a question of scientific criteria that must be applied in a human way. An architect must possess enormous technical knowledge and be informed on the latest technical advances so that his architecture may be capable of assimilating them without rendering them visible. I believe that a sustainable architecture is one that's capable of arriving at such a balance. _ Renzo Piano, *Sustainable Architectures,* Corte Madera: Ginko Press, 1998

We are in the middle of a new historical time: after the drunkenness with cement and steel [Piano is referring to the Modern Movement], and the liberation from styles, architecture should celebrate the discovery of the fragility of the world. . . . This approach is not merely naturalistic, it is also social. _ Fulvio Irace, ed., "Dialog on Cities," in *Renzo Piano: Visible Cities,* Rome: Electa, 2007

This recent discovery that the world is fragile is going to be probably the single most inspiring element for the new century for architecture. Not in terms of morality or consuming less energy but finding a new language that is actually the language of building that breathes. . . . _ Renzo Piano, Jean Nouvel, Zaha Hadid, and Frank Gehry interview by Charlie Rose, *Charlie Rose,* June 5, 2008

**BUILDING IN NATURE** The act of building can be brutal. When I build on a site in nature that is totally unspoiled, it is a fight, and attack by our culture. In this confrontation, I strive to make a building that will make people more aware of the beauty of the setting, and when looking at the building, a hope for a new consciousness to see the beauty there as well.

I think sometimes I have a deal with the climate, the nature, and the topography. It is important to get a dialogue between nature and creative life. . . . It's curious to say it, but at the same time the dialogue between the past and the present also has to be manifested. _ Sverre Fehn interview by Bonnie Churchill, *Christian Science Monitor,* April 14, 1997; "Pritzker Winner Sverre Fehn Offers Insights for Young Architects," *Architectural Record,* May 1997

# SVERRE FEHN

**BORN:** August 14, 1924, Kongsberg, Norway; Died: February 23, 2009

**EDUCATION:** State Architectural Diploma, Oslo School of Architecture, Oslo, Norway, 1949

**OFFICE:** Fastingsgate, Oslo 0358 Norway

**PROJECTS FEATURED:** The Aukrust Center, Alvdal, Norway, 1995; The Norwegian Glacier Museum, Fjaerland, Norway, 1991; The Hedmark Cathedral Museum, Hamar, Norway, 1979; Nordic Pavilion in the Venice Biennial, Italy, 1962

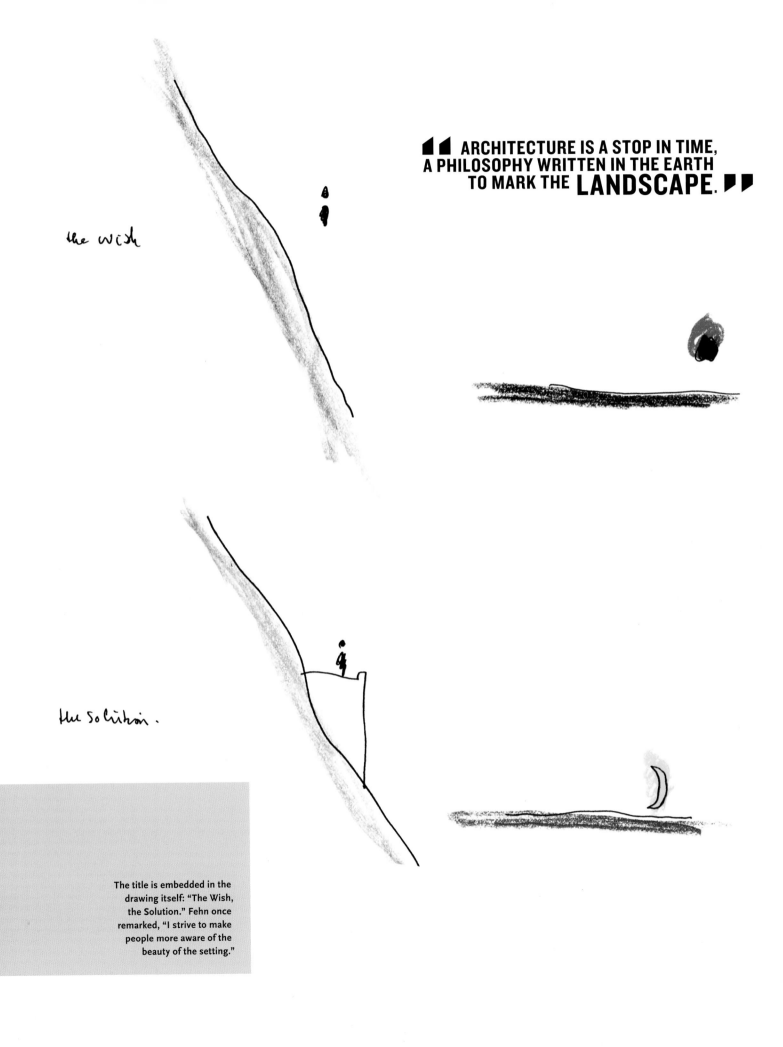

the wish

the solution.

**ARCHITECTURE IS A STOP IN TIME, A PHILOSOPHY WRITTEN IN THE EARTH TO MARK THE LANDSCAPE.**

The title is embedded in the drawing itself: "The Wish, the Solution." Fehn once remarked, "I strive to make people more aware of the beauty of the setting."

### HAMAR 1979
## THE HEDMARK CATHEDRAL
## MUSEUM

I am an eternal wanderer in the world of architecture. I roam in and out of buildings and cities, admiring plazas and parks. Everything seems to belong to a far and near past. Spaces open and close around me, impressions fill my head and empty it. My footprints wash away behind me. The plan of the museum expresses some of this free movement between heaven and earth. A landscape without a horizon is created. There is no separation between the outer and inner world, outer and inner space, exterior and interior. . . . The basic architectural concept has been to create a museum form that preserves the existing remains of Hamar Bishop's

Manor and the large barn and offers the possibility of giving the archaeological excavations as much importance in the museum as the exhibited objects have. The structural elements of the new museum have no physical contact with any of the medieval walls or ruins. _ "The Hedmark Museum in Hamar, Norway," *Living Architecture*, no. 12, 1993

They [the ruins] must remain unchanged for they tell the old tragic story of wars, bishops, and history. . . . You confront the past and have to work with it. It has made a great impression on my work. _ Sverre Fehn interview by Bonnie Churchill, *Christian Science Monitor*, April 14, 1997

The concept of the "suspended museum" offers the possibility of experiencing history not as words in a book, but as it emerges in the world of archaeology. Fehn's important building captures an important theme of his, that "we are the eternal passers-by."

"The museum will not be restricted to the walls and roof of the buildings. Its rhythm and traffic will by means of ramps be directed in such a manner that the public will constantly be in contact with the archeological discoveries and the future excavations also around the building." _ "Sverre Fehn," *GA Document 11*, September 1984

## THE TENSION BETWEEN NATURE AND INTERVENTION

*A consistent theme in Fehn's work is creating a sense of place. While he is sensitive to nature, it does not always mean that nature is tread upon gently. Instead, each project is fundamentally concerned with man's presence in nature and his imprint on the landscape.*

Architecture is an orchestration, which appeals to your movement, your temperament. One can say that the nature reveals your temperament. The architect's role is to find the secret of the place. It is a profession. A signal to other people. But the architect must also identify with the needs of others, their wishes and dreams. But of course, there should also be resistance in architecture. _ Sverre Fehn interview by Henrik Sten Møller, *Living Architecture*, no. 15, 1997

## HUMAN SCALE, CITY, AND LANDSCAPE

I think one must at all times refer to a simple starting point, be able to read the language of the landscape as precisely as possible, and be familiar with the dimension of the body to obtain a human scale in one's architecture. _ "Interview with Sverre Fehn." *A + U: Architecture and Urbanism*, January 1999

Each material has its own shadow. The shadow of stone is not the same as that of a brittle autumn leaf. The shadow penetrates the material and radiates its message. You converse with material through the pores of your skin, your ears, and your eyes. The dialogue does not stop at the surface, as its scent fills the air. Through touch, you exchange heat, and the material gives an immediate response. Speak to a stone and it

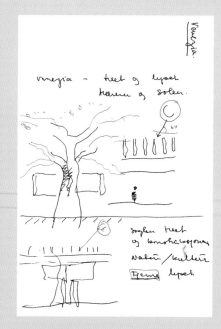

### NORDIC PAVILION AT THE VENICE BIENNIAL, 1962 "In this field as in others, I think you have to fight against indifference. You have to integrate yourself precisely and voluntarily in the site. Never consider nature in a romantic way. Always try to create a tension between nature and your intervention. This is how architecture gains in readability and architects discover the story they have to tell." _ "Musée glaciaire à Fjaerland," *L'Architecture d'Aujourd'hui*, June 1993

gives resonance's mystic. Speak to a mountain ledge, and it gives sound a mirror. Listen to a snow-covered forest, and it offers the language of silence. The great master in the use of wood as a material is a musical instrument maker. His ear gives each piece its dimension. _ "Has a Doll Life?" *Perspecta*, no. 24, 1988

Humans are not rational and logical—they are full of surprises, bizarre dreams, poetry, lies, and humor. Architecture must supply answers and create a dialogue with the people around it. _ Sverre Fehn interview by Henrik Sten Møller, *Living Architecture*, no. 15, 1997

Cities have the strangeness, fear, the grand urban architecture, density, symbols, the difference between architecture and culture. And most of all, the city possesses a calmness. Out in the country it is never calm. There are fields to be tended, cows to be milked, chickens to be fed, but the city possesses a great calm and a sense of waiting. The city is a waiting room, the soldier that waits for his girlfriend, the sailor that waits for the arrival of the ship . . . compared to this, nature is one great prison, and as a child I experienced nature itself confined in a prison. _ Sverre Fehn interview by Henrik Sten Møller, *Living Architecture*, no. 15, 1997

Structure is my mode of expression, a language. It is like a poet who must weed out excesses to reveal the essence. _ Sverre Fehn interview by Henrik Sten Møller, *Living Architecture*, no. 15, 1997

**❝ I HAVE SAID TO MY STUDENTS THAT IF, WHEN LOOKING AT A BUILDING, THEY NOTICE A BEAUTIFUL TREE, THEN THE BUILDING IS A GOOD PIECE OF ARCHITECTURE, BECAUSE THE DIALOGUE BETWEEN NATURE AND ARCHITECTURE MAKES THE TREE BEAUTIFUL. ❞**

## ALVDAL 1995
# THE AUKRUST CENTER *The Aukrust Center is a museum dedicated to Kjell Aukrust (1920–2002), the famous Norwegian illustrator and humorist.*

I explain [that] building a home for a man is like making his self-portrait. You create a kind of poetry around your client or project. _ Sverre Fehn interview by Bonnie Churchill, *Christian Science Monitor,* April 14, 1997

The project fell into place when we recognized the importance of the plateau for the image of the landscape, and it seemed natural to raise a line of monumental pillars against the untouched valley beyond. _ Bjørn Larsen, *Byggekunst: The Norwegian Review of Architecture,* no. 2, 1997

The Aukrust Center lies like a line in the landscape. Like a dam, the large wall along the length of the building gathers up Kjell Aukrust's drawings, with motifs from the rural community he once left. Between the large wooden pillars, the impulsive world of the artist flows continuous into the spaces. _ Bjørn Larsen, *Byggekunst: The Norwegian Review of Architecture,* no. 2, 1997

The road to the site ran through the forest of the Østerdalen valley, with the morning light filtering through the pine trees, the river Glomma flowing gently through the soft valley floor, the water creating clear mirrored surfaces over quiet sand banks, and the stone walls around church graveyards. . . . At the end of the journey the building had found its materials; stones for the dry walls, sand for the structural concrete elements and the ground concrete floor, pine for the woodwork. Between all this, the glass stretches like a transparent skin. You turn around, look back, and imagine that the architecture sets the stage for the landscape. It presents the sunset from the promenade that lies in the cornfield, and the changing light on the great ridge of Trond Mountain. _ Bjørn Larsen, *Byggekunst: The Norwegian Review of Architecture,* no. 2, 1997

The architect once said of his work in relationship to nature that it "is a fight, an attack by our own culture on nature...I strive to make a building that will make people more aware of the beauty of the setting." The long concrete wall acts as a border; the other side, wood columns or pillars, relate to the Norwegian woods.

## LIFE AND DEATH: "ARCHETYPES OF LIGHT AND DARKNESS"

*Fehn's architectural theory is driven by dualities. Along with themes of irrationality and rationality, and the past and the future, Fehn consistently deals with a profound interest in the universal trajectory of life and death.*

I find it very mysterious, my architecture. It is filled with death and mysticism—the archetypes of light and darkness. Here [Norway] the whole winter is dark, and when you're a child you need a big imagination to manage the darkness. Life is not so regular as in the south, where you have the same sun coming and going, and not so different in winter and summer. I am always fascinated by light and shadow and precisely manipulating those forms. The contrasts, the enormity. _ "Pritzker Winner Sverre Fehn Offers Insights for Young Architects," *Architectural Record,* May 1997

The greatest mental construction of all—the one that strikes me as being the most poetic—is the idea mankind has of a possible life after death. To me it seems to have been the motor of the greatest architectural innovations. All the great structures deal with the problem of death—the pyramids, gothic architecture—but at the same time I try to serve the object, to become the object. If museums are just places where things can be stored, then we dishonor objects. An object has to find its place before it can live. _ "Musée glaciaire à Fjaerland," *L'Architecture d'Aujourd'hui,* June 1993

I see materials as letters we use to write our poetic thoughts. . . . We work with letters—an alphabet—we write a story. The story and its structure are inseparable. The poetic idea needs the support of structure to exist. We should have a story to tell. _ "Interview with Sverre Fehn," *A + U: Architecture and Urbanism,* January 1999

## LISTENING TO THE PAST

You'll never reach the past by running after it, but if you manifest the present you'll get a dialogue with the past. _ Sverre Lyngstad, *Scandinavian Review,* Winter 1997/1998

## FEHN'S WORK: "A THRESHOLD OF MISUNDERSTANDING"

I have never cultivated business acquaintances or politics. It has never interested me. . . . I had my breakthrough by winning competitions, I became known even though the projects were seldom realized. And when they were, they were heavily criticized. I have always been hurt by this threshold of misunderstanding. Just about everything I built was subject to public criticism. On the other hand, I could travel abroad with my projects and they were often published in professional journals. Fortunately I had a job teaching, and this kept me alive, but one cannot say that society supported me or wanted my buildings, and I had no connections, so in this way I am somewhat antisocial. _ Sverre Fehn interview by Henrik Sten Møller, *Living Architecture,* no. 15, 1997

**❝❝ ONLY BY REINCARNATING THE MOMENT CAN WE BEGIN A DIALOGUE WITH THE PAST. ❞❞**

---

### FJAERLAND 1991
# THE NORWEGIAN GLACIER MUSEUM

The awareness of a glacier as a physical element had a great influence in the design phase of the Norwegian Glacier Museum. This enormous mass of ice and snow lies like a huge bluish blanket over a vast land area. The ice masses conceal many secrets from the past encased in the glacier's transparent invisibility. A glacier has an animal-like character: the slow gliding movement that leaves deep impressions on the surface of the earth, and the damp litter left behind to build new land areas as it seeks the sea. _ "The Hedmark Museum in Hamar, Norway," *Living Architecture,* no. 12, 1993

**Objects Are Remnants of the Past** A traditional museum seeks to create an awareness of objects as remnants of the past. Today we feel the need for museums that make us aware of that we cannot see. Our future is bound to elements of our past. The atmosphere that we have breathed through the ages has left its trace in the glacier's ice masses. In the

The Glacier Museum is a stellar example of the architect working *with* the landscape rather than charging or imposing something foreign. Here the museum is logically placed like "a fissure," as Fehn has said, at the base of the two mountains.

"An altar in the landscape"—S.F.

The Norwegian Glacier Museum is located at the end of Norway's longest fjord. The building is considered one of Fehn's masterpieces.

decreasing in intensity as one ventures deeper into the space; the pitch of the roof, which gives the space a false perspective; the exterior with the sloping concrete surfaces, which seem to converse with the steep mountain walls; and the cool glass bays that break free of the heavy concrete walls and give associations to the ice-blue chunks on the sides of the valley at the foot of the glacier. _ "The Hedmark Museum in Hamar, Norway," *Living Architecture*, no. 12, 1993

When I was asked to design the Glacier Museum at the base of the Sognefjord, there was an incredible abundance of nature. So I shaped concrete like a stone altar that was strong enough to create a dialogue with those fantastic surroundings. I was afraid of what I was doing, but it ended up succeeding. If I had made a building with a sod roof in search of harmony, it would've been a fiasco. I find counterpoint to be vastly more interesting than harmony. _ Sverre Fehn interview by Henrik Sten Møller, *Living Architecture*, no. 15, 1997

incomprehensible tranquility of the iceberg lie hidden reservoirs of water, which after a few degrees' increase in temperature, could inundate the fertile plains of the earth. The architecture of the museum tries to reflect some of these thoughts: the upward movement to a plateau realized by the two monumental stairways; the entrance, which lies like a cleft between the stringers of the two large stairways; the interior, lit from a crack in the roof; the light

# ORIGINS, INFLUENCES, AND INSPIRATION

## NORWAY

As a youth, I always imagined I was getting away from traditional Norwegian architecture. The more I study, the more I realize I was operating within its context. My interpretation of the site, the light, the materials have a strong relationship to my origins. _ Sverre Fehn interview by Bonnie Churchill, *Christian Science Monitor*, April 14, 1997

## ARCHITECTS

I must admit that I have never had a favorite, not Mies, not Utzon, not even Aalto, but I have, of course, felt the great inspiration that emanates from these architects. Yet I have always looked for answers in my own character. I have tried to express my poetry and buildings. _ Sverre Fehn interview by Henrik Sten Møller, *Living Architecture*, no. 15, 1997

## JEAN PROUVÉ, LE CORBUSIER, CARLO SCARPA

In 1953, I got a French scholarship and chose to study in Jean Prouvé's office in Paris. His original solutions on technical questions related to construction fascinated me. The first meeting with Jean Prouvé was at the C.I.A.M. congress at Aix. The housing project I presented at the congress had nothing to do with Jean Prouvé. It was a result of a teamwork between Jørn Utzon, Geir Grung, and myself. (By the way, Jean Prouvé found the drawings very interesting.)

It was my own initiative. As concerning Le Corbusier, I visited his atelier the first time in the period when he worked with the habitat at Marseille in 1947. I remember he had a big blackboard in his drawing room where he designed in 1:1 the detailing of the balcony. Later, when the design of Chandigarh filled his atelier in rue Sèvres 35, I had good contact with the work. I had no direct discussion with the great master, but I was very thankful for being able to visit his office. _ "Interview with Sverre Fehn," *A + U: Architecture and Urbanism*, January 1999

I met Carlo Scarpa early, when I was in Venice in 1959, in connection with the pavilion construction work. Scarpa was very skeptical of Nordic architecture, but I managed to establish a kind of friendship with him, and it was clear that, for me, as a Norwegian, he was a great revelation. He never allows materials to meet without something decisive happening. Something very decisive. Concrete and wood, but separated by the steel. He is an architect who tells great tales of life and death. _ Sverre Fehn interview by Henrik Sten Møller, *Living Architecture*, no. 15, 1997

## ARNE KORSMO AND FEHN'S EXPOSURE TO EUROPEAN AND AMERICAN ARCHITECTS

I was in one of the first classes to start at the architecture school in Oslo, and there I met architect Arne Korsmo, who came to be a great inspiration. . . . At that point, just after the war, there was a strong nationalistic attitude in Norway. . . . Arne Korsmo was the only one I knew who was above this questionable nationalism. He looked toward Europe and the United States, and through him I met personalities like Jørn Utzon, Aldo van Eyck, and Allison and Peter Smithson, who became my friends. I was soon aware that there was a world outside of Norway, and I was fortunate enough to get to Paris, where I worked for Jean Prouvé, and experienced this technological metropolis. . . . At that time in Paris, it was possible to visit Le Corbusier's studio every evening to see what was happening. I did this often. . . . Later, I was enchanted by the work of Ray and Charles Eames, which is something for which I can also thank Korsmo and his creative anti-national attitude. . . . Korsmo was my true master. _ Sverre Fehn interview by Henrik Sten Møller, *Living Architecture*, no. 15, 1997

**"I have managed to continue my life-drawing exercises as an extremely effective form of practice throughout my career."** _ Sverre Fehn interview by Henrik Steen Møller, *Living Architecture*, no. 15, 1997

**CONTINUITY** The city is thus understood as an "open game," a version of solitaire in which we add new cards that transform—but don't destroy—the models and standards of their predecessors. Our work as architects modifies the field of play—the city, the buildings—and prepares it for the next move, for those who will follow us. To my understanding, the admission of the specific condition of a work of architecture, something that we learn both from studying a building's situation in the city as much as we do from the building itself, is crucial for the architect, and refers us to the specific logic for a work of architecture, as a means of knowing this singular notion of continuity. _ *A + U* Lecture, July 2007, courtesy of Rafael Moneo Architect

# RAFAEL MONEO

**BORN:** May 9, 1937, Tudela, Spain

**EDUCATION:** Titulo [Title], Technical University of Madrid, 1961

**OFFICE:** José Rafael Moneo, Miño 5, Madrid, 28002 Spain
Tel: +34 915-642-257, Fax: +34 915-635-217

**PROJECTS FEATURED:** Prado Museum Expansion, Madrid, 2007; Cathedral of Our Lady of the Angels, Los Angeles, 2002; Audrey Jones Beck Building at The Museum of Fine Arts, Houston, Texas, 2000; Kursaal Auditorium and Congress Center, San Sebastián, Spain, 1999; Pilar and Joan Miró Foundation, Palma, Spain, 1992; National Museum of Roman Art, Merida, Spain, 1986

**"** TO EXPERIENCE AND UNDERSTAND A BUILDING IS TO REALIZE THE CONTINUITY IT PROPOSES BETWEEN AN IDEA OF THE WORLD AND **THE CONSTRUCTION ITSELF. "**

**National Museum of Roman Art, Merida, 1986**
Rafael Moneo wanted to build a museum that would allow people to experience the sense of an ancient Roman town. The choice of the brick was central to the concept of the project.

# ❝❝ THE CONSCIOUS USE OF MATERIAL
## ALLOWS A MUCH MORE COMPLEX
### AND RICH ARCHITECTURE. ❞❞

A sketch of the nave of the building.

**Buildings as "Radical Solitude"** My point of view . . . is that this durability, this condition of being, built to last is very powerful. One must still fight for that. Of course, I understand that I am going against the mainstream in this, but I believe that from many points of view, it would be favorable to have more stable cities, more stable architecture, more durable and less ephemeral constructions. _ "The Idea of Lasting—A Conversation with Rafael Moneo," *Perspecta*, no. 24, 1988

When I speak of lasting and permanence . . . I mean only to emphasize the actuality of the building as its lasting domain. . . . I see architecture as always addressing the same questions throughout history. _ "The Idea of Lasting—A Conversation with Rafael Moneo," *Perspecta*, no. 24, 1988

Architecture arrives when our thoughts about it acquire the real condition that only materials can provide. It is in accepting and bargaining with the limitations and restrictions conveyed by the active construction that architecture becomes what it really is. _ Rafael Moneo, *The Solitude of Buildings, Kenzo Tange Lecture, March 9, 1985*, Cambridge: Harvard University Press, 1986

The building itself stands alone, in complete solitude—no more polemical statements, no more troubles. It has acquired its definitive condition and will remain alone forever, master itself. I like to see the building assume its proper condition, living its own life. . . . I prefer to think that architecture is the air we breathe when buildings have arrived at their radical solitude. _ Rafael Moneo, *The Solitude of Buildings, Kenzo Tange Lecture, March 9, 1985*, Cambridge: Harvard University Press, 1986

## MERIDA 1986
# NATIONAL MUSEUM OF ROMAN ART

In essence, I wanted to achieve two things: first, to be more abstract, and thus more distant from the Roman; and second, to use brick in a way that allowed a better appreciation of Roman archaeological fragments. . . . The conscious use of material allows a much more complex and rich architecture. I try in my work to take advantage of this. _ "The Idea of Lasting—A Conversation with Rafael Moneo," *Perspecta*, no. 24, 1988

The first intention of the project was to build a museum that would offer to people the opportunity to understand the lost presence of the Roman town. Moreover, it was important that the museum building achieve the character and presence of a Roman building. . . . The walls are constructed by a procedure not far from the Roman manner—a massive masonry-bearing wall and filled with concrete—a manner of building that allows the materiality of the Roman brick wall to become, finally, the most important feature in the architecture and museum. _ *GSD News 13*, no. 3, January–February 1985, Harvard University Graduate School of Design

In this particular project, the choice of the brick was fundamental to its nature. It would not be the same in another material. . . . In this sense, distance—or if you prefer, the sensation of closeness—depends on material. . . . This means that the intended material of the building must be present at its conception. _ "The Idea of Lasting—A Conversation with Rafael Moneo," *Perspecta*, no. 24, 1988

Roman brickwork always exhibits a much thicker mortar joint than I have pursued at Merida. I have worked very hard to do away with this joint altogether. . . . This lack of a joint makes the museum's wall much more abstract. At the same time, this wall provides a support for the archaeological pieces, a wall which is much more beautiful being, as it is, less contaminated by the presence of the joint. _ "The Idea of Lasting—A Conversation with Rafael Moneo," *Perspecta*, no. 24, 1988

## CRITIQUING CONTEMPORARY ARCHITECTURE

*Having dedicated a great deal of his professional career to teaching, Rafael Moneo's role as a professor of architecture has made him hugely influential upon future generations of architects. One of his most significant contributions to academia was as chairman of the Department of Architecture at Harvard University's Graduate School of Design from 1985 to 1990. The following texts offer some of Moneo's critical views on the status of contemporary architecture.*

A lot of recent architectural dialogue calls for things to be taken from French philosophers . . . or from translating what has been read in physics or music or whatever. I like to see architects being influenced by the fields around them, by the culture around them, but I would still insist on trying to center intellectual research in architecture on a more disciplinary feel. . . . A building isn't a piece of music. The critical tools and instruments to judge buildings should come from architecture itself. _ Rafael Moneo interview by Kieran Long and Marcus Fairs, *Icon 009,* January 2004

. . . In architecture, true novelty is very difficult. You ask me what I think about this trend of creating single icons—these icons happen very rarely in the history of architecture. But there are many buildings of tremendous subtlety and interest that do not compete madly for your attention. I think very good architecture happens to be this way. _ Rafael Moneo interview by Kieran Long and Marcus Fairs, *Icon 009,* January 2004

. . . Everyone wants to do their own thing, to be different. There is no attempt at architects coming together to try to work for society, to give things to the people rather than simply create monuments to the self and to strive for sensation. There is this feeling that architects want to be artists. _ Rafael Moneo interview by Kieran Long and Marcus Fairs, *Icon 009,* January 2004

Architecture as a profession is a long way from satisfying anyone who loves the discipline. It has lost the importance that it had in society in the past. _ Rafael Moneo, *The Solitude of Buildings, Kenzo Tange Lecture, March 9, 1985,* Cambridge: Harvard University Press, 1986

## AN ARCHITECTURE OF COMPACTNESS

*In a 1998 lecture, Rafael Moneo defined his theory of "Compactness," which he has applied to many of his building designs.*

Compactness is not a discovery but an enduring way of approaching architecture. Compactness as a way of answering to a double-edge reality: one the urban fabric, the other an autonomous inner world. Therefore, my buildings have been conceived in an attempt to reply appropriately to what could be called the urban fabric. All these projects try to be respectful of the site and pretend to be included in it, creating a new perception of the given conditions. _ Rafael Moneo, "End of the Century Paradigms, Fragmentation and Compacity in Recent Architecture," *El Croquis,* no. 98, 2000

Compact architecture gives rise to saturated, dense floor plans that make use of the interstitial spaces to encourage movement, and it can permit surprising liberty in the disposition of architectural programs. _ Rafael Moneo, "Raoul Wallenberg Lecture, April 13, 2001," in Brian Carter and Annette W. LeCuyer, ed., *The Freedom of the Architect, Rafael Moneo,* Ann Arbor: The University of Michigan Press, 2002

## ON SITE

The site is an expectant reality, always awaiting the event of a prospective construction on it, through which will appear its otherwise hidden attributes. _ Rafael Moneo quoted by Robert Campbell, "Thoughts on José Rafael Moneo," www.pritzkerprize.com

The shadow of anywhere is haunting our world today . . . architecture claims the site from anywhere. . . . Architecture is engendered upon it. . . . The site is where architecture is. It can't be anywhere. _ Rafael Moneo quoted by Robert Campbell, "Thoughts on José Rafael Moneo," www.pritzkerprize.com

## ON DRAWING

. . . When buildings enter into the realm of materiality, they become much more unpredictable. . . . In this moment the transference occurs that brings buildings from drawings to reality. I think this is one of the more exciting moments for the architect. _ "The Idea of Lasting—A Conversation with Rafael Moneo," *Perspecta,* no. 24, 1988

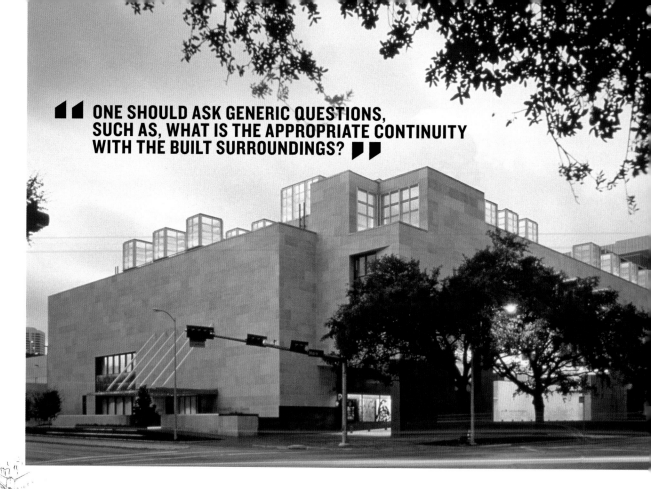

> ❛❛ ONE SHOULD ASK GENERIC QUESTIONS, SUCH AS, WHAT IS THE APPROPRIATE CONTINUITY WITH THE BUILT SURROUNDINGS? ❜❜

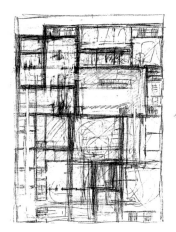

A concept sketch of the museum.

"The Museum of Fine Arts of Houston was built in 1924, following the design of the architect William Ward Watkin. Much later, Mies van der Rohe built extensions, first in 1958 and again in 1974." _ Rafael Moneo, "Raoul Wallenberg Lecture, April 13, 2001," in Brian Carter and Annette W. LeCuyer, ed., *The Freedom of the Architect, Rafael Moneo,* Ann Arbor: The University of Michigan Press, 2002

### HOUSTON 2000
## AUDREY JONES BECK BUILDING AT THE MUSEUM OF FINE ARTS

The Museum of Fine Arts is a clear example of this [Moneo's theory of "compactness"] way of understanding architecture. The floor plan of a museum is "broken" into a series of rooms and galleries connected by means of the hidden path that, without being imperious, guides the visitor's steps. The museum makes intense use of natural light that illuminates the rooms and galleries from above. _ Rafael Moneo, "Raoul Wallenberg Lecture, April 13, 2001," in Brian Carter and Annette W. LeCuyer, ed., *The Freedom of the Architect, Rafael Moneo,* Ann Arbor: The University of Michigan Press, 2002

The variety of the galleries is reflected in the fragmented and broken outline of a roof that becomes the most characteristic image of the museum showing the importance given to light, the real protagonist of an architecture whose substance is found in the interior space. _ Rafael Moneo, "Raoul Wallenberg Lecture, April 13, 2001," in Brian Carter and Annette W. LeCuyer, ed., *The Freedom of the*

*Architect, Rafael Moneo,* Ann Arbor: The University of Michigan Press, 2002

In placing the principal façade on this street [Main Street], homage is paid to the museum of Mies van der Rohe and a relationship is established that is absolutely necessary. _ Rafael Moneo, "Raoul Wallenberg Lecture, April 13, 2001," in Brian Carter and Annette W. LeCuyer, ed., *The Freedom of the Architect, Rafael Moneo,* Ann Arbor: The University of Michigan Press, 2002

### SAN SEBASTIAN 1999
## THE KURSAAL AUDITORIUM AND CONGRESS CENTER
To our way of thinking, it is crucial that the Kursaal area retain its condition as a site of geographical accidents. Our proposal for the auditorium and the conference hall, the key programmatic elements of the scheme, are conceived as separate autonomous volumes, as two gigantic rocks stranded at the mouth of the river, forming part of the landscape rather than belonging to the city. _ Rafael Moneo, *Assemblage,* no. 14, April 1991

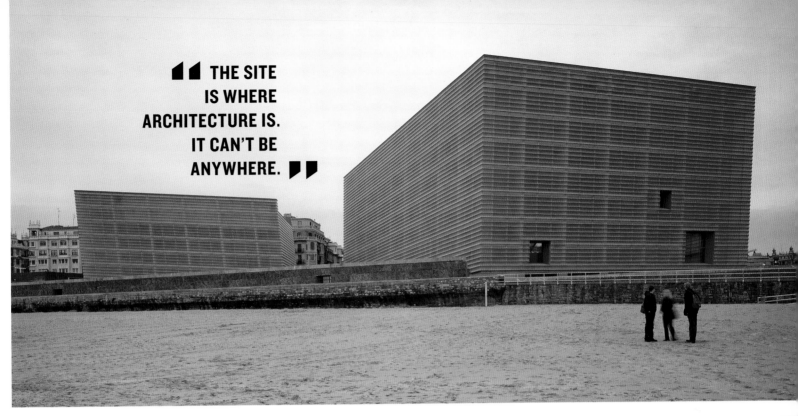

**"THE SITE IS WHERE ARCHITECTURE IS. IT CAN'T BE ANYWHERE."**

For the Kursaal, it was essential to establish a compact yet fragmented set of volumes. Once the ground rules of a project are in place, there may be an almost dialectical development of contrasting moves, and these can enrich a scheme. _ Rafael Moneo interview by William J. R. Curtis, *El Croquis 98*, 2000

Our response to the Kursaal site is simple: No building should be erected that violates the presence of the Urumea River. _ Rafael Moneo, *Assemblage*, no. 14, April 1991

Outside, the glass services protect against salt-laden winds from the sea, making the volume a dense, opaque, yet changing mass by day, and a mysterious and dazzling source of light by night. _ Rafael Moneo, "Raoul Wallenberg Lecture, April 13, 2001," in Brian Carter and Annette W. LeCuyer, ed., *The Freedom of the Architect, Rafael Moneo*, Ann Arbor: The University of Michigan Press, 2002

The asymmetry is oriented in such a way that a visitor entering the foyer is unconsciously led toward the highest level, where Mount Urgull and the sea and all of its splendor can be contemplated from a single window. This window punctures the buildings' double wall, composed of the steel frame clad inside and out

with special laminated glass panels. The result is a neutral and luminous interior space. The only contact with the outside world is through the foyer window. _ Rafael Moneo, "Raoul Wallenberg Lecture, April 13, 2001," in Brian Carter and Annette W. LeCuyer, ed., *The Freedom of the Architect, Rafael Moneo*, Ann Arbor: The University of Michigan Press, 2002

People in San Sebastian are privileged to enjoy these marvelous surroundings in this interplay between city and nature. I wanted to provide them with a very different experience, to do with humidity, with wetness and water—almost a feeling of going under the sea. . . . Kursaal does not have to do with the Miesian way of just establishing total continuity between indoors and outdoors. Instead, it is related to stimulating awareness of inside and outside by architectural means. _ Rafael Moneo interview by William J. R. Curtis, *El Croquis 98*, 2000

The Kursaal Auditorium is on a site in San Sebastian affected by hills, mountains, and, top, beaches. Moneo said he envisioned the two buildings as two rocks on the shores of the Urumea River and the Bay of Biscay. The walls have flat glass on the interior, above, and curved glass on the exterior that work together to muffle sound. *Left:* A concept sketch by Moneo.

### PALMA 1992
## PILAR AND JOAN MIRÓ FOUNDATION
The visitor following the entry path will be surprised to find a beautiful, ample square. From here he can go on to explore the garden. _ Rafael Moneo quoted by Robert Campbell, "Thoughts on José Rafael Moneo," www.pritzkerprize.com

Sharp and intense, the volume ignores its surroundings or, better still, answers with rage the hostile buildings that have worn down the previously beautiful slope. _ Rafael Moneo quoted by Robert Campbell, "Thoughts on José Rafael Moneo," www.pritzkerprize.com

### MADRID 2007
## PRADO MUSEUM EXPANSION
When you are in the extension, you don't feel you are in another building—you feel you are in the Prado. That has to do with the fact that you can see the

For the Miró Foundation, Moneo had to contend with the location of the building in which Miró's paintings were to be housed as well as the south-facing degraded slope in Mallorca. One of the many unique features is the floating pool on the roof, shown above, which is meant to convey the presence of the sea that has been diminished by overdevelopment.

shoulder of the old building (the apse of the basilica hall) from the new foyer. If something good can be said of the extension, it is that it doesn't fall in with other canonical solutions. When the Venturis built at the National Gallery in London, for example, they talked about their building as something that was added—a sort of aggregation. We have tried to make an extension that has a more symbiotic relationship with the building it joins. _ Rafael Moneo interview by Ellis Woodman, Building Design, The Architects' Website, www.bdonline.co.uk, November 2, 2007

The façade is very contained and respectful—I don't want to use the word classical—but Cristina's door [the massive bronze doors are by Spanish artist Cristina Iglesias] relaxes it and draws people's attention. In a way, the façade becomes what architecture very often used to be—just the frame for other things to happen. _ Rafael Moneo interview by Ellis Woodman, Building Design, The Architects' Website, www.bdonline.co.uk, November 2, 2007

The extension maintains the longitudinal nature of the old building and establishes a transverse axis from the Velázquez gate [the main entrance in the

**YOU COULD THINK OF IT AS A ROSARY OF DIFFERENT EPISODES.**

original Prado museum design] all the way to the cloister. _ Rafael Moneo interview by Ellis Woodman, Building Design, The Architects' Website, www.bdonline.co.uk, November 2, 2007

I see the buildings of the past conveying another reality which I would like to reach. I am pushing to think about what this reality is as the first theoretical question of today. In the past, the act of construction itself was conveying—or implying—the form and image of the building as one. That provides the feeling of authenticity. . . . _ "The Idea of Lasting—A Conversation with Rafael Moneo," *Perspecta*, no. 24, 1988

The Prado Museum addition has given us as many headaches as the cathedral for Los Angeles [Cathedral of Our Lady of the Angels, 2002]. Both projects were won in rigorous competitions, a fact that would seem to guarantee a degree of settlement through the jury's selection. But the truth is that once the

project is presented to the public, disagreeing voices multiply. . . . These are inevitable consequences any time anyone has to work with such an iconic public institution. . . . That is not an entirely negative situation, nor does it bother me. . . . I know that the presence of diverse opinions will eventually enrich the project. The project does not suffer, it simply follows its evolution, gradually becoming more reconciled with its objectives. To speak of the architecture for the Prado Museum addition as a reconciliation, I consider a virtue. _ Carlos Jiménez, "A Talk with Rafael Moneo," *Cite*, no. 47, Spring 2000

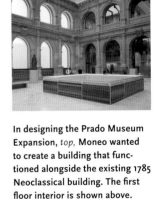

In designing the Prado Museum Expansion, *top*, Moneo wanted to create a building that functioned alongside the existing 1785 Neoclassical building. The first floor interior is shown above.

# ◀◀ ...AN **EPIPHANY** OF LIGHT... ▶▶

those achieved by architects of the Baroque. _ Rafael Moneo, "Raoul Wallenberg Lecture, April 13, 2001," in Brian Carter and Annette W. LeCuyer, ed., *The Freedom of the Architect, Rafael Moneo*, Ann Arbor: The University of Michigan Press, 2002

### LOS ANGELES 2002
# CATHEDRAL OF OUR LADY OF THE ANGELS
Light is the origin of the Cathedral of Our Lady of the Angels. On the one hand, the light captured by the large windows and reflected from the chapels orient us along the path of the ambulatories that takes us to the nave. This light is not very different from that found in Romanesque churches. On the other hand, the light filtered through the alabaster creates a luminous, diffuse, and enveloping atmosphere in which the constructed element floats in ensuring a spatial experience close to that of various Byzantine churches. Finally the glass cross which presides over the apse lets us understand light as a mystic metaphor of the presence of God. This presence is manifested in the rays of sunlight that come through the cross, bringing about an architectural experience similar to

When I began to think about the cathedral, I tried to recall in which modern architectures the presence of the sacred could be felt. The church in Turku by Erik Bryggmann [1941] and the chapel at Ronchamp by Le Corbusier [1954] come to mind. They are the two contemporary churches that have impressed me the most, and I would say they both share the importance of light. I understand light as the protagonist that tries to recover the sense of the "transcendent." It is the vehicle through which we are able to experience what we call sacred. _ Rafael Moneo, "Raoul Wallenberg Lecture, April 13, 2001," in Brian Carter and Annette W. LeCuyer, ed., *The Freedom of the Architect, Rafael Moneo*, Ann Arbor: The University of Michigan Press, 2002

**Moneo said that as he worked on the design of the Cathedral of Our Lady of the Angels, top, he thought about modern churches that most impressed him.** *Top:* **The cathedral nave and, bottom, the column wall.**

## REFLECTIONS ON HIS WORK

*Unlike his "starchitect" colleagues whose signature styles reflect their personas, Rafael Moneo produces refreshingly varied and timeless architecture. His studied architectural approach is concerned with broad and important issues like the continuity of history and site, the experience of space, and architecture's role in society. He considers his architecture not a reflection of himself, but as singularly standing in its own presence.*

. . . The good thing about my work is that it can be explained. I am able to give reasons for what I did. And probably that offers to others the hope that knowledge can be a way of entering into architecture. That I hope could be my contribution. _ Rafael Moneo interview by Kieran Long and Marcus Fairs, *Icon 009*, January 2004

It is always that prizes make you think about where you are. Thoughts about time and life. But as you can imagine, I am still working with the same eagerness. _ Rafael Moneo interview by Kieran Long, *Icon 001*, April 2003

Architecture implies the distance between our work and ourselves, so that in the end the work remains alone, self-supported, once it has acquired its physical consistency. Our pleasure lies in the experience of this distance, when we see our thought supported by a reality that no longer belongs to us. _ Rafael Moneo, *The Solitude of Buildings, Kenzo Tange Lecture, March 9, 1985,* Cambridge: Harvard University Press, 1986

I believe the presence of the architect quickly disappears and that, once completed, buildings take on a life of their own. . . . I am certain that once the construction is finished, once the building assumes its own reality and its own role, all those concerns that occupied the architects and their efforts dissolve. _ Rafael Moneo, *The Solitude of Buildings, Kenzo Tange Lecture, March 9, 1985,* Cambridge: Harvard University Press, 1986

## THE ARCHITECT IN SOCIETY

Today an architect is certainly aware of the key elements of construction, but he or she is not in full dominion of all the technical imperatives. Nonetheless, the ultimate definition of the role of the architect still centers around the notion that the architect must assume responsibility for what is built . . . the study of contemporary formal problems, the ability to build within a variety of urban mediums, the knowledge of new programs, a keen knowledge of technical issues, and, lastly, a deep investment in the world of culture while grasping the pregnancy of a moment. All of these things are essential in the making of an architect, and all of these things comprise the reasons why we can still talk about the indispensable role that the architect continues to play in our society. _ Carlos Jiménez, "A Talk with Rafael Moneo," *Cite*, no. 47, Spring 2000

## "A SLOW AND REFLECTIVE PRACTICE"

News, films, TV, advertising—everything pushes us toward a life understood as a continuous consumption of information received through images. No wonder that architecture, in today's world, no longer represents power. The media are the vehicle of power. _ Rafael Moneo quoted by Robert Campbell, "Thoughts on José Rafael Moneo," www.pritzkerprize.com

. . . Time is converted into a highly pressured commodity, one in which architecture is pushed to reduce the margins between the beginning of an idea and its eventual execution. . . . It leads to the thinking that architecture must somehow be imbued with this immediateness, or that it might be produced with the same speed at which images appear and disappear in front of our eyes. But the act of construction continues to demand enormous time and vigilance. The great effort and cost that it takes to build leads one to view the design process as a slow and reflective practice. _ Carlos Jiménez, "A Talk with Rafael Moneo," *Cite*, no. 47, Spring 2000

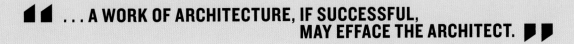

## ▐▌ . . . A WORK OF ARCHITECTURE, IF SUCCESSFUL, MAY EFFACE THE ARCHITECT. ▐▌

I wanted the material and substance of the building to be seen from the beginning. . . Concrete is also a very original material if you consider the earthly conditions of the site. We are studying very carefully the performance over time of this material. The color is another interesting aspect: Getting the yellowish color we are looking for is proving to be a painstaking but extremely gratifying task. Concrete can give this double-edged condition indoors and outdoors—continuity between walls within and without that enables the building to be seen and understood as a homogenous whole. _ Rafael Moneo interview by William J. R. Curtis, *El Croquis 98, 2000*

**THE VIRTUE OF SIMPLICITY** The aim of my design is, while embodying my own architectural theories, to impart rich meaning into spaces through such things as natural elements and the many aspects of daily life. Such things as light and wind only have meaning when they are introduced inside a house in a form cut off from the outside world. The isolated fragment of light and air suggests the entire natural world.

The forms I have created have altered and acquired meaning through elements of nature (light and air), which give indications of the passing of time and the changing of the seasons, and through connections with human life. Although many possibilities for different kinds of development are inherent in space, I prefer to manifest these possibilities in simple ways. Furthermore, I like to relate the fixed form and compositional method to the kind of life that will be lived in the given space and to local regional society. In other words, I select solutions to problems in reaction to the prevailing circumstances.

_ Tadao Ando, *Japan Architect,* May 1982

# TADAO ANDO

**BORN:** September 13, 1941, Osaka, Japan

**OFFICE:** Tadao Ando Architect & Associates, 5-23 Toyosaki 2-Chome, Kita-ku, Osaka, 531-0072 Japan
Tel: +81 06-6375-1148, Fax: +81 06-6374-6240

**PROJECTS FEATURED:** Modern Art Museum of Fort Worth, Texas, 2003; Pulitzer Foundation for the Arts, St. Louis, Missouri, 2001; Naoshima Contemporary Art Museum (Benesse Art Site Naoshima), Naoshima Island, Japan, 1992; Church of the Light, Osaka, Japan, 1989; Church on the Water, Hokkaido, Japan, 1988; Chapel on Mount Rokko, Kobe, Japan, 1986

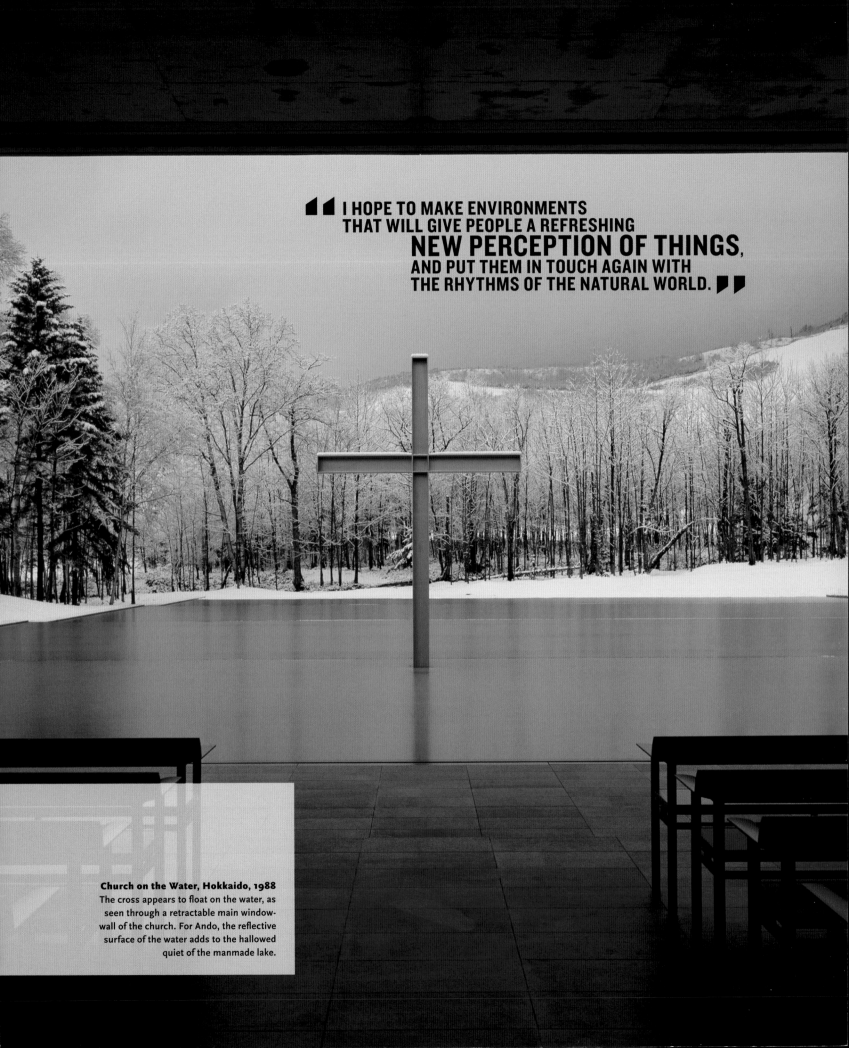

" I HOPE TO MAKE ENVIRONMENTS
THAT WILL GIVE PEOPLE A REFRESHING
**NEW PERCEPTION OF THINGS,**
AND PUT THEM IN TOUCH AGAIN WITH
THE RHYTHMS OF THE NATURAL WORLD. "

**Church on the Water, Hokkaido, 1988**
The cross appears to float on the water, as
seen through a retractable main window-
wall of the church. For Ando, the reflective
surface of the water adds to the hallowed
quiet of the manmade lake.

> **WATER IS OFTEN USED TO REFLECT LIGHT, BUT ALSO TO RELEASE THE IMAGINATION OR TO INDUCE TRANQUILITY. WATER IS A KEY ELEMENT IN MANY OF MY SCHEMES.**

**FORT WORTH 2003**
## MODERN ART MUSEUM OF FORT WORTH

*Ando has spoken a great deal about his philosophy and approach to building the museum in Texas. The extended discussion that follows provides, in effect, the anatomy of the building and analysis of his approach.*

Ando said that the pavilions for the Modern Art Museum of Fort Worth were inspired by those of the nearby Kimbell Museum in Fort Worth. This is the exterior view of the building, lit up at night.

**The Kimbell Art Museum as Inspiration** The surrounding context of any site is very important, and in this case the most prominent feature of the site is not the topography but the proximity of the Kimbell [in Forth Worth]. . . . I have tried to create a design that has a sympathetic dialogue with the Kimbell. . . . This project has been a way to offer Mr. Kahn my gratitude and respect. The pavilions for the Modern are partly inspired by the pavilions at the Kimbell. _ Michael Auping, *Seven Interviews with Tadao Ando*, Fort Worth: Modern Art Museum of Fort Worth, 2002

**"A Swan Floating on Water"** I envision this building as a swan floating on the water. From a distance, it is the image I think you will see. There is a famous temple in Kyoto, Byodo-in Temple in Uji. It looks like a phoenix, a legendary swan that is a reflection in the

water. The Fort Worth project is part of this image.
_ Michael Auping, *Seven Interviews with Tadao Ando*,
Fort Worth: Modern Art Museum of Fort Worth, 2002

**"An Arbor for Art"** You will always be aware of nature in this building. I think of it as an arbor for art. . . . This is all made possible by this unique site. We can build the natural into and around the building and situate the building correctly to take advantage of every viewpoint and the movement of light. _ Michael Auping, *Seven Interviews with Tadao Ando*, Fort Worth: Modern Art Museum of Fort Worth, 2002

**The Soul of the Building** The interior of this building is its soul. You pay as much attention as you can to the pouring of the concrete, but if you don't pay the same attention to the granite and wood floors, it will not complete the vision. _ Michael Auping, *Seven Interviews with Tadao Ando*, Fort Worth: Modern Art Museum of Fort Worth, 2002

**Fort Worth Metal Panels—A Shoji Screen of Sorts**

I see the metal [panels] like a shoji screen. Relative to the gravity of the concrete, it is like a paper screen— something that creates a space but is very light. The Western concept of a wall is always something very strong, powerful, and thick. In the East, we have a number of ways of approaching the concept of a wall. _ Michael Auping, *Seven Interviews with Tadao Ando*, Fort Worth: Modern Art Museum of Fort Worth, 2002

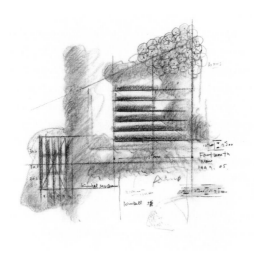

**Sacred and Secular Space** The art museum, like the church, creates a special space in people's lives. Day-to-day life is very busy, very hectic. At the museum, although it is an extension of your life, you are allowed, by facing the art and the environment, to reclaim yourself. If you can be with yourself and your thoughts in a serene place for even just one hour, then this place can provide a special point of energy. I don't want people to come to be entertained, but to come to reclaim and nourish their spirit and soul. _ Michael Auping, *Seven Interviews with Tadao Ando*, Fort Worth: Modern Art Museum of Fort Worth, 2002

Ando saw the interior of the building as its soul. *Top left:* a space for Anselm Kiefer's artwork "Book with Wings," part of the permanent collection. *Left:* Ando's conceptual sketch studying the relationship between the Kimbell Museum and the Modern Art Museum of Fort Worth. One of the many places he paid homage to the Kimbell is the large staircase, leading to the gallery.

## JAPANESE CONCEPTS

*Ando frequently references various Japanese concepts that he consciously adapts to the architecture he designs.*

### ENGAWA

I am interested in the ambiguous space which exists between inside and outside and which I refer to with the traditional term *engawa*, which means roughly "veranda." So many of my buildings set out to serve everyday life by establishing these transitional zones. . . . _ William J. R. Curtis, "A Conversation with Tadao Ando," *El Croquis*, no. 44+58, 2000

### SUKIYA

I prefer not to deal in the actual forms themselves, but in their spirits and emotional contents. . . . On a small scale, *sukiya* can refer to a single isolated tea-ceremony house. . . . Although *sukiya* itself is not the property of ordinary people, the aesthetic awareness and emotion evident in it is fundamental to the Japanese people as a whole. . . . *Sukiya* uses shoji panels to contain light and simultaneously separates and connects the inner and outer garden walls by means of fences. _ Tadao Ando, *Japan Architect*, May 1982

### MINKA: THE JAPANESE FARMHOUSE

Another traditional Japanese architectural style that attracts me strongly is that of the old-fashioned farmhouse *(minka)*. . . . These farmhouses have a simplicity of composition evolved through years of struggle and amity with nature, and which reflects a settled and tranquil way of life that is distinctive of people who till the soil.

Unlike *sukiya*-style buildings, farmhouses had frameworks assembled as spatial totalities that determined everyday life. The simplicity of the inhabitants' way of life accounts for the power of the simple farmhouse's framework. _ Tadao Ando, *Japan Architect*, May 1982

## ◀◀ IF YOU GO TO A JAPANESE TEMPLE, YOU SEE THAT
# NOTHING IS DISREGARDED.
## YOU COULD SAY THAT EVERY MATERIAL, EVERY JOINT, IS SACRED. ▶▶

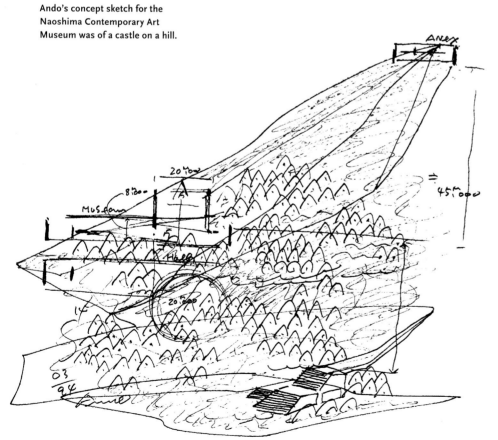

Ando's concept sketch for the Naoshima Contemporary Art Museum was of a castle on a hill.

### NAOSHIMA ISLAND 1992
# NAOSHIMA CONTEMPORARY ART MUSEUM
I always have an image in mind when I begin. . . . In Naoshima, the image I had was to build a castle. This was the first impression I had—a castle on a hill on an island—a dream image that was accessible for people, especially for children. . . . It was an image that I thought could inspire their imagination as soon as they saw it from the water. _ Michael Auping, *Seven Interviews with Tadao Ando*, Fort Worth: Modern Art Museum of Fort Worth, 2002

**Site and Memory** A site possesses its own physical and geographical character; at the same time it has layers of memory imprinted on it. I always listen to that whispering voice of a given place. I think of it comprehensively with all of its forces—the visible characteristics as well as the invisible memories to do with the interaction between a locality and humankind. And I try to integrate these into my building

which shall carry that spirit on to later generations.

For example, the site of Minamidera on Naoshima Island, located among old row houses where a temple once stood, possesses this strong spirit and this unique urban memory that one hopes to awaken through the creation of the new building. _ William J. R. Curtis, "A Conversation with Tadao Ando," *El Croquis*, no. 44+58, 2000

**Ruins** I like ruins because what remains is not the total design, but the clarity of thought, the naked structure, the spirit of the thing. It is this that provides inspiration, and one can learn a great deal from it. _ William J. R. Curtis, "A Conversation with Tadao Ando," *El Croquis*, no. 44+58, 2000

An aerial view of the Benesse House of the Naoshima Contemporary Art Museum showing the building merged into the landscape. *Inset, left to right:* An interior view of the cylindrical gallery and a view of the Oval Court.

## SPACE:
## BRINGING SPIRITUAL MEANING TO SPACE

A space is never about one thing. It is a place for many senses: sight, sound, touch, and the unaccountable things that happen in between. Working with space and form is about working with as much of the human intellect and spirit as possible. _ Michael Auping, *Seven Interviews with Tadao Ando*, Fort Worth: Modern Art Museum of Fort Worth, 2002

Architecture consists of two elements. An intellectual element in that we have to create a space that is logical and clear, that has a logical or intellectual order. At the same time, you have to use your senses to imbue the space with life. These are the two main aspects of creating architectural space. One is practical and theoretical; the other is sensory and intuitive. . . . When you say order, people often imagine limitations and containment, but I think of a geometry that expands to the spirit of the living person who enters the building. The order must feel expansive. _ Michael Auping, *Seven Interviews with Tadao Ando*, Fort Worth: Modern Art Museum of Fort Worth, 2002

In a way, I want the surface to disappear and become a space, a space that stimulates thinking. If the surface does not speak too loud, then people will begin to think about themselves. They bring the meaning to the space. _ Michael Auping, *Seven Interviews with Tadao Ando*, Fort Worth: Modern Art Museum of Fort Worth, 2002

## WALLS

A good wall, as you call it, is a matter of its physical relationship to people and the way it can create space around us, a system of spatial relationships. It is very basic, but something that people, including architects, often forget. . . . If you look at one wall in front of you, you can perceive it as an object. If you see it from the side, you understand that it divides space. If it then connects with another wall, you begin to see it as a container of space. At that point, the wall functions as a shelter, protection, a sense of security from the elements. This is the most primitive function of a wall, but it is a part of any important architecture. Creating spaces that inspire a sense of well-being is the main goal of building walls. . . . A wall must assert its presence in terms of its form and materiality, to make you understand that it has its own power or presence, but it must do so in a way that inspires and does not force or intimidate. . . . It's important to be forceful without being intimidating or overly elaborate. . . . The wall is the most basic tool of architecture. _ Michael Auping, *Seven Interviews with Tadao Ando*, Fort Worth: Modern Art Museum of Fort Worth, 2002

## ST. LOUIS 2001
# PULITZER FOUNDATION FOR THE ARTS
Initially, this building was designed to house part of the collection of the family of the founders of the Pulitzer Prize, as well as to become a cultural hub for the area. . . . Given the surrounding site conditions and the programmatic requirements, the design . . . should have a residential-scale character. . . . The building is composed of two rectangular volumes, placed parallel to each other on either side of a water garden. The two volumes are each given different heights. . . . With regard to the interior of the exhibition rooms, by actively bringing in natural light to enhance this interior-exterior continuity, the intention was to create spaces that breathe nature by integrating the changing effects of time and season.

From the planning stage onward, the artists Ellsworth Kelly and Richard Serra, who have provided works for this foundation, participated in the design process, which progressed as the architects and artists exchanged opinions and proposals. . . . Although our opinions sometimes came into conflicts the quality of the architecture steadily increased through uncompromising dialogues between us and with the client. This collaborative work with them was extremely significant, making us think about the very basic elements of art museums. _ Courtesy Tadao Ando Architects & Associates

Ando at right with artist Richard Serra. For the architect, natural light was a "must" in his concept of the Pulitzer building—even on the darkest days the use of artificial light in certain areas is prohibited. The space is like a sanctuary, a continuing homage to art, as seen in Ellsworth Kelley's Blue Black, opposite, specially commissioned for the new building, and even the water garden, opposite top left.

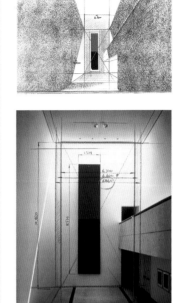

**❝ ORDER MUST FEEL EXPANSIVE. ❞**

## CONCRETE

*The use of concrete brings out the poet in Ando.*

I tend to think of concrete as being very hard and sharp. I like the sharp edges and planes that can be made with concrete. When they come into contact with nature they are like a powerful foil. The precise order in contrast to nature can make both elements more dynamic. However, over the years of using this material, I have come to see different qualities of concrete. Depending on the space I am trying to construct, I may see it as just the opposite: softer and less severe. _ Michael Auping, *Seven Interviews with Tadao Ando,* Fort Worth: Modern Art Museum of Fort Worth, 2002

I began as a craftsman and a builder working with my hands. I still miss that now. Working with your hands and muscles is important. It is very important, very important to understand scale and weight and the voice of materials. I don't want to design impractical things that a human being cannot build. Working with your hands teaches you very basic concepts of beauty. For example, I like concrete because it is handmade compared to some other types of modern building methods. _ Michael Auping, *Seven Interviews with Tadao Ando,* Fort Worth: Modern Art Museum of Fort Worth, 2002

## WHAT CONCRETE IS (OR ISN'T)

It appears to be a very common material that is available everywhere, and because it is generally used in only one way we think of it as being very one-dimensional. However, concrete possesses many variables. Every concrete mix and pour has a different character. It is not like steel or glass, which has a more consistent nature. Concrete can vary greatly. Concrete has a depth of expression that changes with every use. Le Corbusier used concrete as if it were clay. He used its plastic quality almost as if he were sculpting. Louis Kahn used concrete as if it were hard steel. The same material—two very different effects. _ Michael Auping, *Seven Interviews with Tadao Ando,* Fort Worth: Modern Art Museum of Fort Worth, 2002

There is also the rebar—the reinforcing bar—and this is very important. The rebar is like the bones of a human body. The concrete is like the flesh. I think of a poured-concrete building as a metaphor of the human body. If you have a thick bone and not enough muscle and skin, the bone will start to stick out. Or if you have too much skin with no sense of bone, the building will look fat and bloated. It is very important to maintain the precise space, the right amount of space between the rebar. . . . Poured-in-place concrete is a kind of handmade building. _ Michael Auping, *Seven Interviews with Tadao Ando,* Fort Worth: Modern Art Museum of Fort Worth, 2002

As you know, there are wide variations in color from white to gray to black. Concrete can be very rich in color. I see color there in terms of depth rather than surface. The gradations of color create a sense of depth. If you only look at color in terms of projecting out from the surface, then you fail to see the depth. _ Michael Auping, *Seven Interviews with Tadao Ando,* Fort Worth: Modern Art Museum of Fort Worth, 2002

I am among a number of architects who use concrete because of the freedom it allows me. I like concrete because I can invent forms, which allows me to create new kinds of spaces. . . . Concrete gives the illusion that it is easy to work with because you can pour a long wall relatively quickly rather than having to build it brick by brick. _ Michael Auping, *Seven Interviews with Tadao Ando,* Fort Worth: Modern Art Museum of Fort Worth, 2002

> ❝ **NO MATERIAL FUNCTIONS EXCLUSIVELY ON ITS OWN. IT IS ALWAYS AFFECTED BY THE CONTEXT OF OTHER MATERIALS AND NATURAL CONDITIONS.** ❞

### KOBE 1986
# CHAPEL ON MOUNT ROKKO

The chapel's theme is progression through shadow and light—the contrast of light and darkness. A post and beam form an inverted cross in dividing a large window on the left; intercepting the sunlight, they cast a distinct cruciform shadow in the floor. This monochromatic space, restricted in its materials, draws the exterior greenery inside to become an interior scenery, and underscores nature's depth. _ Courtesy Tadao Ando Architects & Associates

**Darkness** Shadows and darkness contribute to serenity and calmness. In my opinion, the darkness creates the opportunity to think and contemplate. . . . But areas of darkness are critical, and I think they relate to deep metaphorical levels of creation. _ Michael Auping, *Seven Interviews with Tadao Ando,* Fort Worth: Modern Art Museum of Fort Worth, 2002

The Chapel on Mount Rokko plays on shadow and light. Ando divided a large window so that a cruciform would be cast on the floor. The portico is at bottom, right.

> **IT SEEMS TO ME THAT, AT PRESENT, CONCRETE IS THE MOST SUITABLE MATERIAL FOR REALIZING SPACES CREATED BY RAYS OF SUNLIGHT.**

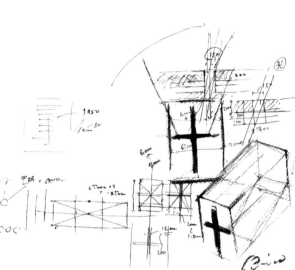

Budgetary concerns ultimately led to a highly elegant, spare design featuring a cross cut into the front wall.

## OSAKA 1989
# CHURCH OF THE LIGHT
*Ando describes how budget played an active role in determining the simplicity and design of this religious building.*

Because of the limited budget, the building was unavoidably a simple box shape. How to bring forth a sacred space within this box, appropriate for a place where people gather and pray? After thinking hard for more than a year, I arrived at a composition in which a concrete wall diagonally cuts through the box, dividing the entrance from the single-space worship hall, which has a descending stepped floor. Without heating or cooling equipment, the bare concrete hall contains only pews and a pulpit made of simple, untouched materials. With absolutely no ornamental elements, it is a naked space reduced to the limit. Only a cross-shaped incision in the front wall projects the symbol of the church into this gloomy space: Church of the Light.

The idea was to take advantage of the severity of the given conditions, but the real difficulty of the project was in the next stage, the process of actually constructing the building. Somehow, once construction had started, the lack of funds became conclusive, and construction was finally stopped after the walls had been completed. I even had to consider an alternative plan for an open-air worship hall without a roof. However, construction was completed due to the enthusiasm of the believers and the response this drew from the construction company, who have produced something worthy of pride. The process of producing this small work of architecture is great proof that human will can sometimes transcend economic issues. _ Courtesy Tadao Ando Architects & Associates

## INFLUENCES:
## OSAKA CHILDHOOD HOME

As a child, I used to go looking at the construction sites near my home in Osaka. I always thought the carpenters were important people. They looked so great to me, a young boy with so much interest toward making things by my own hands. They would put the frames up before the siding was put on, and they were so confident and proud that the house they were building would stand for one hundred years . . . . They would tell me that a building must be built with confidence and pride—materials alone do not make a building great or strong. . . . The combined effect of beginning to understand a carpenter's confidence, and the pride of a craftsman, made me think that this could be a way for me to contribute to society in some way. . . .

We all have had certain experiences in our childhood that have stayed with us for our entire lives. The house that I grew up in was very important for me. It is an old, Japanese, small wooden house partitioned into several units—a Nagaya row house. It is very long, and when you come in from the street you walk through a corridor and then into a small courtyard and then another long space that takes you deeper into the house. The courtyard is very important because the house is very long and the amount of light is very limited. Light is very precious. When you live in a space like that you realize how important light is to interior space. _ Michael Auping, *Seven Interviews with Tadao Ando*, Fort Worth: Modern Art Museum of Fort Worth, 2002

## BOXING AND ARCHITECTURE:
## STEPPING INTO THE UNKNOWN

*For many years Ando was a professional boxer. His interest in architecture began when a series of boxing matches took him to Bangkok, Thailand. There, Ando visited Buddhist temples and became fascinated by their design. This led to several years of traveling to observe architecture in Japan, Europe, and the United States. He then abandoned his boxing career to pursue self-education by apprenticeship in architecture.*

They are of two different worlds—architecture in the realm of the creative and boxing in the realm of the purely physical. The one thing I can say is that in boxing you have to be courageous and take some chances, always taking one step deeper into your opponent's side. You must

risk moving into a dangerous area in order to fully take advantage of your skills and eventually win the match. Creating something in architecture—not just building something but creating something—also requires courage and risk, moving into areas that are not so known, taking that extra step forward. If you stay in your day-to-day lifestyle, just building buildings without thinking about why you build buildings and never questioning yourself, it doesn't require courage. To create a form of architecture, something that may not look familiar, you have to take that extra step into the unknown. _ Michael Auping, *Seven Interviews with Tadao Ando*, Fort Worth: Modern Art Museum of Fort Worth, 2002

## BASIS FOR
## ARCHITECTURE

One way, for example, of learning how to make architecture is to go to school. This is the conventional way. . . . However, I did it in a different way. I did it through my body. I worked around craftsmen and builders, who I thought of as artists. So the basis of my relationship with architecture is related to this physicality. The physical presence of architecture is the foundation of my sensibility. _ Michael Auping, *Seven Interviews with Tadao Ando*, Fort Worth: Modern Art Museum of Fort Worth, 2002

## FROM BUILDING TO ARCHITECTURE

It was a gradual process. It did not happen at a fixed moment. The period when I decided to travel around Europe in 1965 was critical. I saw the Parthenon in Greece, the Pantheon in Rome, and many works of Le Corbusier. That was when I knew that architecture could be a creative force, that a building represented something more than a protection from the weather. That took me to a higher level of thinking about architecture. _ Michael Auping, *Seven Interviews with Tadao Ando*, Fort Worth: Modern Art Museum of Fort Worth, 2002

## ANDO'S ROLE AS AN ARCHITECT

All I can do as an architect is consider the diversity of people on this planet and how architecture can help bring them together; not just as a meeting place, but a space of inspiration. As an architect, this is all I can do—to create a dialogue between diverse cultures, histories, and values. We can learn so much from each other and our past. _ Michael Auping, *Seven Interviews with Tadao Ando*, Fort Worth: Modern Art Museum of Fort Worth, 2002

# 19 94

**CONSTANT EVOLUTION** . . . all my projects reflect an evolution, related not so much to taste but to the idea of architecture as a cultural and formal presence. An idea of architecture as determining space. I would say I design objects in relation to space rather than the other way around. . . . I admire people who were system-builders like Johann Sebastian Bach. But I am not like them. My example would be like Picasso or even Frank Lloyd Wright, people who evolved throughout their lives, relating to time and its passing. You have the Wright of the turn of the century, and then you have the Wright of Art Deco and the Wright of fifties' modernism. Extraordinary. He was always himself, but he never failed to respond to the problems of his time. The same goes for Picasso. They were travelers as opposed to system-builders. Some things in my work are systematic, but as far as form goes, I like to be constantly evolving. I try to avoid worshipping an ideal style, and am always trying to escape my own mannerisms—which can be difficult. _ Christian de Portzamparc interview by Yoshio Futagawa, *GA Document Extra No. 4, Christian de Portzamparc, 1995*

# CHRISTIAN DE PORTZAMPARC

**BORN:** May 5, 1944, Casablanca, Morocco

**EDUCATION:** Diplôme d'Architecture, École Nationale Supérieure des Beaux-Arts, Paris, 1969

**OFFICE:** 38, rue La Bruyère, Paris, 75009
Tel: +331-40-64-80-00, Fax: +331-43-27-74-79
www.christiandeportzamparc.com

**PROJECTS FEATURED:** Luxembourg Philharmonic, Luxembourg, 2005; French Embassy, Berlin, 2003; Crédit Lyonnais Tower, Lille, France, 1995; Cité de la Musique, Paris, France, 1995; Nexus II, Fukuoka, Japan, 1991; Paris Opera Ballet School, Nanterre, France, 1987

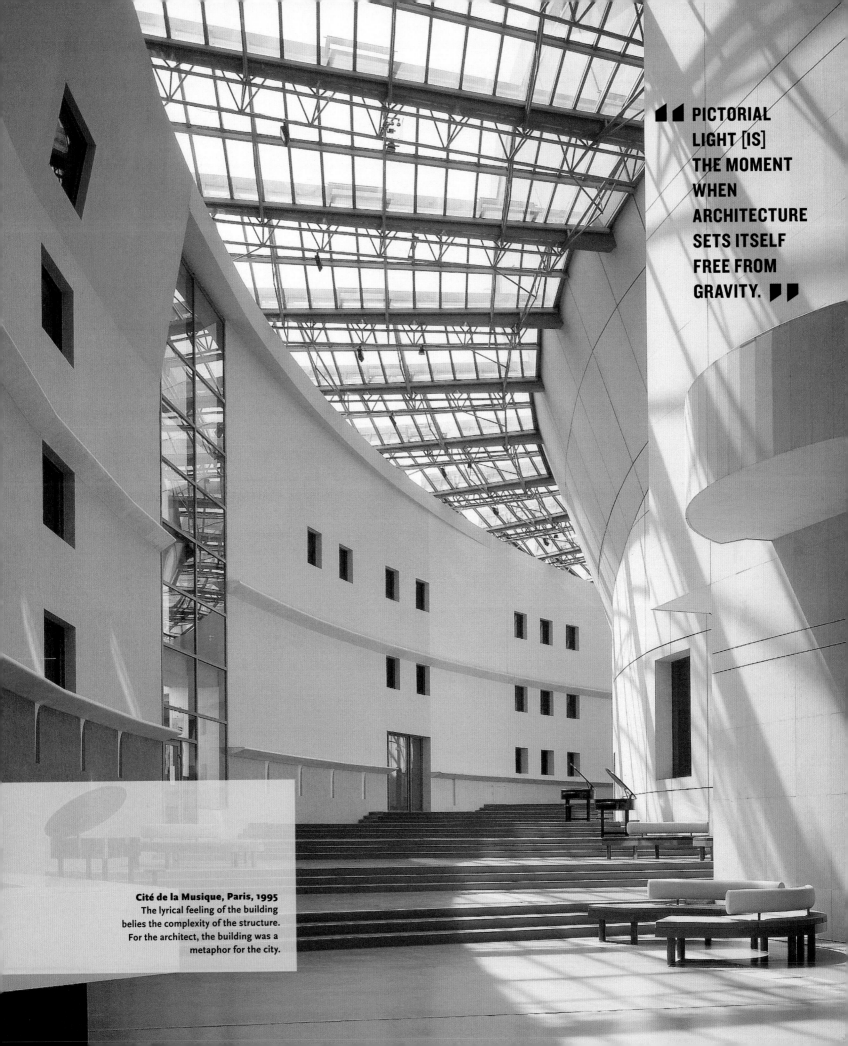

**PICTORIAL LIGHT [IS] THE MOMENT WHEN ARCHITECTURE SETS ITSELF FREE FROM GRAVITY.**

**Cité de la Musique, Paris, 1995**
The lyrical feeling of the building belies the complexity of the structure. For the architect, the building was a metaphor for the city.

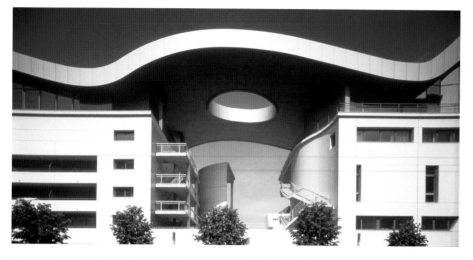

space. In fact, the project became a sort of laboratory for my work. On the one hand, the program was highly specific, but on the other, many of my general architectural themes were integrated into the project. _ Christian de Portzamparc interview by Yoshio Futagawa, *GA Document Extra No. 4, Christian de Portzamparc,* 1995

## PARIS 1995
# CITÉ DE LA MUSIQUE
The fact is that the emotion triggered by spaces is masked by all manner of contingencies. In the long run, the habit of place dilutes its sensations. Music is on a par with emotion, unencumbered by habit, economy, and the burden of space. It is wonderfully free of contingency. Apparently, its rules are intrinsic to it. That is the great lesson of music, and the architect who, encumbered by material and technical difficulties of his craft, is always liable to lose sight of the poetics of space should bear this in mind. _ Michel Jacques with Armelle Lavalou, eds., *Christian de Portzamparc,* Basel, Switzerland: Birkhäuser, 1996

## ▌▌ MUSIC IS LIKE A BURN, A POWERFULLY FELT EVENT. ▐▐

There is a lot to say about the Cité de la Musique because there were thousands of problems to solve: a highly complex program, functional questions, the urban context, the events I wanted to unfold inside the building, and the quality of forms and

I was trying to make several buildings in one, in which the sense of inside and outside would be ambiguous—a clear metaphor of the city. _ Christian de Portzamparc interview by Yoshio Futagawa, *GA Document Extra No. 4, Christian de Portzamparc,* 1995

**Integrating "Families of Music"** So I had two very different types of problems. The conservatory part— the West Wing—had to be organized into precise relationships . . . to accommodate the various types of musical activity: dance, jazz, classical, electronic, and so on. . . . . The other side, the East Wing, is for different uses, with a concert hall, a museum, the headquarters of an orchestra, some lodgings, a laboratory for music, and an entrance café. . . . The various elements are disconnected and quite independent. . . . In a way there are distinctive buildings within the building. _ Christian de Portzamparc interview by Yoshio Futagawa, *GA Document Extra No. 4, Christian de Portzamparc,* 1995

Among the design elements, Cité de la Musique was an integration of several buildings. *Opposite:* One of the rehearsal rooms.

The idea of the families of music, with each family having its own home inside, made it important not to design anything too static, symmetrical, or repetitive. I didn't want it to be seen as a state institution. I wanted there to be an experience of discovery. . . . For this reason, the shapes, volumes, and colors are all different, and this is something you realize when you enter, whereas the outside constitutes a unified whole. So you have the contrast between the experiences of inside [and] outside. _ Christian de Portzamparc interview by Yoshio Futagawa, *GA Document Extra No. 4, Christian de Portzamparc*, 1995

I wanted a well-asserted rhythm effect between dark and light places. This was because of my experience at the Nanterre dance school, whose light struck me as too homogeneous. I said to myself that what was lacking there was the beautiful, poetic dimension of shadow—the sort of thing you have at the Palais Garnier for example. Light is always a phenomenon of relative contrast, between brightness and darkness . . . _ Christian de Portzamparc interview by Henri Ciriani, "Guided Tour of the Cité de la Musique," *L'Architecture d'Aujourd'hui*, April 1991

## "THE CITY AS 'SCENARIO'"

The cinema of Antonioni, of Godard, showed us the town of today, its present nature, with that of the past, as being the totality of our contemporary experience. _ Courtesy Christian de Portzamparc

Half my mind was involved with theory and the other half gradually became concerned with building. At the beginning of the seventies I saw that form, space, and the visual had to be related to people's lives. . . . But who would be the one to relate the dimensions of one building to the next, and give form to place?

Technological thinking alone couldn't lead the world, even if it was governing more and more of the world. I felt that architecture could begin to approach technology in another way, to be conscious of it but not submerged by it. _ Christian de Portzamparc interview by Yoshio Futagawa, *GA Document Extra No. 4, Christian de Portzamparc*, 1995

Architecture should not be a personal gesture. It belongs to the city. But it needs an artistic investment. _ "Designing Frenchman," *Newsweek*, May 9, 1994

## FRANCE IN THE 1960s

In Paris, during the sixties, town planners anticipated demolishing two thirds of the town center, and rebuilding it. These were modern times, the dawn of a new age, and all this excited us. Soon, however, I began to doubt the wisdom of this vision. Razing the city center seemed improbable. This unlikely idea stemmed from a misunderstanding of the profound nature of the city. The city had to be understood as an entity existing in time, as well as in space. _ Courtesy Christian de Portzamparc

Architecture and the voids created by it can produce movement, but it must all be seen in context. I always consider a building as part of the whole, a piece which creates a collective performance, which is the city. _ Thomas D. Sullivan, *The Washington Times*, May 2, 1994

You have to remember that in the sixties architectural work in France was all about the improvement of the cities and the building of the postwar urban fabric. At the beginning of the sixties I believed strongly in the new urbanism. We were convinced that 70 percent of Paris would be completely rebuilt, creating a completely modern city—at least that was the official plan. Around 1966 I began to do exercises on this idea of inventing new neighborhoods and the idea of sequences which I depicted in drawings and photographs. I was also interested in the relationships between the city and the movies—the city as "scenario." _ Christian de Portzamparc interview by Yoshio Futagawa, *GA Document Extra No. 4, Christian de Portzamparc*, 1995

From about 1966 on . . . I began to feel that architecture alone was dry and unrelated to real life in the city. At this time we became more and more politically involved in contesting the old methods of teaching. In 1967 I rejected the idea of becoming an architect altogether. Symbolically, I gave away all my paintings and drawings to my sister. _ Christian de Portzamparc interview by Yoshio Futagawa, *GA Document Extra No. 4, Christian de Portzamparc*, 1995

I think it had partly to do with the seven months I spent in New York in 1966. I went there thinking I would be working or looking at architecture, but I ended up hanging around writers, poets, and musicians, reading, going to exhibitions. I stopped drawing because I thought pictorial architecture was too reductive. I started writing. By the end of my stay my interests had changed to a mix of literature, poetry, and cinema. I now considered architects as technocrats. _ Christian de Portzamparc interview by Yoshio Futagawa, *GA Document Extra No. 4, Christian de Portzamparc*, 1995

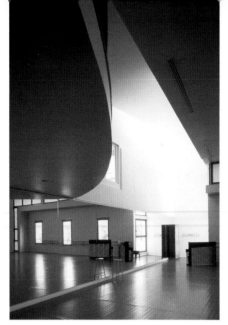

The Paris Opera Ballet School is the oldest ballet school in the Western world and the cradle of classic academic ballet. Architecture, like dance, the architect says, is a celebration of space.

### NANTERRE 1987
# PARIS OPERA BALLET SCHOOL

The design results from the idea of setting in movement not only the eye, but the whole body. Seen to move, moving to see. Like architecture, dance is a celebration of space. Place suggests movement, and movement occurs within the stability of place.
_ Christian de Portzamparc, Courtesy Atelier Christian Portzamparc

A school for children—adolescents. The rhythms of the twenty-four-hour cycle. Lessons in the morning, dance in the afternoon. Then play, supper, sleep. A boarding school in fact.

The three times of day. Three universes, three buildings in a centrifugal movement. Three interlocking registers.

Dance: light and movement. Dance has a backdrop, volume, wall, cardinal points. A dance studio is a painter's canvas, a blank sheet of paper, waiting for the first stroke of the pencil. _ Christian de Portzamparc, *De la Danse: École du Ballet de l'Opera de Paris à Nanterre,* Paris: Editions du Demi-Cercle, 1990

The project is *extraverted;* intervals are extended, generating highly differentiated *loci*. Elongations, rotations, elevations, planilinearities, architectural *promenade,* transparency, polarization, etc. It cannot be grasped in a single gaze; each façade, each space is highly specific, and one is forced to move: architectural *promenade,* the free movement of dance.
_ Christian de Portzamparc, *De la Danse: École du Ballet de l'Opera de Paris à Nanterre,* Paris: Editions du Demi-Cercle, 1990

**❝ THE ARRIVAL OF A FRESH EYE OFTEN MAKES IT POSSIBLE TO FIND ORIGINAL SOLUTIONS THAT INDIGENOUS ARCHITECTS, USED TO THE STEREOTYPES OF THEIR OWN COUNTRY, NO LONGER PERCEIVE. ❞**

**FUKUOKA 1991**
# NEXUS II

*Nexus II is a housing project consisting of thirty-seven apartments in four different units. Arata Isozaki designed the master plan within which Nexus II is situated.*

Collective housing has been our training ground for the urban question. . . . Hands-on, case-by-case confrontations with the city—one can no longer simply draw up plans without first reflecting on the range of possible heights, interstices, views, and lighting configurations. The perfect unit is no longer a credible goal.

Equal conditions for all are an illusion, unless it be mediocrity for all. Volumetric parameters are decisive—one has to work with the site, exploiting optimal conditions depending on positions, orientation, light, and prospect. _ Michel Jacques with Armelle Lavalou, eds., *Christian de Portzamparc*, Basel, Switzerland: Birkhäuser, 1996

It is very invigorating to work abroad. But I have only found myself facing a genuinely "different" culture in Japan when I constructed the housing units in Fukuoka. The design had to be of typically Japanese rooms, but hybrid, since the apartments also included a Western-style kitchen. These experiences outside my own country have above all enabled me to think about housing units much more attractively than in France, where the plans are too often set in stone.

In other countries, it is much more acceptable, for example, to get to a bedroom by crossing the living room, without passing along a corridor, which necessarily limits the space available. _ Christian de Portzamparc interview by Emmanuel Thévenon, French Ministry of Foreign and European Affairs website, http://www.diplomatie.gouv.fr

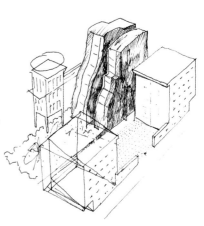

The Nexus II housing project required de Portzamparc to venture outside of Europe and consider a non-Western culture in his design.

De Portzamparc's Crédit Lyonnais Tower in Lille, France, is known as the "ski boot" building.

### LILLE 1995
# CRÉDIT LYONNAIS TOWER

*Portzamparc's iconic tower for Crédit Lyonnais, popularly known as the "ski boot," is part of Euralille, an ambitious urban commercial project, inaugurated in 1994, which reinvigorated a formerly industrial district of the city of Lille. The master plan was designed by Rem Koolhaas.*

In reality, in every city the practice of architecture is like writing an "oulipien" poem with its particular mathematics and formal constraints. It is a matter of constantly adapting to the context, always strange, unique, in which one is working. _ Christian de Portzamparc interview by Emmanuel Thévenon, French Ministry of Foreign and European Affairs website, http://www.diplomatie.gouv.fr

After the war, political, public, and religious institutions went into architectural hiding. Monumentality had become more or less taboo: for the Modernists, it had implied the culpable search for "external effects"; totalitarian regimes largely contributed to its discredit. The international, functionalist architectures of the postwar era were latter-day democratic assertions of this expiation.

Obviously, architecture will always generate "external" and "internal" effects, which work on the senses. All the rational systems in the world can do nothing to prevent this. Repress sensations and they return as symptoms. The problem is to control the perception of certain entities. And thus I became interested in public buildings which give weight to place—fleshing out spaces which in any case will always transcend them. _ Michel Jacques with Armelle Lavalou, eds., *Christian de Portzamparc*, Basel, Switzerland: Birkhäuser, 1996

## LUXEMBOURG 2005
# LUXEMBOURG PHILHARMONIC

I love creating buildings for music. They express the dialogue between hearing and sight. _ Raul Barrenche, *Travel + Leisure,* August 2005

. . . we perceive architecture with our senses and our bodies through motion and the passing of time. This is common to both architecture and music. _ Christian de Portzamparc interview by Yoshio Futagawa, *GA Document Extra No. 4, Christian de Portzamparc,* 1995

## ❝ . . . A CURTAIN OF LIGHT . . . ❞

I wanted the public to populate the walls of the space. . . . It's good for the musicians to see people all around them. And it's good for the audience to feel close to the performers. _ Raul Barrenche, *Travel + Leisure,* August 2005

For the Luxembourg Philharmonic de Portzamparc originally wanted a ring of trees surrounding the hall—to give visitors a promenade to stroll through before they would "enter the realm of music." When he realized he couldn't fit the trees on the site, he turned the façade into a "forest" of 823 columns to create a similar effect.

## THE CITY: A MULTIPLICITY OF ONE

By contrast with a museum, which encloses time, showing us epochs deliberately removed from the present, in the town we are permanently recycling history. An eighteenth-century building rubs shoulders, in a street laid out in the fifteenth century, with a building of the twentieth century. Elegant or ugly, we live with it, we use it, and we transform it. _ Courtesy Christian de Portzamparc

I personally understood the town to represent a vast physical, collective, and intimate memory, of chance events that give dynamism to the present moment, as well as reaching out to the future. _ Courtesy Christian de Portzamparc

## A SPIRIT OF PLACE

A lot of people think that the city is eternal. . . . But I think—and history bears this out—that the city shapes itself like any other manmade work to contingencies of current economy, lifestyles, and techniques, and that because of this it is obviously an evolving entity . . . _ Christian de Portzamparc, "Des Situations Plurielles, Toujours Singulières," *L'Architecture d'Aujourd'hui,* September 1994

We need light and views—close-up and long views at the same time. Mine was a new theory of the block. This is a question of topology, of the relationships between void and objects . . . _ Christian de Portzamparc interview by Yoshio Futagawa, *GA Document Extra No. 4, Christian de Portzamparc,* 1995

Architecture and towns are manifested as physical, sensorial, and material events. We walk in town, the architecture surrounds us. It may repel us or leave us indifferent; it might suddenly excite or dazzle us. The effect of "logos"—the spirit of the place—can make us strangely "present"; a hidden, secret world seems to emerge and may reveal itself to us. _ Courtesy Christian de Portzamparc

When designing a project I think in terms of space, figure, distance, shadow, and light. . . . I am thinking directly in terms of forms and figures. Yet such notions had never been addressed in theory. _ Christian de Portzamparc interview by Yoshio Futagawa, *GA Document Extra No. 4, Christian de Portzamparc,* 1995

### BERLIN 2003
## FRENCH EMBASSY
Here, a rough surface in fragmented concrete, there, a smooth and glossy wall. Over here, a glass partition, and over there, a pure white coating. All of these materials interact and contrast with each other, highlighting opposite directions and enlarging the space. In a German newspaper article, a journalist questioned the fact that I did not use the same type of concrete all over. Although the academics of the time advocated the unity of materials and shapes, the space would have become a cloister if I had used the same type of concrete all over. We have all experienced this phenomenon a thousand times over. Here, the unity relies on a redefined atmosphere. One generally thinks that the unity of a space is solely defined by materials rather than ambience. Most often, the atmosphere cannot be seen. _ Christian de Portzamparc and Eric Reinhardt, *Les Inrockuptibles*, supplement to no. 462, October 2004

The French Embassy in Berlin sits close to the famous Brandenburg Gate. De Portzamparc used a roster of materials and surface treatments so they could interact with one another. The variety allowed the building to feel unencumbered.

. . . the constraints greatly limited the work on the façade, which opens to Pariser Platz, near the famous Brandenburg Gate. I sought to make a very narrow, enclosed plot surrounded by enormous blank walls as habitable and pleasant as possible. To give a feeling of space I could have decided to cover the area between the buildings with [an] atrium—a glass roof. But in Germany, as in other northern countries, people try to get some fresh air whenever the weather permits. I therefore wanted everyone to be able to open their windows to the fresh air, and look out on plants growing everywhere . . . _ Michel Jacques with Armelle Lavalou, eds., *Christian de Portzamparc*, Basel, Switzerland: Birkhäuser, 1996

## "INTERESTED IN THE VISIBLE"

I already liked to draw when I was a little boy. Right from the start, I was very much interested in the visible. _ Christian de Portzamparc and Philippe Sollers, *Writing and Seeing Architecture*, Minneapolis: University of Minnesota Press, 2008

Well, I was already drawing and painting and sculpting. I discovered a book with drawings by Le Corbusier and became interested in the idea of space and scale. I was also interested in the fact that there were different disciplines within architecture, more than in painting. But above all, at first, I was interested in the idea of space. _ Christian de Portzamparc interview by Yoshio Futagawa, *GA Document Extra No. 4, Christian de Portzamparc*, 1995

My use of color comes from my painting—something I've been doing since the early sixties. Gradually, this use of colors and sense of materials brushed off on my architectural work. _ Christian de Portzamparc interview by Yoshio Futagawa, *GA Document Extra No. 4, Christian de Portzamparc*, 1995

## FIGHTING CLASSICAL TRADITION

I enrolled at the Beaux-Arts—already a militant follower of Corbusier and convinced that the old school was too academic. _ Christian de Portzamparc interview by Yoshio Futagawa, *GA Document Extra No. 4, Christian de Portzamparc*, 1995

We had to do analytical drawings of classical buildings, but I was the first to do an analysis of modern buildings—the Maison de Verre by Pierre Chareau and buildings by Le Corbusier. We were proud when such initiatives were rejected, because we were fighting the school and trying to change things; it was an opportunity to assert what we wanted. I think studying at the Beaux-Arts obliged us as students to look for something different, to fight against tradition. The school was very traditional and anti-theory, whereas we read and followed the Structuralists. _ Christian de Portzamparc interview by Yoshio Futagawa, *GA Document Extra No. 4, Christian de Portzamparc*, 1995

## A CONFRONTATION BETWEEN THE OBJECTIVE AND THE SUBJECTIVE

Architecture has never really felt comfortable in its status as art and technology in the city. It vacillates between engineering process, relying on technology to improve life, and art which creates the mysterious. For me, architecture comprises objective responsibilities but also an unpredictable, idiosyncratic, personal, artistic application; it's a confrontation between the objective and the subjective. _ Christian de Portzamparc interview by Yoshio Futagawa, *GA Document Extra No. 4, Christian de Portzamparc*, 1995

## THE PRITZKER PRIZE AND SOCIAL RESPONSIBILITY

In the face of change, with the abolition of doctrines, the [Pritzker] Prize committee has been obliged to adopt another stance, to re-determine the legitimacy of architecture by referring to the achievement, the personal adventure of individual talents. It may be said that our individual responsibility as architects is great, and that we have to become ecologically orientated and urbanistic. _ Courtesy Christian de Portzamparc

I got a realistic idea of a concrete way to understand architecture as a social responsibility. I came to realize that architecture might not be able to create Utopia, but as an architect, I could help change things for the better. _ Thomas D. Sullivan, *The Washington Times*, May 2, 1994

An architect must remember that the people working or living in his building need space—to dream, to be quiet, to find beauty somewhere. _ Bonnie Churchill, *Christian Science Monitor*, May 11, 1994

I always keep in mind that architecture serves a purpose—that it is useful in life. If we want to keep this idea of usefulness not as dry functionality, imagination is crucial. The city is a tool for working and living, but you also experience it like a novel—a novel of your own life, or a movie of your own life. This is the work of the architect. _ Christian de Portzamparc interview by Yoshio Futagawa, *GA Document Extra No. 4, Christian de Portzamparc*, 1995

**◀◀ MY AESTHETIC CHOICES, HOWEVER, NEVER RELATE TO COMMERCIAL PRESSURES. ▶▶**

**ATONAL CONTROL** Architecture must produce tension, and the tension must be created from unstable orders, not from very stable ones. But in the end . . . the final arrangement of elements and parts will still be governed by your sensibility. And, certainly, the sensibility, in my case, is not wild enough: to make a building or a part of one, I still try to compose.

My past work, ten to fifteen years ago, had a more stable image; but even when we look, let's say, at the first phase of the Hillside Terrace project, there are many different elements acting. I was always against a very static totality; and yet I probably still seek stability by activating elements so that they conflict with each other in a way that is under my own rational control.

These are very difficult matters to clarify. For some people, atonal music is without harmony, but in my buildings you still can probably find some kind of harmony. _ Serge Salat, *Fumihiko Maki: An Aesthetic of Fragmentation,* New York: Rizzoli, 1988

# FUMIHIKO MAKI

**BORN:** September 6, 1928, Tokyo, Japan

**EDUCATION:** M.Arch., Harvard University, Cambridge, Massachusetts, 1954; M.Arch., Cranbrook Academy of Art, Bloomfield Hills, Michigan, 1953; B.Arch., University of Tokyo, Tokyo, Japan, 1952

**OFFICE:** Maki and Associates, Hillside West-C, 13-4 Hachiyamacho Shibuya Tokyo, 150-0035, Japan
Tel: +81 3-3780-3880, Fax: +81 3-3780-3881, www.maki-and-associates.co.jp

**PROJECTS FEATURED:** Shimane Museum of Ancient Izumo, Shimane, Japan, 2006; Sam Fox School of Design and Visual Arts, Washington University in St. Louis, Missouri, 2006; Hillside Terrace Complex, Tokyo, 1969–92; Tokyo Metropolitan Gymnasium, Tokyo, 1990; National Museum of Modern Art, Kyoto, Japan, 1986; Spiral (Wacoal Art Center), Tokyo, 1985

**IT IS THE RESPONSIBILITY OF THE ARCHITECT TO LEAVE BEHIND BUILDINGS THAT ARE ASSETS TO CULTURE.**

**Spiral, Toyko, 1985**
Seen from the outside, Fumihiko Maki's Spiral building appears to be an emsemble of forms. This was sleight of hand on Maki's part, for the design was a deliberate evocation of Tokyo's urban landscape.

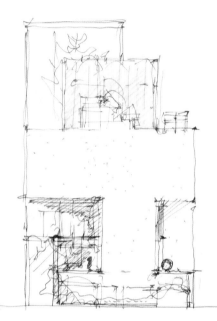

**A nighttime view of Spiral, as well as a concept sketch early on in the formative stage.**

### TOKYO 1985
# SPIRAL

Spiral gives expression . . . to a variety of familiar elements that are products of modern art and architecture. These elements suggest a spiral movement that progresses upward and culminate in the lightning rod. _ Serge Salat, *Fumihiko Maki: An Aesthetic of Fragmentation,* New York: Rizzoli, 1988

The spatial experience consists of a central café with an exhibition space surrounding it. This configuration integrates the café space with the exhibition space. An esplanade leads from the building entrance up to the second floor where large windows offer a panoramic view of the urban activity outside. Chairs are placed in front of the windows to allow the visitors to stop and relax while observing the flow of urban life below. Continuing along the esplanade, there is a terrace, which offers a serene, but surreal, place.

Seen from the outside, the Spiral building appears as an ensemble of forms and a collage of modern icons. This collection of forms is intended to respond to the jumbled urban landscape surrounding the building and to give a message from the outside of the spatial experience on the inside. _ Fumihiko Maki interview by Sangleem Lee, *Space,* November 2006

The façade of Spiral is conceived as a collage of a number of elements. However, unlike an actual collage, various considerations such as matters of urban design, internal functions, and the building's performance as an external skin underlie the composition. The result is a collage that is autonomous even as it reflects such considerations. _ Serge Salat, *Fumihiko Maki: An Aesthetic of Fragmentation,* New York: Rizzoli, 1988

> **" SPIRAL SYMBOLIZES TODAY'S IMAGE OF THE CITY—AN ENVIRONMENT THAT IS FRAGMENTED BUT THAT CONSTANTLY RENEWS ITS VITALITY PRECISELY THROUGH ITS STATE OF FRAGMENTATION. "**

## URBAN ARCHITECTURE

*Maki's definition of architecture involves the city. In the late 1950s, he was a founding member of the Metabolists, a visionary group of young Japanese architects and city planners who explored a theoretical city of the future characterized by large-scale, flexible structures that enabled an organic growth process. Out of this experience, Maki defined his own distinct philosophy of group form, emphasizing individual elements as a genesis of the whole.*

Regarding cities and architecture, the most important aspect of their relationship is that architecture has its own urbanity. When we think about urbanity, what is important is that it should give a sense of familiarity for the public to share. . . . I think buildings that offer this familiarity are necessary for making good cities. _ Fumihiko Maki interview by Sangleem Lee, *Space*, November 2006

The city represents the sum total of paths of journeys repeated every day by individuals. Buildings are in a sense the cross-sections of journeys and together create a place, a genius loci that people share, even if for a short interval. A place is at times a mnemonic device for a group of individuals and is a dramatic stage on which contemporary mythic ceremonies are held. To create architecture in a city is to build places and to give life to "time" (i.e., past, present, and future). _ Serge Salat, *Fumihiko Maki: An Aesthetic of Fragmentation*, New York: Rizzoli, 1988

The ultimate goal of architecture and urban design is place making. People are attracted to places where they find comfort and delight. If there are more of these spaces, then cities will become better places to live and work. _ Fumihiko Maki interview by Sangleem Lee, *Space*, November 2006

## "COLLECTIVE FORM"

*Published in 1962, Maki's* Investigations on Collective Form *has served as the core theories of his architectural practice over his whole career. The following excerpts are taken from this important text.*

We have so long accustomed ourselves to conceiving of buildings as separate entities that we now suffer from an inadequacy of spatial language to make meaningful environments. This situation has prompted me to investigate the nature of "collective form." Collective form concerns groups of buildings and quasi buildings—the segments of our cities. Collective form is, however, not a collection of unrelated, separate buildings, but of buildings that have reasons to be together. . . . I have established three major approaches: Compositional Form, Megastructural/Megaform, and Group Form. _ Fumihiko Maki, *Buildings and Projects*, New York: Princeton Architectural Press, 1977

> **" THE CITY CAN BE SEEN AS THE SUM TOTAL OF COUNTLESS EVENTS BEING GENERATED SIMULTANEOUSLY. "**

. . . the notion of an urban order based on a collection of elements, and [I] believed it offered an alternative to the order, based on enormous structures built on the scale of civil engineering works, that architects and utopians had been proposing since the start of the twentieth century. _ Fumihiko Maki, *Buildings and Projects*, New York: Princeton Architectural Press, 1977

By emphasizing the autonomy of individual architectural elements and deliberately creating weak linkages between them, one enables those elements to become more distinct indices of time and place. I learned that both opposition and harmony in fact characterize relationships on many different levels and that their cumulative effect determines our actual image of the city. _ Fumihiko Maki, *Buildings and Projects*, New York: Princeton Architectural Press, 1977

> **" CREATION IN ARCHITECTURE IS DISCOVERY, NOT INVENTION. IT IS NOT A PURSUIT OF SOMETHING THAT TRANSCENDS THE IMAGINATION BUT A CULTURAL ACT IN RESPONSE TO THE COMMON IMAGINATION OF VISION OF THE TIME. "**

deference to subtle topographical changes, spatial layering, and the creation of protected exterior public space. The success of this project is a result of spatial and architectural means—scale, transparency, etc.— as well the programmatic development of public life. _ Project Description, courtesy of Maki and Associates, www.maki-and-associates.co.jp

. . . the Hillside Terrace project exhibits a series of traditional elements, which includes using trees to mediate the open space between buildings. Also, the entrances to the Hillside Terrace buildings are accessed from the corner, which reflects the entrance style of traditional Japanese housing. One last example is the formation of various spaces within a small area, which recalls the style of open spaces in traditional Japanese cities. In the Hillside Terrace Complex, each of these traditional elements has been completed in the modernist language. _ Fumihiko Maki interview by Sangleem Lee, *Space*, November 2006

# HILLSIDE TERRACE COMPLEX

. . . the project that has left the deepest impression on me as an architect, I would cite the Hillside Terrace Complex, which I have been involved in the design and execution of for the past thirty years. _ Fumihiko Maki interview by Sangleem Lee, *Space*, November 2006

**This ambitious project— executed in seven phases over more than three decades—was a unique opportunity for Maki to engage fully in design for public life. The traditionalist met the modernist in Hillside's successful evolution.**

The Hillside Terrace Complex is a collective form that has developed over seven phases since 1969, corresponding to the continuously changing circumstances of Tokyo. A variety of design strategies are used to create its unique atmosphere, including

For me, the Hillside Terrace project was an opportunity to act as a community architect, which has been an invaluable experience. . . . The Hillside Terrace Complex maintains its original conditions because of good maintenance by the client . . . _ Fumihiko Maki interview by Sangleem Lee, *Space*, November 2006

## JAPANESE HERITAGE

My maternal family was engaged in the construction business. When I was young, I used to visit many completed buildings. Thus, I was raised in an environment where every family member cultivated an interest in architecture. _ Fumihiko Maki interview by Sangleem Lee, *Space*, November 2006

When I started to build my own works in 1965, I began to fully embrace my Japanese heritage. . . . Rather than merely imitating the roof shapes and wooden structural styles of traditional Japanese architecture, I tend to create spatial concepts that permeate through Japanese culture. For instance, I consider unique relationships between interiors and exterior, use trees as mediating devices, or explore techniques and methodologies for expressing the character of wooden structures with metallic materials. As these examples suggest, an important aspect of my career has focused on the issue of expressing traditional Japanese culture through modern architectural styles and techniques. _ Fumihiko Maki interview by Sangleem Lee, *Space*, November 2006

Urban societies that have been forced, as in Japan, to develop within various irregular frameworks of land configuration . . . evolved traditional techniques of spatial formation and perception such as the Japanese concepts of *ma* and *oku*. These techniques serve to create a flexible urban order, one that is amorphous and collage-like, and which ironically is more amenable to the principles of modernism—that is, the higher priority given to space over mass and a concern for an asymmetrical order rather than axiality—than in Western cities. _ Serge Salat, *Fumihiko Maki: An Aesthetic of Fragmentation*, New York: Rizzoli, 1988

*Ma* or *sukima* in English is called a residue. But in a Western sense a residue is a leftover; it does not have a meaningful role in the organization of form and space, as it does for us. We appreciate meaningful void, meaningful leftover. *Ma* to some extent represents that character. _ Serge Salat, *Fumihiko Maki: An Aesthetic of Fragmentation*, New York: Rizzoli, 1988

The National Museum of Modern Art in Kyoto is located in the city's historic district. Maki considered the modernity of the building the most important design theme of the project.

## KYOTO 1986
# NATIONAL MUSEUM OF MODERN ART, KYOTO

The National Museum of Modern Art, Kyoto, is located in the heart of historic Kyoto. As such, the appropriate expression of twentieth-century modern spirit within a sensitive context was considered the most important design theme. . . . A 1.5-meter grid was used for the basic exterior module—representing horizontality and verticality, present and past, transparency and mass, and the duality of Japanese and Western. _ Project Description, courtesy of Maki and Associates, www. maki-and-associates.co.jp

. . . everything takes place in depth, horizontally and not vertically. . . . This is a way of structuring the experience of space that implies the dimension of time . . . _ Serge Salat, *Fumihiko Maki: An Aesthetic of Fragmentation*, New York: Rizzoli, 1988

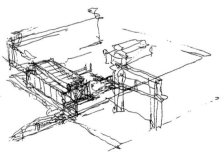

## SPATIAL DEPTH

... we are interested in developing a spatial quality which is not necessarily to be judged in terms of absolute height or length, but rather in terms of a sense of depth in space. In order to achieve that, you have to develop sequences of layers of space or boundaries. _ Serge Salat, *Fumihiko Maki: An Aesthetic of Fragmentation*, New York: Rizzoli, 1988

One does not physically experience urban space by simply gazing at buildings or looking at them from above. Space is experienced only through sequential movement. _ Fumihiko Maki, *Buildings and Projects*, New York: Princeton Architectural Press, 1977

When I was a boy living in Tokyo, I can remember the darkness and invisible centers of many of the neighborhoods. However, it seems that such elements are gradually disappearing in this modern time. Therefore, I think it is important to create architecture that has a sense of spatial depth. _ Fumihiko Maki interview by Sangleem Lee, *Space*, November 2006

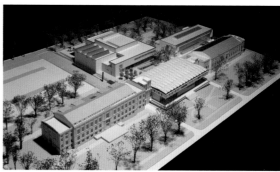

The Sam Fox School of Design and Visual Arts in St. Louis is made up of buildings that form a mini-campus of sorts. The new buildings are limestone with a variety of light glazing elements.

### ST. LOUIS 2006
# SAM FOX SCHOOL OF DESIGN AND VISUAL ARTS
Sam Fox School of Design and Visual Arts consolidates and enhances all facilities and programs related to the study of the visual arts and architecture. The two new buildings, Mildred Lane Kemper Art Museum and Earl E. and Myrtle E. Walker Hall, are arranged in an ensemble with the existing arts buildings to form a "mini-campus" that cloisters a series of outdoor spaces. The Kemper Museum is envisioned as a "center piece" that both establishes a symbol for the visual arts on campus and serves the larger St. Louis community. The building is organized around a vaulted, double-height atrium intended as a symbolic multipurpose space. Three galleries and the library open onto this hall. The Walker Hall houses divisions of the Art School requiring heavy infrastructure. These studios are arranged as open spaces that enable the highest level of flexibility. To maximize open space all fixed core elements are concentrated at the ends of the building. The new buildings are clad in limestone and a variety of light glazing elements. The ensemble of traditional and new materials will create a harmonious dialogue with the existing architectural context. _ Project Description, courtesy of Maki and Associates, www.maki-and-associates.co.jp

Suppose you make three independent buildings and try to relate them to the open spaces between. In Western architecture you have developed quite a number of rules and principles, governed by the laws of geometry, and also perspectives. If you look at Renaissance buildings, you have a very strict rational order through which you could construct their relationship. But we [Japanese architects] make an arrangement as we see fit, without using rational orders as such. _ Serge Salat, *Fumihiko Maki: An Aesthetic of Fragmentation*, New York: Rizzoli, 1988

## SKETCHING

In the early 1960s, when I was still teaching at Harvard, there were a number of architects around who had had experience working for Le Corbusier. Among their various anecdotes concerning Le Corbusier, one that made a particular impression on me was his sketchbook. According to their accounts, he always carried a slim sketchbook that would fit the inside pocket of a jacket and used it for not only architectural design, but various memos. . . . About twelve years ago, I found a sketchbook that was just right. It was 16 centimeters wide, 21 centimeters high, and had a cloth cover. The paper, ruled with a grid, was sturdy, and you could use a felt-tip pen on it without having the ink show on the back. There were about 300 pages to a book, which was very convenient. I continued to use rolls of tracing paper as before, but I got into the habit of drawing the first images of a building in this sketchbook. Eventually, the sketchbook became one of the things I always carry on me, like my glasses and keys. _ Fumihiko Maki, *Selected Passages on the City and Architecture*, Tokyo: Maki and Associates, 2000

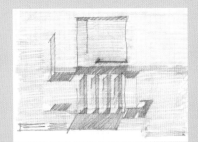

Maki says it took him some time to find the perfect sketchbook to carry with him. "Eventually the sketchbook became one of the things I always carry on me, like my glasses and keys."

Architectural design is an odd process. One sketches not only to give expression to forms and ideas that are already developed or that have just come to mind, but also to call forth new forms and ideas. I am not familiar with the world of dance, but it seems to me the ruled grid of a sketchbook is like a stage where—instead of one gesture inviting the next—one line summons another. It may be somewhat narcissistic, but one must first feel an affection for the lines one draws. _ Fumihiko Maki, *Selected Passages on the City and Architecture*, Tokyo: Maki and Associates, 2000

A sketch leaves things uncertain even to oneself and incorporates areas of emptiness. A sketch is appealing precisely because it records a dream that will not be fulfilled. _ Fumihiko Maki, *Selected Passages on the City and Architecture*, Tokyo: Maki and Associates, 2000

## ❝❝ IT MAY BE SOMEWHAT NARCISSISTIC, BUT ONE MUST FIRST FEEL AN AFFECTION FOR THE LINES ONE DRAWS. ❞❞

### TOKYO 1990
# TOKYO METROPOLITAN GYMNASIUM

Tokyo Metropolitan Gymnasium is located in the outer gardens of Meiji Shrine. Fitting its parklike surroundings, it is designed to include a variety of exterior spaces and a diversity of architectural expressions. Each building (main arena, sub-arena, and indoor pool) maintains its integrity as a large volume, while simultaneously establishing humane exterior spaces for the public. Together, these elements constitute an expression of "collective form." As one's viewpoint shifts, the overlapping of these volumes creates unexpected silhouettes.
_ Project Description, courtesy of Maki and Associates, www.maki-and-associates.co.jp

The overall composition is an attempt to create a new urban landscape by juxtaposing strongly geometric and symbolically charged pieces. The result is a constellation of clearly defined geometric forms that make up an indeterminate cloudlike whole. _ Fumihiko Maki Announcement, www.pritzkerprize.com

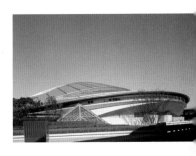

The Tokyo Metropolitan Gymnasium is actually a series of buildings, whose dominant structure is a large arena. The building appears to be all roof because its walls rise just a few stories from the plaza. When viewed from above, the roof is composed of two symmetrical leaflike shapes, leaning against each other.

In keeping with materials historically significant to Shimane, Maki chose corten steel for its similarity to the traditional *Tatara* steel.

SHIMANE 2006
# SHIMANE MUSEUM OF ANCIENT IZUMO
Adjacent to the eastern side of the approach to Izumo Taisya Shrine, the site expands along the shrine's north-south axis, blessed with a "borrowed landscape" of the Kitayama Range in the background. The exterior view of the building is compact in expression. A pair of folded roofs blends the mass of the building with the surrounding scenery to create a lifting skyline. The eye is drawn from the roofs in the foreground to the gentle undulation of the garden and further on to the placid image of the mountains in the background, creating scenic harmony. Corten steel on the exterior walls is reminiscent of "Tatara steel," an important material in the history of Shimane. In a marked contrast with the transparent glass surface, the corten steel expresses a concise yet dynamic texture. _ Project Description, courtesy of Maki and Associates, www. maki-and-associates.co.jp

## DESIGN PROCESS

*The hallmark restraint of Maki's architecture can also be found in his published writings and texts. Yet how he thinks about architecture is surprisingly intuitive and nonrational, as seen in his thoughts about his design process.*

The characteristics of each project may look systemized, which is partly due to functional similarities or geographic conditions. As for what is coherently featured in my projects it would be difficult to explain logically, as I think it is attributable to my personality. _ Fumihiko Maki interview by Sangleem Lee, *Space*, November 2006

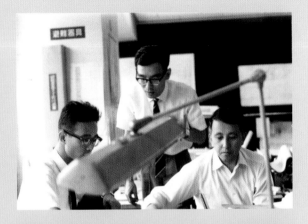

Quite often I shift the axis of buildings. But I don't use 45 degrees or 30 degrees. I just use my eyes and mind for such an operation. It's probably a matter of feeling. In the same way, when I try to place two or three buildings to make one complex, often I use models. But the models, again, are used in such a way that the final decision will be made by just shifting and juggling. _ Serge Salat, *Fumihiko Maki: An Aesthetic of Fragmentation*, New York: Rizzoli, 1988

When I start to design, quite often I have ideas, not just on the whole, but on parts. I play with that, and gradually the total picture comes out. In some cases, as in classical buildings, you start with the totality, or a clear whole, then you begin to make the parts to be fitted within this frame. _ Serge Salat, *Fumihiko Maki: An Aesthetic of Fragmentation*, New York: Rizzoli, 1988

Architects are like movie directors. . . . The most important thing in a movie is what kind of scene or scenery he wants to produce at the critical moment. Then to justify those sceneries he uses a story or he makes up a story. . . . As an architect, I'm very much interested in a particular situation, almost a scenery or a scene, and one of them in the case of Wacoal [the Spiral] was a roof or an atrium for a procession. That is very important. Out of that, we begin to construct the rest of the building. _ Serge Salat, *Fumihiko Maki: An Aesthetic of Fragmentation*, New York: Rizzoli, 1988

If architecture is an art, I think we have to confront it with each and every inner landscape, regardless of the rationality that the architecture commands. The image is something we cannot just extract: the image is very deeply associated with your inner landscape. _ Serge Salat, *Fumihiko Maki: An Aesthetic of Fragmentation*, New York: Rizzoli, 1988

I was never attracted to the idea of a large organization. On the other hand, a small organization may tend to develop a very narrow viewpoint. My ideal is a group structure that allows people with diverse imaginations, that often contradict and are in conflict with one another, to work in a condition of flux, but that also permits the making of decisions that are as calculated and objectively weighed as necessary for the creation of something as concrete as architecture. _ Fumihiko Maki Biography, www.pritzkerprize.com

Architects should produce architecture derived from their own long-held ideals rather than from short-term trends. _ Fumihiko Maki interview by Sangleem Lee, *Space*, November 2006

I don't want to become an architect who reaches his peak quickly then disappears. I want to work steadily with long-term goals while demonstrating a certain architectural presence to the younger generation. _ Fumihiko Maki interview by Sangleem Lee, *Space*, November 2006

# ❝ ARCHITECTURE IS LIKE A
# MARATHON,
### NOT A 100-METER RACE. ❞

**19**
**92**

## THE FLEETING IMAGE

I don't work within any theoretical framework nor do I offer a key as to how you should understand my work. What I am interested in is projects that anticipate new developments that one hardly has a name for yet and which exploit the potential of a specific place—the culture that prevails there and the resulting tensions and conflicts. I look for proposals that go beyond any passive notion of just giving material form to an idea, that, by trying to grasp all the facets simultaneously, refuse to impose limits on reality. The point, then, is always to avoid static images and a linear development in time. With every design you need to make a serious attempt to capture one concrete moment of a fleeting image in all its aspects. In concrete terms that means that a project begins for me as soon as I assess the situation on the site itself. . . . I let all kinds of elements work on me; they may be vague but that doesn't mean they are any less important.

_ Alvaro Siza Vieira interview by Ole Bouman and Roemer van Toom, alvarosizavieira.com

# ALVARO SIZA

**BORN:** June 25, 1933, Matosinhos, Portugal

**EDUCATION:** Degree in Architecture, University of Porto, Porto, Portugal, 1955

**OFFICE:** Rua do Aleixo, 53-2, Porto 4150-043 Portugal
Tel: +22 6167270, Fax: +22 6167279
www.sizaviera.pt

**PROJECTS FEATURED:** Iberê Camargo Foundation, Porto Alegre, Brazil, 2007; Santa Maria Church and Parochial Center, Marco de Canavezes, Portugal, 1997; Faculty of Architecture, University of Porto, Portugal, 1993; Serralves Museum of Contemporary Art, Porto, Portugal, 1997; Borges & Irmão Bank, Vila do Condo, Portugal, 1986; Swimming Pools, Leça da Palmeira, Matosinhos, Portugal, 1966; Boa Nova Tea House, Leça da Palmeira, Matosinhos, Portugal, 1963

**"** FOR MYSELF I LIKE TO SACRIFICE MANY THINGS,
TO SEE ONLY WHAT IMMEDIATELY ATTRACTS ME,
TO WANDER AT RANDOM, WITHOUT A MAP
AND WITH AN ABSURD SENSATION
OF BEING AN EXPLORER. **"**

**Boa Nova Tea House,
Leça da Palmeira, 1963**
This was one of Alvaro Siza's first
built projects. It rises from the rocks
along the Atlantic Ocean like a natural
extension of the landscape. The kitchen,
at the back of the building, is virtually
underground because Siza wanted to
hide what was unnecessary from view.

The Boa Nova Tea House sits on the rocks not far from where Siza grew up. Its roof hugs the concrete building, which keeps the restaurant cool in summer and protects it from the crashing waves and storms of winter.

## LEÇA DA PALMEIRA 1963
# BOA NOVA TEA HOUSE
The visual relationship with the Atlantic is mediated by a rocky outcrop, through which the sea enters, transforming the shape of the landscape according to the weather conditions and the tides. _ Antonio Angelillo, *Alvaro Siza—Writings on Architecture,* Milan: Skira, 1997

. . . the vernacular tradition had an importance in our education at this time, but so did its opening, our meeting with European, Italian, and Spanish influences. The reconstruction in France, the reconstruction in England, the programs of new towns and new schools: It was a moment of the convergence of many influences. And if you look at the Boa Nova Restaurant, which was in a sense my first work . . . you will notice, I am sure, many influences of the architecture that was strong in Europe at that time, these mixed with the Portuguese vernacular. _ Dawne McCance, *Mosaic: A Journal for the Interdisciplinary Study of Literature,* December 2002

[For] the Boa Nova Tea House . . . I designed all the furniture, and I have always felt the need to think about the movements of people—and we need furniture. To make a chair, for instance, I would make a prototype, which might be some boxes in the office, and check the measurements. I know there are books with all these rules, but the rules never tell you everything if you want to create special forms, special expressions of furniture. _ C. C. Sullivan, *Architecture—New York and Washington—American Institute of Architects,* vol. 93, no. 7, 2004

The Boa Nova Restaurant is in a beautiful place, and it is natural that the influence of the surroundings should have been important on conceiving the project. The attention to the surroundings was very intense, mimicking the profile of the rocks. In the two Swimming Pools at Leça and Matosinhos, the relationship between construction and landscape is quite different. The construction is strongly determined by its geometry. This is not a purely mimetic relationship, but a transformation of the landscape, though the attitude is still within that logic of the landscape. _ Alejandro Zaera, *El Croquis,* no. 68–69, 1994

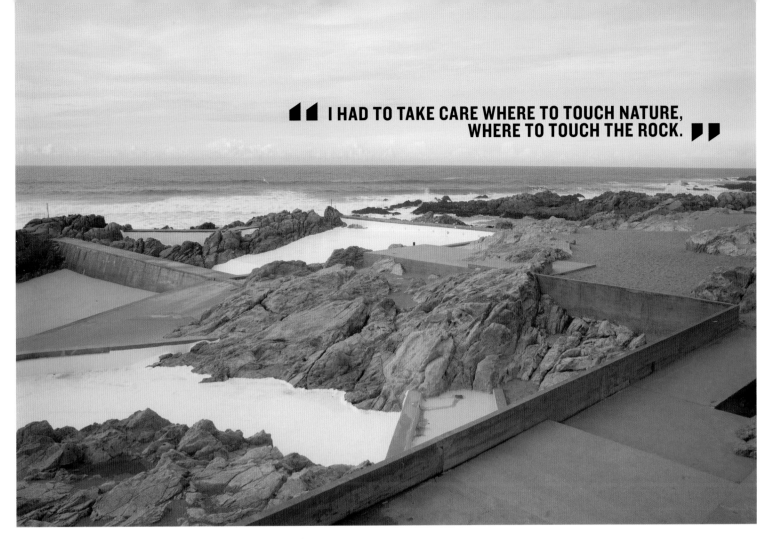

**I HAD TO TAKE CARE WHERE TO TOUCH NATURE, WHERE TO TOUCH THE ROCK.**

## LEÇA DA PALMEIRA 1963
# SWIMMING POOLS
The area for the swimming pool was created from natural contours of the rocky outcrop which serves as its support, with the paths and the resting places being cleared from these and the few constructions (platforms, steps, concrete walls).

The relationship between nature and design is less circumstantial and more precise than it is in the Boa Nova Restaurant, and therefore more open to the broad lines of the landscape than to the site it immediately occupies. _ Antonio Angelillo, *Alvaro Siza—Writings on Architecture,* Milan: Skira, 1997

The Atlantic is like a rock, and there is this sensation of space. And you cannot separate it from Portuguese culture and life. . . . I made my first two works by the sea—the tea house and, three years later, the swimming pool—and that was a fantastic experience because the materials I had—in fact, the rocks and the sea, which has a very strong life—conditioned everything. _ C. C. Sullivan, *Architecture—New York and Washington—American Institute of Architects,* vol. 93, no. 7, 2004

My intention was to say: Do not do a geometric swimming pool, but use the rocks, then we only have to put a wall here and another there. The limit of the pool will be the rocks. . . . Then I made the building for cloakrooms very low, so that the people here could always see the sea, the beach. I made it rather dark so that we could go down in a ramp, and there is not much light, and then we go outside, and there is a wall, and we turn and—pop!—we are in the open. This was the idea . . . _ "Architects Do Not Invent, They Just Transform Reality," *Oris,* vol. 8, no. 41, 2006

When I put something here, it had to be completely autonomous, strictly geometric. But I had to take care where to touch nature, where to touch the rock. _ "Architects Do Not Invent, They Just Transform Reality," *Oris,* vol. 8, no. 41, 2006

The Leça Swimming Pools are located in a small town near Porto, Portugal, and were the first Siza project to win global acclaim. These seaside pools follow the landscape with man-made concrete walls that meld seamlessly with the natural rock. The changing rooms, above, are in a pavilion of concrete with wood roofs. The visitor travels through dark corridors before emerging into light from an opening that looks out to the sea.

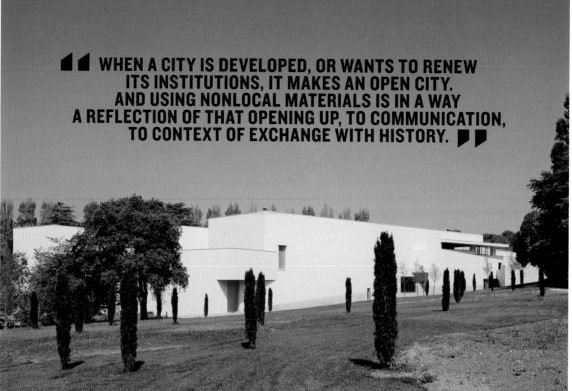

For the Serralves Museum, Siza had to contend with a property having a large house surrounded by meadows and gardens. The exterior walls are covered with stone or stucco. The white walls have occasional openings, which are meant to provide unexpected views of the garden. Siza had the building's granite-clad base follow the natural slope of the land.

**PORTO 1997**

# SERRALVES MUSEUM OF CONTEMPORARY ART

With Serralves, above all, it was the immense importance of the site, the park around it, the historic house, et cetera. Another huge consideration was the atmosphere of *fear* surrounding any kind of intervention on the site. In this case, it wasn't so much my own fear, but rather the fear of the client—which became almost paralyzing to me. But at the same time, the project was a great challenge both because of the irregular shape of the park—its borders—and because of how enormous the project itself was—14,000 square meters. We ran the risk of creating meaningless residual spaces, illegible spaces, spaces without form. . . . The building will never be seen in its totality—it will always appear as a fragment. And I wanted these fragments to have a very precise, keen line in contrast to the nature around it. This is very important, and we'll only really be able to appreciate it in one hundred years because the trees are still too small today. The building is quite hard and strong in contrast to the softness of the trees, the leaves, the branches. It is this combination of light and shadow and reflection that I wanted to see through the whiteness of the building. . . . There was a case to be made for introducing a nonlocal material to an exceptional building in an exceptional part of the city. We shouldn't be afraid of that. _ Alvaro Siza interview by José Antonio Aldrete-Hass, *BOMB*, Summer 1999

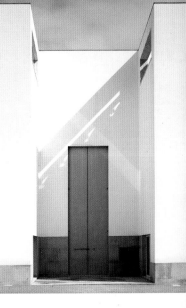

## MARCO DE CANAVEZES 1997
# SANTA MARIA CHURCH AND PAROCHIAL CENTER

The new buildings are arranged to complement the existing built environment and with it to form a special space in front of the church door, called an *adro* [churchyard—a modest church square or meeting place]. The church is sited at the center of the composition, with the ancillary buildings mediating between it and the scale of the surroundings. _ *Courtesy the office of Alvaro Siza*

I had a Catholic education as a child: I went to church every Sunday and had many memories, childish sensations, like being uncomfortable because the church was very dark, sad, and closed; the need to go outside during the priest's speech and gradually to smoke cigarettes as adults did, but secretively. All these things came back—how mysterious in my mind those church windows were. Because of all these mysteries and passions, it made sense to put the windows very high. . . . The horizontal window . . . this is on a high place overlooking the wonderful valley. The other idea was the need I had for the freedom to go outside for a moment, to have a view of that. _ "Architects Do Not Invent, They Just Transform Reality," *Oris,* vol. 8, no. 41, 2006

**The Cross** I think a symbol is not something you create. It is something that is made concrete through life and experience. . . . I decided to make one myself. . . . My first tries with sketches were a disaster. . . . The church was opened with a borrowed cross, because I was not able to make one. . . . I tried many things for two years. In the end, it is a golden piece, when you see it you have the feeling of a body there. _ "Architects Do Not Invent, They Just Transform Reality," *Oris,* vol. 8, no. 41, 2006

Santa Maria Church is part of an overall complex that creates a small urban square. Siza, as he does with many of his buildings, also designed the furniture and the fixtures, including the 400 wooden chairs that lead to the altar.

## PORTO 1993
# FACULTY OF ARCHITECTURE, UNIVERSITY OF PORTO

Siza had to set the buildings for the Porto architecture school on a terraced triangular site, hemmed in on three sides by highway exits, existing roads, and the former estate of Quinta da Povoa. The main building on the north side was designed to provide visual and acoustic protection from the road.

**The "Idea of a Park"** What I see in fragmentation . . . is just a strategy for some types of work. If you look from the other side of the river at the Faculty of Architecture, at the site, you will see what I mean. You will see a number of towers that embody the idea of beauty for the 60s and 70s. This is where I had to build. And I wanted to integrate these towers into the landscape and into the ambience of the site. I thought of it as a park-garden in the English tradition (in fact, most of the English colony in Oporto lived there). It's a very good site; to the south it is very beautiful. So I looked on it as a park, with these buildings already in place, and I wanted to add another part to it with my fragments in the landscape. But these fragments are related, in a way, around a kind of patio, and you can read them as forming a whole—indeed, they must be read as a whole, as a school or public building, and as related to the landscape. While it is difficult to put architects' work together and into relation, I wanted, with this project, on which I was working alone, to contribute to the larger work in place, and to affect this convergence through the idea of a park. _ Dawne McCance, *Mosaic: A Journal for the Interdisciplinary Study of Literature,* December 2002

I became aware of these relations in the end, after the evolution of the project. The large building began as a single volume and was subsequently fragmented and distributed such that in the end I noticed an open courtyard had been established with separate pieces more or less in the geometric form of the pavilion. This was not a preestablished idea, but emerged after an evolution dependent upon other problems. The program, the desire to maintain some preexisting stone walls, and the difficulties of the topography all led to a form which suggested the pavilion itself months before [these] were also used in the definition of the architecture of the complex. There really was a continuity in the process of this project. In the end, due to specific reasons and not because it was thought of as a method, there are affinities or similarities between the complex and the small pavilion that made the pavilion serve as a support for the development of the architecture of the complex as a whole. _ Peter Testa, *Harvard Architecture Review,* vol. 7, 1989

## "ARCHITECTURE IS ART"

Architecture is Art or it is not Architecture. It is not mother of the Arts because it does not give rise to them, being like them autonomous and contrary to dispersal. _ Antonio Angelillo, *Alvaro Siza—Writings on Architecture*, Milan: Skira, 1997

I was very interested in [Antonio] Gaudí because when I compared the buildings in real life to the photographs of this famous architecture I said this was like sculpture. In fact I think I was more interested in it as sculpture than as architecture. When I arrived and saw it with my own eyes, I saw that this sculpture was actually houses and had all of the elements of a regular house: doors, windows, baseboards. So this in a way opened the world of architecture up to me. Before I could see the work as sculpture, but now I could see it as architecture. _ Alvaro Siza interview by Yukio Futagawa, *GA Document Extra 11*, 1998

## INTENTION TO BE A SCULPTOR

My intention was to become a sculptor, but my family didn't like that idea. My father was an engineer, and I had no interest in being one. So I went to a school where they offered painting, sculpture, and architecture together, with a plan to switch from architecture to sculpture. But I didn't—I discovered architecture. And it was at a very stimulating moment, just following the war: It had been a beaux-arts school, but things were changing, and a younger generation of teachers was taking power. _ C. C. Sullivan, *Architecture—New York and Washington—American Institute of Architects*, vol. 93, no. 7, 2004

. . . architecture belongs to the same human wish and motive that painting or sculpture or cinema or writing literature is about. It belongs to the human need to understand and to express. _ Dawne McCance, *Mosaic: A Journal for the Interdisciplinary Study of Literature*, December 2002

## VILA DO CONDO 1986
## BORGES & IRMÃO BANK

The building has a rotational character; the interior spaces and the connecting staircases emphasize this, apart from the more obvious curves of the banking counter, profiled ceiling, exterior end walls, and ramp. Little of the bank is given away on the exterior, though similarly, little remains totally private on the interior: All floors are visually related in section, recalling Le Corbusier's Carthage Villa. _ *Courtesy the office of Alvaro Siza*

In the Borges & Irmão Bank at Vila do Condo, the curve had another origin: The clients wanted a building with a certain presence, but the front of the site was too small to do anything significant. The curve continues to produce a magnification of the scale of the house front by means of its extension toward the lateral wall. It is also necessary to create access to a new square, and the curve served to produce an opening in the urban space. _ Alejandro Zaera, *El Croquis*, no. 68–69, 1994

The curve employed in Siza's design of the Borges & Irmão Bank was central for enhancing the impact of the bank. The curved interior creates a visual flow throughout the building.

The Iberê Camargo Foundation building is on an awkward site, sandwiched between a cliff and a busy street. The museum is relatively small at just 88,000 square feet, but Siza made it look bigger by creating ramps and varying the height of the gallery floors. The entry plaza, *right,* plays with the idea of openness and enclosure. *Opposite:* A concept sketch showing the foundation sited in the Porto landscape.

## PORTO ALEGRE 2007
# IBERÊ CAMARGO FOUNDATION

The principal volume is carved out against the cliff vegetation, occupying its concave space, and results from the superposition of four floors with an irregular form, including a ground floor at the platform level. This volume is delimited by a straight and almost orthogonal wall on the south and west, and by an undulating wall on the north and east.

_ *Courtesy the office of Alvaro Siza*

This undulating wall, which rises the entire height of the building, delimits the access atrium, which is surrounded by the exhibition halls (an equal sequence, on the three floors above, of three rooms of varying dimensions) and by the reception, coatroom, and bookstore on the ground floor. Permanent and temporary exhibition spaces are not differentiated, opting for a flexibility appropriate to the actual functioning of museums. _ *Courtesy the office of Alvaro Siza*

## DESIGN PROCESS: COMMUNICATING

He [Siza is referring to himself] does not draw from the requirements from Architecture. He draws for pleasure, necessity, and as a vice. _ Sketchbook entry by Alvaro Siza dated March 1, 1994, in Antonio Angelillo, *Alvaro Siza—Writings on Architecture*, Milan: Skira, 1997

As well as being a valuable tool of communication and analysis, design provides the possibility of capturing atmospheres with a potential to free us from preconceived ideas and open up unexpected areas of exploration. . . . _ Enrico Morteo, *Domus*, February 1993

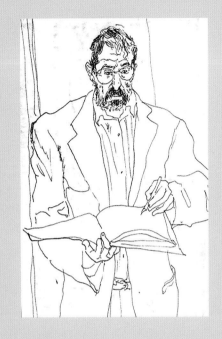

. . . periodically, during the process of a project, I take home the drawings and I need to concentrate not only on designing and sketching things, but on really knowing the building, really knowing the project. I have to be able to walk through the whole building mentally without looking at the drawings, you know? I have to be able to sit and imagine walking through the building, going down each hall, entering the bathroom, washing my hands, going to the kitchen if it is a house. . . . But I make every effort to study the project as it develops. _ Dawne McCance, *Mosaic: A Journal for the Interdisciplinary Study of Literature*, December 2002

[Design is] a process that unfolds in an unsystematic way because my experiences in recent years have taught me not to exclude a priori any element from a project, because architecture has to do with everything. It's a syncretic activity, which though it may seem vague at the beginning acquires density as problems come up. _ Enrico Morteo, *Domus*, February 1993

## ❝ IT IS JUST THAT ALL OF US CAN DRAW AND NEED TO DRAW. ❞

### "A GOOD ARCHITECT WORKS SLOWLY"

But no matter what machinery you devise there are quite simply no shortcuts one can take in the process of finding solutions for architectural problems. . . . The wealth of mutual relations between all the different aspects—for instance, the precise articulation of the spaces—that's something that doesn't just happen by itself. . . . A good architect works slowly. _ Alvaro Siza Vieira interview by Ole Bouman and Roemer van Toom, alvarosizavieira.com

As far as I'm concerned, when I think of architecture, I think primarily of stability, serenity, and presence. . . . You have to define your position in the midst of this glut of information. The more information I can assimilate, the more serene my architecture becomes. _ Alvaro Siza Vieira interview by Ole Bouman and Roemer van Toom, alvarosizavieira.com

### ❝ EVERY COMMISSION NEEDS IDEAS TO BRING IT TO LIFE AND IDEAS TAKE TIME TO RIPEN. IT'S AS SIMPLE AS THAT. ❞

It is not a curve but a modulation . . . because I had to build a whole, and I had there a big river, like the sea. The space was reduced, with a big difference in levels. It was wonderfully invaded by the greenery, by plants. I said I did not want to touch that, because it was impossible to remake that beautiful whole. The difficulty in this was that I had to have access to the exhibitions on the hillside, but I could not make the access to the exhibition on the hillside, . . . so I had to do a movement parallel with the access. . . . When I was designing it and thinking of a big motorcar going there, the curve appeared very strong. Afterwards, the ramps came. I made the big interior space. You say—and it is true—it is like the Guggenheim. But half of the ramp is inside, half is outside, and the rooms are rectangular. In the exterior, you can see the small windows. They are small, but in fact, you see the river and there is an angle where you see the whole town. _ "Architects Do Not Invent, They Just Transform Reality," *Oris*, vol. 8, no. 41, 2006

**INTUITIVE CRAFTSMANSHIP** I often refer to what I liked as a child. The configuration of the back door of the house I grew up in—you will find in the front door of my mother's house, and now that door is all over the world. And it's in the entrance of the Sainsbury Wing of the National Gallery. The vivid multicolored terracotta on the exterior of the Philadelphia Museum of Modern Art which I loved as a child has influenced our museum in Seattle. And so I find I have respected my early intuitions—acknowledged what I liked, and I think artists might go wrong when they fail to monitor their intuitive likes and dislikes and when they think in terms of what they should like, or they adapt an ideology they think they should adapt. . . . From the beginning, we haven't ever thought in terms of "We're going to be leaders, we're going to be great, we're going to be original." As an architect you are a craftsman, and you just try to do your best every day, and if it turns out you become a leader, if you become original and revolutionary or whatever, it's incidental. _ Robert Maxwell, "Robert Venturi and Denise Scott Brown: Interview with Robert Maxwell," *Architectural Design*, vol. 62, no. 5–6, 1992

# ROBERT VENTURI

**BORN:** June 25, 1925, Philadelphia, Pennsylvania

**EDUCATION:** M.F.A., A.B., Princeton University, Princeton, New Jersey, 1950, 1947

**OFFICE:** VSBA, 4236 Main Street, Philadelphia, Pennsylvania 19127
Tel: +1 215-487-0400, Fax: +1 215-487-2520
www.vsba.com

**PROJECTS FEATURED:** The Anlyan Center for Medical Research and Education, Yale University School of Medicine, New Haven, Connecticut, 2003; Seattle Art Museum, Washington, 1991; Sainsbury Wing, National Gallery; London, 1991; Gordon Wu Hall, Butler College, Princeton University, New Jersey, 1983; Best Products Catalog Showroom, Langhorne, Pennsylvania, 1978; Vanna Venturi House, Chestnut Hill, Pennsylvania, 1964

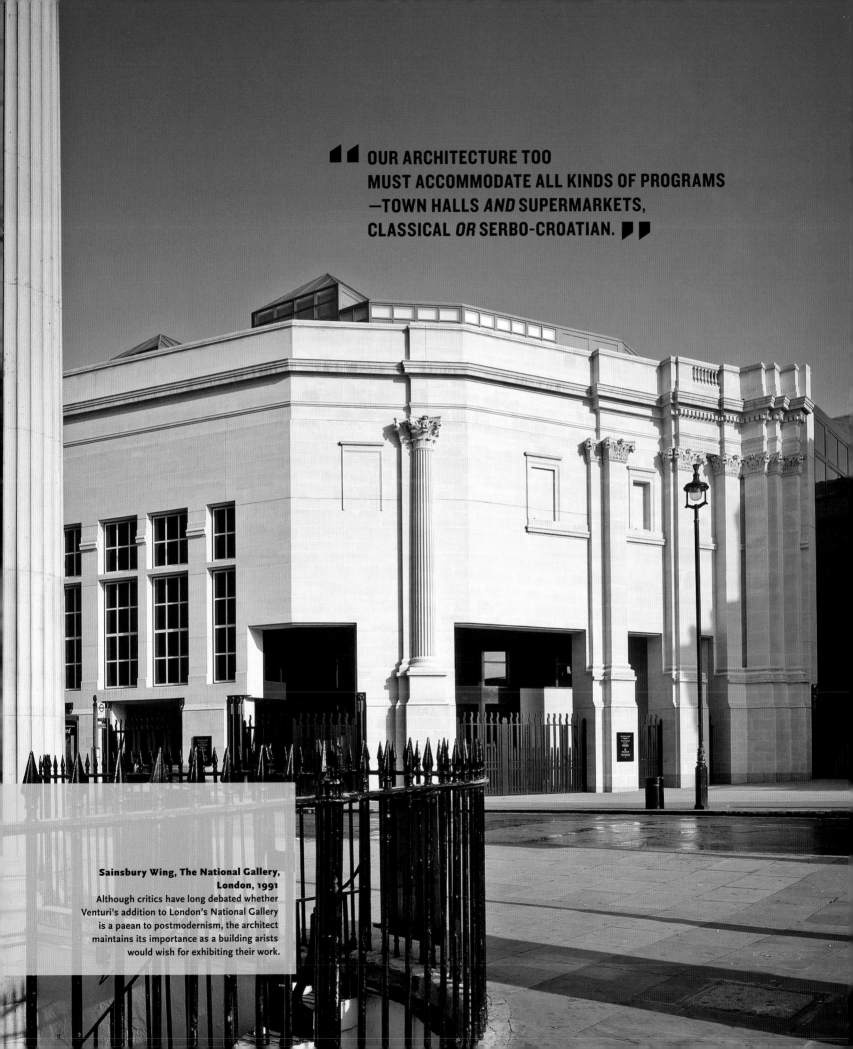

**"OUR ARCHITECTURE TOO MUST ACCOMMODATE ALL KINDS OF PROGRAMS —TOWN HALLS *AND* SUPERMARKETS, CLASSICAL *OR* SERBO-CROATIAN."**

**Sainsbury Wing, The National Gallery, London, 1991**
Although critics have long debated whether Venturi's addition to London's National Gallery is a paean to postmodernism, the architect maintains its importance as a building arists would wish for exhibiting their work.

Steve Izenour [former principal at VSB] and I were standing in Trafalgar Square, on the second day of thinking about the project, and the contextual limitations, which are very important, guided us immediately. The idea of using the metal colonnettes, and an 1830s elemental which Wilkins doesn't use, comes from the need to get small detail down at the base. _ Robert Venturi, David Vaughan, and Charles Jencks, "National Gallery—Sainsbury Wing," *Architectural Design*, vol. 6, no. 5–6, 1991

## LONDON 1991
# SAINSBURY WING, THE NATIONAL GALLERY

Our wing is like an organism separate from the older building, which has glandular problems where some of its elements must serve the whole complex. _ Robert Venturi, David Vaughan, and Charles Jencks, "National Gallery—Sainbury Wing," *Architectural Design*, vol. 6, no. 5–6, 1991

Classical elements from the Wilkins façade, including its characteristic pilasters, are replicated on the new building, but they are used in new and unexpected ways, alongside elements that contrast with the older building—for example, large square-cut openings to accommodate late-twentieth-century museum attendance and small metal columns to create small-scale interest at eye level. The chief elements of the façade, especially the pilasters, create a jazzy rhythm that calms down as it evolves toward Pall Mall South. _ Stanislaus Von Moos, *Venturi, Scott Brown & Associates: Buildings and Projects, 1986–1998*, New York: Monacelli, 1999

We acknowledged the client wanted something that paralleled the original setting the painters might have anticipated for their art. The sense of place was important. Also it is thrilling to see art in the real world, rather than in a museum: if you go to someone's house and they have a great painting in their living room, there is something *more* wonderful about it than if you see it in a museum—it's in the real world. At the same time you have to acknowledge the museum as an institution for accommodating high security and great crowds, so what we did was to place occasional windows in the galleries. A window indicates that you are part of the living world. Also you can look through it—and the magic you've been experiencing looking at great paintings becomes more magical after it is interrupted by the real world; it's like intermissions between acts at the theater. _ Robert Venturi, David Vaughan, and Charles Jencks, "National Gallery—Sainsbury Wing," *Architectural Design*, vol. 6, no. 5–6, 1991

Venturi used large square-cut openings to contrast with the older building that made up the National Gallery. He also placed the occasional window in the gallery so visitors could enjoy the artwork but also connect with the world outside the museum.

Now in designing the popular museum in terms of its aesthetic lyrical-ornamental dimension as well as its downtown location and its didactic and communal program, we are working within an established tradition. By sensuous I have meant appealing directly to the senses via color and rhythm to make this architecture immediately attractive to the ordinary person. But it must be attractive not only to the naïve or to children, but also to the sophisticate for whom this is to be a kind of cultural temple containing significant icons. _ Robert Maxwell, "Robert Venturi and Denise Scott Brown: Interview with Robert Maxwell," *Architectural Design*, vol. 62, no. 5–6, 1992

The idea seems so simple: an "at home" experience for viewing art. In fact, it was a revelation.

## "I GET THE IDEAS OUT IN WORDS RATHER THAN BRICKS AND MORTAR"

I have done my share of talking and writing; indeed, some of my writing has had some influence on the content of current talking and the tendency to talk. I write out of frustration. When my ideas about building exceed my opportunities to build, I get the ideas out in words rather than bricks and mortar. I wrote more when I was young than I do now because, luckily, we have more work now, although, as you will see, it is still relatively modest in scale and extent. Much architectural writing today is by young architects, probably for the same reason. But there is no justification for bad writing. When I read current architectural literature, I am often distressed by its pretension, confused by its obscurity, or bored by its banality. Yet when I look at everyday things I am not bored, and when I look at architectural history books I continue to learn. _ Peter Arnell, Ted Bickford, and Catherine Bergart, eds., *A View from the Campidoglio: Selected Essays 1953–1984 Robert Venturi and Denise Scott Brown*, Cambridge, Mass.: Harper & Row, 1984

I have always loved history, and if I hadn't been an architect, I would have been an art historian—no more dealing with contracts, public relations, marketing, insurance, partners, codes, bureaucrats, lawyers, clients, and meeting the payroll. I was just born with an interest in the history of architecture. _ Philippe Barrière and Sylvia Lavin, "Interview with Denise Scott Brown and Robert Venturi," *Perspecta*, no. 28, 1997

*Robert Venturi's writings have been hugely influential to generations of architects. Through them, Venturi has best expressed controversial and critical views of modern architecture. He wrote his first "gentle manifesto,"* Complexity and Contradiction, *in 1966.*

. . . at the American Academy in Rome, I had two years to just look at history. [Venturi won the Rome Prize in 1954.] In our day we had a bias toward the Baroque and piazzas. And we looked at form and space rather than symbol and meaning. But during my last months in Rome, I realized that Mannerist architecture was what really meant most to me, and I reexamined a lot of Italian historical architecture for its Mannerist qualities. This was important when I came to write *Complexity and Contradiction* in the following years. _ Philippe Barrière and Sylvia Lavin, "Interview with Denise Scott Brown and Robert Venturi," *Perspecta*, no. 28, 1997

**❦❦ AS ARCHITECTS, OUR THEORY, TO A GREAT EXTENT, SHOULD DERIVE FROM OUR PRACTICE. ❦❦**

## COMPLEXITY AND CONTRADICTION, 1966

I write, then, as an architect who employs criticism rather than a critic who chooses architecture, and this book represents a particular set of emphases, a way of seeing architecture, which I find valid. . . . As an architect, I try to be guided not by habit but by a conscious sense of the past—by precedent, thoughtfully considered. . . . As an artist, I frankly write about what I like in architecture: complexity and contradiction. From what we find we like—what we are easily attracted to—we can learn much of what we really are . . . _ Robert Venturi, *Complexity and Contradiction in Architecture*, New York: The Museum of Modern Art, 1966

For the young Venturi, the Chestnut Hill home designed for his mother was a sort of testing ground of his emerging design aesthetic—the fundamentals of what constitutes a house.

### CHESTNUT HILL 1964
# VANNA VENTURI HOUSE
The little house for a close friend or a relative is usually a first opportunity to test theories and expand them. If [the architect's] practice is slack, this at least allows him to put his heart and soul and a full work week into developing this one small idea, which is always a deepening experience. The years spent refining can be in the nature of a personal odyssey for the architect. It is an opportunity literally to seclude himself in order to focus his thinking. _ Frederic Schwartz, ed., *Mother's House: The Evolution of Vanna Venturi's House in Chestnut Hill,* New York: Rizzoli, 1992

Some have said my mother's house looks like a child's drawing of a house—representing the fundamental elements of shelter—gable roof, chimney, door, and windows. I like to think this is so, that it achieves another essence, that of the genre that is house and is elemental. _ Peter Arnell, Ted Bickford, and Catherine Bergart, eds., *A View from the Campidoglio: Selected Essays 1953–1984 Robert Venturi and Denise Scott Brown,* Cambridge, Mass.: Harper & Row, 1984

The house started out more like Kahn. After all, I was young and he was influential. The design was my way of learning, and it was a wonderful experience. But I wasn't satisfied with the house, and it didn't turn out the way I wanted it to be. In a way, I was lucky that the budget made the house change, and it got much better. My intuition told me what to draw and took control of my hand. It told me what to do, and it came out very quickly in the end. _ Frederic Schwartz, ed., *Mother's House: The Evolution of Vanna Venturi's House in Chestnut Hill,* New York: Rizzoli, 1992

My mother loved the house. At first she thought the marble floor in the dining room was pretentious, but she was proud of it. She was a widow living alone, and she enjoyed showing the house to a lot of handsome young architects; she would sit them down at the dining room table and talk about Bernard Shaw—I assumed this was their price of admission. _ Frederic Schwartz, ed., *Mother's House: The Evolution of Vanna Venturi's House in Chestnut Hill,* New York: Rizzoli, 1992

## LEARNING FROM LAS VEGAS, 1972

*The publication* Learning from Las Vegas, *written by Robert Venturi, Denise Scott Brown, and Steven Izenour, originated from The Las Vegas Studio, a 1968 architectural studio at Yale University. At the time, Izenour, who was Venturi and Scott Brown's teaching assistant, and twelve students accompanied the architects on a research expedition to document the Las Vegas "Strip." The analytical results were a revealing analysis and critique of the "ugly and the ordinary" commercial landscape. At the time of his unexpected death in 2001, Steven Izenour was a principal at Venturi, Scott Brown & Associates, and led the firm's exhibition and graphic design, project presentations, research, and office organization.*

The Las Vegas described here is the commercial strip of c. 1968, not the scenographic Disneyland configurations of Las Vegas today. _ Robert Venturi and Denise Scott Brown, *Architecture as Signs and Systems, for a Mannerist Time,* Cambridge, Mass.: The Belknap Press of Harvard University Press, 2004

[Our] first reaction was that the Strip has a quality and a vitality—a significance—that Modern-designed urban landscapes don't have . . . . _ Peter Arnell, Ted Bickford, and Catherine Bergart, eds., *A View from the Campidoglio: Selected Essays 1953–1984 Robert Venturi and Denise Scott Brown,* Cambridge, Mass.: Harper & Row, 1984

In *Learning from Las Vegas* we analyzed commercial roadside building as one model for a symbolic architecture and illustrated our Football Hall of Fame Competition entry [unbuilt, Rutgers University, New Brunswick, New Jersey, 1967], which we called a billdingboard. From these sign-appliqués we developed the idea of the decorated shed as a building type and as a vehicle for ornament in architecture. _ Peter Arnell, Ted Bickford, and Catherine Bergart, eds., *A View from the Campidoglio: Selected Essays*

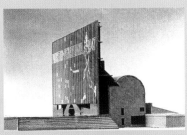

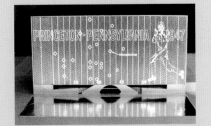

*1953–1984 Robert Venturi and Denise Scott Brown,* Cambridge, Mass.: Harper & Row, 1984

The architecture connected with "symbolism" and "iconography" is derived a lot from . . . *Learning from Las Vegas,* where we analyzed the landscape of architectural quality that drives signage in a greater extent. As we made an analysis of that, we studied the history of Western architecture, European and American, and we came to realize that symbolism, iconography, and graphics were elements that were very important in the whole history of architecture. _ Sangleem Lee, "Robert Venturi & Denise Scott Brown," *Space,* January 2006

## ❝ WE HAD AN EXHILARATING FEELING OF REVELATION IN LAS VEGAS IN THE SIXTIES . . . ❞

As we had learned from the spaces of Rome, we learned from the symbolism of Las Vegas. We soon learned that if you ignore signs as "visual pollution," you are lost. . . . It is when you see the buildings as symbols in space, not forms in space that the landscape takes on quality and meaning. _ Peter Arnell, Ted Bickford, and Catherine Bergart, eds., *A View from the Campidoglio: Selected Essays 1953–1984 Robert Venturi and Denise Scott Brown,* Cambridge, Mass.: Harper & Row, 1984

**For students of architecture and admirers of Robert Venturi and Denise Scott Brown, the publication of *Learning from Las Vegas* was of major importance. It was also highly formative for Venturi and Scott Brown's work. *Learning from Las Vegas* helped inspire Venturi's entry into the Football Hall of Fame Competition, bottom photographs.**

**" . . . THE BIGGEST SHOWER CURTAIN IN BUCKS COUNTY! "**

### LANGHORNE 1978
## BEST PRODUCTS CATALOG
## SHOWROOM . . . conventional generic [loft]
as decorated [shed] . . . a storage/showroom whose
porcelain-enameled panel façades are ornamented
with pretty flower patterns and graphics whose scale
is big enough to be read from a highway, yet are in
the context of a parking lot. This design became
known as the biggest shower curtain in Bucks
County! _ Robert Venturi and Denise Scott Brown,
*Architecture as Signs and Systems, for a Mannerist
Time,* Cambridge, Mass.: The Belknap Press of Harvard University Press, 2004

Many architects act as if we were still living in the
industrial age and had to build offices made of steel
and glass that look like factories. What we ourselves
do is try to make use of the advertising and entertainment industries as sources of ideas. _ Hanno
Rauterberg, *Talking Architecture: Interviews with
Architects,* Munich: Prestel, 2008

There is an irony that our buildings are often seen as
not flashy enough. But at other times they say we are
too flashy in a vulgar and commercial way, not in an
architecturally expressionistic way. _ "VSBA Today,"
*Architectural Record,* February 1998

**Advertising with appeal: Venturi's
façade for the Best Products
Catalog Showroom was a brilliant
coup and quickly became
a populist icon.**

## IN PRAISE OF THE ORDINARY

For most people, modern architecture is much too abstract. They want vitality that's more ordinary, that's not so difficult to understand. _ Hanno Rauterberg, *Talking Architecture: Interviews with Architects*, Munich: Prestel, 2008

. . . in [the] twentieth century . . . architecture was about space. I think that's fine for abstract aesthetics. However, it is no longer space, but iconography—signage and symbolism. _ Sangleem Lee, "Robert Venturi & Denise Scott Brown," *Space*, January 2006

What we are trying to say is that abstract art is over. Let's get back to the great tradition in which art can engage symbolism, and can tell you stories, and can build that. _ Sangleem Lee, "Robert Venturi & Denise Scott Brown," *Space*, January 2006

There's a long tradition of art that observes ordinariness and gets ideas from it. _ Hanno Rauterberg, *Talking Architecture: Interviews with Architects*, Munich: Prestel, 2008

One of the ways to define a great architect was through the fact that he used a personal, recognizable vocabulary. I would say that today the definition of a great architect would be the opposite: it would be in terms of adaptability and use of multiple vocabularies. This relates to our era's ideas on taste, cultures, heterogeneity, and eclecticism, and to the preference of richness over unity. _ Philippe Barrière and Sylvia Lavin, "Interview with Denise Scott Brown and Robert Venture," *Perspecta*, no. 28, 1997

Another aspect of our work that people seem to have a hard time getting and makes us so opposite of the "original signature genius" is how we value the generic building that allows flexibility over time—the New England mill, the loft, the palazzo. The Italian palazzo was the same for 400 years except for the ornament on it. It was a building that could be used in many different ways, which goes against the Modernist notion of making a glove for the hand rather than a mitten. The related point is that the architectural content comes more from fanfare applied, not form-distorting abstraction. _ "VSBA Today," *Architectural Record*, February 1998

## ARCHITECTURE THAT APPEALS

Well of course you must never forget that the primary purpose of architecture is shelter and background—and much of its aesthetic is a matter of persuasion. One's approach, however, should not involve appealing to a box office via sensationalism which much hype-architecture does today in its trendy evolutions. Perhaps the word *appeal* works better than persuade—appeal appropriately to a wide range of taste cultures today. _ Robert Maxwell, "Robert Venturi and Denise Scott Brown: Interview with Robert Maxwell," *Architectural Design*, vol. 62, no. 5–6, 1992

For us, architecture is above all an art in the background. At least it's in good hands there—it doesn't have to keep pushing itself forward. But there are exceptions, where it can be crazy and egotistical, in Times Square, for example, in the center of New York. _ Hanno Rauterberg, *Talking Architecture: Interviews with Architects*, Munich: Prestel, 2008

## ▟▟ YOU HAVE TO REFER TO A NORM IN THE FIRST PLACE BEFORE YOU BREAK THE RULES. ▜▜

Many people think we're archenemies of modernism. That's nonsense, of course. We love architects such as Alvar Aalto, and hats off to Le Corbusier's Villa Savoye. Though we allow ourselves to observe that this modernism has long since become history, just like the Renaissance and the Baroque. _ Hanno Rauterberg, *Talking Architecture: Interviews with Architects*, Munich: Prestel, 2008

Many architects are intoxicated with their belief in sincerity, in honest buildings that are only what they pretend to be. But there's also honest ornament, building decoration that's employed quite deliberately to give the building meaning. What's hypocritical about that? _ Hanno Rauterberg, *Talking Architecture: Interviews with Architects*, Munich: Prestel, 2008

## SEATTLE 1991
# SEATTLE ART MUSEUM
This building was designed to be a work of art, yet one that does not upstage but instead serves as a background for the art inside. It does not conform to the current trend of the museum as articulated pavilions but to an older tradition—going back to the adapted palaces and grand museums of the nineteenth century and the original Museum of Modern Art in New York—of the museum as generic loft. _ Stanislaus Von Moos, *Venturi, Scott Brown & Associates: Buildings and Projects, 1986–1998,* New York: Monacelli, 1999

. . . the richness of the 10–12 story office buildings built [mainly] in the teens and 20s that are characteristic of downtown Seattle. . . . We can make somthing truly new that reinforces that older tradition. _ David B. Brownlee, David G. De Long, and Kathryn B. Hiesinger, *Out of the Ordinary: Robert Venturi Denise Scott Brown and Associates,* Philadelphia Museum of Art in association with Yale University Press, 2001

. . . you probably gotta have decoration. I'm sorry, but it's true—decoration as abstract pattern involving expres-

sion and/or as referential sign involving meaning. In the Seattle Art Museum the lyrical quality of its exterior surface ornament derives from polychromatic patterns configured by varied terracotta and masonry units which also work to compose rhythm and variety of scale on the façade. _ Robert Maxwell, "Robert Venturi and Denise Scott Brown: Interview with Robert Maxwell," *Architectural Design,* vol. 62, no. 5–6, 1992

When you're planning museums—and we have been designing them in Seattle, San Diego, and Texas—you find that only one-third of the space is dedicated to exhibitions. The rest is given over to didactic use and administrative requirements. _ Robert Venturi, David Vaughan, and Charles Jencks, "National Gallery—Sainsbury Wing," *Architectural Design,* vol. 6, no. 5–6, 1991

. . . the museum is both civic and civil. Civic scale penetrates the interior by means of the grand stair, which is visible from and corresponds to the sidewalk stair outside and which makes the building feel open and accessible. _ Stanislaus Von Moos, *Venturi, Scott Brown & Associates: Buildings and Projects, 1986–1998,* New York: Monacelli, 1999

# THE ANLYAN CENTER FOR MEDICAL RESEARCH AND EDUCATION, YALE UNIVERSITY SCHOOL OF MEDICINE

An enormous architectural complex consisting of flexible lofts. The apparent size and scale is perceptually diminished on the exterior by wall surface patterns in a variety of materials and by an iconographic decorative/sculptural element as fanfare depicting a row of trees on the rear façade which turns a friendly face toward the local town and softens the effect of the security fencing. _ Robert Venturi and Denise Scott Brown, *Architecture as Signs and Systems, for a Mannerist Time,* Cambridge, Mass.: The Belknap Press of Harvard University Press, 2004

## "BUILDINGS PLAIN AND FANCY"

Architecture can be many things, but it should be appropriate. _ Peter Arnell, Ted Bickford, and Catherine Bergart, eds., *A View from the Campidoglio: Selected Essays 1953–1984 Robert Venturi and Denise Scott Brown,* Cambridge, Mass.: Harper & Row, 1984

But a sense of appropriateness should apply not only to a variety of cultural types, but also to a hierarchy of cultural values—not all buildings are equally important; not all buildings should be high art; most landscapes should include buildings plain and fancy. _ Peter Arnell, Ted Bickford, and Catherine Bergart, eds., *A View from the Campidoglio: Selected Essays 1953–1984 Robert Venturi and Denise Scott Brown,* Cambridge, Mass.: Harper & Row, 1984

Someone called our architecture "ugly and ordinary," and we take that as a compliment. . . . We are ugly and ordinary, not heroic and original.

## ❝❝ WE LEARN FROM GAS STATIONS AS WELL AS BORROMINI AND CHARTRES. ❞❞

Ordinary is very good in the sense that there is a good tradition of architecture that essentially derives from a constant system. _ Sangleem Lee, "Robert Venturi & Denise Scott Brown," *Space,* January 2006

You must learn from the past and from your environment. Denise and I are never bored when we travel, even when we take the train between New York and Philadelphia. We look out the window and see beautiful old churches from earlier prosperous blue-collar neighborhoods, great generic industrial loft buildings, very beautiful billboards that enliven the landscape. We learn from gas stations as well as from Borromini and Chartres. _ Martin Filler, "Robert Venturi & Denise Scott Brown," *House Beautiful,* June 2000

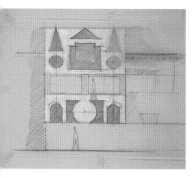

When Venturi designed the Gordon Wu Hall at Princeton University he described it as "a visual hyphen" connecting the existing adjacent dormitories. The drawing, above, identifies the building blocks motif.

## PRINCETON 1983
# GORDON WU HALL, BUTLER COLLEGE, PRINCETON UNIVERSITY

A brick dining hall situated and designed to identify the center of Butler College, made up of existing dormitories all in brick. The entrance enhances the identity of this otherwise recessive building through the bold symbolic pattern adorning it, which refers to Elizabethan/Jacobean motifs often found over fireplaces and appropriate within the context of a quasi-Elizabethan-style precinct of the campus. _ Robert Venturi and Denise Scott Brown, *Architecture as Signs and Systems, for a Mannerist Time,* Cambridge, Mass.: The Belknap Press of Harvard University Press, 2004

The building's design takes important cues from what is around it, but it promotes also an identity of its own. Its long shape and central position make it a visual hyphen that connects the dormitories and unites them. The brick, limestone trim, and strip windows that adhere to the entrance, set off-center and broadside in the building, is marked by a bold marble and gray granite panel recalling early Renaissance ornament and symbolizing the entrance to the college as a whole as well as to the building itself. _ Neil Levine, "The Return of Historicism," in *The Architecture of Robert Venturi,* ed. Christopher Mead, Albuquerque: University of New Mexico Press, 1989

## INFLUENCE AND INNOVATION
## LOUIS KAHN: "I WOULD SEE HIM IN THE ELEVATOR"

I had a summer job with Robert Montgomery Brown, who was a local modern architect. Louis Kahn—whom no one had heard of— was in an office on the floor above. I would see him in the elevator. I also saw the five or six young people who worked for him. They never talked to me because I was young and naïve, but Louis Kahn did; he was very kind. And when I returned to Princeton to finish my Master's thesis I asked Kahn to be on the jury along with George Howe. _ Philippe Barrière and Sylvia Lavin, "Interview with Denise Scott Brown and Robert Venturi," *Perspecta*, no. 28, 1997

Louis Kahn also recommended me to Eero Saarinen, whose office I was in for two and a half years. I was not particularly at home there, but I made some nice friends, and I learned a lot about the running of an office. Then I came back to run my family's fruit and produce business because my father had become ill. For a year and a half, I worked in the family firm—horrified that I might be caught in the business for the rest of my life. At that time, I would visit Kahn's office for sustenance, and he was a good mend. _ Philippe Barrière and Sylvia Lavin, "Interview with Denise Scott Brown and Robert Venturi," *Perspecta*, no. 28, 1997

When I came back [after having received the Rome Prize], I worked for Louis Kahn and also taught at the University of Pennsylvania as his assistant. Later, probably in '61, Holmes Perkins, the Dean of the Architecture School at Penn, asked me to teach a course in the theory of architecture. In a way that course was a preparation for *Complexity and Contradictions*. Denise helped me with the course, and the notes evolved into the book. _ Philippe Barrière and Sylvia Lavin, "Interview with Denise Scott Brown and Robert Venturi," *Perspecta*, no. 28, 1997

## "STUDENTS INFLUENCING MASTERS"

Well, Kahn respected the Las Vegas direction Denise and I took but could not accept it for himself. Also, although his later historicism may have derived from his Beaux-Arts training with Paul Cret at Penn, I think a lot of it came from me. Someone should consider the subject of students influencing masters. _ Philippe Barrière and Sylvia Lavin, "Interview with Denise Scott Brown and Robert Venturi," *Perspecta*, no. 28, 1997

The main lesson I learned from Kahn was the idea of the servant space, a hierarchy of space in which you have a general space and a minor space. And those became a system of building. I think that was and

is very relevant and interesting. In my writings, I have indicated a number of things that he learned from me, but he would never indicate that. People always learn from each other, and you have to acknowledge that when you take young ideas. _ Sangleem Lee, "Robert Venturi & Denise Scott Brown," *Space*, January 2006

## ALVAR AALTO: HE DIDN'T WRITE ABOUT ARCHITECTURE

Alvar Aalto's work has meant the most to me of all the work of the Modern masters. It is for me the most moving, the most relevant, the richest source to learn from, in terms of its art and technique. Like all work that lives beyond its time, Aalto's can be interpreted in many ways. Each interpretation is more or less true for its moment because work of such quality has many dimensions and layers of meaning. . . . But Aalto's most endearing characteristic for me as I struggle to complete this essay is that he didn't write about architecture. _ Peter Arnell, Ted Bickford, and Catherine Bergart, eds., *A View from the Campidoglio: Selected Essays 1953–1984 Robert Venturi and Denise Scott Brown*, Cambridge, Mass.: Harper & Row, 1984

## DENISE SCOTT BROWN: "SHE CORRUPTED ME"

I think it happened that we two people have had a similar approach to life, to ideas, and to art. We met at the University of Pennsylvania, and Denise left Penn and went to California, and she introduced me to Las Vegas. I would like to say she corrupted me. Then we became real partners. I think it is fate that we have a similar approach. We have very different backgrounds. We also have a similar interest in the sociological, social sides of architecture, and that has been from youth pretty much, and we have that in common. So, the unusual things in architecture that we are interested in happened to correspond. On the other hand, we have some differences. I am more into architectural scale, and she is more involved in urban design scale or the city planning stage, but she is still in architecture, and I'm still in planning. _ Sangleem Lee, "Robert Venturi & Denise Scott Brown," *Space*, January 2006

## ❝ WE INEVITABLY HAVE TO WORK TOGETHER. ❞

Some people have trouble understanding us because they think we have to be an individual genius, and that's wrong. There is plenty of creativity that happens as partners in literature, in architecture, especially when so many people have to work in such complexity now. We inevitably have to work together. _ Sangleem Lee, "Robert Venturi & Denise Scott Brown," *Space*, January 2006

**WHERE LINES INTERSECT** Recalling the city still suggests to me a reading not only of my own architecture but indeed of architecture in general. I believe that I have access to a privileged way of looking, of observing. It is a position that is closer to the engineer's than to that of the psychologist or geographer: I like to apprehend a structure in its broad outlines and then think how these lines intersect. This is no different from the experience of life and relationships: the nucleus of a fact is always rather simple, and indeed, the more simple a fact is, the more it is destined to clash with the events which it itself produces. I am reminded of a sentence from Hemingway which I found frightening yet fascinating: "All truly wicked things are born from an innocent moment."

_ Aldo Rossi, *A Scientific Autobiography*, Cambridge, Mass.: MIT University Press, 1981

# ALDO ROSSI

**BORN:** May 3, 1931, Milan, Italy; Died: September 4, 1997

**EDUCATION:** Degree in Architecture, Milan Polytechnic, Milan, Italy, 1959

**PROJECTS FEATURED:** Bonnefanten Museum, Maastricht, Netherlands, 1995; Il Palazzo Hotel, Fukuoka, Japan, 1989; Cemetery of San Cataldo, Modena, Italy, 1984; Teatro del Mondo, Venice, 1979; Elementary School in Fagnano Olona, Varese, Italy, 1976; Gallaratese II Housing, Milan, 1974

**ONE CANNOT MAKE ARCHITECTURE WITHOUT STUDYING THE CONDITION OF LIFE IN THE CITY.**

**Cemetery of San Cataldo, Modena, 1984**
Solemnity and grandeur, elegiac and the personal,
came together in the articulation of Rossi's design.
He was asked to respond to "the blue of the sky."

THE CONFIGURATION OF THE CEMETERY AS **AN EMPTY HOUSE** IS THE SPACE OF LIVING PEOPLES' MEMORIES.

**MODENA 1984**
# CEMETERY OF SAN CATALDO In

April 1971, on the road to Istanbul between Belgrade and Zagreb, I was involved in a serious auto accident. Perhaps as a result of this incident, the project for the cemetery at Modena was born in the little hospital of Slawonski Brod, and simultaneously, my youth reached its end. I lay in a small, ground-floor room near a window through which I looked at the sky and a little garden. Lying nearly immobile, I thought of the past, but sometimes I did not think: I merely gazed at the trees and the sky. This presence of things and of my separation from things—bound up also with the painful awareness of my own bones— brought me back to my childhood. During the following summer, in my study for the project, perhaps only this image and the pain in my bones remained with me: I saw the skeletal structure of the body as a series of fractures to be reassembled. At Slawonski Brod, I had identified death with the morphology of the skeleton and the alterations it could undergo.

The blue sheet-metal roofs were chosen specifically to reflect the band of sky and seasons.

_ Aldo Rossi, *A Scientific Autobiography*, Cambridge, Mass.: MIT University Press, 1981

The Cemetery of Modena is a city for the dead, an abandoned city which resounds of sadness. The object of the competition [held in 1971] was to reconcile the traditional Italian cult of the dead with modern requirements. The three parts of the cemetery are the cone, the cube, and the stepped wings which correspond to the three types of structures. These structures are characteristic of the traditions and norms of the Italian Catholic Cemetery. I have given symbolic meaning to each of these three parts. _ Aldo Rossi lecture at Graham Foundation for Advanced Studies in the Fine Arts in Chicago, March 1, 1979, in "The Works of Aldo Rossi," *CRIT*, no. 5, Spring 1979

The slogan of the competition for which it [the cemetery] was designed was "the blue of the sky," and now when I look at those huge, blue, sheet-metal roofs, so sensitive to day and evening light as well as to that of the seasons, they sometimes seem deep blue, sometimes the clearest azure. The pink stucco of the walls covers the Emilian brick of the old cemetery, and it too displays the effects of

the light, appearing almost white or else dark pink.
_ Aldo Rossi, *A Scientific Autobiography*, Cambridge, Mass.: MIT University Press, 1981

Early in 1979 I saw the first wing of the cemetery at Modena being filled with the dead, and these corpses with their yellowish-white photographs, their names, the plastic flowers offered out of family and public sympathy, gave the place its unique significance. But then after many polemics it went back to being the great house of the dead where the architecture was a scarcely perceptible background for the specialist. In order to be significant, architecture must be forgotten, or must present only an image for reverence which subsequently becomes confounded with memories. _ Aldo Rossi, *A Scientific Autobiography*, Cambridge, Mass.: MIT University Press, 1981

A view within the vast interior of the cube. The exterior is seen on the opposite page.

## THE CITY

*Aldo Rossi's legacy not only as an architect, but as a theorist and writer, is significant. Two books written by Rossi define his approach to architecture:* The Architecture of the City, *published in 1960; and* A Scientific Autobiography, *published in 1984. The first was Rossi's major work of architectural and urban theory. In it, Rossi presented his theory of typology, while arguing against functionalism and the Modern Movement. The second book was Rossi's memoir based on his notebooks, which he had been composing since 1971. Here, Rossi discusses his architectural projects as well as literary and artistic influences on his work and his personal history.*

## THE ARCHITECTURE OF THE CITY

Around 1960 I wrote *The Architecture of the City*, a successful book. At that time, I was not yet thirty years old, and as I have said, I wanted to write a definitive work: It seemed to me that everything, once clarified, could be defined. . . . I scorned memories, and at the same time, I made use of urban impressions: Behind feelings I searched for the fixed laws of a timeless typology. I saw courts and galleries, the elements of urban morphology, distributed in the city with the purity of mineralogy. I read books on urban geography, topography, and history, like a general who wishes to know every possible battlefield—the high grounds, the passages, the woods. I walked the cities of Europe to understand their plans and classify them according to type. Like a lover sustained by my egotism, I often ignored the secret feelings I had

**❝❝ A KNOWLEDGE OF THE CITY ENABLES US NOT ONLY TO UNDERSTAND ARCHITECTURE, BUT ALSO, AS ARCHITECTS, TO DESIGN IT. ❞❞**

for those cities; it was enough to know the system that governed them. Perhaps I simply wanted to free myself of the city. Actually, I was discovering my own architecture. _ Aldo Rossi, *A Scientific Autobiography*, Cambridge, Mass.: MIT University Press, 1981

. . . my one idea about the city and the places where we live: They should be seen as part of the reality of human life. They are like copies of different observations and times: my youthful observation of long workers' scaffolds, of courtyards full of voices, and meeting which I spied on with a sort of fear in my bourgeois childhood had the same fascination as the cabins or, better, as the small houses which came to mind in other situations and places—like the monks' houses at the Certosa in Pavia or those endless American suburbs. _ Aldo Rossi, *A Scientific Autobiography*, Cambridge, Mass.: MIT University Press, 1981

I think that the modern city is very beautiful, or as beautiful as any ancient city, because in a certain sense the modern city, that is, the cities that we see today, is already filled with history and humanity. _ "Interview with Aldo Rossi," *Process: Architecture*, October 1987

The Bonnefanten Museum has become an iconic building in the Maastricht. For Rossi, the dome was both a link to a classical tradition in architecture and response to Holland's surrounding waterways.

MAASTRICHT 1995
# BONNEFANTEN MUSEUM

Perhaps we will end up showing that the museum, like every personal history, every vice and virtue, everything human, is restricted and constricted within the narrow bounds of a marble slate which only the foolishness of the enlightenment wished to measure in meters and centimeters. This museum is a refusal of that foolishness.

The foyer, with its characteristic telescope shape, is the first space the visitor encounters. The telescope is a typical example of a *lichtraum*, found in the "Lichthof" of Zurich University; on the other hand this idea is not typically Nordic but is the major point of contact between grand Castile architecture and the colonial world. . . . This tall space is colored with a light-blue aquamarine material where the light and the color destroy the very materiality that built them.

The foyer leads directly to the live and vital part of the building: The visitor enters the very essence of the museum in trepidation and fear. It is difficult, if not impossible, to define just what the essence of this space is; is the museum a collection of reminders of life or is it a very part of our life? Our architecture leaves this question open, but the essence of the museum remains the beginning and end of our cultural decadence. . . . Let us instead find out what strikes even the most hurried visitor in the museum as a whole. Whoever you ask, the answer will invariably be the dome.

There are two main motives behind the grandiosity of the dome: the first is its link with the purest architectural tradition from the classical world to Turin's Alessandro Antonelli; the second is that it is the beginning and the end of Holland, a reminder of Dutch topography, with its sea and rivers . . .

But now, as if we were crossing the belvedere, let us look at the museum in its unity, a lost unity perhaps, which we recognize only through those fragments of our life, which are fragments of art and of old Europe.

Perhaps we will remember that the *lapidarium romano* lies between the main blocks of the museum, a reminder of how a simple stone slate, a tangible fragment, is a valuable testimony of any past. _ Aldo Rossi, "Bonnefantenmuseum a Maastricht 1990–1991," *Zodiac 6,* March–August 1991

# TEATRO DEL MONDO

The Theater of the World was officially opened in Venice on the 11th of November, 1979 . . . for the Theatre/Architecture Biennale. The idea of the Biennale was to recall the floating theaters which were so characteristic of Venice in the 18th century. The present scheme modified certain features of these theaters, while retaining the concept of building-cum-barque [ship]. Constructed in the Fusina shipyards, the theater was towed across to Venice by tugboat. The building was erected over steel beams, welded together to form a raft. . . . The city of Venice is always visible in the background, creating a perfect sense of depth behind the proscenium space. _ Gianni Graghieri, ed., *Aldo Rossi*, Barcelona: Editorial Gustavo Gili, 1993

There are Greek islands where one can still find the houses of Venetian merchants, villages which reproduce the system of historic Venice. These images, also in their decline or abandon, possess an extraordinary force. Perhaps from such sources or considerations, as well as others, the image of the "Teatro del Mondo" is born. For example, from the great lighthouses of New England. _ "Interview with Aldo Rossi," *Process: Architecture*, October 1987

What pleases me above all is that the theater is a veritable ship, and like a ship, it is subject to the movements of the lagoon, the gentle oscillations, the rising and sinking; so that in the uppermost galleries a few people might experience a slight seasickness that proves distracting and is increased by the sight of the waterline, which is visible beyond the windows. I cut these windows according to the level of the lagoon, the Giudecca, and the sky. The shadows from the little crosses of the window mullions stand out against the wood, and these windows make the theater resemble a house. . . . _ Aldo Rossi, *A Scientific Autobiography*, Cambridge, Mass.: MIT University Press, 1981

I should like to say immediately that in this case the work has made a great impression on me through its life, that is, through its evolution, its construction, and its position in the city, and also through the spectacles performed in it. While I was listening to some music by Benedetto Marcello on opening night and watching people flowing up the stairs and crowding onto the balconies, I perceived an effect which I had only vaguely anticipated. Since the theater stood on the water, one could see from its window the vaporetti and boats passing by just as if one were standing on another boat; and these other boats entered into the image of the theater, constituting a scene that truly was both fixed and mobile. . . . _ Aldo Rossi, *A Scientific Autobiography*, Cambridge, Mass.: MIT University Press, 1981

The tower of my Venetian theater might be a lighthouse or a clock; the campanile might be a minaret or one of the towers of the Kremlin: The analogies are limitless, seen, as they are, against the background of this preeminently analogous city. _ Aldo Rossi, *A Scientific Autobiography*, Cambridge, Mass.: MIT University Press, 1981

It also seemed to me that the theater was in a place where architecture ended and the world of the imagination or even the irrational began. _ Aldo Rossi, *A Scientific Autobiography*, Cambridge, Mass.: MIT University Press, 1981

Only in Venice would Rossi's Teatro del Mondo be so appropriate. Rossi's drawings are always spectacular.

For an architect who has often mined his past, especially his childhood, the Elementary School in Fagnano Olona was an opportunity to further consider the autobiographical. An important aspect of Rossi's design is the courtyard, seen above.

# ELEMENTARY SCHOOL IN FAGNANO OLONA

The central concept of this project is the construction of a little city: This city unfolds around a central square on two levels. This square is treated as if it were a theater with tiers of seats; a theater in which political demonstrations, talks, and meetings can take place.

The road which runs past the school has a symbolic value, being built of brick, like the old factories, a fact which connects the school with the meaning of the industrial landscape surrounding it. _ Gianni Graghieri, ed., *Aldo Rossi*, Barcelona: Editorial Gustavo Gili, 1993

*For Rossi, courtyards are an important and recurring typology based on his careful observations of various places and cities.*

The study of courtyards has always seemed to me to be important in architectural design. In a large part of Europe, courtyards have always been an important feature. . . . It is seen in the architecture of farms and is related to the forms of the old Carthusian monasteries. A typical Carthusian monastery with a large central courtyard bordered by the monk's abodes can be translated into an urban form. _ Aldo Rossi lecture at Graham Foundation for Advanced Studies in the Fine Arts in Chicago, March 1, 1979, in "The Works of Aldo Rossi," *CRIT*, no. 5, Spring 1979

There is no photograph of Fagnano Olona that I love so much as the one of the children standing on the stair under the huge clock which is indicating both a particular time and also the time of childhood, the time of group photos, with all the joking that such photos usually entail. The building has become pure theater, but it is the theater of life, even if every event is already anticipated. . . . Nonetheless, it remains true that I envisaged this theater-school in terms of everyday realities, and the children who were playing there comprised the house of life . . . . _ Aldo Rossi, *A Scientific Autobiography*, Cambridge, Mass.: MIT University Press, 1981

## FILM: "A UNIQUE CAPACITY TO COMMUNICATE"

. . . after dealing with architecture, I would now like to make a film. You should understand that cinematography meant a lot to my generation in Italy in the fifties; film was a basis of our culture. We were emerging from Fascism and the Resistance, and cinema was an aspect of a new world that we could hardly foresee. We were impressed and fascinated by Italian Neo-Realism, by Visconti and Rossellini and later by Clair, Cernet, and the first great American movies. This love has always been growing in me, and now that I am somewhat tired of architecture, I would like to try other techniques, such as cinema or painting. Today, cinema has a unique capacity to communicate; it can affect and express both our personal and collective souls like no other technique. _ "The Architecture of the City: An Interview with Aldo Rossi," *Skyline,* September 1979

I believe that the Canalettos or the Piranesis of our time are the directors, the people of the cinema; they describe the modern city, its center, and its outskirts. _ "Interview with Aldo Rossi," *Process: Architecture,* October 1987

. . . surrealism is a definite part of my architecture. For example, in Luis Buñuel's films, Buñuel shows the reality of the subject, but with a particular eye or from a particular point of view. I think to parallel my work to that of Buñuel's would be most interesting. It is not a revival, but the many points of view in the study of realism. _ "The Works of Aldo Rossi," *CRIT,* no. 5, Spring 1979

## "THE LINE IS NO LONGER A LINE"

All my drawings and writings have seemed to me definitive in two ways: First, they conclude my experience, and second, I then had nothing more to say. _ Aldo Rossi, *A Scientific Autobiography,* Cambridge, Mass.: MIT University Press, 1981

"Thou talk'st of nothing" is a way of saying nothing and everything. I recognize this in many of my drawings, in a type of drawing where the line is no longer a line, but writing. _ Aldo Rossi, *A Scientific Autobiography,* Cambridge, Mass.: MIT University Press, 1981

What surprises me most in architecture, as in other techniques, is that a project has one life in its built state but another in its written or drawn state. _ Aldo Rossi, *A Scientific Autobiography,* Cambridge, Mass.: MIT University Press, 1981

I understand that this is the aim of all techniques: the identification of the object with the imagination of it. But the aim is also to bring the imagination back to its base, to its foundation—to the earth and to the flesh. _ Aldo Rossi, *A Scientific Autobiography,* Cambridge, Mass.: MIT University Press, 1981

## ❝❝ WITHOUT AN EVENT THERE IS NO THEATER AND NO ARCHITECTURE. ❞❞

---

## MILAN 1974
## GALLARATESE II HOUSING

This passion for technique is very important for my projects and my interest in architecture. I believe that my building in the Gallaratese quarter of Milan may be significant, above all, because of the simplicity of its construction, which allows it to be repeated. _ Aldo Rossi, *A Scientific Autobiography,* Cambridge, Mass.: MIT University Press, 1981

The design of my building in the Gallaratese development in Milan reflects another typology—that of a gallery . . .

The plan is very simple. What gave me the most difficulty was the design of the large two-story portico which serves as the public space of the building. It can be used for an open-air market, or a place for children to play. _ Aldo Rossi lecture at Graham Foundation for Advanced Studies in the Fine Arts in Chicago, March 1, 1979, in "The Works of Aldo Rossi," *CRIT,* no. 5, Spring 1979

An early project in Rossi's career, the Gallaratese housing project was a model of his typology and views about urban space. The long colonnade extends the whole of the block.

**FUKUOKA 1989**
## IL PALAZZO HOTEL
The most important feature of this project is undoubtedly its siting. . . . The hotel stands, set back a little, on a base which forms the public square. . . . The main entrance is on the square, which, as in many Italian cities, forms part of the architecture of the building. . . . The square affords a view of the building's façade and the banks of the river. The architecture here, as in the past, is a point of reference for the city's inhabitants and the tourists, who are drawn close to admire and study the building's beauty.

The square is paved with Roman travertine; the façade is of reddish travertine from Iran. Its color changes with the changing light, from a brilliant red to gold. The façade which looks onto the square is inset with a series of architraves of green-painted iron which mark the levels of the different floors. The two side façades, also of stone, are bare of decoration except for the rhythmic sequence of the windows of the hotel rooms. _ Gianni Graghieri, ed., *Aldo Rossi*, Barcelona: Editorial Gustavo Gili, 1993

Color—bright, dynamic, playful— and shape are often identified as telling features of Il Palazzo.

## DEFORMATION AND EVOLUTION

Perhaps the observation of things has remained my most important formal education; for observation later becomes transformed into memory. Now I seem to see all the things I have observed arranged like tools in a neat row; they are aligned as in a botanical chart, or a catalogue, or a dictionary. But this catalogue, lying somewhere between imagination and memory, is not neutral; it always reappears in several objects and constitutes their deformation and, in some way, their evolution. _ Aldo Rossi, *A Scientific Autobiography*, Cambridge, Mass.: MIT University Press, 1981

Ever since my first projects, where I was interested in purism, I have loved contaminations, slight changes, self-commentaries, and repetitions. _ Aldo Rossi, *A Scientific Autobiography*, Cambridge, Mass.: MIT University Press, 1981

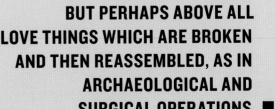

Whenever I followed the progress of my few realized projects, I liked the errors made on the construction site, the little deformations, the changes which became remedial in some unexpected way. Indeed, they amazed me because they began to seem the life of the structure. As a matter of fact, I believe that any original order is open to practical changes, and that it allows for all the failures of human weakness. Because of this belief, my commitment has always been fundamentally different from that of my contemporaries and professors . . . _ Aldo Rossi, *A Scientific Autobiography*, Cambridge, Mass.: MIT University Press, 1981

## ". . . THE LIFE OF ARCHITECTURE IS ALWAYS IMPORTANT."

When I was a student at the Politecnico, I was always cited by the professors as an example not to follow! This means, undoubtedly, that my architecture provoked something passionate and something hateful, and I don't know frankly why. But I believe every one of us expresses himself in his own work, and there is something personal in my work, which is passed along. _ "Tradition, Form and Typology," *Japan Architect,* January 1985

. . . I believe that the major importance of life is based on moral and poetic principles. I always think of several moments and memories. The memory of the city is very important; the collective memory, not the personal memory. In this sense, I find the life of architecture is always important. _ "Tradition, Form and Typology," *Japan Architect,* January 1985

The emergence of relations among things, more than the things themselves, always gives rise to new meanings. _ Aldo Rossi, *A Scientific Autobiography*, Cambridge, Mass.: MIT University Press, 1981

Because every aspect of the building is anticipated, and because it is precisely this anticipation that allows for freedom, the architecture is like a date, a honeymoon, a vacation—like everything that is anticipated so that it can occur. Although I also love what is uncertain, I have always thought that only small-minded people with little imagination are opposed to discreet acts of organization; for it is only such efforts of organization that in the end permit contretemps, variations, joys, disappointments. _ Aldo Rossi, *A Scientific Autobiography*, Cambridge, Mass.: MIT University Press, 1981

An architectural project is a vocation or a love affair; in either case, it is a construction. One can hold oneself back in the face of this vocation or affair, but it will always remain an unresolved thing. _ Aldo Rossi, *A Scientific Autobiography*, Cambridge, Mass.: MIT University Press, 1981

The houses of the dead and those of childhood, the theater, or the house of representation—all these projects and buildings seem to me to embrace the seasons and ages of life. Yet they no more represent themes than functions; rather they are the forms in which life, and therefore death, are manifested. _ Aldo Rossi, *A Scientific Autobiography*, Cambridge, Mass.: MIT University Press, 1981

**❝❝ I LOVE THE BEGINNING AND THE END OF THINGS; BUT PERHAPS ABOVE ALL I LOVE THINGS WHICH ARE BROKEN AND THEN REASSEMBLED, AS IN ARCHAEOLOGICAL AND SURGICAL OPERATIONS. ❞❞**

**PERSONAL EFFORT** For me and for the people that work for me, in a way what we do is less about the final product and more about achieving the final product, because that's what we spend all of our time doing. So aside from the fact that we all consider ourselves lucky that we're in a position to work with great clients and great consultants, what matters to us most is the process of doing all of it. Not that many people understand what that's all about because they never get the chance to see that side of it. Probably the biggest mistake is to make assumptions—in this case to assume that we never think about function or budget, that we just sit around crumpling paper and we let the computer do the rest, that we're just concerned with creating spectacles to get ourselves on magazine covers. _ Frank O. Gehry, *Flowing in All Directions,* Los Angeles: Circa Publishing, 2003

I consider it a personal effort. I don't think about it in megalomaniac terms of taking over the world. I think maybe what's been successful about it is that I have been able to keep on a sort of personal course. I've had little forays into somebody else's thing, but I pull back and have been intensely involved with keeping it a personal expression. I've been consciously pushing this personal signature, or whatever you want to call it. I don't know what its impact is going to be; it's been so personally satisfying, that that's plenty for me. _ Peter Arnell and Ted Bickford, eds., *Frank Gehry: Buildings and Projects,* New York: Rizzoli, 1985

# FRANK O. GEHRY

**BORN:** February 28, 1929, Toronto, Canada

**EDUCATION:** B.Arch., University of Southern California, Los Angeles, 1954

**OFFICE:** Gehry Partners, LLP, 12541 Beatrice Street, Los Angeles, California, 90066
Tel: +1 310-482-3000, Fax: +1 310-482-3006
www.foga.com

**PROJECTS FEATURED:** Jay Pritzker Pavilion, Millennium Park, Chicago, 2004; Walt Disney Concert Hall, Los Angeles, 2003; The Guggenheim Museum Bilbao, Spain, 1997; Vitra Design Museum, Weil am Rhein, Germany, 1989; Fishdance Restaurant, Kobe, Japan, 1987; Gehry House, Santa Monica, California, 1978

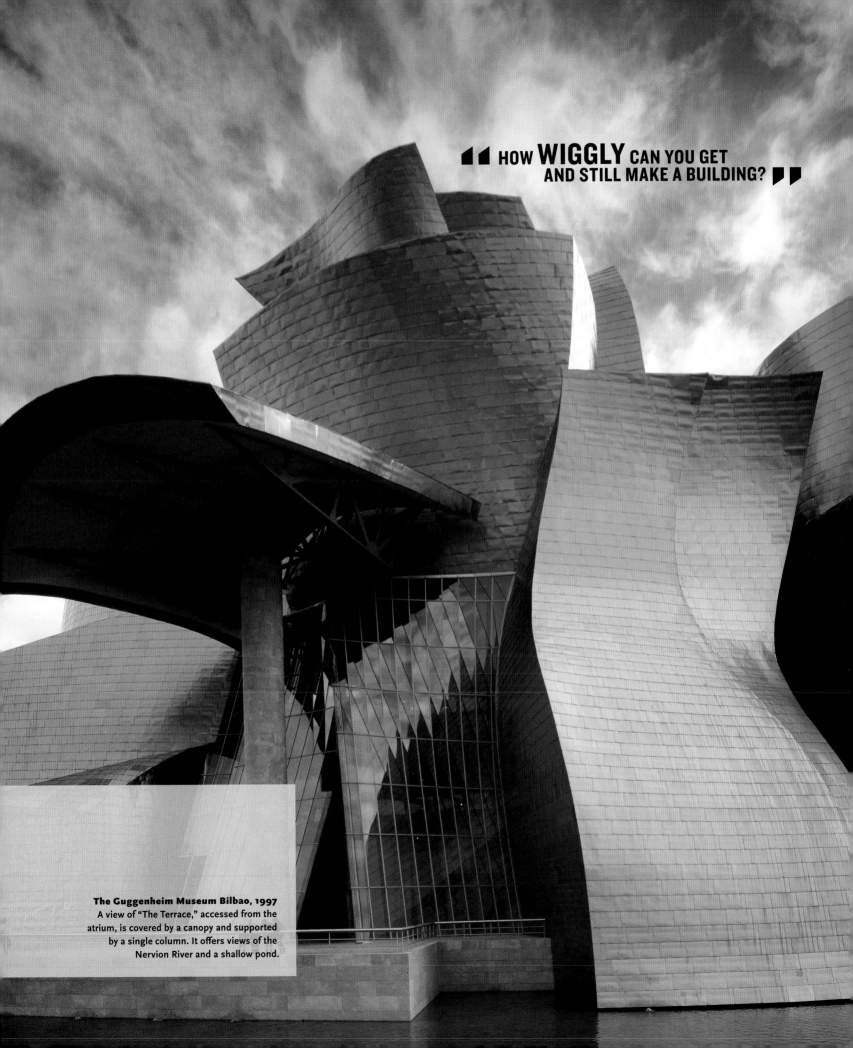

**HOW WIGGLY CAN YOU GET AND STILL MAKE A BUILDING?**

**The Guggenheim Museum Bilbao, 1997**
A view of "The Terrace," accessed from the atrium, is covered by a canopy and supported by a single column. It offers views of the Nervion River and a shallow pond.

## BILBAO 1997
# THE GUGGENHEIM MUSEUM BILBAO

People look at the building and don't know how I did it. They rush to some judgment. I would hope that if somebody looks at the evolution, like the one presented in the book for Bilbao, they would see the evolution of the thinking from the beginning to the end. . . . But instead people continue to see it as though I do some kind of magic trick or something. But in the end, I'm not that self-conscious about all that stuff because the most important thing to me is to build the buildings. _ Frank O. Gehry interview by Yoshio Futagawa, *Studio Talk: Interview with 15 Architects,* Tokyo: A.D.A. Edita, 2002

**For Gehry, Bilbao emerged as "a beautiful thing"—something easily seen in the early concept sketches, opposite.**

. . . when I drew the plan of Bilbao I was so happy, because I realized that it was a beautiful thing. I'd never seen anything like it except in those build-

ings. It just evolved. I didn't consciously do it, but it intuitively evolved. . . I enjoy the complexity of a big project, trying to organize it. . . . Scale is a struggle. How do you make a big monolithic building that's humane? I try to fit into the city. In Bilbao I took on the bridge, the river, the road, and then tried to make a building that was scaled to the nineteenth-century city. _ Mildred Friedman, ed., *Gehry Talks: Architecture and Process,* New York: Rizzoli, 1999

. . . I said to myself, "Artists have trouble with scale in the city because the city is such a large scale. No one ever commissions artists to make sixty-story sculptures, and until one of them makes a sixty-story sculpture, their works will not stand beside the Empire State Building and mean anything." I thought, if you could metaphorically create a city that would allow them to play, that might work.

**" I HAVE A FREEDOM IN MY DRAWINGS THAT I LOVE TO EXPRESS IN ARCHITECTURE. "**

Then I realized that this was an opportunity to make something in the tradition of the great metaphorical cities. And that's what led to what's there, using the ramps and the stairs as a kind of metaphorical city— a metropolis. _ Mildred Friedman, ed., *Gehry Talks: Architecture and Process*, New York: Rizzoli, 1999

I love to go back to Bilbao. They're [the buildings] all part of my family now. _ Mildred Friedman, ed., *Gehry Talks: Architecture and Process*, New York: Rizzoli, 1999

In the end my work is my work; it's not a critic's work. If I had changed my work to conform to a critic's perception or rules about architecture, Bilbao would never have been built. _ Frank O. Gehry interview by Yoshio Futagawa, *Studio Talk: Interview with 15 Architects*, Tokyo: A.D.A. Edita, 2002

## "THERE ARE NO REAL RULES"

I am a *slow* architect; I take a long time to create, so the thought that my building ideas are just tossed in the air and land is the furthest thing from the truth. _ Charles Jencks, ed., *Frank O. Gehry: Individual Imagination and Cultural Conservation*, New York; St. Martin's Press, 1995

For me it's a free association, but it grows out of a sense of responsibility, sense of values—human values. The importance of relating to the community, and all of those things . . . and the client's budget, their pocketbook, the client's wishes. But even within that there's a . . . range of creativity possible, and I think it behooves us to explore that envelope and push at it. It comes out of an intuition, or a learned intuition, I guess. You study a long time 'til you can do it. But it's from looking around you, it's from understanding what's happening in the culture, what's happening in the world. It's a really big picture. Because there are no real rules. _ "Interview: Frank Gehry," *Academy of Achievement*, June 3, 1995

So it became how you took the energy of the idea through the process and ended with a building that had feeling, genuine passion. _ Mildred Friedman, ed., *Gehry Talks: Architecture and Process*, New York: Rizzoli, 1999

I am not a deconstructivist! That term really drives me crazy. _ "American Center: Interview with Frank O. Gehry," *GA Architect 10*, 1993

People insist on putting us in a box. They can't be comfortable with something they can't categorize. It's true that I'm very interested in buildings that are open, that allow people in them. But my buildings have always been that way because I'm interested in openness and accessibility, not just in structural devices. _ "American Center: Interview with Frank O. Gehry," *GA Architect 10*, 1993

I think that the architecture comes out of a lot of exploration. When you're young and you're starting out you need to build things and try things. You need to learn to build. And it's hard. A lot of people don't bother to learn that. They go right into theorizing their design before knowing how to build. Building is its own discipline. The building industry has its own mechanisms, and you have to learn it in order to manipulate it because you're making a three-dimensional object. _ Frank O. Gehry interview by Yoshio Futagawa, *Studio Talk: Interview with 15 Architects*, Tokyo: A.D.A. Edita, 2002

# ❝ …PROBABLY IT'S AS HARD AS ANYTHING I'VE HAD TO DO
## AS A DESIGNER BECAUSE THE FIRST HOUSE [IN SANTA MONICA]
## WAS A DESIGN AROUND A BUILDING. ❞

### SANTA MONICA 1978
### GEHRY HOUSE
I bought an old house, and I put a new house around it. I got interested in the dialogue between the old and the new and trying to sculpturally create a new entity, but that retained the qualities of the new as independent of the old. I set myself goals like that when I started. I kind of pulled it off. I also wanted it to be seamless—that you couldn't tell where it began and where it stopped—and that was very successful, and that was the power of it. In fact, critics would come in and would look at a rain spot on the plaster and say, "Is that on purpose or not?" They thought they were maligning me, and I thought that was just wonderful. That was exactly what I wanted them to worry about. _ "Interview: Frank Gehry," *Academy of Achievement*, June 3, 1995

My house was a turning point; it was my money, and I felt I could use the project for R&D—research and development. I was completely in control—budget, time, the look. But it freaked out my developer clients. _ Peter Arnell and Ted Bickford, eds., *Frank Gehry: Buildings and Projects*, New York: Rizzoli, 1985

The chain link for me was about denial. There was so much chain link being absorbed by the culture, and there was so much denial about it. I couldn't believe it. That's the populism in my work, as opposed to the art. What's wrong with chain link? I hate it, too, but can we make it beautiful? I said, "Maybe, if you make it beautiful—if you're going to use it in huge quantities—you can use it beautifully." _ Mildred Friedman, ed., *Gehry Talks: Architecture and Process*, New York: Rizzoli, 1999

My house was strange. . . . I was fascinated by the denial, and I was trying to humanize it, so that if you are going to use it, find some way to use it right or aesthetically more pleasing. _ "Interview: Frank Gehry," *Academy of Achievement*, June 3, 1995

. . . whatever I did the first go-around couldn't be quantified, couldn't be talked about. I couldn't say, "This is what I was trying to do, and this is what I did." I started out to do something, and then I followed the end of my nose. _ Mildred Friedman, ed., *Gehry Talks: Architecture and Process*, New York: Rizzoli, 1999

You were never sure what was intentional and what wasn't. It looked in-process. You weren't sure whether I meant it or not. There was something magical about the house. And I knew that the thing a lot of people hated or laughed at was the magic. _ Mildred Friedman, ed., *Gehry Talks: Architecture and Process*, New York: Rizzoli, 1999

The built-in challenge of designing a new house around an existing one came early in Gehry's career.

## "ARCHITECTURE IS SURELY AN ART"

I used to be a symmetrical freak and a grid freak. I used to follow grids, and then I started to think, and I realized that those were chains, that Frank Lloyd Wright was chained to the 30-60 grid, and there was no freedom in it for him, and that grids are an obsession, a crutch. You don't need that if you can create spaces and forms and shapes. That's what artists do, and they don't have grids and crutches, they just do it. _ Mildred Friedman, ed., *Gehry Talks: Architecture and Process*, New York: Rizzoli, 1999

The moment of truth, the composition of elements, the selection of forms, scale, materials, color, finally, all the same issues facing the painter and the sculptor. _ Frank O. Gehry Pritzker Prize acceptance speech, May 18, 1989

When I saw the Combine show at the Met [Metropolitan Museum of Art, New York, 2005–6], it reminded me how much I learned from Bob Rauschenberg in the early years. And how much everybody learned from Bob. _ Frank Gehry interview by Charlie Rose, *Charlie Rose*, April 10, 2006

## ❝ ARCHITECTURE IS SURELY AN ART, AND THOSE WHO PRACTICE THE ART OF ARCHITECTURE ARE SURELY ARCHITECTS. ❞

I was interested in what the artists were doing, how they were working with materials and craft, and consequently learnt a lot from them. I wanted to deal with the craft, I wanted to deal with the people who were *making* the buildings, I wanted to engage them—which is not the way we are trained as architects. I wanted to break down those barriers—which will take two more lifetimes. _ Charles Jencks, ed., *Frank O. Gehry: Individual Imagination and Cultural Conservation*, New York: St. Martin's Press, 1995

Painting and sculpture influence my work. For instance, when I had the Bellini picture with the Madonna and Child, I originally thought of it as the Madonna-and-Child strategy for architecture. You see a lot of big buildings with a lot of little buildings, little pavilions in front. I attribute that to the Madonna-and-Child composition. _ Mildred Friedman, ed., *Gehry Talks: Architecture and Process*, New York: Rizzoli, 1999

Painting had an immediacy that I craved for architecture. _ Frank O. Gehry Pritzker Prize acceptance speech, May 18, 1989

## "THE MOMENT OF TRUTH"

My artist friends—people like Jasper Johns, Bob Rauschenberg, Ed Kienholz, Claes Oldenburg—were working with very inexpensive materials—broken wood and paper—and they were making beauty. These were not superficial details, they were direct—it raised the question of what was beautiful. I chose to use the craft available and to work with the craftsmen and make a virtue out of their limitations. . . . I explored the processes of raw construction materials to try giving feeling and spirit to form. In trying to find the essence of my own expression, I fantasized the artist standing before the white canvas deciding what was the first move. I called it the moment of truth. . . .

I'm an architect. . . . I've hung around with a lot of artists, and I'm very close to a lot of them. I'm very involved with their work; I think a lot of my ideas have grown out of it, and that there's been some give and take. So sometimes I get called an artist. Somebody'll say, "Oh, well, Frank's an artist." I feel in a way that's used like a dismissal. I want to say I'm an architect. My intention is to make architecture. _ Peter Arnell and Ted Bickford, eds., *Frank Gehry: Buildings and Projects*, New York: Rizzoli, 1985

### KOBE 1987
# FISHDANCE RESTAURANT *The form and analysis of fish have been central in Gehry's design process and specifically in the design of the Fishdance Restaurant.*

I was looking for movement earlier, and I found it in the fish. The fish solidified my understanding of how to make architecture move. The fish form that I designed for the Walker exhibition—I cut off the tail,

cut off the head, cut off everything, and you still got a sense of movement—was really powerful for me. [Gehry's *Standing Glass Fish* was commissioned by the Walker Art Center in Minneapolis in 1986.] _ Mildred Friedman, ed., *Gehry Talks: Architecture and Process*, New York: Rizzoli, 1999

You know, I got very angry when other architects started making buildings that look like Greek temples. I thought it was a denial of the present. It's

a rotten thing to do to our children. It's as if we're telling them there's nothing to do but look back. It's like there's no reason to be optimistic about the future. So I got angry. That's really when I started drawing the fish, because the fish has been around for thousands and thousands of years. It's a natural creature, very fluid. It's a continuous form, and it survives. And it's not contrived. To tell you the truth, I didn't intend for it to become a central form when it first occurred to me. It was an instinctive thing.
_ "American Center: Interview with Frank O. Gehry," *GA Architect 10,* 1993

The fish evolved further: I kept drawing it and sketching it, and it started to become for me like a symbol for a certain kind of perfection that I couldn't achieve with my buildings. _ Peter Arnell and Ted Bickford, eds., *Frank Gehry: Buildings and Projects,* New York: Rizzoli, 1985

Also, when I was a kid I used to go to the market with my grandmother on Thursdays. We'd go to the Jewish market, we'd buy a live carp, we'd take it home to her house in Toronto, we'd put it in the bathtub, and I would play with this goddamn fish for a day until the next day she'd kill it and make gefilte fish. I think maybe that has something to do with it.
_ Peter Arnell and Ted Bickford, eds., *Frank Gehry: Buildings and Projects,* New York: Rizzoli, 1985

## ❝❝ THE FISH SOLIDIFIED MY UNDERSTANDING OF HOW TO MAKE ARCHITECTURE MOVE. ❞❞

Fishdance Restaurant in Kobe, Japan, has a dramatic four-story-high fish sculpture at the entrance. For Gehry the fish form played a key role in his design development, most evidently expressed in the Kobe structure.

## THE IMPORTANCE OF DIGITAL TECHNOLOGIES

*Like some of his contemporaries, Gehry has a love-hate relationship with the computer, though he has come to see it as a necessary tool. This first comment below was made prior to the formation in 2002 of Gehry Technologies, which Gehry founded in order to bring technology into wider use in the architecture and building industries.*

I don't like the computer, except as a gadget to explain myself to the contractors. But I did, in the course of working with it, get into trying to design on it, even though I hate the imagery. I likened it to putting my hand in the fire and seeing how long I could keep it there before I pulled it out. So I would sit at the thing. It took about three minutes before the fire got too hot and I'd pull it out. _ "Interview: Frank Gehry," *Academy of Achievement,* June 3, 1995

We started to use the computer because of Vitra [Vitra Design Museum]. I had a stairway on the backside that I couldn't build. If you look at it you

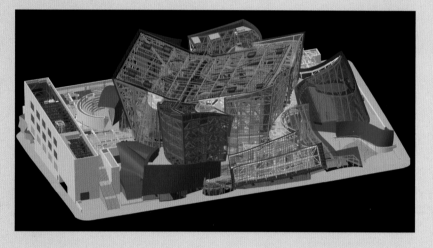

can see that it's a spiral with an awkward bend in it, kind of a funny kink. I couldn't do it, and I was very frustrated. So Jim Glymph [a partner at Gehry Partners, LLP, and CEO of Gehry Technologies] got the computer, and then it became easy to do it. It gave me freedom to make forms differently. That was a big change, and it's changed the work a lot. _ Frank O. Gehry interview by Yoshio Futagawa, *Studio Talk: Interview with 15 Architects,* Tokyo: A.D.A. Edita, 2002

In the last few years they've [Dassault Systèmes in France] been working on making the system [CATIA] fit our way of working. So they now have a new enhanced CATIA that they're going to install here, which backs us up even more and allows us to control the architectural processes to within seven decimal points of accuracy. That's what I like about it. They've tuned in to understanding that this can change the way architecture is practiced and can make new buildings possible—more exciting sculptural shapes in the landscape instead of just plain boxes. _ Mildred Friedman, ed., *Gehry Talks: Architecture and Process,* New York: Rizzoli, 1999

## MATERIAL EXPLORATION

I used metal to make three-dimensional objects. I explored metal: how it dealt with the light in Boston on the 360 Building [a former office building at 360 Newbury Street, 1989, recently reopened as residences], and in Toledo [University of Toledo Art Building, 1992], where I used lead copper. The lead copper in Toledo is just beautiful. It does beautiful things with the light. The first time I used the metal pillow surface was on the Aerospace Museum [California Aerospace Museum, Los Angeles, 1984]. The big metal piece that hangs out is pillowed. I started out to do it otherwise, but I realized that you couldn't control it flat. Flat was a fetish, and everybody was doing that. I found out that I could use metal if I didn't worry about it being flat; I could do it cheaper. It was intuitive. I just went with it. I liked it. Then when I saw it on the building, I loved it. I used it again on Irvine [Computer Science Building at University of California at Irvine, 1986, now demolished]. And then at Herman Miller [Herman Miller Facilities, Rocklin, California, 1985], I used it even thinner. Bilbao [The Guggenheim Museum Bilbao, 1997] is a lot thinner because it's titanium. You couldn't use it at the same thickness as the others—wouldn't be able to afford it. We prefer titanium because it's stronger; it's an element, a pure element, and it doesn't oxidize. It stays the same forever. They give a hundred-year guarantee! _ Mildred Friedman, ed., *Gehry Talks: Architecture and Process,* New York: Rizzoli, 1999

But I was trying all kinds of things . . . I did a building with plaster. I did another with metal. I did one that had roofs. I think I tried everything. Maybe I went wrong. I think the issue is that I explored a lot of ideas, which I think was very healthy. I didn't think I was destroying the architectural fabric of the world by doing it. I thought I was being quite personal. _ Frank O. Gehry interview by Yoshio Futagawa, *Studio Talk: Interview with 15 Architects,* Tokyo: A.D.A. Edita, 2002

**A CAD of the Walt Disney Concert Hall. Californians have long had an affinity with water, and given Gehry's interest in sailing, the Disney Concert Hall is apt expression: the metal skin looks especially lyrical.**

## LOS ANGELES 2003
# WALT DISNEY CONCERT HALL

The project got resurrected after Bilbao. When Bilbao was built the same people said: "Oh, he can build that." So then they came to me and said: "Now we understand you can build it, so we want it." And that's how it went on again. _ Frank Gehry interview by Vladimir Paperny, www.paperny.com, December 16, 2004

Originally Disney Hall was to be stone. Then the client saw the American Center [The American Center in Paris, 1994], which wasn't sealed and not maintained, and the stone got dirty, so everybody was worried about it. They thought I didn't know what I was doing. They were all out to get me here because I'm the local guy, and they think I'm "chain-linking." So they started a barrage coming at me. Finally I said, "I don't care if it's toothpicks. If you really want me to look at it in metal, I'll do it." So I just took two weeks off and designed it in metal, and they all love it now. It saved ten million dollars, so they're all happy, and I like it better. _ Mildred Friedman, ed., *Gehry Talks: Architecture and Process,* New York: Rizzoli, 1999

When I was working on Disney Hall I got excited about movement. I got into sails and the luffing of the sails. When you're sailing, the wind catches the sail and it's very tight, and it's a beautiful shape. Then, as you turn, the wind is coming at you when you're going forward—the wind is actually coming at an angle. When you turn into the wind slightly, the wind is on both sides of the sail. At that moment, the sail luffs—flutters. And when it flutters, it has a beautiful quality that was caught in the seventeenth century by Dutch painters such as the van de Veldes [Baroque painter Willem van de Velde the Elder (1611–1693) and his sons Adriaen van de Velde (1636–1672) and Willem van de Velde the Younger (1633–1707)]. But I didn't have the guts to do it. So everything is tight in Disney Hall. Later, when I saw Sluter [Dutch sculptor Claus Sluter (1350–1406)], it was luffing all over the place; it was very much like Greek drapery. It gave me courage. _ Mildred Friedman, ed., *Gehry Talks: Architecture and Process,* New York: Rizzoli, 1999

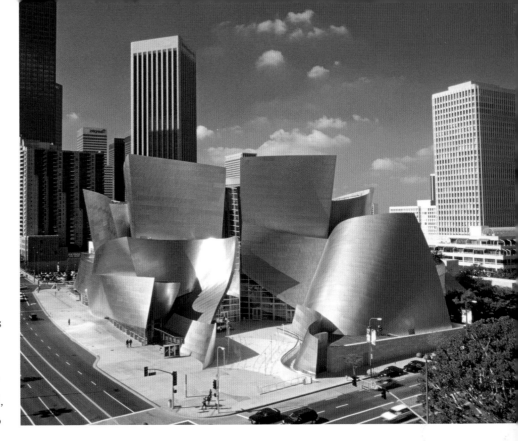

**❝❝ IT'S ONE OF THE FEW BUILDINGS, OTHER THAN MY HOUSE, THAT I ACTUALLY USE. ❞❞**

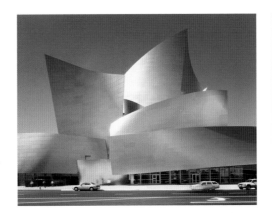

## "WE START WITH SHAPES, SCULPTURAL FORMS"

The models are a way of studying. It's the way of working I feel most comfortable with. That's how I design. I ask someone in my staff to start for me, they will bring it in, and then I'll fold something here, cut something there. They'll work on it some more and bring it in again. The model lets me have a dialogue with my staff. _ Frank O. Gehry interview by Yoshio Futagawa, *Studio Talk: Interview with 15 Architects*, Tokyo: A.D.A. Edita, 2002

And I make a value out of solving all those problems, dealing with the context and the client and finding my moment of truth after I understand the problem. If you look at our process, the firm's process, you see models that show the pragmatic solution to the building without architecture. Then you see the study models that go through, leading to the final scheme. We start with shapes, sculptural forms. Then we work into the technical stuff. _ "American Center: Interview with Frank O. Gehry," *GA Architect 10*, 1993

We agonize about every little part of it, and I stare for hours and then I move something just a little bit, and I stare some more, and then slowly it starts to take shape. _ Frank O. Gehry, *Flowing in All Directions*, Los Angeles: Circa Publishing, 2003

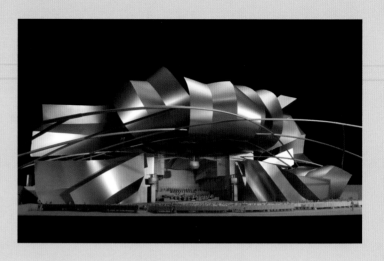

The Jay Pritzker Pavilion stands 120 feet high and Gehry gave it a billowing headdress of brushed stainless steel. Ribbons of metal frame the stage and connect the overhead trellis to a lattice of steel pipes. The trellis supports a sound system that was designed to mimic the acoustics of an indoor concert hall—even for those in the lawn seats farthest away.

### CHICAGO 2004
### JAY PRITZKER PAVILION, MILLENNIUM PARK
How do you make everyone—not just the people in the seats, but the people sitting 400 feet away on the lawn—feel good about coming to this place to listen to music? And the answer is, you bring them into it. You make the proscenium larger; you build a trellis with a distributed sound system. You make people feel part of the experience. _ Frank Gehry on the Jay Pritzker Pavilion, http://www.millenniumpark.org

## CLIENTS: "A REAL INTENSE RELATIONSHIP"

"I need a personal connection. I need to feel like it's not a love-in but it's like somebody I'm talking to and they're involved." _ Frank Gehry interview by Charlie Rose, *Charlie Rose*, April 10, 2006

I'm probably more contentious with a client than most. I find myself questioning their programs, questioning their intentions. . . . I get into a real intense relationship, which finally ends up synergistically giving more positive results, I think, because the client's spent more time thinking about the program and what they want—they get more involved. _ Peter Arnell and Ted Bickford, eds., *Frank Gehry: Buildings and Projects*, New York: Rizzoli, 1985

What I'm telling them [the clients] is, "I'm bringing you into my process. Watch it, get involved, understand that I'm not stopping here."

_ Mildred Friedman, ed., *Gehry Talks: Architecture and Process*, New York: Rizzoli, 1999

If the client doesn't feel married to the project, you're dead. If the client buys in, you're home free, because then no matter what happens the client will go along with you. My success has been that, and it makes for better buildings. _ Mildred Friedman, ed., *Gehry Talks: Architecture and Process*, New York: Rizzoli, 1999

But most importantly you have to work with people who fully understand how you work. And in the end that's not a lot of people. We have to be allowed to work the way we want to work and be paid accordingly. It actually limits the kind of work you do. That's why I don't have a lot of big courthouses or high-rise buildings, airports, or things like that. _ Frank O. Gehry interview by Yoshio Futagawa, *GA Document*, no. 68, March 2002

## WEIL AM RHEIN 1989
# VITRA DESIGN MUSEUM
It was a tiny little workshop kind of museum he [Rolf Fehlbaum, CEO of Vitra] had in mind for exhibits of special chairs. He only had 200 chairs in the collection when we started. He thought he needed one room for a rotating collection, and then he'd have a room where he'd hold interior systems symposiums, so he wanted two galleries. _ Mildred Friedman, ed., *Gehry Talks: Architecture and Process,* New York: Rizzoli, 1999

The Vitra Design Museum was meant to trace the history of the Vitra company as well as accommodate the CEO's collection of miniature chairs.

[Fehlbaum] had a lot of pleasure with the design of the museum, and it became exuberant. He felt that people going into the factory would be short-changed if they didn't have a nice entrance. So the sculptural entrances to the factory started to happen, and I started playing with something that I was interested in, which was the urban quality that I could create out in the field, the urban quality between the museum and those entrances.

I was also interested in the play between my building and Nicholas Grimshaw's earlier high-tech factory, and I didn't want to preempt Grimshaw's high-techness. I thought it was good that he maintained that, and that I should either go way out forward or . . . . Well, I didn't have the money to go way out forward with the factory, so I just cut big holes in the walls, and it looked like an old-fashioned factory. When it was built, the factory part looked like it was there before Grimshaw's. _ Mildred Friedman, ed., *Gehry Talks: Architecture and Process,* New York: Rizzoli, 1999

## "INDIVIDUAL EXPRESSION"

I believed that just becoming an architect was an act of social responsibility; when I got out of school with a planning background, I did not want to do the rich guys' houses, I only wanted to work on big plans. _ Charles Jencks, ed., *Frank O. Gehry: Individual Imagination and Cultural Conservation*, New York: St. Martin's Press, 1995

But it really began with my mother taking me to see galleries and to listen to music when I was a child. She tried to expose me to those kinds of things. That was very personal, and I think very important to me. I still go very often. I always go to concerts and listen to music, classical music. I'm not a scholar, but I'm a fan. I need that kind of inspiration. I've continued to study art history on my own, wherever I go. _ Frank O. Gehry interview by Yoshio Futagawa, *Studio Talk: Interview with 15 Architects*, Tokyo: A.D.A. Edita, 2002

I'm a craftsman. I took woodcraft classes when I was a kid, but I wasn't the greatest at it. My father had a furniture factory, and I used to help him. It seems to me that when you're doing architecture, you're building something out of something. There are the social issues, there's context, and then there's "how do you make the enclosure and what do you make it with?" _ Mildred Friedman, ed., *Gehry Talks: Architecture and Process*, New York: Rizzoli, 1999

I went to work as a truck driver. I had just finished high school and was seventeen or eighteen. . . . I went to night school. I couldn't afford to go to a university. _ Frank O. Gehry interview by Yoshio Futagawa, *Studio Talk: Interview with 15 Architects*, Tokyo: A.D.A. Edita, 2002

. . . these architects [Gregory Ain, Garrett Eckbo, Seymour Eisenberg, and Calvin Straub] who had been influenced by all of this architecture they saw in Japan were teaching us. They were enamored with Japanese technology and construction. It made sense to them because it was so beautiful and could be made out of wood. Wood was plentifully available here, and all houses here were being made out of wood, so it was a good fit with the wood and the Southern California climate. Some of my early buildings look like they came from Japan. _ Frank O. Gehry interview by Yoshio Futagawa, *Studio Talk: Interview with 15 Architects*, Tokyo: A.D.A. Edita, 2002

I didn't like Frank Lloyd Wright because of his politics. I didn't think his writings were very democratic. I liked the work, but I had trouble with the person. In fact when he came to give a lecture at USC, I didn't even go. Years later, after I went to Harvard [Gehry studied city planning at Harvard University's Graduate School of Design in 1956 and 1957] and came back to Los Angeles I passed through Taliesin West. The flag was up, which meant that Mr. Wright was there. I was with my wife and two daughters, and they wanted a dollar for each person to enter. I said, no thanks. _ Frank O. Gehry interview by Yoshio Futagawa, *Studio Talk: Interview with 15 Architects*, Tokyo: A.D.A. Edita, 2002

There certainly wasn't much theory. We didn't study theory. I myself came at it from the arts, and I was always interested in painting and sculpture. I was different from the other architects in that way, although I didn't realize it when I was a student. I only realized that I was different later on in my career _ Frank O. Gehry interview by Yoshio Futagawa, *Studio Talk: Interview with 15 Architects*, Tokyo: A.D.A. Edita, 2002

Actually, I think if somebody really spent some time with me they'd find out that I'm very conventional. I even go to Brooks Brothers. I'm intense about my work, and I spend every waking hour on it. I love my kids, my wife, but I'm so intensely involved with my work that I forget birthdays, anniversaries—I never remember anything personal. On the other hand, my projects come in on time, on budget— really on budget—I really take those kinds of things seriously. _ Peter Arnell and Ted Bickford, eds., *Frank Gehry: Buildings and Projects*, New York: Rizzoli, 1985

I think all of us are, finally, just commenting in our own way about what's going on in our cone of vision. I tend to have this particular way of looking at it. . . . I don't look for the soft stuff, the pretty stuff. It puts me off because it seems unreal. I have this socialistic or liberal attitude about people and politics. I think of the starving kids and that do-gooder stuff I was raised on. _ Peter Arnell and Ted Bickford, eds., *Frank Gehry: Buildings and Projects*, New York: Rizzoli, 1985

I see what I'm doing as the only thing I could do. I'm intensely involved with it; I don't understand anything else. _ Peter Arnell and Ted Bickford, eds., *Frank Gehry: Buildings and Projects*, New York: Rizzoli, 1985

But I don't think architecture should be pulled in any one direction. It's a democracy. Lots of people have different ideas, and it's exciting. _ Frank O. Gehry interview by Yoshio Futagawa, *GA Document*, no. 68, March 2002

**A FEEL FOR LOGIC** I believe, and I've told anybody who will listen to me, that an architect should see as many things that are designed or have designs, whether they're natural, paintings, sculpture, graphics, architecture. He should see as much as he can. He should spend as much time in a museum looking at great art as looking at buildings. My elementary theory is that our brain, a computer, absorbs all this whether we're aware of it or not. When you get down to doing some work, the more you see, the more this computer may throw out. You don't say, "I want to do the cathedral at Chartres." You'll just subconsciously have more choices than you would if your computer was half-empty because you didn't see anything but architecture. _ "Gordon Bunshaft Interview—On SOM," in *SOM Journal 3*, Ostfildern, Germany: Hatje Cantz Publishers, 2004

# GORDON BUNSHAFT

**BORN:** May 9, 1909, Buffalo, New York; Died: August 6, 1990

**EDUCATION:** M.Arch., B.Arch., Massachusetts Institute of Technology, Cambridge, Massachusetts, 1935, 1933

**PROJECTS FEATURED:** National Commercial Bank, Jeddah, Saudi Arabia, 1983; Joseph H. Hirshhorn Museum and Sculpture Garden, Washington, D.C., 1974; Beinecke Rare Book & Manuscript Library, Yale University, New Haven, Connecticut, 1963; Manufacturers Hanover Trust, New York, 1953; Lever House, New York, 1952

**❝ I LIKE MY ARCHITECTURE TO SPEAK FOR *ME* . . . ❞**

**Beinecke Rare Book & Manuscript Library, Yale University, 1963**
"The thing about the Beinecke that's interesting is the outside is cold and severe," said Bunshaft, "and you walk inside and it's very warm and rich."

## I'VE HAD LADIES WRITE ME ABOUT THE BEINECKE, SAYING THAT THEY JUST SHIVERED WHEN THEY SAW IT.

NEW HAVEN 1963
# BEINECKE RARE BOOK & MANUSCRIPT LIBRARY, YALE UNIVERSITY
*At the time that Bunshaft was first meeting with the Beinecke brothers, Eero Saarinen was designing a dormitory and Paul Rudolph was doing the Art and Architecture Building at Yale.*

The Beinecke Library started with Paul Rudolph [Dean of Yale University School of Architecture, 1958–64] calling me one afternoon and asking if I would be willing to do a competition. . . . I told Paul immediately that I would have no part of it, that is not the way to do a good building. I explained that when you do a competition, you're given a two- or three-page program of what the building is to be, and from that, without talking to any of the people who are going to use it, you produce a solution. . . . So you start making alterations, and the ultimate thing is a compromise. I believe one of the most important things in doing a building is writing a program, and that entails almost living with the people who are going to use the build-

**What Bunshaft called "a large number of beautiful books" is in fact the main repository at Yale for literary papers and related manuscripts in such fields as literature, theology, history, and the natural sciences.**

ing, finding out how they hope to work in it, not listening to their solutions but listening to their needs. With that data you start a building. Getting a program on a piece of paper is silly. _ "Gordon Bunshaft Interview—On SOM," in *SOM Journal 3*, Ostfildern, Germany: Hatje Cantz Publishers, 2004

As soon as we got the job I started thinking about a rare book library, and there isn't much to know about it. It's a huge vault, a secure place with tremendous humidity and temperature control, and stacks of books. In addition to that, there are some offices for curators, a reading room for a few scholars, and some exhibit space for books. . . . I happen to love books, especially bindings, and I thought it ought to be a treasure house and express that by having a large number of beautiful books displayed behind glass. _ "Gordon Bunshaft Interview—On SOM," in *SOM Journal 3*, Ostfildern, Germany: Hatje Cantz Publishers, 2004

The structure would be covered with onyx, and these big panels would be translucent onyx. The idea came from seeing what I thought was onyx in a Renaissance-type palace in Istanbul. . . . The model lit up, and it was a fabulous thing. It was made out of real onyx shaved down to less than an eighth of an inch. . . . They loved the model. I don't know if we told them the estimate, but I think Fuller did. [The Fuller Construction Company was a leading builder in New York at the time, including Lever House.] It was eight million. From then on it was a beautiful affair. . . . I thought of onyx because books cannot be exposed to direct sunlight. This model looked like a treasure casket. It was held up by four corner columns. The whole pattern of the exterior is a structural truss. . . . I had the idea of onyx from the very beginning because it admits soft light, but no sunlight. It's like being in a cathedral. . . . _ "Gordon Bunshaft Interview—On SOM," in *SOM Journal 3*, Ostfildern, Germany: Hatje Cantz Publishers, 2004

The thing about the Beinecke that's interesting is the outside is cold and severe, and you walk inside and it's very warm and rich. When the sun pours in, it's quite nice with the rich books. Everybody loves to go into a great space. That's what makes people love to see cathedrals. . . . That's what the public likes. However, I didn't think of the public. Our space isn't that size, and it's got a big bulk in the middle. But if they're handsomely done, great spaces give an emotional experience to people. I've had ladies write me about the Beinecke, saying that they just shivered when they saw it. _ "Gordon Bunshaft Interview—On SOM," in *SOM Journal 3*, Ostfildern, Germany: Hatje Cantz Publishers, 2004

I think perhaps this building will be associated with me more than any other building I have designed, and it's going to be there a long time. I don't know if that means it's great, but in the long haul a building becomes important by the judgment of future generations. _ "Gordon Bunshaft Interview—On SOM," in *SOM Journal 3*, Ostfildern, Germany: Hatje Cantz Publishers, 2004

**❝❝ EVERY BUILDING THAT I'VE BEEN INVOLVED IN, THE MAIN PURPOSE OF THAT BUILDING IS FOR THE PEOPLE USING IT. ❞❞**

## SOM: "WE NEVER HAD TO SELL MODERNISM TO ANYBODY . . ."

*In 1990, on behalf of the Chicago Architects Oral History Project, Betty J. Blum conducted an oral history with Gordon Bunshaft, which is catnip for anyone interested in knowing what mattered to the great architect when he was at ease and willing to talk. Although by nature a man of few words—Bunshaft's Pritzker Prize acceptance speech in 1988 consists of fifty-eight words and four sentences, making it the shortest delivery by a Pritzker laureate thus far—at the time of this interview Bunshaft was a loquacious eighty-year-old. As he remarked to Blum, "I'm old. And I can reminisce for the next ten years."*

So in 1947, I was thirty-seven years old, and the United States, especially in New York, was starting on a building boom. Clients wanted modern architecture, and here I was at the right age, excited about modern, and fortunate enough to join Skidmore, Owings & Merrill in 1937 when it consisted of [Nathaniel] Owings in Chicago and [Louis] Skidmore in New York with a couple of men. . . . From there, the firm had no place but to go up. That's my point about being excited about having been born in 1909. _ Gordon Bunshaft interview by Betty J. Blum, *Oral History of Gordon Bunshaft*, Chicago: The Art Institute of Chicago, 1990

We never had to sell modernism to anybody. . . . It was a unique and marvelous thing, the situation after the war. Lots of young architects, disciples of Mies and Corbusier, had just finished their training and were anxious to do something new. At the same time, the heads of these big corporations needed new facilities, and they all wanted something new looking. They all wanted buildings they could be proud of. _ Carol Herselle Krinsky, *Gordon Bunshaft of Skidmore, Owings & Merrill*, New York: The Architectural History Foundation, 1988

When history is written in future centuries, Skidmore, Owings & Merrill will probably not be the greatest creative architects of this century but will be the most important of this century because they didn't anticipate, had nothing, no philosophy. . . . The firm had one basic thing—I think all the people involved were sound, logical thinkers. They were not dreamers. SOM exists today because they could service the needs of the building public. Half the jobs they get, nobody else could do. SOM grew with the times. _ "Gordon Bunshaft Interview—On SOM," in *SOM Journal 3*, Ostfildern, Germany: Hatje Cantz Publishers, 2004

## ❝❝ I DIDN'T THINK THERE WAS ANYTHING UNIQUE IN LEVER HOUSE. WE JUST DID THE BEST WE COULD. ❞❞

You know, some people like to say that Lever House is Corbu [Le Corbusier]. Others says it's Mies because it has thin mullions. And they're both full of baloney. It's modern and probably influenced by Corbu's pilotis and other things, period. But it's an insult to Le Corbusier. He would do a much more interesting building than Lever. _ "Gordon Bunshaft Interview—On SOM," in *SOM Journal 3*, Ostfildern, Germany: Hatje Cantz Publishers, 2004

*Lever Brothers was headquartered in Cambridge when the president, Charles Luckman, decided to move it to New York. Soon after, he hired SOM, where Gordon Bunshaft had just been made a partner, to design its new headquarters.*

Luckman offered the job of doing an office building for a thousand people, and it should be a distinguished building. . . . He also put a condition that Raymond Loewy would do the interiors. That's how we got the job. _ Gordon Bunshaft interview by Betty J. Blum, *Oral History of Gordon Bunshaft*, Chicago: The Art Institute of Chicago, 1990

## ❝❝ LEVER WAS THE FIRST REALLY CONTEMPORARY BUILDING, THE FIRST MAJOR ONE. ❞❞

### NEW YORK 1952
### LEVER HOUSE
*In designing Lever House, Gordon Bunshaft created what many consider to be the quintessential modern corporate office building. As the pinnacle of this American building type, Lever House was imitated worldwide. Though Bunshaft claimed no adherence to any specific ideology, the building's design has been compared to the principles laid out by the 1932 International Style exhibition as well as by both Le Corbusier and Mies van der Rohe's prewar visions of the glass skyscraper.*

**In recognition of its significance and forty years after it was completed, Lever House was designated an official landmark in 1992.**

The first thing you do on a site is find out the zoning limitations, the air space you can't intrude on, and how big a building you could build on that site. . . . There were certain air slopes. We wanted to build a glass building. We wanted to be as avant-garde as possible. Twenty-five percent of the site produced a floor of 7,500 square feet. . . . Of course we wanted something new, so we put it on stilts. _ "Gordon Bunshaft Interview—On SOM," in *SOM Journal 3*, Ostfildern, Germany: Hatje Cantz Publishers, 2004

# MANUFACTURERS HANOVER TRUST

Manufacturers Trust, at that time, had a new president who had been given a set of complete working drawings for a branch bank on 43rd and 5th Avenue, which had been turned over to him by the previous president. Evidently, he didn't think much of it. He asked his good friend, Lew Crandall, who was on the board of Manufacturers, and one of the biggest contracting firms in the city, what he should do. Crandall called me and said that he had this set of drawings. We were friends because Crandall built Lever House. . . . He said, "I'm going to send over a set of drawings for a bank. I want you to look at it and see if you can save at least the structural drawings and make a decent design out of it." . . . I called him back and said, "Look, if you're going to do a new bank, saving a few engineering drawings that will limit exploring a good building is ridiculous. If you want a good building, you have to start new." . . . He was the first of many future clients that became close friends of ours. He was a marvelous person. We had a wonderful time working with him. My wife and I would go down to see progress of the building at night, and we'd find him with his wife wandering around. He was a real charmer. He said to me once, "If this doesn't work"—because it was quite a change to an all-glass bank—"we'll both have to leave town." Anyhow, it worked. He had wonderful opening parties, and their business rapidly expanded and he was very pleased. _ Gordon Bunshaft interview by Betty J. Blum, *Oral History of Gordon Bunshaft,* Chicago: The Art Institute of Chicago, 1990

Well, in the course of doing the building, there was a lot of art. It was the first building where we talked clients into using art up in the executive floors. . . . _ Gordon Bunshaft interview by Betty J. Blum, *Oral History of Gordon Bunshaft,* Chicago: The Art Institute of Chicago, 1990

## An SOM internal competition for only $50

There were three or four young designers in the firm and he [Louis Skidmore, founding partner of SOM] said, "If you fellows want to work on the weekend, if you want to do a sketch for a bank, I'll give a prize of $50 to the winner." So he got four fellows working a whole weekend coming up with an idea for $50. Charlie Hughes [who won] was a very nice man—his grandfather was the chief justice [Charles Evans Hughes, Sr., served as Chief Justice of the United States from 1930 to 1941]. [Hughes came up] with a rough idea of a glass box. We would have done a glass box because that was the thing to do. . . . Then Skid said to me, "You take it over." _ Gordon Bunshaft interview by Betty J. Blum, *Oral History of Gordon Bunshaft,* Chicago: The Art Institute of Chicago, 1990

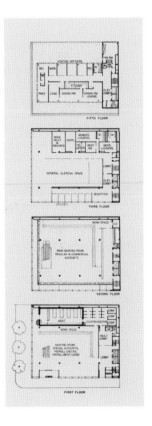

Banking was never as transparent as when Bunshaft designed the modernist Manufacturers Hanover Trust: even the bank vault was visible. As with Lever House, the building's historical significance was recognized when in 1997 it was made a New York City Landmark.

## **[A] LARGE PIECE OF FUNCTIONAL SCULPTURE . . .** 🔳🔳

WASHINGTON, D.C. 1974
# JOSEPH H. HIRSHHORN MUSEUM AND SCULPTURE GARDEN
It's probably the only museum in the world that doesn't have a third of its construction taken up with lobbies and monumental architectural doodads. It's all for art. . . . I am a believer in artificial light for museums.
_ Carol Herselle Krinsky, *Gordon Bunshaft of Skidmore, Owings & Merrill*, New York: The Architectural History Foundation, 1988

*In addition to structural method, the choice of building material was extremely important to Bunshaft. He decided to clad the museum with sandblasted concrete for two primary reasons; it weathered well and was the appropriate material to best articulate the building's cylindrical shape. When the General Services Administration requested that he clad the building in limestone, Bunshaft maintained his position.*

[Limestone would] look the same in sunshine, shade, or anything, and . . . contribute absolutely nothing to the building. _ Carol Herselle Krinsky, *Gordon Bunshaft of Skidmore, Owings & Merrill*, New York: The Architectural History Foundation, 1988

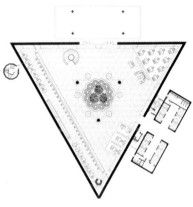

". . . gardens in the air . . ."
_ Gordon Bunshaft biography,
pritzkerprize.com

## JEDDAH 1983
## NATIONAL COMMERCIAL BANK

The only building that I think has a major concept that's unique and my own is the [National Commercial Bank] in Jeddah. It is a totally new approach to solving an office building in an extremely hot and dry climate. _ "Gordon Bunshaft Interview—On SOM," in *SOM Journal 3*, Ostfildern, Germany: Hatje Cantz Publishers, 2004

Lever is a fine building, but it's in the discipline of the whole modern movement of Le Corbusier. This [the National Commercial Bank] is not in anybody's discipline. This is a unique solution for a unique part of the world. _ Gordon Bunshaft interview by Betty J. Blum, *Oral History of Gordon Bunshaft*, Chicago: The Art Institute of Chicago, 1990

Because of the peculiarity of the site and the development of a parking garage, and from exploring the concept of an inward-facing office, we came up with a triangle. That enabled us to open the courtyards in two directions and gave a change of view to people who move through the building. . . . The question of solving a relatively high building in an extremely hot, unpleasant environment has never been attacked in a fundamental way. . . . All the buildings I worked on in the past were part of currents in international architecture; this building isn't a current of anything. _ Carol Herselle Krinsky, *Gordon Bunshaft of Skidmore, Owings & Merrill*, New York: The Architectural History Foundation, 1988

Not only was the Hirshhorn Museum designed to accommodate the modernist art collection of Joseph Hirshhorn, Bunshaft needed to consider its relationship to other existing buildings that were part of the Smithsonian. *This page*: Jeddah's National Commercial Bank was designed as an "inward-facing" office due to the extremely dry, hot climate. For the architect, the triangle was key to the design.

## WORKING WITH CLIENTS

Another thing about our approach, especially mine, is the owner is a joint part of the venture. When we got Banque Lambert [1959–62], I told the mother who was the Baroness Lambert, "Hiring an architect is like getting married for four years without sex." That's what it is. _ Gordon Bunshaft interview by Betty J. Blum, *Oral History of Gordon Bunshaft,* Chicago: The Art Institute of Chicago, 1990

# IF AN ARCHITECT CAN'T ADD TO WHAT A CLIENT WANTS, HE ISN'T DOING MUCH.

So in 1947 you had this boom of clients wanting to build buildings. It was easily more of a Golden Age than the Renaissance with the Medicis. When I say clients, they were mostly corporations. The heads of them were men who wanted to build something that they'd be proud to have representing their company, whether it was a bank or whatever. In the corporations in those days, the head man was personally involved and personally building himself a palace for his people that would not only represent his company, but his personal pleasure. They were the new Medicis, and there were many of them. _ Gordon Bunshaft interview by Betty J. Blum, *Oral History of Gordon Bunshaft,* Chicago: The Art Institute of Chicago, 1990

I think when a building is done, the client initially is happy. If he's happy after he's been there three or four years—when I say client, I mean the head man I work with—and the people in there are happy, and the best judgment of that is if it's maintained meticulously. That means pride is involved. That's the most important thing of all, without question. The second most important thing for me, and the thing that's given me the greatest pleasure in my whole architectural life, is that most of my clients were people I liked and they've liked me and they've become lifelong friends. _ Gordon Bunshaft interview by Betty J. Blum, *Oral History of Gordon Bunshaft,* Chicago: The Art Institute of Chicago, 1990

## IN THE BEGINNING: "IGNORANCE WAS BLISS"

*Despite his education and career laurels—his schooling at MIT, his Rotch Traveling Fellowship, his forty-two years at SOM—Bunshaft credited his parents for giving him the foundation that propelled him through life.*

Perhaps the most important thing that ever happened to me was that I born on May 9, 1909, with parents who had just come from Russia a year before I was born. . . . My father, David, and my mother, Yetta, were both Bunshafts before marriage. They were first cousins. They were poor when they arrived, but my father worked very hard and saved money and eventually sent me through MIT as if I were the son of a very rich man. _ Gordon Bunshaft interview by Betty J. Blum, *Oral History of Gordon Bunshaft,* Chicago: The Art Institute of Chicago, 1990

Whatever they made, they saved a part of it, regardless of whether they made two dollars a week or a hundred dollars a week. . . . Their pleasures never occurred to them. . . . It was the family and the devotion to education." _ Gordon Bunshaft interview by Betty J. Blum, *Oral History of Gordon Bunshaft,* Chicago: The Art Institute of Chicago, 1990

I was born into what you'd call today a slum [in Buffalo, New York]. . . . I was sickly when I was young, and I had diphtheria a couple of times. The second time I must have been eight years old. . . . I guess like any kid you make little drawings of a house or something. Any kid does that. You don't have to be a potential architect. He [the Bunshaft family doctor] saw them and said to my mother, "Gordon should be an architect." I don't think my mother knew what that meant, and later on I didn't either. . . . I must have been around twelve or so when I decided to be an architect and go to MIT. . . . It was sort of through ignorance that I picked that. I couldn't draw. I never could draw well, but in the seventh grade I had a nice teacher and I got the catalogue for MIT. . . ." _ Gordon Bunshaft interview by Betty J. Blum, *Oral History of Gordon Bunshaft,* Chicago: The Art Institute of Chicago, 1990

I set up a little woodworking place down in the basement of our house. With my allowance I'd buy Stanley tools. I was not a boy who ran around with the guys and got into trouble or chased girls. You could say I was a sissy or kind of a jerk. _ Gordon Bunshaft interview by Betty J. Blum, *Oral History of Gordon Bunshaft,* Chicago: The Art Institute of Chicago, 1990

I think I was an odd duck—I'm not being modest—as far as being a regular guy. A regular guy didn't spend his high school evenings and weekends—not every time but quite a bit—making furniture. . . . Before I went to college, I made furniture, including a bed and cabinets and all that. With my allowance I'd go buy lumber. . . . I didn't go out with girls. I don't think I ever kissed a girl until I was twenty-two. My father used to worry that I didn't drink. _ Gordon Bunshaft interview by Betty J. Blum, *Oral History of Gordon Bunshaft,* Chicago: The Art Institute of Chicago, 1990

**Influences: "Mies was the Mondrian of architecture and Le Corbusier was the Picasso."** But we, as students [at MIT], were looking in the library. I wasn't, but my pals were. I used to wait for them to bring the books up, and then I'd look at them. We were looking at Le Corbusier. Le Corbusier, in my opinion, was the person who created worldwide modern architecture as a standard through his books. . . . All the southern countries all through the world were all concrete countries, and Le Corbusier's stuff came to them naturally. He was the main teacher of architecture through his books. . . . Mies didn't publish as early as Le Corbusier, and also Mies didn't blossom really until he came to this country. _ Gordon Bunshaft interview by Betty J. Blum, *Oral History of Gordon Bunshaft*, Chicago: The Art Institute of Chicago, 1990

I think Mies was a really great architect, and he built three or four magnificent buildings: the Tugendhat House, the Barcelona Pavilion, and the greatest office building built at any time, his Seagrams Building. I think he got too many commissions afterward and they got a little repetitious. I think he was a man that should have built few buildings, and, of course, those three he built are so wonderful and will endure. There are very few architects who have three great buildings. _ Gordon Bunshaft interview by Betty J. Blum, *Oral History of Gordon Bunshaft*, Chicago: The Art Institute of Chicago, 1990

**The Intrinsic Modernist** *In 1935, Strunk & White wrote their now-famous* Elements of Style, *which contained reams of good advice, still relevant today. Their disregard for pretension is apt for the plainspoken no-nonsense Bunshaft: "Avoid the elaborate, the pretentious, the coy, and the cute. Do not be tempted by a twenty-dollar word when there is a ten-center handy, ready, and able."*

I don't read books. I mean, I read a lot of novels and things, or biographies, but I very seldom read architectural books at all or art books. I look at the pictures or the drawings. _ Gordon Bunshaft interview by Betty J. Blum, *Oral History of Gordon Bunshaft*, Chicago: The Art Institute of Chicago, 1990

## ❝ I DIDN'T KNOW REALLY TOO MUCH OF WHAT ARCHITECTURE IS EXCEPT FOR BUILDING. ❞

I think what has helped me for the rest of my life was a sort of logic, common sense, and doing it. I didn't hesitate. I never hesitated. _ Gordon Bunshaft interview by Betty J. Blum, *Oral History of Gordon Bunshaft*, Chicago: The Art Institute of Chicago, 1990

Fundamentally a building has to work. Now there are a lot of buildings by great architects that don't work at all. The Guggenheim is a disaster. It is no more a museum than I am Napoleon. _ Gordon Bunshaft interview by Betty J. Blum, *Oral History of Gordon Bunshaft*, Chicago: The Art Institute of Chicago, 1990

Buildings don't stay forever unless the goddamn historical people preserve every junky building in the city. _ Gordon Bunshaft interview by Betty J. Blum, *Oral History of Gordon Bunshaft*, Chicago: The Art Institute of Chicago, 1990

I try to do the best I can with the personality that I have, good or bad. The simplest thing I can say is I'm very pleased with what I did with my life. I think it was due to several things. One, that I had a dedicated family that saw that I had every opportunity to learn and be educated. Two, that I think I had a fairly sound mind that was not too poetic but had a good deal of logic. And, three, that I lived at the right time as far as architecture was concerned. There are probably more reasons, but perhaps the most important thing of all is that I persevered stubbornly on what I believed. Last—and probably more important than any of them—is that I was very lucky. _ "Gordon Bunshaft Interview—On SOM," in *SOM* Journal 3, Ostfildern, Germany: Hatje Cantz Publishers, 2004

**ECSTASY** I have always confronted life as an unwavering rebel. After reading Sartre, I viewed life as an unfair and unrelenting tragedy. When I was a young man of only fifteen, I was anguished to think of man's destiny, doomed as we are to total abandonment, and defenseless against it. I was frightened by the idea of someday disappearing forever. Like everyone else, I have tried to erase such thoughts and instead take advantage of the pleasures of this brief and joyful passage on earth that fate grants us without our consultation. I have felt the ecstasy of the fantastic natural world around us, and, arm-in-arm with my friends, I cast aside the disturbing thoughts that so afflicted me when I was alone. I wore a mask of youthful optimism and contagious good humor. I was known as a high-spirited and spontaneous personality, a lover of the bohemian lifestyle, while deep inside I nursed a tremendous sorrow when I thought about humanity and life. _ Oscar Niemeyer, *The Curves of Time: The Memoirs of Oscar Niemeyer*, London: Phaidon, 2000

# OSCAR NIEMEYER

**BORN:** December 15, 1907, Rio de Janeiro, Brazil; Died: December 5, 2012

**EDUCATION:** Architect Engineer, National School of Fine Arts, Rio de Janeiro, Brazil, 1934

**OFFICE:** 3940 Avenida Atlantica, Rio de Janeiro, Brazil

**PROJECTS FEATURED:** Niterói Contemporary Art Museum, Rio de Janeiro, Brazil, 1996; Latin America Memorial, São Paulo, Brazil, 1987; Metropolitan Cathedral of Brasília, Brazil, 1970; Itamaraty Palace, Brasília, Brazil, 1960; National Congress, Brasília, Brazil, 1958; Church of Saint Francis of Assisi, Pampulha, Brazil, 1943

**MOUNTAINS/WAVES/WOMEN =CURVES**

**Church of Saint Francis of Assisi, Pampulha, 1943**
The tile-clad façade of the four undulating concrete parabalas is by Portuguese artist Cāndido Partinari.

## "I AM ATTRACTED TO FREE-FLOWING, SENSUAL CURVES."

*Niemeyer admires reinforced concrete for the plasticity he strives for in his buildings. His unabashed preference for curves illustrates the creative expression and surprise he seeks in all his buildings. To Niemeyer, the curve is as logical a form as a straight line—and far more beautiful.*

I am not attracted to straight angles or to the straight line—hard and inflexible—created by man. I am attracted to free-flowing, sensual curves. _ Oscar Niemeyer, *The Curves of Time: The Memoirs of Oscar Niemeyer,* London: Phaidon, 2000

In architecture, as in any work of art, the most important thing is astonishment. It's for a person to look and see that it's something different. Architecture is all about curiosity. _ Oscar Niemeyer interview with Brian Mier, *Index Magazine,* http://www.indexmagazine.com/interviews/oscar_niemeyer.shtml

Architecture is invention. It must offer pleasure as well as practicality. If you only worry about function, the result stinks. _ Jonathan Glancey, *The Guardian,* August 1, 2007

Each architect has his own style. It's true that the climate in Brazil caused me to change certain things. It's a lighter architecture—simpler, more transparent than what you can make in colder climates. _ Oscar Niemeyer interview with Brian Mier, *HUNCH,* Berlage Institute Report, Issue 4, 2001/2002

## "TOTAL PLASTIC FREEDOM"

First were the thick stone walls, the arches, then the domes and vaults—of the architect, searching out for wider spaces. Now it is concrete-reinforced that gives our imagination flight, with its soaring spans and uncommon cantilevers. Concrete, to which architecture is integrated, through which it is able to discard the foregone conclusions of rationalism, with its monotony and repetitious solutions. _ Oscar Niemeyer, Pritzker Prize acceptance speech, May 23, 1988

Today we enjoy total plastic freedom. Reinforced concrete has made new and unpredictable forms possible, beginning with Pampulha in the 1940s. _ Oscar Niemeyer, *The Curves of Time: The Memoirs of Oscar Niemeyer,* London: Phaidon, 2000

It has been my hobby and one of my greatest joys to devise new and creative forms suggested by reinforced concrete. I have sought to discover them, multiply them, and combine them with state-of-the-art technology to achieve an architectural spectacle. _ Oscar Niemeyer, *The Curves of Time: The Memoirs of Oscar Niemeyer,* London: Phaidon, 2000

Of course, I have given my engineers some headaches over the years, but they go with me. I have always wanted my buildings to be as light as possible, to touch the ground gently, to swoop and soar, and to surprise. _ Jonathan Glancey, *The Guardian,* August 1, 2007

---

# **❚❚ . . . THE PAMPULHA PROJECT, THE FIRST REAL CHALLENGE TO RATIONALIST ARCHITECTURE. ❚❚**

### PAMPULHA 1943
### CHURCH OF SAINT FRANCIS OF ASSISI

My architectural oeuvre began with Pampulha, which I designed in sensual and unexpected curves. This was the beginning of the plastic freedom that reinforced concrete unleashed. _ Oscar Niemeyer, *The Curves of Time: The Memoirs of Oscar Niemeyer,* London: Phaidon, 2000

The project was an opportunity to challenge the monotony of contemporary architecture, the wave of misinterpreted functionalism that hindered it, and the dogmas of form and function that had emerged, counteracting the plastic freedom that reinforced concrete introduced. I was attracted by the curve—the liberated, sensual curve suggested by the possibilities of new technology yet so often recalled in venerable old baroque churches. _ Oscar Niemeyer, *The Curves of Time: The Memoirs of Oscar Niemeyer,* London: Phaidon, 2000

At that time, architecture did not do justice to concrete. It was rigid. The right angle predominated. I thought it should be otherwise because when one wants to do a project in concrete the curve is always there. So the highlight of the Pampulha project was a church that had curves everywhere. A new architecture, but more like the old churches—a bit baroque. _ Oscar Niemeyer interview with Brian Mier, *Index Magazine,* http://www.indexmagazine.com/interviews/oscar_niemeyer.shtml

Critics never tired of attacking it, but the wind was knocked out of their sails when the journal *Brazil Build* highlighted its [the church's] architectural importance. . . . The criticisms did not bother me at all. . . . Le Corbusier alone refused to jump on the bandwagon. I remember him once remarking, "Oscar, what you are doing is baroque, but it's very well done." And again, several years later, "They say my work is baroque, too." _ Oscar Niemeyer, *The Curves of Time: The Memoirs of Oscar Niemeyer*, London: Phaidon, 2000

### Le Corbusier: "Architecture . . . A Free Creation of the Mind"

When Le Corbusier came to Rio, I helped him out designing some projects. So when I first embraced the profession I was already doing the architecture that I liked. I learned a lot from my contact with Le Corbusier and from reading his theories. The only direct influence I had from him, however, was on the day that he told me "architecture is universal." Then I started my architecture. It all started in Pampulha in 1942. It was there that I found out that architecture would have to be different. _ Oscar Niemeyer interview with Brian Mier, *Index Magazine*, http://www.indexmagazine.com/interviews/oscar_niemeyer.shtml

I worked with him; I helped him on some projects. The main influence I got from him was when he told me that architecture is a mental invention, a free creation of the mind. _ Oscar Niemeyer interview with Brian Mier, *HUNCH*, Berlage Institute Report, Issue 4, 2001/2002

I remember him today with the same enthusiasm I felt the first time we met, forty years ago [now sixty years ago—Ed.], when we went to pick him up at the airport. He seemed to be an architect-genius come down from heaven. If, on the one hand, he was sometimes overly eager to make his own architecture, on the other hand I always felt he was a human being who carried a message, a paean to beauty that could not be silenced. Accept and understand him: that is what I always tried to do. _ Oscar Niemeyer, *The Curves of Time: The Memoirs of Oscar Niemeyer*, London: Phaidon, 2000

It was obvious that my architecture had influenced Le Corbusier's later projects, but this factor is only now being taken into account by critics of his work. _ Oscar Niemeyer, *The Curves of Time: The Memoirs of Oscar Niemeyer*, London: Phaidon, 2000

For Niemeyer, material meets shape in the Church of Saint Francis of Assisi. *Below:* A concept sketch of the church.

## SÃO PAULO 1987
# LATIN AMERICA MEMORIAL

. . . in São Paulo, at the Memorial da América Latina, my design radically follows advanced construction techniques. There are no minor details, only 70 to 90-meter beams and curved shells. These form the great free spaces recalled by the project's theme. The memorial is a work whose monumental size corresponds to the greatness of its objective: to unite the people of an oppressed and exploited Latin American continent. _ Oscar Niemeyer, *The Curves of Time: The Memoirs of Oscar Niemeyer,* London: Phaidon, 2000

Thus, to represent Latin America, I designed a large, concrete, open-palmed hand, its fingers slightly bent to convey despair, and a trickle of blood running down to its wrist. To explain the spirit of my sculpture, I wrote, "Sweat, blood, and poverty have marked our disjointed and oppressed Latin America. Now it is crucial that we readjust this continent, unite it, and transform it into an untouchable monolith capable of insuring its independence and happiness."

Thus the 25-foot-tall hand was erected. It represented a critique and a forewarning rather than a provocation. It brings to mind a shadowed past and future full of hope and doubt. _ Oscar Niemeyer, *The Curves of Time: The Memoirs of Oscar Niemeyer,* London: Phaidon, 2000

The choice of a hand—so primary and gestural—was a brilliant decision of Niemeyer's. It immediately telegraphed the humanity of the memorial. The Niterói Contemporary Art Museum, *opposite,* is a majestic response to a spectacular setting.

## "I BECAME A COMMUNIST"

I was born into a middle-class family. My grandfather was a federal cabinet minister; we were more or less well off. But when I went out into the world, I felt that it was unfair. So if you ask me what I like in my work, it is that I sided with the poor, that I tried to work with them. I joined the Communist party. . . . The most important thing for the youth is to become part of the struggle, to be ready to react. _ Oscar Niemeyer interview with Brian Mier, *HUNCH*, Berlage Institute Report, Issue 4, 2001/2002

I was always something of a rebel. Having left behind all the old prejudices of my Catholic family, I saw the world as unjust and unacceptable. Poverty was spreading as if it was only natural and inescapable. I joined the Communist party and embraced the thinking of Marx, as I still do today. _ Oscar Niemeyer, *The Curves of Time: The Memoirs of Oscar Niemeyer*, London: Phaidon, 2000

I do not know why I have always designed large public buildings. But because these buildings do not always serve the functions of social justice, I try to make them beautiful and spectacular so that the poor can stop to look at them and be touched and enthused. As an architect, that is all I can do. _ Oscar Niemeyer, *The Curves of Time: The Memoirs of Oscar Niemeyer*, London: Phaidon, 2000

Many of my buildings have been political and civic monuments, but perhaps some of them have given ordinary people—powerless people—a sense of delight. _ Jonathan Glancey, *The Guardian*, August 1, 2007

## RIO DE JANEIRO 1996
# NITERÓI CONTEMPORARY ART MUSEUM

The natural setting is beautiful, so that helped the project. It was really good for Niterói because today the museum has become a kind of flag for the city. . . . The landscape was great, and I didn't want to hide nature. I had to go up, opening up. So the building stands out like a flower in space. Nature is glorified on the ground. When you arrive there you see the building, the view. You see the buildings going by, you see the Sugar Loaf across the bay in Rio de Janeiro. When this happens you notice that the program of architecture is linked to the place where it is performed. It must preserve what is beautiful in the area. _ Oscar Niemeyer interview with Brian Mier, *Index Magazine*, http://www.index-magazine.com/interviews/oscar_niemeyer.shtml

During this phase . . . the prevailing idea was to manifest not only the plastic freedom of my architecture but also the advancements in engineering in Brazil. _ Oscar Niemeyer, *The Curves of Time: The Memoirs of Oscar Niemeyer*, London: Phaidon, 2000

". . . from it [the central support], the architecture arose spontaneously like a flower." _ Oscar Niemeyer interview with Brian Mier, *Index Magazine*, http://www.indexmagazine.com/interviews/oscar_niemeyer.shtml

**❝❝ THE BUILDING STANDS OUT LIKE A FLOWER IN SPACE. ❞❞**

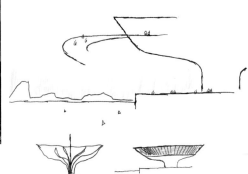

## "I LIVE FOR BRASÍLIA"

*Brasília is the relatively new capital city of Brazil, designed by architect Oscar Niemeyer and urban planner Lucio Costa. In 1957, construction began on the complex, and on April 21, 1960, Brasília was inaugurated as the new capital of Brazil, although construction of the city was not yet complete. The idea of monumentality was embodied in its simplistic master plan and individual buildings. Soon after its completion, though, the ideal vision of Brasília emerged as two cities: the monumental city of government and the low-income satellite towns, or favelas, where the workers of Brasília lived and commuted from. Despite Niemeyer's left-wing politics, Brasília became a city socially divided by class distinction. Nonetheless, Brasília was hugely influential in defining international as well as Brazilian modernism through its architectural purity and structural logic.*

There has never been a city built so far away from everything. Brasília was built at the end of the world. There were no telephones, nothing. There were no roads. Everything had to be flown in. The few roads that existed were dirt. Transportation was a serious problem. _ Oscar Niemeyer interview with Brian Mier, *Index Magazine*, http://www.indexmagazine.com/interviews/oscar_niemeyer.shtml

During automobile trips to Brasília, my greatest distraction was to observe cloud formations in the sky. What numerous and unexpected possibilities they suggested! Now they formed mysterious, towering cathedrals—most certainly, the cathedrals of Saint-Exupéry; now, ruthless warriors or Roman charioteers crossing the skies; now, outlandish monsters racing swiftly with the wind; and, more often (because I always looked out for them), lovely and vaporous women reclining on the clouds. _ Oscar Niemeyer, *The Curves of Time: The Memoirs of Oscar Niemeyer*, London: Phaidon, 2000

From Pampulha [1943] to Brasília [1956–70], my work followed the same trajectory of plastic freedom and architectural inventiveness, and I became aware of the convention of defending it against the limitations of constructive logic. Thus, if I designed a different shape, I had to have arguments to explain it. Every time I designed

a curved block standing alone on a site, for instance, I presented it with accompanying sketches showing the existing curved topography itself had suggested it. . . . In this way I defended my architecture and my fantasies, creating new forms and architectural elements that over time were added to the plastic vocabulary of our architecture. . ." _ Oscar Niemeyer, *The Curves of Time: The Memoirs of Oscar Niemeyer*, London: Phaidon, 2000

I must confess that when I started my work in Brasília I was already weary of providing so many explanations. I knew that I was experienced enough to be rid of such justifications, and I could not care less about the inevitable criticism my designs were sure to raise. _ Oscar Niemeyer, *The Curves of Time: The Memoirs of Oscar Niemeyer*, London: Phaidon, 2000

## ARCHITECTURE AND STRUCTURE: "TWO THINGS THAT MUST BE BORN TOGETHER"

*Niemeyer regards Brasília as the second phase in his career. The key building in the first phase was his 1943 design for the Church of Saint Francis of Assisi in Pampulha.*

Then came Brasília, where I glorified structure, inserting architectural style into it. By the time the structure was finished, architecture and structure were there as two things that must be born together and that together enrich each other. _ Oscar Niemeyer, *The Curves of Time: The Memoirs of Oscar Niemeyer*, London: Phaidon, 2000

. . . a feeling of protest possessed me in Brasília. It was no longer the imposition of the right angle that angered me, but the obsessive concern for architectural purity and structural logic, the systemic campaign against the free and creative forms that attracted me and which were viewed contemptuously as gratuitous and unnecessary. _ Oscar Niemeyer, *The Curves of Time: The Memoirs of Oscar Niemeyer*, London: Phaidon, 2000

Until Brasília, I regarded architecture as an exercise to be practiced in a sporting spirit and nothing more. Now I live for Brasília. _ "Art: The Architect of Brasília," *Time*, July 28, 1958

## BRASÍLIA 1958
# NATIONAL CONGRESS

It was the president's idea to build Brasília. He thought it was an important thing to do—to bring progress to the interior of the country. And I did my kind of architecture. _ Oscar Niemeyer interview with Brian Mier, *Index Magazine,* http://www.indexmagazine.com/interviews/oscar_niemeyer.shtml

I was the architect responsible for Brasília and—as everybody knew—I had worked there since the beginning, honestly, without a break, for next to nothing. I was a member of the steering committee appointed by Congress . . . _ Oscar Niemeyer, *The Curves of Time: The Memoirs of Oscar Niemeyer,* London: Phaidon, 2000

I designed the remaining buildings with the same degree of architectural innovation. In the National Congress complex, the dome and the saucer-shaped building were hierarchically arranged . . . . _ Oscar Niemeyer, *The Curves of Time: The Memoirs of Oscar Niemeyer,* London: Phaidon, 2000

Now when I visit Brasília I feel that our effort was not in vain; that Brasília marked a heroic period of labor and optimism; that my architectural design duly reflects my state of mind and my courage to expose that which touched me most deeply. In my design I honored the volumes and free spaces of Lucio Costa's master plan—its extraordinarily well-conceived characteristics that produced a monumental and hospitable city. _ Oscar Niemeyer, *The Curves of Time: The Memoirs of Oscar Niemeyer,* London: Phaidon, 2000

This view of the National Congress in Brasília, the new capital of Brazil, shows the two main design elements—the dome and saucer-shaped building.

## "I PREFER TO LOOK AT WHAT'S STILL LEFT TO BE DONE."

Architecture for me has always begun with drawing. When I was very little my mother said I used to draw in the air with my fingers. I needed a pencil. Once I could hold one, I have drawn every day since. . . . When I have looked at the site for a building, considered its budget and thought of how it might be built, and what it might be, the drawings come very quickly. I pick up my pen. It flows. A building appears. _ Jonathan Glancey, *The Guardian,* August 1, 2007

I think that I entered school because I liked to draw. And drawing brought me to architecture. . . . I had my own ideas. I wanted a smoother architecture with more freedom, and that's what I did and that's what I still do. I think that in the end, intuition always prevails in architecture and art. The important thing is to want to do something. _ Oscar Niemeyer interview with Brian Mier, *HUNCH,* Berlage Institute Report, Issue 4, 2001/2002

*When he was 100 years old, Niemeyer married for the second time. His bride was his longtime assistant, 60-year-old Vera Lúcia Cabreira.*

I think of myself as no more than 60. . . . What I could do at 60, I can still do now. _ Jonathan Glancey, *The Guardian,* August 1, 2007

I never thought that I was going to live so long, but I confess that it is still not enough. I don't look much to the past; I prefer to look at what's still left to be done. _ Oscar Niemeyer interview by Pedro de la Hoz, *Granma Daily,* August 7, 2006

When people ask me if I take pleasure in the idea of someone looking at my buildings in the future, I tell them that this person will vanish, too. Everything has a beginning and an end. You. Me. Architecture. We must try to do the best we can, but must remain modest. Nothing lasts for very long. _ Jonathan Glancey, *The Guardian,* August 1, 2007

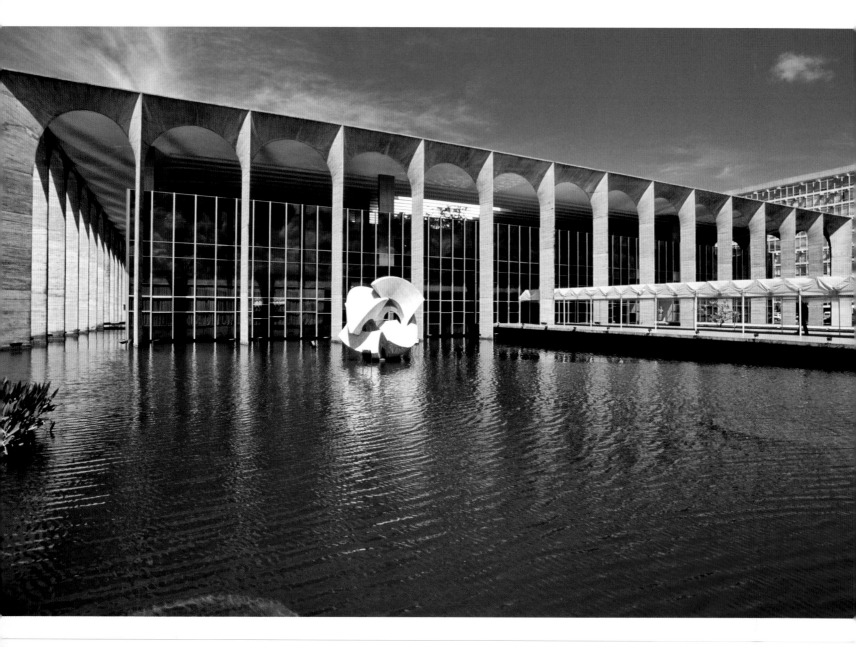

The long bridge, seen above at far right, extends over the ornamental pool and leads to a superb collection of Brazilian art. The carved marble sculpture, *Meteor*, by Bruno Giorgi, symbolizes the union between the five continents. The gardens are by Roberto Burle Marx.

### BRASÍLIA 1960
# ITAMARATY PALACE

In my opinion, it was up to architects to anticipate structural problems, so that by combining their imagination with technical sophistication they could create an architectural spectacle responsive to current trains of thought. _ Oscar Niemeyer, *The Curves of Time: The Memoirs of Oscar Niemeyer,* London: Phaidon, 2000

I decided to follow this line of thinking for the palaces of Brasília. They would be characterized by their own innovative structural form. As a result, minor details typical of rationalist architecture would recede against the dominant presence of the new structures. _ Oscar Niemeyer, *The Curves of Time: The Memoirs of Oscar Niemeyer,* London: Phaidon, 2000

Anyone who observes the National Congress complex and the palaces of Brasília immediately realizes that once their structural framework was built, the architectural design was already in place.

I sought to experiment with reinforced concrete, primarily with the supports that tapered to very slender ends, so thin that the palaces seemed to barely touch the ground. _ Oscar Niemeyer, *The Curves of Time: The Memoirs of Oscar Niemeyer,* London: Phaidon, 2000

## METROPOLITAN CATHEDRAL OF BRASÍLIA

The search for an unusual solution fascinated me. . . . I avoided conventional solutions, which had produced the old dark cathedrals reminding us of sin. On the contrary, I designed a dark entrance hall leading to the nave, which is brightly lit—colorful—its beautiful, transparent stained-glass windows facing infinite space. I always received understanding and support from the clergy, even from the Papal Nuncio, who could not contain his enthusiasm upon visiting the cathedral: "This architect must be a saint; only a saint could devise such splendid connection between the nave, heaven, and God." _ Oscar Niemeyer, *The Curves of Time: The Memoirs of Oscar Niemeyer*, London: Phaidon, 2000

Brasília begins a new phase in my work—more geometrical, more simple, more monumental. _ "Art: The Architect of Brasília," *Time*, July 28, 1958

The four bronze sculptures seen here represent the Evangelists. Inside, the baptistry is covered in ceramic tiles.

**ARCHITECTURAL REALITY** Architectural creation is a special form of comprehending reality. It works upon and transforms reality. . . . Artistic form . . . has the two-fold quality of both mirroring and enriching reality. . . . We contemplate and mold outer reality through the image which has been shaped by the method of architectural creation, through inner reality. . . . This is the logic of architectural creation. . . . Two points attract our attention when we look back upon the development of contemporary architecture from a worldwide viewpoint. On one side, there has been the tendency toward universalization and internationalization in the forms of expression. . . . On the other side, there has been an individualistic, specific, and person-subjective tendency in modern architecture. . . . We then become aware that the expression of some of our architectural works has been influenced by the traditional passive attitude, and we begin to see the need for taking a positive stand to overcome it. . . . The development of methods in contemporary architecture is not a mere handing down of traditional methods but can be promoted only by bringing architecture face to face with today's reality.

_ Kenzo Tange, "Creation in Present-Day Architecture and the Japanese Tradition," *Japan Architect,* June 1956

# KENZO TANGE

**BORN:** September 4, 1913, Imabari, Shikoku Island, Japan; Died: March 22, 2005

**EDUCATION:** Ph.D., M.Arch., B.Arch., University of Tokyo, Tokyo, Japan, 1959, 1945, 1938

**OFFICE:** Tange Associates, 1-6-18 Minami Azabu, Minato-ku, Tokyo, 106-0047 Japan
Tel: +81-3-3452-8818, Fax: +81-3-3452-8808
www.tangeweb.com

**PROJECTS FEATURED:** Tokyo City Hall, Japan, 1991; Kuwait International Airport Terminal, Farwaniyah, Kuwait, 1979; Saint Mary's Cathedral, Tokyo, 1964; National Gymnasium for the Tokyo Olympics, Japan, 1964; Hiroshima Peace Memorial Museum, Japan, 1952

"I FEEL VERY FORTUNATE TO HAVE WITNESSED THE TRANSFORMATION OF JAPAN FROM WAR DEVASTATION TO THE AFFLUENCE OF TODAY."

**Hiroshima Peace Memorial Museum,
Japan, 1952**
This view frames the Tange-designed memorial
Cenotaph for the A-Bomb Victims, as well as
the Genbaku Dome, known colloquially as
the "A-Bomb" Dome, an exhibition hall that
survived largely intact the nuclear bombing of
Hiroshima in August of 1945.

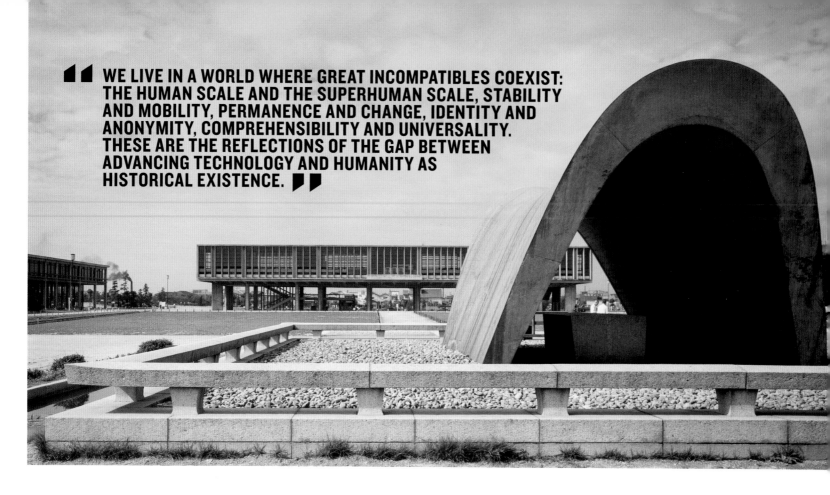

> **WE LIVE IN A WORLD WHERE GREAT INCOMPATIBLES COEXIST: THE HUMAN SCALE AND THE SUPERHUMAN SCALE, STABILITY AND MOBILITY, PERMANENCE AND CHANGE, IDENTITY AND ANONYMITY, COMPREHENSIBILITY AND UNIVERSALITY. THESE ARE THE REFLECTIONS OF THE GAP BETWEEN ADVANCING TECHNOLOGY AND HUMANITY AS HISTORICAL EXISTENCE.**

## HIROSHIMA 1952
## HIROSHIMA PEACE MEMORIAL MUSEUM

*Kenzo Tange was in charge of the reconstruction of Hiroshima after World War II, and in 1949 he won a competition for the Hiroshima Peace Memorial Museum, which came to include the museum, an auditorium, conference center, exhibition gallery, library, offices, and hotel on approximately 122,100 square meters. Amazingly, the public square defined by these buildings could accommodate as many as 50,000 people at one time around the arched cenotaph of the memorial. Tange's design would define postwar modern architecture in Japan: the Peace Center demonstrated a deep understanding of traditional culture while at the same time was a signpost in the search for modern architecture in Japan.*

Our major topic of interest in the 1950s had been devising a way to make contemporary architecture take root in the severe conditions of postwar Japan. _ Kenzo Tange, "Development of Design Concept and Methodology," *Japan Architect*, August–September 1996

From my standpoint, the Hiroshima project has both great significance as architecture and consider-able meaning above architectural considerations. Its design was proposed immediately after World War II—a time of various restrictions. Nonetheless, going beyond issues of good or bad, it has transcended time to become a symbol of Hiroshima. _ Kenzo Tange, "Creating a Contemporary System of Aesthetics," *Japan Architect*, January 1983

The earliest phase of my development as an architect is the years between the Hiroshima Peace Center (1946) and the 1950s. During that time . . . I was trying to find ways to make contemporary architecture take root in Japan. Undeniably, during that time, the discussions of Japanese traditionalism and the masses of the people that appeared in architectural journalism stimulated me. _ Kenzo Tange, "Development of Design Concept and Methodology," *Japan Architect*, August–September 1996

. . . Hiroshima project will remain an example of the maintenance of architectural monumentality. _ Kenzo Tange, "Creating a Contemporary System of Aesthetics," *Japan Architect*, January 1983

Tange's heroic response to the bombing of Hiroshima also served to introduce modern architecture in Japan.

# ❝❝ TRADITION MUST BE LIKE A CATALYST
## THAT DISAPPEARS ONCE ITS TASK IS DONE. ❞❞

## TRADITION AND CREATIVITY

*Tange's architecture was a unique synthesis of tradition and modernism. His approach to modern architecture included overcoming tradition while confronting it, as well as a critique of modern functionalism; he felt that the consideration of function was overstated. Tange's antidote to function was creativity.*

The realities of present-day Japan [post–World War II], while part of a historically conditioned worldwide reality, are at the same time given their unique shape by the traditions of Japan. Living within this reality, yet also trying always to comprehend it afresh in a forward-looking spirit, these traditions force themselves insistently upon our attention. . . . Only those who adopt a forward-looking attitude realize that tradition exists and is alive. It is therefore only they who can confront and overcome it. This means neither elaborating grandiose schemes for the future nor being fatefully involved with the past, but awareness that the most vital task of today is creatively to elevate both past and future. _ Kenzo Tange, "Creation in Present-Day Architecture and the Japanese Tradition," *Japan Architect,* June 1956

## ❝❝ I HAVE NO DESIRE WHATEVER
## TO HAVE MY WORKS
## APPEAR TRADITIONAL. ❞❞

Even when I was most sincerely interested in tradition, I was strongly moved to find ways to sever my ties with it. Tradition could be compared to a catalyst triggering chemical change but disappearing after the chemical action is performed. _ Kazuo Shinohara, "After Modernism, A Dialogue Between Kenzo Tange and Kazuo Shinohara," *Japan Architect,* November–December 1983

I do not believe that tradition as such can either be preserved or converted into creative drive. . . . If the smell of tradition is noticeable in my works . . . it is because our creative abilities have not flowered, because we are still in the transition toward creativity. _ Robin Boyd, *Kenzo Tange,* New York: George Braziller, 1962

Our contemporary projects are not always related to tradition, but lie rather in the reality in which we live. An attitude that fails to realize that

tradition is within our inner selves or simply refuses to face the fact of tradition does not result either in the negation or overcoming of tradition in a true sense. _ Kenzo Tange, "Creation in Present-Day Architecture and the Japanese Tradition," *Japan Architect,* June 1956

## TECHNOLOGY AND HUMANITY

It is always impossible to think about technological things or technological advance separately from social advance. Accordingly, we cannot take out technological things only. We have to think simultaneously as to how the social change affects architecture. _ John Peter, *The Oral History of Modern Architecture: Interviews with the Greatest Architects of the Twentieth Century,* New York: Harry Abrams, 1994

## ❝❝ CREATIVE WORK
## IS EXPRESSED IN OUR TIME AS A UNION OF
## TECHNOLOGY
## AND HUMANITY. ❞❞

Inconsistency itself breeds vitality. . . . [The greatest] arises from the confrontation of technology and human existence. _ Robin Boyd, *Kenzo Tange,* New York: George Braziller, 1962

It is a problem of technology versus humanity, and the task of today's architects and city planners is to build a bridge between these two things. _ Robin Boyd, *Kenzo Tange,* New York: George Braziller, 1962

## CONCRETE, THE MATERIAL OF REALITY

*It is worth noting that Tange made this statement around 1960.*
We have to choose material according to realities. As far as Japan is concerned, concrete is currently the most favorable and basic material. It is cheaper than iron and is capable of making freer forms. . . . In the past, I wanted to use steel for my works, but under the circumstances in Japan it was too early to do that. I felt I could not fully express or make forms that I wanted. Therefore, I have heavily depended on concrete . . . . _ John Peter, *The Oral History of Modern Architecture: Interviews with the Greatest Architects of the Twentieth Century,* New York: Harry Abrams, 1994

## TOKYO 1964
# SAINT MARY'S CATHEDRAL *When*
*Tange designed the projects Saint Mary's Cathedral and the National Gymnasium for the Tokyo Olympics, his interest and research in "the powerful feeling in spaces" led him to visit several medieval Gothic cathedrals.*

**Saint Mary's Cathedral in Tokyo was built to replace the original church that was destroyed by fire in World War II. The roof creates a cross that is visible not only from the sky, but from inside as well.**

After experiencing their heaven-aspiring grandeur and ineffably mystical spaces, I began to imagine new spaces and wanted to create them by means of modern technology. _ Kenzo Tange biography, The Pritzker Architecture Prize, www.pritzkerprize.com/laureates/1987/bio.html

In about 1960 . . . I began sensing what I can figuratively describe as viscosity or a glue-like stickiness in spaces that formerly had been crisp and clean. In other words, I developed an increasingly powerful feeling that spaces, which I had formerly interpreted as something created by tearing physical things apart, have glue-like power to adhere. This change in viewpoint can be compared to something like photographic negative and positive. Gradually I came to interpret space not as empty but as something supremely adhesive, to which other things cling. _ Kazuo Shinohara, "After Modernism, A Dialogue Between Kenzo Tange and Kazuo Shinohara," *Japan Architect*, November–December 1983

## A PLAN FOR TOKYO

*"A Plan for Tokyo, 1960," was Kenzo Tange's influential urban manifesto that responded to the city's rapid economic expansion. Tange's utopian design featured extending the growth of the city out over Tokyo Bay with a mega-structural network of bridges, manmade islands, and floating parking. This unbuilt project is important in understanding Tange's desire to create projects sensitive to the changing needs of a populous future in Tokyo.*

. . . the Plan for Tokyo, 1960, was more a methodological approach to the optimum nature of a large city and an experimental attempt to clarify the importance of the concept of structure in methodologies for architecture and cities than a proposal for the specific city of Tokyo. In the plan, Tokyo is provided with a civil axis as a structure along which growth and change of the city are possible. But this same civil axis has a symbolic meaning too. We came to see that identification of functional units can be sublimated to a symbolic level and that structural bodies themselves are bathed in *symbolism*. _ Kenzo Tange, "Development of Design Concept and Methodology," *Japan Architect*, August–September 1996

There is only one way to save Tokyo, and that is to create a new urban structure which will make it possible for the city to perform its true basic functions. _ Kenzo Tange, "A Plan for Tokyo, 1960: Toward a Structural Reorganization," *Japan Architect*, April 1961

Our plan, in effect, would provide for architecture which would be compatible with the speed and scale of the times, but which at the same time would permit the continuation of our historical urban life. _ Kenzo Tange, "A Plan for Tokyo, 1960: Toward a Structural Reorganization," *Japan Architect*, April 1961

Until only recently, Japan was constantly under the control of an absolute state, and the cultural energy of the people as a whole—the energy with which they might have created new forms—was confined and suppressed . . . Only in our own times has the energy of which I speak begun to be released. It is still working in a confused medium, and much remains to be done before real order is achieved, but it is certain that this energy will do much to convert Japanese tradition into something new and creative. _ Kenneth Frampton, *Modern Architecture, A Critical History*, London: Thames & Hudson, 1980

## TOKYO 1964
# NATIONAL GYMNASIUM FOR THE TOKYO OLYMPICS

Typification *is a term coined by Tange to replace* function. *Typification encompassed the requirements and functions of a building that are the "most human, most essential, and most future-oriented."*

*While Tange designed the gymnasium as a symbol, the building was also a brilliant structural design. The elliptical volumes of the gymnasium were covered by catenary steel roofs hung from concrete beams that also supported the upper tiers of the raked seating.*

**The monumental meets the human in Tange's architecture. As he once said, "creative work is expressed in our times in a union of technology and humanity."**

When this kind of typification identification is accompanied by a spiritual content, it reaches the dimension of the expression of *symbol*. I think we can be said to have begun giving thought to this

issue with the design of the National Gymnasium for the Tokyo Olympics, located in Yoyogi, Tokyo, and the Tokyo Saint Mary's Cathedral. _ Kenzo Tange, "Development of Design Concept and Methodology," *Japan Architect*, August–September 1996

On the surface, the client imposes various requirements, and we rethink them from the viewpoint of the citizens. In connection with this process, we employ the words *typification of function;* and, by them, we indicate, selecting from among the many requirements and functions proposed for buildings of this kind, the ones that are most human, most essential, and most future-oriented. _ Kenzo Tange, "Development of Design Concept and Methodology," *Japan Architect*, August–September 1996

# ◀◀ 'TO DESIGN' IN ITSELF MEANS TO BE ABLE TO READ AHEAD. ▶▶

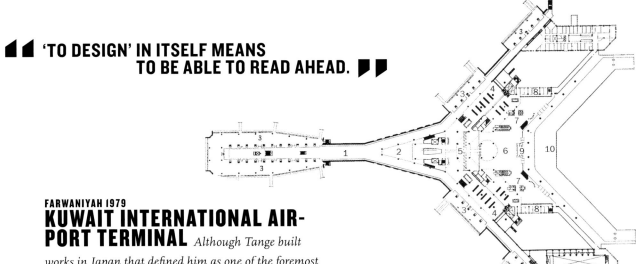

**FARWANIYAH 1979**
# KUWAIT INTERNATIONAL AIRPORT TERMINAL
*Although Tange built works in Japan that defined him as one of the foremost architects of his time, he was also commissioned to build several foreign buildings in the 1970s and 80s. The most successful, architecturally, of these was the Kuwait airport, which along with the Hiroshima Peace Memorial is considered by many to be Tange's major, crowning achievement.*

. . . as a landmark in the vast desert location—the air terminal was aesthetically created as a symbolic entrance into the country, in an effort to create a strong impression to incoming visitors from the immense outer space. _ Kenzo Tange obituary, *The Times* (London), March 25, 2005

The projects in which we engaged began to spread out into various regions: We did work in America, Europe, and the Middle East, as well as in Japan. These regions have their own contemporary characteristics and historical climates. _ Kenzo Tange, "Development of Design Concept and Methodology," *Japan Architect*, August–September 1996

As part of the plan to upgrade the area, the Kuwaiti royal family commissioned Tange to build a grand airport. It was a symbolic entrance into the Arab city.

I have two masters, Michelangelo and Le Corbusier. _ "Architecture: Japanese Kenzo Tange Dies Aged 91," *ANSA English Media Service*, March 22, 2005

I am in love with Rome, which I have visited at least 150 times after the war. _ "Architecture: Japanese Kenzo Tange Dies Aged 91," *ANSA English Media Service*, March 22, 2005

I appreciate most highly Corbusier's works. I also highly appreciate Mies's works, but as he has set limits to his work, I think no one can develop it further. Therefore, I appreciate Mies because he has approached the ultimate goal on one line. I do not know in what way it will be developed after this point. It might be impossible. In this connection, Corbusier still continues to walk freely, leaving various possibilities. As a teacher of architecture, I highly appreciate Gropius. All of them are our great teachers, and I respect them very much. But, as a friend, I most appreciate Saarinen. _ John Peter, *The Oral History of Modern Architecture: Interviews with the Greatest Architects of the Twentieth Century*, New York: Harry Abrams, 1994

Architects today tend to depreciate themselves, to regard themselves as no more than just ordinary citizens without the power to reform the future. I feel however, that we architects have a special duty and mission . . . [to contribute] to the sociocultural development of architecture and urban planning. _ Maggie Jackson, "Japan's New Architecture Is an Expression of Freedom," *The Associated Press, International News*, November 22, 1987

I feel very fortunate to have witnessed the transformation of Japan from war-devastation to the affluence of today. Although I consider myself to have been quite privileged, I am grateful for the opportunities I have had to work in such exciting projects. There are still many things I want to accomplish. I do not wish to repeat what I have done. I find that every project is a springboard to the next, always advancing forward from the past to the ever-changing future. That is my next challenge. _ Kenzo Tange website, www.ktaweb.com/profile/en_index.html

Tokyo City Hall is actually a complex of three buildings that serve as the seat of government not just for the city, but also for the governor. The complex includes the Metropolitan Assembly Building and a tower that houses the 127 members of the assembly and their staff.

## TOKYO 1991
# TOKYO CITY HALL

Our methodology began with a certain criticism of functionalism. People require many different functions from many different standpoints. We entertained doubt that it was our responsibility to pursue all of these arbitrary functions and give them form. For instance, in the case of a building for a city hall, it is often true that all kinds of demands from many different standpoints—beginning with that of the mayor and including those of the people who work in the building, the citizens who use it, and the city council member who represents those citizens—are imposed. When we come to grips with all of these demands, the question of which one is the true function of the city hall becomes a matter of great significance for our methodology. _ Kenzo Tange, "Development of Design Concept and Methodology," *Japan Architect*, August–September 1996

## "COMMUNICATION SPACE"

My philosophy of architecture is to think about what design is the ideal expression of the information society. . . . Modern architecture used to be the expression of industrial society, where space was considered a place for function. In the information society, space should be considered a communication field. . . . Some people say that with electronic communication, we don't need to move around. On the contrary, with these electronic devices, more direct communication will be needed. The telephone is just a tool to make appointments. _ Douglas C. McGill, *New York Times*, March 19, 1987

. . . In the 1950s, Japan dashed head-long into the industrialized society with the result that we found our daily lives brought into close contact with new technologies of kinds we had not previously even imagined. . . . Consequently, while using the latest technology in expressions conforming to the industrialized society, we all seriously attempted to find ways to enable architecture to respond to the actuality of violent growth and change. _ Kazuo Shinohara, "After Modernism, A Dialogue Between Kenzo Tange and Kazuo Shinohara," *Japan Architect*, November–December 1983

Structures exist in several dimensions. There are physical structures of dynamic relations. There are structures according to which things are given associations. Space itself transmits messages to people. In terms of written language, structure establishes the grammar of those messages. Moreover, it is the channel by means of which people can participate in a communication space. _ Kenzo Tange, "Development of Design Concept and Methodology," *Japan Architect*, August–September 1996

. . . the word *structural* in this case is the same as the one in the phrase *social structures*. . . . In other words, I mean ways of connecting spaces by means of communications spaces. _ Kazuo Shinohara, "After Modernism, A Dialogue Between Kenzo Tange and Kazuo Shinohara," *Japan Architect*, November–December 1983

In architecture, the demand was no longer for boxlike forms, but for buildings that have something to say to the human emotions. That new demand has had an effect on the designs of everything, from small window displays to streetscapes to buildings. Technological considerations are of great importance to architecture and cities in the informational society. The development of so-called intelligent buildings is a natural consequence and today's society will demand that whole districts and cities themselves become "intelligent" in the same way as the individual buildings. . . . A society that places great stress on communications, relationships with the surroundings probably deserve as much consideration as the functional sufficiency of the individual building.

I believe the development of a new architectural style will result from further study and work on the three elements that I have discussed: human, emotional, and sensual elements; technologically intelligent elements; and social-communicational structure of the space. _ Kenzo Tange biography, The Pritzker Architecture Prize, www.pritzkerprize.com/laureates/1987/bio.html

In the 1970s, because of the energy crisis, our values—at least in Japan—shifted from material things to the nonphysical and even spiritual considerations. That shift took place not just in architecture, but in daily life, as people tended to prefer the immaterial to the material. With de-emphasis on industrialization and the advent of the "information-communication society," the fundamentally rational and functional philosophy of the preceding period changed, and people sought things that appeal to the emotions and the senses. _ Kenzo Tange, Pritzker Prize acceptance speech, May 2, 1987

## HARMONY

In the early part of the 1970s, the world began with a powerful swing in a new direction. . . . The speed of economic growth during the sixties had caused intense pollution that still threatens to destroy the natural environment and the historical environment as well. Quite naturally, a popular movement has arisen to offer fierce resistance to such destruction. . . . I was deeply impressed with the need for harmony between the natural and the manmade environments and between the contemporary and the historical. Furthermore, I was convinced of the need to create such harmony. _ Kenzo Tange, "Development of Design Concept and Methodology," *Japan Architect*, August–September 1996

**NATURAL CONTINUITY** Especially after World War II, we have cut wide gashes into the fabric of our cities the world over—we put great traffic arteries through them and erected buildings whose function, shape, size, materials, and colors had no bearing on the existing urban environment.

It is therefore important today to heal these wounds, retaining the positive aspects, and re-establishing the necessary cohesion of the urban environment so that we can once more experience the natural sense of community which we so admire when strolling through old cities. . . .

I don't overestimate the influence of architecture on people, but I am sure that the physical alienation of our cities contributes to our inability to live together harmoniously. . . .

A building is a human being's space and the background for his dignity, and its exterior should reflect its contents and function. New buildings should fit naturally into their surroundings, both architecturally and historically, without denying or prettifying the concerns of our time. You cannot just quote from history and above all you cannot take it out of context, in however humorous a fashion. On the contrary, history has a natural continuity that must be respected. _ Gottfried Böhm, Pritzker Prize acceptance speech, April 17, 1986

# GOTTFRIED BÖHM

**BORN:** January 23, 1920, Offenbach am Main, Germany

**EDUCATION:** Art Prize Berlin, Academy of the Arts, Berlin, Germany, 1974; Master of Architecture, Technical University, Munich, Germany, 1946

**OFFICE:** Architekturbüro, Auf Dem Römerberg 25, 50968 Cologne, Germany
Tel: +49 0-221-8882470, Fax: +49 0-221-342864
www.boehmarchitektur.de

**PROJECTS FEATURED:** Public Library, Ulm, Germany, 2003; Peek & Cloppenburg, Berlin, 1995; Züblin AG Headquarters, Stuttgart, Germany, 1985; Civic Hall with Theater, Bergisch Gladbach, Germany, 1980; Parish Church of the Resurrection of Christ and Youth Center, Cologne-Melaten, Germany, 1970; Neviges Pilgrimage Church, Velbert, Germany, 1968;

**" I HAVE NO EXPRESSION OF MY OWN OTHER THAN TO CREATE BUILDINGS THAT ARE AS GOOD AS POSSIBLE, AND BEAUTIFUL. "**

**Neviges Pilgrimage Church, Velbert, 1968**
For Böhm, the construction of churches was a visible manifestation of man's desire to bring God down to earth and make Him part of his world.

The stark, angular exterior of the Neviges Pilgrimage Church is in contrast to the light-filled sanctuary. Accommodations for the pilgrims are in the unfolding series of rooms leading to the church.

VELBERT 1968
# NEVIGES PILGRIMAGE CHURCH

The church in Neviges is situated on a slope, which, in conjunction with a flanking development, we turned into a great processional way for pilgrims. This route leads to an open forecourt in front of the church and continues into the space within, the altar area representing the culmination of this path.
_ Svetlozar Raèv, ed., *Gottfried Böhm: Lectures Buildings Projects*, Zurich: Karl Krämer Verlag, 1988

. . . it is the altar itself that is the goal, from where one's eyes are diverted upwards. In the interior of this church the desire to create a structural and spatial unity of walls and ceilings is particularly evident.

Situated in front of the church to one side of the path of pilgrimage is the pilgrims' house, containing welfare and service facilities and sleeping cells on the upper floor. In summer the forecourt approach is also used as an outdoor space for major events. Tent-like roofs can be spanned over part of its area.
_ Svetlozar Raèv, ed., *Gottfried Böhm: Lectures Buildings Projects*, Zurich: Karl Krämer Verlag, 1988

How light a whole room then seems! The walls can be kept thin . . . pillars become slender rods . . . and

I feel this is most important, [it] provides a whole raft of new possibilities for living and monumental designs in reinforced concrete. _ Wolfgang Voigt, ed., *Gottfried Böhm*, Frankfurt: Jovis, 2006

The construction of churches is a visible manifestation of the desire in man to bring God down from heaven and make Him part of man's world. Regardless whether one was a believer, a doubter, or a dissenter, the erection of a church was always a very special event for a town. My church building work is of course deeply indebted to that of my father.
_ Svetlozar Raèv, ed., *Gottfried Böhm: Lectures Buildings Projects*, Zurich: Karl Krämer Verlag, 1988

*The Neviges Pilgrimage Church demonstrates Gottfried Böhm's progression in his work and architecture from that of his father, Dominikus Böhm. Gottfried's architectural vision emerged in the grim years immediately following the Second World War in Germany; he had completed his architectural studies and was experimenting with concrete. Early intentions to be a sculptor figured largely in Böhm's development as an architect. The concept of "fabric ceilings," a new application of concrete, was the result of his studies. The structures fundamentally changed the nature of space.*

**❝ I SIMPLY WANTED TO BUILD A BEAUTIFUL CHURCH. ❞**

**COLOGNE-MELATEN 1970**
# PARISH CHURCH OF THE RESURRECTION OF CHRIST AND YOUTH CENTER

... a series of individual-built volumes to form an ensemble. In view of our ideas of creating a folded structure, I felt it would be more consistent to unite the ceilings and walls in this structure to form a single spatial entity.
_ Wolfgang Voigt, ed., *Gottfried Böhm*, Frankfurt: Jovis, 2006

It must also be possible to create a festive space with new buildings. _ Wolfgang Voigt, ed., *Gottfried Böhm*, Frankfurt: Jovis, 2006

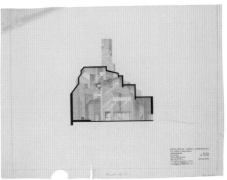

The Parish Church, along with Neviges, quickly established Böhm's importance and sculptural use of concrete.

377

## "APPROPRIATE MATERIAL"

What does one mean by the "appropriate material" or the "appropriate form of construction" nowadays? Brickwork, in the conventional sense of that word, no longer exists. The brick walls we build today are at best a half-brick skin of facings, behind which are thermal insulation, a cavity, and concrete or occasionally a further layer of brickwork. . . . External rendering today is usually a plastic coating no more than a few millimeters thick and applied to expanded polystyrene, behind which all manner of things are concealed. . . . _ Svetlozar Raèv, ed., *Gottfried Böhm: Lectures Buildings Projects*, Zurich: Karl Krämer Verlag, 1988

## "DRAWING ATTENTION TO DETAILS"

Reinforced concrete seems to me to be a relatively clear-cut material in terms of the legibility of the structure. One sees a column that is really a load-bearing column. . . . A column system . . . lends itself to prefabrication. The use of prefabricated concrete elements is not a new method of construction, but it has acquired a bad reputation on account of its generally insensitive execution. One must therefore ask oneself whether and in what way the method could be improved—in other words, how one could use it to build in a more attractive manner. Molded by the philosophy of functionalism as we are today, how can we liberate ourselves from a false understanding of utility—as something that merely strives for technical perfection—which has made our cities so sterile, indeed dead? For a long time people believed they could safely "pack" buildings in the cheapest and most simple-to-maintain forms, completely ignoring the question of giving expression to content and structure.

Fine buildings in earlier times were also functional, but they were not impoverished. The façades of Schinkel's buildings, for example, are quite simple systems. [Karl Friedrich Schinkel, 1781–1841, was a prominent German neoclassical architect whose work and theories were a great influence on Mies van der Rohe.] But he knew how to enrich them by drawing attention to details that were derived from the function and construction. He accentuated the windows, the doors, the edges of walls, the quoins, and thus celebrated their function. Or he would articulate the function between roof and wall with a slight exaggeration. _ Svetlozar Raèv, ed., *Gottfried Böhm: Lectures Buildings Projects*, Zurich: Karl Krämer Verlag, 1988

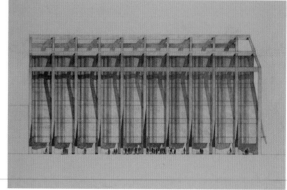

Böhm's spectacular churches displayed an inventive use of reinforced concrete; the same innovation is on view in Berlin's Peek & Cloppenburg store, this time with the unique glass sheeting for the façade.

**BERLIN 1995**
# PEEK & CLOPPENBURG
One can emphasize things in a very subtle, restrained manner; nevertheless one wishes to feel something of the event that is taking place. "Less" is not always in itself "more." A certain innate strength has to exist in the first place. When this is presented in a restrained manner, then it can become "more." _ Svetlozar Raèv, ed., *Gottfried Böhm: Lectures Buildings Projects*, Zurich: Karl Krämer Verlag, 1988

> ## IT SEEMS TO ME A GOOD THING WHEN A BUILDING HAS NOT BEEN DESIGNED ENTIRELY ON A MOMENT'S INSPIRATION. 🔳🔳

**ULM 2003**

## PUBLIC LIBRARY
Our cities don't need just new buildings. They need buildings that help make connections. What we admire in great cities is that all of their parts connect. I believe that architecture and urban planning can encourage a sense of community among human beings, and even influence their relations among one other. _ Douglas C. McGill, *New York Times*, April 18, 1986

The Public Library in Ulm draws on features from other buildings in the Old City. The pyramid point borrows from the pointed gables of the Late Gothic and Renaissance buildings in the area. The red spiral staircase is a distinguishing feature at the core of the library. The overall impression—of openness and light—conveys Böhm's intention to invite the public to experience learning.

### STUTTGART 1985
## ZÜBLIN AG HEADQUARTERS

There is nothing ordinary about the Züblin administration building. Böhm was sensitive to the materials used on buildings in the area; he designed the glass hall as an atrium that could also be for local gatherings and entertainment; and he even planted vines in an abandoned vineyard surrounding the headquarters.

The site for the administrative headquarters of the Züblin concern is in a suburb of Stuttgart. The city is surrounded by a great number of smaller suburbs, in this case for example, Möhringen and Vaihingen, both of which have their own highly individual character. These suburbs are growing together more and more, however. So far as the planning is concerned, the problem is that of finding a way to connect them without blurring the distinctions. One would like to be able to tell where one place begins and another ends, or at what point they are linked. One of the special features of this site is that it is adjoined by other developments only to the east and west. To the north and south it borders on relatively unspoiled countryside.

In the Züblin project we created two linear office blocks with a linking hall spanned between them. The development is laid out in such a way that the urban structures of the suburbs of Möhringen and Vaihingen are brought to a halt at this point but are also joined by a visible connecting link. The two green zones to north and south of the site are also linked in the lateral direction by the hall, which is in the nature of a large transparent space that draws in the landscape from both sides and unites it in its own special way. _ Svetlozar Raèv, ed., *Gottfried Böhm: Lectures Buildings Projects*, Zurich: Karl Krämer Verlag, 1988

The hall itself can be the arena for many different kinds of activities. Linked to it at ground-floor level are the lecture hall, library, canteen, and other facilities, including rooms for functions that can overflow into the hall. In addition, exhibitions can be held there and other festivities, for the people of Stuttgart know how to celebrate. Small concerts can be performed in this hall, and it is planned to stage an opera there, which I imagine could be an extremely beautiful occasion, in view of the wealth of possibilities that the space as a whole has to offer. _ Svetlozar Raèv, ed., *Gottfried Böhm: Lectures Buildings Projects*, Zurich: Karl Krämer Verlag, 1988

On one side of the hall the picture in the screed has the characteristics of an "old city," and on the other side, those of a "new city" with the church of Neviges, erected twenty years previously by the same construction company. _ Svetlozar Raèv, ed., *Gottfried Böhm: Lectures Buildings Projects*, Zurich: Karl Krämer Verlag, 1988

In the choice of materials one will always seek a point of reference in the immediate vicinity, especially when surrounding developments are of a more or less homogeneous construction. In the case of the Züblin complex, however, no single material predominated in the area. In the neighboring developments one can find all kinds of materials—brickwork, concrete, rendering, and many others. It therefore seemed sensible to us to allow the constructional constraints to determine the materials. _ Svetlozar Raèv, ed., *Gottfried Böhm: Lectures Buildings Projects*, Zurich: Karl Krämer Verlag, 1988

The formwork was struck and the surface was sprayed down after a number of hours, bringing out the true grain and color of the concrete. The color and texture become more and more attractive with time. There are few materials that age so well. _ Svetlozar Raèv, ed., *Gottfried Böhm: Lectures Buildings Projects*, Zurich: Karl Krämer Verlag, 1988

The two towers at the ends of the hall will be overgrown by plants from spacious planting boxes. The headquarters of the firm were hitherto situated near a vineyard, and in memory of this we planted these troughs with vines. In crossing from one strip of offices to the other, one passes through an arbor of vine leaves, where one can withdraw and find some peace and quiet, or where two people can meet. That is also part of life in a big firm. _ Svetlozar Raèv, ed., *Gottfried Böhm: Lectures Buildings Projects*, Zurich: Karl Krämer Verlag, 1988

### BERGISCH GLADBACH 1980
# CIVIC HALL WITH THEATER

For us architects . . . the task remains to give buildings that house representatives of the people, or at least the council chamber itself, a certain dignity that exceeds and differs from that of a bank or an insurance building. _ Svetlozar Raèv, ed., *Gottfried Böhm: Lectures Buildings Projects,* Zurich: Karl Krämer Verlag, 1988

**On his choice of materials, Böhm said simply, "I use different kinds of materials on different kinds of projects. Today we can do things with steel and glass that we could not do before."**

A cathedral, such as that in Reims, creates the impression that heaven has been drawn down to earth and firmly implanted there. City halls dating from the same period, such as those in Aachen or Bremen, are very similar to churches, so far as the dignity of the outer shell is concerned, but they appear to be raised from the ground, as if removed from the bustle of the city to a sphere that is closer to heaven, where there are fewer errors and weaknesses.

_ Svetlozar Raèv, ed., *Gottfried Böhm: Lectures Buildings Projects,* Zurich: Karl Krämer Verlag, 1988

*Bergisch Gladbach marked a major change in the materials used by Böhm, from molded concrete to glass and steel.*

I use different kinds of materials on different kinds of projects. Today we can do things with steel and glass that we could not do before. _ Gottfried Böhm, Pritzker Prize acceptance speech, April 17, 1986

## "CREATING CONNECTIONS"

It is clearly important to keep its integrity in mind when designing a building, but it is especially necessary today to consider its neighbors and to find out what they might have in common. _ Gottfried Böhm, Pritzker Prize acceptance speech, April 17, 1986

I believe the future for architects does not lie so much in continuing to consume ever more areas of open countryside with building, but in mending and restoring order to existing towns and villages by creating links between functions, structures, materials, and so on. _ Svetlozar Raèv, ed., *Gottfried Böhm: Lectures Buildings Projects*, Zurich: Karl Krämer Verlag, 1988

The 1920s and in particular the age of Mies van der Rohe taught us to regard elemental things as something important, if not absolute. In Mies's case a wall is an element in itself, one that marks a division. The floor and the ceiling are also self-contained elements in their own rights; so too is a column. Every element has its own character and would seem neither to be dependent on the others, nor to wish to enter into a relationship with them. The connections are almost coincidental, and they are hidden from sight as far as possible behind shadow joints and the like, as if it were somehow embarrassing that they were necessary at all. In classical architecture this was different. A Greek column also represents an elemental component of support. At the same time it seeks a linking role, a context. It stands boldly upright. The link with the ground is strongly underlined by the base. The same applied to the capital: the connection with the entablature is celebrated as a special event. . . .

The concept of purity of the 1920s was not confined to architecture alone. One also finds it in painting, in music, and above all in urban planning, where it has both very positive and very negative effects. . . . One merely has to think of the total segregation of pedestrian and vehicular traffic so widely implemented in recent times. In most cases this has had disastrous results, not only for the vehicular routes that have been relegated to mere "delivery streets," but in particular for the pedestrian zones themselves. . . . In the realm of urban planning, a "clean" separation of elements has brought not merely advantages but a great many disadvantages for the urban environment. I recognized the tremendous virtue in wishing to represent basic elements in a pure form; and in returning to this subject in the context of the connecting detail, it is because I think we should retain our feeling for elementary things at all costs. Nevertheless, we should also see the value of creating connections that we do not need to hide. _ Svetlozar Raèv, ed., *Gottfried Böhm: Lectures Buildings Projects*, Zurich: Karl Krämer Verlag, 1988

The problem seems to me to be that, if one tries too hard to make the details visible, one is in danger of inventing things that are seemingly essential, but to which one is not in a position to give an entirely convincing architectural form, and this in turn results in a reduction of the force of the elemental qualities. It is not important simply to make buildings richer in detail. (Various attempts in this direction can be found nowadays, including the meaningless use of historical motifs.) What is of relevance today is to allow the stimulating quality of connections, of combinations to become an event in itself. That applies as much to small details as to the general context in our cities. _ Svetlozar Raèv, ed., *Gottfried Böhm: Lectures Buildings Projects*, Zurich: Karl Krämer Verlag, 1988

## LOOKING BACK, LOOKING FORWARD

*Gottfried Böhm comes from a family of architects. He began his practice in 1947, after working for his father, Dominikus Böhm, whose Roman Catholic churches and ecclesiastical architecture were respected internationally. Gottfried Böhm cites his father as the most significant influence of his architecture. The legacy continues: Three of Gottfried Böhm's four sons are also architects.*

Even as a student I was very enthusiastic about these buildings of my father's. What fascinated me was how richly one could articulate space with weblike constructions.

The church in Riehl, Cologne, for example, with its centralized form, dates from the 1930s. Its spatial concepts, which were modern for the time, and its concrete structure were something of a sensation then. _ Svetlozar Raèv, ed., *Gottfried Böhm: Lectures Buildings Projects*, Zurich: Karl Krämer Verlag, 1988

Anyone who does not have the strength to sin will not necessarily be a saint or a good architect—more likely a bore. _ Svetlozar Raèv, ed., *Gottfried Böhm: Lectures Buildings Projects*, Zurich: Karl Krämer Verlag, 1988

I think the future of architecture does not lie so much in continuing to fill up the landscape as in bringing back life and order to our cities and towns. _ Carleton Knight III, *Christian Science Monitor*, April 25, 1986

After World War II, we cut wide gashes into the fabric of our cities the world over. As my wife tells our sons, "Our generation has built a lot, but your generation will have to work hard to heal all that." _ Bonnie Churchill, *Christian Science Monitor*, May 9, 1996

**ANTI DOGMA** When I sort of chimed in, I think there was a dogma about functionalism. . . . This opened us up to a more widespread interpretation, which told us that we could go in several directions. There was not one truth, but several truths. . . . Because at that time function was thought to be everything which was dealing with material function—but there were psychological functions, and other functions . . . also we started to branch out not within the restricted realm of architecture proper, but from architectural design to urban design, to product design, or to stage design. There were no specific borders between these. It was a fluid thing. I always had this fluidity that could sort of spread into different restricted areas and intrude into them. The same is true for the relationship between art and architecture because first, architecture is also an art. Second, you can be an artist and an architect. Today, at the end of the twentieth century, a number of artists, sculptors, and painters went into architecture. Which I think is an absolutely valid sort of proposition.

_ Hans Hollein interview by Sangleem Lee, *Space*, November 2007

# HANS HOLLEIN

**BORN:** March 30, 1934, Vienna, Austria; Died: April 24, 2014

**EDUCATION:** M.Arch., University of California, Berkeley, California, 1960; Mag.Arch., Academy of Fine Arts, Vienna, Austria, 1956

**OFFICE:** Atelier Hollein, Argentinierstrasse 36,1040 Vienna, Austria
Tel: +43 1-505-51-96, Fax: +43 1-505-88-94
www.hollein.com

**PROJECTS FEATURED:** Vulcania, Auvergne, France, 2002; Austrian Embassy, Berlin, 2001; Generali Media Tower, Vienna, 2000; Museum of Modern Art, Frankfurt, Germany, 1991; Museum Abteiberg, Mönchengladbach, Germany, 1982; Retti Candle Shop, Vienna, 1966

**I AM COMPLETELY AGAINST ARCHITECTURE BEING NEUTRAL.**

**Vulcania, Auvergne, 2002**
Natural light floods the museum through two 37-meter-high tapering shells, which are lined with gold, shimmering, stainless-steel scales.

## ❝ UNDERGROUND
## IS WHERE THE MOST POSSIBILITIES
## FOR DIFFERENT STATES OF EXISTENCE
## ARE OPENED UP. ❞

Hollein says Vulcania should be seen as a sculpted park, hollowed out from the flows of lava in Auvergne, France. He wanted people to imagine a world underneath the earth, a place where the eye is in contact with the horizon, instead of above it.

### AUVERGNE 2002
### VULCANIA
The idea of a descent into the Earth has always fascinated me. We know of Dante's descent into the inferno, and at the Vulkan-Museum presentation I deliberately used collages of Gustave Doré's illustrations to Jules Verne's *Journey to the Center of the Earth.* But for the architecture, the decisive thing is the conceptual difference. On the one hand, the tectonic construction process, the fitting together of parts, and on the other, the subtractive process, the taking away. _ Hans Hollein interview by Dietmar Steiner, *Domus,* February 1999

Vulcania is a sculpted park hollowed from flows of basaltic lava. There is no borderline with the surrounding countryside. _ Hans Hollein, arcspace.com, www.arcspace.com/architects/hollein/Vulcania

There's a very deep incision. You descend into the mountain—what is a huge cone on the ground—and suddenly you emerge out of a situation which you know is underground, and nevertheless find yourself in the open air. You lose the feeling of being above

ground or below ground. Here too there was a discussion on the legal aspects: where is ground level? At the top, or in the open air down below? That was important even for placing the emergency exit routes. Or take Piranesi's *Carceri:* do you know if they're above or below ground? _ Hans Hollein interview by Dietmar Steiner, *Domus,* February 1999

**"We must learn to think subterranean"** I come from a family of miners and smelters, all of whom were people who spent much of their lives underground. _ Hans Hollein interview by Dietmar Steiner, *Domus,* February 1999

We must learn to think subterranean. Buildings like an Imax cinema don't need any light. And with today's machines and technologies, a cubic meter of space costs the same whether it's above or below ground, and you save the expense of maintaining the façade. The important thing is thinking in new situations, psychological situations, which allow pointwise eye contact with the zero-line, the horizon. _ Hans Hollein interview by Dietmar Steiner, *Domus,* February 1999

## ▟◢ ONE PASSES THROUGH THE MUSEUM AS THROUGH A LANDSCAPE. ◤▜

Space can be freely developed in all directions. Because what Gehry has done in Bilbao may be magnificent, but it is a form of expensive sculpture. Underground, you are not constrained to create a new room above every load-bearing ceiling. You don't have these tectonic caesuras. Here, you can develop a much greater freedom, both of the life inside and of movement and possible space-formation. _ Hans Hollein interview by Dietmar Steiner, *Domus*, February 1999

When I design a subterranean building, I can create different spaces. If I excavate a space in a specific form, the next one can be set above it to the left, for example, and assume an entirely different shape. Such spaces do not have to be cubic or layered on top of each other, in contrast to conventional buildings that consist of architectonic stacking and layering. This different form principle can be conceptualized in terms of suddenly acquiring the ability to swim in all directions, like a fish in water. _ Hans Hollein interview by Susanne Titz and Chantal Jacobi, *Art of the Eighties and Seventies*, Frankfurt: Revolver, 2006

### MÖNCHENGLADBACH 1982
# MUSEUM ABTEIBERG
I did this museum in Mönchengladbach in Germany, which actually started a new idea about museums. When I did that, no architect was interested in museums; they were considered outdated operations you shouldn't be concerned with. But at Mönchengladbach I introduced a new idea of the museum as a concept building—I even used titanium zinc, and since then museums have been clad in metal. . . . Frank Gehry said at the press conference for the opening of Bilbao that without Mönchengladbach, Bilbao couldn't have happened. _ Hans Hollein interview by Justin McGuirk, *ICON 018*, December 2004

One more thing—I started using metal as a building material and as a façade material very early on and so too in Mönchengladbach. There the façades of the exhibition halls are clad in titanium zinc. . . . After Mönchengladbach, interestingly enough, the majority of museums now have sheet-metal façades.

_ Hans Hollein interview by Vera Grimmer, Sasa Bradic, and Andrija Rusan, *Oris*, vol. 7, no. 31, 2005

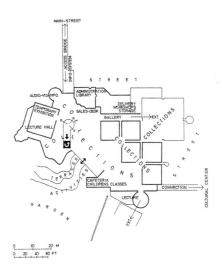

The museum in Mönchengladbach has become renown as a high point of postmodern design—the various corners, niches, array of vistas are complemented by the then-innovative use of titanium zinc.

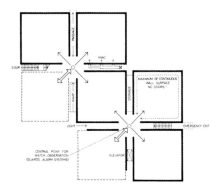

What I tried to avoid . . . is passing in a straight line from halls 1 to 20. This is what I absolutely didn't want, because I believed that this linear connection is not always a given, especially not in modernism. I simply selected a matrix, and various paths exist within that matrix. The primary idea was that one passes through the museum as through a landscape. _ Hans Hollein interview by Vera Grimmer, Sasa Bradic, and Andrija Rusan, *Oris*, vol. 7, no. 31, 2005

### "A Complex Heterogeneity and Contextualism"

The museum in Mönchengladbach . . . is based on ideas which were developed in the years before, when all the other people had been working in the neo-Corbusian or functionalist mode. These ideas spring from a belief in what I call a complex heterogeneity. Buildings had a complex content. By this I do not mean only physical content, but a content which may infer a spiritual meaning. One can divide buildings into such hierarchies in this way. When a design works in a specific setting, or "context" as it is called now, one works in a complex environment. . . . As well, the building is made up of smaller parts that refer to the neighboring buildings in the environment. In doing this they refer to certain parts of the genius loci of the area by regarding other buildings which have a metaphorical value, a metaphorical function in the community. I did this also because this notion was appropriate to its adjacent environment. _ "Interview: Hans Hollein," *Transition*, April/July 1984

Although it wasn't yet called contextualism, I think it is a perfect example of contextual consideration, i.e., how to integrate a new building into an old structure and how to integrate tendencies which are perhaps already apparent in a place into the new building without making the building look like the old ones, and so forth. This is not historicism but rather a way to find continuity within the historical situation of a given site. _ Hans Hollein interview by Matsunaga Yasumitsu, *Japan Architect*, October 1984

The interior galleries and walkways offered a completely new way to experience art—as though "through a landscape," according to Hollein.

# MUSEUM OF MODERN ART FRANKFURT
The concept of the Museum of Modern Art in Frankfurt represents a further development of my considerations regarding the construction of a museum and is based on my concrete experiences with projects realized by us before. It is further based on my involvement in fine arts, both as a receiver and as a creator of art. So a compact, triangular, chiefly symmetric building has been created. The apex of the triangle is conceived as a succinct solitaire, although integrated into the building proper. Visibility from long distances and noticeability of the design media are significant prerequisites. . . . A significant feature was to elevate the main action area of the entrance hall from a direct relationship to the street outside and also from the secondary functions like reception design and cloakroom. _ Hans Hollein, *Museum für Moderne Kunst Frankfurt am Main*, Frankfurt: Ernst & Sohn, 1991

. . . I accepted the site, the very dense site, the shape of the site, that made a triangular building. I could have made a composition of scattered pavilions of different sizes or materials. Actually, a number of the contestants did. [Hollein won the commission in a 1983 competition.] I thought this was wrong. In this case the design responded to the basic force of this simple condition of the site and I worked on it, elaborated it, and made it more complex, but not with a complexity through fracturing the building into . . . different pavilions. So I also think this is a question of how to respond to a certain task. _ "Interview: Hans Hollein," *Transition*, April/July 1984

The building is articulated by small recesses and notches as well as by the selection of materials. The main building materials are—in compliance with the characteristic style of public buildings in Frankfurt—red sandstone and plaster for the walls, copper (and aluminum) for the roofs. The stepped apex of the building is like a sculpture on an urban scale, both allowing for the urban planning aspect and assuming the function of escape route. _ Hans Hollein, *Museum für Moderne Kunst Frankfurt am Main*, Frankfurt: Ernst & Sohn, 1991

An unusual site called for an unusual approach, in this case a largely triangular shape, neatly wedged among Frankfurt's densely packed city.

## "TEACHING" ARCHITECTURE

*Teaching is an activity that Hollein very much enjoys, driven by his conviction that each aspiring architect develop a singular vision. Hollein has taught twice at Washington University in St. Louis, in 1963 to 1964 and in 1966. From 1967 to 1976, Hollein was a professor in the Academy of Fine Arts in Düsseldorf. Since then, he has been a professor at the University of Applied Arts Vienna.*

History should be understood. You should learn history, digest it, and come up with something of your own. Originality is important with me. _ Lawrence Von Bamford, "Hans Hollein: An Exclusive Interview," *Dimensions*, vol. 3, 1989

I got an invitation from Washington University in St. Louis that then was a very interesting melting pot of ideas. People like the Team Ten, Sert, Woods, Frei Otto, and Fumihiko Maki from Japan were there. _ Hans Hollein interview by Matsunaga Yasumitsu, *Japan Architect*, October 1984

You cannot teach a student how to become an important architect. It is stupid. A lot of students come because they think you have a special secret. _ Lawrence Von Bamford, "Hans Hollein: An Exclusive Interview," *Dimensions*, vol. 3, 1989

There is no secret; it's work and it's ideas, both. I prefer to teach at the academy in Vienna in small groups, and I don't give lectures. I try to be specific with each student and try to help generate their own ideas and to define his or her own departure point. This is different for each person. _ Lawrence Von Bamford, "Hans Hollein: An Exclusive Interview," *Dimensions*, vol. 3, 1989

. . . it is always individual architects who have set clear precedents that mass-produced architecture has then followed. Without Foster or Pei's wonderful towers in Hong Kong there would no doubt never have been such a skyscraper boom in Southeast Asia. It is always singular architects who set a precedent that investors and real estate developers follow. That is also part of the seismographic capacity of architects—to feel that there are new social and economic tasks that can become a precedent, a building. _ Hans Hollein interview by Dietmar Steiner, *Domus*, December 1996

## HUMAN NEEDS:
## "ARCHITECTURE IS NOT FOR BUILDINGS ONLY"

. . . architects have different tasks, not only to design buildings. In designing a house, for instance, I think that you can clearly see that the architect is not just concerned with the structure, but with the furniture and other environmental issues. _ Lawrence Von Bamford, "Hans Hollein: An Exclusive Interview," *Dimensions*, vol. 3, 1989

In a metaphoric context you might say that Abraham Lincoln was the architect of the new America. We use the term "architect" in many different ways. Architecture is not for buildings only. _ Lawrence Von Bamford, "Hans Hollein: An Exclusive Interview," *Dimensions*, vol. 3, 1989

I still see the architect, and my view has been confirmed by the history of this century, as an "all-rounder," someone capable of bringing together many different developments—social, technological, three-dimensional, and pictorial—and combining them in a concrete shape. Clear authorship of the architect for a project still exists. Utzon's Sydney Opera House is an historical example of how it is possible for an architectural form to become a symbol in its own time for an entire city. _ Hans Hollein interview by Dietmar Steiner, *Domus*, December 1996

**" . . . ARCHITECTURE IS A TOTAL ENCOMPASSING ENTITY WITHOUT STRICT BORDERS AND WALLS . . . "**

For each of the embassy's three principal functions the architect essentially made three design sections. The public area is located on the ground level, whereas departmental offices and reception areas are above.

### BERLIN 2001
# AUSTRIAN EMBASSY
*The Austrian Embassy in Berlin achieves a careful balance of expressionism and contextualism. It is a composition of sculptural and individualistic buildings that are also contextually aware of the surrounding architecture. The building's cubic and curvilinear volumes house the consular department, the embassy offices, and the ambassador's residence. The cubic blocks are in stucco and stone while the curved structure is clad in copper.*

Today's architecture speaks in structures that are geometrically rectangular and organically related to the surrounding landscape and point forward into the next millennium. _ Hans Hollein, *Structurae*, http://en.structurae.de/structures/data/index.cfm?id=s0005219

Hollein wanted the Generali Media Tower, opposite, to fit seamlessly into the Vienna skyline.

## VIENNA 2000
# GENERALI MEDIA TOWER

The high-rise is a category unto itself. . . . But this simply is a type that has always interested me. . . . The question is what the top of a skyscraper or high-rise can be like. The Generali Media Tower is complexly shaped, from various formal blocks which are thereby very narrowly tied into the integration with the city surroundings. A high-rise building was to emerge in an environment of houses from the nineteenth century, and so I continued this block matrix in part. Close by is the so-called Bundesländergebände from the first generation of tall buildings in Vienna. I reacted to this with a metal "box," pulled back from the building line, which in turn created a public space. The glass structure, which is slanted toward the top, points to the future. This was not just about an individual building, but about [an] object integrated into the urban fabric. _ Hans Hollein interview by Vera Grimmer, Sasa Bradic, and Andrija Rusan, *Oris*, vol. 7, no. 31, 2005

A living city is in constant transformation, so certain things have to change, but to make the right transition, the right kind of intervention, that is the task for many of the European cities. _ Hans Hollein interview by Justin McGuirk, *ICON 018*, December 2004

## THE HUMAN ENVIRONMENT —"WHAT MATTERED WAS SPACE"

*A persistent theme in Hollein's work has been space, both conceptually as a medium for experimentation and as interior design. In the June 1980 issue of the Italian architectural journal* Domus, *James Stirling referred to Hans Hollein as "the greatest interior designer anywhere."*

I have long been interested in using nonbuilding media to create space. I think sound can create space. To me, one of the most interesting experiences I've had was at an underground pharaoh's tomb in Egypt. I passed through a dark corridor, and experienced the reflection of sound. Suddenly, there exists a completely different sense of acoustics, and you sense this enormous space . . . _ Lawrence Von Bamford, "Hans Hollein: An Exclusive Interview," *Dimensions*, vol. 3, 1989

I think there is no difference between exterior and interior architecture. The interior of the building is as important as the exterior. You must consider the exterior and interior equally while you are designing a building. The interiors are the spaces in most areas of this world where the people live and spend most of their time. The creation of the interior and the mood which you have created are of utmost importance. _ Lawrence Von Bamford, "Hans Hollein: An Exclusive Interview," *Dimensions*, vol. 3, 1989

. . . in the United States when I gave lectures, Richard Meier said to me, "Hans, show buildings, but don't talk about and show slides of interiors, because interiors here in the U.S. are for interior decorators."

Today, the situation has changed completely. All the famous American architects—Michael Graves, Richard Meier, and others—want to design interiors, furniture, tableware, and so on. I have designed interiors for many years as a matter of fact, just coinciding to what my understanding of what human environment is. It was not a decision to follow what was acceptable as a fashion or a fad. _ Lawrence Von Bamford, "Hans Hollein: An Exclusive Interview," *Dimensions*, vol. 3, 1989

Retti Candle Shop was perhaps an unusual debut for Hollein but it was conceptually a brilliant success. The limitations of the project—chiefly size—required the architect to devise a number of solutions, including the illusionistic use of mirrors.

### VIENNA 1966
# RETTI CANDLE SHOP

**"An Architectural Manifesto"** . . . my first commission, which was a candle shop, came eight years after my diploma and then subsequently came some other smaller commissions in the form of shops, or others like the Feigen Gallery in New York (1967–69). The candle shop was a minute object, only 14 square meters large. I, of course, wanted to design a shop because that was the use of it, but I also thought it had to be an architectural manifesto. So I consciously put all my energy and ideas into this little nutshell, which addressed a series of my concerns about architecture that I had developed in the years I was not able to realize buildings, and was thinking about not only specific buildings, but about architecture in general and the background. The candle shop is an extremely functional building, including its materials, which are also extremely functional. For instance, the materials used there are materials that were just starting to be used in architecture at that time. Aluminum was one of the things that were part of this manifesto: I would not build in brick and stone, but in new materials in metal. _ Hans Hollein interview by Sangleem Lee, *Space*, November 2007

I think the illusionistic aspect of architecture is a very real component. In the creation of space, it isn't necessarily the question of building. I demonstrated this in . . . the Retti Candle Shop, by the use of mirrors. The mirrored space is altered space that you see, but, of course, cannot walk through. A planned illusion in the candle shop occurs when you come in the front and experience a cylinder in front of a mirror. What you see is half a cylinder; one half is real and one half is an illusion because of the mirrors. You comprehend the whole. _ Lawrence Von Bamford, "Hans Hollein: An Exclusive Interview," *Dimensions*, vol. 3, 1989

## "AN ARTIST AS WELL"

Unfortunately, my father died very early in my life. Through my mother I was confronted with the arts, not only with the visual arts but also with music. As a child, I was already very much interested in art, but there was no artist or architect in my family. There were engineers and specialists in steel, some of them very progressive. . . . Trying to decide whether I wanted to become a painter or an architect, I thought as an architect I could have more impact on society, and more possibility to leave something behind, standing in the middle of the city or somewhere to be seen by other generations—without having to go to a museum—and be part of their day life in the future, like the way the Gothic towers or the Baroque palaces were part of my life and my childhood. I also thought as an architect I could have the possibility to be an artist as well. I wanted to be an artist also, not just an engineer or a builder, or a building contractor. _ Hans Hollein interview by Sangleem Lee, *Space*, November 2007

## THE UNITED STATES, 1958

I have a strong affinity for America. I don't think of myself as specifically Austrian. I'm a native Austrian, of course, having experienced all the influences of this culture but have never made a point to refer to myself as Austrian. _ Lawrence Von Bamford, "Hans Hollein: An Exclusive Interview," *Dimensions*, vol. 3, 1989

In late 1958 I decided to go to the United States for two reasons: One, to get to know the United States in general—the architecture, the people, everything. Two, I had a fellowship to study in the United States. I had the option to study at Harvard, Yale, or at several other distinguished universities. However, I decided I did not want to be in an Ivy League, ivory tower atmosphere. Also, I wanted to know the everyday life of people in a large city. Because of this and because of my interest in the work of Mies van der Rohe, I selected the Illinois Institute of Technology to attend, and Chicago as the city in which to live. I stayed there for a year and then decided to go to California, where I enrolled in the University of California, completing my master's at Berkeley.

I traveled a lot during my two years in the United States, covering about 60,000 miles in my car. I saw most of the buildings that Frank Lloyd Wright had designed. Then, I did some special research on Rudolph Schindler, who at the time had not been covered at all by the publications. I also was very interested in the buildings of the American Indians, especially the Pueblos. . . . To me landscape is a very evocative element in terms of generating architectural ideas. This phase was very important for my growth as an architect. _ Lawrence

Von Bamford, "Hans Hollein: An Exclusive Interview," *Dimensions*, vol. 3, 1989

The Viennese have a very dualistic approach to life, or rather, view of life. The Viennese spirit is not only a merry and friendly one but also very mean and death oriented. This is also exemplified in the spirit of the Baroque buildings, an approach which, I think, is very characteristic of my architecture. _ Hans Hollein interview by Matsunaga Yasumitsu, *Japan Architect*, October 1984

Landscape has always been a great influence on me, but so have people—my mother, my wife, friends or teachers in the widest sense of the term, comrades-in-arms—often only encounters and experiences that lasted for seconds or minutes. _ Dirk Meyhöfer, ed., *Architectural Visions for Europe*, Braunschweig: Vieweg, 1994

## ❝❝ ARCHITECTURE ON ONE SIDE IS A RITUAL THING AND ON THE OTHER SIDE IS A MEANS OF PRESERVING THE BODY TEMPERATURE. ❞❞

I think that erotic—let's say erotic elements—are a very important part of life and a very important part of art. I don't think there can be life without eroticism. Of course you should not have blatant eroticism. You can have it in a very hidden way and to me it has a very ritual implication. I always give this example as a short definition of architecture: architecture on one side is a ritual thing and on the other side is a means of preserving the body temperature. _ Hans Hollein interview by Matsunaga Yasumitsu, *Japan Architect*, October 1984

Michelangelo had an abstract block of stone in front of him, and took something away from this given material until David appeared. Things can go wrong: maybe the neck is too long or the foot too short. But all the same, spatial imagination is essential for this task. One also needs an idea of the building in one's head. That's the way I think and work too. _ Hans Hollein interview by Dietmar Steiner, *Domus*, February 1999

I want to be remembered as an architect—and an artist—who has contributed something to architecture and to the places where my work is placed. I try to encompass many issues and also accept that architecture is not only a piece of art, but architecture is something that, besides fulfilling its material function, also has its cultural function. _ Hans Hollein interview by Sangleem Lee, *Space*, November 2007

**LIGHT AND SPACE** . . . in describing my own aesthetic, mine is a preoccupation with light and space . . . space whose order and definition are related to light, to human scale, and to the culture of architecture. Architecture is vital and enduring because it contains us; it describes space, space we move through, exit in, and use. I work with volume and surface, manipulating forms in light, changes of scale and view, movement and stasis. . . . Mine is an attempt to find and redefine a sense of order, to understand, then, a relationship between what has been and what can be—to extract from our culture both the timeless and the topical. This, to me, is the basis of style: the decision to include or exclude—choice—the final exercise of the individual will and intellect. In this way, one might say that my style is something that is born out of culture, and yet is profoundly connected with personal experience. But to gain any sense of my involvement, it is necessary to consult the work. Fundamentally, my meditations are on space, form, light, and how to make them. My goal is presence, not illusion. I pursue it with unrelenting vigor and believe that is the heart and soul of architecture.

_ Richard Meier, Pritzker Prize acceptance speech, May 15, 1984

# RICHARD MEIER

**BORN:** October 12, 1934, Newark, New Jersey

**EDUCATION:** B.Arch., Cornell University, Ithaca, New York, 1957

**OFFICE:** Richard Meier & Partners, Architects LLP, 475 Tenth Avenue, 6th Floor, New York, 10018
Tel: +1 212-967-6060, Fax: +1 212-967-3207
www.richardmeier.com
mail@rmpla.com

**PROJECTS FEATURED:** Ara Pacis Museum, Rome, 2006; The Getty Center, Los Angeles, 1997;
Museum of Decorative Arts, Frankfurt, Germany, 1984; High Museum of Art, Atlanta, 1983;
The Atheneum, New Harmony, Indiana, 1979; Smith House, Darien, Connecticut, 1965

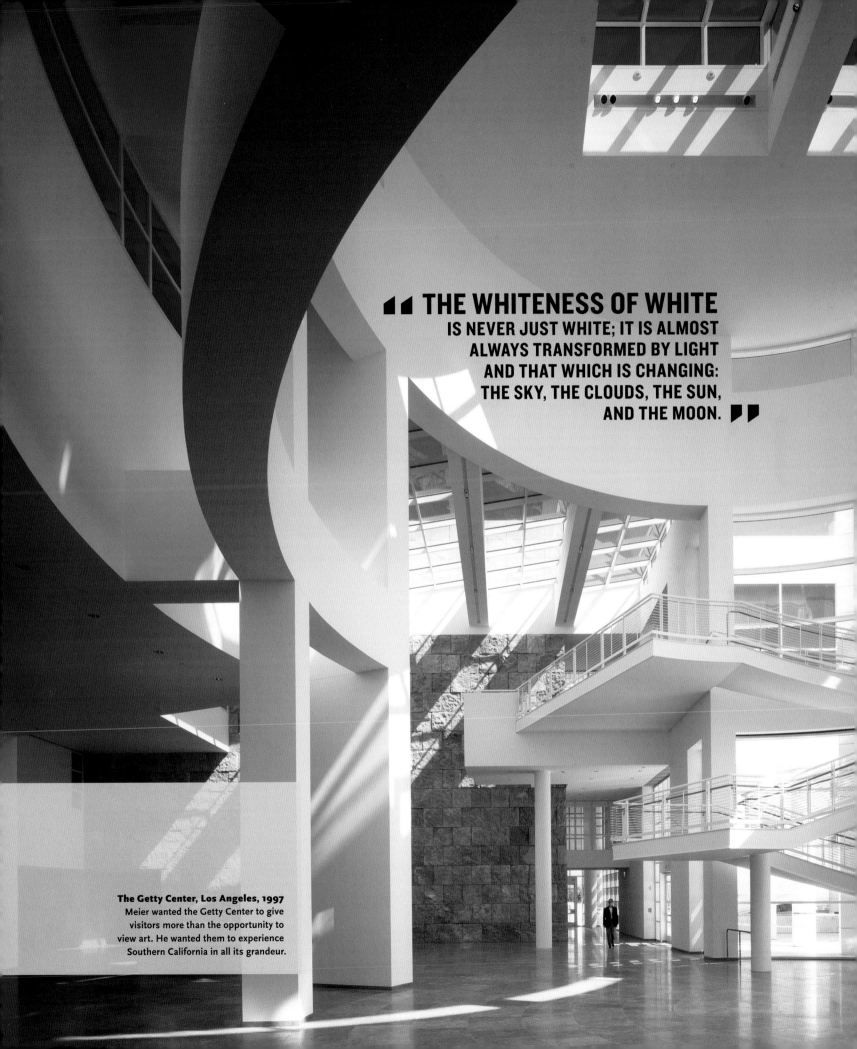

**" THE WHITENESS OF WHITE** IS NEVER JUST WHITE; IT IS ALMOST ALWAYS TRANSFORMED BY LIGHT AND THAT WHICH IS CHANGING: THE SKY, THE CLOUDS, THE SUN, AND THE MOON. **"**

**The Getty Center, Los Angeles, 1997**
Meier wanted the Getty Center to give visitors more than the opportunity to view art. He wanted them to experience Southern California in all its grandeur.

## LOS ANGELES 1997
# THE GETTY CENTER
This is *not* a white building, and for many reasons—the site, the climate, the nature of the program, etc. So inevitably it will be very different from any of my previous buildings.

_ Richard Meier, *Richard Meier: Buildings and Projects 1979–1989*, New York: St. Martin's Press, 1990

The Getty is not conceived as a giant compendium dominating the hillside. It's humanly scaled, it's diverse, and complex. And it is not some awesome presence, but rather a village-like structure of quality and distinction. Above all it is not intended to be an imperial presence. _ Richard Meier, *Richard Meier: Buildings and Projects 1979–1989*, New York: St. Martin's Press, 1990

Most villages grow over time with different architects. This is quite different—like a tiny university—a frag-

ment being planned at *one* time. It's even more like a college—The "Getty College." . . . The Getty Center is analogous to a small college campus. It's a cluster of buildings, all of which have their different identity.

_ Richard Meier, *Richard Meier: Buildings and Projects 1979–1989*, New York: St. Martin's Press, 1990

The Getty, it seemed, needed a material with a strong sense of permanence and stability, and stone seemed the right thing to mix with porcelain and glass. We also wanted a stone that wasn't too familiar, one you wouldn't associate with some other building complex. . . . It's a split-faced travertine, and we must have looked at every stone in the world before we chose it. . . . Travertine isn't unusual, of course, but this way of treating it—making it rough instead of smooth—is. We invented a new process to make it look old.

_ Richard Meier interview by Stanley Abercrombie, *Interior Design*, October 1996

Meier's stunning response to a challenging site and superlative and large collection was several years in the making. The travertine surface was unexpected and used to great effect. Light, a prerequisite of Southern California life, is encountered in all areas of the Getty, especially inside.

The experience of viewing art is part of the experience of viewing the world . . . at every turn there is an invitation here to *move out,* an invitation to look at the real world, to take in the panorama of downtown Los Angeles and the Pacific Ocean. . . . When the visitor comes to the Getty it will not be just for the experience of viewing art, but it will be to experience the grandeur of Southern California as well.

_ Richard Meier, *Richard Meier: Buildings and Projects 1979–1989,* New York: St. Martin's Press, 1990

The outdoor museum café takes advantage of the spectacular views, including the Pacific Ocean.

## LIGHT: "A TRANSITORY ELEMENT"

You can't work with light as though it were a real or solid material. It's a transitory element. . . . Some people find my architecture too open, too transparent, too light-saturated. As far as I'm concerned, there can never be enough light. That's just impossible. . . . But there are days like today, gray and overcast, a typical New York day. In my opinion it's important to be aware of the fact that it's gray. It means you enjoy the less gray days all the more. Not having the possibility of perceiving the changes in light, color, and mood of the outside world would be an extraordinary loss of quality of life for me. _ "Richard Meier: Light as a Transient Medium," *Architectural Design,* March–April 1997

It most effectively reflects the passing colors of nature: the green grass, the blue sky, the autumn leaves. It is in that sense then that white is all colors. . . . In architectural terms white is the color that most easily allows the fundamentals of building—space, volume, material—to be expressed in the most direct and clear way. . . . The whiteness allows one to perceive the difference between transparent, translucent, and opaque surfaces more easily. . . . The whiteness creates a neutral surface on which to build an experience of a space. . . . Ultimately, the use of that "white-light whiteness" allows me to pursue my basic concerns of creating space, form, and light in architecture. _ Richard Meier, *Thirty Colours,* Blaricum, The Netherlands: V+K Publishing, 2003

**❝ I AM FASCINATED BY THE WORLD OF LIGHT AND SHADOW THAT EXISTS FREE OF ASSOCIATIONS WITH SPECIFIC COLORS OR MATERIALS. ❞**

A particular challenge for me as an architect is not so much the question of how I light spaces, but of how, under the given circumstances and conditions, I light both the interior as well as the exterior spaces. It's not a question—and this is very important—of balance or equilibrium but of relationship or dialogue . . . . _ "Richard Meier: Light as a Transient Medium," *Architectural Design,* March–April 1997

Architecture deals with space, the thoughtful and meaningful making of spaces. Natural light gives mood to space and by the nuances of light changing throughout the day and changing throughout the seasons of the year natural light modifies and articulates space, space that is calm yet brimming with life. _ Yoshio Futagawa, *Studio Talk: Interview with 15 Architects,* Tokyo: A.D.A. Edita, 2002

## "WHY WHITE?"

The question I am most often asked by students of architecture following a lecture is "Why white?" . . . For me, white encompasses all colors.

. . . whiteness has been one means of sharpening perception and heightening the power of visual form. _ Richard Meier, Pritzker Prize acceptance speech, May 15, 1984

Superimposition of color would create a whole new spatial environment that I felt would be destructive to the building in relation to the landscape. _ Richard Meier, *Richard Meier: Buildings and Projects 1979–1989,* New York: St. Martin's Press, 1990

**❝ THERE CAN NEVER BE ENOUGH LIGHT. ❞**

I can't speak for all architects; I can speak only for myself. I wear a white shirt every day. Why? Because I like white. Does that mean that everyone should wear a white shirt? No. People have to do what they want to do. _ Yoshio Futagawa, *Studio Talk: Interview with 15 Architects,* Tokyo: A.D.A. Edita, 2002

... the project was conceived so as to sit between two trees very close to the base of the building. It was very important to us that it be sited this way, and we took many precautions to insure that these trees not be lost during construction. We did this with a simple ambition: to preserve the landscape which had prompted its inhabitation. But we could not have anticipated the precise way in which those trees have grown and affected the house over time. They have, in fact, created a virtual umbrella over both sides of the building, filtering light differently depending on the time of day and year and modeling its colors in ways much more intricate than we could ever have planned. I believe the success of the house lies in its capacity to absorb and enter into a dialogue with these temporal phenomena of light and context. They are, in the end, its material. _ "Essay: Richard Meier," *Perspecta*, no. 24, 1988

The Smith House, in a way, was my first building; whereas my parents' house was a project that helped me work out a lot of different things. If you look at Corbusier's work with Chaux de Fonds [Le Corbusier's Villa Jeanneret-Perret in Chaux de Fonds, Switzerland, built in 1912, which, like the Smith House, was a first commission and also for his parents], you can see that it's interesting, but he's still searching. For me, ... my whole Wrightian view of the world shifted dramatically after my parents' house. I also had to work out my whole relationship with my parents in that house, which made it a very complicated project. So the Smith House was my first architectural endeavor in the sense of finding my way as a designer. _ Yoshio Futagawa, *Studio Talk: Interview with 15 Architects*, Tokyo: A.D.A. Edita, 2002

These houses [Smith House and the Douglas House in Harbor Springs, Michigan, 1973] are not meant to look like concrete or appear like anything other than what they are: white-painted wood. The reason that the overlap joint has been eliminated, in terms of the horizontal clapboard, is very obvious: in order to get a planar reading of the surface. _ Richard Meier, *Richard Meier: Buildings and Projects 1979–1989*, New York: St. Martin's Press, 1990

**❝❝ THE DISTINCTION BETWEEN PUBLIC AND PRIVATE DOMAINS HAS BEEN A CENTRAL THEME IN MANY PROJECTS, PARTICULARLY IN MY HOUSES. ❞❞**

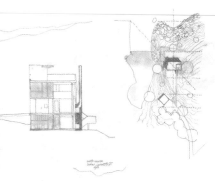

An aerial plan of Smith House and the actual residence. For Meier, the house was a sort of testing lab for various of his ideas.

### DARIEN 1965
# SMITH HOUSE
*House commissions were important in Meier's early career. In 1963 Meier launched his architectural practice, working out of his New York City apartment on a commission for a residence in Essex Falls, New Jersey, for his parents. Yet it was another residential commission, the 1965 Smith House in Darien, Connecticut, that thrust Meier into national prominence.*

I enjoy houses. . . . A house goes quickly compared to a public building. And you can do different things with houses, such as explore energy conservation by making use of location, climate, orientation to the site. _ Richard Meier interview by Robert Ivy, *Architectural Record*, September 2002

# FRANKFURT 1984
# MUSEUM OF DECORATIVE ARTS

*Richard Meier applies his rigorously high standards to a diverse range of building types, yet the museum building type has special meaning for him, going back as much as nearly twenty years ago when the comment below was made. Meier's many museums have made significant contributions to the art of museum design.*

Not too long ago someone asked me if I could choose the one building type that I preferred to do the rest of my life—what would it be? My answer was museums. Someone up there was listening, for I got my wish. _ Werner Blaser, ed., *Richard Meier: Building for Art,* Basel, Switzerland: Birkhäuser, 1990

The museum is really the most important non-secular community space that exists in the world. You see a whole cross section of people you never see in any other situation. There's no finer type of institution one can design for. _ Richard Meier interview by Stanley Abercrombie, *Interior Design,* October 1996

. . . we were invited to take part in a competition in Frankfurt for a new museum of decorative arts. Three foreign architects and three German architects were invited . . . myself, Robert Venturi, and Hans Hollein. Fortunately, I won, because it was a very important building for me. And at the same time we were working on the museum in Frankfurt, we were interviewed to do another museum in Atlanta. All we could show the committee from the High Museum in Atlanta at that time were the drawings and models for Frankfurt. On that basis we were selected to do the High Museum. So we worked on those two museums, which are both about the same size, at more or less the same time. The museum in Frankfurt had a schedule of six years, from start to completion, and the museum in Atlanta had a schedule of three years. So the High Museum was actually finished first, although it was begun afterward. _ Yoshio Futagawa, *Studio Talk: Interview with 15 Architects,* Tokyo: A.D.A. Edita, 2002

The Frankfurt museum is actually an addition to an existing building. It happens to be nine times the size of the existing Villa Metzler, but the problem was still

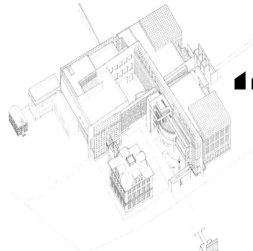

**❚❚ MY INVOLVEMENT WITH ART AND WITH MUSEUMS HAS BEEN LIFELONG. ❚❚**

how to add on to the Villa Metzler without touching it, because it's a historic monument. The solution is a series of connected pavilions, which are based on the size, scale, and dimensions of the existing villa. . . . There were a lot of aspects to what we were dealing with in Frankfurt, not least of which was that we had to preserve all the trees, which are a hundred years old. _ Yoshio Futagawa, *Studio Talk: Interview with 15 Architects,* Tokyo: A.D.A. Edita, 2002

Meier's passion for building museums allows the architect to engage with the public through the aperture of culture. Here the telltale elements of his exterior design are apparent—grid-based, glass and metal exteriors. And always the clean beauty of white.

For the High Museum of Art in Atlanta, Meier drew inspiration from the Guggenheim Museum.

### ATLANTA 1983
# HIGH MUSEUM OF ART
*Pritzker Prize laureates Richard Meier and Renzo Piano have become the most sought-after architects of museums in the world, and the High Museum of Art was able to have both architects design for them. Richard Meier was the architect for the original building, which was completed in 1983, and Renzo Piano the architect for the museum's 2006 expansion.*

It's perfectly appropriate for one architect to add onto another architect's work. That's the history of architecture, the way it's always been. _ Richard Meier interview by Stanley Abercrombie, *Interior Design*, October 1996

So the main challenge in the design of the High Museum was to determine how to house a rather diverse collection, which includes decorative art, contemporary art, and nineteenth-century art, in a museum which also has a social function. . . . As a solution, I looked at the Guggenheim Museum [1959] and decided to straighten out Frank Lloyd Wright's spiral organization of exhibition space. _ Yoshio Futagawa, *Studio Talk: Interview with 15 Architects*, Tokyo: A.D.A. Edita, 2002

. . . by separating the circulation system of the ramp from the gallery spaces, which are flat floors off the ramp, I feel that I took something of that wonderful, central, light-filled space of the Guggenheim and reinterpreted it. We have this fabulous space with the ramp, which allows you to move through the museum; and at the same time, the gallery space is kept adjacent to the circulation space. You can look from gallery to gallery, or from the gallery to the atrium space, but you don't feel that you're part of the circulation space when you are in the galleries. _ Yoshio Futagawa, *Studio Talk: Interview with 15 Architects*, Tokyo: A.D.A. Edita, 2002

> ❝ ROME IS BEAUTIFUL, BUT IT HAS TO BE A LIVING CITY, NOT SIMPLY A MUSEUM. ❞

## ROME 2006
## ARA PACIS MUSEUM

Rome is a city of light, and light here is intoxicating. So you think about . . . how do you bring light in in different ways? How do you see out, how do you see the city that surrounds you? And then in terms of materiality, this is the first modern building in Rome since Mussolini, since WWII. And as a modern building, there should be an openness, a transparency, a lightness, a use of modern materials. But at the same time, it's Rome and Rome is a city of stone, of travertine. . . . But since the Ara Pacis was moved to this site, since it was taken from another location and relocated here, it seemed appropriate to also then look back at where it was. . . . That we're not only relating to the present situation of the Ara Pacis. _ "Interview with Richard Meier, Designer of the New Ara Pacis Museum," *Musei in Comune Roma Museo dell'Ara Pacis,* September 4, 2008

Significantly, Meier's Ara Pacis Museum was going to be the first modern building constructed in Rome since World War II. The demands of the site, the public, the needs of the museum (auditorium, bookshop, additional exhibition space), and the historical surround all impacted Meier's design.

# THIS IS AS CLOSE TO A SUPER-MATERIAL THAT I'VE FOUND.

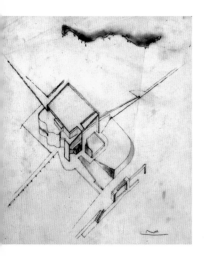

Meier's consistent design vocabulary for museums is well on display here: precision, exact planes and shapes, ramps, and a sense of self-containment. The two-dimensional plan is what Meier says is "the most convincing and fundamental expression of design ideas." The Atheneum in New Harmony, Indiana, above, was the first building to be actually constructed with porcelain and steel panels. It sits on the Wabash River and Meier's use of ramps, glass walls, and columns is reminiscent of the work of French architect Le Corbusier.

### NEW HARMONY 1979

## THE ATHENEUM
I never really thought of this before, but my work in certain geographical areas has defined periods in my career. For instance, there was a time when I worked in Middle America—Michigan and Indiana. I began my career in New York, I have worked in Europe for some time, and at present I'm doing a lot on the West Coast. I suppose you could categorize my work that way. The 70s happened to be the Midwest period. _ Yoshio Futagawa, *Studio Talk: Interview with 15 Architects,* Tokyo: A.D.A. Edita, 2002

The Atheneum didn't have to look like the historic buildings, because physically and conceptually it stood at a distance from them. It therefore could be a contemporary building, expressive of what it was. . . . So the building became like the town, as it were . . . _ Yoshio Futagawa, *Studio Talk: Interview with 15 Architects,* Tokyo: A.D.A. Edita, 2002

The Atheneum is surrounded by nature, but the site has multiple characteristics. The side by the river is different from the side with the woods. You have a closed side and two open sides; there is also the road side and the town side. They're all different, and the building has to express not only itself but also the differences among those sides. . . . So the design has to do with each particular place. _ Yoshio Futagawa, *Studio Talk: Interview with 15 Architects,* Tokyo: A.D.A. Edita, 2002

. . . the path of circulation is the primary spatial protagonist in this building, and within that the ramp is clearly the most vital element. It passes from an orthogonal setting to a 5-degree diagonal grid, putting the entire building into motion. _ Richard Meier, *Richard Meier: Buildings and Projects 1979–1989,* New York: St. Martin's Press, 1990

The Atheneum was the first building to be actually constructed with porcelain steel panels . . . _ Richard Meier, *Richard Meier: Buildings and Projects 1979–1989,* New York: St. Martin's Press, 1990

### "Super-Material": Metal Panels
I have experimented with various types of metal panel construction . . . it was the parts of the building, not its volumes, that were articulated. . . . [The] structural grid is the building's unifying element. . . . Separate functional systems can thus be read as juxtaposed layers.

The thin-skin wall is the most expressive part of the building . . . and accurately reflects the meaning of the whole building. . . . We found that there was only one company in America that could make it. . . . So we found ways of doing what had been done years ago with more or less the same technology. _ Richard Meier, *Richard Meier: Buildings and Projects 1979–1989,* New York: St. Martin's Press, 1990

## MODERNISM: "THE BABY WITH THE BATHWATER"

I see myself as part of the continuation of modern architecture, because there are valid explorations that still have to be made in its syntax. _ Richard Meier, *Richard Meier: Buildings and Projects 1979–1989*, New York: St. Martin's Press, 1990

## MODERNISM DOESN'T HAVE TO THROW OUT THE BABY WITH THE BATHWATER.

I don't think that everything has to be conceived as being new and different just for difference's sake. I do believe that architecture is related to the past, that the present is related to the past, and that we learn from the past in order to move into the future. . . . I would like to think that I can learn from Bernini and Borromini, and Bramante, as well as I can from Le Corbusier, Frank Lloyd Wright, and Alvar Aalto. _ Richard Meier, Courtesy of Richard Meier & Partners, Architects

I don't think we reinvent architecture every Monday morning with a new project. _ Yoshio Futagawa, *Studio Talk: Interview with 15 Architects*, Tokyo: A.D.A. Edita, 2002

. . . I believe that ultimately it [my work] is integrated. I believe in integration. I don't believe in collision, although I do believe that Frank Gehry works as hard at his collisions as we work at our integration. _ Richard Meier, *Richard Meier: Buildings and Projects 1979–1989*, New York: St. Martin's Press, 1990

## MEIER ON MEIER

Architecture is not the product of a natural process. It simply *is* what you make it. _ "Essay: Richard Meier," *Perspecta*, no. 24, 1988

Architecture which enters into a symbiosis with light does not merely create form in light, by day and at night, but allows light to become form. _ "Richard Meier: Light as a Transient Medium," *Architectural Design*, March–April 1997

## THE INFLUENCES OF MARCEL BREUER, GORDON BUNSHAFT, AND MUSIC

I liked to read about buildings when I was young, and I remember having a drafting table in the basement and a place where I made models. I worked one summer in an architect's office, and I worked on construction sites when I was in high school. I worked as a roofer, putting shingles on roofs. Somewhere along the line I just decided I wanted to be an architect. _ Yoshio Futagawa, *Studio Talk: Interview with 15 Architects*, Tokyo: A.D.A. Edita, 2002

As a young architect, Richard Meier developed his modernist approach to architecture in the offices of Skidmore, Owings & Merrill, under Gordon Bunshaft, and at Marcel Breuer. Breuer (1902–1981) was an influential modernist architect who studied and taught at the Bauhaus in the 1920s and emigrated to the United States in the 1930s. He taught at Harvard's architecture school, where he had such students as I.M. Pei, Philip Johnson, and Paul Rudolph. His best-known works range from specific objects (the tubular steel Wassily Chair, 1925) to such buildings as the Whitney Museum of American Art in New York, 1966.

When I was in Rome, I received a letter from Breuer's office saying that they had an opening. This was early in my travels, so I wrote back telling them I would like to come work but that I was not ready to do so at the time. I hoped that the job would still be open when I got back to America. Well, four months went by, and when I came back to New York the job was gone. So I went to work for Skidmore, Owings & Merrill for a while. After six months I got a call from Breuer's office and they said if I wanted to come I could. _ Yoshio Futagawa, *Studio Talk: Interview with 15 Architects*, Tokyo: A.D.A. Edita, 2002

I was very lucky to get the chance to work under Gordon Bunshaft. . . . I didn't really have much responsibility, but it was a very interesting office to work in and was very educational for me. But it wasn't the kind of office I was interested in. So I went to work for Marcel Breuer for three years. _ Yoshio Futagawa, *Studio Talk: Interview with 15 Architects*, Tokyo: A.D.A. Edita, 2002

## ARCHITECTURE IS THE MOTHER OF THE ARTS.

I listen to Beethoven a lot. Sometimes I play all nine symphonies in order, from the earliest to the latest, and I'm amazed by the continuity and thoroughness and beauty of his development as an artist. If you think of Mies van der Rohe, you feel the same amazement, a sense of wonder at the consistency with which his work developed over his life. If someone were to find that sense of continuity in my work, I would be very happy. _ Yoshio Futagawa, *Studio Talk: Interview with 15 Architects*, Tokyo: A.D.A. Edita, 2002

**LIVING FORCE** I belong to that generation of American architects who built upon the pioneering perceptions of the modern movement, with an unwavering conviction in its significant achievements in the fields of art, technology, and design. I am keenly aware of the many banalities built in its name over the years. Nevertheless, I believe in the continuity of this tradition, for it is by no means a relic of the past but a living force that animates and informs the present. . . . Architects by design investigate the play of volumes in light, explore the mysteries of movement in space, examine the measure that is scale and proportion, and above all, they search for that special quality that is the spirit of the place, as no building exists alone. . . . I believe that architecture is a pragmatic art. To become art it must be built on a foundation of necessity. Freedom of expression, for me, consists in moving within a measured range that I assign to each of my undertakings. How instructive it is to remember Leonardo da Vinci's counsel that "strength is born of constraint and dies in freedom." _ I.M. Pei, Pritzker Prize acceptance speech, May 16, 1983

# I.M. PEI

**BORN:** April 26, 1917, Canton, China

**EDUCATION:** M.Arch., Harvard University, Cambridge, Massachusetts, 1946; B.Arch., Massachusetts Institute of Technology, Cambridge, Massachusetts, 1940

**OFFICE:** Pei Cobb Freed & Partners, Architects LLP, 88 Pine Street, New York, 10005
Tel: +1 212-751-3122, Fax: +1 212-872-5443
www.pcf-p.com

**PROJECTS FEATURED:** Suzhou Museum, China, 2006; Grand Louvre, Paris, 1993; Morton H. Meyerson Symphony Center, Dallas, 1989; The Bank of China, Hong Kong, 1989; East Building of the National Gallery of Art, Washington, D.C., 1978; National Center for Atmospheric Research, Boulder, Colorado, 1967

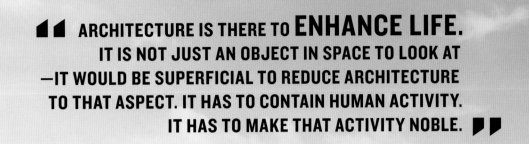

**"ARCHITECTURE IS THERE TO ENHANCE LIFE.**
**IT IS NOT JUST AN OBJECT IN SPACE TO LOOK AT**
**—IT WOULD BE SUPERFICIAL TO REDUCE ARCHITECTURE**
**TO THAT ASPECT. IT HAS TO CONTAIN HUMAN ACTIVITY.**
**IT HAS TO MAKE THAT ACTIVITY NOBLE."**

**Suzhou Museum, China, 2006**
The gray and white palette was in
keeping with traditional colors used
in ancient Suzhou to complement the
area's superior gardens, nine of which
are listed as World Heritage Sites.

### SUZHOU 2006
# SUZHOU MUSEUM
When this commission came, it was very special. I was reared in Suzhou, a city not very far from Shanghai. . . . The location [of the building site] could not be more exciting. It's a very special site, surrounded by a wonderful garden. I thought the project would touch on my relationship with my past, my ancestors, my old home. _ Robert Ivy, *Architectural Record*, June 2004

There is a difference between the Suzhou Museum on the one hand and the Fragrant Hill Hotel [Beijing, 1982] and many other projects in regard to the third dimension. They all have flat roofs. I have given the Suzhou Museum a volumetric solution, and this is a major change. _ Philip Jodidio and Janet Adams Strong, *I.M. Pei Complete Works*, New York: Rizzoli, 2008

*The main garden of the Suzhou Museum was influenced by Pei's family garden in Suzhou, the Lion Forest Garden.*

My family garden started in the Yuan Dynasty with Taoist priests. Taste declined over time, and my great-uncle changed it. He selected rocks from Lake Tai, which is not far away. They call what they do there rock farming. Volcanic rocks are selected and left to erode in the water for periods of fifteen or twenty years. They cut a hole and put it back into the water and let it erode more until it becomes a beautiful thing. This is how these rocks, quite typical of Suzhou, are made. Rocks became very important in gardens. They are like sculptures. Poets and painters worked on rock gardens beginning in the Yuan Dynasty, but they don't have painters and poets who do this anymore. . . . I sent a young architect to Shandong Province (near Korea), where there are many stone quarries. . . . Forty or fifty slices of rock were brought to Suzhou. I selected about thirty of them, and then in 2005, I went there and they were all on the ground, so I sat in the middle of what is now the pond at the table and looked at that wall. . . . There was a crane there—so they put pieces up and down as I wished. I did that for about a week and finally got something that looked reasonably good . . . _ Philip Jodidio and Janet Adams Strong, *I.M. Pei Complete Works,* New York: Rizzoli, 2008

I was not aware that I learned anything from my experiences in Suzhou until much later. When I think about it in retrospect I must say that, yes, it did have an influence on my work. It made me aware of the complementarity of man and nature, not of just nature alone. Somehow, the hand of man joined with nature becomes the essence of creativity. _ Gero Von Boehm, *Conversations with I.M. Pei: Light Is the Key,* New York: Prestel, 2000

## "A MUSEUM FOR SHANGHAI"

*In the early 1940s as a student under the tutelage of Walter Gropius at the Graduate School of Design at Harvard University, Pei questioned the universality of modern architecture. He proposed that differences in life and culture should be explored in modern architecture.*

. . . I said I would like to prove something to myself—that there is a limit to the internationalization of architecture. The reason why I said that was because there are differences in the world such as climate, history, culture, and life. All these things must play a part in the architectural expression. . . . Gropius said, "Well you know my views. But if you think you're right, go ahead and prove it. It would be very interesting." So I chose a subject, which was to design a museum for Shanghai. _ Gero Von Boehm, *Conversations with I.M. Pei: Light Is the Key,* New York: Prestel, 2000

sance to the nineteenth century, was mostly commissioned to celebrate the power of the church and the state. The art of the Orient, by which I mean China, Korea, and Japan, on the other hand, was created largely for private enjoyment. Important paintings, for example, were not hung on a wall for long periods of time. Rather, they were unrolled, looked at and enjoyed, and rolled back up again. _ Gero Von Boehm, *Conversations with I.M. Pei: Light Is the Key,* New York: Prestel, 2000

Architecture is an art form, there is no question about that. Not surprisingly, my interest in Cubism arose about the time when I sensed a certain symbiosis between it and architecture. Le Corbusier's work undoubtedly influenced me in that regard. _ Gero Von Boehm, *Conversations with I.M. Pei: Light Is the Key,* New York: Prestel, 2000

## ❝ THESE DIFFERENCES IN LIFE AND CULTURE MUST HAVE THEIR EFFECTS ON THE DESIGN OF MUSEUMS TO CONSERVE AND EXHIBIT ART. ❞

I made my design—it was quite Cubist in a way—and presented it to the faculty. Marcel Breuer thought it was the most important project that Harvard had ever produced. _ Gero Von Boehm, *Conversations with I.M. Pei: Light Is the Key,* New York: Prestel, 2000

[The Museum for Shanghai] was really a container for art objects that are very different from Western art objects. European art, from the Renais-

## "THE MUSEUM HAS BEEN A CONSTANT . . ."

I have always been most interested in civic work, and in my opinion the best civic project is a museum. The museum has been my preference because it sums up everything. . . . I learn a great deal when I build a museum, and if I don't learn, I can't design. _ Philip Jodidio and Janet Adams Strong, *I.M. Pei Complete Works,* New York: Rizzoli, 2008

### PARIS 1993
# GRAND LOUVRE

It was a total surprise that they approached me to do the project. You know the French, not to mention the Parisians—they see the Louvre as their monument, so to come to an American for a project like that is something I never expected. . . . [President François] Mitterand was a student of architecture; he had done a lot of research before he called me. He said, "You did something special at the National Gallery of Art in Washington—you brought the new and the old together."

I didn't accept the project right away, excited though I was. Instead, I told Mitterand that I needed four months to explore the project before I could accept it. For eight hundred years the Louvre has been a monument for the French—the building mirrors their history. . . . In those four months, I studied. I asked for four visits to the Louvre, one visit each month. . . . Mitterand agreed to all this. You cannot defend your design without knowing what you're designing for.

_ Robert Ivy, *Architectural Record,* June 2004

I understood that it was impossible to create a break in the architecture of the Louvre because it has such a strong identity that the eye would reject any addition to the building immediately. This is why I decided to work as a landscape designer rather than as an architect. Le Nôtre [André Le Nôtre, 1613–1700, French landscape architect] more than anyone else

By any standard, the commission to design the Grand Louvre was considerably challenging. Within the vastness of the Louvre complex, the pyramid was a bold and brilliant concept.

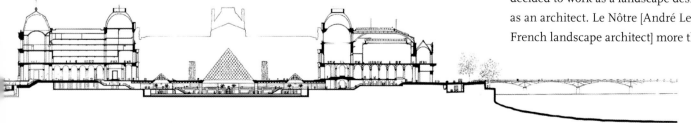

**"THE LOUVRE IS A CHALLENGE THAT YOU GET ONLY ONCE IN A LIFETIME."**

inspired me. . . . The glass reflects the Louvre and the sky. . . . I like to imagine that it is a French spirit that gives life to the fountains, to the Pyramid—even if they were designed by an American. _ Philip Jodidio and Janet Adams Strong, *I.M. Pei Complete Works*, New York: Rizzoli, 2008

Why a pyramid? . . . Formally, it is the most compatible with the architecture of the Louvre, especially with the faceted planes of its roofs. . . . As it is constructed of glass and steel, it signifies a break with the architectural traditions of the past. It is a work of our time. . . . The pyramid assumes the function of a symbolic entry to a huge complex of meandering interconnected buildings which had no center.
_ Gero Von Boehm, *Conversations with I.M. Pei: Light Is the Key*, New York: Prestel, 2000

## CONSIDERING LIGHT

[Marcel Breuer] was my best friend and teacher at Harvard. My wife and I traveled with him and his wife Connie to Greece twice. . . . While on board we rarely talked about architecture. He was very much interested in light—light which brings in shadows. He kept talking about light and shadow. If there is anything special in Greece, it is that special quality of light. So I became much more aware, let's say through his way of looking at light, of the importance of light on architecture. _ Gero Von Boehm, *Conversations with I.M. Pei: Light Is the Key*, New York: Prestel, 2000

Light continued to play a very important role in my work. Early Cubist sculpture, which I am very fond of, would be impossible to appreciate without light. As a matter of fact, almost any sculpture is impossible to appreciate without light. Therefore you can extend that to architecture. I would like to think that when I design buildings light is one of my first considerations. _ Gero Von Boehm, *Conversations with I.M. Pei: Light Is the Key*, New York: Prestel, 2000

### WASHINGTON, D.C. 1978
## EAST BUILDING OF THE NATIONAL GALLERY OF ART

This building had to relate to the other public buildings whose ensemble was first planned by L'Enfant [Pierre Charles L'Enfant 1754–1825, French-born American architect and civil engineer] in 1789 and elaborated by McMillan [Senator James McMillan, principal backer for the redesign of the monumental core of Washington, D.C.] in 1900. I felt that the new building needed to relate to the existing ensemble, especially to the West Wing by John Russell Pope. This is not unlike relationships among people in a community. Equally important, to my mind, it had to be an architecture of its time. Maybe it is the Chinese in me to give such deference to harmony: It is due to a belief that

this is a place where the whole is greater than its parts. _ Gero Von Boehm, *Conversations with I.M. Pei: Light Is the Key*, New York: Prestel, 2000

The site is a triangle. It's not an equilateral triangle, so therefore we have a problem of facing a new classic neighbor, a sister building, which is the West Building, which is a perfectly symmetrical site—east/west and north/south—and here we are: we have to join, we have to become part of the ensemble. So therefore the axis must start with the old building, and then when you go to your irregular site you have to find the one triangle that fits that, and then the leftover becomes the other triangle. And that's how it started—it's really to find an axial relationship with the sister building, and then what's left over is

another triangle. _ I.M. Pei interview by John Tusa, bbc.co.uk/radio3, August 18, 2008

### Baroque Sources: "The Secret Was in the Curvilinear Surfaces"

This site is a triangle. In the beginning I felt very uneasy about it. I felt that there was a restriction which I was obliged to overcome. Sometimes when you are trying to solve a problem, you may hit on an idea that turns the problem into an asset. That idea had to do with perspective. I had visited many great buildings, especially in Europe, which taught me the lesson of movement and perspective. . . . The most convincing example is the church I found last, a pilgrimage church called Vierzehnheiligen, in southern Germany. There I found the sensuality of church design, the voluptuousness of it. . . . At that moment I didn't know what it meant. But when I was confronted with the triangle, I thought of the church in Germany. . . . What was the secret? I think the secret was in the curvilinear surfaces found in those churches, which were the direct descendants of Borromini [Francesco Borromini, Baroque architect], animated by ever-changing light. _ Gero Von Boehm, *Conversations with I.M. Pei: Light Is the Key*, New York: Prestel, 2000

Curvilinear surfaces . . . have endless points. When you move in such a space, the perspective changes constantly. Most buildings are designed with an orthogonal grid that has only two vanishing points. A triangular grid, on the other hand, has three. It was this lesson that taught me to turn the constraint of the triangle into an asset. _ Gero Von Boehm, *Conversations with I.M. Pei: Light Is the Key*, New York: Prestel, 2000

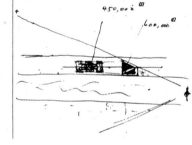

Pei needed to make the East Building of the National Gallery of Art in Washington relate to the other buildings around it, especially the West Building of the National Galley.

## "RECOGNIZING THE FORCES OF NATURE"

Nature and man working together—that is in my blood, and I brought it from China. That is why working with nature helped me to overcome the loss of my country to a certain extent. _ Gero Von Boehm, *Conversations with I.M. Pei: Light Is the Key,* New York: Prestel, 2000

. . . she [Pei's mother] was a devout Buddhist, and I remember her taking me with her to one of her regular retreats in a monastery. I had to sit there over long periods in silent meditation. That is among the things my mother taught me: to listen to the silence. _ Gero Von Boehm, *Conversations with I.M. Pei: Light Is the Key,* New York: Prestel, 2000

If I use light in my buildings it is using the forces of nature. If I use geometric structures to give some rigidity to, let's say, a huge high-rise building like the Bank of China in Hong Kong, I am recognizing the forces of nature. It seems so natural, so fundamental, and yet to be sensitized to it takes time. _ Gero Von Boehm, *Conversations with I.M. Pei: Light Is the Key,* New York: Prestel, 2000

## "WHY USE TWO STROKES WHEN ONE WILL DO?"

Why use two strokes when one will do? . . . You need to recognize and accept the constraints of a project and prioritize them so that you can get to the crux of the matter. . . . In other words, before you can deal with form, space, light, and movement—the things that go into architecture—you need to reduce very complicated requirements down to their essence. This is not easily accomplished. It takes time. You have to peel away the less significant and abstract. I learned this from Lao Tse, who eliminated words until only the essential remained; my approach is also to simplify. . . . Thus the process starts out very complicated, becomes simpler, simplest, and then returns to complexity in the development and detailing of the completed building. _ Philip Jodidio and Janet Adams Strong, *I.M. Pei Complete Works,* New York: Rizzoli, 2008

From the beginning of a design idea, through construction, to the completed building, takes many years. The process often reminds me of rock farming. _ Gero Von Boehm, *Conversations with I.M. Pei: Light Is the Key,* New York: Prestel, 2000

that problem is not to fight nature, but to join with it. _ I.M. Pei interview by John Tusa, bbc.co.uk/radio3, August 18, 2008

When I went there to explore the place I thought a lot about harmony. I recalled the places I had seen with my mother when I was a little boy—the mountaintop Buddhist retreats. There in the Colorado mountains, I tried to listen to the silence again—just as my mother had taught me. The investigation of the place became a kind of religious experience for me. And the project gave me the opportunity to break away from the Bauhaus approach. That exactly was my goal. _ Gero Von Boehm, *Conversations with I.M. Pei: Light Is the Key,* New York: Prestel, 2000

### BOULDER 1967
# NATIONAL CENTER FOR ATMOSPHERIC RESEARCH

. . . when you build a building at the foothills of the Rocky Mountains, you cannot do a fragile building—it has to be a building that can stand up to that kind of a scale. It shouldn't be like a fortress, because it has to be human, but at the same time it must be strong enough to be there. And I found the best way to solve

[Dr. Walter Roberts, founding director of NCAR and Pei's client] said, "I don't want an efficient building, I want an inefficient building" . . . "I'll tell you why," he said. "You know, scientists like to meet each other in corridors, and talk and talk and talk, and then when they finish talking they want to be away from people—they don't want to meet people, they want to be isolated." In other words, don't give me long corridors with rooms one, two, three, four, give me a build-

## ❝ I HAVE A GREAT LOVE FOR NATURE. ❞

ing that people can meet and talk—chance meeting is very important—and be isolated when he wants to. So it's a completely new set of rules—for me anyway. And so from that point on I was delighted; I said that's exactly what I would like to try. _ I.M. Pei interview by John Tusa, bbc.co.uk/radio3, August 18, 2008

The reason I was attracted to him, and I think to a certain extent he was attracted to me, is because of my love of nature. This site was on the foothills of the Rocky Mountains, and you have this huge mountain behind you, and you are to build a building there. A building's only this small, and the mountain's incredible. We talked about that a lot, as to how to deal with it, how to put a building on a site of that kind—and this was where my interest in nature came in to help me. _ I.M. Pei interview by John Tusa, bbc.co.uk/radio3, August 18, 2008

I want to join with nature, so I used a stone, from one of the mountains and built this building with stone. . . . When I use that stone—in a new way of course, not lay it, you know, stone on stone, no not at all, but pour into concrete—the color of that building turned out to match the color of the mountains. As I said to

Dr. Roberts, I said, "If you made [this] a million years [ago], it would look the same; it would be the same color." Of course that's an exaggeration, but that way the building blends with the nature. I learned that from American Indians. They build that way; they fit so well. Why? Because they're part of nature. The buildings almost blend into nature. _ I.M. Pei interview by John Tusa, bbc.co.uk/radio3, August 18, 2008

Mesa Verdes could have come out of a Cézanne painting, with its cubistic forms. The National Center for Atmospheric Research is a piece of cubistic work. _ Gero Von Boehm, *Conversations with I.M. Pei: Light Is the Key,* New York: Prestel, 2000

The naturally massive foothills of the Rocky Mountains led to Pei's apt observation, "You cannot do a fragile building." The color of the building blended with the color of the mountains. *Opposite bottom:* Pei with Dr. Walter Roberts.

## ARCHITECTURE AND MUSIC: "CONSTRUCTIONS OF THE MIND"

In China, we didn't know much about Western music. My first experience with it was at the symphony hall in Boston, which is one of the finest concert halls in the United States. I was deeply moved by the performance, which was one of Beethoven's symphonies. _ Gero Von Boehm, *Conversations with I.M. Pei: Light Is the Key,* New York: Prestel, 2000

I knew Chinese music. My mother was a flutist. Western classical music was new for me, strange as it may seem. In Shanghai I knew jazz music, but that is not classical music. So when I was first exposed to Beethoven, Mozart, Bach, and Schubert, it was all new to me, and I took to it just like a fish takes to water. _ Gero Von Boehm, *Conversations with I.M. Pei: Light Is the Key,* New York: Prestel, 2000

Architecture and music are both constructions of the mind. They need structure to give them form, which becomes the physical evidence of an idea. Then there is the element of time, which demands sequential experience within the construct which is space. Music and architecture both engage the senses with form, structure, color, and space. _ Gero Von Boehm, *Conversations with I.M. Pei: Light Is the Key,* New York: Prestel, 2000

### DALLAS 1989
# MORTON H. MEYERSON SYMPHONY CENTER

When I was interviewed for that commission, I was already in my seventies. I mentioned to the committee that I loved music, but I knew very little about music. _ Gero Von Boehm, *Conversations with I.M. Pei: Light Is the Key,* New York: Prestel, 2000

I was very frank; I told the building committee that I'd never designed a concert hall before and that, in fact, I didn't know much about them, but that I wanted to do a great one before I died. _ Philip Jodidio and Janet Adams Strong, *I.M. Pei Complete Works,* New York: Rizzoli, 2008

Pei's concept sketch shows how the architect adapted the music center to the needs of the "shoebox" acoustic shape.

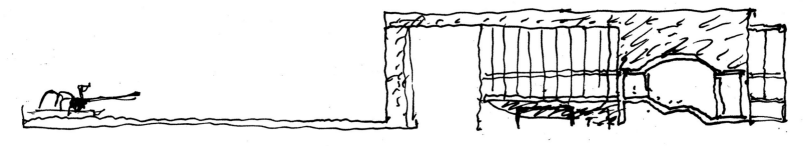

## ❝ ... AS THE SPACE UNFOLDS, YOU'RE DRAWN IN. ... THERE'S MYSTERY, SURPRISE. ❞

When I entered the scene to accept the commission the acoustician was already selected. They had already agreed that the best halls in the world are the prototypes like Vienna and Boston, which is like a double-cube shoebox. That was a given. . . . Then the question was, what I have to work with besides surrounding the hall and the interior. . . . I was very, very conservative. I wanted to be more eighteenth and nineteenth century in spirit because of the music being played there. As for the outside of the hall, I felt the need to be free. Therefore, to wrap another form around the shoebox, I started to use curvilinear forms . . . Baroque [forms]. It does have

some spatial excitement in that space for that reason. _ Gero Von Boehm, *Conversations with I.M. Pei: Light Is the Key,* New York: Prestel, 2000

Meyerson is not a better building than the East Wing [East Building of the National Gallery of Art] but spatially it is more complex. The curvature in Dallas makes the space more fluid and sensuous. You cannot just look and understand it. You have to walk and, as the space unfolds, you're drawn in. . . . There's mystery, surprise. _ Philip Jodidio and Janet Adams Strong, *I.M. Pei Complete Works,* New York: Rizzoli, 2008

"Spatial excitement" is how Pei describes the interior of the center—something not easily sensed from the outside.

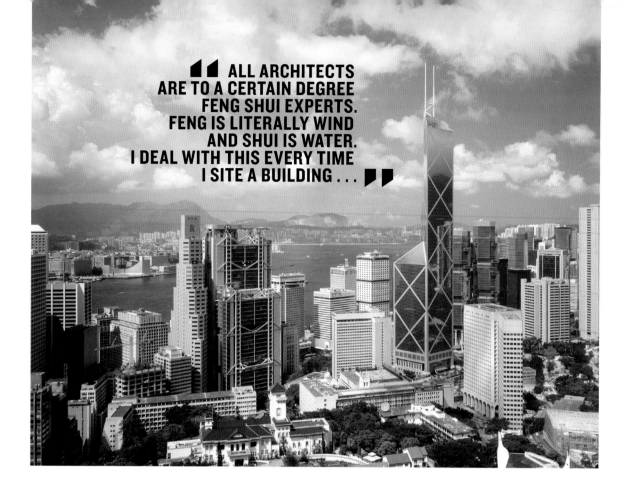

> **ALL ARCHITECTS ARE TO A CERTAIN DEGREE FENG SHUI EXPERTS. FENG IS LITERALLY WIND AND SHUI IS WATER. I DEAL WITH THIS EVERY TIME I SITE A BUILDING . . .**

I.M. Pei's father had once been general manager at the Bank of China. He had actually initiated the construction of the old Bank of China building in downtown Hong Kong. Out of respect, Chinese officials asked Pei's father if they could try to convince his son to build their modern headquarters in Hong Kong.

## THE BANK OF CHINA

In 1982, two representatives of the bank came to see my father because he was once general manager of the bank. . . . These two representatives . . . asked my father for permission to persuade me to design this building. It was a very Chinese kind of gesture of respect. . . . He said that designing their building was my decision, and they should ask me. That's what they did, and I accepted. Incidentally, my father initiated the construction of the old Bank of China building in Hong Kong in the twenties. He was the manager at that time. _ Gero Von Boehm, *Conversations with I.M. Pei: Light Is the Key*, New York: Prestel, 2000

*While the Bank of China commission had personal relevance to Pei, the project came to him with many obstacles already in play, most significantly the site conditions. Pei accepted the Bank of China commission based on a land swap and a new road. In addition to the public feng shui criticism, the Bank of China commission was fraught with controversy. Nonetheless, as a client, the Bank of China supported him throughout the process.*

This site is surrounded, girdled, by flyovers, highways, and consequently the noise of the cars moving around is a concern to us. . . . That is why we put the water gardens on both sides of the building. _ I.M. Pei in conversation with Bernhard Leitner, May 1985, "Oases of Sound in Traffic Noise" *Daidalos*, no. 17, 1985

[Feng shui] has its roots in the worship of the forces of nature, which sometimes degenerated into a form of superstition. When you design buildings in Hong Kong, you cannot get away from that problem. . . . As soon as we made our design public, I was immediately attacked—just as fiercely as I was attacked for the Louvre, but for entirely different reasons. For instance, they attacked our building because it had too many sharp corners. They said, "The corners are like the blades of a sword, which will bring bad luck to one's neighbors." There were many other objections. Fortunately, my client supported me to the end. _ Gero Von Boehm, *Conversations with I.M. Pei: Light Is the Key*, New York: Prestel, 2000

## FROM EAST TO WEST

In Suzhou I was very much conscious of the past, but in Shanghai I saw the future or the beginning of the future. The new buildings that went up in Shanghai obviously had an influence on me. I was quite taken, as a matter of fact, that they were able to build taller and taller buildings. That was very unusual. In Suzhou we had only one-, two-, or three-story buildings and that was all, but in Shanghai they were building ten, twenty, and thirty stories. So I became interested in architecture, largely because of that. _ Gero Von Boehm, *Conversations with I.M. Pei: Light Is the Key*, New York: Prestel, 2000

I almost never missed a film by Buster Keaton, Harold Lloyd, Charlie Chaplin, or Bing Crosby. Crosby's films in particular had a tremendous influence on my choosing the United States instead of England to pursue my education. College life in the United States seemed to me to be mostly fun and games. Since I was too young to be serious, I wanted to be part of it. _ Gero Von Boehm, *Conversations with I.M. Pei: Light Is the Key*, New York: Prestel, 2000

I did study with Walter Gropius [at Harvard University], the former director of the Bauhaus, but I was never a disciple like many others. His theories never struck an inward chord, which is why I turned to Mies van der Rohe as well, once I'd graduated. That may sound obvious to you—that's how people do it nowadays, going from one thing to another. But it was different then. If Gropius had got wind I was going to Mies, he'd have been beside himself. You had to stick to a single school of thought. _ Hanno Rauterberg, *Talking Architecture: Interviews with Architects*, Munich: Prestel, 2008

After MIT and Harvard, I was ready to go home, but the country was at war—civil war. I was ready to return, but my father told me to stay. That was the best advice I had ever received. I am deeply grateful to him for that. _ Gero Von Boehm, *Conversations with I.M. Pei: Light Is the Key*, New York: Prestel, 2000

## "ARCHITECTURE IS AN OLD MAN'S BUSINESS"

When two of my sons wanted to be architects, which is in fact what they are now, I was rather negative about it. I said that it is a rather difficult life. To be an architect you have to have a great love for the profession that you are entering into, and success does not come early. It is an old man's business. You have to work for many years before you are recognized or given the opportunity to do work on your own. We are dealing with a fairly large investment of capital. People don't just choose a twenty-five-year-old to design an office building. A small house perhaps, if you are lucky. . . . I did not encourage them to study to become architects, nor did I discourage them. When they said that they wanted to, I said, "Alright then, go ahead." _ Gero Von Boehm, *Conversations with I.M. Pei: Light Is the Key*, New York: Prestel, 2000

. . . I'd like to be a sculptor. I envy them their freedom . . . . _ Hanno Rauterberg, *Talking Architecture: Interviews with Architects*, Munich: Prestel, 2008

. . . if I start with only form-making, I would be a sculptor; I wouldn't be an architect. For an architect you have to put all these things together before you invent a form. You have to take many things into consideration at one time. But form is not unimportant—in fact . . . it's not the be all and end all. You don't just start with the form and fit function in willy-nilly—that I don't do, and you cannot be successful if you do that. _ I.M. Pei interview by John Tusa, bbc.co.uk/radio3, August 18, 2008

. . . to me China has never totally disappeared. I've been living in America for sixty-eight years now, and I feel Chinese. Isn't that odd? I got myself a new skin but inside everything was already there. . . . Sometimes I feel inspired by the traditions of Chinese calligraphy and sometimes by a Western artist such as Anselm Kiefer, whom I consider one of the greatest painters. _ Hanno Rauterberg, *Talking Architecture: Interviews with Architects*, Munich: Prestel, 2008

## COMPLETING A CIRCLE

When has it ever been possible for one architect to learn so much and build in so many places? When was it possible for a Chinese to go to America and then subsequently design buildings for Europe? Or for Asia, where now, at the end of my life, I'm building a museum, in my hometown. _ Hanno Rauterberg, *Talking Architecture: Interviews with Architects*, Munich: Prestel, 2008

## ARCHITECTURE AS SOCIAL RESPONSIBILITY

You know the experience of being excited and encouraged and delighted by a successful building. You see photographs of a building, you read about it, you have art history lectures about it, and your reaction is so-so. Then you visit it, and suddenly you surprise yourself—you are surprised by the reaction you have to the building. You can be absolutely overwhelmed. You see it for a moment, and that's it for life—you never see the building in that way again—but you know you've had a great moment. That's one way. The other way is to wear the building like an old shoe, and it gives you a lifetime of pleasure.

That's where the process of design begins. It begins really with the user and the viewer. You have two people who are involved: the people who use and the people who pass by, the people who see it every day and the people who see it once or are conscious of it as a part of their cultural heritage. _ Kevin Roche, "A Conversation," *Perspecta,* no. 19, 1982

# KEVIN ROCHE

**BORN:** June 14, 1922, Dublin, Ireland

**EDUCATION:** B.Arch., National University of Ireland, Galway, Ireland, 1945

**OFFICE:** Kevin Roche John Dinkeloo and Associates LLC, 20 Davis Street, P.O. Box 6127, Hamden, Connecticut, 06517-0127
Tel: +1 203-777-7251, Fax: +1 203-776-2299
www.krjda.com

**PROJECTS FEATURED:** Bouygues SA Holding Company, Paris, 2006; Knights of Columbus Headquarters, New Haven, Connecticut, 1969; Oakland Museum of California, 1969; Ford Foundation Headquarters, New York, 1968; The Metropolitan Museum of Art, New York, 1967–2007; IBM Pavilion, New York World's Fair, New York, 1964

**THE GREATEST REWARD IN BUILDING IS ...THE OPPORTUNITY TO SERVE.**

**Ford Foundation Headquarters, New York, 1968**
Roche transformed the lobby of a postwar office building into a living design element. He built a 12-story, glass-roofed garden. His decision to do so came at a time when public space in New York was disappearing.

**❝ . . . THIS IS NOT JUST ANOTHER OFFICE BUILDING, BUT AN ENTIRELY NEW ANIMAL. ❞**

NEW YORK 1968
## FORD FOUNDATION HEADQUARTERS

In the Ford Foundation, I was trying to explore several different things. I was convinced that as buildings got bigger and bigger they simply could not be a multiplication of an interior grid such as the Seagram Building [New York office building designed by Mies van der Rohe, completed in 1958]—such has happened everywhere all over the country when almost every building was a box. I was convinced that one had to introduce a series of scales as existed in traditional architecture, starting with the human scale which was brought up to the next level, and so on to a final scale which is suitable for the whole building and a scale suitable for the parts.

The importance of what Roche calls "the human scale" factored into the elegant headquarters of the Ford Foundation.

That was one interest; the other was the method of construction. I was attempting to construct the building in the same way as highway engineers construct bridges, to use concrete for bearing and steel for spanning, so the columns are all poured and have bearing pockets into which the spanning steel beams are inserted. _ Francesco Dal Co, *Kevin Roche*, Milan: Electa, 1985

. . . the Ford Foundation is a much more ambitious building on many levels because it begins to address the problem of encouraging people relationships. The sense of community. The sense of family, which is the purpose of the building. _ Francesco Dal Co, *Kevin Roche*, Milan: Electa, 1985

## "I'D LIKE AN ENGAGEMENT DEALING WITH PEOPLE"

The beginning of design in a project is "the user." What is the user going to expect, what is the user going to experience, and how is the user going to be rewarded from the building? So I start there, not with the structure, not with the axes, not with the plans, and not with the colors. I start with individuals—"the psyche." Because that's an architect's charge. That is our social responsibility. That's what we can contribute to society. _ "Kevin Roche," *Space*, July 2006

I like to start not with the person who is hiring us, but with the person who is intimately going to be using the building—in the case of an office building, the office worker. I have interviewed thousands and thousands of office workers, laboriously asking them, "What do you want? What do you see? What do you care about?" and it is a very humbling experience. I recommend it to you when you are practicing architecture, to really talk and understand and listen, because we as architects tend not to. We tend to decide, "This is what is going to be," but we should never start that way. We should start with the person who has to use the building. _ "A Way of Saying 'Here I Am': *Perspecta* 40 Interviews Kevin Roche," *Perspecta*, no. 40, 2008

Ultimately, a building—a great building—touches in all ways; it touches in the local language, the precise and technical, and it touches in the universal language, which is the emotional and intellectual. The skill is to create a language that the scholar and the artist and the common man understand without being conscious of the structure or the form and syntax; to penetrate to the ideas and emotion is the circumstance of all great art. _ Francesco Dal Co, *Kevin Roche*, Milan: Electa, 1985

Architecture isn't an abstraction. It's very much involved in the day-to-day life of people. It's a very utilitarian art, if I may say. _ "Kevin Roche," *Space*, July 2006

## PARIS 2006
# BOUYGUES SA HOLDING COMPANY

While I may have a reputation for designing many corporate headquarters, in fact, I wish I had had an opportunity to do more. It is rather like having a reputation for being a great lover, one only wished it were true. . . . I really like to do such buildings because corporations are tremendous clients and because there are great opportunities to exercise one's sense of social responsibility, even in some cases where there are unsympathetic management attitudes, although that is the exception. _ Francesco Dal Co, *Kevin Roche*, Milan: Electa, 1985

. . . we introduced the idea of these living rooms into large buildings. I draw the analogy that an office building is the same as a home. It has the same elements: a front door, which identifies it; a living room, which is the community space; a dining room, which is also a communal space; and a garage. It has many of the same elements. The family gets together in the kitchen or in the dining room or in the living room, and it is in that act of getting together that the family establishes relationships between people. _ Francesco Dal Co, *Kevin Roche*, Milan: Electa, 1985

**❝ WE SHOULD START WITH THE PERSON WHO HAS TO USE THE BUILDING. ❞**

The Bouygues Building may look small from the front, but it contains an auditorium, offices, and dining rooms with garden views.

## THE ARCHITECT AS "HANDYMAN"

The role of an architect is service. You are a servant of the community. You are in a way a "handyman." _ "Kevin Roche," *Space*, July 2006

. . . my passion is to build buildings where you can control the interior as well as the exterior and where you have an opportunity to provide an environment for people that are working, because I'm mostly concerned about the awful boredom. It's almost like paid slavery. It's not something that humans are capable of, so there are many possible kinds of excitement. You end up in an office, punching in like factories seen in Charles Chaplin's movie about the twentieth century, *Modern Times*. I'd like to think that we can do something, and I'd like an engagement dealing with people. _ "Kevin Roche," *Space*, July 2006

Remember that very often the greatest reward in building is not the pleasure of designing, but the opportunity to serve which the building gives you. It makes me apprehensive, though, when I design a factory and I think of the guy standing there eight hours a day at the machine. It's hard not to look away from him. You put a little skylight up there, but the guy is still standing at the machine, and you haven't done anything for him. What you really do is walk away from the problem when you can't deal with it; so often that happens. You can't solve all the problems, but you can have a desire to deal with people's needs, to deal with the heart of the matter, as best you can. _ Kevin Roche, "A Conversation," *Perspecta*, no. 19, 1982

The Knights of Columbus is in keeping with Roche's interest in older American cities, and gives him the opportunity to refine the regional skyline.

## NEW HAVEN 1969
## KNIGHTS OF COLUMBUS HEAD-QUARTERS

Now, in New Haven, we were confronted with the problem that we had a site along the highway . . . a very small site for a relatively large building of some 300,000 square feet. So we automatically got into a high-rise building. . . . It seemed to be a building which would be seen from all directions. And, I think that's justified, particularly if you drive on the highway. You are conscious of the sense of movement around this tower. _ John W. Cook and Heinrich Klotz, *Conversations with Architects*, Westport, Conn.: Praeger Publishers, 1973

**"A Power Plant"** [The building has] nothing to do with medieval Europe, nothing to do with Louis Kahn. At that time we were working on the Fine Arts Center for the University of Massachusetts [1975], which is in Amherst, and I had to drive there quite frequently. . . . There was a power plant which had four large chimneys, which were braced together by some steel trusses. After passing it several times, I was impressed by the extraordinarily strong, arresting form that these four cylinders produced and the wonderful bridging quality of the steel between.

Before we ever got the commission for the Knights of Columbus, I made a sketch of a high-rise building which would have four cylinders with spanning steel in between. I was just so struck by the image. _ Francesco Dal Co, *Kevin Roche*, Milan: Electa, 1985

**Scale** Monumental architecture is something I don't want any part of. I don't believe in it. I don't think it has any part in our society. . . . That is certainly not the intention of the Knights of Columbus Building in terms of design. _ John W. Cook and Heinrich Klotz, *Conversations with Architects*, Westport, Conn.: Praeger Publishers, 1973

I have spent a great deal of time thinking about scale and studying it, and on the one level it is really an investigation to understand the nature of scale and how it affects buildings and how it affects people, and I have deliberately overscaled things just to see what the effect is in real life. _ Francesco Dal Co, *Kevin Roche*, Milan: Electa, 1985

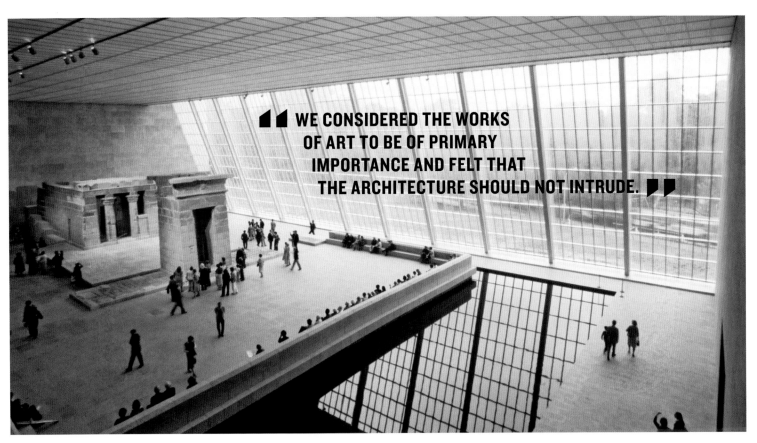

**WE CONSIDERED THE WORKS OF ART TO BE OF PRIMARY IMPORTANCE AND FELT THAT THE ARCHITECTURE SHOULD NOT INTRUDE.**

### NEW YORK 1967–2007
## THE METROPOLITAN MUSEUM OF ART

*It was more than four decades ago that Kevin Roche John Dinkeloo and Associates began master planning for The Metropolitan Museum of Art. The first phase, starting in 1967, was the redesign of the urban plaza in front of the museum. Since then, the firm has designed some of the museum's most important additions: The Lehman Pavilion, The Sackler Wing for the Temple of Dendur, The Michael C. Rockefeller Wing, The New American Wing, and The Wallace Galleries for Twentieth Century Art.*

. . . when the building and landscaping are entirely finished, you will begin to see the original intended effect of urban architecture and park architecture forming one building. We were being sympathetic to the park [Central Park]. We were trying to not extend the ponderous formal architecture of the original street building (which would be inappropriate) into the park. . . . We considered the works of art to be of primary importance and felt that the architecture should not intrude. And when we do make an archi-

tectural expression, it is in the garden courts, which are not gallery spaces. . . . These are the areas that I consider to be the public community space. They are places to rest and to relax and to get away from the intense experience of the museum, and so were introduced for that purpose. These spaces are where we make our architectural statement. The rest of the space is background for the collections. _ Francesco Dal Co, *Kevin Roche*, Milan: Electa, 1985

When designing additions to The Metropolitan Museum of Art, Roche said he didn't want to extend "the ponderous formal architecture of the original street building" into the green space.

# ❝ . . . IT WAS VERY 'CALIFORNIAN,' . . . THE RELAXED QUALITY. ❞

Roche designed everything at the Oakland Museum of California very low in order to offer select views all around. He combined stairs with side walls and got "miles of seats," rather than inserting benches.

### OAKLAND 1969
## OAKLAND MUSEUM OF CALIFORNIA

We discovered almost immediately that there was really no client, in a way. There was no program. Everybody wanted to build a museum, but nobody had stopped long enough to think about exactly what that meant. So it was a unique opportunity. _ John W. Cook and Heinrich Klotz, *Conversations with Architects*, Westport, Conn.: Praeger Publishers, 1973

Eero Saarinen had died in September of 1961, and John Dinkeloo, my partner, and I were interviewed at the end of that month. . . . We were completely unknown to them; we had no reputation, so it was very brave of them to select us. . . . We were suddenly confronted with the question of what a museum should be, and what role it should play in the community. _ John W. Cook and Heinrich Klotz, *Conversations with Architects*, Westport, Conn.: Praeger Publishers, 1973

. . . recognizing the need for some greenery, and interlocking these various museum uses, creating this space to which people would actually come, and making a sort of general-purpose public space,

which would not be a big, draft plaza—all these things came together in the idea of stepping the levels of the museum. You have art on the higher end, then cultural history in the middle, and natural history at the lower end. There are offices related to each of these areas, as well as special gardens, a changing gallery, an auditorium, classrooms, a lecture hall, and a restaurant.

In a museum, one's attention span is short, especially for children. You really should be able to get out and look at something outside. You can walk out onto a lawn which slopes away from the window so that you can see more green than if it were level . . . _ John W. Cook and Heinrich Klotz, *Conversations with Architects*, Westport, Conn.: Praeger Publishers, 1973

. . . everything in it is designed very low, in order to make possible a better view. All these walls are designed to be sat upon. They are all 20 inches high. All over the place, we combined the stairs with side walls and got miles of seats, rather than getting into the bench world. _ John W. Cook and Heinrich Klotz, *Conversations with Architects*, Westport, Conn.: Praeger Publishers, 1973

## INFLUENCES: EERO SAARINEN, MIES VAN DER ROHE, AND CHARLES EAMES

*Kevin Roche spent a semester studying with Mies van der Rohe at the Illinois Institute of Technology, but it was his eleven years in the office of Eliel and Eero Saarinen in Bloomfield Hills, Michigan, that profoundly developed and sharpened Roche's views about architecture and the notion of service.*

### "NEVER GIVE UP"

Everything I know, I learned from Eero really. And his approach to things: How to work, the consistency, and the endless "never give up" sort of attitude; you keep at it, keep at it, keep at it, until you feel that you've got it right. And then the whole craft of how to explain that to a client; because as you know most architects aren't very good at explaining or communicating . . . in terms that are understandable for the layman. _ Kevin Roche interview by Ellen Rowley, *Irish Journal of American Studies*, Issue 1, Summer 2009

I was there for eleven years. . . . The firm was expanded to about one hundred people and a whole variety of different projects were undertaken. My role really began to be one of being as we are sitting here, having a conversation with Eero as he designed. We would have conversations about the project, and I would translate it to people who were actually working on the project and supervise them. . . . What I was fond of him for was his ability to take a fresh look at what the nature of the problem was and to draw solutions from that. And those solutions gradually applied to the buildings very practically. The buildings function economically, but at the same time they also became a representative architecture of our time. _ "Kevin Roche," *Space*, July 2006

And since I was an unreconstructed Miesian and had very firm ideas and could argue with him, he [Saarinen] liked to argue with me. I became a very close family friend. As a bachelor, I was always available, almost an adopted son. He was extraordinarily generous to me as he was to many people. In the middle fifties the office got bigger and he was beginning to release control over some projects because, even though Eero wanted to embrace everything, his mind worked like a concentrated beam. _ Francesco Dal Co, *Kevin Roche*, Milan: Electa, 1985

There was a great kind of intellectual intercourse, as if one were part of a world community. Eero, in a sense, was the opposite of Mies in his ambition to embrace everything. Mies wanted to pull back all the layers and get to the heart. Eero wanted to embrace the entire body. _ Francesco Dal Co, *Kevin Roche*, Milan: Electa, 1985

### "AN ABSOLUTIST ENVIRONMENT"

*Before working for Eero Saarinen, Kevin Roche emigrated to the United States in 1948 from Ireland to study with Mies van der Rohe at the Illinois Institute of Technology in Chicago.*

I had a brief encounter with Mies where I learned that there is a right and a wrong way, and the wrong way was any way other than his. But Eero didn't have a right and a wrong way. He had an almost research approach to his buildings. _ "A Way of Saying 'Here I Am': *Perspecta* 40 Interviews Kevin Roche," *Perspecta*, no. 40, 2008

Mies was a wonderful teacher. He didn't speak very much because his English wasn't that great, but he had such a formidable presence. _ "Kevin Roche," *Space*, July 2006

Mies had a perspective on architecture that was absolutely black and white. There was nothing in between. It was either his way or the wrong way. For Mies, if you put things together incorrectly, you were totally out. It was very unforgiving, but very good. I am exaggerating, of course, but I would recommend that all young architects try to find and immerse themselves in an absolutist environment for a period of time. It is a very, very good thing for a young architect to experience. Nothing is better for a young person than to meet somebody who has total conviction about their architecture. _ Kevin Roche interview by Jeffrey Inaba, *Volume*, no. 13, 2007

### "CHARLES HATED ARCHITECTS"

One of the people who always interested me was Charles Eames. Charles hated architects and all their pretensions. He had an ability to address the heart of the problem as he saw it. He dealt with process always, very carefully and methodically; he searched and searched. He had no preconceptions, but just worked his way through. _ Kevin Roche, "A Conversation," *Perspecta* no. 19, 1982

IBM's pavilion at the World's Fair in New York featured a large ellipsoid stamped with the company's well-known logo. An elevation, seen opposite, of the pavilion.

# IBM PAVILION, NEW YORK WORLD'S FAIR

*Initially, Eero Saarinen and Charles Eames were commissioned to design the IBM Pavilion. Saarinen died in 1961, leaving Kevin Roche and John Dinkeloo, both associates in his office, to complete the outstanding projects, which included the IBM Pavilion and working with Eames.*

About the same time, also, IBM was beginning to think of their 1964 World's Fair Pavilion. Eero and Charles Eames had been requested by IBM to design it some months prior, but Eero died before they had done any work. Charles was not at all sure that he wanted to continue the project with us; however, after some deliberation he and IBM agreed to proceed with us, and this again was a significant statement of confidence.

_ Francesco Dal Co, *Kevin Roche,* Milan: Electa, 1985

## "I HAD NO ARCHITECTURAL BACKGROUND . . ."

I had a very happy childhood. After the independence of Ireland, my father was involved in the whole program of putting farmers together. And when I was young, my parents had wood and metal workshops, so I could work in these. I got a very good education in carpentry, metalwork and welding, and all these things. _ "Kevin Roche," *Space,* July 2006

I had no architectural background in my family, no references at all. I did grow up in a small town with about 2,000 people in the south of Ireland. Not Dublin. There was a castle built by English settlers. I can't say they had much influence on me, but architecture, designing buildings, was something I always wanted to do. I don't know why, even in the early ages. _ "Kevin Roche," *Space,* July 2006

I decided to come to the United States, and I applied to IIT where Mies was, to Harvard, and to Yale. I got accepted by all three. I decided to go to Mies because I felt that he was the person. . . . _ "Kevin Roche," *Space,* July 2006

## CULTIVATED ARCHITECTURE

An architect can have some of the sculptor genes, some of the painter genes, some of the performance genes, and some of the genes of the reformer—the reformer, in the sense of someone who strives to do better—or the genes of the person who wants to serve. You can have all of those and all are useful and indeed necessary to a successful practice. _ Kevin Roche interview by Jeffrey Inaba, *Volume,* no. 13, 2007

I do not particularly think in terms of style. One lives in one's time, however, and there are many people investigating many ideas and all of this is in the air and one is part of that, but I am not attempting to be a leader in a stylistic movement; I have no interest in that. _ Francesco Dal Co, *Kevin Roche,* Milan: Electa, 1985

Architecture is not an isolated activity. It's very much a part, even an appendage, of the general movement of society. Sometimes we architects would like to think that we lead, but of course we don't. _ John W. Cook and Heinrich Klotz, *Conversations with Architects,* Westport, Conn. Praeger Publishers, 1973

. . . it's a great profession, it really is. The only regret that I have is that as a group, we architects don't take the responsibility of service to the community as seriously as we should. We could contribute just as much to the well-being of the community and the human condition as the medical profession if we could create the right kinds of living environments and respect nature. . . . Modern architecture never really produced a livable environment. Building a livable environment isn't the foremost objective of architecture today. It should be. It should be our reason for being architects. _ Kevin Roche interview by Jeffrey Inaba, *Volume,* no. 13, 2007

# 19 81

**DEFYING DEFINITIONS** For many architects working with the abstract vocabulary of modern architecture—Bauhaus, International Style, call it what you will, this language has become repetitive, simplistic, and too narrowly confining, and I, for one, welcome the passing of the revolutionary phase of the Modern Movement. . . . Today we can look back and again regard the whole of architectural history as our background, including, most certainly, the modern movement—High Tech and all. Architects have always looked back in order to move forward, and we should, like painters, musicians, and sculptors, be able to include "Representational," as well as "Abstract" elements in our art. . . . So, freed from the burden of utopia but with increased responsibility, particularly in the civic realm, we look to a more liberal future, producing work perhaps richer in memory and association in the continuing evolution. . . . [In] addition to Representational and Abstract, this large complex I hope supports the Monumental and Informal, and the Traditional and High Tech. _ Robert Maxwell, ed., *James Stirling, Writings on Architecture*, Milan: Skira, 1998

# JAMES STIRLING

**BORN:** April 22, 1926, Glasgow, Scotland; Died: June 25, 1992

**EDUCATION:** B.Arch., University of Liverpool, Liverpool, United Kingdom, 1950

**PROJECTS FEATURED:** Number 1 Poultry Office Development, London, 1996; Arthur M. Sackler Museum, Harvard University, Cambridge, Massachusetts, 1985; Neue Staatsgalerie, Stuttgart, Germany, 1983; Hall of Residence, University of St. Andrews, Scotland, 1968; Faculty of History, University of Cambridge, England, 1967; Department of Engineering, University of Leicester, England, 1963

**" I'VE ALWAYS BEEN A DESIGNER WITH WIDE-RANGING INTERESTS AND PERHAPS ECLECTIC TENDENCIES . . . "**

**Neue Staatsgalerie, Stuttgart, 1983**
James Stirling's design for the addition to the
Alte Staatsgalerie combined references to the
monumental style of the nineteenth century
and the vocabulary of functionalist architecture.
This view shows the open-air rotunda.

## ❝ ALL PUBLIC BUILDINGS SHOULD DO TWO THINGS AT LEAST: THEY SHOULD SATISFY THE CLIENT, AND MAKE A GIFT TO THE CITY. ❞

The u-shaped galleries echoed those in the original museum, though here Stirling's wave of windows introduced an element of playfulness. Above, Stirling placed a pedestrian walkway that cut diagonally across the property.

**STUTTGART 1983**

### NEUE STAATSGALERIE It could be
said that nearly all our projects are vernacular. . . .
You could actually say that the Staatsgalerie was
vernacular in its relationship to other historic
museums in Germany in the context of Stuttgart,
the materials used, and so on. You might say it
had a kind of vernacular relationship to the neo-
classical buildings which abound in that part of
Germany. _ Robert Maxwell, ed., *James Stirling,
Writings on Architecture,* Milan: Skira, 1998

When I've had the job of designing a museum, what
interests me are not so much the pictures which
might be there as the problem of creating a space or

ambience for looking at pictures. _ James Stirling,
"Architecture in an Age of Transition," *Domus,*
September 1992

If you place modern sculpture on a concrete terrace, in front of a plate glass window, this is a very
abstract ensemble. I didn't want that. I wanted to
place the art in a more familiar scene, and for this
reason we used planting with ivy and growies all
over. _ "James Stirling, sa conception de musée,"
*Techniques et Architecture,* October–November 1986

The building is now overgrown with ivy and creep-
ers, and it looks much more like a ruin than when it
was new. _ "James Stirling, sa conception de musée,"
*Techniques et Architecture,* October–November 1986

# LEICESTER 1963
# DEPARTMENT OF ENGINEERING, UNIVERSITY OF LEICESTER

Architects are in a difficult position with buildings of a highly scientific nature as they don't have the specialist knowledge to query the "brief"; with this particular building you would have needed a degree in about four subjects to have been able to dissect it. In this situation it is essential to propose a generalized solution which can take change and has inherent flexibility. We regarded the workshop shed in this way; the only expressed units of accommodation are those we understood at the level of our own experience and felt reasonably confident would not change—lecture theaters, staircases, etc. . . . The tapering section of the tower and building derives from the way circulation has organized the building form. There are about three hundred students in the building and, by making it like an iceberg, the bulk of student movement is limited to the lower three levels, where large numbers are changing lessons on the hour every hour. _ Robert Maxwell, ed., *James Stirling, Writings on Architecture*, Milan: Skira, 1998

There is no attempt visually to relate any of the rooms to each other when the activity which takes place in them is different. _ Robert Maxwell, ed., *James Stirling, Writings on Architecture*, Milan: Skira, 1998

The university magazine did an issue on the building—staff, students, and visitors wrote articles. There was some criticism at the level of taste (color, shape) but all the contributors ended by saying it was tremendously stimulating to be in the building, and they felt intensely alive working and studying there. This is the ultimate compliment for the architect, as it is his unique responsibility to raise the human spirit by the quality of the environment which he creates, whether in a room, a building, or a town. _ Robert Maxwell, ed., *James Stirling, Writings on Architecture*, Milan: Skira, 1998

How does an architect approach having to design for a specialized audience? For Stirling, framing his concept was a matter of connecting to the building, in this case through the various general requirements as well as the lively interplay of the students.

## "A ROUTINE FUNCTIONALIST"

In modifying and even rejecting principles on which the New Architecture [Stirling is referring to the Modern Movement] was founded, it is necessary to replace them with working rules and methods which are realistic in a situation of low cost and expediency. _ Robert Maxwell, ed., *James Stirling, Writings on Architecture,* Milan: Skira, 1998

## ❝ . . . FOR ME, RIGHT FROM THE BEGINNING, THE 'ART' OF ARCHITECTURE HAS ALWAYS BEEN THE PRIORITY. ❞

We might also like to use high-tech curtain walls plus the familiarity of domestic-type windows in the same building, so that the façade is made of different scales with differing associations in different places. _ "James Stirling, sa conception de musée," *Techniques et Architecture,* October–November 1986

I regard myself as a routine functionalist. By this I mean using patterns of logic which involve producing a building solution which is relevant to the times we live in and which is inherent in the problems as it is presented—the site, the functions, the materials, the cost. But functionalism is not enough. The building must also be expressive. You ought to be able to look at it and recognize its various component parts where people are doing different things. _ Robert Maxwell, ed., *James Stirling, Writings on Architecture,* Milan: Skira, 1998

## "WHERE IS THE STIRLING STYLE?"

Like music, architecture should have a whole repertoire. Though with the work of Norman Foster, it seems possible to make a very refined architecture out of one note. For me, however, that's not musical enough. _ "James Stirling, sa conception de musée," *Techniques et Architecture,* October–November 1986

At a low journalistic level, surprise is often expressed that every building I do seems different from the previous one. . . . Where is the Stirling style, where is the consistency, what will he do next? This is partly a fallacy of the Modern Movement. With Mies van der Rohe and those Bauhaus architects, you knew what you were getting. But you can cite just as many modern masters—Le Corbusier, Frank Lloyd Wright, and so on—whose work was always changing and moving on. _ Hugh Pearman, *The Sunday Times* (London), April 14, 1991

## "THE MODERN MOVEMENT, A BIT THIN"

It was only in the twentieth century that architects like Gropius threw out the baby with the bathwater. In eighteenth century, and indeed in every century, you find references to Rome, Egypt, or classical, gothic, etc. With the coming of the Bauhaus, architects began to throw away the past. Now we have to retrieve it a little I think. _ "James Stirling, sa conception de musée," *Techniques et Architecture,* October–November 1986

I think high-tech architects have put their eggs in one basket. It's rather limited, like the Modern Movement, a bit thin. _ "James Stirling, sa conception de musée," *Techniques et Architecture,* October–November 1986

## "THE MULTIPLE LAYERS OF HISTORICAL PRECEDENT"

In any case, I am more interested in the architecture of the past than in architecture which calls itself modern. Being specific, the virtues I like in neo-classical architecture are the obvious ones of geometry and abstraction. Even more specifically, I like the very particular period of the late neo-classicism, the transition to Victorian architecture toward the end of the nineteenth century. It is the period of Soane, Weinbrenner, Schinkel, Gilly, and then of the early Victorian architects like Gibbs or Thompson, called *the greek.* _ James Stirling, "Architecture in an Age of Transition," *Domus,* September 1992

Well, nowadays one can draw equally, without guilt, from the abstract style of modern design and the multiple layers of historical precedent. _ Robert Maxwell, ed., *James Stirling, Writings on Architecture,* Milan: Skira, 1998

. . . my fascination with the Modern Movement never really got more recent than early Corbusier and the Constructivists, and in the early 50s I developed an interest in all things vernacular, from the very small—farms, barns, and village housing—to the very large—warehouses, industrial buildings, engineering structures, including the great railway and exhibition sheds. _ Robert Maxwell, ed., *James Stirling, Writings on Architecture,* Milan: Skira, 1998

## ❝ YOU SHOULD STARVE TO DEATH IF YOU RELIED ONLY ON THE LANGUAGE OF THE MODERN MOVEMENT. ❞

## LOUIS KAHN
## "PROFOUNDLY RENEWED MODERN DESIGN"

I think Louis Kahn was the last great master of recent times. . . . He was able to add a dimension of grandeur to the vocabulary of architecture through his historical perception, which, added to the abstract and geometric styles of the 1920s, enriched the whole architectural scene. . . . What was new in his thinking profoundly renewed modern design, and I would like to think that those aspects are present sometimes in our works. _ James Stirling, "Architecture in an Age of Transition," *Domus,* September 1992

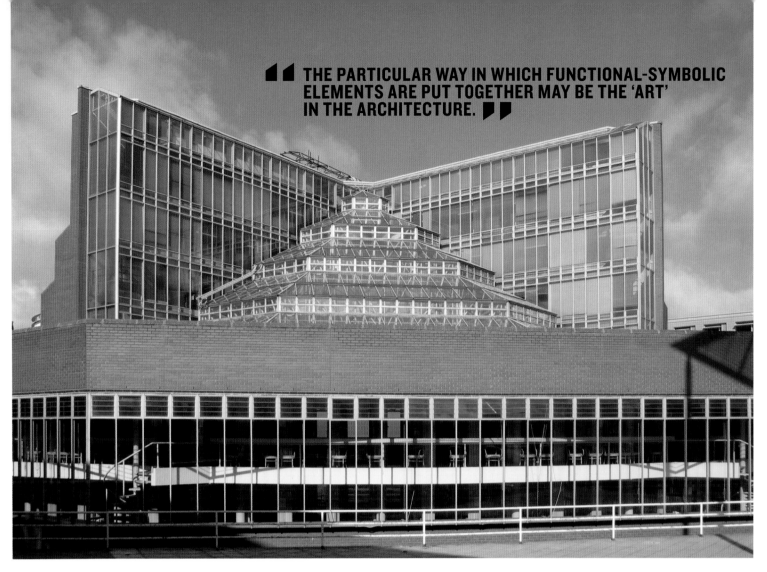

> **THE PARTICULAR WAY IN WHICH FUNCTIONAL-SYMBOLIC ELEMENTS ARE PUT TOGETHER MAY BE THE 'ART' IN THE ARCHITECTURE.**

## CAMBRIDGE 1967
## FACULTY OF HISTORY, UNIVERSITY OF CAMBRIDGE

This building also has a tapering section. The reading room (280 students) has the greatest density of occupation and, therefore, is at ground level. Staff and student common rooms are at first- and second-floor level and above are the seminar rooms; staff rooms are on the two top floors. Student movement around the lower levels is by stairs, with the lift relatively free for staff to get to the top.

The circulation is the primary organizing element, and the corridors around the upper floors are designed as tiers of galleries. These appear under the roof lantern which lights the reading room: as you move along them you may be seeing out across the roof, and the next moment you are alongside it looking in, seeing the mechanics of the building. _ Robert Maxwell, ed., *James Stirling, Writings on Architecture,* Milan: Skira, 1998

Glass buildings are, I think, appropriate in the English climate. We are, perhaps, the only country where it is seldom too hot or too cold and, on a normal cloudy day, there is a high quality of diffused light in the sky. A glass covering keeps the rain out and lets light through. . . . I think of glass rather like polythene, to be pushed in and out, enveloping the shape of the rooms, which are considered as always having an ideal shape according to their use. It is necessary to maintain the shape of rooms at their most functional without compromise by forcing them into an overall constricting form, and in designing a building one compiles these various room shapes to become the complete assembly. This can then be covered with a membrane of glass, not structurally a difficult thing to do.
_ Robert Maxwell, ed., *James Stirling, Writings on Architecture,* Milan: Skira, 1998

Given the significance of the reading room at Cambridge, Stirling went forward with one of his well-known points: "The shapes of a building should indicate—perhaps display—the usage and the way of life of its occupants."

**" ... THE ARCHITECTURE WE DO ...
HAS ALL THESE DISJUNCTIONS, COMPLEXITIES, AND DIFFERENCES IN SCALE
BECAUSE THAT KIND OF ARCHITECTURE IS MORE INTERESTING TO ME
—AND I THINK TO THE PUBLIC. "**

### ST. ANDREWS 1968
# HALL OF RESIDENCE, UNIVERSITY OF ST. ANDREWS
There are 250 students in each residence (both sexes) and the students' bedrooms are positioned in the fingers, which are pointed toward a magnificent view of the North Sea and the Scottish mountains. The nonrepetitive accommodation (i.e., dining hall, game rooms, etc.) is located in the web where the fingers join. There is a glazed promenade level about halfway up the building and, from this, internal staircases give access up or down to the students' rooms. This promenade is the main artery of circulation and is intended to be the major element of sociability. . . . _ Peter Arnell and Ted Bickford, ed., *James Stirling, Buildings and Projects, 1950–1980*, New York: Rizzoli, 1985

Stirling used prefabricated concrete modules for Andrew Melville Hall at the university. The students were gifted with dormitories that afforded each of them with a view of the North Sea and neighboring St. Andrews golf links.

## CAMBRIDGE 1985
# ARTHUR M. SACKLER MUSEUM, HARVARD UNIVERSITY

I hope that visitors moving through the Sackler will experience a succession of minor shocks or jolts. Firstly, they have to go down instead of up to enter the building. Then, entering through the glass lobby between the columns, the cross axis of the entrance hall immediately creates a stop movement: across the hall the staircase reverts to the axis on which they entered and, when the gallery at the top is reached, its axis is again at right angles, and so on. In a short staccato walk, the reorientation of stop/go axis changes is a substitute for the transitional vestibules in a Baroque sequence. _ Robert Maxwell, ed., *James Stirling, Writings on Architecture*, Milan: Skira, 1998

. . . usually one thinks of the grand stair as a feature in a continuous sequence. But I prefer to think of this staircase as an event in itself. The circulation flow in the Sackler is interrupted by a series of contra axes and stop movements as you move from the entry hall and up the stair to the top-floor galleries. The in-between transitional elements normally found in Baroque ensembles, such as vestibules and anterooms, are here excluded, making for an abrupt juxtaposition of basic elements. The staircase is therefore more a picturesque and less a sequential element in the spatial whole. _ Robert Maxwell, ed., *James Stirling, Writings on Architecture*, Milan: Skira, 1998

It was our feeling that these rooms should have a view of the street and an involvement with campus activities around the building. _ Robert Maxwell, ed., *James Stirling, Writings on Architecture*, Milan: Skira, 1998

In some parts I hope there is the quality of ambiguity that you sometimes see in Soane (who devised ceilings that float and introduced light from mysterious sources) [architect Sir John Soane, 1753–1837]. For instance, in the Ancient Greek gallery, when looking back to where you entered from the staircase, you cannot see the recessed door. People will just appear in the gallery, as it were from the midst of the wall; alternatively, one moment they will be there

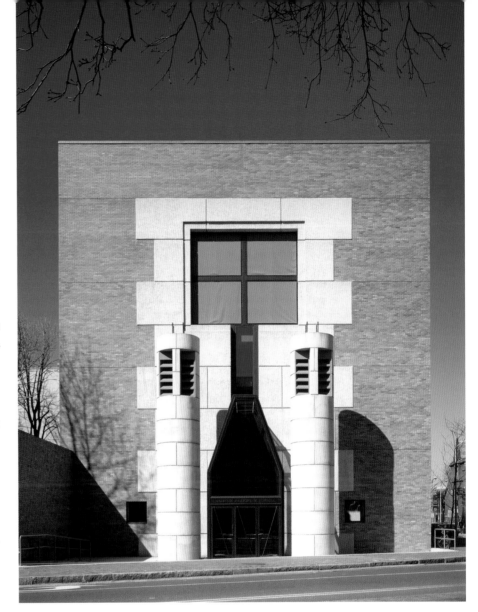

and, when you look again, they will have disappeared without a trace. _ Robert Maxwell, ed., *James Stirling, Writings on Architecture*, Milan: Skira, 1998

The galleries are intended to have a more public though not monumental persona, to have an ambience verging on the domestic, especially when the ancient, Islamic, and oriental objects are installed in the galleries, and if arranged with the charm and slightly idiosyncratic layout I associate with the Fogg [Fogg Art Museum, Harvard University], the domestic character should be reinforced. The galleries will, I hope, be more personal, more like those annex rooms of grand houses that display the owner's private collection than galleries in a public institution. _ Robert Maxwell, ed., *James Stirling, Writings on Architecture*, Milan: Skira, 1998

The Sackler Museum at Harvard University includes a monumental entrance with a stone form. Its shape takes its cues from the collection inside: The museum houses Oriental, ancient, and Islamic art.

There is a certain tinge of the poetic in considering Stirling's comment that Number 1 Poultry is the "Quintessence of London," for it has indeed come to be regarded as justly deserving the declaration. It was his last building.

### LONDON 1996
# NUMBER 1 POULTRY OFFICE DEVELOPMENT
*Although Number 1 Poultry Office Development was constructed posthumously, it was thought to potentially be one of Stirling's best designs, finalized in 1988. Prior to Stirling's proposal for the same site was a 1967 Mies van der Rohe design for a completely different kind of building, a steel and glass tower with a plaza. Mies's design was vetoed in 1985.*

I always thought—right up to the last moment—that Poultry stood a 50-50 chance. I do regard this site as being very special, at this spider's web intersection surrounded by all those heroes like Lutyens and Hawksmoor and Dance. It's the quintessence of London. _ Hugh Pearman, *The Sunday Times* (London), April 14, 1991

All of which contrasts with this (he says, pulling out a photo of the Mies tower with its sheer, unbroken façade). I supported it, and I still would. I would have liked to see a Mies building in the city, but it's only one aspect of modern architecture. _ Hugh Pearman, *The Sunday Times* (London), April 14, 1991

### "I WORK VERY INTUITIVELY"

We follow a very linear route. We try to avoid any idea that looks like a blinding flash. Rather, it's a linear process where we very definitely have first priorities and less important ones. So a form, a plan, is worked out in the head, which you might doodle on paper but which has nothing to do with materials. It's just a form. Only later, when the entire concept is worked out, do you start to have feelings about the most appropriate structure to hold it up and the most suitable building materials. _ James Stirling, "Architecture in an Age of Transition," *Domus*, September 1992

It's a combination of what's coming out of the ends of my fingers and what I'm thinking of at the same time. I generally do that in office, sometimes at home, sometimes in airplanes. First I do that alone, then I talk to people about it and ask them to take the concepts and continue with the process—it becomes interactive. _ Robert Maxwell, ed., *James Stirling, Writings on Architecture*, Milan: Skira, 1998

## " MORE THAN TENNIS, IT'S [ARCHITECTURE] LIKE A GAME OF CRICKET WITH ALL THE PLAYERS AROUND THE BATSMAN, WHO IS KNOCKING THE BALLS IN SEVERAL DIRECTIONS. "

### USING MODELS

In the two months of working out the scheme, we start on the proper drawings, the plans, and axonometric down-and-up drawings. We never really use models in the design process: we do sketches, axonometrics, other types of drawings, but models are not part of our way of working. We do make models, usually at the end of the schematic design, for a presentation to journalists, a planning authority, or university committee. In those cases, a model is very useful, but the design is over. _ James Stirling, "Architecture in an Age of Transition," *Domus*, September 1992

### "THE ELEGANCE OF FUNCTIONAL DRAFTSMANSHIP"

. . . going back to the beginning, to my mother who was a Scottish/Irish schoolteacher and who early on perceived that I had no heart for my father's wish that I should follow him in going to sea—my father was the archetypal Scottish chief engineer. Ironically it was my discovery of his "apprenticeship" drawings—beautiful blue and pink wash sectional drawings of machine parts, turbines, ships' engines—that first opened my eyes to the elegance of functional draftsmanship. _ Robert Maxwell, ed., *James Stirling, Writings on Architecture*, Milan: Skira, 1998

I've always been a designer with wide-ranging interests and perhaps eclectic tendencies; as a young man I did not work in an office or through the English system of being an articled pupil— a practice which seemed to be dying out (about 1945) just as I went to architectural school— so my problem was not one of working for a master or of getting out from under the influence of one. _ Robert Maxwell, ed., *James Stirling, Writings on Architecture*, Milan: Skira, 1998

## " I NEVER HAD THE BAUHAUS TYPE OF EDUCATION "

My generation grew up with the cinema, just as present generations grow up with rock groups and pop music. But when I was young, it was the cinema that was the big attraction. If I could, I went two or three times a week; I was obsessed by it, and so it must have had an influence on me. _ James Stirling, "Architecture in an Age of Transition," *Domus*, September 1992

During my first visits to the United States, I was also aware of the incredibly high finish and "way out" aspect of New York Art Deco buildings such as the Chrysler Tower. It seemed to me we had nothing to come near them. _ Robert Maxwell, ed., *James Stirling, Writings on Architecture*, Milan: Skira, 1998

For architects to create buildings as monuments to their own aesthetic feelings is a worthless occupation, always. Today we have to create practical, logical, and appropriate organizations out of the problems of society—at the big level of the city and town right down to the smallest level, which is the street or individual house. _ Robert Maxwell, ed., *James Stirling, Writings on Architecture*, Milan: Skira, 1998

I would hope for drama and also refinement and quietness in a building. Places where the architecture is very dramatic, and places where it is very subdued. _ "James Stirling, sa conception de musée," *Techniques et Architecture*, October–November 1986

*Considered among the most influential architects of the second half of the twentieth century, Stirling's premature death at the age of sixty-six in 1992 was viewed as a great loss for architecture. Just before his death, Stirling had been given a knighthood, which he only reluctantly accepted because he thought it would be "good for the office."*

## BEAUTY IN ARCHITECTURAL SIMPLICITY

My architecture is autobiographical. . . . Underlying all that I have achieved, such as it is, I share the memories of my father's ranch where I spent my childhood and adolescence. In my work I have always strived to adapt to the needs of modern living the magic of those remote nostalgic years. The lessons to be learned from the unassuming architecture of the village and provincial towns of my country have been a permanent source of inspiration. Such as, for instance, the whitewashed walls; the peace to be found in patios and orchards; the colorful streets; the humble majesty of the village squares surrounded by shady open corridors. And as there is a deep historical link between these two squares surrounded by shady open corridors. And as there is a deep historical link between these teachings and those of the North African and Moroccan villages, they too have enriched my perception of beauty in architectural simplicity.

_ Luis Barragán, Pritzker Prize acceptance speech, June 3, 1980

# LUIS BARRAGÁN

**BORN:** March 9, 1902, Guadalajara, Mexico; Died: November 26, 1988

**EDUCATION:** Civil Engineer, Free School of Engineers, Guadalajara, Mexico, 1923

**PROJECTS FEATURED:** Gilardi House, Chapultepec, Mexico City, 1977; Los Clubes Subdivision, Mexico City, 1961–72; Los Arboledas Subdivision, Mexico City, 1958–63; Chapel in Tlalpan, Mexico City, 1960; Barragán House, Tacubaya, Mexico City, 1948

**SOLITUDE
IS GOOD COMPANY,
AND MY ARCHITECTURE
IS NOT FOR THOSE
WHO FEAR OR SHUN IT.**

**Gilardi House, Mexico City, 1977**
The brightly colored pink wall shooting
up from the indoor pool is just there for
decoration. "It doesn't support anything,"
the architect said. "It's a bit of color in
the water, for pleasure's sake."

## COLOR AND LIGHT

In my activity as an architect, color and light have always been a crucially important constant. Both are basic elements in the creation of an architectural space, given that they can vary the conception of the latter. _ Danièle Pauly, *Barragán: Space and Shadow, Walls and Color*, Basel, Switzerland: Birkhäuser, 2002

Color is a complement to the architecture. It serves to enlarge or reduce a space. It's also useful for adding that touch of magic a place needs. _ Danièle Pauly, *Barragán: Space and Shadow, Walls and Color*, Basel, Switzerland: Birkhäuser, 2002

I use color, but when I draw I don't think about it. I usually define it when the space is constructed. Then I constantly visit the location at different times of the day and begin to "imagine the color," to imagine colors ranging from the craziest to the most credible. _ Danièle Pauly, *Barragán: Space and Shadow, Walls and Color*, Basel, Switzerland: Birkhäuser, 2002

For the pleasure of seeing them [colors]; to revel in them. _ Danièle Pauly, *Barragán: Space and Shadow, Walls and Color*, Basel, Switzerland: Birkhäuser, 2002

## ◀◀ I AM A SYMBOL FOR ALL THOSE TOUCHED BY BEAUTY. ▶▶

## PAINTERS AND ARCHITECTS

I think that if painters can change an entire canvas, architects must do this with their own work. The act of building is, in itself, a creative process. _ Danièle Pauly, *Barragán: Space and Shadow, Walls and Color*, Basel, Switzerland: Birkhäuser, 2002

## ◀◀ I UNDERLINE THE STUDY OF COLOR ABOVE ALL. ▶▶

I am a devotee of Surrealism (I have always taken the side of people with imagination). _ Federica Zanco, ed., *Luis Barragán: The Quiet Revolution*, Milan: Skira, Barragán Foundation, Vitra Design Museum, 2001

In him [Giorgio de Chirico] I found the magic I've always sought. When I saw his painting I thought: "This is what I can also do in the architecture of landscape . . ." _ Danièle Pauly, *Barragán: Space and Shadow, Walls and Color*, Basel, Switzerland: Birkhäuser, 2002

## "WITHOUT TOUCHING A SINGLE PENCIL"

When I start a project, I usually begin it without touching a single pencil, without any drawing. I sit down and try and imagine the wildest things. . . . After imagining those ideas, I let them settle in my mind for a couple of days, sometimes longer. I go back to them and start to draw little sketches in perspective, I frequently do them on a sketchpad, seated on a chair. I don't draw on a laptop or drawing board. Later, I give these sketches to a draftsman, and we start drawing the floor plans and elevations. We almost always make cardboard models and work on these, making continual changes. _ Danièle Pauly, *Barragán: Space and Shadow, Walls and Color*, Basel, Switzerland: Birkhäuser, 2002

## MEXICO CITY 1977
## GILARDI HOUSE

I'll tell you a secret: the swimming pool has a pink wall or column that doesn't support anything. It's a bit of color in the water—for pleasure's sake—to bring light to the space and to improve its overall proportions. _ Danièle Pauly, *Barragán: Space and Shadow, Walls and Color*, Basel, Switzerland: Birkhäuser, 2002

. . . that column needed to be there in order to form one more color in the composition. _ Danièle Pauly, *Barragán: Space and Shadow, Walls and Color*, Basel, Switzerland: Birkhäuser, 2002

The corridor prepares the journey through the house to reach an important space: the dining room with a covered pool. Without warning, from the pool there emerges a pink wall that curtails the water and almost reaches the ceiling. That wall gives meaning to the space, makes it magical, creates a surrounding tension. From the ceiling a small skylight bathes the wall in light and emphasizes its role. _ Danièle Pauly, *Barragán: Space and Shadow, Walls and Color*, Basel, Switzerland: Birkhäuser, 2002

The Gilardi House is a testament to Barragán's love of color and its importance in his architecture.

Color and light are seductive tools in the Barragán kit, especially when used to achieve spiritual contemplation. The "appearance" of silence is profound.

### MEXICO CITY 1960
## CHAPEL IN TLALPAN
I attentively studied light and color, because I wanted to create an atmosphere of stillness and spiritual meditation. The idea of semi-darkness was very important in this project. _ Danièle Pauly, *Barragán: Space and Shadow, Walls and Color,* Basel, Switzerland: Birkhäuser, 2002

Religion and myth. It is impossible to understand art and the glory of its history without avowing religious spirituality and the mythical roots that lead us to the very reason of being of the artistic phenomenon.

Without the one or the other there would be no Egyptian pyramids, nor those of ancient Mexico. Would the Greek temples and Gothic cathedrals have existed? _ Luis Barragán, Pritzker Prize acceptance speech, June 3, 1980

I am a fervent Catholic, as you know: I love cathedrals, I love the austerity of convents, I love St. Francis of Assisi, but I am not very fond of confessionals. What seems intolerable to me is noise. _ Federica Zanco, ed., *Luis Barragán: The Quiet Revolution,* Milan: Skira, Barragán Foundation, Vitra Design Museum, 2001

## WALLS

*For Barragán, the wall is an architectural structure of emotional significance. In some cases he is known to have moved walls more than once to adjust to what he considers the elements of solitude and serenity, another signature Barragán concern.*

**❝ THE WALL IS
'AN ARCHITECTURAL STRIPTEASE.' ❞**

I've continually worked with right angles. At all moments of my work I've taken the horizontal and vertical planes, and the angles of intersection, into account. This explains the frequent use, in my architecture, of the cube. _ Danièle Pauly, Barragán: *Space and Shadow, Walls and Color,* Basel, Switzerland: Birkhäuser, 2002

Even in buildings where there's nothing neighboring them, just the surrounding landscape, you also need to have some walls to create corners with an intimate atmosphere, and it's possible that all this grows out of the need we have—being the mammals we are—for bits of shadow. These shadows can also be considered a basic human need, a kind of spiritual concern represented by the idea of meditation. And this meditation ought not to only refer to experiences of a religious sort, but simply to a person being able, at certain times, to take stock of himself, his problems, and his own dreams. _ Danièle Pauly, *Barragán: Space and Shadow, Walls and Color,* Basel, Switzerland: Birkhäuser, 2002

I can say that streets, limited by walls, are not objectionable, provided these walls are treated satisfactorily from a plastic point of view with trees, vines, and flowers as if they were vertical gardens. _Luis Barragán, "Gardens for Environment," *Journal of The American Institute of Architects,* April 1952

**❝ HUMAN LIFE DEPRIVED OF BEAUTY
IS NOT WORTHY OF BEING CALLED SO. ❞**

Architecture, besides being spatial, is also musical. That music is played with water. The importance of walls is that they isolate one from the street's exterior space. The street is aggressive, even hostile: walls create silence. From that silence you can play with water as music. Afterwards, that music surrounds us. _ Tim Street-Porter, *Casa Mexicana,* New York: Stewart, Tabori & Chang, 1989

## SERENITY, SILENCE, SOLITUDE, AND JOY

*In addition to his ideas about walls, Barragán imbued a spiritual quest and importance to having the three Ss (serenity, silence, and solitude) present in his architecture.*

It is alarming that publications devoted to architecture have banished from their pages the words Beauty, Inspiration, Magic, Spellbound, Enchantment, as well as the concepts of Serenity, Silence, Intimacy, and Amazement. All these have nestled in my soul, and though I am fully aware that I have not done them complete justice in my work, they have never ceased to be my guiding lights. _ Luis Barragán, Pritzker Prize acceptance speech, June 3, 1980

Serenity is the great and true antidote against anguish and fear, and today, more than ever, it is the architect's duty to make of it a permanent guest in the home, no matter how sumptuous or how humble. Throughout my work I have always strived to achieve serenity, but one must be on guard not to destroy it by the use of an indiscriminate palette. _ Luis Barragán, Pritzker Prize acceptance speech, June 3, 1980

**❝ THE IDEAL SPACE
MUST CONTAIN ELEMENTS OF
MAGIC, SERENITY, SORCERY,
AND MYSTERY. ❞**

Silence. In the gardens and homes designed by me, I have always endeavored to allow for the interior placid murmur of silence, and in my fountains, silence sings. _ Luis Barragán, Pritzker Prize acceptance speech, June 3, 1980

Solitude. Only in intimate communion with solitude may man find himself. Solitude is good company, and my architecture is not for those who fear or shun it. _ Luis Barragán Pritzker Prize acceptance speech, June 3, 1980

How can one forget joy? I believe that a work of art reaches perfection when it conveys silent joy and serenity. _ Luis Barragán Pritzker Prize acceptance speech, June 3, 1980

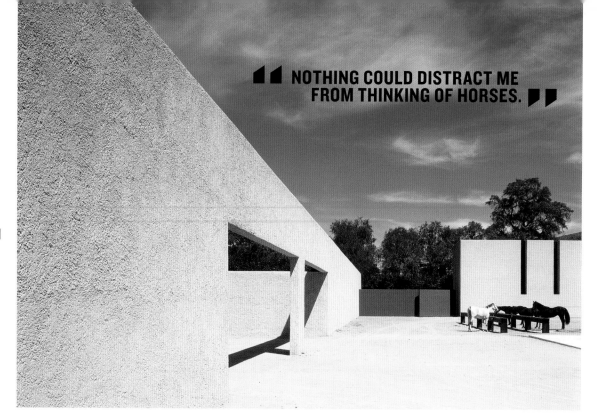

**❝ NOTHING COULD DISTRACT ME FROM THINKING OF HORSES. ❞**

**❝ A FOUNTAIN BRINGS US PEACE, JOY, AND RESTFUL SERENITY.... ❞**

My love of landscape and animals in the landscape, and for the horse in particular, goes back to stables, fountains that in reality are troughs or horse baths; from here come the walls that protect the horses. _ Federica Zanco, ed., *Luis Barragán: The Quiet Revolution*, Milan: Skira, Barragán Foundation, Vitra Design Museum, 2001

I spent my youth on horseback, looking at houses that sang over the earth, passing by popular festivals; I remember the play of shadows that always fell over the walls as the late sun was weakening, and no matter how much the shadows changed the angles were either attenuated or the lines were cut off. From here also comes my fixation with aqueducts. At Mexican ranchos you always see streams of water; you would never have a house or an architectural ensemble without a pond, or a stream, or a fragment of an aqueduct. Nothing could distract me from thinking of horses. _ Federica Zanco, ed., *Luis Barragán: The Quiet Revolution*, Milan: Skira, Barragán Foundation, Vitra Design Museum, 2001

**MEXICO CITY 1961–72**
## LOS CLUBES SUBDIVISION

Barragán was an accomplished horseman. As a result, ranches, horses, and haciendas influenced his work and designs. His fountains were inspired by the troughs from which his beloved horses drank.

San Cristóbal . . . combines the elements I've always looked for: the stable, the pool, the drinking trough for the horses, the house. _ Danièle Pauly, *Barragán: Space and Shadow, Walls and Color*, Basel, Switzerland: Birkhäuser, 2002

A fountain brings us peace, joy, and restful sensuality and reaches the epitome of its very essence when by its power to bewitch it will stir dreams of distant worlds. _ Luis Barragán, Pritzker Prize acceptance speech, June 3, 1980

# LOS ARBOLEDAS SUBDIVISION

I think there's mystery when you see the top of a tree behind a wall. _ Danièle Pauly, *Barragán: Space and Shadow, Walls and Color*, Basel, Switzerland: Birkhäuser, 2002

I believe that architects should design gardens to be used, as much as the houses they build, to develop a sense of beauty and the taste and inclination toward the fine arts and other spiritual values. _ Muriel Emanuel, ed., *Contemporary Architects*, New York: St. Martin's Press, 1980

"The construction and enjoyment of a garden accustoms people to beauty," Barragán once said.

## "MODERNITY" IN LATIN AMERICA

It is astonishing that modern architecture has not produced an example of work which expresses the attraction of a place. This would fulfill spiritual desires and create confidence in the inhabitants. I do think there is more "modernity" in Latin America than in Europe. That is, everything being built here—and if not all, most of it—is contemporary architecture. And the main clients (government and civil authorities, religious leaders, industrialists and people who want their residences done, rich and poor), they all want contemporary architecture. That is, they follow the tradition that says we should use the architecture of our time. It can be successful. There can be beauty in it, also ugliness; but I consider the Latin American spirit as being more modern and progressive than the European. _ Damian Bayon, "An Interview with Luis Barragán," *Landscape Architecture*, November 1976

For me, true tradition consists of creating contemporary architecture, not trying to create what the Mayas or the colonial architects achieved. _ Enrique X. de Anda Alanis, *Luis Barragán: Clasico Del Silencio (Colección Somosur)*, Bogotá-Colombia: Escala, 1989

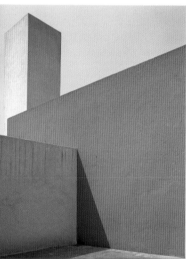

The spare space is not about paring down but of reaching for something more cerebral. Barragán's color canvasses convey emotional heat as well as define architectural elements.

### MEXICO CITY 1948
## BARRAGÁN HOUSE
In 1943 I designed the house in which I live. It is a house which expresses my own tastes and my sense of nostalgia and the idea of comfort. Four of five other houses followed in a similar style. I wanted to feel that I was living here in Mexico, and I rejected all the false and overly decorated imported "French" styles then in vogue. _ Enrique X. de Anda Alanis, *Luis Barragán: Clasico Del Silencio (Colección Somosur)*, Bogotá-Colombia: Escala, 1989

Man also needs his hideaway, a place to withdraw to, to isolate himself in. . . . Here I had a picture window; after a few months I realized it was disturbing me and I blocked it off; over there, between the dining room and this room we're in, there wasn't a division, from where we're sitting I saw the garden, and it also managed to affect me: I didn't need so much light; I erected a wall and next to the wall I put these seats we're sitting on. I immediately felt better. I think closed-in spaces give you a feeling of tranquility. _ Danièle Pauly, *Barragán: Space and Shadow, Walls and Color*, Basel, Switzerland: Birkhäuser, 2002

## PERSONAL FRAMEWORK

When I was a student there was no special preparatory training as there is now. In due course I entered the school of engineering [Free School of Engineers, Guadalajara, Mexico] to study civil engineering. The school did not have any proper program for training architects . . . _ Enrique X. de Anda Alanis, *Luis Barragán: Clasico Del Silencio (Colección Somosur)*, Bogotá-Colombia: Escala, 1989

I became very interested in houses and the life which is lived inside them and in particular, the Arab style of housing. _ Enrique X. de Anda Alanis, *Luis Barragán: Clasico Del Silencio (Colección Somosur)*, Bogotá-Colombia: Escala, 1989

But there was no work for architects in those years in Guadalajara, and I subsequently decided to try and make some money in other activities. I then went to the United States. I started to design houses and small buildings in Guadalajara on my return, between 1936 and 1940. But once again I decided to abandon architecture and devote myself to real estate activities, up to around 1945, although I did some landscaping of gardens. It was my work in gardens that gave me a certain reputation, for example, in the case of El Pedregal [Luis Barragán's Gardens of El Pedregal, 1945–1953]. _ Enrique X. de Anda Alanis, *Luis Barragán: Clasico Del Silencio (Colección Somosur)*, Bogotá-Colombia: Escala, 1989

a kind of liberation because it allowed me to see the importance of the imagination and to free myself from a lot of traditional ideas. And so I came to appreciate the importance of creating certain kinds of atmospheres which allow people to live comfortably as well as functionally within their homes. This is what Mathias Goeritz [Mexican painter and sculptor of German origin, 1915–1990] later called "emotional architecture." _ Enrique X. de Anda Alanis, *Luis Barragán: Clasico Del Silencio (Colección Somosur)*, Bogotá-Colombia: Escala, 1989

It is very important for humankind that architecture should move by its beauty; if there are many equally valid solutions to a problem the one which offers the user a message of beauty and emotion, that one is architecture . . . . _ Source unknown

The construction and enjoyment of a garden accustoms people to beauty, to its instinctive use, even to its pursuit. . . . _ Muriel Emanuel, ed., *Contemporary Architects*, New York: St. Martin's Press, 1980

❝ **MY ARCHITECTURE IS AUTOBIOGRAPHICAL.** ❞

I base myself a lot on intuition and on the observations made during my readings and my travels. _ Danièle Pauly, *Barragán: Space and Shadow, Walls and Color*, Basel, Switzerland: Birkhäuser, 2002

### EMOTIONAL ARCHITECTURE

*Before he turned to architecture, Barragán was a considerably gifted gardener and landscape architect. The love of gardens, of what he saw as beauty in nature, later became a cornerstone of his approach to architecture.*

It is essential to an architect to know how to see—to see in such a way that vision is not overpowered by rational analysis. _ Luis Barragán, Pritzker Prize acceptance speech, June 3, 1980

I believe in emotive architecture. _ Danièle Pauly, *Barragán: Space and Shadow, Walls and Color*, Basel, Switzerland: Birkhäuser, 2002

As regards my ideas on architecture, I can only say that I have never had any particular method; I have always preferred to let myself be guided by intuition. _ Enrique X. de Anda Alanis, *Luis Barragán: Clasico Del Silencio (Colección Somosur)*, Bogotá-Colombia: Escala, 1989

. . . there was my discovery of the magical gardens of Ferdinand Bac [French architect and illustrator, 1859–1952], a discovery which was in fact

## A STYLE TO SUIT THE JOB

It is strange to recall my Saul/Paul conversion to modern architecture almost a half century ago. I was, before that, a student of philosophy and the classics, interested—but only interested—in architecture. . . . The moment of conversion came in 1929 when I read an article by Henry-Russell Hitchcock on the architecture of J. J. P. Oud. From that moment, it was only modern and only that kind of modern architecture that enthralled me. . . . I am, in spite of speeches to the contrary, a functionalist; but, perhaps in contradiction, also an eclectic. "Eclectic" means to me that I am free to roam history at will, and that brings with it a new sympathy for the "style-to-suit-the-job" attitude. . . . We live in a time of flux. There seems to be no consistency of style. . . . Sensibilities change fast, but in what direction? There are no regional prides, no new religions, no new Puritanism, no new Marxism, no new socially conscious morality that can give discipline, direction, or force to an architectural pattern. Today we know too much too quickly. It takes moral and emotional blinders to make a style. One must be convinced one is right. Who can stand up today and say: "I am right!" Who, indeed, would want to? _ Philip Johnson, *Writings,* New York: Oxford University Press, 1979

# PHILIP JOHNSON

**BORN:** July 8, 1906, Cleveland, Ohio; Died: January 25, 2005

**EDUCATION:** B.Arch., A.B., Harvard University, Cambridge, Massachusetts, 1943, 1930

**OFFICE:** Philip Johnson Alan Ritchie Architects, 330 West 42nd Street, New York, 10036
Tel: +1 212-319-5880, Fax: +1 212-777-1530
www.pjar.com

**PROJECTS FEATURED:** AT&T Corporate Headquarters (now Sony Plaza Building), New York, 1984; Transco Tower (now Williams Tower), Houston, Texas, 1983; Museum for Pre-Columbian Art (now Philip Johnson Pavilion), Dumbarton Oaks, Washington, D.C., 1963; The Four Seasons, New York, 1959; Glass House, New Canaan, Connecticut, 1949

**" ARCHITECTURE IS ART, NOTHING ELSE. "**

**Glass House, New Canaan, 1949**
Johnson's celebrated Glass House was designed in the early part of his career and was his home until he died at the age of 98.

## ❝ ... THIS BUILDING KEEPS SURPRISING ME, IT KEEPS GIVING ME PLEASURE EVERY DAY. ❞

Even after his death, Johnson's Glass House remains in the public eye.

### NEW CANAAN 1949
# GLASS HOUSE
*As the first Pritzker Prize winner, Philip Johnson was arguably the most influential architect of the latter two-thirds of the twentieth century. In the early part of his career, Johnson was primarily a critic and curator, serving as the first director of the Department of Architecture at the Museum of Modern Art in New York. In this position, he was largely responsible, along with Alfred Barr, Jr., and Henry-Russell Hitchcock, for arguing the aesthetic side of architecture in the hugely important 1932 exhibition "Modern Architecture—The International Style." Receiving an architecture degree relatively late in his life, Johnson pursued an illustrious, yet controversial, career as a practicing architect for the remainder of his long career. His celebrated Glass House, designed when he had been an architect for less than a decade, was his home until his death at the age of 98.*

I consider my own house not so much as a home (though it is that to me)—as a clearinghouse of ideas which can filter down later, through my own work or that of others. _ Selden Rodman, *Conversations with Artists,* New York: Devin-Adair Co., 1957

Well, I did buy the land because of the site and its narrow, rocky promontory that stuck out. I chose the site because of the famous Japanese idea: always put your house on a shelf, because the good spirits will be caught by the hill that's behind the house; the evil spirits will be unable to climb the hill below the house. Frank Lloyd Wright put it differently. He said never, never build on top of a hill. _ Hilary Lewis and John O'Conner, *Philip Johnson: The Architect in His Own Words,* New York: Rizzoli, 1994

It was only a five-acre plot. It's now forty. So it has developed over the fifty years that I've been working on it. . . . It's really a forty-year architectural design. It's a continuing process. The house and that promontory were the first part I landscaped. But since then, I've bought all this land, and I keep extending it outward, like an English landscape. _ Hilary Lewis and John O'Conner, *Philip Johnson: The Architect in His Own Words*, New York: Rizzoli, 1994

It's a 1920s house. The furnishings are all Mies. . . . I've done chairs, but they're just terrible. Take the masterworks. Why reinvent the spoon? _ Hilary Lewis and John O'Conner, *Philip Johnson: The Architect in His Own Words*, New York: Rizzoli, 1994

**Viewing the House** I just sit outside the house—a sitting place under a tree. It faces the slope down, and you can turn and look up. Then you look over and see the sculpture gallery and painting gallery. _ Hilary Lewis and John O'Conner, *Philip Johnson: The Architect in His Own Words*, New York: Rizzoli, 1994

. . . the snow comes down at night, and the building floats. If the snow comes down at an angle, then it's as if you're in an elevator going up that way. It isn't going straight up, because the snow never comes straight. You're being levitated, and that impressed me—really fantastic. It had very little to do with architecture. _ Hilary Lewis and John O'Conner, *Philip Johnson: The Architect in His Own Words*, New York: Rizzoli, 1994

in this Glass House, it changes as the light of the day changes. It changes as the wind and as the seasons. So, we're adding, instead of a beautiful décor—let's say, like a Rococo, which I of course love—we have the seasons changing through glass walls. _ John Peter, *The Oral History of Modern Architecture: Interview with the Greatest Architects of the Twentieth Century*, New York: Harry Abrams, 1994

The cylinder made of the same brick as the platform from which it springs, forming the main motif of the house, was not derived from Mies but rather from a burnt wooden village I saw once where nothing was left but the foundations and chimneys of brick. _ Hilary Lewis and John O'Conner, *Philip Johnson: The Architect in His Own Words*, New York: Rizzoli, 1994

**Architecture's Fourth Dimension** The fire is not only a warmth—it touches so many senses, the fire and the flicker. The heat the fireplace gives you. Water gives you the noise, the flicker, and light. This is the depth and deepening of architecture which formerly could be given by the handcrafts of decoration which we are no longer able and maybe we don't want. It's a matter of time. I do feel that you have to introduce the fourth dimension into architecture. Times change. That is one thing that my "wallpaper" does

**Glass House vs. Farnsworth House** You see, in this house, the processional into where we're sitting now, in the living room, is much more complicated than the Farnsworth. [Mies van der Rohe's Farnsworth House, completed in 1951, is also a glass house.] The Farnsworth is a single-unit space. Here, there's a very important vestibule outlined by the chimney and the kitchen before you debouch into the living room. I think I'm more elaborate perhaps. You get out of your car, which is the entrance to the building, and you make many turns. Of course, it comes from a definition of the Parthenon that you always approach a building at an angle. That kind of development very consciously influences me. There's always that sense of processional space that may make a line in my work, I hope. _ John Peter, *The Oral History of Modern Architecture: Interviews with the Greatest Architects of the Twentieth Century*, New York: Harry Abrams, 1994

The interior furnishings are all designed by Mies van der Rohe. Johnson said he had designed chairs but they were "terrible."

**Criticism of Glass House** . . . they went so far as publishing in a magazine, "People that live in glass houses should ball in the basement." But I don't have a basement, so I don't ball in the basement. But much more important than exhibitionism is the interface of architecture and the desire for all kinds of sexual experiments. . . . The idea of a glass house, where somebody just might be looking—naturally, you don't want them to be looking. But what about it? That little edge of danger in being caught. _ Hilary Lewis and John O'Conner, *Philip Johnson: The Architect in His Own Words,* New York: Rizzoli, 1994

[Erich] Mendelsohn once wrote that architects are remembered by their one-room buildings. How true. _ John Peter, *The Oral History of Modern Architecture: Interviews with the Greatest Architects of the Twentieth Century,* New York: Harry Abrams, 1994

**❰❰ YOU SEE, I HAVE NO CONVICTIONS, BUT DO HAVE TASTE. ❱❱**

DUMBARTON OAKS 1963
**MUSEUM FOR PRE-COLUMBIAN ART (NOW PHILIP JOHNSON PAVILION)** . . . this was the most interesting job I ever had; it was a joyous pleasure to work. I mean, I had none of those troubles I had with other buildings . . . _ Hilary Lewis and John O'Conner, *Philip Johnson: The Architect in His Own Words,* New York: Rizzoli, 1994

There was no budget. No budget at all. The critic Peter Blake once figured out it was the most expensive building per square foot ever built. _ Hilary Lewis and John O'Conner, *Philip Johnson: The Architect in His Own Words,* New York: Rizzoli, 1994

Yes, well, I had my partner, Mrs. Bliss. . . . Very few times you get a perfect client with a perfect program with all the money in the world. There's one or two—Mies and the Tugendhat House, for example. _ Hilary Lewis and John O'Conner, *Philip Johnson: The Architect in His Own Words,* New York: Rizzoli, 1994

## HISTORY AND BREAKING LOOSE

Architecture should adorn and uplift—it doesn't need meaning. It's not politics or philosophy. . . . Anyone who wants to solve the many problems of mankind shouldn't be an architect but a politician or scientist. Or become a developer and build accommodations for the poor and sick—with the help of a good architect, I hope. . . . As far as I was concerned, modernism was mainly a style. What appealed to me was the radically new forms. I liked the revolutionary mutation, the change. . . . I don't think ideology has anything to do with architecture. . . . You see, I have no convictions, but do have taste. _ Hanno Rauterberg, *Talking Architecture: Interviews with Architects,* Munich: Prestel, 2008

There's very little passion around. Without passion, you shouldn't go into architecture. _ "Philip Johnson Gets Real: The Godfather on Influence, His Heirs, and What Makes Him Weep," *Metropolis,* November 1998

Now I'm not telling you that you have to go and do International Style work. Let them break away if they can. Let them even try to bend the style, by so much as the crook of a finger, as [Eero] Saarinen is trying to do, which I am trying to do. Any architect worth his salt is trying to break loose. _ John Peter, *The Oral History of Modern Architecture:*

*Interviews with the Greatest Architects of the Twentieth Century,* New York: Harry Abrams, 1994

I see my work in a sequence of history, and I see no contradiction between that and modern. _ Hilary Lewis and John O'Conner, *Philip Johnson: The Architect in His Own Words,* New York: Rizzoli, 1994

. . . I have a peculiar approach to history, no doubt about it, and I use it a lot more. Eisenman [American architect Peter Eisenman, born 1932], for instance, knows his history perfectly, but he wouldn't think of using it. _ Hilary Lewis and John O'Conner, *Philip Johnson: The Architect in His Own Words,* New York: Rizzoli, 1994

I believe in history. I mean by tradition, the carrying out, in freedom, the development of a certain basic approach to architecture which we find upon beginning our work here. I do not believe in perpetual revolution in architecture. I do not strive for originality. As Mies once told me, "Philip, it is much better to be good than to be original." I believe that. _ Philip Johnson, "The Seven Crutches of Modern Architecture," informal talk to students, School of Architectural Design, Harvard University, December 7, 1954

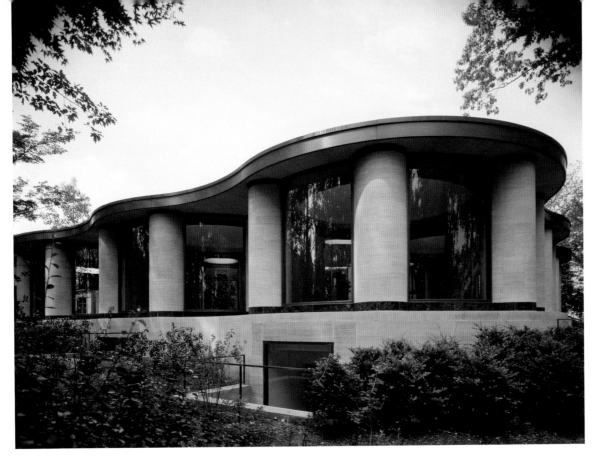

I was inspired by the Madrasa (school) across the street from Sinan's great mosque in Istanbul—it looked very much like this. In fact, the idea of clustered domes came straight from Istanbul. And, of course, it didn't hurt that Dumbarton Oaks is a Byzantine institute. _ Hilary Lewis and John O'Conner, *Philip Johnson: The Architect in His Own Words*, New York: Rizzoli, 1994

There was really no attempt on my part to study Islamic architecture. I just remembered that the feeling of repeated domes was a rather delicious way to organize space in a module. It's modular. _ Hilary Lewis and John O'Conner, *Philip Johnson: The Architect in His Own Words*, New York: Rizzoli, 1994

In Dumbarton Oaks the axis is classical, of course. And the domes are Islamic. But I think you can do anything you want. To me they were just new. I never thought about where I got things from. _ Hilary Lewis and John O'Conner, *Philip Johnson: The Architect in His Own Words*, New York: Rizzoli, 1994

The idea I was after was woods enclosed, because the worst thing in a museum is glass. The last thing you want is for your eyes to keep wandering away from the art. _ Hilary Lewis and John O'Conner, *Philip Johnson: The Architect in His Own Words*, New York: Rizzoli, 1994

But the minute you take an inside view you see what the idea is. It's a purely "inside" building. It has no façades at all. _ Hilary Lewis and John O'Conner, *Philip Johnson: The Architect in His Own Words*, New York: Rizzoli, 1994

**Museums** The one building that's viable in America as a symbol of the importance of their town has become the museum. _ John Peter, *The Oral History of Modern Architecture: Interviews with the Greatest Architects of the Twentieth Century*, New York: Harry Abrams, 1994

My main group of work is in museums. I think it's the most important job of the day for the simple reason that there is no more possibility of having churches as the monument building of a community. _ John Peter, *The Oral History of Modern Architecture: Interviews with the Greatest Architects of the Twentieth Century*, New York: Harry Abrams, 1994

The curved glass walls are a response to the Dumbarton Oaks landscape whereas the columns reflect Johnson's interest in Islamic architecture.

**NONE OF THESE BOYS WHOM I TALK ABOUT AS PATRONS ARE JUST AFTER MONEY.**

## WEALTH AS INDEPENDENCE

*Philip Johnson was born into a wealthy family. While Johnson was a student at Harvard College, his father divided a large amount of his fortune between his children. Johnson was given stock in Alcoa Aluminum, which ensured his lifelong financial independence and also factored into his great success. For example, Johnson had the luxury of building his thesis project as an architecture student at the Graduate School of Design at Harvard University (House on Ash Street, Cambridge, built in 1943) as well as serving as his own client on Glass House.*

You know, money is a terrible thing to have. It was glorious. If you have a passion, you can indulge it. What more do you wish in the world? If you want leisure to paint or leisure to write poetry, how are you going to do it if you're not—you have to marry—it's the same in architecture. You marry the rich daughter, rich daughter of an industrialist, or you have money yourself. There's no other way to do architecture. _ Frank Gehry and Philip Johnson interview by Charlie Rose, *Charlie Rose*, aired on January 27, 2005

I'm always afraid someone'll come and tap me on the shoulder and say, "Johnson, you've spent a lifetime in architecture and you're wealthy enough so you don't have to worry; why aren't you better?" I still have the big building to do. [Johnson was eighty-six when he said this.] _ "Philip Johnson Gets Real: The Godfather on Influence, His Heirs, and What Makes Him Weep," *Metropolis*, November 1998

I like to work. I like to be considered—I like fame. I like power—well, the normal things. People who say they don't are lying. _ Frank Gehry and Philip Johnson interview by Charlie Rose, *Charlie Rose*, aired on January 27, 2005

---

HOUSTON 1983
# TRANSCO TOWER (NOW WILLIAMS TOWER)
*In this project and the following, AT&T Corporate Headquarters, the professional relationship between Philip Johnson and developer Gerald Hines was significant.*

He [Gerald Hines, developer] and Bowen [Jack Bowen, CEO of Transco] both wanted the building to end all buildings. And somehow, they can always find the money when they get that desire strong enough. It's so funny. . . . None of these boys whom I talk about as patrons are just after money. _ Hilary Lewis and John O'Conner, *Philip Johnson: The Architect in His Own Words*, New York: Rizzoli, 1994

Jack Bowen of Transco was very interested in glory. He was the head of a large company, and he was interested in art. In fact, he turned one of the lobbies in the Transco Tower into an art gallery. Gerry Hines [developer] thought that the suburban area now known as the Galleria district was the beginning of a new, great commercial development. Thank God the real estate bust came—and it came just in time—otherwise the Transco Tower would be surrounded by other tall buildings. . . . I like it alone. I don't want any other buildings around it. Gerald Hines was going to build another building right there. He thought it was wonderful land for development. I said, "Gerry, it is not! It is right in your front door. Why don't you just tell Transco to develop that as a park." . . . Well, Gerry's thinking was that we'll all make money on this eventually, but in the meantime, maybe for the next twenty years, let's do something to attract people to this part of town, to make that area really develop. _ Hilary Lewis and John O'Conner, *Philip Johnson: The Architect in His Own Words*, New York: Rizzoli, 1994

The feature that really makes the Transco Tower stand out, besides not having any other buildings around it, is its very slender proportions. It's a needle-like skyscraper. _ Hilary Lewis and John O'Conner, *Philip Johnson: The Architect in His Own Words*, New York: Rizzoli, 1994

**Waterwall** The whole thing was to be water. . . . When you think of the cost of that fountain! It was just unbelievable. But Gerry built it anyhow . . . _ Hilary Lewis and John O'Conner, *Philip Johnson: The Architect in His Own Words*, New York: Rizzoli, 1994

◀◀ I AM A WHORE, AND I AM PAID VERY WELL FOR HIGH-RISE BUILDINGS. ▶▶

Transco Tower in Houston, opposite page, was supposed to be "the building to end all buildings." Or at least that was Johnson's instruction when he was commissioned to do it.

## YOU CAN'T DO A PROMINENT BUILDING LIKE THAT WITHOUT BEING MORE HATED THAN LOVED. 

The AT&T building is one of the most recognized sites in New York. The pink stone and pediment, above and opposite, further distinguishes it on the Manhattan skyline.

### AT&T CORPORATE HEADQUARTERS (NOW SONY PLAZA BUILDING)

The space was basically tailored to AT&T—it is an imperial space. Madison Avenue is a shopping street, not an imperial street, [but] AT&T didn't want lingerie stores in the lobby. They said, "Make it the front door into our empire. Let's make it so you'll be impressed when you go by." _ Hilary Lewis and John O'Conner, *Philip Johnson: The Architect in His Own Words,* New York: Rizzoli, 1994

DeButts [John DeButts, then – AT&T chairman and Johnson's client] said to me, "Now, look, I don't want just another building. We'd like to make the next step in tall building architecture since the Seagram Building—just go to it." We thought we'd use pink stone, and he was overwhelmed with delight, so we did it, that's all. _ Hilary Lewis and John O'Conner, *Philip Johnson: The Architect in His Own Words,* New York: Rizzoli, 1994

## "ARCHITECTURE SHOULD TRIGGER OFF AMAZEMENT"

My main interest in life is to build buildings that people are going to have a pride in. It becomes a building with overtones of art, magnificence, monumentality, emotion . . . One thing that I really think runs as a thread is my passionate interest in processional space, space as apprehended by walking through it. It isn't just a space. It is the procession of the appreciation of space. This I get a little bit from Mies. Then I got interested in more complex processionals. _ John Peter, *The Oral History of Modern Architecture: Interviews with the Greatest Architects of the Twentieth Century,* New York: Harry Abrams, 1994

. . . architecture should trigger off amazement . . . it should give people pleasure, cheer them up, or even move them to tears. In my case, that's what happened when I visited Chartres Cathedral with my mother when I was thirteen. . . . If an architect can do that, or even just a bit, he's good. How he achieves it is irrelevant. _ Hanno Rauterberg, *Talking Architecture: Interviews with Architects,* Munich: Prestel, 2008

I feel about it [a fountain] the way I do about processionals. It's an emotional feeling that's in space—the way to decorate that space to enhance it, that is unique. _ John Peter, *The Oral History of Modern Architecture: Interviews with the Greatest Architects of the Twentieth Century,* New York: Harry Abrams, 1994

I am into water and light. Anything that moves, anything that makes a focal point, anything that is existing in time. _ John Peter, *The Oral History of Modern Architecture: Interviews with the Greatest Architects of the Twentieth Century,* New York: Harry Abrams, 1994

My philosophical outlook dates from a time and a way of thinking that differs from the liberal, acceptable, politically correct line that we all subscribe to today. To me, Plato was the worst—living the good and the true and the beautiful. There's no such thing as the good or the true or the beautiful. I'm a relativist. I'm a nihilist. _ Hilary Lewis and John O'Conner, *Philip Johnson: The Architect in His Own Words,* New York: Rizzoli, 1994

They were an imperial company, and they thought of themselves that way. Chairman DeButts was a one-man democracy. He wanted to build. Nobody on the board wanted to build a building. _ Hilary Lewis and John O'Conner, *Philip Johnson: The Architect in His Own Words,* New York: Rizzoli, 1994

There are two things that were done intentionally—the enormous columns, and the top—there's no top like that in New York, although it's not as visible as the tops of tall buildings like the Chrysler. It's unique in that when you do catch sight of it, you don't forget it. That's what I told DeButts. I said, "If we don't do something very striking on top, you won't know your building is up there." _ Hilary Lewis and John O'Conner, *Philip Johnson: The Architect in His Own Words,* New York: Rizzoli, 1994

I was looking at early Romanesque, of course. I don't think I got it looking at specific buildings or books. I look at McKim [Charles Follen McKim (1847–1909) of McKim, Mead & White, a prominent architecture firm at the turn of the twentieth century]. _ Hilary Lewis and John O'Conner, *Philip Johnson: The Architect in His Own Words,* New York: Rizzoli, 1994

**The AT&T Controversy** Oh, naturally, postmodernism was very much in the air. Bob Stern used the word first, and I went along with it out of sheer fatigue with the International Style. So the reaction at AT&T was that the building was to be people-friendly. I must have been out of my mind, but it was understandable and was received well. Well, it was and wasn't. You can't do a prominent building like that without being more hated than loved. _ Hilary Lewis and John O'Conner, *Philip Johnson: The Architect in His Own Words,* New York: Rizzoli, 1994

It surprised me. . . . The only really bad response was *New York* magazine. They made a list of the buildings New Yorkers love to hate, and they ranked AT&T with that one at [2] Columbus Circle [Built in 1964, 2 Columbus Circle was originally the Gallery of Modern Art. It was designed by architect Edward Durell Stone (1902–78)]. But most people come up to me when I walk by there and say, "Thank you for this great building." _ Hilary Lewis and John O'Conner, *Philip Johnson: The Architect in His Own Words,* New York: Rizzoli, 1994

Despite early controversy, the AT&T building has emerged as an oasis in midtown, especially the glass atrium.

## NEW YORK 1959
# THE FOUR SEASONS

*The Four Seasons Restaurant is located in the Seagram Building, which was designed by architect Mies van der Rohe and completed in 1958. Philip Johnson had played a significant role in the Seagram Building, not only as collaborating architect, but as the liaison between Mies and his client. Phyllis Lambert, daughter of Samuel Bronfman, owner of the Seagram Company Ltd., had consulted Johnson, then director of architecture at the Museum of Modern Art, on her search for an architect to design the new headquarters building. Johnson recommended Mies van der Rohe and the result was the Seagram Building.*

**The cool elegance of the Four Seasons Restaurant was a modernist rebuke to fancy French restaurant décor at the time. Two large square rooms are connected by a travertine corridor, and the white marble pool anchors the center of the main room.**

We had this empty space—we didn't know it was going to be a restaurant. So we thought, "Well, it's going to be a Cadillac showroom." And then Phyllis Lambert [director of planning for the Seagram Building] said, "Look, what are we going to do in this space?" A restaurant couldn't pay the rent for the space; it was not on the ground floor. You couldn't make it a shop; that would be inappropriate. So Mr.

Bronfman and Phyllis decided that the space should be subsidized. _ Hilary Lewis and John O'Conner, *Philip Johnson: The Architect in His Own Words*, New York: Rizzoli, 1994

Oh, Mies got tired. "For God's sake, I don't want to sit here and do a restaurant. You do it." He wanted to go back to Chicago. That's where his girlfriend, and life, were. _ Hilary Lewis and John O'Conner, *Philip Johnson: The Architect in His Own Words*, New York: Rizzoli, 1994

Restaurants are very tricky. And usually, there's never enough money. But there was here. That was the cheapest way we could use that space. Of course, no restaurant would have done what we did—it would have been tinsel. The Four Seasons, now that is architecture. _ Hilary Lewis and John O'Conner, *Philip Johnson: The Architect in His Own Words*, New York: Rizzoli, 1994

## "ARCHITECTURE IS A TERRIBLY FOOLISH PROFESSION"

You can't learn architecture any more than you can learn a sense of music or of painting. You shouldn't talk about art, you should do it. _ Philip Johnson, "The Seven Crutches of Modern Architecture," informal talk to students, School of Architectural Design, Harvard University, December 7, 1954

I think it would be very interesting to have time to run an atelier. I think it would be very interesting to have students following the way I think and being free to leave at any time. Teaching becomes a personal thing—as all art always has been. _ "Interview: Johnson and Eisenman," *Skyline*, February 1982

Architecture is a terribly foolish profession to go into. I think most students know that. At least I always tell them. _ John Peter, *The Oral History of Modern Architecture: Interviews with the Greatest Architects of the Twentieth Century*, New York: Harry Abrams, 1994

## BILBAO AND ROBERT A. M. STERN

I have a very simple rule: Does it make me cry when I step in? . . . Bilbao did. I've been back, too, and I said it wouldn't happen again, because I've learned now. But it did: I burst into tears. That's not easy to do. Gehry is so far the greatest architect that you almost can't talk about the rest. But the man of influence . . . is Stern [Robert A. M. Stern, American architect, born 1939]. I noticed that when he was a student of mine. I said, this is the brightest kid that ever worked for me—I didn't say "designer"—I said [he had] an influence for the good, through his knowledge of history, his personality, everything you can come up with. And he did become powerful. He did exactly what I thought he would. When he was my student, I said, "You are going places, young man." And, boy, did he go places. _ "Philip Johnson Gets Real: The Godfather on Influence, His Heirs, and What Makes Him Weep," *Metropolis*, November 1998

My measuring stick is the great architect who does great buildings that will go down in history with the cathedrals of the past. Bilbao [The Guggenheim Museum in Bilbao, by Canadian-American architect and 1989 Pritzker Prize winner Frank Gehry] is the only building like that built in this century. . . . The whole century. There's nothing that Frank Lloyd Wright ever did that has that emotive power. You walk into Bilbao—have you been? . . . Well you better get your ass over there. That is the important building of our generation and of our time. _ "Philip Johnson Gets Real: The Godfather on Influence, His Heirs, and What Makes Him Weep," *Metropolis*, November 1998

## BECOMING AN ARCHITECT: "IT HAPPENED IN EXACTLY THREE HOURS"

When I was eighteen years old I read an article in the old *Arts Magazine* on architecture. I was a major in college in Greek. I picked up this magazine article by [Henry] Russell Hitchcock on the work of J. J. P. Oud, one of the Dutch pioneers. That afternoon as I finished the article—it was practically illegible, but the pictures were there—I decided that I was going to change my career and I'd be an architect. It happened in exactly three hours. I had never thought of being an architect before that time. _ John Peter, *The Oral History of Modern Architecture: Interviews with the Greatest Architects of the Twentieth Century*, New York: Harry Abrams, 1994

## "I'M DIFFERENT"

I don't think I am a big-time original architect. I'm no Frank Gehry; I'm different. I think everybody has said bad things about me, and they're usually right. But they don't bother me. I'm not an intellectual in their sense of the word. I may be bright enough—no way I can tell. _ Hilary Lewis and John O'Conner, *Philip Johnson: The Architect in His Own Words*, New York: Rizzoli, 1994

I'm proud of my architecture. . . . I don't know the judgment of history. I'm not as good as—I know I'm not a Frank Lloyd Wright. I know I'm not a Mies van der Rohe. But, my God, there's a long range of excellence in between that. _ Frank Gehry and Philip Johnson interview by Charlie Rose, *Charlie Rose*, aired on January 27, 2005

It's change I want. When I'm designing a building, it gives me an opportunity to change myself, try out something new. I think that's the quintessence of life. And if I can't sense that, I needn't bother to get up any more. _ Hanno Rauterberg, *Talking Architecture: Interviews with Architects*, Munich: Prestel, 2008

Death is nothing, you see—it just happens and that's the end. I just want to finish some more buildings. _ "Philip Johnson Gets Real: The Godfather on Influence, His Heirs, and What Makes Him Weep," *Metropolis*, November 1998

I certainly will be remembered as an architect, but only one kind. . . . As a person that's in the middle of the maelstrom, the whirligig that is architecture, rather than for my formal greatness. I'll never be remembered for the Seagram building. I'll never be a "Great architect," quote-unquote, capital G. _ "New York's Godfather, Now We Are 80," *Blueprint*, March 1987

# PHOTOGRAPHY AND TEXT CREDITS

## PHOTOGRAPHY CREDITS

The laureates, their offices, institutions, and photographers around the world have generously granted us permission to reproduce photographs, drawings, and plans for this publication. The following is the most accurate and complete listing of sources.

AENA (Manuel Renau): 136 above right; Aker/Zvonkovic Photography, LLP: 260 main; © Alburtus/Yale News Bureau: 344; Courtesy Amateur Architecture Studio: 79 below right, 80, 82 below, 83 below, 84 all, 85, (Lv Hengzhong) 75, 78 above left and right, top left, 82 above left and above right, 83 above, (Zeng Han) 78 below left, 79 above, (Zhu Chenzhou) 74; Bridgit Anderson: 51, 58 above left and above right, 59; Courtesy Tadao Ando: 266, 269 center, 270, 271 inset right, 272, 273 inset top to bottom, 275 main and inset below, 276 center, 277; arcaid.co.uk: (Richard Bryant) 137 both, 399 above, 430 top left and bottom, 435, 436 both; (Richard Einzig) 431 both, 433 below right; (John Gollings) 180–181, 183; (Tim Griffith) 202, 203; (Michael Harding) 332; (Gavin Jackson) 410 left; (Nicholas Kane) 140 below; (Marcel Malherbe) 182 left above; (Photoservice Electa/Marco Covi) 135, 207 both; (Florian Monheim) 324 above; (Bildarchiv Monheim) 324 below; (Rainer Kiedrowski/Bildarchiv-Monheim) 400 both; (Alan Weintraub) 357 above; Alejandro Aravena: 35 bottom, 36; Courtesy of Architecture Foundation of Australia: 190, 192 below, 195; Manuel Armand: 386 right; Aspen Art Museum (Derek Skalko): 54 above and bottom, (Michael Moran/OTTO) 54 middle; Iwan Baan: 66, 76, 199, 201 above; Shigeru Ban Architects: 50, 58 below; Richard Barnes: 213 above left; Collection of the Barragán Foundation, Switzerland: (Ursula Bernath) 443, 447; (Leopold Soto) 438; © Barragán Foundation, Switzerland/Prolitter, Switzerland/ARS: (Armando Salas Portugal) 444 both, 445 right; Hélène Binet: 109, 110 main, 113 left, 116 all, 118 above; Reiner Blunck: 188; Nicholas Borel: 278, 279, 280 all, 281, 282 all, 283 above left and above right, 284 both, 286 right; Augusto Brázio: 90; Anthony Browell: 196 above; © Burkhardt: 41 middle right; Adrian Carter: 182 above and bottom left; Collection Centre Canadian

d'Architecture/Canadian Centre for Architecture, Montreal: (Aldo Rossi fonds) 325 below; (James Stirling/Michael Wilford fonds) 437; www.chocolate-fish.net (© Oliver Ross): 359 main and below left, 362 both,363 below; Provided by The Chugoku Shimbun: 365; Citiscape: 138 right; Tyler Cohen: 403; Justin W. Cook: 322, 323; Hans Danuser: 113 right; Paulo Mendes da Rocha: 144 below, 146 below left, 148 center, 149 above and bottom; Marlies Darsow: 389 above right; Gitty Darugar: 286 above left; Lucie Debelkova: 184 above, 185; © Gautier Deblonde: 166; Sylvain Deleu: 62, 73 above left; Michel Denancé: 134 below, 236 right, 237, 243 center and below; Christian de Portzamparc: 283 below, 286 center and below; Deutsches Architekturmuseum, Gottfried Böhm Archiv: 377 right, 378 right, 382 below right; Felipe Díaz Contardo: 33 above and middle; Carolyn Djanogly: 222; Javier Lorenzo Domínguez: 14; Steve Double: 164, 176; Andrew Dunn: 433 above; Todd Eberle: 198; Gerry Ebner, www.gerryebner.com: 108; John Edward: 395; © Elemental: 28 below, 29 middle, 30 above, 31 below left and top right, 32, 37 all; © Esto: (Ezra Stoller) 345, 346, 349 above, 350 both, 351main, 352, 366, 398 above, 402 above, 411 above, 412 above, 453 both; (Luca Vignelli) 320; Marloes Faber: 106 all, 327; Guy Fehn: 255; Sverre Fehn, The National Museum of Art, Architecture and Design: 247, 250 above; Luis Ferreira Alves: 87, 88 all, 89 all, 91 all, 93 all, 94 all, 96 all; © George Fessey: 124, 125 both; Leonardo Finotti: 146 below right; floto + warner: 104 above left and right; © Norman Foster: 224, 225 right, 228, 231 below, 232 center and below; Foster + Partners: 233 bottom; (© Nigel Young) 223, 225 center, 227 above, 229 center, far right, and below, 232 above, 233 from the top, 1-4; Klaus Frahm: 420 right; Gianni Berengo Gardin: 234, 238 left, 239 left above and below, right, top to bottom, 243 above, 244; Gehry Partners, LLP: 333 both, 338, 339 above, 340 both; Dominik Gigler: 210; © Dennis Gilbert/VIEW: 231 center; goerner-foto.de: 229 left center; Stina Glømmi: 252; Ingbet Gruttner: 404; Fujita Gumi: 149 center; Fernando Guerra/FG + SG: 300 below left, 301 below, 303 all, 304 both, 305 below left and right, 306 all; Wojtek Gurak, www.bywojtek.net: 139 above and below right, 168 main, 169 above, 342; Courtesy Zaha Hadid Architects: 165, 167, 168 left, 169 below, 170, 171 bottom, 172 bottom, 175 below; © Roland Halbe: 105 all, 112 all, 117 all, 121,

122 both, 123, 127 all, 128 above, 129 all, 132, 136 above left, 154, 155 left and right, top to bottom, 157 all, 160 both, 161 both, 171 left, and right, top to bottom, 172 above left and center, right, 173 all, 175 above and middle, 204, 211, 212, 226 all, 261 above, center, and below, 263 above and right, 264 all, 302all, 339 center and below, 341 all, 401 all, 416 left, 429; Mark Hanauer: 152; © Naoya Hatakeyama: 69 middle, 70 above right, 71 middle; Jiri Havran: 248, 251 all, 254 both; © Herzog & de Meuron: 201 below; Hester + Hardaway Photographers: 454 all; Henrik Hille: 253 below right; Hiroyuki Hirai: 52, 53, 56 all, 60 all; Atelier Hollein (Sina Baniahmad): 384, 385, 386 left, center, and below, 387 below right, 388 to left, 389 below left, below right, 390 above, bottom, and right, 393; Koji Horiuchi: 408 above, 409 above; Franz Hubmann: 387 left, 388 center and bottom, 392 both; © Ishiguro Photgraphic Institute: 65 all; Kerun Ip: 405, 406 above, 407; Philip Johnson Glass House/National Trust for Historic Preservation: 450 below; © Christine Kanstinger: 39, 43 all; © Ai Katazawa: 130; Dean Kaufman: 99, 100 above, 101; Bas Kegge: 326 above; Katsuhisa Kida/FOTOTECA: 133, 134 above; Nelson Kon: 144 above, 145 all, 146 above, 150 both, 151 both, 358 right, 361; Ilpo Koskinen: 335 all; Søren Kuhn: 186 right, 187 above; Morten Krogvold: 246; Paul Kulig: 321; Ian Lambot: 230; Nic Lehoux: 153, 205 all, 238 main; Armin Link/OMA: 216; Lu Wenyu: 79 above right, 81 all; Arne Magnussen: 178; Vibeke Maj Magnussen:179; Melissa Majchrzak: 330, 343; Fumihiko Maki: 288, 290 left, 293 below, 294 left and right, 295 above, 297 both; (ASPI) 292 (top); (Toshiharu Kitajima) 289, 292 above left and right, 293 left and right,295 right, 296 both; (Kaneaki Monma) 292 below; (Nikkei Architecture) 295 center; (Robert Pettus) 294 below; Duccio Malagamba: 262 above, 331, 363 above; Mitsuo Matsuoka: 268; 269 above left, above right and below, 271 main and inset left, 273 above left and below, 276 below left and right; © Thomas Mayer, www.thomasmayerarchive.com: 107 all, 114 center, 47 above; Elizabeth McEnaney: 299, 300 right, 301 above; Ben McMillan: 417; Florian Medicus: 156; Richard Meier: 398 below; Richard Meier & Partners Architects: 399 below, 402 left; Rudi Meisel, Berlin: 229 above; Miyagi Prefecture Sightseeing Section: 68; Courtesy of Rafael Moneo: 256, 258, 259, 260 left, 261 bottom, 262 center, 263

bottom, 265; (Didda Biggi) 257; (Francisco Ontañón) 262 below; David Montgomery: 428; Michael Moran: 55 all; Courtesy of Morphosis: 155 bottom, 158, 163 above and below; José Moscardi: 148 above and below left; Maurizio Mucciola:290 right, 369 main, 370, 372 left and right; Glenn Murcutt: 191 both, 196 left, 197 bottom right; Courtesy of Glenn Murcutt & Associates (John Gollings): 197 above and center; Nacása & Partners, Inc: 156; Oscar Niemeyer Foundation Collection: 357 below, 358 above left and below, 359 below right, 360; (Michel Moch) 355; (Juliana Zuccoloto): 354; Jean Nouvel Atelier: 128 below; Occhiomagico: 325 above and center; Oerlimans: 389 left; Tomio Ohashi: 67 above left and above right, 275 inset above; Takashi Okamoto: 98; © OMA: 41 right center and below, 42 above, 215 bottom, 216 all, 217, 218 left, 219 below; (Rory McGowan) 215 left, above right and center; (Hans Werlemann) 218 main, 220 all; Grace Ong Yan: 213above right; 449, 451 both; Klemens Ortmeyer, courtesy Wilkhahn: 48, 49 all; © Archive Frei Otto: 46, 47 above and center; © Frei Otto: 40, 41 top and middle left, 45, 47 bottom; Ana Ottoni: 142; Cristobal Palma: 26, 28 above, 29 above left and above right, 30 left, 31 top left, 33 bottom, 34, 35 above; Richard Payne, FAIA: 414 above; I. M. Pei Architect/Pei Partnership Architects: 406 below; Pei Cobb Freed & Partners: 408 below, 409 below, 411 middle and below, 414 below; © Serge Picard: 287; Eugeni Pons: 21 middle right; Robert Prat: 24 above left; Philippe Rault: 131 both; © RCR Arquitectes: 18 bottom, 20 middle, below left, 22 below, 23 all, 24 center; © RPBW: 235, 236 left, 239 below right, 240 left center and below, 242 below left and center, 243 below left and bottom; (Fregoso & Basalto) 245; (Yoshio Hata) 240 above left; (Paul Hester) 241, 242 below right; (Alistair Hunter) 242 above; (Shunji Ishida) 240 center left, 242 middle left; (Kawatetsu) 240 right; Richter: 390 left center, 391; Georg Riha: 387 above right; Dominic Roberts: 249 all; Kevin Roche John Dinkeloo and Associates: 418, 419, 420 all, 421 both, 422 both, 423 all, 424 all, 425, 426 both, 427 both; Rogers Stirk Harbour + Partners: 136 center, 138 left, 139 below left; Arved von der Ropp: 376 both, 377 above and center, 382 above and left; Courtesy of Charlie Rose: 221; Charles Rhyne: 396 all, 397; Manfred Sack: 374, 383; SANAA: 100 below, 102 all, 103, 104 below left, 104; Pietro Savorelli: 114 above left and right; © von Schlaich: 38;

Karl Hugo Schmölz: 380, 381 both; Richard Schulman, www.schulmanphotography.com: 410 right, 448, 450 above, 452, 456 right, 459; Seier + Seier: 250 below, 375; Mark Seliger: 394; Yoshio Shiratori: 267; Alvaro Siza, Architect: 298, 300 above left, 305 above, 307 both; Skidmore, Owings & Merrill LLP: 349 right, 351 right; Jennifer Calais Smith: 458; © Eduardo Souto de Moura: 89 bottom, 91 top right and below right, 92, 94 above, 96 both, center; Margherita Spiluttini: 209; Annette Spiro: 143 all; Dan Stevens: 132; © Tim Street-Porter: 227 below; Dennis Stock © Magnum Photos: 231 above; Hisao Suzuki, 15, 17, 18 above left and above right, 20, 21 top and middle left, 22 above and middle both, 24 above right, 25 all; Koichi Suzuno: 189, 192 left above and center, right, 193 all, 194 all; Tange Associates: 371 center, 372 below left; © Christophe Petit-Tesson: 34; Courtesy TIAA: 62, 67 bottom, 69 above and 69 below, 70 above left, 71 above right, 72, 73 above right; Tomio Tominaga: 364, 373; Tonk: 208; University Corporation for Atmospheric Research: 412 below, 413 both; Courtesy of University of St. Andrews:434 below; Christano Urban: 329; Utzon Archives/Danish Architectural Press: 186 left, 187 below; Courtesy Jan Utzon: 180 left, 184 left; Courtesy of Venturi, Scott Brown and Associates, Inc.: 308, 309, 310 all, 311, 312 both, 313 all, 314, 315, 316 all, 317 both, 318 both, 319; © Nina Vidic: 27; Isabel Villac: 147; Johan Vipper: 214 second, third, and fourth from the top, 348, 456 left, 457 both; Takahiro Watabe: 337 all, 368; © Paul Warchol: 415 both, 416 right; Courtesy of WikiArchitectura.com: 326 below; You-are-here.com: 378 left, 379 all; Reiner Zetti: 163 center; Wade Zimmerman: 285 both; Andrew Zuckerman: 140 above, 141; Peter Zumthor: 110 below, 114 below, 115, 118 below, 119; © Kim Zwarts, Maastricht: 159 both, 162 all, 439, 440 all,442 both, 445 left, 446 both; source unknown: 177 all, 253 main, 369 center and below, 371 right above and below.

## TEXT CREDITS

### RAFAEL ARANDA, CARME PIGEM, RAMON VILALTA
Descriptions for several projects and themes. Reprinted courtesy RCR Arquitectes.

Excerpts from Pritzker announcement videos "Nature," "Materials," and "Collaboration" (2017). Copyright © Hyatt Foundation. Reprinted with permission. Excerpts from "Special Issue 542," *A + U: Architecture and Urbanism* (November 2015). Reprinted with permission.

### ALEJANDRO ARAVENAA
Descriptions for several projects and themes. Reprinted courtesy Elemental.

### FREI OTTO
Excerpts from *Frei Otto: On His Career and Pritzker Prize, February 2015*. Copyright © Hyatt Foundation. Reprinted with permission.

Excerpts from *Frei Otto: Spanning the Future*, documentary, 2016. Reprinted by permission.

Juan Maria Songel and Frei Otto, excerpts from *A Conversation with Frei Otto*. Copyright © 2008 by Juan Maria Songel and Frei Otto. Reprinted by permission.

### SHIGERU BAN
Descriptions for several projects and themes. Reprinted courtesy Shigeru Ban Architects.

### TOYO ITO
Excerpts from "The Building After: Toyo Ito Interviewed by Julian Rose," from *Artforum* (September 2013). Copyright © 2013. Reprinted by permission.

### WANG SHU
Descriptions for several projects and themes. Reprinted courtesy Amateur Architecture Studio.

Rafael Magrou, excerpts from *L'Architecture d'Aujourd'hui 375* (December 2009). Reprinted with the permission of Archipress & Associés.

### EDUARDO SOUTO DE MOURA
Descriptions for several projects and themes. Reprinted courtesy Souto Moura Arquitectos.

### KAZUYO SEJIMA + RYUE NISHIZAWA
Edan Corkill, excerpt from "Kazuyo Sejima & Ryue Nishizawa: Successes stack up for Tokyo design duo," the *Japan Times* (January 6, 2008). Copyright © 2008. Reprinted with permission.

Christina Diaz Moreno and Epran Garcia Grinda, excerpt from interview with Kazuyo Sejima & Ryue Nishizawa from *El Croquis* 121/122 (2004). Copyright © 2004. Reprinted with permission. Juan Antonio Cortés, excerpt from interview with Kazuyo Sejima & Ryue Nishizawa from *El Croquis* 139 (2008). Copyright © 2008. Reprinted with permission.

Kristin Feireiss, ed., excerpt from *SANAA: Kazuo Sejima and Ryue Nishizawa—Zollverein School of Management and Design, Essen, Germany*. Copyright © 2006. Reprinted with permission.

Augustin Pérez Rubio, excerpt from *Houses: Kazuyo Sejima + Ryue Nishizawa, SANAA*. Copyright © 2007. Reprinted with permission.

### PETER ZUMTHOR
Peter Zumthor, excerpts from *Lecture: Teaching Architecture, Learning Architecture, 1996* (Lars Müller Publishers, 1998). Reprinted with permission of Atelier Peter Zumthor & Partner.

Peter Zumthor, excerpts from *Peter Zumthor Works: Buildings and Projects 1979–1997*. Reprinted with permission of Atelier Peter Zumthor & Partner.

Peter Zumthor, excerpts from *Atmospheres: Architectural Environments—Surrounding Objects*. Reprinted with permission of Birkhäuser GmbH, Publishers for Architecture, Basel.

### JEAN NOUVEL
Conway Lloyd Morgan, excerpts from *Jean Nouvel: The Elements of Architecture*. Copyright © 1998. Reprinted with permission of Rizzoli International Publications, Inc.

Excerpts from "Jean Nouvel 1987–2006," *A + U: Architecture and Urbanism* (April 2006). Reprinted with permission.

Excerpt from *GA Document* 93 (2006). Reprinted with permission.

Jean Nouvel, excerpt from "Real/Virtual," *Lotus* 84 (1994). Reprinted with permission.

### RICHARD ROGERS
Yoshio Futagawa, excerpts from interview with Richard Rogers from *GA Document Extra* (1995). Reprinted with permission.

### PAULO MENDES DA ROCHA
Paulo Mendes da Rocha, excerpts from *Paulo Mendes da Rocha 1957–2007, Fifty Years*. Copyright © 2007. Reprinted with permission of Rizzoli International Publications, Inc.

Excerpts from "Concrete Poetry," *Domus* (May 2006). Reprinted with permission.

Annette Spiro, excerpts from *Paulo Mendes da Rocha Works and Projects*. Reprinted with permission of Verlag Niggli AG, Sulgen, Switzerland.

### THOM MAYNE
Jeffrey Inaba, excerpts from "Ambition Then and Now," *Volume* 13 (2007). Reprinted with permission.

Vladimir Paperny, excerpt from interview with Thom Mayne. Reprinted with permission.

Excerpts from *Charlie Rose* (December 2, 2005). Reprinted with permission.

Thom Mayne, excerpts from *Morphosis*. Copyright © 2003. Reprinted with permission of Phaidon Press.

### ZAHA HADID
Excerpt from "Architecture and the Museum," a conversation between Zaha Hadid and Alice Rawsthorn, conducted as part of Frieze Talks, held at Frieze Art Fair, October 21, 2005. An edited version of this interview is included in "Frieze Projects: Artists' Commissions and Talks 2003–2005," published by Frieze.

Excerpts from "Zaha Hadid," *Perspecta* 37, "Famous" (January 8, 2005). Reprinted with the permission of *Perspecta*, The Yale School of Architecture.

Terry Gross, excerpt from interview with Zaha Hadid from *Fresh Air* (NPR, May 26, 2004). Copyright © 2004 by *Fresh Air*. All rights reserved.

Yukio Futagawa, excerpts from *Zaha M. Hadid*, edited and photographed by Yukio Futagawa (Tokyo: A.D.A. Edita, 1999). Reprinted with permission.

Excerpts from Zaha Hadid interview with Alvin Boyarsky in *Zaha Hadid, Planetary Architecture Two* (London: Architectural Association, 1983). Reprinted with permission.

Excerpt from *GA Document Extra* 03. Reprinted with permission.

**GLENN MURCUTT**
Yoshio Futagawa, excerpt from interview with Glenn Murcutt from *GA Houses* 75 (May 2003). Reprinted with permission.

Excerpts from "Spirit and Sensibility," *Architecture* 87, no. 10 (October 1998). Reprinted with permission of Hanley Wood, LLC.

Excerpts from *AA (Australian Architecture)* (September/October 1992). Reprinted with permission.

Cynthia Davidson, excerpts from "Raised to Observe: Glenn Murcutt," *Log* (Summer 2006). Reprinted with permission of Anyone Corporation.

**JACQUES HERZOG & PIERRE DE MEURON**
Cynthia Davidson, excerpts from "Interview with Herzog & de Meuron," *ANY* 13 (1996). Reprinted with permission of Anyone Corporation.

Jacques Herzog and Pierre de Meuron, excerpts from *A + U: Architecture and Urbanism* (February 2002): 120, 122. Reprinted with permission.

Rita Capezzuto, excerpts from "Herzog & de Meuron and Phenomenological Research," *Domus* 823 (February 2000). Reprinted with permission.

Jacques Herzog and Pierre de Meuron, excerpts from Gerhard Mack, *Herzog & de Meuron 1989–1991: The Complete Works, Volume 2*. Reprinted with the permission of Birkhäuser GmbH—Publishers for Architecture, Basel.

Ulrike Knöfel and Susanne Beyer, excerpts from interview with Jacques Herzog, translated from the German by Christopher Sultan from *Spiegel Online International* (July 30, 2008). Reprinted with permission of *Der Spiegel* and Jacques Herzog.

Aaron Betsky, excerpts from "Interview with Jacques Herzog," Diana Ketcham, et al., *The de Young in the 21st Century* (New York: Thames & Hudson, 2005). Reprinted with permission of the Fine Arts Museums of San Francisco.

Lynnette Widder, excerpts from "Towards an Intuitive Understanding," *Daidalos* (August 1995). Reprinted with permission.

Dietmar Steiner, excerpts from "Herzog & de Meuron: Tate Modern," *Domus* 828 (July 2000). Reprinted with permission.

**REM KOOLHAAS**
Alejandro Zaera-Polo, excerpts from "Encontrando Libertades: Conversaciones Con Rem Koolhaas," *El Croquis* 31 (February, 1992). Reprinted with permission of Alejandro Zaera-Polo and Rem Koolhaas.

**NORMAN FOSTER**
Robert Ivy, excerpts from interview with Norman Foster from *Architectural Record* 187, no. 7 (July 1999). Copyright © 1999 by The McGraw-Hill Companies. Reprinted with permission of *Architectural Record*, www.architecturalrecord.com

Norman Foster, excerpts from *Reflections*. Copyright © 2005. Reprinted by permission.

Norman Foster, excerpts from "Design in a Digital Age" (previously unpublished text, 2000) in Norman Foster and David Jenkins, *On Foster . . . Foster On* (Munich: Prestel Publishing, 2000). Reprinted with permission of Foster + Partners.

Stefano Casciani, excerpts from interview with Norman Foster from *Domus* 897 (November 2006). Reprinted with permission.

Norman Foster, excerpts from "Reinventing the Airport" (Lecture at the UIA, Barcelona, June 1996) in Norman Foster and David Jenkins, *On Foster . . . Foster On* (Munich: Prestel Publishing, 2000). Reprinted with permission of Foster + Partners.

**RENZO PIANO**
Excerpts from "Dialog on Cities: An Interview with Fulvio Irace and Renzo Piano," *Renzo Piano Building Workshop: Visible Cities*, (Rome: Triennale Electa, 2007). Reprinted with permission.

Excerpts from *Renzo Piano Building Workshop: Architecture and Music* (Milan: Lybra Immagine, 2002). Reprinted with permission.

Renzo Piano, excerpts from *Sustainable Architectures*. Reprinted with permission of Editorial Gustavo Gili SA.

**SVERRE FEHN**
Excerpts from "The Hedmark Museum in Hamar, Norway," *Living Architecture* 12 (1993). Reprinted with permission.

Henrik Steen Møller, excerpts from "Sverre Fehn—an interview with the Norwegian architect," *Living Architecture* (1997). Reprinted with permission.

**RAFAEL MONEO**
Excerpts from "The Idea of Lasting— A Conversation with Rafael Moneo," *Perspecta* (1988). Reprinted with permission of *Perspecta*, The Yale School of Architecture.

Rafael Moneo, excerpts from "Raoul Wallenberg Lecture, April 13, 2001" in Brian Carter and Annette W. LeCuyer, eds., *The Freedom of the Architect, Rafael Moneo*. Reprinted with permission of the A. Alfred Taubman College of Architecture and Urban Planning, The University of Michigan.

Carlos Jiménez, excerpts from "A Talk with Rafael Moneo," *Cite* 47 (Spring 2000). Reprinted with permission.

**TADAO ANDO**
Tadao Ando, excerpt from "From Self-Enclosed Modern Architecture Towards Universality," *The Japan Architect* 301 (May 1982): 446, 447, 448. Reprinted with permission of Shinkenchiku-sha Co., Ltd.

Michael Auping, excerpts from *Seven Interviews with Tadao Ando, November 1989–April 2002*. Reprinted with permission of the Modern Art Museum of Fort Worth.

Project description for several Tadao Ando projects. Courtesy Ando Architects.

**FUMIHIKO MAKI**
Sangleem Lee, excerpts from interview with Fumihiko Maki from *Space* 468 (November 2006). Reprinted with permission.

Project description for several Fumihoko Maki projects. Courtesy of Fumihiko Maki, Maki and Associates, www.maki-and-associates.co.jp

Serge Salat and Françoise Labbé, excerpts from interview with Fumihiko Maki (Geneva, June 24, 1986), from Serge Salat, *Fumihiko Maki: An Aesthetic of Fragmentation*. Copyright © 1987, 1988. Reprinted with permission of Rizzoli International Publications, Inc.

Fumihiko Maki, excerpts from *Selected Passages on the City and Architecture* (Tokyo: Maki and Associates, 2000). Courtesy of Fumihiko Maki, Maki and Associates, www.maki-and-associates.co.jp

**ALVARO SIZA**
Antonio Angelillo, excerpts from *Alvaro Siza: Writings on Architecture* (Skira,1997). Reprinted with permission.

Dawne McCance, excerpts from "An Interview with Alvaro Siza," *Mosaic: A Journal for the Interdisciplinary Study of Literature* 35, no. 4 (December 2002). Reprinted with permission.

C. C. Sullivan, excerpts from "The Sea, the Alhambra, and Port Wine: Alvaro Siza, Portugal's master builder, reflects on five decades of practice," *Architecture* 93, no. 7 (2004). Reprinted with permission of Hanley Wood, LLC.

Excerpt from "Architects do not invent, they just transform reality," *Oris* 8, Issue 41 (2006). Reprinted with permission.

José Antonio Aldrete-Hass, excerpts from interview with Álvaro Siza from *BOMB* 68 (Summer 1999). Reprinted by permission.

**ROBERT VENTURI**
Robert Venturi and Denise Scott Brown, excerpts from Peter Arnell, Ted Bickford, and Catherine Bergart, eds., *A View from the Campidoglio: Selected Essays 1953–1984*. Copyright © 1984 by Robert Venturi and Denise Scott Brown. Reprinted with permission of the Perseus Books Group.

Robert Maxwell, excerpts from "Robert Venturi and Denise Scott Brown: Interview with Robert Maxwell," *Architectural Design* 62, no. 5–6 (July–August 1992). Reprinted with permission of Academy Editions.

Philipe Barriere and Sylvia Lavin, excerpts from "Interview with Denise Scott Brown and Robert Venturi," *Perspecta* 28 (1997). Reprinted with permission of *Perspecta*, The Yale School of Architecture.

Sangleem Lee, excerpts from "Robert Venturi & Denise Scott Brown," *Space* 458 (January 2006). Reprinted with permission.

Hanno Rauterberg, excerpts from interview with Robert Venturi from *Talking Architecture: Interviews with Architects*.

**ACKNOWLEDGMENTS** This updated edition of *Architect* encompasses a timeline of nearly fifteen years, beginning with our work on the project in the early aughts, the original publication in 2010, and now this new edition in 2017.

Our journey has brought us into contact with scores of architects and their staffs, photographers, photo agencies, researchers, foundations, museums, libraries, and estates. It has entailed scouring hundreds of publications, including books such as monographs and architectural surveys, major newspapers, popular and trade magazines, scholarly journals, and privately published documents; and it has meant looking at recordings of public lectures and televised interviews or reading transcripts. The Internet has provided us with access to documents that we otherwise would never have known about or been able to find, in large measure online architectural sites, obscure articles, important blogs, and activities at academic institutions large and small. Our purpose has been single-minded: to discover and document the writings and comments on architecture made by the Pritzker Prize laureates, and to include illustrations in support of these comments.

The cooperation and help we've been shown by the many architects and their staffs have been invaluable. We know that the people who work in the communications and archive departments in any large architecture firm are beleaguered with requests, so to each person who has been forthcoming, who has sent us material and communicated with us over the past years, we extend heartfelt thanks. For those laureates who work with modestly sized staffs, the commitment to help us is indeed laudable. To each of these laureates and their staffs, our deepest gratitude and appreciation.

Our original team in New York included Donna Torrance, of Eight Communications, who brought vigor, humor, and clarity to our efforts, and whom we dearly miss to this day. Liz McEnaney and Julie Powell, the photo researchers for the original publication, were dedicated and thorough. Thank you to John Kerner for research assistance for this current edition. We are grateful to Johan Vipper, our caring designer from the outset, who graciously returned as art director for the updated edition. We have been further aided in our research by many fine universities and museums, including the Fisher Fine Arts Library at the University of Pennsylvania, in Philadelphia, and the Avery Architectural & Fine Arts Library of Columbia University and the Watson Library of the Metropolitan Museum of Art, both in New York.

Thank you to all the photographers and their agents who worked with us and who provided us with stellar visual material.

At the Pritzker Architecture Prize of the Hyatt Foundation, that great bastion of architectural excellence, we were aided first by Bill Lacy, a former executive director of the Prize and colleague, who supported the premise of this book and put us into contact with Martha Thorne, the current executive director. In Martha we are blessed with having a steady and wise partner: she allowed us great latitude in shaping this book but aided us considerably as needed, and in all ways led us to believe that we had a project worthy of the laureates themselves. We look upon her as a mentor and are proud to have her as a friend. Also at the Hyatt Foundation we thank Allen Turner, whose early support was significant, and more recently Edward Lifson, who extended us every possible courtesy and help needed, and Eunice Kim along with the rest of the staff in Chicago. Above all, our special thanks and gratitude to Cindy Pritzker and her son and daughter-in-law, Tom and Margot Pritzker, whose endorsement and support are invaluable.

To our other colleagues, friends, and family, thank you for indulging us in this most enjoyable enterprise.

Ruth Peltason and Grace Ong Yan

THE GRAND LOUVRE
WILL HOLD THE FIRST PLACE
IN MY LIFE AS AN ARCHITECT.
I.M. PEI

LANDSCAPE HAS ALWAYS BEEN A GREAT INFLUENCE ON ME, BUT
SO HAVE PEOPLE—MY WIFE, FRIENDS OR TEACHERS
IN THE WIDEST SENSE OF THE TERM, COMRADES-IN-ARMS—
OFTEN ONLY ENCOUNTERS AND EXPERIENCES
THAT LASTED FOR SECONDS OR MINUTES.
HANS HOLLEIN

IN THE END MY WORK IS MY WORK;
IT'S NOT A CRITIC'S WORK.
IF I HAD CHANGED MY WORK
TO CONFORM TO A CRITIC'S PERCEPTION
OR RULES ABOUT ARCHITECTURE,
BILBAO WOULD NEVER HAVE BEEN BUILT.
FRANK GEHRY

I REGARD MYSELF AS A
ROUTINE FUNCTIONALIST.
JAMES STIRLING

EVEN AS A STUDENT, I WAS VERY ENTHUSIASTIC
ABOUT THESE BUILDINGS OF MY FATHER'S.
GOTTFRIED BÖHM

THERE A
SO THE V

HIROSHIMA PROJECT WILL REMAIN AN EXAMPLE
OF THE MAINTENANCE
OF ARCHITECTURAL MONUMENTALITY.
KENZO TANGE

I LIKE THE GUGGENHEIM—BECAUSE OF THE ABILITY
TO SEE DIFFERENT PERSPECTIVES
ALL AT THE SAME TIME.
ZAHA HADID

BOTH OF US—FILM DIRE
INVENT S

EVERYBODY WAS SAYING
THE POMPIDOU WAS MORE LIKE A FACTORY
THAN LIKE A MUSEUM,
AND WE WERE VERY PLEASED ABOUT THAT.
RENZO PIANO

THE MUSEUM IS REALLY THE MOST IMPORTANT
NON-SECULAR COMMUNITY SPACE
THAT EXISTS IN THE WORLD.
RICHARD MEIER

OR THE
THE PE

LE CORBUSIER WAS THE PICASSO.
THAT'S VERY SIMPLE.
GORDON BUNSHAFT

HISTORY HAS A NATURAL CONTINUITY
THAT MUST BE RESPECTED.
GOTTFRIED BÖHM

AS A TEENAGER
I DISCOVERED THE VERY DIFFERENT WORLDS OF
FRANK LLOYD WRIGHT AND LE CORBUSIER—IMAGINE
THE CONTRAST OF A HOME ON THE PRAIRIE
WITH A VILLA AND A PARIS BOULEVARD.
NORMAN FOSTER

I THINK
QUITE A

I SEE MY WORK IN A SEQUENCE OF HISTORY,
AND I SEE NO CONTRADICTION
BETWEEN THAT AND MODERN.
PHILIP JOHNSON

EVERYTHING I KNOW,
I LEARNED FROM EERO REALLY.
KEVIN ROCHE

HISTORY SHOULD BE UNDERSTOOD.
YOU SHOULD LEARN HISTORY, DIGEST IT,
AND COME UP WITH SOMETHING OF YOUR OWN.
ORIGINALITY IS VERY IMPORTANT WITH ME.
HANS HOLLEIN

FRANK LLOYD WRIGHT WAS CHAINED TO THE 30-60 GRID,
AND THERE WAS NO FREEDOM IN IT FOR HIM...
GRIDS ARE AN OBSESSION, A CRUTCH. YOU DON'T NEED THAT
IF YOU CAN CREATE SPACES AND FORMS AND SHAPES.
THAT'S WHAT ARTISTS DO,
AND THEY DON'T HAVE GRIDS AND CRUTCHES,
THEY JUST DO IT.
FRANK GEHRY

ALL NOSTALGIA ABOUT THE CITY IS UNDERSTAN
BUT ONE CANNOT LIVE IN ANOTHER AGE.
JEAN NOUVEL

IS C

I'M PROUD OF MY ARCHITECTURE. . . .
I'M NOT AS GOOD AS—I KNOW I'M NOT A FRANK LLOYD WRIGHT;
I KNOW I'M NOT A MIES VAN DER ROHE.
BUT, MY GOD, THERE'S A LONG RANGE OF EXCELLENCE
IN BETWEEN THAT.
PHILIP JOHNSON

WELL, NOWADAYS ONE CAN DRAW EQUALLY,
WITHOUT GUILT, FROM THE ABSTRACT STYL
MODERN DESIGN AND THE MULTIPLE LAY
OF HISTORICAL PRECED
JAMES STIRL

I THINK MY FATHER, A BUILDER,
WAS THE MOST INFLUENTIAL.
RENZO PIANO

PARADOXICALLY, ARCHITECTURE IS ALWAYS LINKED
TO A PRECEDENT, EVEN ARCHITECTURE
THAT LOOKS TO HAVE A MEANING IN THE FUTURE.
JEAN NOUVEL